History of The New York Times

1851-1921

By ELMER DAVIS
Of The New York Times Editorial Staff

ILLUSTRATED

NEW YORK
The New York Times
1921

PRESS OF J. J. LITTLE & IVES CO.
NEW YORK

CONTENTS

LIST OF ILLUSTRATIONS

LIST OF ILLUSTRATIONS

FACSIMILE PAGES OF "THE NEW YORK TIMES"

INTRODUCTION

THIS historical sketch of *The New York Times* was prepared in commemoration of the quarter-centenary of the present management, which occurs on August 18, 1921, and of the seventieth anniversary of the first issue of the paper, which falls on September 18, 1921. It was written by a member of the editorial staff, Mr. Elmer Davis, with such advice and assistance as other members of the staff could give. Mr. Davis joined the staff of *The Times* in 1914, after his graduation from the University of Oxford, England, which he attended as a Rhodes Scholar from his native State, Indiana. He modestly disclaims any idea that his work is to be regarded as an ideal or definitive treatment of the subject. Most of the material of Part I has been drawn from the articles in *The Times Jubilee Supplement* of 1901, and from Augustus Maverick's "Henry J. Raymond and the New York Press." The second part has been compiled with the coöperation and assistance of many members of the staff. Without aspiring to a wholly detached point of view, which could hardly be achieved by men who have faith in and affection for the institution they serve, Mr. Davis believes that he has at any rate tried to tell the story impartially. However, it is but just to say that the unflagging industry and the literary skill with which Mr. Davis has executed his

task command the sincere admiration of his associates.

The New York Times's peculiar position in the esteem of the public may make its history of interest not only to working newspapermen and students of journalism but to many readers who are unfamiliar with the technique of newspaper-making and unacquainted with the personnel of *The Times*. Some episodes, particularly controversial episodes, have been treated with a certain reserve, as it was felt that it would not be wholly fair to present only one side of the case. But in no instance has accuracy been sacrificed to brevity, and it is the belief that nothing relevant to the history of *The Times*, or to its interpretation, has been omitted.

With respect to my own sentiments on the occasion of the twenty-fifth anniversary of the present management of *The Times*, I can do no better than to repeat here the following article, which appears in *The Times* of August 18, 1921:

Today — twenty-five years ago — August 18, 1896 — *The New York Times* passed to my management and has ever since been under my unrestricted control. So it may be fitting that I render an account of my stewardship to those who have made *The New York Times* of today possible — its readers — and take occasion to make clearer the forces that are truly directing and influencing its conduct. I am reluctant to strike the personal note that may manifest itself in this recital of the history of *The New York Times*, as it has been my endeavor to have the public as well as those who are associated in creating the paper regard it as an institution and,

so far as possible and feasible, make impersonal the treatment of news and its interpretation. The human element, however, enters into all man's activities and it fortunately exists in the conduct of newspapers. A newspaper if possible freed from the frailties of humanity, with no sense of responsibility, no sympathies, no prejudices, no milk of human kindness, would be a nuisance and a plague, an excrescence on the bodies social and politic, and would be despised and shunned and consequently without influence and altogether an unnecessary evil. We have made an effort to make *The New York Times* a creditable human institution. To what extent we have succeeded we are confident we can leave to others to say; whether this effort has contributed to the general welfare and to gaining respect for the honesty, integrity and patriotism of American newspapers.

I am pleased to be able to say that *The New York Times* is firmly established as an independent conservative newspaper, free from any influence that can direct or divert its management from a righteous and public-spirited course. It is within itself financially independent and in the enjoyment of a large and increasingly profitable legitimate income from circulation receipts and advertising revenue — in the aggregate probably the largest income of any newspaper in the world. The net result of its operations is beyond the earlier dreams of those who are its chief beneficiaries, and fortunately they know no interest they can serve that can give them greater joy, satisfaction and comfort. I wish that thought could find lodgment in the minds of those who may

be inclined to believe that some ulterior object may at times influence the policy of *The New York Times*, so that they may understand that, being free from pecuniary necessity or personal greed, no sane man would voluntarily forfeit the confidence and good-will of intelligent people by degrading himself through loss of his self-respect or the surrender of his independence. Persons may disagree with *The New York Times*—with its treatment of news and its views thereon—but there is no ground on which they can attribute to it base or improper motives for such differences of opinion. *The New York Times* is an open book and may be taken at its face value; it is no worse than it may seem to appear; its faults are those of human fallibility and we cherish the knowledge that at least in purpose it is better than we have been able to make it appear.

On this occasion of the twenty-fifth anniversary of the present management I wish first to make our grateful acknowledgments to the several hundred thousand readers of *The New York Times* who have expressed by their patronage their endorsement of the kind of newspaper we are endeavoring to produce. We are fully sensible of the fact that our editorial position on public questions has not always had the unanimous approval of our readers; many honestly differ from us; but whether we are right or wrong our views are not directly or indirectly presented with any thought that they may please or displease a reader. We do not now nor have we ever sought readers because of our favorable or unfavorable attitude toward men or measures. So we flatter ourselves that the third of a million persons who

daily purchase *The New York Times* and the more than half a million who purchase it on Sunday do so because they approve of our kind of newspaper, and that is the inspiration to which we owe such success as we enjoy.

To the advertisers who have paid many millions of dollars for space in the advertising columns of *The New York Times* we are grateful for generous patronage and the many evidences of sympathy and encouragement they have manifested, and especially do we appreciate this proof of their understanding of the potency and value of newspaper circulation among those who find such a newspaper as *The New York Times* to their taste. *The New York Times* has been forced to steadily increase its advertising rates, and the difficulty was minimized because its discriminating advertisers have realized that the increases were not out of proportion to the increased service tendered. We have great pride in the high business standing of our advertisers. It is of the rarest occurrence that a high-class advertiser does not place *The New York Times* first on his list. In this connection it can be stated positively that no advertiser influences, or ever has influenced, the conduct of *The New York Times* or has been encouraged to seek any favors that are not accorded any good citizen. If in the past twenty-five years there has ever appeared an improper line written for the purpose of holding or securing advertising patronage, it was without the knowledge or consent of the management.

Words fail me when I try to express the obligation and gratitude I feel to the capable, earnest,

loyal men who have been associated with me in making *The New York Times.* I am proud of the fact that we have been able to obtain and retain such men in the service of the paper. No newspaper organization in the world has or has ever had, as a group, so many experienced newspaper men with love and pride of profession giving enthusiastically and indefatigably their best thoughts and service to informing honestly the public of the happenings and occurrences of the day; who in their relations with each other are gentlemanly and courteous and all united in working harmoniously and with a common purpose for giving unselfishly their very best ability to making a newspaper that is enterprising, reliable and trustworthy, and at the same time decent and dignified; men who find joy in their work and have profound sympathy with the general policies of *The New York Times*, giving such zeal and devotion to their respective duties as to create a character and form a power that make *The New York Times* the great newspaper it is; men of almost every shade of political and religious opinion and belief, of every variety of sympathy and conviction, all working together in the belief that they are serving a newspaper that tolerates no tampering with the news, no coloring, no deception, and in the making of which no writer is required, requested or even invited to express any views that he does not honestly entertain. With such men and under such conditions the building up of *The New York Times* was a pleasant task. No publisher ever had more faithful and efficient assistants. I hesitate to make invidious distinctions among the army of men who have aided

me in creating a newspaper, not so complete as I hope it may yet become as we are better enabled to take advantage of its opportunities, but which I believe, nevertheless, now to be the most complete in the world.

I wish, however, to select the notably conspicuous figures whose great contributions to the success of *The New York Times* I desire publicly to acknowledge, and to express my sense of obligation for their able support of my efforts to make *The New York Times* the best newspaper in the world:

To CHARLES R. MILLER, who from the beginning has been my editor-in-chief, whose whole-hearted sympathy with my opinions and my aims and purposes with *The Times* has been an inspiration. His scholarly attainments, his facility and lucidity of expression, broad vision, extraordinary knowledge of public affairs, having a statesman's conception of their proper conduct, and his lofty patriotism have made the editorial page of *The New York Times* consulted and respected throughout the world, and distinguished it as the foremost exponent of enlightened American public opinion.

To CARR V. VAN ANDA, who has been managing editor of *The New York Times* for the past eighteen years; to whose exceptional newspaper experience, genius for news-gathering and marvelous appreciation of news value and fidelity to fairness and thoroughness, knowing no friend or foe when presiding over the news pages of *The Times*, the greatest measure of credit is due for the high reputation it has attained for the fullness, trustworthiness and impartiality of its news service. His vigilance and

faithfulness to the very highest and best traditions of newspaper-making make him a tower of strength to the organization.

To LOUIS WILEY, the business manager, who has been associated with me almost from the beginning, particularly devoting himself to the circulation and advertising departments that have furnished the bone and sinew to the business, and has, while maintaining the very highest standards of business ethics, extended the greatest courtesy and painstaking attention to all having occasion to have transactions with *The Times*. Of unusual ability, alert, indefatigable and agreeable, and in full accord and sympathy with the policies of *The Times*, he has been one of my most useful and valuable assistants. No one has been more earnest and faithful to the duties that come under his management — and these have been multifarious — and he has made himself, as he is, an integral part of the institution.

Because of the loyal support and skillful aid of these three men, each preëminent in his particular and important field of responsibility, the publisher of *The New York Times* is free from some of the many problems and anxieties that are associated with newspaper-making for the reason that the reputation of the newspaper is in safe and prudent hands. There are others who have been of noteworthy aid in creating this great newspaper and their exceptional ability unstintingly given me was helpful and of enduring value, and their contribution is indelibly impressed in the results that have been achieved: Edward Cary (deceased), in the editorial department; John Norris (deceased), in the business and

mechanical departments; William C. Reick, Henry Loewenthal, and Arthur R. Greaves (deceased), in the news department. The work of these men was constructive and an inspiration, and conspicuously helpful in the building of the newspaper. I dare not go further in the personnel of the splendid men and women who have so ably, unselfishly and enthusiastically aided in the work of bringing *The New York Times* to its high eminence in public favor, for fear of not properly and adequately estimating their individual contribution to that end. Suffice it that to their ability, devotion to duty, kind sympathy and confidence, credit is due in great measure for what has been accomplished. With such men and women to assist, almost any deserving enterprise should be a pronounced success. They are all entitled to share in whatever praise may be accorded *The Times* as a newspaper.

Now as to the ownership of *The New York Times*. It is owned by a corporation with $1,000,000 common and $4,000,000 preferred 8 per cent stock (the latter recently issued as a stock dividend). I and the immediate members of my family own and control 64 per cent of the shares of the company free and unencumbered, and not one share of our holdings is pledged or hypothecated; 25 per cent more of the shares is held by those who are or have been employed by *The Times*, and the remaining 11 per cent of the shares is distributed among twenty-eight individuals or estates (all Americans) who acquired the stock by exchanging for it shares of the old company, the largest individual holder of the latter group holding only one-quarter of 1 per cent of the

capital stock. The New York Times Company has real estate and paper-mill properties costing more than $5,000,000, and on these properties there are unmatured bonds and mortgages amounting to $1,500,000, constituting the sum total of the indebtedness of the company except its current monthly accounts payable. The cash reserves of the company are more than sufficient to pay its total funded indebtedness and leave free a large and sufficient working capital. So it can be said that The New York Times Company is virtually free of indebtedness. It has a gross annual income exceeding $15,000,000, and only about 3 per cent of its gross annual income is distributed to its shareholders; the remainder of its income is employed in the development and expansion of its business. This result has been achieved in a business that twenty-five years ago was running at a loss of $1000 a day, by the investment of only $200,000 of new capital. It is the result of the application of practical common sense by experienced newspaper-makers who undertook the management of a newspaper of long and good reputation — temporarily crippled by mismanagement and untoward universal financial conditions — in the firm belief that a clientele existed in the greatest city in the world for a newspaper edited for intelligent, thoughtful people. At the time *The Times* passed to its present management — 1896 — the rapidly increasing circulation and advertising of the sensational newspaper indulging in coarse, vulgar and inane features, muck-raking and crusades of every character were creating a widely extending impression that otherwise a newspaper

would be dull, stupid and unprofitable. It was this situation that caused *The New York Times* to hoist its legend of "All the News That's Fit to Print." The wiseacres of journalism prophesied an early failure; the motto was made sport of and ridiculed. It was this prevailing impression that proved a valuable factor in the growth of *The Times*, for in the field it was trying to cover it met no serious competition and thus was for a considerable time left to its full benefit. The neglected non-sensational departments of news of the other daily morning newspapers were quietly and unostentatiously improved in *The New York Times* and made as far as possible complete — such as financial news, market reports, real estate transactions, court records, commercial and educational news; the news of books, the routine affairs of the National, State and City Governments; and there were also attractively presented decent and trustworthy pictures of men, women and events. Altogether the task undertaken in this direction was to tell promptly and accurately the happenings and occurrences that were not sensational but of real importance in the affairs of the people. This supplemented the general news of the day intelligently and quietly presented and with editorial interpretation that was fair and informative. The columns of *The Times* were open without money and without price for the presentation of views honestly differing with the opinions of *The Times*, and this was practiced to an extent never theretofore done by a newspaper. All of this soon gave *The Times* the reputation that its readers could expect full and trustworthy information regarding

any and all angles of the news. In the very first political campaign during the régime of the present management such was the fairness and impartiality of *The Times* news reports that at its close both the Democratic and Republican managers of the National Committees voluntarily sent letters of thanks and appreciation to *The Times* management.

We began on August 18, 1896, with a daily issue of 18,900, over half of which were returned unsold, and, as said before, with a deficit of $1000 a day. The gross income for the first year was $561,423, and at the end of the year the deficit was $68,121.67. The second year the deficit was $78,559; but in the third year the balance was $50,252 on the right side and has been so increasingly every year since. The gross income for the period of twenty-five years has been, in round figures, $100,000,000, every dollar of which, less an average of $125,000 a year withdrawn from the business and distributed as dividends, has been expended in making *The Times* what it is today. Not one dollar of the $100,000,000 was a gift or a gratuity, but every cent a legitimate newspaper income. It is a fortunate outcome for those who own the shares of The New York Times Company and who have been hopeful and patient for so many years, but it has also been a happy and encouraging result for the country and particularly for American journalism.

There was a time when it was no secret in financial circles that The New York Times Company had limited resources and that it was an active borrower, and this gave rise to speculation as to where the necessary funds were obtained. As a result wild

and stupid conjectures were given currency whenever it suited the purpose of malevolent persons to attempt to discredit the newspaper. Among the stories were these: That there was English or foreign capital in *The Times;* that traction interests were owners or controllers; that certain political factions were "backing" it; that department stores were financially interested; that well-known Wall Street concerns directed its policy, and variations ad libitum. The truth is that from the day I assumed the management of *The New York Times* — twenty-five years ago today — I have been in absolute and free control, and no man or interest was ever in a position to direct or demand of me to do anything with *The Times*, and no one ever attempted to do so. So far as the management of *The New York Times* is concerned we can say, without fear of any contradiction from the thousands who in the past twenty-five years have been employed on *The Times*, that never a line appeared in its columns to pay a real or imaginary debt or to gain expected favors. *The New York Times* owes no man or interest any support or goodwill that it does not owe to every good man and worthy cause.

The operation of so large an enterprise, including real estate transactions and large building construction, of course required capital, and the general impression that the newspaper business is extra-hazardous, and the personal equation the all-important factor, made financing no easy task; so it cannot be surprising to know that we had many and continued financial problems made more than ordinarily difficult as we scrupulously avoided the

easiest way, knowing full well that in that direction the enterprise would be imperiled and robbed of the attraction that made the work a joy, an inspiration and opportunity for public service. The financing, however, was always done on a strictly business basis. Not a dollar was borrowed at less than the prevailing rate of interest, and principal and interest were paid to the last cent. In no single instance did we receive any financial accommodation for a selfish motive, and never in a single instance was it predicated on any personal benefits, direct or indirect, asked or expected.

I was reluctant to go at such length into the business and financial history of *The New York Times*, but think this occasion is the time once and for all to make the indisputable facts clear.

I do not wish to overemphasize the material progress of *The New York Times*, as like results may be obtained in any well-conducted business in the world's greatest metropolis, for on this twenty-fifth anniversary of the present management we prefer to be appraised by the product we are offering the public for their information and guidance, and to have it judged by the highest standards of honesty, fairness and cleanliness, and public service applied in making newspapers. We present the nine thousand and thirty-one issues of *The New York Times* that have appeared during the past twenty-five years for review and criticism. They are not without faults and shortcomings and not altogether what we should have wished them to be, but they are our best under the circumstances of their construction. We have little to regret for what has appeared

therein, but in no issue was principle ever surrendered or subordinated to expediency. We have not yet reached our ideal of a newspaper in contents or make-up and may never be able to achieve it, but we shall continue to improve, and to that end we hope to merit a continuance of our pleasant and profitable relations with intelligent men and women.

With respect to the principles and policies of *The New York Times* that represent our platform and our guide I can do no better than to repeat what was announced would be the policies of *The Times* when assuming its control and management, and shall leave to others to say how well we have lived up to that declaration. The following was the salutatory appearing in the issue of *The New York Times* of Wednesday, August 19, 1896:

ANNOUNCEMENT

To undertake the management of *The New York Times*, with its great history for right doing, and to attempt to keep bright the lustre which Henry J. Raymond and George Jones have given it, is an extraordinary task. But if a sincere desire to conduct a high-standard newspaper, clean, dignified and trustworthy, requires for success honesty, watchfulness, earnestness, industry, and practical knowledge applied with common sense, I entertain the hope that I can succeed and maintain the high estimate that thoughtful, pure-minded people have ever had of *The New York Times*.

It will be my earnest aim that *The New York Times* give the news, all the news, in concise and attractive form, in language that is permissible in good society, and give it as early, if not earlier than it can be learned through any other reliable medium; to give the news impartially, without fear or favor, regardless of party, sect, or interests involved; to make of the columns of *The New York Times* a forum for the consideration of all ques-

tions of public importance, and to that end to invite intelligent discussion from all shades of opinion.

There will be no radical changes in the personnel of the present efficient staff. Mr. Charles R. Miller, who has so ably for many years presided over the editorial page, will continue to be the editor; nor will there be a departure from the general tone and character and policies pursued with relation to public questions that have distinguished *The New York Times* as a non-partisan newspaper — unless it be, if possible, to intensify its devotion to the cause of sound money and tariff reform, opposition to wastefulness and peculation in administering public affairs, and in its advocacy of the lowest tax consistent with good government, and no more government than is absolutely necessary to protect society, maintain individual and vested rights, and assure the free exercise of a sound conscience.

ADOLPH S. OCHS.

NEW YORK CITY, *August 18, 1896.*

The foregoing was our invitation for public favor twenty-five years ago, and I reaffirm it today in the full conviction based on my experience that these are the proper principles that should be maintained in the conduct of a representative American daily newspaper.

ADOLPH S. OCHS.

NEW YORK CITY, *August 18, 1921.*

HISTORY OF THE NEW YORK TIMES

PART I

CHAPTER I

Beginnings of The Times, 1851-1859

IN a sense *The New York Times* is the result of an accident, or of a sequence of accidents. Sooner or later Henry J. Raymond and George Jones would have become partners in the production of a newspaper; and wherever or whatever that newspaper might have been, its character would have been fixed by the common ideals which these men held, as its prosperity would have been insured by their unusually fortunate combination of talents. But it was only a chance that this Raymond-Jones newspaper, whose early years established the standard and the character which *The Times* strives to maintain today, was *The New York Times* and not *The Albany Evening Journal*; and it took more accidents to bring Raymond and Jones together in 1851.

The acquaintance and friendship of the two men who directed *The Times* for the first four decades of its history began in the early forties, in the office of *The New York Tribune*. Jones, a native of Vermont, had come to New York and gone into business, and had been invited by Horace Greeley to become his partner in the establishment of *The Tribune* in 1841. Whether from a failure to realize the wider field for newspaper enterprise which was opening in New York, or from a well-grounded distrust of

CHAPTER I

Beginnings of The Times, 1851–1859

IN a sense *The New York Times* is the result of an accident, or of a sequence of accidents. Sooner or later Henry J. Raymond and George Jones would have become partners in the production of a newspaper; and wherever or whatever that newspaper might have been, its character would have been fixed by the common ideals which these men held, as its prosperity would have been insured by their unusually fortunate combination of talents. But it was only a chance that this Raymond-Jones newspaper, whose early years established the standard and the character which *The Times* strives to maintain today, was *The New York Times* and not *The Albany Evening Journal;* and it took more accidents to bring Raymond and Jones together in 1851.

The acquaintance and friendship of the two men who directed *The Times* for the first four decades of its history began in the early forties, in the office of *The New York Tribune.* Jones, a native of Vermont, had come to New York and gone into business, and had been invited by Horace Greeley to become his partner in the establishment of *The Tribune* in 1841. Whether from a failure to realize the wider field for newspaper enterprise which was opening in New York, or from a well-grounded distrust of

Greeley's business judgment, Jones refused; but he did take a place in the *Tribune* business office, and there not only acquired a thorough familiarity with what may be called the alimentary system of a newspaper, but formed a friendship with Raymond, who was Greeley's principal editorial assistant. Presently Raymond went over to *The Courier and Enquirer*, then edited by General James Watson Webb, and Jones later moved to Albany, where he engaged in the business of redeeming bank notes. In those days, when almost anybody could start a bank and issue paper money which might or might not have a solid reserve behind it, this was a somewhat hazardous occupation, but Jones made it profitable. His business ability commended itself to Thurlow Weed, who had become acquainted with Raymond both as a newspaperman and as a rising young Whig politician. In 1848 Weed wanted to get out of *The Albany Evening Journal*, and offered to sell it to the two friends. Raymond and Jones were willing, but one of Weed's partners would not let go, so the enterprise came to nothing. But it had shown Raymond and Jones that they were not alone in thinking that they could get out a pretty good newspaper. For the moment Raymond's chief attention was diverted to politics; he was elected to the Assembly in 1849 and became its Speaker two years later. But the idea of a Raymond-Jones newspaper never died thereafter.

In 1850 General Webb went to Europe and left Raymond in temporary charge of *The Courier and Enquirer*. Raymond not only failed to use his political influence to promote Webb's brief Senatorial

boom, but incurred his chief's disfavor by speaking out some plain truths on the slavery question in connection with the compromise proposals of that year. Raymond was not then, and never was till well along in the Civil War, an abolitionist; but he did not think that the more urgent question of the slave power in politics could be cured by ignoring it or by tame surrender. His independence got him into Webb's bad graces, and when Raymond went to Albany for the legislative session that winter he was eager to get away from Webb and start out for himself.

Jones was somewhat more reluctant to give up a business which he had made profitable, but it happened that a bill was then before the legislature which proposed to regulate the rate of bank-note redemption so severely that it would make the business entirely too hazardous for men of integrity. One day early in 1851, Jones and Raymond were walking across the Hudson on the ice when Jones observed that he had heard that *The Tribune* had made a profit of $60,000 — in those days an enormous sum — in the past year. This renewed Raymond's enthusiasm, and before they reached the other shore he had obtained Jones's promise to join him, if the redemption bill passed, in the establishment of a new daily in New York. The bill did pass. Jones closed up his business, and he and his business associate, E. B. Wesley, prepared to put their money, with Raymond's experience, into the new venture.

But if this series of accidents led directly to the establishment of *The Times*, it is nevertheless true that essentially the paper was brought into being to

fill a keenly felt want in the New York journalism of the day. The conditions which made possible the prosperity of *The Times* in the fifties were in general the conditions which opened the way for the spectacularly successful reconstruction of *The Times* in the nineties. In each case New York newspapers, numerous and varied as they were, had none the less left vacant a large and profitable part of the newspaper field; and in each case the demand for a certain kind of paper — a paper characterized under Raymond as under Ochs by the somewhat unpretentious but still popular qualities of moderation and decency — created the supply. In the fifties as in the nineties there were many newspaper readers in New York who wanted a paper which first of all gave the news, but which was not distorted by eccentricities of a personal editorial attitude or tainted by excessive attention to folly, immorality and crime. The character which Raymond gave to *The Times* — excellence in news service, avoidance of fantastic extremes in editorial opinion, and a general sobriety in manner — is the character which *The Times* has retained ever since, and which those now engaged in producing the paper hope it still retains.

There was a field for a sane and sensible newspaper in New York in 1851. The city had not yet recovered from its surprise at finding itself a great metropolis, with more than half a million people, already far beyond its old rivals of the Atlantic seaboard and obviously destined to still greater growth in the future. It was spreading rapidly, sprawlingly, with little attention to the manner of its extension;

its government was execrable, its civic beauties few and well concealed, its spirit still affected by the old small-town tradition. But it was growing; it was attracting new men by the thousands, ambitious young men like Raymond, from up-state; like Jones and others, many others, from New England. Those men were beginning the work of making New York, to which their most active and able successors of more recent times have done little more than add a few embellishments.

Both the old spirit and the new were reflected in the newspapers of New York. There still survived some excellent examples of the type of newspaper which had prevailed in the earlier decades of the century — the so-called blanket sheets, literally big enough to be slept under, especially by those who had tried to read them. They were massive, expensive, and dull; dignified if not respectable; content with a small circulation among gentlemen who had plenty of time, if not much inclination, for reading, and were willing enough to get around to this morning's news about the middle of next week. The new era began with the establishment of *The Sun* in 1833 — a paper which for the first time in America discovered the rudimentary literacy of the lower classes. *The Sun* of 1833, or even of 1851, was nothing like *The Sun* as made famous by Dana long afterward; it was filled for the most part with trivialities, and according to Augustus Maverick, Raymond's biographer, was read in 1851 chiefly by "domestics in quest of employment, and cartmen dozing at street corners in waiting for a job." But it had opened up a new field, and this field was

entered two years later by a much more interesting and much better newspaper, James Gordon Bennett's *Herald*.

Bennett was the inventor of almost everything, good and bad, in modern journalism. He was the first editor who gave his chief attention to the collection of news, and before long his competition had compelled all newspapers which made any pretension to influence to undertake unheard-of expenditures and to compete with him in the utilization of the railroad, the steamship, the telegraph and other new inventions just coming into use. In his salutatory to the public he disclaimed, among other things, "all principle, as it is called." His enemies and professional rivals — in the early days of *The Herald* the two terms were synonymous — would have said that he had merely rejected all good principles. Tammany Hall and slavery usually found *The Herald* on their side. Moreover, Bennett invented yellow journalism; he discovered and encouraged the popular taste for vicarious vice and crime, and before long respectable citizens who would have liked to read *The Herald* for the news felt constrained to exclude it from their homes for fear of its effect on the somewhat sensitive morals of the Victorian family.

It must be admitted that this "obscene" *Herald* which was regarded with such horror in the middle of the nineteenth century was not so very terrible, judged by the more elastic standards of our time. Every page of every issue bears the mark of Bennett's powerful and eccentric talent, and it undoubtedly did give more space to news of crime and human

error than its rivals; but it respected certain reticences which had passed into history before many of the night city editors of 1921 were born. However, moral standards were more exigent in those days, and Bennett's frank and premature cynicism probably contributed to the ill repute of his paper. In the forties good principles were exemplified by few, but professed by everybody but Bennett; and it was the shrinking of virtuous citizens from the loathsome newspaper whose editor dared to talk as most people acted that opened the way for Greeley's success with *The Tribune*.

When Greeley established *The Tribune* in 1841 Bennett had things pretty much his own way. Of the heavier and more conservative sheets *The Courier and Enquirer* was kept in the foreground by the aggressive and pugnacious personality of James Watson Webb, but none of these papers could vie with Bennett in popularity or financial success. *The Sun* had long since been beaten in its own field, and no one then foresaw its ultimate revenge in that recent and curious transaction wherein *The Herald* swallowed *The Sun*, and emerged from the process so exactly like *The Sun* as to furnish perhaps the best exemplification in history of the proverb, "Man ist was man isst." But Greeley soon gave Bennett real competition. In the first place, *The Sun* and *The Herald* leaned toward the Democrats, and Greeley first came forward to offer a cheap newspaper to the Whigs. Moreover, *The Tribune* as a newspaper was about as good as *The Herald*, and it carefully avoided all *The Herald's* offenses against the taste of the time. Yet *The Tribune* itself

soon incurred moral disapproval because of Greeley's advocacy of the principles of Fourieristic Socialism.

The chief characteristic of *The Tribune* under Greeley was an aggressive and even ostentatious purity. "Immoral and degrading police reports," and any notices of the existence of the theater, whether in news or advertising, were at first scrupulously excluded. Greeley appealed to man as he likes to pretend to be, Bennett to man as he is occasionally compelled to admit he really is. Greeley promoted temperance with a zeal equaled only by that other eminent moralist of the time, P. T. Barnum, and professed an intention to make *The Tribune*, though a penny paper, "a welcome visitor at the family fireside." Heads of families soon found it rather startling that a paper with such an ambition was becoming the vehicle of doctrines whose logical application would make the family obsolete. Greeley's Socialism was no doubt sincere — he seems to have been the type of man who was so sincere in everything he did as to make the impartial observer somewhat more tolerant of judicious hypocrisy — and certainly his observation of the panic of 1837, and of the struggles between Tammany and the local Whig machine for the control of the city government, might have justified him in concluding that no political and economic organization of society could be much worse than that which actually obtained. Fourierism was popular; Brook Farm, the Oneida Community, New Harmony, and hundreds of less known and less successful communistic experiments were being attempted in various parts of the country. Greeley's advocacy of the reorgani-

zation of society on the basis of the "social phalanx" was not hampered by any consideration of the difficulty of fitting a metropolitan newspaper with a large circulation into a state of phalangites, but doubtless he was taking only one step at a time, and saw no reason for crossing this bridge before he came to it. In the meantime Albert Brisbane, father of the better known Arthur Brisbane, and an eminent apostle of what Mr. Wells would doubtless call the Neanderthal type of Socialism, was allowed the run of *The Tribune*, and enjoyed the esteem of its editors.

Greeley, to be sure, was no more than what would now be called a parlor Bolshevik, but it was only natural that his professional and commercial rivals, in that acrimonious age, should suspect him of a willingness to acquiesce in the logical extension of his doctrines to other parts of the house. Despite his protests and denials, it suited the other newspapers of the city to regard him as the advocate of free love; and the controversy found fullest expression in the autumn of 1846, in an editorial warfare between Greeley and his old employé Raymond, then on *The Courier and Enquirer*. A dozen or so long articles were written on each side, and Raymond succeeded in proving, to the entire satisfaction of everybody who agreed with him, that the doctrines advocated by *The Tribune* not only would be destructive of property right, family affection, and political association, but were contrary to the teachings of revealed religion — an assertion which he evidently regarded as crushing, and which in 1846 undoubtedly was.

The Tribune prospered in spite of these handicaps; but there were a great many people who wanted the news as *The Tribune* printed it, without the sensational matter to be found in *The Herald*, and equally without the questionable and subversive doctrines which might be seen lurking beneath the chest-thumping morality of *The Tribune's* editorial page. To its enthusiasm for Socialism, moreover, *The Tribune* added a vigorous propaganda for Irish freedom, and the growing power of the Irish element in Tammany Hall had already aroused a certain reluctance, readily intelligible today, to allow New York City to be used as an overseas base for this hardy perennial conflict. To this public Raymond and Jones decided to appeal — not only because it was there and waiting for a paper suited to its taste, but also because its taste happened to be the taste of Raymond and Jones.

Raymond went to Europe for a vacation in the summer of 1851, after drawing up with Jones and Wesley the plans for the new paper. His own expression in a letter to his brother, dated from London in June, 1851, is modest enough — "Two gentlemen in Albany propose to start a new paper in New York early in September, and I shall probably edit it." This was undoubtedly the way it seemed to Raymond at the time, but it was Raymond's personality that made the paper's character at the outset, and in the Jubilee Supplement of *The Times*, issued in 1901, it was set down as the measured judgment of the editors of the paper that "*The Times* has always been at its best when its conduct approached most nearly to his ideal of a daily news-

paper." After Raymond's death circumstances compelled Jones to discover and display for a time his own very great talent as supervisor of the editorial policy of *The Times;* but for the eighteen years from its establishment to Raymond's death it was known to the country as Raymond's newspaper. Its virtues were largely his; its weakness was chiefly due to his one uncontrollable defect, an addiction to politics.

Raymond was born on a farm near Lima, N. Y., in 1820, and graduated from the University of Vermont in 1840. For a few months thereafter he supported himself in New York as a free lance newspaperman, but was about to give it up in despair and become a school teacher in North Carolina when Greeley, for whom he had done some writing on space, offered him a salary of eight dollars a week. It was Greeley who in later years, when Raymond was a rival editor, bestowed on him the title of "the Little Villain" — a mild enough epithet according to the standards of journalistic courtesy in the fifties; but Greeley in his more moderate moments liked Raymond, and said that "a more generally efficient journalist I never saw," and that Raymond was the only man who ever worked for him whom he had had to reprove for working too hard.

After three years with Greeley, Raymond went over to *The Courier and Enquirer*, and remained with that paper till plans had been made for the establishment of *The Times*. By that time, though only thirty-one, he was one of the best known and ablest newspapermen in New York. He was a small man, but pugnacious, as editors had to be in those

days. Though it was Raymond's fortune to begin his independent career after the close of the period when editors went about in momentary expectation (or meditation) of personal violence, he had occasion more than once to display not only moral but physical courage in defense of his principles. As a reporter and editorial writer he was remarkably gifted; his writing was rapid, his style clear; a rarer virtue in those times, his copy was legible. A feat recorded by his biographer, Maverick, who says he was an eyewitness, is here cited without comment: on the day of Daniel Webster's death Raymond wrote, in the late afternoon and early evening, sixteen columns of the obituary — in longhand, and without the aid of such material as a newspaper "morgue" now furnishes.

In his views on public questions Raymond was if anything too well balanced. He often lamented a habit of mind which inclined him to see both sides in any dispute. This may have hampered him as a politician, but on the whole it probably did *The Times* more good than harm. There were plenty of infuriated and vituperant newspapers in those days, and the success of *The Times* in the fifties showed that a considerable part of the public approved a measure of temperance in opinions on public affairs. To a certain extent, however, Raymond was really ahead of the time. His attitude toward the problems which led to and arose out of the Civil War, for example, is in almost every detail that which is approved by the judgment of history in so far as that judgment can ever be set down with certainty. He was a Whig in the early fifties, but not a bigoted Whig. He was not an abolitionist, but he believed that the domi-

nation of the federal government by the slave states in the interest of slavery — the domination of a majority by a minority — must be ended. In the middle of the decade he became a free-soil man and then one of the founders of the Republican party. During the war he was a bitter-ender, even in the dark days when better advertised patriots were willing to accept a peace without victory; but when the end was reached Raymond did his best to remove the bitterness. It would have been infinitely better for the whole country if Raymond and not Thaddeus Stevens had been allowed to lay down the reconstruction policy, and though Raymond went astray in thinking for a time that Andrew Johnson was all that a man in his position, with his enemies, ought to have been, the soundness of the principles which Raymond held and which Johnson rather spasmodically tried to apply has been demonstrated by the subsequent course of history.

There can be no doubt, however, that Raymond's preoccupation with politics distracted much of his attention from *The Times*, and the paper suffered heavily, though not for long, from his unpopularity in the early days of reconstruction. In the fifties it was not yet realized that the editor of a successful New York paper was a bigger man than the Speaker of the Assembly, or even the Lieutenant-Governor; yet it was characteristic of Raymond that when some of his friends wanted to put him up for Governor, in 1856, he refused for fear his aggressive record as a Whig might stand in the way of the rapprochement of free-soil Whigs and free-soil Democrats in the new Republican party.

Raymond has perhaps too hastily been called a political follower of Thurlow Weed and William H. Seward, and some writers have even regarded Weed as a sort of man behind the throne on *The Times*. It is a curious foible of a certain type of mind that it is unable to imagine a newspaper editor as one who may, on some public questions, honestly have the same view as that held by other persons. Unless he is absolutely unique and eccentric in his political opinions, he is presumed by certain critics to be bought or otherwise controlled by the people who agree with him. Raymond did indeed have a great respect for Weed's political judgment, a general agreement with Weed's political views, and a friendly relation with Weed himself. In his early political career he was in a sense a follower of Weed, just as he was a "follower" of Seward in 1860 to the extent of supporting him for the presidential nomination. But on many matters he disagreed with these gentlemen, and while their relative rank in political affairs was considerably higher than his in the fifties, Raymond's vigorous support of Lincoln gave him a personal influence during the Civil War that was due to Raymond alone. In 1864, as chairman of the Republican National Committee, he could hardly be described as a follower of anybody but Lincoln, who fully recognized his immense value in that year to the party and the nation.

Weed often and naturally came into the *Times* office to talk politics with Raymond, and no doubt to offer occasional thoughts on political journalism; but Raymond knew a good deal about politics and a good deal more about journalism, and would have

known it if he had never seen Weed in his life. For a short time just after the Civil War Weed was a contributor of political articles to the paper; but there seems to be no foundation for the theory that he was ever its dominating influence, or ever tried to be. Raymond was not so inhuman as to have no friends, or so original as to have no political associates, but he and he alone was editor of *The Times*.

On August 5, 1851, the association which was to publish the new paper was formed under the name of Raymond, Jones & Company. In August, 1860, the name was changed to H. J. Raymond & Company; and in July, 1871, after Raymond's heirs had sold out their holdings, to The New York Times. The stock was divided into a hundred shares, the nominal par value of which seems to have been set by tacit agreement at $1000. Raymond received twenty shares "as an equivalent for his editorial ability." Jones and Wesley had forty shares each "as an equivalent for their capital and business ability," but the actual cash investment then made was only $40,000, each man putting up half. When the paper was established in the following month the cash investment seems to have totaled $69,000. Jones and Wesley had already found it necessary to increase their own investment, and to give up some of the stock which was to have been an equivalent for their business ability in return for cash. At the outset Jones and Wesley held 25 shares each; J. B. Plumb, Daniel B. St. John, and Francis B. Ruggles five shares each, and E. B. Morgan and Christopher Morgan two shares each. The Morgan

interest, small as it was, has a considerable place in the *Times* history, for at a later crisis in the affairs of the paper (during the fight against Tweed), E. B. Morgan came in and bought the stock of the Raymond estate, thereby giving Jones invaluable security in his struggle with Tammany.

Raymond chose for the new paper the name of *The New-York Daily Times*, which had been borne in the thirties by a publication so short-lived that for all practical purposes the name was as good as new. A prospectus was already in circulation and had been published (as an advertisement) in the other dailies of the city. On the whole, and inevitably, the prospectus contained blameless generalities; *The Times* was going to include all that was good in both conservatism and radicalism, while avoiding the defects of either; it announced in firm tones its belief in the doctrines of Christianity and republicanism, which nobody in the United States except the Indians would in that day have denied; and it declared the intention of the publishers "to make *The Times* at once the best and the cheapest daily family newspaper in the United States." But along with these routine announcements there were one or two which meant something. *The Times* "is not established for the advancement of any party, sect or person." "It will be under the editorial management and control of Henry J. Raymond, and while it will maintain firmly and zealously those principles which he may deem essential to the public good, and which are held by the great Whig Party of the United States more nearly than by any other political organization, its

New-York Daily Times.

VOL. I.....NO. 1. | NEW-YORK, THURSDAY, SEPTEMBER 18, 1851. | PRICE ONE CENT.

New-York Daily Times.

THE NEW-YORK DAILY TIMES IS PUBLISHED EVERY MORNING (Sunday excepted,) at the office, No. 113 NASSAU-STREET, between Beekman and Ann, just behind the Old Park Theater, and delivered to subscribers in the city, Brooklyn, Williamsburgh and Jersey City for six cents a week; or, when they prefer they can pay in advance at the Desk for six months or a year at the same rate. Single copies, ONE CENT. Mail subscribers, FOUR DOLLARS a year.

THE NEW-YORK EVENING TIMES IS PUBLISHED EVERY EVENING, (Sundays excepted,) on the same terms as the Morning Edition.

THE NEW-YORK WEEKLY TIMES, A VERY LARGE NEWSPAPER FOR THE COUNTRY, is published every Saturday Morning, at the low price of $2 per annum. Ten copies for $15, or twenty copies for $20, will be sent to one address, and the paper in no case continued beyond the time for which payment is made.

Payment in all cases must be paid in advance.

RAYMOND, JONES & CO., Publishers.

New-York Daily Times.

THE NEWS FROM EUROPE.

ARRIVAL OF THE EUROPA'S MAILS.

AFFAIRS IN ENGLAND.

The Election in France—Arrests, &c.

APPREHENDED DISTURBANCE IN AUSTRIA.

SOUTHERN EUROPE.

The Royal Mail Steamer *Europa* arrived at Boston yesterday morning, at about 6 o'clock. Her mails were sent on by the New Haven Railroad train, which left at 8 o'clock, and reached this city at an early hour last evening.

By this arrival we have received our regular English and French files, with correspondence, circulars, &c., to Saturday, September 6th—the *Europa's* day of sailing.

The news by this arrival has considerable interest, though it is not of startling importance.

In ENGLAND, political affairs are quiet. The *Humboldt* arrived at Southampton on Thursday, the 4th, with the news of the execution at Havana of the fifty men under Col. Crittenden's command. The details of the news are given at length in the London papers.

In FRANCE attention is chiefly absorbed with speculations on the approaching Presidential election. The Prince de Joinville is clearly to be a candidate, and will doubtless be a more formidable opponent of Louis Napoleon than any other that could be selected.

Another "Conspiracy" has been discovered in Paris, forty-seven arrests have been made by the Police.

In AUSTRIA hostility to the government still smoulders under the surface with occasional outbreaks. An affray took place near Gross-Waradin, between a rustic wedding party and several *Gendarmes*, of the most brutal character.

In PORTUGAL attention is absolved by an accusation of a Cabinet Minister of bribery. He has resigned and come before the courts of law.

The news of KOSSUTH's release is confirmed, but the time is now said to have been the 13th of September. It is said that he proposes to go first to England and provide there for the education of his children and then proceed to the United States.

The money market presents no feature of marked interest.

GREAT BRITAIN.

The Queen was absent on her visit to Scotland where she had been very enthusiastically received. The Exhibition continues to attract numerous visiters. The attendance and receipts were:

Tuesday, ...	40,866 persons—	£2,407,15s.
Wednesday, ...	41,917 persons—	2,080,12s.
Thursday, ...	44,209 persons—	2,137,18s.

The necessity of reducing prices is strongly urged.

In Dublin it is stated that the Government intend to send four additional regiments of infantry from England, to enforce obedience to the law. The correspondent of *The Times* denounces this as simply preposterous.

The Freeman's Journal announces the death of one of the celebrities of the memorable year 1843, namely, the Rev. Thomas Tierney, one of the two clergymen included in the monster indictment of the then Attorney General, Mr. A. B. C. Smith. Up to 1843 he was one of the most active supporters of the Repeal movement headed by O'Connell.

DUBLIN, Sept. 4.—The weather has been extremely fine during the present week, and the agricultural reports from all parts of the country are proportionably favorable. In the south, harvest operations are nearly

the stern, the very act of the water in rising to supply the displacement would aid the impetus on the body of the vessel; and experiment tended to justify that expectation. The make of the *America*, we understand, is quite the *reverse* of that just described: the bows are sharp, and the breadth of beam, which is considerable, is greatest about parallel to the mainmast; so far coinciding with the other model. But the draught of water at the bows is trifling—about three feet; and it deepens to three times as much toward the stern.

The make is not conducive to great freightage capacity; yet its origin is commercial. American shippers have inclined lately to prefer speed to large capacity; as they find that rapidity, by facilitating certainty of movement and a multiplicity of voyages within a given time, returns a larger profit than slower and more uncertain voyaging with greater bulk. The model of the *America* is the result.

The good luck of the discovery has first fallen to the United States; but there is no room either for chagrin or dismay. Ship-building in this country is not stagnant; a considerable number of ships are made annually, and there can be no doubt that any well-tested model will soon find its way to our docks. We shall not therefore, be much behind in the practical progress of ship-building. Nor is it to be assumed, that because empiricism has beaten science, that the latter is to yield in despair. On the contrary, empiricism has always been the jackal to theoretic science, and every discovery by the working shipwright only brings us nearer to the desideratum—a scientific rule. We have heard an American express the hope that England, by beating America, would give the impulse for a new effort, which should again give his country a new triumph. Such friendly emulation is not rivalry: it is but the pride of him, who for the moment gets foremost in the search for the common good. A more invidious feeling would have kept the *America* at a distance from our waters: as it is, our friends hasten over, with a natural pride, to make us a party in the new idea.

From the London Examiner, Aug. 30.

The American challenge stipulating for at least a six-knot breeze, proves that the *America* must be a wholesome as well as a fast craft. A six-knot breeze with a dead beat in a head sea would be too much for many of our crack yachts, which, if they are brought to reducing sail, are overwhelmed by the excess of their masts and spars in a sea way.

The truth is, they are built for the inside of the Isle of Wight, and for owners who take to yachting for fashion's sake, knowing nothing about the matter, having no real taste for the sea, subject to sickness, and confining their trips to Hurst Castle to the west, Ryde and Portsmouth to the east, and preferring to them the Southampton water if a weather-tide raises a popple on the gentle Solent. The great pleasure of these gentlemen is to swagger about in sea-toggery, and to have boats'-crews in smart equipment dangling after them. Many a yacht hardly stirs from its moorings at Cowes in a whole season; but to make up for that inaction, there is plenty of boat-work, rowing backwards and forwards, hailing and signalling. There are exceptions; there are some score of the two hundred members of the Royal Squadron Club who are good seamen, ay, and competent navigators to boot but the great majority are unskilled. The other Clubs contain a much larger proportion of seamen among their members, because with them it is not a matter of fashion so much as it is with the aristocratic Squadron. Some years ago a member of the Thames Club undertook to man his yacht (between 60 and 70 tuns) with gentlemen, members of the Club, exclusively, not employing a single working-man, and to sail her against any vessel of the Squadron, manned in like manner; but the challenge fell to the ground. And well it might, for though there are some few members of the Royal Yacht Squadron who know whether a gaff-topsail is properly set or not, we have our doubts whether there is one who could go aloft and lace it to the topmast. But no matter how shallow the taste is, or how much is mere fashion, the fashion is a good one, and has excellent consequences susceptible of further improvement, which we trust the present lesson of the *America* will stimulate.

The veteran yachter, the Marquis of Anglesea, upon seeing the *America*, is reported to have remarked, "If she is right, we are all wrong."

It is to be borne in mind, however, that something besides speed is to be considered in the yacht. A yacht must have stowage and accommodation, and both these points are in the *America* sacrificed to speed. Still we have no doubt that something may be learnt from a craft which requires a six-not breeze, and beats our clippers; and it is her model, not her canvass, that must be looked to for the lesson.

Kossuth and Austria.

From The London Daily News, Sept. 2.

This is the day on which the Sultan promised to liberate Kossuth, Perczel, Bathyani, and the illustrious prisoners of Kutahia. Since the fact was first announced, as it was by us some weeks back, a regular fire of menace has been kept up by all the organs, or would-be organs of the great military governments. They would break with the Porte, the ambassadors should be withdrawn, retaliation taken by re-exciting the Bosnian

President will probably be left to the Assembly, which is not by any means well-disposed towards the present President.

The number of councils-general, which up to the present time have recorded resolutions in favor of the revision of the Constitution amounts to about sixty. Out of this number about fifteen have declared themselves in favor of the prolongation of the Powers of the President.

The council of war of Marseilles has just pronounced judgment on five men belonging to the 11th regiment of dragoons, who were tried for having excited their comrades to insubordination and revolt, in June last, at Orange. Four of them have been condemned to death, and the fifth acquitted.

P. S. 6½ o'clock.—For several days vague rumors of a plot, discovered in Paris, have prevailed. Last night a number of arrests were made, in relation to which I have just heard the following account. It has for some time been known to the police that Ledru Rollin and Mazzini's Central European Committee were in correspondence, through the Central German Committee of London, with a German committee sitting in Paris. A man named Meir was the delegate employed to transmit instructions to the Paris committee from the two committees in London. Besides this, an advocate, named Maillard, formerly secretary to Ledru Rollin, was instructed by the latter to organize an insurrectional committee in Paris, ready to take arms at a signal to be given by the Central European Committee of London. Such was the activity of Maillard that he had formed the nucleus of a society that had put itself in communication with the departments, and had made such progress as to be able to send to London within the last few days to take Ledru Rollin's final instructions.

It was on the return to Paris of the emissary sent on this occasion that the Prefect of Police informed the authorities that the time had come for putting a stop to all these proceedings. Warrants were issued simultaneously to arrest persons designated at St. Amand. Forty-seven arrests have been made. All the prisoners have been sent to the prison of Mazas, and this explains the reason why the Prefect of Police has within these few days sent away several prisoners who were there, in order to have vacant cells at his disposition.

The most prominent among the persons arrested are M. Dallcau, the director of *The Voix du Proscrit*, and M. Maillard, the advocate. The rest are obscure individuals, principally journeymen, tradesmen, and mechanics. One of them named J. J. Cherval, a lithographer, is described as an "Irish subject." Last night, at about 9 o'clock, 60 "Sergens de Ville" marched to the Café de la Haute-Saône, Rue Grenelle St. Honoré, where they arrested a dozen persons. Several brigades of police were sent in the night to different quarters of Paris, wich instructions to execute warrants of arrest. As many as 80 prisoners have already been sent to the Mazas prison.

It is said at the Palais de Justice that most important papers, emanating from the London Committees, have been seized.

Paris is absolutely quiet, and no alarm or even excitement has been produced in the public mind.

AUSTRIA.

VIENNA, Aug. 27.—The decrees of the Emperor on the responsibility of the ministers, and on the revision of the constitution, *octroyée* in March, 1849, amount to a complete retrogression to absolutism.

In Italy, Radetski fears an outbreak, and the army is said to be reinforced for the third time—ten thousand men are to march to the Piedmontese frontier. There is a report that the dissensions between the Croat and Hungarian soldiers are daily increasing, and that they led to a bloody conflict in the neighborhood of Verona. The papers remain silent on such events, but the letters from Italy mention it as a fact. In Hungary the gendarmerie had had several conflicts with the peasants, and a tragedy which in the month of June happened at Szent Maria, near Gross-Waradin, is soul-stirring, like an episode of a French novel. I relate it as I had it from an Hungarian gentleman of the Bihar county, who happened to be at Vienna.

At a peasant's wedding, when the procession of the betrothed was moving toward the church, the gendarme approached the bride and summoned her immediately to divest herself of the red, white and green ribbons which she had in her tresses, according to the custom of the country girls, saying that these colors were revolutionary. The bridegroom objected, saying that after the ceremony the bride would comply with the desire of the gendarme, but that now they could not keep the priest waiting at the altar. The gendarme retired, the procession proceeded to the church, but at the moment the bride was kneeling at the steps of the altar to receive the benediction, the gendarme rushed forward and cut her tresses and ribbons with scissors from her head. In Hungary it is considered a great insult to a female to cut her hair; it conveys the notion of infamy. Naturally an affray took place; the gendarme was assailed by the bridegroom, other gendarmes arrived in aid of their fellow-official, the people, though without arms, rushed upon them, and the result was the slaughter of seven men, three gendarmes and four peasants,

Von Flottwell, who made a speech in his capacity of royal commissioner. Count Arnim Boitzenburg, Marshal of the Diet, and chief of the party of the extreme right in the second chamber of Prussia, replied to M. Von Flottwell.

A letter from Berlin of the 29th ult., states that the minister of state, Von Thill, is dangerously ill. The Diet of the province of Prussia will meet on the 11th inst.

ITALY.

The Genoa Gazette announces from Cagliari that the levy of recruits in the Island of Sardinia has been effected without the slightest resistance, but that a serious affair occurred in the north of the island. It appears from this account that Major de Sant Elia, one of the recruiting commissaries, while on his way to Nulvi, with an escort of twelve dragoons, was attacked by a party of bandits, who fired four shots at him; his horse was wounded, and the flap of his coat pierced with a ball. Three of his escort were also wounded. The bandits have not been arrested.

The King of Naples, says *The Brussels Independent*, has just appointed a commission for the reform of the prisons in his kingdom. His Majesty, in order that the truth may be known, has requested several members of the *corps diplomatique* to follow the labors of this commission, and to visit, with its members, the different prisons in the city of Naples.

The Pope is about to erect the city of Hamburg into a bishopric.

The Opinione of Turin announces military evolutions on a large scale, representing the battle of Montenotte, which, in 1796, opened Italy to the invasion of the French. General La Marmora is entrusted with the general direction of the evolutions.

LOMBARDY.

The Milan Gazette of the 28th ult. announces that the brigadier of carabineers, who, in 1849, arrested Ugo Bassi, (the priest who acted as chaplain to Garibaldi's troops, and was shot by the Austrians,) has been assassinated at Comacchio.

TUSCANY.

The Tuscan Monitore publishes a series of regulations issued by the minister of worship at Florence on the 28th ult., concerning the right of censorship reserved to the bishops by the new concordat. By these regulations every bishop has the right of censorship over ecclesiastical works to be published within his diocese; a work rejected by one bishop cannot be approved by another, and there is no appeal from the decision of a bishop in such matters.

THE PAPAL STATES.

A dissolution of the Ministry has taken place, we learn, at Naples, and another Cabinet been formed. The names of the members of the new Administration had not been made public at the date of the last advices. [*Galignani.*

SWITZERLAND.

According to letters from Berne of the 29th ult., the damages caused in the canton by recent inundations are valued at 2,400,000 fr., or about £96,000. Subscriptions are open all over Switzerland to cover the losses of the inundation. The city of Berne has already subscribed 12,000fr.

ICELAND.

The Diet of Iceland was opened on the 5th July at Reikiavik. Amongst the bills presented was one enacting that from the 15th June, 1852, foreign vessels shall be allowed to enter the port of Reikiavik without passports of the authorities of the island, and shall be treated as Danish vessels.

Fugitive Slave Riot in Lancaster Co., Pa.

Our readers will be already advised of the occurrence of a lamentable riot and loss of life at Christiana, Lancaster Co., Pa., on the 9th inst.,—growing out of the attempted capture of two fugitive slaves by their owner.

In order to give the conclusion of this affair in an intelligible shape, a brief summary of the circumstances of the case may be necessary.

A party composed of Edward Gorsuch, of Baltimore county, Md., his two sons, Dickerson Gorsuch and Joshua Gorsuch, Dr. Thomas Pierce, Henry C. Kline, a Deputy Marshal, and two police officers from Philadelphia, started from Philadelphia, with a warrant issued by Edward D. Ingraham, United States Commissioner, to ... fugitive slaves

its severest penalty by the law of Pennsylvania. I am very proud that the first steps to detect and arrest these offenders have been taken by Pennsylvania officers.

Permit me, gentlemen, having thus removed all just cause of anxiety from your minds, respectfully to suggest that the idea of rebellion or "insurrectionary movement" in the county of Lancaster, or anywhere else in this commonwealth, has no real foundation, and is an offensive imputation on a large body of our fellow citizens. There is no insurrectionary movement in Lancaster county, and there would be no occasion to march a military force there, as you seem to desire, and inflame the public mind by any such strange exaggeration. I do not wish our brethren of the Union to think that, in any part of this State, resistance to the law goes undetected or unpunished, or that there exists such a sentiment as treason to the Union and the constitution.

The alleged murderers of Mr. GORSUCH, whose crime is deep enough without exaggerating it, have been arrested and will be tried, and they and their abettors will be made to answer for what they have done in contravention of the law. But in the meantime, let me invite your coöperation, as citizens of Pennsylvania, not only to see that the law is enforced, but to add to the confidence which we all feel in the judicial tribunals of the land, by abstaining from undue violence of language, and letting the law take its course. Depend upon it, gentlemen, there is in Lancaster county a sense of duty to the laws of the land, manifested in the easy and prompt arrest of these offenders, which will on all occasions shew itself in practical obedience.

The people of that county are men of peace and good order, and not easily led aside from the path of duty which the constitution prescribes. They and every Pennsylvanian love the constitution and the Union. They will detect, as they have done in this case, and arrest and punish all who violate the laws of the land. There is no warrant, depend on it, for representing the men of Lancaster county as traitors and participants in an "insurrectionary movement." You do them, unintentionally, I have no doubt, great injustice.

I am deeply indebted to you for affording me the opportunity of expressing my views. But for your communication, I might not have been able to do so. You, and my fellow citizens at large, may be assured of my firm determination at all hazards and under all circumstances, to maintain the supremacy of the constitution, and enforce obedience to the law, alike of the United States and of this commonwealth.

In order that I may be sure that my answer may reach its destination (your letter having but accidentally come to my hands,) I have requested Mr. White to put it in the hands of Mr. John Cadwallader, whose signature, I observe, is first. I am, with great respect,

your obedient servant,

WM. F. JOHNSTON.

The Baltimore Sun of yesterday, learns from a private source, that the Executive of Maryland, Gov. LOWE, will take immediate action upon the official information which he has received relative to the riot. A special messenger has already been despatched to the President with a communication on the subject.

A mulatto man, supposed to be the slave Pinkney, owned by Mr. Garsuch, was seen yesterday on the hills near Lancaster, and several citizens had gone in pursuit of him.

NEW-YORK CITY.

☞ The weather was the theme upon which we hinged an item for our morning edition, but we have been forced to forgo the infliction of it upon the public, by the proceedings of the Boston Jubilee, which our special correspondent has forwarded us. Never mind, the President cannot always be lionising through the country, and as soon as he returns home, we shall endeavor to do this important subject full justice.

DEATH OF A BAPTIST MISSIONARY. We regret to announce the death of Rev. WM. T. BIDDLE, of this city, who departed this life yesterday morning, at the house of Rev. John Dowling, D. D., where he was making a temporary home, in anticipation of his early departure for his field of labor in Burmah, at or near the station lately occupied by Rev. Dr Judson. The intelligence of Mr. Biddle's death will be received with deep regret by a wide circle of friends, who were looking to his future career with large hopes, warranted by the honor with which he acquitted himself at Hamilton University, where he has just graduated. He was married but a few weeks since, and in a few days was to have sailed for his future home in India. The funeral exercises were held at the Berean Baptist Church, cor. of Bedford and Downing streets, and were attended by a large and deeply affected audience.

☞ The Board of Assistant Aldermen closed their session for September, last evening. Our sketch of the proceedings is driven out by the Foreign News, but we are consoled by the reflection that our readers will find a full record of their doings in *The Evening Times*, which will be published at 4 o'clock this afternoon.

☞ The Fountain in Washington Square gets on towards completion with moderate speed. It is to be a very large circular basin, with a central jet and several side jets. The excavation is made, the wall around the border of the basin is nearly done, and the workmen were yesterday laying a bottom of hard plaster. The fountain will be a very fine one, and will increase greatly the attraction of this beautiful park.

NEW STEAMBOAT LINE.—The staunch little steamer, the C. Durant, has been placed on the East River, to run between this city and Flushing, touching at Astoria and Strattonport, by Mr. Flanner, the enterprising proprietor of the latter village. The fare has been reduced to one shilling, and the boat is to make two trips each way a day, and is to be a permanent arrangement. We hail with pleasure every new enterprise that will bind the Metropolis and the quiet and beautiful rural districts in its closer contact.

DEATH IN A CELL.—At a late hour on Tuesday night, policeman Coulter, of the Fourth Patrol District, found an unknown female, aged 35 years, lying in Madison-st., laboring under the effects of delirium tremens, and apparently lifeless. A dray was procured, and the poor woman was conveyed to the Station-house, where she seemed to somewhat revive, but was yet under the influence of strong drink, and was accordingly placed in a cell in the female department, where she was found a corpse in about two hours after. Yesterday morning the Coroner held an inquest on the remains, and the jury rendered a verdict of "Death by an apoplectic fit."

DEATH FROM CONVULSIONS.—The Coroner held an inquest yesterday, at the Bellevue Hospital, upon the body of a young woman named Sarah Carr, born in New-York, and aged 21 years, who, it appears, was admitted into the above institution on the 15th inst., in a fit of convulsions, and after lingering a few hours, died from the effects of the same. A verdict was rendered in accordance with the foregoing facts.

☞ A Bloomer Costume made its appearance in Sixth-avenue day before yesterday. A crowd of "Conservatives" manifested their hostility to this progressive movement by derision. "New ideas" are compelled to wage fierce battle in this world before they obtain recognition and favor. Two Bloomers appeared in Broadway and two in Washington square yesterday.

☞ It has been stated that Senator Douglass was too ill to fulfil his engagement, to deliver the oration at the State Fair. We understand that he has so far recovered from his indisposition, that he left for Rochester last evening.

FALSE ALARM.—The Hall bell rang an alarm at 9 o'clock last evening for the Sixth District, but our item gatherer failed to discover the first spark of a fire.

ANOTHER.—About 2 o'clock there was an alarm in the Second District—but the fire was not visible.

WOMAN POISONED.—Coroner Geer was called yesterday to hold an inquest on the body of a married woman by the name of Mrs. Eliza Knecht, lying dead at her late residence, No. 204 Seventh-street. A jury was was empanneled, and the first witness sworn was Mr. Leonard Smith, a resident of the same house, who deposed that deceased had been married about nine months, and that the husband only lived with her the first four weeks after they were united, since which time he had been absent until Sunday afternoon last, at 4 o'clock, when he called upon his wife and remained with her during the night; he then states that she was seized with violent pains and cramps at 11 o'clock that (Sunday) night, and was in great distress; her husband remained with her till Tuesday morning and then left, at which time she was apparently beyond all hopes of recovery, and continued to labor under severe convulsions. Dr. Ruppenrecht, residing at No. 21 Avenue B., was next called, and deposed, in substance, as follows: I was called, on Tuesday morning, to visit deceased, and was informed that she was on the eve of confinement; but upon examination, found that no symptoms of that nature exhibited themselves, but discovered that she was laboring under severe and repeated convulsions, and all efforts to save her life proved of no avail, and she died at 5½ o'clock on Tuesday evening. I then made a *post-mortem* examination and found the stomach in a high state of inflammation, and all her internal organs exhibiting signs of poison. The medical gentleman then closed his testimony, by saying,

columns will be free from bigoted devotion to narrow interests." For a party politician and office-holder to admit that his party could conceivably fall short of perfection was a novelty in the fifties.

Moreover, "while it will assert and exercise the right freely to discuss every subject of public interest, it will not countenance any improper interference, on the part of the people of any locality, with the institutions, or even the prejudices, of another."

There was a reason for this. During the summer there had been many rumors about the new paper, and the motive of its founders was set down as almost everything but what it really was — to establish a new paper that would publish, as a later motto of *The Times* put it, "all the news that's fit to print," a phrase which exactly expresses the intentions of Raymond and Jones. It suited Raymond's political and journalistic enemies to accuse him of being an abolitionist, and the apprehensive rivals of the new paper tried to discredit it by asserting in advance that it was going to further the doctrine of abolition, or the presidential candidacy of General Scott, or the presidential candidacy of some other dignitary, or anything else that might seem likely to bring it into disrepute. The motive of this was clear enough even at the time; for the established newspapers made the same efforts to hamper the circulation of *The Times* that had been tried successively on *The Sun*, *The Herald*, and *The Tribune* — and with no more effect. New York was growing so fast that the extraordinary prosperity which attended *The Times* almost from the outset brought no real injury to any of its important rivals;

for years thereafter they all grew and prospered together.

These attacks had given the paper a good deal of free advertising, which was soon turned to good account. Raymond had collected the nucleus of an excellent staff — several reporters and editors, and a dozen employés of the mechanical departments, left the *Tribune* in a body to come over to the new paper — and despite the unreadiness of the building at 113 Nassau Street which had been rented as the first home of the paper, it appeared eventually only two days later than the date promised in the prospectus. "On the night of the 17th of September [1851]," says Maverick, "the first number of *The Times* was made up, in open lofts, destitute of windows, gas, speaking tubes, dumb waiters, and general conveniences. All was raw and dismal. The writer remembers sitting by the open window at midnight, looking through the dim distance at Raymond's first lieutenant, who was diligently writing brevier" [editorial copy, so called from the name of the type in which it was set] "at a rickety table at the end of the barren garret; his only light a flaring candle, held upright by three nails in a block of wood; at the city editor, and the news-man, and the reporters, all eagerly scratching pens over paper, their countenances half lighted, half shaded, by other candles; at Raymond, writing rapidly and calmly, as he always wrote, but under similar disadvantages."

The first number of *The Times* on the streets the following morning contained an editorial article (by Raymond, of course) headed "A Word About

Ourselves," and beginning with the declaration: "We publish today the first number of *The New York Daily Times*, and we intend to issue it every morning (Sundays excepted) for an indefinite number of years to come." This salutatory contained a promise which was soon justified by performance: "We do not mean to write as if we were in a passion, unless that shall really be the case; and we shall make it a point to get into a passion as rarely as possible. There are very few things in this world which it is worth while to get angry about; and they are just the things that anger will not improve." There was rather more anger than was needful in most of the New York papers of that period, especially in their editorial controversies with each other. Yet it is pleasant to record that editorial ethics in this city have shown a steady improvement. In the earlier decades of the nineteenth century editors were compelled by public opinion to back up their tirades against each other by appearances on the field of honor. By the time of Greeley and Bennett this practise, which made an already hazardous occupation somewhat too troublesome for comfort, was dying out, and the ethics of the period permitted rival editors to fight out their quarrels with walking sticks or horsewhips when they met on Broadway, instead of taking to pistols and the Weehawken ferry. And in 1851 even horsewhipping was beginning to go out of fashion. No doubt an argument could be made out for this custom, in theory, but as a practical measure it did not seem to moderate editorial passions, though not everybody was as unconcerned as Bennett, who published

the account of one of his own unfortunate personal encounters in *The Herald* under the heading, "Horse-whipped Again."

By 1851, however, the traffic on Broadway had become so heavy that it was impossible to hold it up while rival newspaper proprietors belabored each other with malacca sticks, and emotion had to be expressed on the editorial page. There, to be sure, it flourished with intensity; "vile wretch," "profligate scoundrel," and "infamous reprobate" were terms commonly employed as designations of professional colleagues, and for decades thereafter the newspapers gave a good deal more editorial attention to each other's misfortunes and shortcomings than the relative importance of the topic deserved. Today, aside from one or two publications whose ethical standards are palaeolithic in other respects as well, the newspapers of New York usually have sufficient self-restraint to conceal their opinions of each other, and devote such editorial reference as they make to criticisms of specific views of a contemporary rather than to animadversions on its editor's personal appearance and moral character. No doubt this mollification of manners is all for the best, but veteran editorial writers complain that it has taken a good deal of the fierce joy out of the newspaper business.

The Times was by no means wholly free from controversies with its rivals, but except in one or two instances it did not carry this practise so far as was the custom, and thereby gave a pleasing instance to New York newspaper readers of the possibility of filling up a newspaper without recourse to the

material of personal quarrels. Raymond was only once challenged to fight a duel (by an indignant Irish patriot) and a little diplomacy got him honorably out of that.

This paper which was produced under the difficult conditions described by Maverick consisted of four pages, of six columns each. The page was about a third shorter and a third narrower than a page of today's *Times*. There were morning and evening editions — the latter published at one and three o'clock in the afternoon; but there was only one *Times*. Neither the office files nor the memory of the oldest living members of the staff furnish much information about these evening editions, but apparently they contained merely the news arriving after the paper went to press at midnight, with the editorial, advertising and other features persisting in all editions. The evening editions, in other words, took the place of, and in time were supplanted by, the second, third and later editions which the improvement of newspaper mechanics presently made it possible to issue before daylight.

There was also in the beginning, and for years thereafter, a *Weekly Family Times*. Every daily paper had to have a weekly in those days for circulation on the farm, and in the case of *The Tribune* at least the weekly was largely responsible for Greeley's great influence. But with the extension of railroads it eventually became possible to get the daily paper circulated over a much larger part of the country than was possible in 1851, and after a long and respectable career the weekly edition of *The Times* was finally discontinued in the late seventies.

A *Semi-weekly Times*, chiefly for rural readers, lasted some years longer.

There was, besides, in the early days, a *Times for California*, put together whenever a mail boat happened to be sailing for San Francisco; and a *Campaign Times* issued in presidential years. *The Times for California* passed away with the rise of the California press, and the campaign edition, which was a weekly, died out for the same reason as *The Weekly Family Times*.

From the beginning *The Times* was a good newspaper. The first page of the first number is a good specimen of the art of newspapermaking as understood in 1851. In the first column, under the "masthead" containing the terms of subscription, and so on, is the heading, "The News from Europe." Single-column headlines were the invariable rule then, of course, as they were until a much later period; and the descriptive headline had not yet been invented. "The news from Europe" is preceded by a short summary, the opening lines of which illustrate the method of obtaining foreign news in that day:

> The Royal Mail steamer *Europa* arrived at Boston yesterday, at about six o'clock. Her mails were sent on by the New Haven railroad train, which left at 9 o'clock, and reached this city at an early hour last evening.
>
> By this arrival we have received our regular English and French files, with correspondence, circulars, etc., to Saturday, September 6 — the *Europa's* day of sailing.

> The news by this arrival has considerable interest, although it is not of startling importance.

Then follows a brief summary of the news, and after that the news itself, under the headings "Great Britain," "France," etc. — most of it taken from the London papers. There are some three and a half columns of European news; then a column about a fugitive slave riot at Lancaster, Pennsylvania; the rest of the page is filled with brief local items, ending with perhaps a quarter of a column from Brooklyn. At the head of the local news is this paragraph:

> The weather was the theme upon which we hinged an item for our morning edition, but we have been forced to forego the infliction of it upon the public, by the proceedings of the Boston Jubilee, which our special correspondent has forwarded us. Never mind, the President cannot always be lionizing through the country, and as soon as he returns home we shall endeavor to do this important subject full justice.

Other local items include the announcement that "the fountain in Washington Square gets on toward completion with moderate speed," and reports of the appearance of the bloomer costume in Greenwich Village. Two or three fires are chronicled, and under the heading of "False Alarm" *The Times* announces:

> The Hall bell rang an alarm at 9 o'clock last evening for the Sixth District, but our item-gatherer failed to discover the first spark of a fire.

It must be recorded with regret that *The Herald's* "item-gatherer" did find that fire; but this did not establish a precedent. *The Times's* merits soon forced its way to recognition, and the circulation soon began to approach that of *The Herald* and *The Tribune*. Reviewing the first year of the paper on September 18, 1852, Raymond said that "it has been immeasurably more successful, in all respects, than any newspaper of a similar character ever before published in the United States." So far as public esteem was concerned that was unquestionably true, but if Raymond had stopped to consult Jones and Wesley he might have said "in all respects but one." *The Times* was not yet paying its way. Fifty thousand dollars had been spent at the outset for mechanical equipment. Newsprint paper was then as now the heaviest drain on the treasury (though, as paper, it was a good deal better in those days); of *The Times's* first-year expense more than half — $40,000 — was spent for paper; $25,000 for the wages of the mechanical and business departments; $13,000 on correspondents, editors, and reporters. The circulation at the end of the year was more than 26,000 — a figure highly creditable, in the circumstances; but the small size of the paper restricted the space available for advertising, rates were accordingly high, and advertisers saw no reason for paying extra to appear in *The Times* when they could reach as many readers for less money in the *Tribune*, *Sun* or *Herald*.

The stipulations of the articles of incorporation as to the division of profits were so far a mere exercise in fantasy. Raymond as editor of the paper

HENRY J. RAYMOND.

received a salary of $2500 a year; Jones and Wesley had had only the privilege of putting in more money. But with the second year *The Times* took the plunge and doubled its size. It also doubled the price, going up to two cents a copy, and the circulation at once shrank from 26,000 to 18,000. But the extra pages gave room not only for more advertising, but for more news, and before long the loss in circulation had been more than made up. In 1857 *The Times* claimed a circulation of 40,000.

Jones had managed the business during the first year, but then was constrained to take a trip to Europe on account of his health. Wesley had charge of the business office for some time thereafter, but in 1853 Fletcher Harper, Jr., was installed as publisher, having purchased some of Jones's and some of Wesley's stock. Harper, it seems, did not get along with the other partners, and in 1856 he sold out to them. By that time the paper was prospering; it appeared in some litigation in connection with this sale that the dividends were $20,000 a year, and Jones and Wesley paid $1666 a share for Harper's stock, the par value of a share being $1000.

Wesley sold out his interest in September, 1860, to Raymond and Leonard W. Jerome, the latter of whom served as "consulting director" until 1870. After Harper's departure, however, Jones had resumed the management of the business office, and the prosperity thus early established continued unbroken, under his direction, for more than a quarter of a century.

The Times's reputation for balance was almost upset only three months after its establishment,

when Louis Kossuth came to New York to find in America, if he could, "material aid" for the renewal of the Hungarian struggle against Austria. Magyar-Americans of today may be surprised to learn that in 1851 the *Times* was the principal champion in America of the Magyar cause, but the Hungary of 1849 was not the Hungary of 1914. Raymond's enthusiasm over Kossuth — whose reception everywhere in America was remarkably favorable, and whose progress excited almost as much public interest as the movements of Joffre in 1917 — was unquestionably genuine, and sprang from a love for the principles of liberty and nationalism, for which Hungary had lately fought so gallantly. Also, it must be admitted, the arrival of Kossuth was the first big local news story after the foundation of *The Times*, and it was necessary to show New York what the new paper could do. As a result readers of *The Times* often found that of their twenty-four columns of news and advertising three or four would be devoted to a speech by Kossuth (sometimes with the postscript, "Remainder tomorrow") and another column or so to an account of his doings.

Nevertheless, the virtual adoption of Kossuth and Hungary by *The Times* was probably a good thing for the paper. Kossuth himself, after his return to Europe, acted for a time as London correspondent; and during his stay here Raymond was enabled to defend him — a grateful labor it must have been, too — against James Watson Webb, whose newspaper had taken on itself the function of advocate of the Hapsburgs and Romanoffs. The conflict between the two came to a head at a dinner given

by the city to Kossuth on December 11, 1851, where Raymond had been appointed to respond to the toast: "The Press — the organized Voice of Freedom — it whispers hope to the oppressed, and thunders defiance at the tyrant." As Raymond rose to respond to the toast and express the sentiment of the company, Webb also rose, of his own accord. From the editorial attitude of his paper it was clear that he was going to whisper hope to the tyrant, and thunder defiance at the oppressed. There was a good deal of confusion, and Webb was finally suppressed by the police. Raymond delivered his speech, and then entreated the audience to hear Webb on the other side; but Webb's remarks were drowned by hisses and hoots, and he was compelled to save them up and print them in his paper next day.

On another occasion in that first year Raymond's aggressive personality brought himself and his paper into prominence. The Whig National Convention met at Baltimore in June, 1852. Like the national conventions of both parties for years past, it was dominated by a vigorous and truculent group of southern leaders who were determined that neither the platform nor the candidate should be suspected of hostility to the extension of the "peculiar institution." Fillmore was generally favored by the southern delegates, General Winfield Scott by the northern; with a little group of willful men sticking to Daniel Webster.

The southerners had their way in every detail of organization and in the writing of the platform, but the northern leaders expected that their complaisance in this respect would be met by southern

acceptance of Scott's candidacy. Raymond, who was present as the chief correspondent of *The Times*, mentioned this expectation in a dispatch to the paper during the balloting, and added, "If Scott is not nominated, they will charge breach of faith on the South." This was promptly telegraphed back to James Watson Webb from his paper in New York, and Webb at once gave the dispatch (which had somewhat misrepresented Raymond's language) to some of the southern leaders. The balloting for a candidate was interrupted on the last day by a demand for the expulsion of Raymond from the convention as the author of an infamous and false attack on the integrity of the delegates.

For Raymond was by this time a delegate, having been chosen by the New York representatives to take the place of a man who had gone home. At the time this was represented as a mere accident; but it appears to have been done with intent. Some of the northern leaders were disgusted and ashamed at their continual humiliations at the hands of the southern fire-eaters; and knowing Raymond as a brilliant orator of unquestioned courage, they had told a delegate from Oswego to go home and give his seat to Raymond. The offending dispatch and the intrusive Webb were consequently more or less accidental provocatives of a fight already arranged, to which both sides were looking forward — the southerners with confidence, the New Yorkers with trepidation.

Raymond's speeches on this occasion were a good example of his manner. At the beginning they were mild, conciliatory, almost evasive; he disclaimed any intention to charge a bargain between North

and South; he had merely expressed his own opinion. But then he exploded into a declaration that he would assert and continue to assert his opinion that if the South did not meet the North halfway its delegates would be justly open to charge of a breach of faith, and he, Raymond, would charge them with it "here and everywhere." Then he turned on one Cabell, of Florida, a veteran bravo of the debating platform, who had volunteered to "put the Abolitionist in his place." In a moment Raymond had Cabell indignantly declaring to the chairman, "Sir, I cannot, I shall not, submit to language of that kind." Raymond replied, "Permit me to tell the gentleman from Florida that when he puts words into my mouth which I have not used, for the purpose of founding an accusation upon me, he will submit to whatever language I may see fit to use in repelling his aspersions."

It was the first time in many years that a northerner had dared to use such language toward a representative of the southern oligarchy. According to southerners present, this speech "not only annihilated Cabell at the convention, but he never got rid of its damaging effects when he got home." And a writer, evidently an eyewitness, who gave an account of the episode in *The Albany Evening Journal* after Raymond's death, observed:

> From that hour the Whig Party assumed a new character, and its representatives (with a few disgraceful exceptions) a bolder attitude. . . . Mr. Raymond's clarion voice, on that memorable occasion, sounded the opening notes in the death knell of slavery.

This incident deserves some notice for the reason that in those early years Raymond's career was so largely identical with the history of *The Times*. But it was not altogether so. In 1854 the Kansas-Nebraska Act had begun to split both parties at the North, and was preparing the way for the great organization which carried Lincoln to the White House only six years later. Raymond was nominated for Lieutenant-Governor by the Whig state convention in 1854 (to the great disgust of Greeley, who had wanted the office), but he had already been present as a delegate at an Anti-Nebraska convention, which accepted the regular nominations that had been forced largely by its threat of secession. The Whigs carried the state by a few hundred votes, and Raymond ran a few hundred more ahead of the gubernatorial candidate; but the editorial attitude of *The Times* was reserved during the campaign, and it certainly was never used to promote its editor's political fortunes.

Two years later Raymond's friends wanted him to become a candidate for Governor, but, as already related, he refused. Whigs and Democrats were uniting in the organization of a new party to prevent the further extension of slavery, and Raymond did not want his personality, or any recollection of old animosities either between parties or among Whigs, to stand in the way of that movement. The Republican party, as a national organization, had been established at an informal convention held at Pittsburgh in February, 1856, a convention which gave the call for the Philadelphia convention in June that nominated Fremont. Raymond was

at Pittsburgh and wrote the long confession of faith on which the Republican party was established — an able and convincing document, which showed no sympathy with the abolitionists, but did express the determination of moderate northerners to end the domination of public life by southern terrorism. This declaration, some 10,000 words in length, was telegraphed from Pittsburgh and published in *The Times*, but there was little in the paper about the doings of the Pittsburgh convention, and no editorial comment till long after Raymond's return. In the campaign of 1856 *The Times* and Raymond took a prominent part, and from that time on for twenty-eight years *The Times* stood in the front rank of the Republican journalism of the country; but whatever neglect the institution might have been able to charge against its editor when he strayed aside into politics, it could never have accused him of making the paper an instrument of propaganda or a means to personal advancement.

Newspaper mechanics was an infant art in the fifties, and the papers of those days of course differed greatly in contents and make-up from those of today. Whether all the changes have been for the better or not is to be doubted. Considering the conditions, *The Times* in the fifties was an excellent newspaper — so for that matter were *The Herald* and *The Tribune*. The telegraph was coming into more and more general use, but still was something of a novelty, and an expensive novelty. "The latest by telegraph" was a heading apt to stand over a column or two of brief and heterogeneous items

from everywhere, with most of the details coming along later by mail.

Local news was written much more in the editorial manner than is common today. If a reporter was writing about a spade he called it a spade, instead of describing it generally as an agricultural implement, or referring the responsibility for calling it a spade to the District Attorney. Sometimes, naturally, he was apt to apply the offensive designation of spade to something which was a mere trowel, and the local news probably lost in impartiality what it gained in piquancy. The editorial page was more opinionated, and more violent in the expression of opinion, than civilized editorial pages today. But, allowing for the different manners of the time, it can hardly be doubted that, however primitive the newspapermen of that time may have been, they had a keen scent for news.

An example from the early history of *The Times:* In September, 1854, the steamer *Arctic* was sunk in a collision in the North Atlantic, with a loss of several hundred lives. Rumors of the disaster had been prevalent for several days, after the steamer's failure to arrive had excited apprehension, but not till the night of October 10th did these rumors become precise. Even then nobody could find responsible authority for the report that the *Arctic* had been sunk, and the night city editor of *The Times,* having "put the paper to bed," climbed on a horse car to go home in the early morning hours, thinking that nothing more could be done. By one of those pieces of good luck which do happen to newspapermen more often than a skeptical world believes,

The New-York Times.

VOL. VII......NO. 2155. NEW-YORK, TUESDAY, AUGUST 17, 1858. PRICE TWO CENTS.

THE OCEAN TELEGRAPH.

VICTORY AT LAST!

THE FIRST MESSAGE.

ENGLAND GREETS AMERICA

QUEEN VICTORIA TO PRESIDENT BUCHANAN.

THE PRESIDENT'S REPLY.

TRIUMPHANT COMPLETION OF THE GREAT WORK OF THE CENTURY.

The Old World and the New United.

GLORIA IN EXCELSIS.

The Message of Queen Victoria to President Buchanan.

To the Honorable the President of the United States.

Her Majesty desires to congratulate the President upon the successful completion of this great international work, in which the Queen has taken the deepest interest.

[NOTE.—The above Message was received by the President, with some doubts as to its authenticity; but the matter was relieved of all doubt by the following message from the Superintendent of the Newfoundland Line:]

TRINITY BAY, Monday, Aug. 16—7 P. M.

for the *Niagara*. As soon as the substance of the Queen's dispatch was known, there was a display of fire-works from the Pewter Mug.

How the News Was Received Elsewhere.

WASHINGTON, Monday, Aug 16.

The intelligence of the reception of the Queen's Message rapidly spread throughout the city, and this evidence of the successful working of the Atlantic Telegraph occasioned much rejoicing. In some quarters, however, its authenticity was questioned, until a dispatch from the General Agent of the Associated Press removed all doubts. The first information on the subject to the President was communicated through Senator BIGLER, from information obtained from the Washington Associated Press Agency, when the President returned to the city from the Soldiers' Home, and received at the White House the message from Her Majesty Queen VICTORIA. He then prepared a suitable reply.

The Mayor of Washington, this afternoon, sent a message to the City Councils recommending that measures be taken to celebrate the success of the Atlantic Telegraph. Special Committees are appointed to agree on the programme.

BOSTON, Monday, Aug. 16.

The successful working of the Atlantic Telegraph will be celebrated in this city to morrow, as follows: One hundred guns will be fired on the Common, at noon, and all the bells in the city rung. In the evening, the trees on the Common will be hung with French and Chinese lanterns; all the city buildings will also be illuminated, and four bands of music will discourse music on the Common. The citizens generally will also illuminate their residences.

ALBANY, Monday, Aug. 16—10½ P. M.

There is immense excitement here owing to the receipt of the Queen's Message. As soon as the intelligence reached the city, rockets were fired from opposite the telegraph office, bonfires blazed in all the streets, and the greatest rejoicing prevailed. Cannons are now being fired and the bells are ringing.

PHILADELPHIA, Monday, Aug. 16.

A salute of one hundred guns will be fired here at seven-o'clock to-morrow morning, and all the bells rung, in honor of the successful working of the Ocean Telegraph.

NEWBURG, N. Y. Aug. 16—10 P.M.

The news of the successful working of the Atlantic Cable and of the receipt of the Queen's Message was received here with frantic demonstrations of joy. The bells were rung, cannon fired, steam whistles blown, and the most jubilant excitement prevailed.

UTICA, N. Y., Monday, August 16th.

There was a general exultation here on the receipt of the Queen's Message. Cannons and bells and cheers gave utterance to the general joy, while bonfires were lighted everywhere. The *Herald* office was brilliantly illuminated, and the whole city is alive with enthusiasm and rejoicing.

BUFFALO, N. Y., Monday, August 16.

The receipt of the Queen's Message caused great excitement throughout the City. St. Paul's chimes, together with all the church and fire bells are ringing. Crowds congregate in the streets, and immense enthusiasm prevails. Preparations for a grand illumination are in progress.

ELMIRA, Monday, Aug. 16—10 P. M.

Bells are ringing, cannons firing, and manifestations of joy are on the lips of every man, woman

the first fruit of the united labors of the American and English naval officers.

JOSEPH DAYMAN,
Com. of H. M. S. S. Sloop *Gorgon*.

HALIFAX, Saturday, Aug. 14, 1858.

C. T. MCCLENACHAN, Secretary of Committee of the Common Council, New York.

SIR: Your telegraphs of yesterday have both reached me. I am much flattered by the invitation of the Common Council of the City of New York to be present at the celebration of that great and most important achievement which has just been accomplished, and it is with much regret that I find myself compelled to decline the distinguished honor, my duties demanding my services elsewhere. With respect to the *Gorgon*, I have already signified to Mr. FIELD my inability to interfere in any way with Capt. DAYMAN'S proceedings. He is not under my orders; I have no notice whatever concerning him, and he has instructions direct from the Admiralty, by which he must be guided. I beg you will convey my grateful acknowleogments to all the members of the Common Council, together with my cordial good wishes for the successful issue of their intention to commemorate an event which I earnestly hope will materially tend to cement those feelings of amity and good-will which ought ever to prevail between the United States and Great Britain.

HOUSTON STEWART.

Messrs. LILIENDAHL and HADFIELD were present, and said they could not agree as to which of them should display the centre piece of fireworks in front of the City Hall. Neither of them was willing to exhibit in any other situation, nor could they combine to display the same evening at the same place.

Alderman MCSPEDON said that, prior to any offer having been made by either of these gentlemen, the Committee, in view of the short time originally expected to transpire before the arrival of the Queen's message, had ordered of Mr. EDGE a certain quantity of fireworks, displaying peculiar designs and mottoes, and had paid for, or were liable to pay for them. It was to be regretted that these voluntary offers of pyrotechnic displays had not been made to the Committee a little earlier, as it would have saved expense.

A communication was received from F. GENIN, Jr., desiring the Committee to use show-wagons with proper emblems in the procession. Ordered on file.

The Committee then adjourned until next day, having first allowed Messrs. LILIENDAHL and HADFIELD to arrange their dispute respecting their fireworks as they themselves might best be able.

Celebration at Fairfield, Conn.—Speech of the Rev. Dr. Osgood, of New-York.

From the Bridgeport Advertiser.

A large and enthusiastic meeting was held in Fairfield on Thursday evening, August 12, in honor of the laying of the great Cable that now binds together the two hemispheres. The festivities began early with the ringing of bells and the firing of cannon. A spacious platform had been erected in front of the Fairfield House, so as to command the beautiful square, which was brilliantly illuminated with bonfires. The building was thronged with a genial company of ladies and gentlemen, and the street and square were all alive with the eager assembly.

JOHN H. GLOVER called the meeting to order, and nominated for President of this meeting Colonel ROBERT C. WETMORE, which was confirmed by acclamation, when the following gentlemen were elected Vice-Presidents: John Gould, Esq., Wm. R. Talbot, Esq., Henry M. Smith, Esq., Henry J. Beers, Esq., Dr. J. T. Dennison, Wm. S. Smith, Esq., and Frederick L. DeForest, Charles H. Isham, Secretaries.

On taking the Chair, Col. WETMORE stated the object and importance of the meeting, in a few stirring words, and called upon the Rev. Mr. MCLEAN, of the Congregational Church, to invoke the Divine blessing upon the occasion. After an eloquent and very appropriate prayer, Dr. OSGOOD, of New-York, who spends his Summers in Fairfield, was then introduced, and spoke at some length upon the momentous bearings of the new communication between the Old World and the New. He began by drawing a picture of Fairfield as it was seventy-nine years ago, when it was invaded by British troops, under Gov. TRYON. Eighty-five houses, two churches, fifteen stores and fifteen workshops, were burned to the ground, and the British name was a curse in the mouth of every man, woman and child. He contrasted that Summer of 1779 with this Summer of 1858, and the joy at the approach of British intercourse now with the aversion to everything British then. He then went to speak of the influence of the Great Telegraph, in the first place, as a triumph of man over nature, or mind over matter; then as a new step in the alliance between man and man; and, last of all, as a majestic movement towards the fulfillment of the Divine plans for the union of the whole human race under the mighty laws of mutual industry, active

LATEST BY TELEGRAPH.

ONE WEEK LATER FROM EUROPE.

The Arabia off Cape Race.

Collision Between the Europa and Arabia.

The Europa at St. Johns, N. F.

COTTON UNCHANGED—PROVISIONS LOWER

ST. JOHNS, N. F., Sunday, Aug. 15.

The Royal Mail steamship *Europa*, Capt. LEITCH, from Boston, *via* Halifax, for Liverpool, arrived at this port at 1 P. M. to-day. She was run foul of on Saturday, 14th inst., at 10½ P. M., by the Royal Mail steamship *Arabia*, from Liverpool on the 7th inst., bound to New-York. The *Arabia*, it appears, mistook the lights of the *Europa* for Cape Race light. The *Europa* lost her cutwater, and had her stem knocked off, besides receiving other damage, which will have to be repaired here.

The *Arabia*, after boarding the *Europa*, lay by her for some time, and then proceeded for New-York. She is not so much injured as the *Europa*.

The *Arabia's* dispatches for the Press were not put on board the *Europa*, but we have Liverpool advices to the 7th, the *Arabia's* day of sailing.

The steamship *Fulton*, from New-York 24th ult., arrived at Southampton Aug. 5.

The political news by the *Arabia* does not seem, at a glance, to be particularly important or interesting.

The news of the successful laying of the Atlantic Cable was received on 'Change with glorious enthusiasm, and the declaration that the electric union of Great Britain and America will lead to the unity of all nations.

[The announcement of the arrival of the *Agamemnon* is not in the paper to hand, but if we can possibly gather the particulars of her trip, they shall be forwarded.]

The rebellion in Central India had been effectually put down, and CANNING'S proclamation says that no hopes of pardon need be entertained by any persons immediately connected in the murder of British subjects.

There was still expectations at Paris that the *Crédit Mobilier* would wind up its affairs, and make a fusion with the discount bank of M. DE ST. PAUL.

Vienna advices report the concentration of an Austrian corps of 33,000 men on the Danube, in Southern Hungaria, and on the points nearest Turkey, on the Bosnian and Servian frontiers.

It was again reported that M'lle. PICCOLOMINI has been engaged by BARNUM for America.

Mr. DISRAELI favors the repeal of the paper tax if the Exchequer will spare the income resulting therefrom.

There had been a large embarkment of troops for India.

Commercial Intelligence.

LIVERPOOL COTTON MARKET.

LIVERPOOL, Aug. 6.—Confidence is increasing in force in our COTTON market. The sales of the week foot up 69,340 bales. To-day the demand has been regular, but not extensive, and the sales were 7,000 bales, at previous rates, including 1,000 bales on speculation and for export. American descriptions are in general request, and have been taken largely by speculators and the trade. The quotations for fair qualities authorized by the Committee of Brokers, are for Uplands 7¾d., Mobiles 7 7-16d., Orleans 7⅞d., an advance of ⅛d. on each of the the two first named, and 3-16d. on the latter. The lower and middle qualities have been freely taken by buyers, and have advanced ⅛d.@¼d. Brazils command full prices. Egyptians have advanced ⅛d., and East India is scarce and in good request at last week's prices. During the week 9,470 bales of American were taken on speculation, and 4,244 bales for export. The sales of American are in detail: 400 bales Sea Island, Ga., at 11½d.@18d.; —— Upland, at 5d.@7½d.; 37,300 New-Orleans, at 6½d.@9d.; 9,700 Mobiles, at 5⅛d.@7¾d.

STATE OF TRADE.

MANCHESTER, Friday, Aug. 6.—The market continues steady, and though the demand is quiet, a good business is being done.

INTERESTING FROM WASHINGTON.

New York Custom House Lists in the Treasury Department.

Gen. Harney—The Canvass in Indiana—Indiana Politics—The Nicaragua Treaty—Mail Contract Decision, &c.

Special Dispatch to the New-York Times.

WASHINGTON, Monday, Aug. 16.

Gen. HARNEY is not yet ordered to the Pacific. A command will be assigned to him to-morrow. Gen. CLARK may continue to conduct the Indian War.

Senator BRIGHT left to-day for the West. He thinks the Democracy will unite and sweep Indiana.

It is understood that the Hon. RICHARD W. THOMPSON, of Indiana, will stump Illinois in support of a bargain between the Fillmore Americans and DOUGLAS.

There is a prospect that the President will accept the amendments proposed by MARTINEZ to the Cass-Yrissari Treaty.

The President is in excellent health, and will hold the first Cabinet Council of the month to-morrow.

General WALBRIDGE and JOHN COCHRANE had an interview to-day on the New-York appointments. Both gentlemen will be candidates for Congress this Fall, and the President takes a lively interest in their success.

General CASS attended at the State Department to-day in his usual health.

Comptroller MEDILL decided to-day against CORMICK & RAMSEY'S mail claim of $1,800,000. The claimants made a conditional contract, in 1853, for the conveyance of the mail from Vera Cruz to Acapulco. The claim was for five years' pay and damages. A.

[FROM THE REPORTER FOR THE ASSOCIATED PRESS.]

WASHINGTON, Saturday, Aug. 14.

The New-Granadian Minister had an interview with Secretary CASS this morning at the State Department, and communicated to him the Cass-Herran Treaty as modified by the Congress of that country. There is only one alteration therein, and not three as heretofore, and that refers to the naval coal dépôt. But the treaty is accompanied by two propositions in the nature of explanations.

Mr. ERSKINE, the new Secretary of the British Legation, has arrived here. Mr. RUSSELL, one of the *attachés*, left this afternoon to take passage in the *Persia* for England.

Our Washington Correspondence.

RETURN OF THE PRESIDENT—COLLECTOR SCHELL SUMMONED TO AN INTERVIEW—EXTRACTS FROM CUSTOM-HOUSE LISTS IN THE TREASURY DEPARTMENT, AC., AC.

WASHINGTON, D. C., Sunday, Aug. 15, 1858.

The return of the President will have at least the one desirable effect of bringing the troubles which distract your City Democracy to some definite result. Mr. SCHELL has been summoned to a private interview at the White House, to take place to-morrow; while the opponents of that gentleman are already here in force, and armed with statistics, documents and records which fasten (as they profess) on your Collector the responsibility of all City dissensions in the Democratic family.

Mr. BUCHANAN has been very unreserved and emphatic in pronouncing that this ulcer must be healed, either by balm or burning. He is weary, he says, of being ceaselessly tormented and occupied by the wrangles and remonstrances which pour in on him from all sides in connection with your Custom-House patronage. He desires to take account with Mr. SCHELL as to the execution of the instructions originally given to that gentleman with reference to the "rotation-rule being first made to operate against the enemies of the Democratic Party."

I have seen at the Treasury Department—(and let

mittee of Tammany Hall, it appears, in order to raise funds for the necessary expenses of last City election, assessed Mr. SCHELL in the sum of $300, and asked leave from him to apply to his subordinates (as of old custom) for contributions towards the common good in proportion to their respective salaries. Mr. SCHELL declined paying his own assessment—on what grounds we are at a loss to conjecture—and refused to allow any applications to be made to his subordinates, on the ground that "they were all too poor to afford it."

Now, why are they so poor in this particular Administration? It has long, we know, been the custom of that illustrious Captain, ISAIAH RYNDERS, to make monthly collections for the purpose of "burying" mysterious Democrats, who, as they had lived unknown, were attended to the grave by no other mourner or spectator than the said Captain of Great Fame, whose tears bedewed the pearly sod, over which no monument was ever raised, and beneath which, (as the wicked suggested) no skeleton was ever destined to repose. But Messrs. MCINTYRE, BIXBY & Co. seem to have made a fourfold improvement on this grand original idea, and, for the monthly needs of the gallant Captain, the poor "subs" round Poverty Corner have now to endure weekly or bi-weekly assessments, at a large percentage, for objects (real or supposed) which the despotic assessors do not even deign to communicate! Let Mr. THOMAS MONROE be questioned on this point. He may not be such an adept at swearing as some others but the facts in his possession should have forbidden any prudent men to drive him to despair.

In my next I will continue the list of Custom-House officers marked "A. A." on the private list; and likewise give you—if the same can any way be compassed—the marrow and pith of your Collector's interview with the President.

SIGMA.

THE ILLNESS OF GENERAL CASS—A RETROSPECTIVE VIEW OF HIS LIFE AND PUBLIC SERVICES—HIS PERSONAL PECULIARITIES.

WASHINGTON, Monday, Aug. 16, 1858.

The illness of General CASS of course excites alarm. The seventy-seventh year is a mortal enemy to all mankind. Few politicians survive his attacks. On the first rumor that the venerable Secretary of State was unable to attend to business at the Departments, paralysis was in the mouths of an anxious crowd; a minority were disposed to compromise on apoplexy. The General's illness does seem to have been serious.

Mr. BUCHANAN does the hard work of the Departments, except Mr. COBB'S, the heaviness of which he admits to be too much for him by letting it alone. Yet the loss of the Premier would be a severe blow to the President. GOETHE'S mother, who was but seventeen at his birth, used to say of him, "We have been young together." Their mutual youth was a bond of sympathy between them. And so of these old statesmen—their age is a ligament which unites them.

Gen. CASS is a wonderful old man. He has not survived his immortality. He was born a soldier, became a pedagogue, and graduated as a backwoodsman. Taking to politics as his natural element, and to office as his inheritance, he emerged from frontier life as a Cabinet Minister, and in due course of progression became a courtier. Through his varied experiences caution, timidity, the middle safe course, have been guiding stars to Gen. CASS and his chosen pathway. Adulation has always been a stepping-stone to his ambition. While quietly voyaging about northern lakes, making treaties with Indians, Gen. CASS was writing private letters to Mr. CLAY, congratulating him on his vindication from Mr. BUCHANAN'S charges of corruption. I have been told by his companions in these excursions among the dreary wilds of the northwest, that never did a word escape him in those exciting times indicating a preference for a man or a party. In private he congratulated Mr. CLAY, because Mr. CLAY had the actual power; but he knew that JACKSON was the man of the coming time, and reserved himself.

True to the *in medio tutissimus*, when JACKSON removed the deposites, Secretary CASS paced the floor of his private office in an agony of doubt. The thunders of the opposition and the terrors of impeachment were around and before him. He dared say neither yea nor nay. JACKSON knew his man, and sent General CASS to Paris. Here was another instance of his unfailing luck and his tact. JACKSON would have crushed to powder another man who had hesitated in that emergency, but he only introduced General CASS to LOUIS PHILLIPE.

His whole life has been luck. When he left Detroit to take the War Department, he gave orders to his agent to sell a large tract of land adjoining the town. He was to sell it for $30,000. After some time, the agent wrote that he had been offered $33,000. Gen. CASS instantly replied "Don't sell till further orders." He would have quickly taken his own fixed price, but being offered more, he must look further. The property is now covered by the best part of a flourishing city and is worth $1,000,000. Gen. CASS is a millionaire. While

The President's Reply.

WASHINGTON CITY, Aug. 16, 1858.

To Her Majesty VICTORIA, *Queen of Great Britain:*

The President cordially reciprocates the congratulations of Her Majesty, the Queen, on the success of the great international enterprise accomplished by the science, skill, and indomitable energy of the two countries. It is a triumph more glorious, because far more useful to mankind, than was ever won by conqueror on the field of battle.

May the Atlantic Telegraph under the blessing of Heaven prove to be a bond of perpetual peace and friendship between the kindred nations, and an instrument destined by Divine Providence to diffuse religion, civilization, liberty and law throughout the world In this view will not all nations of Christendom spontaneously unite in the declaration that it shall be forever neutral, and that its communications shall be held sacred in passing to their places of destination, even in the midst of hostilities? (Signed)

JAMES BUCHANAN.

Message from the British to the American Directors.

To the Directors of the Atlantic Telegraph Company, New York:

Europe and America are united by telegraph. Glory to God in the highest; on earth peace and good will towards men.

(Signed)

DIRECTORS ATLANTIC TELEGRAPH COMPANY.

GREAT BRITAIN.

The Excitement About the Queen's Message

From the time the first message concerning the operation of the Atlantic Telegraph Cable was received yesterday, until 10 o'clock at night, when the various bulletins gave what purported to be an abstract of the Queen's dispatch to President BUCHANAN, there were crowds of people on the TIMES Square, waiting, with more or less impatience, for the announcement of the Simon Pure message. They had been hoaxed by the *Herald*, in relation to the working of the line, and in relation to the whereabouts of the *Niagara*, and were determined not to swallow anything more that came through Plum Gut, unless its correctness should be vouched for by some reliable establishment. They waited, and the the longer they waited the more the excitement increased. Whenever anything later was placed upon the TIMES bulletin, they would crowd around it in admirable disorder—those in the periphery of the circle shouting to those nearer the centre of attraction, to read it aloud; and those near the centre shouting to the periphery, to hold its tongue and listen. While thus engaged, the newsboys would ventilate some old papers, and announce the Message. The eager crowd would buy them up rapidly, and rush under a lamp to peruse them, and discover that they had been sold. Then another bulletin would appear, and another rush would be the result. And so they kept it up until a late hour. When exhausted by their efforts, they were obliged to retire before having seen the President's reply.

Elsewhere there was considerable feeling exhibited. On the Battery there were large assemblages, until a late hour, looking out anxiously and unsuccessfully

... illuminated. The firemen are out in torch-light procession, headed by the Hornellsville Brass Band. Engine bells and whistles are also sounding their jubilee.

ITHACA, N. Y., August 16—10 P.M.

Upon the receipt of the Queen's Message, the Telegraph-Office here and other buildings were brilliantly illuminated. Cannon are now firing, flags flying, bonfires blazing, bells ringing, and WHITLOCK's brass band is playing English and American national airs in front of the Telegraph-Office.

WILKESBARRE, Pa., Monday, Aug. 16—11 P. M.

The news of the successful working of the Atlantic Telegraph Cable, and the receipt of the Queen's Message, produced the wildest excitement among our citizens. Grand preparations are being made for a celebration to-morrow.

SCRANTON, Pa., Aug. 16—10 P.M.

The announcement of the receipt of the Queen's Message to President BUCHANAN was received here with the greatest enthusiasm. Guns were fired, bells rung, music, &c. Extensive arrangements are completed for illuminating, &c., on Tuesday evening.

BALTIMORE, Monday, Aug. 16.

The Mayor has issued a proclamation congratulating the citizens of Baltimore on the success of the Atlantic Telegraph, and recommending the firing of a salute of two hundred guns, the ringing of all the bells in the city, and displaying of flags from the public buildings and shipping, between 12 and 1 o'clock to-morrow.

LOUISVILLE, Ky., Monday, Aug. 16.

The reception of the Queen's Message was announced by a grand display of fireworks by the Directors of the National Telegraph Company. The greatest enthusiasm prevailed, and all doubts respecting telegraphic communication across the Atlantic are thoroughly dispelled. The City authorities are making great preparations to celebrate the event.

NASHVILLE, Tenn., Monday, Aug. 16.

The receipt of the Queen's Message here occasioned a tremendous excitement. Large bodies of men headed with bands of music paraded the streets this evening, bonfires were lighted, and bells were rung for half an hour in honor of the great event.

UNITED STATES HOTEL,
LONG BRANCH, N. Y., Monday, Aug. 16.

All hail to the complete success of the "Wonder of the Age," the Ocean Telegraph. We are celebrating it by fireworks, music, and dancing.

NEW-ORLEANS, Monday, Aug. 16.

The Queen's Message was received by the National Telegraph Line at 7 o'clock this evening.

It caused much excitement, and the disbelievers are now satisfied.

Joint Committee on the Telegraph Cable—Letter from Com. Stewart and Captain Dayman.

The Joint Committee assembled for the fifth occasion on Monday, in the City Hall, Alderman THOS McSPEDON in the Chair.

A telegraphic communication was received from Commander JOSEPH DAYMAN, of H. M. steam-sloop *Gorgon*, accepting the proffered hospitality of the Corporation on the forthcoming celebration. Ordered to be printed in the minutes.

A communication was received by telegraph from Admiral HOUSTON STEWART, of the British Navy, declining such hospitality, from the pressure of other and professional engagements. Ordered to be printed.

They are as follows:

ST. JOHNS, N. F., Saturday, August 14th, 1858.

Chas. T. McClenachan, Sec. Committee of Common Council, N. Y.:

SIR: I beg that you will convey to the Common Council of the City of New-York the best thanks of myself and of the officers of this ship for the honor they have conferred upon us by their kind invitation of this day, which it will give us the most sincere pleasure to accept, if the permission solicited from the Admiralty should arrive in time. If not, we shall carry back with us to England this kind message as

... said that the two peoples were in some respects alike. They think pretty well of themselves, and so do we. They moreover are under petticoat government, and so are we. There one Queen is on the throne, while we have one to every household, and we have learned, like the English, to settle down very quietly under our bonds. Great is the power of the petticoat, and its shadow is not at present likely to be less.

After the national anthem of England, "God save the Queen," had been sung by the choir, the Chairman introduced to the meeting Mr. BUNCH, H. B. M. Consul for the States of North and South Carolina, who replied to the sentiment of the Rev. Dr. OSGOOD in substance as follows: He stated that he had become so accustomed, during a residence of nearly ten years in the United States, to hear sentiments in honor of his Sovereign proposed by Americans and received by Americans with a cordiality scarcely inferior to that which would have characterized Englishmen under similar circumstances, that he could scarcely say that the present demonstration had taken him by surprise, or that it appeared to him as at all unusual. Nay, he would go a step farther, and add that it had never been a matter of surprise to him that the name of the Queen should be greeted by Americans, since there was no gentleman, wherever born or whatever his political creed, who did not owe allegiance to the virtues and graces that centre in a perfect woman, or who did not feel that he could reconcile the purest devotion to his own country with an affectionate regard for one who, in all the private relations of life, as daughter, wife or mother, had given a bright example to her sex and to the world. This fact alone, he said, would suffice to account for the respect for the Queen entertained by the great body of the American people. He considered, however, that that there was another and a still more powerful reason for this regard and respect to be found in the reflection that the Queen of England was the recognized Ruler and Representative of a great and kindred people, from whom his hearers were themselves for the most part descended, and to whom they were bound by the nearest and dearest ties. He then proceeded to expatiate at some length upon the manifold advantages to be derived from that close alliance and zealous coöperation between the Governments and peoples of England and America, which were amongst the unmistakable signs of the times, and which were so essential to the carrying on of the great work of spreading the gospel, extending commerce, and promoting civilization, which could only be effected by two such great and powerful nations. That such an alliance was a natural one no one could doubt; as well might you seek to stem with a handful of rushes the course of some noble river hurrying its impetuous waters to the ocean, as to prevent two peoples, united upon all the great doctrines of human progress, from blending into one harmonious whole their destiny and their future. This was a current which no rocks of prejudice or shoals of jealousy could withstand; it must flow on for ever. Mr. BUNCH proceeded to assure his hearers of the cordial respect and affection with which the United States were regarded in England by all classes of society, and of the good wishes which accompanied their onward course. He considered that all such feelings would be greatly enhanced and improved by the great event which they were met to celebrate; he then explained shortly the construction and component parts of the electric cable, and drew from these last a lesson for the guidance of his hearers in their relations with the mother country; he thought that like its gutta percha they should be ready to bend and yield reciprocally whenever differences of opinion might happen to arise, as must necessarily be the case occasionally between nations meeting at so many points of contact; that like its wire, they should ever be ready to receive and to convey from one to the other the electric flashes of courtesy and good-will; and that like its solid encasing steel, they should sink the great chain of international comity deep into the bottom of their hearts. After drawing a sketch of the probable fate of any solitary Englishman who might have happened to present himself eighty years ago upon the same spot where he then stood, calling upon the then residents of Fairfield to join him in marks of deference and of loyalty towards the sovereign of England, and contrasting it with the security which he himself enjoyed, and the enthusiastic welcome with which he was greeted as an official representative of that sovereign, Mr. BUNCH concluded by a tribute to the eminent qualities and virtues of the President of the United States, who, he said, was almost as well known in England as he was in America, and proposed that the meeting should receive his name with every honor, which was at once done in the most satisfactory manner.

After the enthusiastic cheers that were called out by this sentiment, the choir sung "Hail Columbia," with excellent effect. Cheers were then given for the speakers, CYRUS W. FIELD, Capt. HUDSON, PETER COOPER, Prof. MORSE, Col. WETMORE, and the ladies.

During Mr. BUNCH's speech, a large delegation, with torches and music, marched in from Southport, and took their stand among the auditors.

"ATTEMPTED EXTORTION."—Mr. Hiram P. Horton, of Washington Market, desires us to state that he is not the person alluded to in the paragraph published under the above heading in yesterday's papers. The supposition is that some vagabond, with the intention of obtaining money, as alleged, used a name to which he was not entitled. There is but one other person bearing that name in the Directory, and both are far above suspicion of having been concerned in any such transaction.

... BACON, at a reduction of 1 ℔ cent. The demand was increasing.

LIVERPOOL PRODUCE MARKET.

SUGAR was firm. COFFEE steady. Congou was held at ½d. higher, viz.: 10d.@10½d. RESIN—a large business doing; sales of 2,000 bbls. common cold. at 4s.; 2,500 medium to fine, at 10s. to 19s. ℔ cwt. TURPENTINE—Rough, 9s. 3d. ASHES, 33s.@34s. 6d. TALLOW steady, at 50s. 6d.@51s.

LONDON MARKET.

LONDON, Friday, Aug. 6.—SUGAR is active, and has advanced 1s. on the week; refined is in request; Grocery lumps 53s. COFFEE steady. TEA in increasing demand; Common Congou 10½d. SALTPETRE higher, 47s 6d. RICE very firm. TALLOW 48s. 6d. on the spot, and 49s. for the last three months of the year. LINSEED OIL 34s. 3d. INDIGO firm. There is little alteration in other articles.

The Baltimore and Ohio Road and the New-York and Erie and New-York Central Railroads.

BALTIMORE, Monday, Aug. 16.

The New-York roads, persisting in their ruinous reduction of rates to Cincinnati and the regions more legitimately connected with Baltimore, the Baltimore and Ohio Railroad has recently made a decided retaliatory stroke, by reducing the rates of freight between New-York and Cleveland, Chicago and the Lake country, to thirty cents per one hundred pounds less than by the Erie and Central Roads, for first and second-class goods. With the present immense equipment and good condition of the Baltimore and Ohio Road, aided by its connections, this additional trade can readily be accommodated.

Boiler Explosion at Pawtucket.

BOSTON, Monday, Aug. 16.

The boiler of DEXTER & BROTHER's cotton mill, at Pawtucket, R. I., exploded at an early hour this morning, tearing the building into fragments, nearly destroying a grocery store, and making a complete wreck of an adjoining drug store. The mill took fire and was totally destroyed. A boy was taken out of the ruins seriously injured. The amount of damage is not known.

Steamboat Accident.

BOSTON, Monday, Aug. 16.

The steamer *Nelly Baker*, which plies between Boston and Nahant, was run into this afternoon, while at the wharf, by the Philadelphia steamer *Phineas Sprague*, striking the former forward of the wheel, and cutting eight feet through the guards and deck, and otherwise seriously injuring her. The damage is about $3,000. Although the *Nelly Baker* was crowded, no passengers were injured.

Accident to the Steamer Long Branch.

SANDY HOOK, Monday, Aug. 16.

The steamer *Long Branch*, on her trip to Red Bank from New-York, to-day, ran ashore on Sandy Hook Point, and lays well up.

The Canadian Parliament Prorogued.

TORONTO, Monday, Aug. 16.

The Canadian Parliament was prorogued to-day. The Governor made the following speech:

HONORABLE GENTLEMEN: I congratulate you on having closed the session, and am happy to find that the subjects which have been recommended to your consideration have received attention at your hands. The act of abolishing imprisonment for debt and preferential assignments, in Upper Canada, will tend to the assimilating of the laws of the two sections of the Province, and must be of benefit in its operation. Our steam communication with Europe has continued to work successfully, and I have little doubt that you have done well in providing for the regular mail service by steam during the season, to Gaspe and the lower Provinces. The appropriation for a postal line to Red River will open a continuous mail route under the control of the Canadian Government, from that settlement to Nova Scotia. I am glad to find that the customs tariff has undergone your revision, and regret that I cannot speak of the commercial crisis which has passed over the country as something that has entirely. I earnestly pray that the complete restoration of our prosperity may not long be delayed. I propose, in the course of the recess, to communicate with her Majesty's Government, and with the Governments of the sister colonies in another matter of very great importance. I am desirous of inviting them to discuss with us the principles of which a bond of a federal character uniting the Provinces of British North America, may, perhaps, hereafter be practicable. I now release you by proroguing the present Parliament.

Death of George Watson.

CHICAGO, Monday, Aug. 16.

GEORGE WATSON, Superintendent of the Great Western Railroad, died at Springfield, Ill. at 7 o'clock yesterday morning.

... has been drawing pay, the parties he was first appointed to gratify, his antecedents at the time of that appointment, and all such subsequent political action on his part as may have come to the ears of those watchmen who are zealous for the maintenance of party efficiency and union.

This list,—from which to-day I had only time to make a few hurried extracts, but which I purpose thoroughly explaining and reporting on before many days,—is in very truth one of the most curious and startling political documents it has ever been my fortune to obtain the privilege of inspecting. Opposite nearly every third or fourth name the letters "A. A." are pencilled,—this standing, as I learn, for Anti-Administration, while the great majority of such are either fossil Whigs of the Taylor *régime*, or open Black Republicans who have been in their present offices during periods which give an average of *eleven years and eight months* to every man!

Among those so marked on this list I had only time to note the following,—somewhat less than a third of the whole; and for the edification of all hungry Democrats, now in eager pursuit of the seats at present filled by these Philistines, I may as well put opposite each name the salary for which these services are "had cheap" by a Democratic Government, I take them at random as they appear on the roll, and you will, therefore, find some of the richest nuggets in the Collector's gift, mixed up with "dry diggings" and "twice-run sand" of far inferior quality.

ANTI-ADMINISTRATION MEN RETAINED BY COLLECTOR SCHELL.

Name.	Salary.	Name.	Salary.
M. L. Clarkson	$1,500	W. H. Thomas	$1,500
S. S. Coleman	1,750	Jas. Campbell	1,750
H. M. Nichol	1,700	R. S. Slocumb	1,095
J. C. Lowber	1,095	A. L. Strong	1,095
J. Z. Hart	1,095	Chas. Decline	1,095
D. T. Baldwin	2,000	M. Burnham	2,000
Jno. Gants	1,500	A. S. Storey	1,095
J. R. Vandewater	1,500	J. L. R. Jennys	1,095
E. M. Evans	1,500	S. E. Ogden	4,000
W. D. Robinson	3,800	Jno. Dunn	700
James Dunn	700	Robt. Parker	700

[John, James and Robert being father, son and son-in-law.]

T. W. Titus	1,100	Jonas Monas	1,200
C. W. Van Nest	1,095	M. H. Cardoza	1,500
Thos. Haye	1,200	T. A. Keebe	1,200
E. W. Baum	1,100	J. H. Hunter	2,500
Jno. Voorhies	1,500	G. A. O'Brien	1,000
J. T. Griswold	1,100	E. Billings	1,500
J. J. Rowen	1,100	J. H. Clark	1,000
H. Brush	1,500	Jesse Brush	1,200

[Father and son.]

E. COZZENS, 1,100; and over eighty or ninety others, whose names I had not time to copy, but who certainly fill some of the most lucrative and desirable places in that happy feeding ground of the "Unterrified," over which Mr. SCHELL should preside like unto "the Angel with a flaming sword," to bid enter all the pure of faith and expel all tainted with political heresy, infidelity and schism.

In view of these incontestible facts and figures let any dispassionate man condemn, if he can, the action taken by Mr. BUCHANAN, through the Treasury Department, with reference to your Collector and his appointments? What man who at all acknowledges the claims of party can blame the Democratic Congressmen from your City for protesting against the removal of such faithful, energetic and reliable Democrats as are a great majority of those on whose necks Mr. SCHELL commenced the operation of his official guillotine? The names of these are marked on the list as having incurred the Collector's death-warrant; but the blood of such martyrs never falls in vain; and for the hard-earned stipends which have been unjustly taken away from them, it shall be returned to them—and before long—with the interest of martyrdom superadded. I refer more especially—and find my notes for the same in the Treasury list—to such active and faithful workers as these:

GOOD DEMOCRATS REMOVED BY MR. SCHELL.

Andrew Myers,	George T. Gallagher,
T. Van Tyne,	Wm. Murray,
Thomas Dunlap,	J. W. Lamb,
Azel Freeman,	J. M. Freeland,
S. W. Van Ostrand,	Peter Burroughs,
John Quinn,	Thomas Munroe,
Stephen Cornell,	Manus Kelly,
Joseph Shaw,	O. S. Hibbard,

and a hundred others who have esteem and influence in their respective localities, and have always thrown the weight of their exertions, purse and character in favor of the Democratic cause.

Speaking of "purse" in that last paragraph, I am reminded of one trait in Mr. SCHELL's administration which JAMES BUCHANAN will be the last man in the United States, either to overlook or forget—though unhappily it did not come to his knowledge until after your Collector's confirmation. The General Com-

... morning during the halcyon days of JOHN TYLER, walked up to the Treasury, presented his claim, and brought away the $67,000 in gold.

Studious and scholarly, he writes well, and has a taste for classical and elegant things. In Paris, he turned diplomacy over to his secretaries, and wrote a book of elaborate eulogy on LOUIS PHILLIPPE, which is really a very fine biographical memoir. To further employ his leisure he took possession of the flag-ship of the American squadron in the Mediterranean, and with his family, explored the blue Ægean, and meditated amidst the ruins of Greece, Italy, and Ionia. He exploded, by a protest, the Quintuple Treaty, and returned home to quarrel with Mr. WEBSTER, enter the Senate, invent non-intervention, and run for the Presidency. In this last enterprise, Gen. CASS' luck failed for the first and only time in his life. His star paled before the meteor of Buena Vista. Yet, it was characteristic of the canny thrift of this veteran politician, that pending the contest with Gen. TAYLOR, he had appointed a *locum tenens* to keep his seat in the Senate warm, and when he wished to return to it he had this old conveniency appointed to the care of a Light-house on Lake Michigan. Obedient to his will, the Michigan Legislature promptly returned him to his old position.

Personally Gen. CASS is an exemplary man of the world. He is very rich, and is careful of his own. No man looks better after his own household. Politically, he is an infidel. He believes nothing; that is, he has no convictions. In his lukewarm, languid way, he doubtless regards the Democratic Party as the best able to govern the country, but he adheres to it only because he feels it to be safe and profitable to belong to the strong side.

Without intending it I have indited an ante-mortuary memorial upon the Secretary of State. It may stand; and should it live till he dies, I believe impartial men will pronounce it candid and just.

A.

Departure of the Vanderbilt.

To the Editor of the New-York Times:

As guardians to some extent of the public usages and manners, allow me to call your attention to the manner in which a large number of citizens were treated on the occasion of the sailing of the steamship *Vanderbilt* on Saturday last.

For some reason, the steamer was anchored in the stream before her sailing hour, and passengers conveyed to her by a lighter. Those coming to take leave of friends who had gone on board were told at each successive trip that it was the last, and that they were not wanted on board, and if they persisted in going upon the lighter, were treated in a manner that caused them to withdraw.

There are privileges connected with this matter of leave-taking, which I think are universally extended, if from no other motive than mere civility; and why not in the case of this line? Can we not learn something of courtesy in such matters from our English neighbors.

PUBLIC.

Case of Miss Susan Lyle Cross.

To the Editor of the New-York Times:

In your City Article of Saturday last, there occurs an error which it is desirable should be corrected. It is stated therein, in reference to the death of Miss SUSAN LYLE CROSS, from yellow fever, that "she was in the habit of bathing every evening, and in making frequent excursions among the shipping," and as such remarks have a tendency to impute indiscretion to the character of the lady, and hurt the feelings of her bereaved and afflicted relatives and friends, I desire to state that the extent of her bathing and boating excursions were as follows: She went into the water at a point one mile below Vanderbilt's Landing eight times during a sojourn of two months on Staten Island, and about as many times took a sail in a row-boat from the same point along the beach to the New Fort and back again, without coming near the shipping.

The deceased was a modest and amiable lady, and the insertion of the above facts will be but an act of justice to her memory and to the feelings of her relatives, and indeed all who know her.

Very Respectfully Yours, D. McL.

Card from R. H. Isham.

To the Editor of the New-York Times:

The undersigned requests the public to suspend judgment with respect to the charge brought against him until the facts are fully known. He has parted with Bonds to a very large amount, receiving notes purporting to be FREDRICKS' in payment, which, with the exception of the one delivered by himself to, and now in the hands of the magistrate, are in his own possession still.

The transaction is not connected in any way with any of his friends or business connections. Being a private operation entirely, he feels it his duty to make this explanation in order to assure the public that no one has suffered pecuniarily but himself, and the facts, when disclosed, will fully exonerate him from the charge.

R. H. ISHAM.

The President's Reply.

Washington City, [illegible] 1858.

To Her Majesty Victoria, Queen of Great Britain:

The President cordially reciprocates the congratulations of Her Majesty the Queen on the success of the great international enterprise accomplished by the science, skill, and indomitable energy of the two countries. It is a triumph more glorious, because far more useful to mankind, than was ever won by conqueror on the field of battle.

May the Atlantic Telegraph, under the blessing of Heaven, prove to be a bond of perpetual peace and friendship between the kindred nations, and an instrument destined by Divine Providence to diffuse religion, civilization, liberty and law throughout the world. In this view will not all nations of Christendom spontaneously unite in the declaration that it shall be forever neutral, and that its communications shall be held sacred in passing to their places of destination, even in the midst of hostilities?

JAMES BUCHANAN.

Message from the Directors to the American Directors.

To the Directors of the Atlantic Telegraph Company, [illegible]:

Europe and America are united by telegraph. Glory to God in the highest; on earth peace and good will towards men.

(Signed)

Directors Atlantic Telegraph Company, Great Britain.

The Celebration [illegible]

[illegible]

[illegible]

though not so often as the harassed reporter could desire, the editor's attention was attracted to a befuddled passenger on the horse car who was attempting to tell the conductor all about the terrible disaster at sea. The conductor, no doubt, was not so attentive as could be desired, nor was the narrator entirely clear in thought and speech. The editor did his best, but could overhear only a few disjoined phrases, among which were "Herald" and "bottle of wine." The first of these told him where the news had gone, and the second warned him that the prudent *Herald* staff had done what they could do to make it impossible for anybody else to get a coherent story from their informant.

But there was another way out. The editor hurried back to the *Times* building and had the presses stopped. *The Herald* was already on the press, beyond doubt; and a man from the *Times* press room, in whose ability to do difficult things everybody seems to have had confidence, was told to go to the *Herald* building and get the first copy printed. He returned presently and reported that the *Herald* press room was locked up and that the carriers who ordinarily distributed the paper before daylight had been shut out. *The Herald*, having a big exclusive story, had sent out its mail circulation, but had determined to hold up the papers for the city until an hour after all its competitors were in the hands of their readers — when the appearance of *The Herald* with this huge beat would be the more impressive.

The pressman was promised fifty dollars if he could get a copy of *The Herald* in spite of these

obstacles; and by means not recorded by the ancient chroniclers, he did it. And there was the full story of the *Arctic* disaster by the first returning survivor, George H. Burns. *The Times* composing room staff was hastily reassembled — no doubt some of them were found in near-by and easily accessible gathering places such as the vigilance of Mr. Volstead has now abolished — and *The Herald's* story was reset and injected into the first page of *The Times.*

The *Times* city edition was circulated at the usual time the next morning, and no doubt when *The Herald* appeared an hour later many worthy citizens thought with contempt that it had merely lifted Burns's story from *The Times.* The next day a number of survivors arrived, and Raymond himself turned reporter and put himself under the city editor's orders for a task which, considering the limited facilities of the day, was about as hard as that which the *Times* staff confronted after the *Titanic* was sunk — and which was met as successfully.

Maverick, in recording this episode, appears to think it necessary to forestall criticism by saying that of course Burns had undoubtedly given his story to *The Herald* in the supposition that it would at once be communicated to all the other papers, and that in lifting it *The Times* was merely carrying out his wishes and thwarting an iniquitous competitor. Maybe so. At any rate, the night city editor was raised five dollars a week, which was quite a lot of money in those days.

The front page of a New York newspaper in the fifties was usually devoted for the most part either

to telegraphic news of the doings of Congress and the administration, or to European news, of which a much larger amount was printed in proportion to the size of the paper than was dreamed of in recent years, until the war. In August, 1858, New York was in a frenzy of excitement over the successful laying of the first Atlantic cable, but that fragile connection survived barely long enough to endure some polite interchange of felicitations between Queen Victoria and President Buchanan, and then became unworkable. Not till almost a decade later was permanent cable communication established, and even in the Franco-Prussian War cable news consisted of little but a collection of brief official dispatches and announcements, with most of the news conveyed by mail.

In the fifties it all came by mail, and an ingenious and elaborate technique had been evolved to get it as quickly as possible. Correspondents of papers and news associations in Europe sent their letters, their digests of current happenings, and the latest English or French papers by the last mail to the transatlantic steamers, which were met off Cape Race by pilot boats which took off the news dispatches. These were then taken ashore and telegraphed to New York, when this was possible; usually only the briefest skeleton of the latest news could be sent by wire, and the bulk of it had to come by train. More than once *The Times's* dispatches during the war in Italy in 1859 were published in a fragmentary condition, with the explanation that a telegraph operator at some relay point between New York and the Nova Scotian coast

had closed his office and gone home for the night, leaving news dispatches to wait till tomorrow.

The news thus arriving would be headed somewhat as follows:

THREE DAYS LATER FROM EUROPE

Arrival of the "City of Paris"

THE NEW ENGLISH CABINET

And so on.

Other overseas mail correspondence to which much space was given was the news from California, where men who had gone to dig wealth from the ground were preparing the way for a race which should develop new possibilities in the exercise of the free imagination, and from Central America, where William Walker and his associates were valiantly trying to repeat the exploits of Pizarro and Cortez, and create the Golden Circle which would compensate the slave states for the prospective loss of control of the Federal government.

On the second and third pages were book reviews, and general articles something like those now appearing in newspaper magazine sections. The fourth page, editorial, began with a summary of the day's news, and usually included dramatic and musical news and critiques, besides leading articles. Very late telegraphic news was often put on the editorial page, or the page opposite. Local news and advertisements occupied much of the fifth, sixth, and seventh pages, and the last page was devoted chiefly to financial and commercial news and advertising. This is of course a generalized description, and any

given issue of any paper might depart considerably from the type; but substantially this seems to have been the idea of a good newspaper in the fifties. And, allowing for the handicaps imposed by the immature mechanical development of the time, it is a pretty good newspaper even yet.

Raymond is credited with the invention of the display headline in 1856, but ideas of display were more modest in those days, and found sufficient exercise within the limits of a single column. Even in the Civil War single-column heads sufficed. *The Times* on April 4, 1865, for example, told of the capture of the Confederate capital under a single-column head as follows:

GRANT

RICHMOND
and
VICTORY

This was in the first of the six columns; in the last was the story of the effect of the news in New York, of course with its own head; and the four columns between were filled in with a cut of the American eagle, somewhat precariously grasping his thunderbolts, his olive branch, and Richmond all at the same time. Lee's surrender was displayed with a single-column head, and so was Lincoln's death—which *The Times*, for the guidance of its readers, described in the top line of the head as an "Awful Event." On great occasions the telegraph editor sometimes found it desirable to attract attention by beginning his head with the admonitory

line, "Highly Important News," but not till the days of the Tweed ring, when *The Times* had the biggest local exclusive story that had ever come to a New York paper, did the headlines go beyond a single column. However, display headlines, and even descriptive headlines, are an acquired taste, as is evident from the fact that most of the world outside the United States still gets along without them. The newspapers of the fifties afforded little consolation to those who want to read the headlines because they lack the time or the intelligence to read the news; they were published for people who had time to spend on finding out what was going on. It may be that our generation prefers to read the headline "Manning, Elevated to Bishop, Voices Curb on Radicalism" (to select a recent example, not from *The Times*), rather than look into the article in the hope of finding out exactly to what, and in what sense, Dr. Manning was elevated, and just how a curb may be voiced. Perhaps this preference is natural and inevitable, an outgrowth of the spirit of the time, whatever that is. If so, as Henry Adams said about life, one may accept it without feeling the necessity of pretending to admire it.

The Times was never (with the conspicuous exception of its campaign against Tweed) a crusading paper. It has on occasion done its share in exposing conditions that needed correction, but it does not select this one out of many activities of a good newspaper as a life work. It crusaded occasionally and mildly in the fifties, but after the time of Kossuth it never lost its balance. In 1856, for example,

it gave a good deal of attention to the condition of the streets, and seemed much encouraged when public indignation was aroused and an attempt was made to compel the city government to give back a little service in return for unlimited opportunity of peculation. They had much to learn in the fifties; not for forty years were New York streets to be measurably improved, and the art of snow removal is far from perfection even yet.

In 1857 James W. Simonton, then Washington correspondent of *The Times*, exposed a magnificent scheme of land-stealing and corruption in connection with the extension of railroads into Minnesota. The affair seems to have been conducted in the grand manner, very much as the similar enterprise described in "The Gilded Age." The House of Representatives was outraged in its finest sensibilities by Simonton's charges that four of its members were corruptly involved, and he was summoned before a Congressional committee for proper rebuke. By the time the committee had finished with Simonton it had been compelled to admit that he was telling the truth, and to recommend that the four guilty men be expelled.

Soon after Simonton was sent across the plains with General Albert Sidney Johnston's expeditionary force against the Mormons. To the regret, perhaps, of certain persons, among them newspaper editors eager to show how ably they could cover a war, Brigham Young came down as promptly as Davy Crockett's coon. Simonton went on to California and was lost to *The Times*. But another and greater war was on hand, and *The Times* added

greatly to its prestige by its efficiency in giving the news of the war in Italy in 1859.

Raymond covered that war himself, ably assisted by his Paris correspondent, Dr. W. E. Johnston, who, following a custom prevalent then and till much later, wrote over the pen name of "Malakoff." The most brilliant incident of Raymond's career as a war correspondent was his eyewitness account of the battle of Solferino, perhaps the best of many admirable pictures of the war which *The Times* published. Solferino displayed not only Raymond's ability as a writer but his talent as a news editor. In those days the press of the world was divided into two classes. In Class I, alone and unapproachable, stood *The London Times;* the other newspapers of Europe and America differed only in their degree of inferiority — at least, in the public estimation. A *London Times* correspondent was of course at Solferino, apparently as essential a part of the battle as the three sovereigns who honored it with their personal attention; and Raymond knew that when *The London Times* with this man's account reached New York every editor would feel that the definitive and decisive story had arrived. Raymond decided not only to have as good a story as *The London Times,* but to beat it to New York — a feat which of course would have to be accomplished by mail. Through "Malakoff's" influence Raymond's dispatch, written among the wounded in Castiglione while the guns still sounded a few miles away, was taken to Paris with Napoleon's own dispatches by a French military messenger, and given to Mrs. Raymond, then at a Paris hotel. With it were

GEORGE JONES.

directions from her husband to put it on the first steamer leaving either England or France for New York. Mrs. Raymond seems to have been a pretty good reporter herself, in emergencies; thirty hours later she put her husband's dispatch on the Liverpool mail boat with her own hands. At that moment *The London Times*, whose story had come up from Italy by the same messenger, was just appearing on the streets in London; but it missed the New York mail and arrived ten days after Raymond's account of the battle had been published.

Solferino may serve as an illustration of the slowness with which European news reached New York in those days before the cable. The battle was fought on the 24th of June. On July 7, under the heading "The War in Italy—Advices Three Days Later," *The Times* published the batch of news brought on a steamer leaving Ireland on June 26. The beginning of the two columns of news announced that the steamer had been "boarded off Cape Race by the news yacht of the Associated Press," which took off "the synopsis of news prepared by our Liverpool agent." This reached St. John's, Newfoundland, on July 4, and managed to get to New York by telegraph on the 6th. "Our Liverpool agent's" synopsis closed on June 23, and consisted mainly of official announcements in Vienna and Paris that a battle might be fought, would be fought, but had not yet been fought. Down below all this, an inch or two above the bottom of the column, appeared a modest item dated in Paris, on June 25, and headed "The Very Latest by Telegraph to Galway." It contained Napoleon's dis-

patch to Eugenie announcing the decisive victory at Solferino.

This dispatch, of course, had been mentioned in the headline — three or four banks below the top — and it was handled editorially with a due sense of its importance. The leading article was an admirable analysis of the campaign and drew from very scanty material inferences fully justified by the event. But the custom of printing the news first received at the top of the column and letting the later dispatches follow in chronological order had a strong hold on newspaper tradition. Not till the seventies did it occur to some enterprising journalist that it might be a good idea to put the latest or most important news at the head of the column. The next mail boat brought Raymond's and "Malakoff's" dispatches, which *The Times* published on July 12 — again with the first dispatch first, and the story of Solferino trailing along toward the end. *The Times* that day gave up two of its eight pages to news and correspondence from the war. As early as 1852 it had devoted seven of its 24 columns to the news of the final day in the famous Whig convention at Baltimore (and this without any undue prominence for Raymond); and in 1856 nine columns of the 48 (including the whole front page) were one morning given up to the publication of the full text of correspondence in a diplomatic dispute with England. Whether these displays were disproportionate is a matter of taste.

Raymond's feats, however, were not the only source of distinction for *The Times* in the Italian war. Quite as much attention was aroused by an

exploit on the internal front which tradition ascribes to William Henry Hurlburt, whom Raymond had left in charge of the editorial page. On the morning of July 15, 1859, this gentleman was one of a party who saw a friend off on a steamer. The party spent an enjoyable morning, and then Hurlburt went to the office to write an editorial about the Quadrilateral, the famous Austrian fortress group to which the armies of Francis Joseph retired after the defeat at Solferino. Apparently his mind wandered from time to time — now to the cabinet crisis in England, now to the new fortifications of Paris, and now to the social morning just ended. The result appeared on the *Times* editorial page the next morning under the heading, "The Defensive Square of Austrian Italy." Future sociologists of this well prohibited republic are commended to a study of this article.

The *Times* proofroom was then regarded as the best in New York, but a few days before that a proofreader had ventured to change a word in one of Hurlburt's editorials, and had been ordered, with much indignation, never to do so again. He read this article on the Quadrilateral, and found therein such expressions as the following: "If we shall follow the windings of the Mincio, we shall find countless elbows formed in the elbows of the regular army." . . . "If we follow up the course of the Mincio, we shall find innumerable elbows formed by the sympathy of youth." . . . "Notwithstanding the toil spent by Austria on the spot, we should have learned that we are protected by a foreign fleet suddenly coming up on our question of citizenship. A canal cuts Mantua in two, but we

may rely on the most cordial cabinet minister of the new power in England." . . . "The Adige is deep and swift at Verona; Paris is strong in her circle of fortifications." Along with much else which was plausible and often accurate.

Whereupon the proofreader remembered that he had been forbidden to touch a word of Hurlburt's copy, and the article was printed as written.

Next day it was reprinted as it ought to have been written, with an apologetic note that "by a confusion of manuscripts sent up at a late hour" a regrettable error had occurred; which, *The Times* admitted, had furnished "a happy occasion for airing a little envy, malice, and uncharitableness to the less respectable among the daily journals." A friend of Raymond's reports that when he read this article in Paris, weeks later, he "denounced it," as was natural enough; but did not disavow it. This generosity is praiseworthy, but it would have been rather late for a disavowal by that time.

So by the opening of the Civil War *The New York Times* (the "Daily" had been dropped from the title in 1857) had already won itself a place as one of the great papers of America. Also, it had prospered. As early as 1855 it claimed the honor of being second only to *The Herald* in circulation, and by the end of its first decade nobody in the *Times* office would admit that it had any superior.

The original quarters were long since outgrown. As early as 1854 *The Times* had begun to think of moving, but when plans for a new home became more definite the paper had reached such a degree of

prosperity that it was possible to build on a more magnificent scale than could have been hoped a few years earlier. The first Times Building — first, that is, of those which the paper built for itself—into which the paper entered on May 1, 1858, occupied the triangle between Park Row and Nassau and Beekman Streets, on the spot where the second Times Building, erected in 1888, still stands. The growth of the paper in recent years led to the erection of the Times Building in Times Square, and then of the Times Annex in West 43d Street, which already is uncomfortably small; and each of the four homes of *The Times* has in its turn been the finest newspaper building in the country.

The structure which seemed so magnificent in the fifties would of course be somewhat commonplace today, but in its time it was far superior to anything ever built for the accommodation of an American newspaper. For its erection a sixty per cent assessment was levied on the stock, and all profits above twenty per cent a year were set aside for the time being for a building fund. *The Times* was making money — enough money to justify its owners in what then seemed to some of their contemporaries a rather hazardous investment in unnecessary luxury. The five stories of the Times Building rose to the dizzy height of eighty feet above City Hall Park, and from the windows of the top floor, as Maverick wrote, "the upper part of New York is spread out before the eye in one grand panoramic view."

CHAPTER II

Civil War and Reconstruction, 1860–1869

RAYMOND, as has been said, seems to have been somewhat ashamed of his ability, even rarer in that day than at present, to see both sides of a question, and felt that it sometimes gave him an appearance of irresolution. Probably the fault was more evident to him than to others. Certainly in the great crisis that led up to the Civil War, and throughout the war itself, there was nothing irresolute or Laodicean about either Raymond or his paper; and the disfavor into which both fell for a time in the early days of reconstruction was due to the fact that Raymond happened to be right when the majority was wrong.

The oldest living member of the present *Times* staff dates his connection with the paper from some years after the close of the Civil War. Probably every member of the staff of 1860 is dead; certainly all the men who contributed to the formation of an editorial policy which in all its essentials was directed by Raymond himself. Present workers on *The Times* may be pardoned, then, for expressing a somewhat impersonal admiration for the manner in which the paper met the crisis. It was firm in a time when there was a great deal of irresolution; but what was a rarer virtue, it saw the issues clearly in a period when loose thinking was even more

have opened fire on Fort Sumpter, the remainder are held in reserve for the expected fleet.

Two thousand men reached this city this morning and embarked for Morris Island and the neighborhood.

CHARLESTON, Friday, April 12.

The bombardment of Fort Sumpter continues.

The Floating [illegible]ttery and Stephens Battery are operating freely, and [illegible]mpter is returning the fire.

It is reported that three war vessels [illegible]tside the bar.

CHARLESTON, Friday, April 12.

The firing has ceased for the night, but will be renewed at daylight in the morning, [illegible]less an attempt is made to reinforce, which am[illegible] arrangements have been made to repel.

The *Pawnee*, *Harriet Lane*, and a thir[illegible]eamer are reported off the bar.

Troops are arriving by every train.

LATER DISPATCHES—HOSTILITIES STILL PROG[illegible]ING.

CHARLESTON, Friday, April 12.

The bombardment is still going on every twent[illegible] minutes from our morters. It is supposed that Major ANDERSON is resting his ment for the night.

Three vessels of-war are reported outside. They cannot get in. The sea is rough.

Nobody is hurt. The floating battery works well. Troops arrive hourly. Every inlet is guarded. There are lively times here.

CHARLESTON, Friday, April 12.

The firing on Fort Sumpter continues.

There are reviving times on the "Palmetto coast."

CHARLESTON, Friday, April 12—3 A. M.

It is utterly impossible to reinfofce Fort Sumpter, to-night, as a storm is now raging.

The morter batteries will be playing on Fort Sumpter all night.

FROM ANOTHER CORRESPONDENT.

CHARLESTON, Friday, April 12.

Civil war has at last begun. A terrible fight is at this moment going on between Fort Sumpter and the fortifications by which it is surrounded.

The issue was submitted to Major ANDERSON of surrendering as soon as his supplies were exhausted, or of having a fire opened on him within a certain time.

This he refused to do, and accordingly, at twenty-seven minutes past four o'clock this morning Fort Moultrie began the bombardment by firing two guns. To these Major ANDERSON replied with three of his barbette guns, after which the batteries on Mount Pleasant, Cummings' Point, and the Floating Battery opened a brisk fire of shot and shell.

Major ANDERSON did not reply except at long intervals, until between 7 and 8 o'clock, when he brought into action the two tier of guns looking towards Fort Moultrie and Stevens iron battery.

Up to this hour—3 o'clock—they have failed to produce any serious effect.

[illegible] force of men than was supposed. At any rate, he is fighting bravely.

There have been two rain storms during the day, but without effect upon the battle.

Everybody is in a ferment. Some of those fighting are stripped to the waist.

IMPORTANT CORRESPONDENCE PRECEDING THE BOMBARDMENT.

CHARLESTON, Friday, April 12.

The following is the telegraphic correspondence between the War Department at Montgome[illegible] and Gen. BEAUREGARD immediately preceding the hostilities.

The correspondence grew out of the formal notification by the Washington Government, which is disclosed in Gen. BEAUREGARD's first dispatches.

[No. 1.]

CHARLESTON, April 8.

L. P. WALKER, Secretary of War:

An authorized messenger from President LINCOLN, just informed Gov. PICKENS and myself that provisions will be sent to Fort Sumpter peaceably, or otherwise by force.

(Signed,) G. T. BEAUREGARD.

[No. 2.]

MONTGOMERY, 10th.

G. T. BEAUREGARD, Charleston:

[illegible] have no doubt of the authorized character of [illegible]ent who communicated to you the intention [illegible] Washington Government to supply Fort S[illegible] by force, you will at once demand its evac[illegible] and if this is refused, proceed in such man[illegible] you may determine, to reduce it. Answer.

Sign[illegible] L. P. WALKER, Sec. of War.

[No. 3.]

CHARLESTON, April 10.

L. P. WALKER, S[illegible] of War:

The demand will [illegible] to-morrow at 12 o'clock.

Signed, G. T. BEAUREGARD.

Gen. BEAUREGARD, Char[illegible] MONTGOMERY, April 10.

Unless there are especial [illegible] your own condition, it is [illegible]onnected with you should make the demand [illegible] proper that [illegible] hour.

(Signed) L. P. WALK[illegible] [illegible]y of War.

[No. 5.]

CHA[illegible]

L. P. WALKER, Secretary of War, [illegible] 10.

The reasons are special for 12 o'clo[illegible]:

(Signed) G. T. BEA[illegible]

[No. 6.]

CHARLESTON, A[illegible]

L. P. WALKER, Secretary of War:

Demand sent at 12 o'clock. Allowed [illegible] o'clock to answer.

(Signed) G. T. BEAUREGARD.

[No. 7.]

MONTGOMERY, April 11.

Gen. BEAUREGARD—Charleston:

Telegraph the reply of Maj. ANDERSON.

(Signed,) L. P. WALKER, Secretary of War.

to-night by the report of the commencement of hostilities at Charleston this morning at 4 o'clock. The more so because of the previous news of peace and landing of provisions at Fort Sumpter. The news came to-night from the Associated Press agent at Charleston, giving all the particulars of the correspondence between BEAUREGARD and Major ANDERSON, the commencement of the attack by the Secessionists, and ANDERSON'S response from his batteries.

The news was posted at once, in all the hotels, and the wildest scene of excitement ensued. Among the Union men here there was general rejoicing that an issue was made at last, while no advocates of Southern rights were to be found.

Major ANDERSON'S fame is on every one's tongue about the hotels and streets. The news was at once taken to the White House. All visitors will be excluded, and the Cabinet summoned to await further information and act upon it. One thing I am certain of, from positive knowledge—that if this last information proves true, the Administration will support ANDERSON and his course, with the whole power and means of the Government, at all hazards.

A crowd assembled at the telegraph office to await further news.

Everyone had been waiting anxiously all day for the report of an attack upon the Government supply vessels, which it was ascertained last evening would probably approach Charleston harbor some time during the night or this morning. The surprise occasioned by the report from repeated dispatches that they had entered the harbor without molestation, and were landing the supplies without any difficulty, present or apprehensive, created nearly as great an excitement as the later reports of battle. The President was informed by dispatches to three different parties, announcing the safe landing, until he finally concluded that they must be correct, and that better counsels were prevailing among the Southern men.

CABINET COUNCILS.

Mr. LINCOLN summoned the Cabinet together the second time to consult. They had met once at 10 A. M., and now convened again at 1 o'clock P. M. There was general rejoicing at the prospects of peace and final adjustment of our national difficulties, dampened somewhat, however, by fear that it would prove false. LINCOLN said to a friend that if these advices were correct, the crisis had been passed, and the whole question settled without firing a gun. He added that he did not consider the Government at war with the South, and did not intend it should by his act. It was in this view that the provisioning of the fort was ordered to be attempted, unaccompanied by armed demonstration. The President further said, while assuming that the supplies had been landed, that he did not consider maintaining [illegible]upremacy of the Federal Government any victory [illegible] the South, but simply a vindication of the [illegible] he had always reposed in the ultimate good [illegible] and sense of justice among the American [illegible] The War Department did not place any [illegible]ay on the peace dispatches. Secretary [illegible] declared that he saw no escape from [illegible] Forts Sumpter and Pickens.

[illegible] notwithstanding a violent rain-storm, [illegible] thronging the streets, anxious to

FROM ANOTHER CORRESPONDENT.

ANOTHER ACCOUNT OF THE NEWS AT WASHINGTON.

The first dispatches from the seat of war were received in this city about 7 o'clock this evening. The excitement caused by the meagre intelligence was most intense. Bulletins were posted at the principal hotels, where immense crowds gathered to discuss the probable results. It is almost needless to say that while there was but one opinion as to the end, there was an infinite variety of conjectures as to the *modus operandi*. The public sentiment is very decided that in the war inaugurated to-day the Government will prove to be the victor.

NEVER THOUGHT OF EVACUATION.

There is no foundation for the long stories told of the original purpose of the Government to evacuate Fort Sumpter. Mr. LINCOLN has not entertained any such purpose. He has entertained no purpose but to maintain possession of the Government property and enforce the laws. All statements that negotiations were entered upon for the departure of Major ANDERSON'S command were mere *canards* got up for the purpose of covering political defeats. The policy of the Administration never depended upon the contingency of evacuation. It was fixed within ten days after Mr. LINCOLN'S inauguration. If evidence were wanting of this, it would be found in the fact that the Government was prepared to dispatch such quantities of men and material as left the port of New-York within four days.

FORETHOUGHT OF THE ADMINISTRATION—ITS EFFECT.

The rapid shipment of supplies, men and munitions was the result of forethought and previous preparation—the end of means long before matured. The Government continues to receive assurances of the popularity of the measures it has inaugurated. These come from all quarters, and from men of all parties. I was talking with a gentleman from Maryland this evening, who assured me that the steps taken to maintain the supremacy of the General Government had done more to stifle secession in his State than all the compromise propositions. He was at home yesterday when a dispatch was received that a conflict had taken place in the harbor of Charleston. About forty persons were present, including Republicans and "very few" Douglas Democrats and Bell-Everett men. There was a universal expression of hope that the Government would succeed. This feeling pervades the Border States to an extent that surprises all. The stern realities of an actual conflict appear to have sobered the people and brought them to realize the duties of the Government and their own responsibility as citizens.

DEMOCRATIC INDORSEMENT OF MR. LINCOLN'S POLICY.

I met a Democrat to-day, whom I have known all through the excitement of the last election as an out-and-out friend of the Southern Secessionists. He is a New-Yorker, and widely connected with its business, he himself being one of the heaviest dealers in sugars in your City. I was astonished to hear him proclaim unguardedly his approval of the policy of the Administration, his hope that the vigor displayed in the beginning would continue to the end, and his willingness to make all the sacrifices which war imposes upon commercial enterprise. He says that the promi-

Mr. COBB'S experience in the Southern Confederacy does not seem to have improved his judgment at all in the matter of financial estimates, for he continues to come as wide of the mark as ever. In the conversation referred to, he expressed the opinion that the revenues of the Treasury would be only about $1,000,000 per month; that, under this state of facts, the funds would be speedily exhausted, and that, as there is authority to borrow only $27,000,000, which, with the $1,000,000 per month for the ensuing year, would foot up only $39,000,000, while the expenses of the Government must be about $55,000,000, the Treasury must be bankrupted inevitably.

The figures in the Department show, in fact, an increase of revenue over last year, and the revenue is coming in at the rate of $3,000,000 per month, instead of $1,000,000, which Mr. COBB graciously allows. During the two weeks ending April 9, 1860, the receipts in the Treasury were $1,471,241 48. The receipts during the corresponding fortnight of 1861 were $1,500,667 34; increase in 1861 $29,425 81.

It should be remembered, too, that these results are attained at a time when the new Tariff is operating unfavorably towards the Treasury, because goods are withdrawing from bond for consumption in cases where the duty is less under the old Tariff than under the new, while merchandise which can be taken out of bond at *reduced* duties under the new Tariff are allowed to remain. Unless a war shall occur, Government is likely to have abundant means during the coming year.

SUMPTER AND PICKENS CANNOT STAND BOMBARDMENT.

Gentlemen skilled as engineers, and whose judgment is usually sound, express the opinion that neither Pickens nor Sumpter can withstand bombardment, if their assailants are not operated against by land forces. The forts in question were not constructed to sustain a siege, but to defend harbors against hostile fleets. For the latter purpose they are admirably adapted; no "wooden walls" could withstand the fire from their batteries, or do themselves harm; but a well-sustained fire from different points on the adjacent shores, it is maintained, will reduce them both in time,—unless they have men enough and guns enough to promptly demolish the assailing forts.

SWAGGERING NAVAL OFFICERS.

An agent of the Navy Department might be profitably employed in an occasional stroll through the hotel lobbies, at Washington, to notice the language and deportment of some who wear the naval buttons, and yet constantly and publicly swagger about the folly of the Government undertaking to bring the "Southern Confederacy" to terms. It is not often that a naval officer thus dishonors the button,—but when he does, if he has not the manliness to resign, it would be advisable to ship him to sea somewhere where he could do no harm if he should take the notion to turn traitor.

A. B. DICKINSON, on Thursday, formally accepted the mission to Nicaragua.

GUARD DUTY BY THE CLERKS.

It is suggested that the Secretaries of the various departments call upon the clerks to perform guard duty at each Department where they are stationed. In this way all the loyal employes will be very easily discovered, and the shakey ones detected. I have the assurance that the experiment is to be

[illegible] produced sensations of surprise, indignation and rejoicings, according to the nature of the mind to which they were brought. Dispatches were received stating that President DAVIS had, after consultation with his Cabinet, directed Gen. BEAUREGARD to allow unmolested passage of the Federal transports with their loads of supplies for Fort Sumpter, thereby obviating immediate hostilities; others that Maj. ANDERSON and Gen. BEAUREGARD were consulting together, and the probabilities were that the Fort would be surrendered so soon as its supplies were exhausted; and still others announcing that the war had actually begun. The first-mentioned dispatch was generally credited, and the feeling was almost universal that a great moral victory had been achieved by the United States Government.

At 5 o'clock in the afternoon, however, all uncertainty was set at rest. The telegraphic wire brought the long looked-for intelligence that WAR HAS BEGUN, and that the forces of the Confederated Traitors have struck the first blow. Expected as was the news, it produced a most remarkable and wide-spread sensation. Many had hoped the contest might yet be avoided; others thought the Federal Government would back down rather than shed blood; and others were certain that a Divine Providence would interfere to prevent so fratricidal a strife. The bulletin boards were surrounded; the streets near them were blockaded, and the fast-gathering multitude were only satisfied when the self-appointed reader had read himself hoarse in the frequent repetition of the brief announcement of the facts. Hundreds of anxious inquirers besieged the telegraph and publication offices, confident that there might yet be some item of information which was withheld from the masses, and they were only appeased when told that they were in possession of all, and that until this morning's papers were out they could have no more.

"Good, good," exclaimed many a one, as he read the statement, or as it was repeated to him by a friend, "at last we have reached a crisis; something *must* be done." The feeling of rejoicing was everywhere to be met, that Major ANDERSON had not lowered his flag, and that President LINCOLN had determined to sustain, even at so fearful a cost, the honor of the country. Of the very many with whom we conversed, and from whom we heard the freeest expression of opinions, we did not find a single individual who did not respond heartily to the sentiment, "Thank Heaven we have a Government." Speculations and wagers of all kinds were the order of the night, as to the probable effect of this or that battery, of the arrival and probable action of the fleet, and of the result of this first contest; and very long odds were offered and taken that Sumpter would silence Moultrie, and that the fleet, on arrival, would find but little to do. However that may be, the war has begun—the aggressors were the Confederated forces, the Federal post has returned vigorously the fire, and the entire moral support of the North stands about the President in this trying moment, as will the entire physical force stand at his side if a more trying hour should come.

THE PENNSYLVANIA WAR BILL.

HARRISBURGH, Friday, April 12.

The War bill passed both Houses to-night, without amendment. Gov. CURTIN waited at the Executive office to sign it. It is signed.

The Charleston dispatches about hostilities were announced in both Houses, and produced a profound sensation.

Mr. SMITH, a Democratic member of the House, after the Charleston dispatches were received, changed his vote to aye on the War bill. All the Democrats of both Houses voted against it. The bill appropriates $500,000 for the purpose of arming and equipping the militia; authorizes a temporary loan; provides for the appointment of an Adjutant-General, Commissary-General, and Quartermaster-General, who, with the Governor, are to have power to carry the act into effect.

EFFECTS OF THE WAR IN BALTIMORE.

BALTIMORE, Friday, April 12.

The Charleston news was not generally promulgated here until after midnight. It produced a profound sensation, and general expressions of regret at

[*Continued on Eighth Page.*]

shall wage no war except in defense of the constitution and against its foes. But we have a country and a constitutional government. We know its worth to us and to mankind, and in case of necessity we are ready to test its strength."

That sentiment guided the editorial course of *The Times* through the turbulent winter between Lincoln's election and the attack on Fort Sumter. Raymond deprecated, as all sensible men deprecated, any hasty aggression which might provoke to violence men who could still, perhaps, be brought back to reason; but he insisted that as a last resort the union must be maintained by any means necessary. To the proposals for compromise he was favorable, on condition that they did not compromise the essential issue — that they did not nullify the election of 1860 and give back to the slave power the control of the national government which it had lost. Because no other compromise would have been acceptable the issue inevitably had to be fought out, and from Sumter to Appomattox *The Times* was unwavering in its support of Lincoln and its determination that the Federal union must and should be preserved. Its editorial comment on Lincoln's first inaugural address was an index of its position in the weeks just before war broke out. After reviewing Lincoln's program *The Times* observed: "If the dangers of the hour can be averted and the Union can be saved, this is the basis on which alone it can be accomplished. If the Union cannot be saved on this basis and consistently with these principles it is better that it should not be saved at all."

Raymond's letters to Yancey took up several columns each, but they were worth it. The editor of the paper certainly did not allow it to become in any sense a personal organ; on March 1, 1861, it published an address which he had delivered some days before on the policy of the Republican party, but with an apologetic note that it was inserted "perhaps to the exclusion of more interesting matter." It was as a matter of fact an illuminating statement on the prospective course of the new administration, from a man who spoke with some authority — and with an authority which was to increase from year to year. Besides directing *The Times* in the war years, Raymond engaged in a good deal of active work for the Republican party in state and nation. He became one of Lincoln's most valued political helpers, and in 1864 was the chairman of the New York delegation at the national convention. He had a good deal to do with the composition of the platform, and was largely responsible for the vice-presidential nomination of Andrew Johnson, a gentleman in whom Raymond not only had a personal confidence which he eventually admitted was misplaced, but whom he valued as a representative of the Union minority in the South, and a sort of living symbol that the Union had not been and would not be disrupted.

Raymond was presently made chairman of the Republican National Committee and directed the campaign that reëlected Lincoln. Unfortunately, he also allowed himself to be a congressional candidate in New York City. In 1863 he had received some votes for the Senatorship, but not enough.

He was elected to the lower House, however, and took his seat in March, 1865. His course, as will be related presently, was highly creditable to his judgment and principles, but temporarily unfortunate not only for his own political repute but for the welfare of *The Times*.

During the war, however, *The Times* made an excellent record not only as an organ of opinion but as a medium of the news. And the Civil War, it is hardly necessary to recall, effected a great transformation in American journalism. For the first time in American history since the invention of the railroad and telegraph a situation had arisen in which the public wanted to know what had happened yesterday rather than some man's opinion on what had happened last week. Before hostilities had begun papers which previously had printed not more than two or three columns of telegraph news a day were printing two or three pages. Correspondence by mail still existed, but was accepted only with reluctance, when nothing better could be obtained. Even in the fifties, New York papers, maintaining regular correspondents in Washington, could depend for news from the rest of the country for the most part on brief telegrams to the Associated Press, supplemented by details from the local papers when these arrived by mail, and occasionally by letters from correspondents who as likely as not were volunteers. But by 1860 every New York newspaper that wanted to deserve that name had to maintain a large staff of its own correspondents in the southern states. Thanks to their exer-

tions, the North knew pretty well what the South was thinking in that critical year; and the South might have been better off if its knowledge of the North had been as extensive.

The work of these correspondents involved a good deal both of difficulty and of danger. When secession came to be a fact and civil war was visibly just around the corner, northerners in the South were under suspicion. The hazards that attended journalism under these conditions may be illustrated by the case of "Jasper," the *Times* correspondent in Charleston. From the secession of the state until the beginning of the war, Jasper sent every day full, and apparently fair, dispatches giving the news from Charleston and the sentiments of South Carolina. The reactions of some indignant readers of *The Times* were of the sort with which *The Times* became familiar during the recent war. Honest citizens felt that only news which they liked could be true. It was assumed that because *The Times* printed news which might be favorable to the rebels it, or its correspondent, Jasper, was consequently in sympathy with rebellion. There were demands that this "secessionist" be no longer permitted to spread his propaganda in the columns of *The Times*. To one of these complaints *The Times* replied editorially that "Jasper went to Charleston with instructions to write strictly what was true, and to give the facts as they might fall under his observation, whether favorable to secession or otherwise." It was added that perhaps the desirability of getting his dispatches through the Charleston telegraph office had led Jasper to take a view of some phases

of the situation which would be acceptable to the Carolina censors — a consideration which hampered correspondents in Germany from 1914 to 1917. But that Jasper was doing his best to tell the truth was evident from his later misfortunes. After he had watched the bombardment of Fort Sumter for several hours he was suddenly arrested as a Federal spy and locked up in a jail which, he complained, was fit only for negroes. A day or so later he was released and ordered to take the first train north, and his demand for the restoration of his watch and pocketbook was met by the warning from the Governor that he had better not linger in Charleston, as the authorities would probably be unable to protect him from the mob. Jasper finally escaped to Washington, in disguise. His experiences differ in degree rather than in kind from those of any newspaperman who tries to tell the truth as he sees it about a question on which there is violent difference of opinion; but they were not unusual in 1861. A number of northern correspondents had narrow escapes from lynching.

When the war actually began these men who knew the South for the most part became correspondents with the armies. Raymond, with some assistance from the *Times* Washington bureau, covered the first battle of Bull Run himself. As at Solferino, he saw most of it — or most of the earlier phase of it. At two o'clock, convinced that the victory was complete and that McDowell's army had nothing more to do but to march on to Richmond, Raymond went back to Washington to file his dispatch. Returning to the battlefield toward

sunset he suddenly encountered much of the army and all of the spectators in precipitate retreat. The correspondent who had written and filed the story of a great victory now had to set to work to collect the news of a great disaster. Raymond did it; he covered the story all over and sent a substitute dispatch to *The Times*. But there was a censor in Washington that night, and of Raymond's two or three columns only a few disconnected and innocuous sentences ever got into the paper.

This seems to have been Raymond's last appearance as a war correspondent, but the men who followed the Union armies for *The Times* in the East and in the West lived up to the standard which he had set both as a writer and as a gatherer of news.

In the sixties it seems to have been regarded as a natural manifestation of the news instinct to beat the other correspondents on the general's intentions for tomorrow's battle, no matter what the injury to the public interests.

According to a rumor preserved in the army, though not in the *Times* office, one correspondent of the paper was carried away so far by his eagerness for news, during the battle of the Wilderness, that he was lucky to escape with being thrown out of the camp. One night Grant and Meade, being desirous of talking over in the utmost privacy what they thought they could do to Lee the next day, strolled out of the headquarters tent and down to a thicket just beyond the light of the campfire. As they were talking in low tones they heard a movement in the bushes, and making investigation discovered a *Times* correspondent lying on his belly and busily

noting down the strategic plans of the Army of the Potomac. Chased away from headquarters as a result of this, the correspondent made his way to Burnside's corps, and hunted news so diligently there that he came near being shot by an unsympathetic subordinate officer before Grant's leniency permitted him to get off with a reprimand.

A more innocent and certainly more creditable manifestation of newspaper enterprise, made possible by the imperfect communications of those days, was the beating of official reports by the dispatches of correspondents. This happened with such frequency that one suspects that a general pursuing a beaten enemy, or trying to save the remnants of his army from a victorious one, often thought that he might as well wait till tomorrow to tell the War Department what had happened to him, as they would see it all in the papers anyhow. And *The Times* had the felicity, or the prudence, to beat the official reports only in the case of good news. Most expert at this was Major Ben C. Truman, one of the chief *Times* correspondents with the western armies. His story of the repulse of the Confederates at Franklin, Tennessee, reached *The Times* four days before the War Department heard from Schofield, and five days before any other paper had the news. He also accomplished a notable "beat" with an advance notice of Sherman's march from Atlanta to the sea, which luckily had no disastrous effect on the campaign.

Truman, in the opinion of some of his contemporaries, was the most brilliantly successful of all the correspondents of the Civil War. But other *Times* men, including George F. Williams, William

Swinton, and Lorenzo L. Crounse, served the paper almost as well. Swinton and Crounse were the principal *Times* correspondents with the Army of the Potomac. Crounse in particular had his share of the risks of war which correspondents encountered in those days much more often than in modern times when they are allowed to see battles only with infrequency and from a long distance in the rear. He was wounded by a shell in 1862, and later, with some other New York newspapermen, was captured by Mosby's raiders, who let them go after taking possession of their notebooks and carrying their news back for publication in the southern papers —a fact which suggests that newspapermen in those days must have taken much more legible notes than is the rule at present.

Called back from the front for a time, Crounse served as night editor of the paper in the spring of 1864, and his vigilance prevented *The Times* from being deceived by a forged document purporting to be a Presidential proclamation appointing a day of fasting and prayer, which was invented for its effect on the stock market, and was actually published in three New York papers. After this he got back to the Army of the Potomac in time to cover the fall of Richmond and the surrender of Lee.

But not all the hazards of the Civil War were experienced by men in the field. The "internal front" as painfully known in recent years was one of the great facts of the Civil War also, though men had not then given it a name; and the internal front in New York became in July, 1863, one of the liveliest portions of the fighting line when the

JOHN C. REID,
Managing Editor, 1872-1889.

LOUIS J. JENNINGS,
Editor-in-Chief,
1869-1876.

JOHN FOORD,
Editor-in-Chief,
1876-1883.

troops had all gone to Pennsylvania to stop Lee and the draft riots broke out. Raymond was no more afraid of rebellion across the street than of rebellion in the cotton states. Some of the New York papers, congenitally sympathetic not only with the Southern Confederacy but with Tammany Hall and the elements from which that body and the draft riots both derived their chief support, found it convenient as well as congenial to pat the mob on the head. So did some of the public men of the time; the Governor of the State did not think it beneath his dignity, such as it was, to try to conciliate the rioters. But while the mob was burning houses, plundering stores, and shooting policemen, Raymond was writing such lines as these:

> This mob is not our master. It is not to be compounded with by paying blackmail. It is not to be supplicated and sued to stay its hand. It is to be defied, confronted, grappled with, prostrated, crushed.

Warned by the misfortune of *The Tribune*, which had actually been attacked by the rioters and saved only by opportune arrival of a detachment of the overworked police, *The Times* had fortified itself.

The Gatling gun had lately been invented and offered to the War Department, though it was not used either widely or successfully in the war. Two specimens of this gun had been obtained by *The Times*, according to tradition through the President's friendship for Raymond, and were mounted just inside the business office under the command of Leonard W. Jerome. If the mob had not been more interested in attacking those who were unable to

defend themselves, it would have found some trouble waiting for it at the *Times* office, for the entire staff had been armed with rifles; and there was a third Gatling gun on the roof, mounted so that it could sweep the streets in any direction. It is only a malicious invention of jealous rivals that this gun was kept trained on the window of Horace Greeley's office in the near-by Tribune Building.

Raymond insisted that the draft was only the excuse and not the cause of the riot.

> Were the conscription law to be abrogated tomorrow [he wrote] the controlling inspiration of the mob would remain the same. It comes from sources independent of that law, or of any other — from malignant hate toward those in better circumstances, from a craving for plunder, from a love of commotion, from a barbarous spite against a different race, from a disposition to bolster up the failing fortunes of the southern rebels.

Indeed, the only utterance of *The Times* in the period of the riot which was in any degree ambiguous was its editorial comment on Archbishop Hughes's address, which managed, with evident difficulty, to be as polite, as vague, and as noncommittal as the utterances of the prelate himself.

Thirty-two members of the *Times* staff, it may be added, served in the Union armies, and two went south to join the Confederate forces.

Allowing for the curious taste of the time, which dictated such practises as beginning a long series of

dispatches with the oldest of the lot, and burying the latest news at the bottom of a five-column story, the news judgment of war-time editors was pretty good. Now and then, of course, there were exceptions to this rule. On November 20, 1863, for example, *The Times* published an editorial article on two remarkable orations which it printed in full that morning in its news columns. One, which took up two columns of the first page, was Henry Ward Beecher's speech at the Brooklyn Academy of Music, reporting his experiences as a propagandist in England. The other, by Edward Everett, briefly mentioned in the front-page news story where it belonged, was published verbatim on page 2, and took up all of it.

In its editorial comment *The Times* remarked:

> We devote a broadside of this morning's *Times* to the publication of two orations which we are sure will command the attention of the day, and not of this day only. The elaborate and finished discourses of two such men as Edward Everett and Henry Ward Beecher, upon topics of such great national interest as those they discuss, will not be lightly passed over, much less ignored altogether, by any intelligent citizen.

There was another speech in that day's news — a speech which *The Times* printed on the front page because it was part of a front-page story, and in full — it was only two sticks long; printed in full just after the much longer invocation by the officiating clergyman, also given word for word, and

just ahead of the equally detailed list of prominent persons present. That address was received with applause, according to the *Times* report; but the applause was certain, even if not perfunctory, on account of the high position of the orator, and if the news story is to be believed it provoked none of the enthusiasm called forth by Everett's speech on the same occasion. And as for editorial comment, it was not merely lightly passed over, but ignored altogether, not only in the *Times* office but everywhere else. It was the address delivered by Abraham Lincoln at Gettysburg.

The transformations which the war accomplished in newspaper making were not confined to the demand for more news, and an increase in the expense of getting it. The public which reads the newspapers is apt to forget that the mechanical task of getting the news before the public is on the whole as difficult as the obtaining of the news in the first place, and usually a good deal more expensive. The war drove *The Times* to buy additional presses, and to adopt (in July, 1861) the process of stereotyping, which *The Tribune* had already tried out and without which it would have been all but impossible to meet the demands of a rapidly increasing circulation. Typesetting machines were not known until much later, and newspapermen of today may still experience a salutary awe as they contemplate the very respectable results which their predecessors accomplished with such inferior tools.

On April 20, 1861, eight days after the attack on Fort Sumter, *The Times* for the first time was issued

on Sunday. There had long been in existence in New York papers issued on Sunday only, as there are in England today; but New York dailies were driven to the issuance of Sunday editions by the Civil War, as were London dailies in the war lately ended. A newspaper published seven days a week still seems uncongenial to the English temperament; the Sunday issues published occasionally between 1914 and 1919 did not establish a precedent. But the New York morning papers, once committed to the Sunday edition, never gave it up.

At first *The Sunday Times* was issued at the regular price of two cents. Before its first year was ended, however, it had gone up to three cents, to which price the daily paper followed it in 1862. The enormously increased telegraph tolls, the mounting prices of print paper, and the general increase in the cost of everything made this increase inevitable. In 1864 *The Times*, daily and Sunday, went up to four cents a copy, at which price it remained for nineteen years. During the war the Sunday paper was virtually the same as the issue of any other day; but it gradually came to include first of all a considerable literary element, and then more and more of what would today be known as magazine features; so that long before *The Sunday Times* had departed from the daily norm of eight pages it had a character which made it a sort of link between the weekly edition, by that time passing out of favor, and the modern Sunday newspaper with its many departments.

The war brought increased expense, but also increased circulation. On May 2, 1861, while the war

was still a novelty, *The Times* made the editorial declaration that it had gained 40,000 in circulation in the preceding two weeks. It may be noted that one of the few lapses of Raymond's paper from the standard of dignity which he set was a somewhat unworthy controversy with Bennett at the end of 1861 about the relative circulation of *The Times* and *The Herald*. *The Times* offered to put up a forfeit of $2500 for the families of volunteer soldiers in support of its assertion that *The Herald's* circulation did not average more than 100,000, as Bennett asserted, but less than 75,000, and that *The Times's* daily average was more than 75,000. Bennett, perhaps from considerations of prudence, responded in a manner worthy of Greeley that "the practise of betting is immoral; we cannot approve of it." And the consequence was the publication on the first page of *The Times* of two caricatures of Bennett — the first pictorial illustrations ever carried in the paper. Raymond, according to tradition, was afterwards ashamed of this, and certainly the paper which he published was able to stand on its merits without entering into a species of controversy in which *The Herald* was much more experienced.

At any rate, *The Times* gained steadily in prosperity throughout the war, and in December of 1865 took a step which the pressure both of news and advertising had long since made advisable — the enlargement of its page in both directions. It continued for some years thereafter to restrict itself to eight pages, but the pages were now seven columns wide and of the present length. At that time it was the largest paper in the United States, and

equal in size to the ordinary edition of *The London Times*. There were pessimistic newspapermen in 1865 who thought that Raymond and Jones overestimated the possibilities of their business, and that a newspaper of such size could not be supported in New York. They soon learned otherwise.

Shortly after this, however, *The Times* did suffer a serious — though temporary — setback in influence and prosperity as a consequence of Raymond's position in politics. Raymond took his seat in Congress in the special session called in March, 1865. The rebellion was visibly coming to an end, and the conditions of peace and plans of reconstruction were now the topics of greatest importance in public life. Throughout the war *The Times* had been the strongest of newspaper opponents of any sort of defeatist propaganda or of the influences working for a peace by negotiation. It had, to be sure, looked with favor on Lincoln's conference with the Confederate leaders early in the year, for it knew and trusted Lincoln. It knew that Lincoln would, as he did, refuse to consider a compromise peace. With the volunteer experts in statecraft (of a type with which our generation became familiar in the winter of 1917–18) who would have made peace by some sort of happy magic formula without settling any of the questions that were being fought out, *The Times* had no sympathy, but it did believe, with Grant and Lincoln, that the southerners were our own people, citizens of an indestructible union. It favored the punishment — at least by exile — of the few men whom it regarded as the fomenters of

the rebellion; but it regarded the mass of the southern people as led astray by its leaders.

Raymond's views had been expressed in outline in the course of a speech at Wilmington, as early as November, 1863. In the last months of the war they found frequent expression in the columns of *The Times*. On April 13, 1865, for example, *The Times* declared that "if the people lately in revolt choose to accept the result of the war like reasonable men . . . every facility should be accorded them for the speedy repossession of every franchise and privilege existing under the constitution." It insisted, to be sure, that we must wait and see if they were going to accept the result of the war, for at that time Jefferson Davis was still at large and there were die-hards in the South who would have taken to the woods for a guerrilla war. But these extremists found no support; in a few weeks the southern armies had surrendered, the soldiers who might have formed guerrilla bands had gone wearily back home, and the war was at an end. By that time, however, Abraham Lincoln was dead.

The war against secession had been won, but support of the constitutional theory of secession had reappeared in the most unlikely quarter, among the extreme leaders of the Republican party. Thaddeus Stevens, Ben Wade and their colleagues maintained that the southern states had accomplished what no northerner in 1861 would have admitted as possible — that they had cut themselves off from the union. Possibly Lincoln, if he had lived, would by his great prestige have been able to beat down the opposition of these men who, before his death, had re-

The New-York Times.

VOL. XII—NO. 3676. NEW-YORK, MONDAY, JULY 6, 1863. PRICE THREE CENTS.

THE GREAT BATTLES.

Splendid Triumph of the Army of the Potomac.

ROUT OF LEE'S FORCES ON FRIDAY

The Most Terrible Struggle of the War.

TREMENDOUS ARTILLERY DUEL.

Repeated Charges of the Rebel Columns Upon Our Position.

Every Charge Repulsed with Great Slaughter.

The Death of Longstreet and Hill.

Our Cavalry Active on the Enemy's Flank.

THE REBEL RETREAT CUT OFF.

Chambersburgh in Our Possession.

Advance of the Militia under Gen. Smith to Important Positions.

The Rebel Pontoon Bridge at Williamsport Destroyed.

The Contents of the Captured Dispatches from Jeff. Davis to Lee.

A Peremptory Order for the Rebel Ar-

of the enemy's killed and wounded in our hands.

GEORGE G. MEADE, Major-General.

THIRD DISPATCH.

HEADQUARTERS ARMY POTOMAC, July 4—10 P. M.

To Maj.-Gen. Halleck:

No change of affairs since my dispatch of noon.

GEO. G. MEADE, Major-General.

FOURTH DISPATCH.

WASHINGTON, Monday, July 6—12.30 A. M.

The following is the latest official dispatch:

HEADQUARTERS ARMY OF THE POTOMAC, Sunday, July 5—8:30 A. M.

MAJOR-GEN. HALLECK: The enemy retired under cover of the night and the heavy rain, in the direction of Fairfield and Cashtown.

Our cavalry are in pursuit.

I cannot give you the details of our captures in prisoners, colors and arms.

Upward of twenty battle-flags will be turned in from one corps.

My wounded and those of the enemy are in our hands. GEO. G. MEADE, Major-General.

THE PRESIDENT TO THE COUNTRY.

WASHINGTON, D. C., July 4—10:30 A. M.

The President announces to the country that news from the Army of the Potomac, up to 10 P. M. of the 3d, is such as to cover that army with the highest honor; to promise a great success to the cause of the Union, and to claim the condolence of all for the many gallant fallen; and that for this, he especially desires that on this day He, whose will, not ours, should ever be done, be everywhere remembered and reverenced with profoundest gratitude.

(Signed) A. LINCOLN.

THE GREAT BATTLE OF FRIDAY.

Our Special Telegrams from the Battle-Field.

NEAR GETTYSBURGH, Saturday, July 4.

Another great battle was fought yesterday afternoon, resulting in a magnificent success to the National arms.

At 2 o'clock P. M., LONGSTREET's whole corps advanced from the rebel centre against our centre. The enemy's forces were hurled upon our position by columns in mass, and also in lines of battle. Our centre was held by Gen. HANCOCK, with

Thousands of prisoners have been sent to the rear, and yet the conflict still continues.

The losses on both sides are heavy. Among our wounded officers are HANCOCK, GIBBON and a great many others whose names I feel restrained from publishing without being assured that they are positively in the list of casualties.

It is near sunset. Our troops hold the field, with many rebel prisoners in their hands. The enemy has been magnificently repulsed for three days—repulsed on all sides—most magnificently to-day. Every effort made by him since Wednesday morning to penetrate MEADE's lines has been foiled. The final results of the action, I hope to be able to give you at a later hour this evening.

S. WILKESON.

DISPATCH TO THE ASSOCIATED PRESS.

HEADQUARTERS ARMY OF THE POTOMAC, Friday, July 3—6 A. M.

The enemy's guns opened on our left wing at daylight, apparently to feel our position. They found us "at home," and soon suspended operations. They also endeavored to push forward their front on our right, but were driven back with loss.

9:40 *A. M.*—An hour ago, the enemy made a strong infantry attack on our right, and endeavored to break our line. The Twelfth corps, which formed our right, steadily drove them back for half an hour, when the enemy were reinforced, and a portion of the Sixth corps was sent to its support.

Failing in this, the enemy opened a heavy cannonade all along the line. The attack on the right is believed to have been a feint to cover a more formidable flank movement on the left. The cannonading is now heavy in that direction, and appears to be extending.

The Third Corps suffered greatly yesterday. The number of wounded is heavy, with a large number of officers. No estimate can be formed of the killed at this writing.

Heavy musketry has opened now on our right again and cannonading on our left is slackening. The enemy are fighting with the greatest desperation. Nothing can surpass the vigor and precision of our artillery.

Yesterday, the rebels took two of our guns, for want of horses and infantry support, but the division (HUMPHREY's, I think,) rallied and recaptured them. We took one from the enemy.

which they fired being far beyond their original position, and the infantry columns had withdrawn to their covers.

We took upward of three thousand prisoners. The enemy captured but few if any of our men.

The rebel prisoners report that *Gen. A. P. Hill was killed outright upon the field*, and that their officers suffered far greater casualties than in any previous engagement.

So terrific was the enemy's fire that the small house where Gen. MEADE and Staff were quartered, was perforated by several shots. Many of the Staff horses were killed around the house.

Gen. BUTTERFIELD was struck in the breast, and it is feared internally injured, by a piece of shell which exploded in the building. Lieut.-Col. JOSEPH DICKINSON, of the Staff, had his left arm perforated by a flying fragment of shell, and it seemed a miracle that no greater damage was done to life or limb.

Several of our general officers were wounded in the engagement. Gen. HANCOCK was wounded in the leg. Gens. GIBBON, WARREN and HUNT were wounded. In consequence of the excitement and difficulty in ascertaining their locations, the names of many prominent officers reported as killed or wounded cannot be ascertained to-night.

Too much credit cannot be given to our artillerists, who for hours stood to their guns under a broiling sun, and surrounded by the missiles of death, retiring only to give their positions to others, when their caissons and limbers were exhausted of ammunition. The infantry engaged also nobly did their duty, and the enemy to-day at their hands *has received the greatest disaster ever administered by the Union forces.*

All officers award the highest honors to Gen. MEADE for the able generalship he has displayed since he assumed command, and particularly for his coolness, decision and energy on this memorable 3d of July.

Last night, believing it to be his duty to the cause, and to learn how far he would be supported in the approaching conflict, he summoned his corps and division commanders for consultation.

DETAILS FROM OUR SPECIAL CORRESPONDENT.

HEADQUARTERS ARMY OF POTOMAC, Saturday Night, July 4.

Who can write the history of a battle whose eyes are immovably fastened upon a central figure of transcendingly absorbing interest—the dead body of an oldest born, crushed by a shell in a position where a battery should never have been sent, and abandoned to death in a building where surgeons dared not to stay?

The battle of Gettysburgh! I am told that it commenced ... of July, a mile north of the town,

ceased. A silence as of deep sleep fell upon the field of battle. Our army cooked, ate and slumbered. The rebel army moved 120 guns to the west, and massed there LONGSTREET's corps and HILL's corps, to hurl them upon the really weakest point of our entire position.

Eleven o'clock—twelve o'clock—one o'clock. In the shadow cast by the tiny farm house 16 by 20, which Gen. MEADE had made his Headquarters, lay wearied Staff officers and tired reporters. There was not wanting to the peacefulness of the scene the singing of a bird, which had a nest in a peach tree within the tiny yard of the whitewashed cottage. In the midst of its warbling, a shell screamed over the house, instantly followed by another, and another, and in a moment the air was full of the most complete artillery prelude to an infantry battle that was ever exhibited. Every size and form of shell known to British and to American gunnery shrieked, whirled, moaned, whistled and wrathfully fluttered over our ground. As many as six in a second, constantly two in a second, bursting and screaming over and around the headquarters, made a very hell of fire that amazed the oldest officers. They burst in the yard—burst next to the fence on both sides, garnished as usual with the hitched horses of aids and orderlies. The fastened animals reared and plunged with terror. Then one fell, then another—sixteen laid dead and mangled before the fire ceased, still fastened by their halters, which gave the expression of being wickedly tied up to die painfully. These brute victims of a cruel war touched all hearts. Through the midst of the storm of screaming and exploding shells, an ambulance, driven by its frenzied conductor at full speed, presented to all of us the marvelous spectacle of a horse going rapidly on three legs. A hinder one had been shot off at the hock. A shell tore up the little step of the Headquarters Cottage, and ripped bags of oats as with a knife. Another soon carried off one of its two pillars. Soon a spherical case burst opposite the open door—another ripped through the low garret. The remaining pillar went almost immediately to the howl of a fixed shot that WHITWORTH must have made. During this fire the houses at twenty and thirty feet distant, were receiving their death, and soldiers in Federal blue were torn to pieces in the road and died with the peculiar yells that blend the extorted cry of pain with horror and despair. Not an orderly—not an ambulance—not a straggler was to be seen upon the plain swept by this tempest of orchestral death thirty minutes after it commenced. Were not one hundred and twenty pieces of artillery, trying to cut from the field every battery we had in position to resist their purposed infantry attack, and

wet clay I have passionately kissed, and I look up and see Christ spanning this battle-field with his feet and reaching fraternal and lovingly up to heaven. His right hand opens the gates of Paradise—with his left he beckons to these mutilated, bloody, swollen forms to ascend.

INCIDENTS OF THE BATTLE.

Capt. CUSHING, Company A, Fourth Regular artillery, was killed, and his battery suffered severely. The gallantry of this officer is beyond praise. Severely wounded early in the afternoon, he refused to leave his post beside his guns, but continued to pour grape and canister into the advancing columns of the rebels until they had reached the very muzzles of his pieces, and sure of their capture, were attempting to turn them upon our forces, when they were driven off by our infantry. At this moment Capt. CUSHING received his death wound, and fell lifeless to the earth. Heaps of corpses and wounded in front of his battery this morning, told a terrible tale of the effectiveness of its fire.

None of the company were taken prisoners by the rebels. After the battle but one gun of this battery remained uninjured—the rest having been dismounted or destroyed by the terrible fire of the enemy, which for the time was concentrated upon the batteries on this part of the field. In front of this position fell dead the rebel Gen. DICK GARNETT, who was courageously leading his men in this charge upon our batteries on Crow Hill. The rebel Gen. ARMSTEAD was also wounded here while advancing at the head of his brigade.

About fifty yards in front of our batteries was a stone wall, running from our centre in a southwesterly direction, behind which laid several of our regiments, picking off the enemy as they advanced up the slope of the hill. Notwithstanding the terrible fire poured into their ranks from our guns, so impetuous was the charge of the rebels that they drove our men from their position, and were advancing upon our batteries, several of which they captured, but the capture was only temporary. Gen. GIBBON's division, composed of Gens. WEBB's, HARRELL's and HALL's brigades, at the point of the bayonet, drove them back over the stone wall into the plain below.

Gen. GIBBON's division captured fourteen stand of colors and a large number of prisoners. Twenty-eight stands of colors in all were captured by the Second corps.

Gen. ARMISTEAD, when taken prisoner, asked immediately for Gen. MEADE, who was his classmate at West Point.

Col. WARD, of the Fifteenth Massachusetts, was killed.

Corp. HAYDEN, of the First Minnesota, was captured—escaped, seized a musket and seized a rare opportunity, and actually made ten rebels surrender.

HEADQUARTERS ARMY OF POTOMAC,
NEAR GETTYSBURGH, Friday, July 3—8½ P. M. }

Major-Gen. Halleck, General-in-Chief:

The enemy opened at 1 P. M., from about one hundred and fifty guns, concentrated upon my left centre, continuing without intermission for about three hours, at the expiration of which time, he assaulted my left centre twice, being, upon both occasions, handsomely repulsed, with severe loss to him, leaving in our hands nearly three thousand prisoners.

Among the prisoners is Brig.-Gen. ARMSTEAD and many Colonels and officers of lesser rank.

The enemy left many dead upon the field, and a large number of wounded in our hands.

The loss upon our side has been considerable. Maj.-Gen. HANCOCK and Brig.-Gen. GIBBON were wounded.

After the repelling of the assaults, indications leading to the belief that the enemy might be withdrawing, a reconnoissance was pushed forward from the left and the enemy found to be in force.

At the present hour all is quiet.

My cavalry have been engaged all day on both flanks of the enemy, harassing and vigorously attacking him with great success, notwithstanding they encountered superior numbers both of cavalry and infantry.

The army is in fine spirits.

GEORGE G. MEADE,
Maj.-Gen. Commanding.

WASHINGTON, Sunday, July 5—4 P. M.

The latest official dispatch received here, up to this hour, from Gen. MEADE, is dated at Headquarters Army of Potomac, 7 A. M., July 4, which merely states that the enemy had withdrawn from his position, occupied for attack, on Friday. The information in the possession of Gen. MEADE, at that hour, did not develop the character of the enemy's movement, whether it was a retreat or a manœuvre for other purposes.

Reliable information received here to-day asserts that Gen. LEE's Headquarters were at Cashtown yesterday afternoon, and further represents that the rebels were fortifying at Newman's Cut, in the South Mountains, apparently to cover a retreat.

Later official dispatches are expected this evening.

SECOND DISPATCH.

HEADQUARTERS ARMY OF POTOMAC,
July 4—Noon. }

Maj.-Gen. Halleck:

The position of affairs is not materially changed since my last dispatch of 7 A. M.

We now hold Gettysburgh.

The enemy has abandoned large numbers of his killed and wounded on the field.

I shall probably be able to give you a return of our captures and losses before night, and a return

[illegible] and after a furious battle, lasting until 5 o'clock, the enemy were driven from the field, LONGSTREET's corps being almost annihilated.

The battle was a most magnificent spectacle. It was fought on an open plain, just south of Gettysburgh, with not a tree to interrupt the view. The courage of our men was perfectly sublime.

At 5 P. M. what was left of the enemy *retreated in utter confusion*, leaving dozens of flags, and Gen. HANCOCK estimated *at least five thousand killed and wounded on the field.*

The battle was fought by Gen. HANCOCK with splendid valor. He won imperishable honor, and Gen. MEADE thanked him in the name of the army and the country. He was wounded in the thigh, but remained on the field.

The number of prisoners taken is estimated at 3,000, including at least two Brigadier-Generals—OLMSTEAD, of Georgia, and another—both wounded.

The conduct of our veterans was perfectly magnificent. More than twenty battle flags were taken by our troops. Nearly every regiment has one. The Nineteenth Massachusetts captured four. The repulse was so disastrous to the enemy, that LONGSTREET's corps is perfectly used up. Gen GIBBON was wounded in the shoulder. Gen. WEBB was wounded and remained on the field. Col. HAMMELL, of the Sixty-sixth New-York, was wounded in the arm.

At 7 o'clock last evening, Gen. MEADE ordered the Third corps, supported by the Sixth, to attack the enemy's right, which was done, and the battle lasted until dark, when a good deal of ground had been gained.

During the day EWELL's corps kept up a desultory attack upon SLOCUM on the right, but was repulsed.

Our cavalry is to-day playing savagely upon the enemy's flank and rear. L. L. CROUNSE.

FROM ANOTHER CORRESPONDENT.

GETTYSBURGH, Friday, July 3.

The experience of all the tried and veteran officers of the Army of the Potomac tells of no such desperate conflict as has been in progress during this day. The cannonading of Chancellorsville, Malvern and Manassas were pastimes compared with this. At the headquarters, where I write, sixteen of the horses of Gen. MEADE's staff officers were killed by shell. The house was completely riddled. The Chief of Staff, Gen. BUTTERFIELD, was knocked down by a fragment of case-shot. Col. DICKINSON, Assistant Adjutant-General, had the bone of his wrist pierced through by a piece of shell. Lieut. OLIVER, of Gen. BUTTERFIELD's Staff, was struck in the head; and Capt. CARPENTER, of Gen. MEADE's escort, was wounded in the eye.

While I write the ground about me is covered thick with rebel dead, mingled with our own

[illegible] yesterday, the massacre was beyond parallel. Some of the guns were masked, and did not open until the enemy were within canister range.

IMPORTANT SEMI-OFFICIAL DETAILS.

HEADQUARTERS ARMY OF THE POTOMAC,
July 3, 1863. }

The decisive battle has been fought to-day, and the enemy have been repulsed with terrific loss.

At daylight LEE's right wing batteries opened upon our left, and shortly after those of his centre followed. After half an hour's cannonading, doing but little damage to us, the fire slackened, and only occasional shots were exchanged.

Shortly afterward the enemy's left, composed entirely of infantry and sharpshooters, made an attack on our right wing. So sudden and impetuous was it accomplished that our skirmishers and front line were driven back from their intrenchments; but, by the aid of the batteries in the rear, and the indomitable bravery of the Twelfth corps, we regained the first position, capturing a considerable number of prisoners.

Several hours of ominous silence followed this repulse. At 1 o'clock the enemy fired two shots, apparently as signals for the grandest artillery fight ever witnessed on this continent. Before a moment had elapsed it is estimated that at least eighty guns opened upon us. Our batteries returned the compliment with interest. *The air seemed literally thick with iron*, and for more than an hour it seemed impossible that man or beast could live through it. Strange to say the enemy's accuracy of range, as exhibited on the two previous days, was wanting on this occasion. Most of their shells exploded far in the rear of our front, and generally missing our batteries.

Under cover of this *feu d'enfer*, LEE advanced his columns of infantry from the covers, and made several desperate attempts to carry the lines by assault; but each successive attempt was repulsed with terrible havoc to their ranks.

After an hour's incessant cannonading the fire grew less intense for a short time, but was again renewed for a little while, with great spirit. During this period, some of our batteries whose ammunition was expended and the men exhausted, ceased to fire, and on the approach of the reserve batteries, withdrew to the rear. The enemy only seeing the batteries withdrawing, and mistaking this for a retreat, made a massed infantry charge up the hill, and obtained a position in our lines, cutting to pieces and almost annihilating the small infantry supports; but before they had time to rejoice at their imaginary success, the fresh batteries poured in a deadly fire of canister and case-shot. The infantry reserves joined on either flank of the gap, charged them, and added greatly to their destruction. They were completely surprised; and *hundreds of them threw down their arms and asked for quarter.* Nearly the entire brigade of Gen. DICK GARNETT surrendered, and GARNETT himself, wounded, barely made his escape.

Longstreet was mortally wounded and captured. He is reported to have died in an hour afterward.

About 4:30 P. M. the artillery of the enemy slackened and had entirely ceased at 5, the last shots

[illegible] the young and the old blood with which it was bought. The error put us on the defensive, and gave us the choice of position. From the moment that our artillery and infantry rolled back through the main street of Gettysburgh and rolled out of the town to the circle of eminences south of it. We were not to attack but to be attacked. The risks, the difficulties and the disadvantages of the coming battle were the enemy's. Our were the heights for artillery; ours the short, inside lines for manœuvreing and reinforcing; ours the cover of stonewalls, fences and the crests of hills. The ground upon which we were driven to accept battle was wonderfully favorable to us. A popular description of it would be to say that it was in form an elongated and somewhat sharpened horseshoe, with the toe to Gettysburgh and the heel to the south.

LEE's plan of battle was simple. He massed his troops upon the east side of this shoe of position, and thundered on it obstinately to break it. The shelling of our batteries from the nearest overlooking hill, and the unflinching courage and complete discipline of the army of the Potomac repelled the attack. It was renewed at the point of of the shoe—renewed desperately at the southwest heel—renewed on the western side with an effort consecrated to success by EWELL's earnest oaths, and on which the fate of the invasion of Pennsylvania was fully put at stake. Only a perfect infantry and an artillery educated in the midst of charges of hostile brigades could possibly have sustained this assault. HANCOCK's corps did sustain it, and has covered itself with immortal honors by its constancy and courage. The total wreck of CUSHING's battery—the list of its killed and wounded—the losses of officers, men and horses COWEN sustained—and the marvellous outspread upon the board of death of dead soldiers and dead animals—of dead soldiers in blue, and dead soldiers in gray—more marvellous to me than anything I have ever seen in war—are a ghastly and shocking testimony to the terrible fight of the Second corps that none will gainsay. That corps will ever have the distinction of breaking the pride and power of the rebel invasion.

For such details as I have the heart for. The battle commenced at daylight, on the side of the horse-shoe position, exactly opposite to that which EWELL had sworn to crush through. Musketry preceded the rising of the sun. A thick wood veiled this fight, but out of its leafy darkness arose the smoke and the surging and swelling of the fire, from intermittent to continuous, and crushing, told of the wise tactics of the rebels of attacking in force and changing their troops. Seemingly the attack of the day was to be made through that wood. The demonstration was protracted—it was absolutely preparative; but there was no artillery fire accompanying the musketry, and shrewd officers in our western front mentioned, with the gravity due to the fact, that the rebels had felled trees at intervals upon the edge of the wood they occupied in face of our position. These were breastworks for the protection of artillerymen.

Suddenly, and about 10 in the forenoon, the firing on the east side, and everywhere, about our lines,

[illegible] explode. Shells in the yard. The air thicker and fuller and more deafening with the howling and whirring of these infernal missles. The chief of staff struck—SETH WILLIAMS—loved and respected through the army, separated from instant death by two inches of space vertically measured. An Aide bored with a fragment of iron through the bone of the arm. Another, cut with an exploded piece. And the time measured on the sluggish watches was one hour and forty minutes.

Then there was a lull, and we knew that the rebel infantry was charging. And splendidly they did this work—the highest and severest test of the stuff that soldiers are made of. HILL's division, in line of battle, came first on the double-quick. Their muskets at the "right-shoulder-shift." LONGSTREET's came as the support, at the usual distance, with war cries and a savage insolence as yet untutored by defeat. They rushed in perfect order across the open field up to the very muzzles of the guns, which tore lanes through them as they came. But they met men who were their equals in spirit, and their superiors in tenacity. There never was better fighting since Thermopylæ than was done yesterday by our infantry and artillery. The rebels were over our defences. They had cleaned cannoniers and horses from one of the guns, and were whirling it around to use upon us. The bayonet drove them back. But so hard pressed was this brave infantry that at one time, from the exhaustion of their ammunition, every battery upon the principal crest of attack was silent, except CROWEN's. His service of grape and cannister was awful. It enabled our line, outnumbered two to one, first to beat back LONGSTREET, and then to charge upon him, and take a great number of his men and himself prisoners. Strange sight! So terrible was our musketry and artillery fire, that when ARMSTEAD's brigade was checked in its charge, and stood reeling, all of its men dropped their muskets and crawled on their hands and knees underneath the stream of shot till close to our troops, where they made signs of surrendering. They passed through our ranks scarcely noticed, and slowly went down the slope to the road in the rear.

Before they got there the grand charge of EWELL, solemnly sworn to and carefully prepared, had failed.

The rebels had retreated to their lines, and opened anew the storm of shell and shot from their 120 guns. Those who remained at the riddled headquarters will never the crouching, and dodging, and running, of the Butternut-colored captives when they got under this, their friends, fire. It was appalling to as good soldiers even as they were.

What remains to say of the fight? It staggled surlily on the middle of the horse shoe on the west, grew big and angry on the heel at the southwest, lasted there till 8 o'clock in the evening, when the fighting Sixth corps went joyously by as a reinforcement through the wood, bright with coffee pots on the fire.

I leave details to my excellent friend and associate Mr. HENRY. My pen is heavy. Oh, you dead, who at Gettysburgh have baptized with your blood the second birth of Freedom in America, how you are to be envied! I rise from a grave whose

[illegible] low actually threw down his gun and joined the cavalcade, and HAYDEN came in with eleven captives.

Wounded prisoners taken in Gettysburgh this morning report that Gen. BRADLEY L. JOHNSON, of Maryland, was killed in Thursday's attack on our right. He was struck by a shell while charging our lines at the head of his division. Gen. HOOD is also reported to have had his left shot off, and from the effects of which he has since died.

Rebel officers with whom I have conversed frankly admit that the result of the last two days has been most disastrous to their cause, which depended, they say, upon the success of LEE's attempt to transfer the seat of war from Virginia to the Northern Border States. A wounded rebel Colonel told me that, in the first and second days' fight, the rebel losses were between ten and eleven thousand. Yesterday they were greater still. In one part of the field, in a space not more than twenty feet in circumference, in front of Gen. GIBBONS' division, I counted seven dead rebels, three of whom were piled on top of each other. And close by in a spot not more than fifteen feet square lay fifteen "graybacks," stretched in death. These were the adventurous spirits, who in the face of the horrible stream of canister, shell and musketry, scaled the fence wall in their attempt upon our batteries. Very large numbers of wounded were also strewn around, not to mention more who had crawled away or been taken away. The field in front of the stonewall was literally covered with dead and wounded, a large proportion of whom were rebels. Where our musketry and artillery took effect they lay in swaths, as if mown down by a scythe. This field presented a horrible sight—such as has never yet been witnessed during the war. Not less than one thousand dead and wounded laid in a *space of less than four acres* in extent, and that, too, after numbers had crawled away to places of shelter.

The enemy's infantry, saving a small force of sharpshooters, was wholly out of sight at daylight on Saturday morning. There was talk on Friday night, after the battle, of organizing a column of pursuit.

Before the fighting was over—before sunset, considerably—the Signal Officers reported that an immense train of army wagons was going out of Gettysburgh northwest, on the road to Cashtown. Oh! that they could have run against the stonewall of the Harrisburgh army.

PARTIAL LIST OF KILLED AND WOUNDED.

Lieut. Dayton L. Card, commanding Co. E, 108th New York, was killed instantly by a shell. His body presented a ghastly sight. He was struck in the middle of the breast by a missle which exploded and tore him literally in two. Half of his face was also torn away by a fragment of shell.

Charles P. Leclear, Co. E, 108th N. Y.—killed.
J. Wickham, Co. E, 108th N. Y.—wounded.
Sergeant A. B Hadley, do. do.—wounded.
Sergt. M. C. Bryant, Co. E. 108th N. Y.—wounded.
J. D. Ansink, Co. E, 108th New-York—wounded.

Cowen's New-York Battery—Killed.

Privates James Gray, Otis C. Billings, Jacob Y. McIlroy, Edmund Peto.

Wounded.

Lieut. Wm. P. Wright—right breast, probably mortally.

[*Continued on Eighth Page.*]

solved to fight him as bitterly as they afterward fought Johnson. Whether or not Lincoln could have done it, the fight was left in the hands of a President whose defects of personal character and ability brought his principles into discredit; and Raymond, who for a long time stood behind Johnson as he would have stood behind Lincoln, suffered for his defense of the ideas which, if carried out, would have made reconstruction something more than an ironic euphemism.

Raymond was still chairman of the Republican National Committee, a position which gave him prestige sufficient to overcome, to a certain degree, his newness in Congress. Before the end of 1865 he was actively opposing Stevens and the other leaders of the radical Republicans, notably by a speech on December 24. But already it was apparent that the radical control of Congress could not be shaken. At a public meeting in New York in the following February Raymond undertook to defend Johnson for his veto of the Freedman's Bureau bill, and laid the blame for the "increase of ill-feeling" in the South during the past few months to the action of Congress and to the radical Republican press in the North. Raymond favored the immediate acceptance of the state governments which had been set up in some of the border states, and he wanted above all to prevent the reëstablishment of the old sectional antagonism. But the tendency of the time was too strong for him.

Nevertheless, he persisted in spite of repeated setbacks, and finally took a leading part in the "National Union Convention" which met at Phila-

delphia in August, 1866, where for the first time since the outbreak of the war men from all the states, Republicans and Democrats, met to bury the hatchet and try to lay down a program for national reunion. Raymond had had his suspicions that this body might not be of such a character as to command the confidence even of the moderate men in his party; within four weeks before it met he had in a private letter remarked that "it looks now as though it would be mainly in the hands of Copperheads." But evidently he thought, when the convention actually assembled, either that this fear was unwarranted or that his influence might counteract the presence of undesirable members from the North. At any rate, he composed the "Philadelphia Address" which the convention set before the country, declaring that "the results of the war did not either enlarge, abridge, or in any way change or affect the powers the constitution confers on the Federal government, or release that government from the restrictions which it has imposed."

This address and the declaration of principles appended was on the whole a piece of reasoning on constitutional theory not unworthy of the author of the letters to Yancey of 1860. It closed with an enthusiastic endorsement of Andrew Johnson as "a chief magistrate worthy of the nation, and equal to the great crisis upon which his lot is cast." Even then Raymond was not altogether in sympathy with Johnson's course; he supported the constitutional amendments which were eventually grouped into one (the Fourteenth) and thought Johnson unwise in opposing them.

Raymond's only contention was that Congress had no right to make acceptance of them a condition of the "readmission" of any state lately in revolt. He held that the rebellion had been, all along, what Union men considered it in the spring of 1861 — an insurrection and not a dissolution of partnership.

But those views were too advanced for the time. Secession was accepted as a fact by the dominant group in Congress, and under the stress of passion constitutional amendments were put through by unusual, if not absolutely irregular, methods, establishing precedents some of whose harmful effects have been seen within recent years. Raymond was at once furiously assailed by the majority of his party, and was accused of having gone over to the Democrats. He lost his place as chairman of the National Committee for his part in the Philadelphia convention, and the paper lost thousands of readers. Naturally, his journalistic rivals seized the opportunity to try to turn the momentary deviation of *The Times* from the majority opinion to their own financial profit. During the war, and before it, *The Times* and *The Tribune* had been the leading Republican papers of the nation. No doubt Raymond and Greeley had on the whole the same ideals, as in general they upheld the same political principles on the great issues of the Civil War period; but their reactions differed according to their temperaments. Raymond, in the critical months before the war, thought that the suspicions of the South might and should be alleviated by certain prudent concessions from the Republicans, and that Southerners unsympathetic with secession should not be driven into

the arms of the fire-eaters by unconsidered violence; but he insisted that the union must be preserved at any cost, that there must be no tolerance of secession, and that the supremacy of the Federal government must be vindicated. After war had begun he never weakened in the belief that there was no choice between complete victory and ruinous disaster; that peace without victory was peace with defeat; that the war must be fought out to the complete vindication of the Federal authority. But when that result had been accomplished he felt that the interests of the nation required the speediest possible reëstablishment of real national unity.

Greeley, in the period between Lincoln's election and the attack on Sumter, had oscillated between plaintive declarations that "the republic could not be pinned together with bayonets" and insistence on immediate and violent coercive measures which might have put the government in the wrong in the eyes of the border states. When war had come Greeley was a pretty good barometer; he was an enthusiast when things were going well, but after Fredericksburg, and again after Chancellorsville, he was willing to throw up the sponge; and he had that curious conviction that peace might be obtained by some backstairs negotiation on neutral soil and suddenly presented on a platter to a surprised nation, which while it endured furnished valuable moral support to Lee as it later did to Ludendorff.

But when the republic had been pinned together with bayonets, nobody displayed more sanctimonious horror than Greeley at Raymond's adventures in

conciliation. The man who was to go Jeff Davis's bail in 1867, and accept a Democratic Presidential nomination in 1872, in 1866 was accusing Raymond of "acting as a Copperhead" and of betraying the party, because he thought that southern Democrats were still citizens of the United States. The man who, in 1860, thought the South might as well go its way, who early in 1863 was talking of "bowing our heads to the inevitable," and was looking forward gloomily to "the best attainable peace," could in 1866 compare the editor of a competing and more prosperous paper to Judas Iscariot for standing out against vindictive punishment of the South.

But Greeley cherished no unchristian rancor; when Raymond was safely dead, Greeley was magnanimous enough to write that "he was often misjudged as a trimmer and a time server, when in fact he spoke and wrote exactly as he thought and felt." It was true; Raymond was called a trimmer; whereas Greeley acquired a great reputation as a courageous moral leader. The difference seems to have been that Greeley took a certain time off each day to advertise his morality to the public, whereas Raymond was too busy reaching conclusions a year or so ahead of the times.

A moral might be drawn from this, but it could hardly be commended to ambitious young journalists.

Raymond afterward confessed that it would have been worth $100,000 to *The Times* if he had never attended the Philadelphia convention, for great numbers of its loyal supporters promptly turned

away from a paper which they regarded as having gone over to the Copperheads. As it turned out, however, if Raymond had lived a few years longer it might have been worth a hundred thousand to the paper that he had attended the convention; for it had the result of putting him out of politics and turning him back to give his whole attention to *The Times*.

The conservative Republicans among his constituents (it is perhaps needless to observe that the terms "conservative" and "radical" had in the years just after the Civil War a technical significance entirely apart from their ordinary meanings) wanted him to try his chances for renomination to Congress, but in a letter dated only a month after the Philadelphia convention he refused. He denied that he had changed his politics. "With the Democratic party as it has been organized and directed since the rebellion broke out," he assured his friends, "I have nothing in common." But the evils of renewed factional strife which he had attempted to avert were already afflicting the country, and Raymond realized that he could no longer do anything to resist them. And he observed that "a seat in Congress ceases to have for me any attraction, or to offer any opportunity for useful public service." It is easy enough to say that Raymond knew he could not be renominated; the man's whole history is proof that considerations of this sort had nothing to do with his decision.

The last three years of Raymond's life were of great importance to his paper. On the chief of the new issues following the war he had taken the un-

popular side, and was presently forced to admit that he was following an unworthy leader. Johnson's personal shortcomings were largely responsible for compromising the cause of the moderate reconstructionists, but it may be supposed that Raymond's personal feeling had perhaps something to do with the fact that when *The Times* finally repudiated him it was on the question of paying off the national debt with fiat money. The paper opposed the impeachment of Johnson, not so much from love of Johnson as from an estimate of the motives, and a dislike of the methods, of his enemies. In the campaign of 1868 the paper was once more able to be whole-heartedly Republican, for its editors had a great deal of confidence in General Grant and in the policies which the party in that year professed.

But other new questions were arising which were to dominate the generation after the war, and on the chief of these Raymond set a policy which in general was long followed. As Edward Cary, for nearly half a century one of the principal members of the editorial staff of *The Times*, wrote in 1911:

> Apart from his policy regarding reconstruction, he had marked out three lines of discussion for his paper which were of great and lasting importance, and which even now . . . that paper follows with profound respect for the sound brain and loyal heart that set it upon them.

The first of these was the struggle against various forms of easy but unsound money — in the sixties and seventies the Greenback movement, and later free silver. Its insistence on sound money was at

least a minor reason in *The Times's* unwillingness to see any merit in the Presidential candidacy of Tilden, who had given it support in the most spectacular fight of its history; it drove the paper to stand for its principles behind the Gold Democratic ticket in 1896; and it was the first ground for a disbelief in the miraculous powers of William Jennings Bryan for which other reasons in sufficiency were soon discovered.

In Raymond's last days, also, the paper began a campaign for reform of the tariff, a principle to which it has been consistently loyal ever since. David A. Wells and Benjamin F. Tracy were called in to write special articles on this subject under Raymond, and *The Times*, though beaten in its first fight as it has been beaten in many more, began in the later sixties a steady campaign for popular education on this question which it may be hoped has contributed in some degree to the more intelligent views now prevalent. In spite of the genuflections of the present Republican Congress in the house of Rimmon, it is possible to hope that before long the protective tariff as the past generation has known it will be as dead as greenbackism and free silver.

The third of the policies which Raymond laid down for his paper was the fight for the introduction of the merit system into the civil service — a question on which the paper had sometimes expressed itself even in its earliest years, but which it took up in earnest after the Civil War. During the next two decades *The Times* was one of the most insistent and persistent advocates of a reform which

THE FIRST
TIMES BUILDING,
113 Nassau St.,
1851-1854.

THE THIRD
TIMES
BUILDING,
PARK ROW,
1857-1888.

SECOND TIMES
BUILDING,
1854-1857.

BRICK PRESBYTERIAN
CHURCH IN 1840.
Site of the Old Park Row
Building of The Times.

FORMER HOMES OF THE NEW YORK TIMES.

finally triumphed, in principle, and which after two decades more of obstruction by practical politicians of the older sort is now at last beginning to be the rule and not the exception in administration.

It was the enduring faith of *The Times* in all these causes, no less than its conductors' lack of confidence in a man who seemed to embody stiff-necked opposition to most of the needed reforms of his time, which finally led the paper to break away from the Republican party in 1884. Raymond was always a good Republican — best, perhaps, when he was most completely out of harmony with the dominant group in the party — but there can be no doubt that he would have approved of the decision which his partner and successor, Jones, had to make in that campaign.

Local issues, too, were becoming insistent in Raymond's last years. The conduct of the New York City government had always been a scandal, varying only in degree, but by the later sixties the city had fallen into the hands of William M. Tweed and the scandal was becoming unendurable. Tweed had formed an entente, useful to both parties, with the faction of Wall Street manipulators headed by Jay Gould and James Fisk, Jr., which was unable to see any need for going into the long, laborious and expensive process of building railroads when it was so much easier to acquire them already built. In 1868 *The Times* carried on a vigorous fight against the men who were making the Erie Railroad a name notable even in the scandalous chronicle of that period, and before Raymond's death there had already been threats that some of the political instru-

ments of the Wall Street-Tammany inner circle might be used to attack the management of the paper. That Raymond, if he had lived, would have fought the ring as valiantly as did Jones and Jennings cannot be doubted; and no greater tribute can be given them than the statement that not even Raymond could have been more successful.

The setback caused by Raymond's position in 1866 did not long affect the fortunes of *The Times.* It was so good a newspaper that people did not like to go without it, and its return to the outward form at least of party regularity furnished an excuse for a good many Republicans to come back to their old favorite. Some idea of the position which *The Times* held in the estimation of intelligent men at this time can be obtained from "The Education of Henry Adams." Adams had known Raymond in Washington before the war, and some of his letters to Raymond from London had been published in *The Times,* which thus may perhaps claim to have discovered him as a writer. Coming back from London with an experience which in any other country, as he has remarked, would have qualified him admirably for a post in the diplomatic service, he knew that it was hopeless to look for anything of the sort at a time when legations, secretaryships and consulates were ranked with post offices as the reward of political merit; so he thought that the best chance to use his talents and realize his ambitions was in newspaper work. But when Raymond died Adams gave up hope; for him it was *The Times* or nothing. He objected to the political views of *The Tribune;* on *The Herald,* aside from other objections, he thought

there was no room for any important personality but Bennett; and he disliked the "strong dash of blackguardism" which Dana had given *The Sun.* Writing for *The Times,* Adams could have reached a large and influential public; as for any of the other papers which his tastes would have permitted him to consider, he thought that he might as well keep on contributing to *The North American Review.*

Whether Adams would have been permanently satisfied as a newspaper man may be doubted; his case is cited here only as an incidental testimonial to *The Times's* rapid recovery from the misfortune of 1866. Early in 1869 an offer of a million dollars was made, and refused, for the property which had been established eighteen years before on a cash investment of sixty-nine thousand. So before Raymond's death *The Times* had recovered all the ground it had lost even in this department, which Raymond himself would undoubtedly have regarded as the last and least of a good newspaper's claims to eminence. His own material fortunes had risen with those of the paper; at his death he owned a third of the stock. The salary which had been fixed at $2500 a year when *The Times* was founded had been raised to $4000 in 1860. At the beginning of 1869 this was increased to $10,000 — a huge salary for that day — and at the same time an annual salary of $9000 was voted to Jones as business manager. *The Times* could afford it; the dividend that year was eighty per cent.

Had Raymond lived, and kept out of politics, the paper which under Jones's direction became more influential and powerful than ever before, and per-

formed at least one public service which must rank as one of the greatest ever accomplished by an American newspaper, would probably have been still more distinguished. For Raymond was only forty-nine when he died suddenly on June 19, 1869, two months before completing his eighteenth year as editor of the paper. Soon after E. L. Godkin, who had served under him, wrote in *The Nation* that

> *The Times* under his management probably came nearer the newspaper of the good time coming than any other in existence; in this, that it encouraged truthfulness — the reproduction of the facts uncolored by the necessities of a "cause" or the editor's personal feelings — among reporters; that it carried decency, temperance, and moderation into discussion, and banished personality from it; and thus not only supplied the only means by which rational beings can get at the truth, but helped to abate the greatest nuisance of the age, the coarseness, violence, calumny, which does so much to drive sensible and high-minded men out of public life or keep them from entering it.

Certainly Raymond was almost the inventor of the notion that it was possible to believe in a party, to belong to a party, and in general to support that party without being slavishly bound to its policies, right or wrong; and his course in the Civil War showed that this independence of sentiment did not involve any weakening of energies in upholding the truth as he saw it. In Cary's language, he established the corporate conscience of *The Times;* his successors have tried to live up to it.

Yet George Henry Payne, in his "History of Journalism in the United States," seems to think it necessary to account for Raymond's "failure," and does so by explaining that "a journalist can never succeed unless he is fathering popular or moral causes." This extraordinary statement deserves notice because it appears in the most recent book on a subject which has never yet been treated adequately, and because Mr. Payne used to be a newspaperman himself. Without going into metaphysical definitions of success, it may suffice to say that from any point of view Raymond was a brilliant success as a journalist. He was certainly a failure as a politician, if failure means the inability to hold the most powerful political position to which he rose, the chairmanship of the Republican National Committee; but even in this sense he was a failure only because he happened to die, in the prime of life, a few years before the majority came around to his view.

As to Mr. Payne's curious theories on the foundation of newspaper success, it may be observed that *The Times*, which its worst enemies will admit is successful in the sense that it is widely read, influential and prosperous, has never fathered any causes, popular or unpopular, moral or immoral; nor have some others of the most famous and richest newspapers of the world. If "fathering" was a slip of the pen for "furthering," one may wonder what "moral causes" James Gordon Bennett the First ever promoted. Neither abolition nor Fourieristic Socialism could be described as a "popular cause" in New York seventy-five years ago, yet Horace

Greeley made a paper which advocated one of these doctrines, and leaned strongly toward the other, successful in every sense of the word. Nor does this simple definition meet the case of a newspaper which may find prosperity in spite of the furtherance of causes which are both moral and unpopular, or in furthering those which are both popular and immoral. Whatever may be the secret of journalistic success, it can hardly be given away to the world as freely as Mr. Payne seems to think. The art of making a good newspaper is somewhat more than a mere gift for guessing what is going to be popular and moral at the same time; and as can be proved by the examples of Greeley, Raymond, and Bennett (to come no nearer our own time) that art may be exemplified by men who sometimes guess wrong.

CHAPTER III

The Times and the Tweed Ring

THE *Times* had been so emphatically Raymond's paper that a good many people naturally wondered, after his death, what was going to become of it. Raymond's partner, George Jones, had long been in charge of the business office, and was the ranking officer, so to speak, of those who were left. But he had had no experience in the supervision of editorial policy; his life had been spent in the business office, and few outsiders realized how thoroughly the long friendship and partnership between Raymond and Jones had indoctrinated each with the principles of the other. Nor did Jones have anything like a controlling interest in the paper. The Raymond estate, with thirty-four of the hundred shares, was the heaviest stockholder; Jones had or controlled, in 1869, about thirty. And since Raymond's son, then finishing his course at Yale, was preparing to learn the newspaper business from the ground up, it was the general expectation that in time he would succeed his father.

But *The Times* could not wait for him. On July 22, 1869, some five weeks after Raymond's death, the three directors of the company — Jones, Leonard W. Jerome, and James B. Taylor — elected John Bigelow editor. It might have been supposed that this was an excellent selection. Bigelow had for

years been associated with William Cullen Bryant in the editorial direction of *The Evening Post*, and his service as Minister to France had increased his reputation and given him an experience in international politics which at that particular time was extremely valuable. Yet his career as editor of *The Times* lasted only a few weeks, and is interesting chiefly as illustrating the fact that in the equipment of a newspaper editor the wisdom of the serpent is a somewhat more useful quality than the harmlessness of the dove.

The summer of 1869 saw Jay Gould and Jim Fisk and their associates going on from the plunder of a railroad to the more ambitious scheme of cornering the gold supply of a nation in which the resumption of specie payments was still something of a millennial dream. As is well known, they counted on the neutrality of President Grant, who was neither a financial expert nor a connoisseur in human wile, and whose brother-in-law, Corbin, a friend of the Fisk-Gould group, was generally supposed to supply most of the financial information for the White House.

Bigelow, who knew the President well, saw him early in August, and as a result of the interview wrote for *The Times* two editorial articles on Grant's economic policy which were generally understood as representing the views of the White House. At Gould's suggestion, Corbin prepared another editorial article, which a gentleman who was a friend of both Corbin and Bigelow succeeded in persuading the editor was also a reflection of Grant's opinion. This article, headed "Financial Policy of the Ad-

The New-York Times.

VOL. XIV....NO. 4220. NEW-YORK, TUESDAY, APRIL 4, 1865. PRICE FOUR CENTS

GRANT.

RICHMOND

AND

VICTORY!

The Union Army in the Rebel Capital.

Rout and Flight of the Great Rebel Army from Richmond.

Jeff. Davis and His Crew Driven Out.

Grant in Close Pursuit of Lee's Routed Forces.

Richmond and Petersburgh in Full Possession of Our Forces.

ENTHUSIASM IN THE REBEL CAPITAL.

The Citizens Welcome Our Army with Demonstrations of Joy.

RICHMOND FIRED BY THE ENEMY

Our Troops Save the City from Destruction.

front was such that he could not operate with cavalry, and his advance had, therefore, been compelled to fall back. The Fifth Corps was ordered to go to his assistance, in order to relieve it and prevent its withdrawal. Being perceived and taken advantage of by the enemy, Gen. MILES' division of the Second Corps was advanced by the left flank in its front, and it was then withdrawn to the Boydtown road. FOSTER and his staff are in the hottest part of the field, overseeing the assault in person. The General feels, no doubt, that his front is one of the most important positions on the whole line, and from its proximity to the rebel works, most liable to be broken through, except that opposite Fort Steadman, and he is consequently extremely solicitous respecting it. The front at Fort Steadman is ably defended by Gen. WILCOX.

heavy, but at this hour it is impossible to give any estimate. We have succeeded in compelling them to bring their forces from the left and thus opened the way there for SHERIDAN and WARREN to operate successfully. Their force in this front, and which we are now fighting, is Gen. GORDON'S corps, principally Southern troops from Alabama, Ga., and South Carolina. They have fought hard since the attack commenced, and still continue to dispute the ground inch by inch.

and many of their wounded fell into our hands, as well as those of our own that were unavoidably left behind yesterday afternoon.

The attack made on the enemy's line in front of the Twenty-fourth Corps was led by FOSTER'S division, and about two hundred prisoners were brought in, the One Hundred and Forty-eighth New-York taking most of them. Some three hundred or four hundred yards of ground was taken from them, and our picket line so much further advanced.

At 4 o'clock this morning this position was assaulted, and a few of our men captured; but in a very short time it was retaken, with about sixty pris-

THE GLORIOUS NEWS.

Rejoicings in City and Country

Enthusiasm, Solemnity and Thanksgiving.

Business Suspended and Flags Displayed.

The Praise of the Army on Every Tongue.

Great Mass Meetings in Wall Street and at Union Square.

Patriotic Speeches and Patriotic Songs.

The Whole City Aglow with Excitement.

ILLUMINATIONS AND FIREWORKS.

At no time since the Fall of Sumter has the City of New-York been so thoroughly excited as it was yesterday upon the announcement of the occupation of Richmond. The news in the morning journals was sufficient to arouse the most latent patriotism, and cause the hardest heart to beat with gratitude. Scarcely, however, had the people settled themselves at their various avocations when a strange whisper filled the air, penetrating to the counting-room, the workshop and the school, as if by magic, and long before the newspaper extras stamped the joyful news upon the public mind, it was everywhere known that great news had come to hand, and that victory was ours. An interested crowd gathered about the TIMES Bulletin, and as the cheering words were read again and again, great hearty cheers went up from the multitude, and joy beamed from every eye. Soon the nimble feet of the newsboys had sped with the official dispatch throughout the town, and what had been but an intuitive surmise became a patent truth. The manifestations of exhilaration were boundless; flags were flung to the breeze from innumerable stores and dwellings, making Broadway to shine with the Stars and Stripes, and casting a stream of glory upon the harbor. At the ferries, as soon as the announcement was formally made, an order was issued to deck the boats

To Major-Gen. Dix:

The following telegram from the President, announcing the EVACUATION OF PETERSBURGH and probably of Richmond, has just been received by this department:

EDWIN M. STANTON, Secretary of War.

CITY POINT, Va., April 3—8:30 A. M.

To Hon. Edwin M. Stanton, Secretary of War:

This morning Lieut.-Gen. GRANT reports Petersburgh evacuated, and he is confident that Richmond also is.

He is pushing forward to cut off, if possible, the retreating rebel army. A. LINCOLN.

THE CAPTURE OF RICHMOND.

SECOND DISPATCH.

WAR DEPARTMENT, WASHINGTON, D. C., April 3—10 A. M.

To Maj.-Gen. Dix:

It appears from a dispatch of Gen. WEITZEL just received by this Department, that our forces under his command ARE IN RICHMOND, having taken it at 8:15 this morning.

EDWIN M. STANTON, Secretary of War.

THIRD DISPATCH.

WAR DEPARTMENT, WASHINGTON, Monday, April 3—12 o'clock noon.

Maj.-Gen. Dix:

The following official confirmation of the capture of Richmond, and the announcement that the city is on fire has been received.

E. M. STANTON, Secretary of War.

CITY POINT, Monday, April 3—11 A. M.

To Edwin M. Stanton, Secretary of War:

Gen. WEITZEL telegraphs as follows:

"We took Richmond at 8:15 this morning. I captured many guns. The enemy left in great haste. The city is on fire in one place. Am making every effort to put it out. The people receive us with enthusiastic expressions of joy."

Gen. GRANT started early this morning with the army toward the Danville road, to cut off LEE's retreating army, if possible.

President LINCOLN has gone to the front.

T. S. BOWERS, A. A. G.

E. M. STANTON.

OUR SPECIAL ACCOUNTS.

Movements by Gen. Sheridan—His Call for Reinforcements—Four Thousand Prisoners Captured—Operations on the Petersburgh Front—The Gunboat Fleet Doing its Part.

From Our Own Correspondent.

HEADQUARTERS ARMY OF THE POTOMAC, Sunday, April 2—6 A. M.

After we quitted the field on Friday evening the left of the Fifth Corps swung about half a mile further round, and drove the enemy before them. But intelligence being received from Gen. SHERIDAN that the condition of the ground on his [illegible] set out early this morning to support Gen. SHERIDAN, and the divisions of Gen. GRIFFIN and Gen. CRAWFORD followed it about noon. They all formed a junction with Gen. SHERIDAN's Corps at a distance of some five miles from the Mrs. Butler house, and a general engagement commenced there about 3 o'clock.

I was not able to go out, as the distance is too great for me to accomplish anything in time for the mail. I understand, however, that the combined forces of Gens. SHERIDAN and WARREN succeeded, after a hotly contested fight, in putting the enemy to flight. They captured four thousand prisoners, four batteries of artillery, a large train of loaded wagons and a number of cattle. The rebel loss in killed and wounded, as well as our own was very heavy, but I am unable to give any estimate of the number.

On our lines during the day there was no fighting except on the Twenty-fourth Corps front. The rebels assaulted the pickets of that corps, and attempted to retake the picket line, from which they were driven yesterday. They were speedily repulsed with a loss of about twenty-five killed and wounded and sixty-four prisoners. Our loss was fifteen in the aggregate.

In the afternoon our troops were massed at three places in the Ninth Corps front, at two in the Sixth, and one in the Twenty-fourth, one in the Twenty-fifth, and two in the Second, with a view of making several demonstrations on the enemy's works and going through them, if necessary, for the complete development of the plan of attack. In pursuance with this design our artillery opened a furious cannonading along the entire front at about 11 P. M., which was continued with little intermission until 6 o'clock this morning. At 3 this morning, such of our troops as it was deemed proper to send in were got into position in front of our works and held ready to make the assault.

I have not yet had time to ascertain which troops were led to the assault, nor the results at different points, and am only able to speak of the Second Division, Gen. POTTER's, of the Ninth Corps. This division was posted on that part of the line between forts Sedgwick and Davis, and some time before the hour of attack arrived the Brigade Commanders Gens. GRIFFIN and CURTIN, perceiving the opportunity to do so without endangering their own men made a sortie and captured one hundred and thirty-three men and four officers of the rebel pickets.

His picket-line was completely surprised, and only knew of the attack when called upon to surrender At this hour, 6 A. M., there is exceedingly heavy firing along the entire line from Deep Bottom to the Boydtown plank-road, and the fleet of gunboats on the James River are participating in it.

The assault on the enemy's works commenced at 4 o'clock in several places, and is still progressing, but with what success is not yet known. In the front of the Second Division of the Ninth Corps there seems to be more artillery engaged than elsewhere on the line, except at the point where the gunboats are engaged. But Gen. POTTER and his two able Brigade Generals, GRIFFIN and CURTIN, are holding their men well up the work, and the determination is universal throughout the division to go through if required. Gen.

Among the prisoners captured by the Ninth Corps are eight officers, one of them a Major. Col. GOWAN, of the Forty-eighth Pennsylvania, was badly wounded, as also Col. WINSLOW and Major STEINBERGE, of the One Hundred and Sixth New-York; Col. GREGG, One Hundred and Seventy-ninth New-York, badly wounded and reported dead. The fighting was so severe that the loss on both sides must necessarily be very heavy. The rebels fought our men hand to hand when we were about climbing the parapet of the fort, although lying down at the time to avoid the fire of our advancing line. Gen. GRIFFIN, of the Second Brigade of the Division, led the way into their works, and when Gen. POTTER sent to ask if he could hold the works, and if not to fall back, his reply was, "Tell Gen. POTTER I can hold the works. Send me more men if you can; but I will hold the works." He took command of the division on Gen. POTTER being wounded. Gen. CURTIN, of the First Brigade, also behaved with great gallantry, holding his men up to the works till an entrance was effected, and then dashing forward at their head driving the enemy before him. This fight, even if not ultimately successful, proves the old Ninth Corps to be equal to any emergency. The task set for it is the worst this army ever had to do, and so far it has accomplished the object unaided. Everybody here thinks those who are left of us will quarter in Petersburgh to-night, and that the old stars and stripes will wave over the cockade city ere the setting of the sun. In taking Petersburgh we draw the cord that will soon strangle the rebellion in Richmond.

Gen. WILCOX is also in the field with his staff. The lines here are also very close together, and if our forces should be repulsed and disordered, the enemy would have an excellent opportunity to inflict serious damage, and make us pay dearly for the temerity we have evinced in attempting to assault such almost impregnable works as those he occupies along this line.

Gen. HARTRANFT'S Division is engaged in the assault, but I am not able to say at what particular point or with what success. It is composed wholly of new troops who have never been in any engagement but that of the 25th ult., but they behaved so nobly on that occasion that great things are expected of them. And they have such regard for their brave and noble Division Commander that they will no doubt strive hard for the sake of his reputation and their own, Gen. PARKE, the Corps Commander, is also near the scene of action with his staff and within range of the enemy's guns directing the operations. From the present aspect of affairs he will have cause to be proud of his corps ere the day closes as we are no doubt already partially within the enemy's lines, strong as they are, whether we can hold them will soon be known. It is thought here that we can both take and hold them.

1 *o'clock. A. M.*—The demonstration in front of the Second division of the Ninth Corps promises to be a success. We have captured two of their forts, guns and all, and the line of works between and on either flank, and have taken two hundred more prisoners. The fight is still raging furiously. Our loss must be within their line of works and will hold them. By to-night, I hope to write you from Petersburgh.

H. H. YOUNG.

Skirmishing on March 30 Near Supporty Cross-Roads.

From Our Own Correspondent.

DINWIDDIE COURT-HOUSE, Va., Thursday, March 30, Via WASHINGTON, Monday, April 3—8:45 P. M.

The advance of Gen. SHERIDAN'S command crossed Hatcher's Run yesterday, meeting only slight opposition and annoyance at that place from the enemy's cavalry.

W. H. F. LEE's cavalry, three brigades, was in front, but did not see fit to make a stand.

To-day, in an attempt to reach Supporty cross-roads, some of PICKETT'S command and LEE's cavalry formed a line of battle and held the ground. In the skirmish that took place the following named persons were wounded:

KILLED AND WOUNDED.

John Leonard, Company F, Sixth United States Cavalry, left thigh, flesh; James N. Glosswax, Company A, Sixth United States Cavalry, hip; John Thompson, Company M, Sixth United States Cavalry; Henry M. Feelan, First United States Cavalry; Patrick Germon, Company F, Sixth United States Cavalry; John Mooney, Company M, Seventh Michigan; Sergt. Marsh, First Michigan, killed; Sergt. J. L. Cullek, Seventh Michigan, foot; Sergt. R. Harris, Fifth United States Cavalry; J. B. Morril, Company M, Fifth United States Cavalry; Sergt. Thomas M. Welles, Company F, Sixth United States Cavalry; Sergt. James Homer; Corp. E. Leabe, Fifth United States Cavalry, arm, severe; Sergt. J. Miller, Sixth United States; J. Davidson, First Michigan; Maj. Duggin, First Michigan; William Sherburne, Twentieth Pennsylvania; D. Duggin, First Michigan; George Nash; Corp. George Derrick; Sergt. Robert Rordan, Sixth New-York; Corp. George B. Lott, Twentieth Pennsylvania.

E. A. PAUL.

Details of the Victory.

Dispatches to the Associated Press.

HEADQUARTERS ARMY OF THE POTOMAC, Saturday, April 1.

The greater portion of the army has not been engaged with the enemy to-day. The time has been occupied in erecting works on the new line, and repairing the roads connecting the different corps. The late rains had rendered it impossible to move the wagon trains as fast as the troops advanced. One train took forty-eight hours to move five miles with the assistance of one thousand men. But through the untiring industry and perseverance of the officers in charge of the Quartermaster's and Commissary Departments, the army has been almost as well supplied as while in their old quarters.

When the news of SHERIDAN'S repulse reached here last night, a part of the Fifth Corps was at once despatched to his aid, and it is expected that to-night or in the morning we shall receive good news from that quarter.

It appears that SHERIDAN was moving on the road leading to a place called the Three Forks, about three miles from the Southside Railroad, when two cavalry brigades of PICKETT'S division, which had been moved out in a great hurry, came down on a road running from Sutherland Station. As SHERIDAN'S cavalry had most of them passed the junction, this movement of the enemy threatened to cut him off. He, however, discovered his danger in time to get his command back with only a slight loss, at the same time taking about 100 prisoners. Both the LEES were present, but one of them was at a respectful distance.

On being reinforced this morning by the Fifth Corps, the enemy fell back so rapidly that their dead Artillery, is reported wounded and a prisoner.

Three sharpshooters were brought into the Fifth Corps headquarters this morning, sixteen cavalrymen belonging to WM. HENRY LEE's command.

They had been on picket duty and were cut off by the force which went to the assistance of SHERIDAN.

SECOND DISPATCH.

HEADQUARTERS OF THE ARMY OF THE POTOMAC, April 1—Midnight.

A courier from Major-Gen. SHERIDAN has just arrived with the most cheering news.

The combined forces of cavalry and Major-Gen. WARREN'S infantry advanced against the enemy this afternoon, driving them several miles, and capturing about 4,000 prisoners and a number of pieces of artillery.

They retreated to Five Forks, where they were flanked by a part of the Fifth Corps, which had moved down the White Oak road. It was here the large number of prisoners were taken.

The rebels then retreated south along the White Oak road, and were vigorously pursued by Gen. SHERIDAN, while MCKENZIE'S cavalry from the Army of the James, advanced west on the Ford road toward the Southside road, and when the messenger left was only about three miles from it, and would undoubtedly reach it before morning.

Thus the last great line of railroad the rebels have to supply their capital and LEE's army by is about to be severed, and it is firmly believed that they will immediately leave their present position in Petersburgh and Richmond.

Sharp cannonading is now going on near the centre of the line, held by the left of the Sixth Corps.

REPORTS VIA BALTIMORE.

Capture of Forts Hell and Damnation—Heavy Losses.

Special Dispatch to the Evening Telegraph.

BALTIMORE, Monday, April 3.

The latest news here this morning is, that our forces had captured Fort Damnation last night, with all its armament and many prisoners. This fort is near Fort Hell, and one of the strongest and most important rebel forts.

It is also reported that Petersburgh has been captured.

The fighting has been terrible, and the losses heavy on both sides; but the rebel loss thus far is three times more than ours.

It is believed that SHERIDAN by this time has cut the Danville Railroad.

The Flood in the St. Lawrence—Submersion at Montreal—The Victoria Bridge in Danger.

MONTREAL, Monday, April 3.

The river rose several feet on Saturday and was piled with ice to a great heighth. One of the shoves came near striking a tube of the Victoria Bridge.

Yesterday morning, the river rose much higher, flooding William, Wellington and other streets. Between 5 and 6 o'clock in the evening, the ice shoved again and the water rushed over the revetment wall, flooding Commission-street. At about 11 o'clock, it again rose as high as St. Paul and St. Gill streets.

The Grand Trunk Railway track between Bonaventure and the tanneries is inundated.

The river rose a foot higher this morning.

The inundated parts of the city are covered with rafts formed with scows and boats.

At present, by far the greater part of the western end of the city is inaccessible except by boats.

The flood is causing the greatest suffering and distress.

Later—4 O'clock P. M.—The water is now slowly falling.

Fire at Louisville, Ky.

LOUISVILLE, Ky., Monday, April 3.

NUMONT'S dry goods store, on Market-street, was burned this morning. EVERMAN'S bakery and HELBURNE & Co.'s dry goods store, adjoining, were also injured by falling walls and water. The aggregate loss is $60,000, upon which there is very little insurance.

[illegible] South-street and West-street, Broad-street and Beaver-street, with the neighboring marts of traffic, vied in patriotic display with the hotels of Broadway and the mansions of the upper end. The magnetism of delight was upon every man. Not a dismal face, not an averted eye, not a pursed-up mouth was seen, nor a croaking tongue heard. No one suggested an "if" or a "but," but every one accepted the glad tidings as truth from the pen of an "honest man." Hand grasped hand in places where "how much" and "how low," are the ordinary salutation; "glorious news" and "thank God" sprang from lips more accustomed to "buyer sixty" and "seller ten;" hard pebbled spectacles that have weathered the beatings of the world and the buffetings of care for sixty years without a moisture, were wet with tears of gratitude, and men estranged for months grasped each others willing palm, while their hearts beat in harmonious thanksgiving. In the public and private schools as much and as genuine enthusiasm was displayed as in the harsher schools of Wall and William streets. Appropriate addresses were made in several of them by the Principals, and the national hymns were sung with a gusto which only school boys and girls can give. One theme was upon every lip—the boats, the cars, the restaurants, the stages, the streets were full of cheerful, happy, exulting, forgiving people, who waived all ceremony, all points of etiquette, and chatted busily each with his neighbor upon the one great occurrence of the day.

It would be idle to disguise the fact that our people rejoiced particularly over the fact that Richmond, the rebel capital, the home of the Confederate President, the seat of their government, the hub and centre of the contest, was at length occupied by our troops. Atlanta, Savannah, Wilmington and Charleston especially were each in turn the object of public attention and anxiety, but after all Richmond was the point after which the popular heart yearned. There it was that JEFF. and his satellites had reared their temple, there the skill of rebel engineers and the energies of their Gen. LEE had been spent in lines of defence and fortifications of strength. It has been the boast of any Southern man that come what might Richmond was forever theirs; that no power this side of Heaven could take it. For years this kind of talk has been made by the Southern people, and for years the sympathizing newspapers of this city and elsewhere have indorsed it, so that our people have felt within them an irrepressible longing for its possession. They wanted its lines of defence broken and its fortifications captured—they wanted JEFF. DAVIS driven out or hanged at his door post, and Gen. LEE swept from his intrenchments by besom of the Union. At length it came, and came, too, so suddenly, that the people were quite unprepared for it. It took the city several hours to accept the startling fact, to recognize its magnitude; and it is very doubtful if even yet the vast extent of the victory is duly appreciated. As each successive dispatch was placed upon the bulletins of the newspapers, the crowds increased in numbers, but the cup of enthusiasm was too full for further addition. Hardly would the paper be placed upon its board, before its contents would be thundered out to the people by some quick-sighted person, and after cheers were given for the news, he would be called upon for a repetition, and so let up was vouchsafed him until hoarse with shouting and perspiring with exertion, he gave way to a successor, who, in turn, read and reread the stirring dispatches.

Many were the jokes made at the expense of JEFF. and his gray coats; many were the queer suggestions and odd ideas thrown out as to Mr. LINCOLN's probable course. One man, who kept the crowd near our bulletin in a constant uproar, suggested that it would be a good idea if Old ABE would take rooms at the Spottswood House, and issue from thence a proclamation of amnesty to every mother's son in rebeldom, always excepting old JEFF., MASON, and SLI[illegible]

[*Continued on Eighth Page.*]

ministration," was published in *The Times* on August 25. Luckily Caleb C. Norvell, the financial editor, had seen it in proof and had suggested to the surprised Bigelow that it showed evidence of a purpose to "bull gold," presumably in furtherance of the enterprise whose beginnings were already visible to men in Wall Street. The last paragraph was struck out and the article thereby rendered innocuous; but the rest of it was published. Less than a month later came Black Friday, when Grant shattered the final assault of the gold conspirators by opening up the Treasury's reserves; and shortly after that Bigelow left *The Times*.

Jones was justifiably alarmed by this experience, and was consequently forced to set himself, at the age of fifty-eight, to learn something about the editorial management as well as the business affairs of the paper. There seems to have been some surprise among newspapermen of the time when it was discovered that Jones wanted to go on alone. Greeley, for example, attempted to buy *The Times* in the summer after Raymond's death. When *The Tribune* was established Greeley had owned it all, but he was no financier, and at the time of his death retained only one sixteenth of the stock. This coincidence of an editor without a newspaper and a newspaper without an editor suggested to Greeley the idea of buying *The Times*, which he seems to have supposed would be a burden on Jones's hands. But Jones replied that he would never sell out "so long as he was on top of the sod," so Greeley had to stick to *The Tribune*.

After Bigelow's retirement the post of editor of *The*

Times, under Jones's supervision, was given to George Shepard, who for some time had been one of the political editorial writers. In the 1901 Jubilee Supplement of *The Times* Shepard's editorship was thus characterized: "The decorum and solid ability which had long characterized *The Times* were perfectly safe in his hands, but sprightliness was undoubtedly lacking." There were those on the paper, however, who had perhaps an excess of sprightliness, and chief of these was Louis J. Jennings, a man with a great deal of talent, a great deal of temperament, and a character so commingled of opposite qualities that one wonders alternately why he did not achieve brilliant success, and how he managed to get as far as he did. Jennings was an Englishman, who had edited *The Times of India*, served as American correspondent of *The London Times* just after the Civil War, and then written London correspondence for *The New York Times*. He seems to have had an affection for the name, and during Bigelow's brief editorship he had been added to the editorial staff of the paper.

Shortly after Shepard took over the direction of the editorial page, on November 25, 1869, there was a murder in the *Tribune* office. Albert D. Richardson, one of the stockholders in and contributors to that paper, was shot and mortally wounded by a gentleman whose wife had left him for a complex of reasons of which Richardson was one. Mrs. McFarland had obtained a divorce in Indiana, her husband having been served by publication in local papers, and she was married to Richardson on his deathbed. Two or three eminent clergymen signal-

ized their breadth of opinion, if not their literal fidelity to the doctrines of their churches, by defending the relation as an innocent one and turning public sympathy against the injurious husband, if indeed it was not running in that direction already.

This was too much for Jennings's moral principles, especially as it had happened in the office of a rival newspaper. Despite Shepard's hesitation, Jennings succeeded in getting into *The Times* a number of editorials on this case — which indeed was celebrated enough, at the time, to deserve some comment. Beginning with the innocuous and generally acceptable doctrine that newspapermen had no special privilege of seduction, he went on to ask what else could be expected from those who had preached the malignant doctrines of Fourier, destructive of family ties. This must have surprised Greeley, who by that time had almost forgotten his youthful adventures in Socialism, along with other ebullient eccentricities of his earlier years. But nothing was clearer to Jennings than that the infection imported by Brisbane still befouled the *Tribune* office, and that free love, with its consequences of murder or suicide, was the natural result of taking *The Tribune* editorial page seriously.

Jennings had an exceptional talent for stirring up the animals. *The Tribune* presently began to retaliate against these editorial attacks by a counter-offensive; but Jennings being a recent arrival and little known, its editors naturally took for their target the respectable Shepard. After a few weeks of this Shepard told Jones that Jennings could fight his own battles. Shepard retired to his old position

as a writer of political articles and Jennings became editor of *The Times*. In the great battle against Tweed which soon followed Jennings was the leader of the offensive. Jones had the responsibility, and a heavy responsibility it was; John Foord, who had lately joined the editorial staff, handled most of the work of analyzing political and financial evidence that came into the hands of the paper; and equipped with the facts exhumed by Foord, and fortified by the knowledge that Jones was standing behind him, Jennings put his talent for invective to a somewhat more useful employment than annoyance of *The Tribune*.

It is customary, in discussing the Tweed ring, to call attention to the gradual and in the long view quite considerable improvement in the standard of New York municipal politics. Even in the worst scandals of more recent periods the offenders showed a certain regard for outward order and decency. City officials no longer thrust their arms into the city treasury and steal money outright, as Tweed and his associates used to do; modern peculations are measured by thousands where they stole millions, and the unearned increment in the fortunes of certain political leaders of today and yesterday can be traced back to such diverse and subsidiary transactions as taking a percentage from gamblers and prostitutes, or a fortunate and extremely silent partnership in contracting firms dealing with the city or with corporations dependent for franchises on municipal favor.

The percentage of honest men in Tammany Hall is probably higher now than in the days of Croker,

certainly higher than in the days of Tweed or Fernando Wood; and the improvement in public morals has affected even the reform movements. They are no longer, as they were apt to be in the forties and fifties, about as bad as Tammany. They no longer can be bought off by judicious distribution of offices to their leaders, as sometimes happened in the sixties and seventies; nor, in spite of the recent declamations of enthusiastic Republican leaders, are they as likely to make themselves impotent by divisions and quarreling as they were in the eighties and nineties. It is perhaps a matter for dispute whether stupidity and incompetence is an improvement on venality, but there is no doubt that there is a great deal of mere stupidity today where in similar conditions even twenty years ago there would have been corruption.

Still, when all allowance is made for these laudable tendencies, the dispassionate observer can hardly admit that New York would be justified in giving three cheers for itself. Nor does the study of a century of municipal history tend to make converts for the philosophy of Pippa and Pollyanna. It is a painful chronicle of alternating indignation, apathy, and despair; if it teaches anything, it is only the old lesson that the solution of political problems is not to be found in changes of political machinery. In the last hundred years New York has tried about everything. Greater measures of home rule have been introduced as a desperate remedy, in the hope that centralization of responsibility would enable the public to keep officials up to the mark; but it was exactly such

centralization that made possible the enormous stealings of Tweed and his confederates. In reaction from this the city, or that part of it interested in honest government, has from time to time thrown itself on the mercy of the legislature, only to find presently, not exactly that it has exchanged King Log for King Stork, but that between storks the one who spends stolen money at home has at least some advantage over the one who plunders the city for the enrichment of up-state.

In the period of Tweed's supremacy New York had the misfortune of enduring practically all these varieties of political experience, and for some years each new arrangement proved to be worse than what had gone before. The chief accomplishment of *The Times's* exposure of Tweed was the breaking of this ascending spiral. Thievery soon began again, but on a much humbler scale and with considerably more caution. And never since has municipal corruption been anything like so enormous, or so flagrant, as in the period between 1868 and 1871. There have been no more Tweeds; but in view of the lessons of New York City's history, it would be rather venturesome to assert that there will never be another Tweed in the future.

In the fifties and early sixties the dominant figure in Tammany Hall was Fernando Wood, but even then Tweed was doing pretty well for himself. The charter of 1857 had given control of the city's finances to an elective bipartisan Board of Supervisors, twelve in number, on which Tweed managed to obtain a dominant position. Corruption, which had always existed in the city government, rapidly

increased under the benign sway of this virtually irremovable body, but the golden days of graft began only with the election of 1868, when by wholesale naturalizations at the last minute, the voting of cartloads of repeaters, stuffing of the ballot boxes, and other devices now happily gone out of fashion, Tammany elected John T. Hoffman governor of the state and A. Oakey Hall mayor of the city. The legislature was also Democratic by a very slight majority; but the precarious margin could be, and on occasion was, enlarged by the purchase of any necessary number of upstate Republicans. Tweed came into control of both state and city governments on January 1, 1869; his domination was ended in the fall of 1871. It is a tribute both to his ingenuity and to the largeness of his view that estimates of the amount which he and his associates stole in that brief period range from fifty million to a hundred million dollars.

To remove the possibility of inconvenient inquiry into his doings Tweed put through the legislature in 1870 — with the aid of purchased Republican votes — a new city charter. In its preliminary advertising it was proclaimed as a home rule measure; on that understanding it got a good deal of respectable support; even *The Times*, disgusted with the conditions that had arisen under the prevalent system, in the beginning favored the measure. But it presently turned out that the document was full of jokers, and that its real effect, as John Foord has put it, was to turn the city over to the control of four men — the Mayor, Hall; the president of the Board of Supervisors, Tweed; the Controller,

Richard B. Connolly; and the president of the Park Board, Peter B. Sweeney. Heads of departments were appointed by the Mayor, for terms of four or eight years, and during their terms were practically irremovable. This alone would have been enough for moderate men; but for good measure a provision was thrown in that all claims against the County of New York incurred previous to the passage of the act should be audited by Hall, Tweed, and Connolly, and met by revenue bonds payable during 1871.

This board met only once, and then voted that all claims certified by the Board of Supervisors to the County Auditor and presented by him to the Board of Audit should be authorized. In other words, Tweed sent his bills to the Auditor — James Watson, one of his own creatures — and this functionary passed them on to the Board of Audit to receive a blanket endorsement — from Tweed. In this manner some six million dollars was "audited," mainly in connection with work done, or alleged to have been done, on the construction, equipment and repair of the County Court House. Some of the claims were purely fictitious; the others were all set down at far more than the real value of the work; and of it all Tweed and certain of his associates received 65 per cent at first, and eventually 85 per cent.

This was the most scandalous and the most easily visible of the multitudinous thefts promoted by Tweed. Others were of the familiar sort — fraudulent contracts, payrolls padded with the names of dead men, of babes in arms, or of Tammany ward heelers who had to be supported but did not want

CHARLES R. MILLER,
Editor-in-Chief.

to soil their hands with work except on election day; appropriations for the support of non-existent institutions, huge payments to companies in which Tweed or his friends had an interest. But the suspicions which were inevitably aroused by such enormous and ubiquitous peculations were slow in taking definite form. Ostensibly, Tweed was saving money for the city. He reduced the tax rate in 1871, and thereby won the gratitude of tax-payers who had become alarmed at the rapid and unaccountable increase in municipal expenses. Just how much the city was spending or how much it owed nobody knew, but it was evidently a great deal. Tweed's sudden show of economy had its effect in winning support for him among the property-owning classes, and though their suspicions were not killed by any means, a good many respectable and prosperous citizens had become so discouraged with municipal politics, so willing to grasp at any straw of hope, that they were pleased to adopt the policy of the ostrich, and try to pretend that they believed public affairs were being honestly conducted, instead of undertaking the difficult and dangerous process of attempting to find out.

As a matter of fact, Tweed had reduced the tax rate by the very simple process of abandoning the pay-as-you-go plan of municipal finance, and meeting most of the claims which he and his friends presented to the city — together with the comparatively infrequent bills from honest creditors — by the issue of thirty-year bonds; while so far as possible the demands were met by short-term obligations not funded at all. In a city containing

as many competent financiers as New York there were a good many men who saw through this, but none who dared to speak out. The man who did dare to speak was George Jones, and under his direction *The Times* began in September, 1870, a campaign which resulted, after fourteen months, in the complete overthrow of Tweed.

That *The Times* did not begin its attack sooner may perhaps be ascribed to the influence of James B. Taylor, who was one of the three directors of the paper, and one of Tweed's four partners in the New York Printing Company. The history of this organization would alone furnish valuable matter for reflection to political reformers, and some useful hints to thieving politicians; but for the purposes of this narrative it is enough to say that before the exposure of the ring it had received some millions of public money for very slight services, and that Tweed's far-ranging plans looked to making it the sole agency for the printing not only of the city, but of the state and eventually of the nation.

Taylor had been a stockholder in *The Times* since April, 1861, and his associates evidently had a good opinion of him, since though he held only one tenth of the stock he was elected to Raymond's place on the directorate. But that he would have been able to hold back the paper forever from its assault on the ring is a quite untenable supposition, in view of the character of George Jones. Taylor died early in September, 1870, and *The Times's* campaign began soon after; but for the first few months the paper had nothing to go on but its suspicions, and Taylor's objections could well have been, and presumably

were, based on the risk of commencing an attack on the most formidable and best intrenched group of political conspirators the country had ever known without conclusive evidence.

It would be agreeable to suppose that similar considerations of prudence were alone responsible for the fact that the other dailies of the city were at best neutral in the fight, while most of them actually supported Tweed until his guilt was proved beyond any question; but the record shows otherwise. There was a reason why *The Times* had to fight single-handed, except for the support of *Harper's Weekly*, which in Nast's cartoons had a weapon even more powerful than Jennings's vituperation. Enormous sums were being spent for municipal advertising, most of which was quite unnecessary. A good deal of it went to obscure publications either existing solely for the purpose of printing public advertisements, or chiefly maintained by that source of revenue, and owned by various members of the ring; but much of it went to the regular newspapers of the city, and cannot be called anything but a hush fund.

For a while *The Times* received its share of this advertising, which was rejected when it became apparent that it was a hush fund. But Tweed and his subordinates had been wise enough to see that the city was always pretty well in arrears of payment; when *The Times* refused to accept further city advertising, the city refused to pay its bill. *The Times* went to court and got a judgment, but the litigation furnished an excuse by which Mayor Hall tried — though unsuccessfully — to explain the "animus" which the paper eventually displayed by

telling the truth about the city government. In the meantime the account refused by *The Times* was turned over to *The Tribune*, which for some time showed a reluctance to believe, or to publish, anything reflecting on Tweed. In view of the fact that Tweed was at that time the boss of the Democratic party not only in the city but in the state, and was becoming dangerously powerful in his influence on the national leaders of the party, this is an instance of magnanimity toward a political enemy quite without parallel in the history of the period.

The hush fund did its work. When the other papers said anything about Tweed, it was in his defense. *The Sun*, to be sure, did make the ironic proposal of a monument to the "benefactor of the people," the fund to be started by a contribution of ten cents which *The Sun* professed to have received from one of Tweed's admirers. Tweed indeed suspected that Dana was not altogether in earnest, and for this and other reasons refused to accept any such testimonial; but a good many of *The Sun's* readers, as well as some historians of later days, took the suggestion seriously.

The attack was begun by the most obvious method, and the one most readily available in view of the lack of any definite evidence. *The Times* called the attention of its readers to Tweed's sudden and enormous wealth, and asked where he had got it. Again and again the paper called on the respectable leaders of the Democratic party to disown their associate; but just then that would have been somewhat difficult. Tweed could have disowned them and remained a Democrat, but they could hardly

disown the man who had carried the state for the presidential ticket in 1868, and who was still in absolute control of the state organization, without finding themselves out in the cold.

Then *The Times* began to ask for a little information about the city's finances. For a year and a half no statement of them had been published. It was presumed that the Controller, Connolly, was still keeping books, but they were locked away as carefully as the golden plates of the Book of Mormon, despite a law which prescribed that they should be open to the public. For two months the campaign was carried on with all the vigor of which Jennings was capable, but apparently it had little effect. In the fall of 1870 the reform ticket — supported by Republicans, independents, and those Democrats who had turned against Tweed either on principle, or because they had been excluded from the profits that were reserved for the favorites of the inner circle — was beaten by a handsome majority. There was a good deal of reason to suppose that Governor Hoffman and Mayor Hall owed their reelection largely to Tweed's foresight in buying up a good many of the Republican election inspectors; but whatever the reason, they were reëlected.

But *The Times* and *Harper's Weekly* kept on fighting. They kept on despite the discouragement of the election, the evidence that only a minority of New Yorkers took any interest in the continuous and enormous thefts of their own money; despite the opposition of all the other papers, which imputed motives to *The Times* running all the way down from partisan malice against the Democratic leader,

and vindictive efforts to force the payment of the overdue advertising bill, to accusations that the editors of the paper had been bought. In view of the fact that Tweed and his friends could, and eventually did, offer a good deal more for *The Times's* silence than could conceivably be bid by anybody for its continuance of the attacks, this was not a very plausible accusation; but it was often repeated and doubtless believed by a good many who had their own reasons for clinging to their faith in Tweed.

A great many worthy citizens thought that *The Times* was unreasonable and vindictive. There was heard the complaint, since become painfully familiar, that criticisms of the administration were injuring the good name and the credit of the city, and that it was the duty of all good citizens to boost New York — and its officials. Even the reformers of the period were silent. The Citizens' Association had lately been formed for the promotion of higher standards of municipal government. It was organized and intended for reform; it began as a representative of public-spirited taxpayers, and its president was Peter Cooper. But its secretary was soon won over by the gift of a municipal office; and Peter Cooper presently allowed himself to be convinced that Tweed and his friends had stolen as much as they could use, and that hereafter it would be to their interest to turn conservative and save money for the taxpayer.

If this happened to the chief reform organization of the period, it may be surmised how easily Tweed flattered, bribed or terrorized other respectable citizens into giving him at least tacit support. It was

dangerous to oppose him — particularly dangerous for rich men, since Tweed controlled the assessments for taxation and could raise them to any figure that suited him if property owners gave him cause for hostility. And undoubtedly a good many men kept still out of sheer apathy — the apathy begotten of long experience with city governments each of which was more corrupt than its predecessor, and the conviction that even if good citizens got together they would probably be beaten up at the polls by Tammany thugs, or counted out by Tammany election inspectors.

The most amazing instance of Tweed's ability to mobilize the respectability of the city in his support is the famous audit of the Controller's books in the fall of 1870. *The Times* had been calling on Connolly to let the citizens know how much the city was spending, and what it owed. In October Connolly suddenly announced that he would do so, and would submit his books to the inspection of six of the most distinguished and reputable business men of New York — Moses Taylor, E. D. Brown, John Jacob Astor, George K. Sistare, Edward Schell, and Marshall O. Roberts. Their report was published on November 1 — just before the election — and undoubtedly gave to many good citizens a plausible pacifier for the disturbed conscience. For the committee reported that "the account books of the department are faithfully kept. . . . We have come to the conclusion and certify that the financial affairs of the city, under the charge of the Controller, are administered in a correct and faithful manner."

As Foord observes in his "Life of Andrew H. Green":

> These names represent the foremost financial interests of their time, and no group of men could have been selected more likely to command the confidence of the people of New York. Yet, at the very time they certified to the correctness of the Controller's books, those records contained the evidence of direct thefts amounting to about twelve million dollars, while the testimony they bore to indirect stealing was equivalent to many millions more.

Connolly's books, indeed, were "correct." They showed that thus much money had been paid to such and such persons for this and that. When *The Times* later published these records it was at once observed that payments of several hundred thousand dollars to individual carpenters or painters for a month's work seemed somewhat unusual, and that it was curious that three or four men had endorsed all the receipts, no matter in whose names the claims stood; but nothing of the sort seems to have occurred to the six respectable citizens.

Their report, however, was convincing enough to those who wanted to be convinced; but Tweed discovered that there was one man in New York who could not be bought off or scared off. *The Times* continued the fight. Tweed did everything he could to fight back. Two years before, when the paper was fighting the Erie Railroad conspirators, a Tweed-Fisk judge had suggested to the grand jury that it had better indict Raymond and Jones; but the grand jury did not take the advice. Now a new

The New-York Times.

VOL. XIV......NO. 4225. NEW-YORK, MONDAY, APRIL 10, 1865. PRICE FOUR CENTS

HANG OUT YOUR BANNERS

UNION

VICTORY!

PEACE!

Surrender of General Lee and His Whole Army.

THE WORK OF PALM SUNDAY.

Final Triumph of the Army of the Potomac.

The Strategy and Diplomacy of Lieut.-Gen. Grant.

the Richmond and Lynchburgh road to the Farmville and Lynchburgh road, I am at this writing about four miles West of Walter's church, and will push forward to the front for the purpose of meeting you.

Notice sent to me, on this road, where you wish the interview to take place, will meet me.

Very respectfully, your ob'd't servant,
U. S. GRANT,
Lieutenant-General.

APPOMATTOX COURT-HOUSE, April 9, 1865.

General R. E. Lee, Commanding C. S. A.:

In accordance with the substance of my letters to you of the 8th inst., I propose to receive the surrender of the Army of Northern Virginia on the following terms, to wit:

Rolls of all the officers and men to be made in duplicate, one copy to be given to an officer designated by me, the other to be retained by such officers as you may designate.

The officers to give their individual paroles not to take arms against the Government of the United States until properly exchanged, and each company or regimental commander sign a like parole for the men of their commands.

The arms, artillery and public property to be packed and stacked and turned over to the officers appointed by me to receive them.

This will not embrace the side-arms of the officers, nor their private horses or baggage. This done, EACH OFFICER AND MAN WILL BE ALLOWED TO RETURN TO THEIR HOMES, not to be disturbed by United States authority so long as they observe their parole and the laws in force where they reside.

Very respectfully,
U. S. GRANT, Lieutenant-General.

HEADQUARTERS ARMY OF NORTHERN VIRGINIA, April 9, 1865.

Lieut.-Gen. U. S. Grant, Commanding U. S. A.:

GENERAL: I have received your letter of this date, CONTAINING THE TERMS OF SURRENDER OF THE ARMY OF NORTHERN VIRGINIA, as proposed by you. As they are substantially the same as those ex-

pose of arranging definitely the terms upon which the surrender of the Army of Northern Virginia will be received.

Very respectfully, your obedient servant,
U. S. GRANT, Lieut.-General,
Commanding armies of the United States.

April 8, 1865.

GENERAL: I received, at a late hour, your note of to-day, in answer to mine of yesterday.

I did not intend to propose the surrender of the Army of Northern Virginia, but *to ask the terms* of your proposition. To be frank, I do not think the emergency has arisen to call for the surrender.

But as *the restoration of peace should be the sole object of all*, I desire to know whether your proposals would tend to that end.

I cannot, therefore, meet you with a view to surrender the Army of Northern Virginia, but *as far as your proposition may affect the Confederate States forces under my command, and tend to the restoration of peace*, I should be pleased to meet you at 10 A. M., to-morrow, on the old stage road to Richmond, between the picket lines of the two armies.

Very respectfully, your obedient servant,
R. E. LEE,
General, C. S. A.

To Lieut.-Gen. GRANT, Commanding Armies of the United States.

APRIL 9, 1865.

General R. E. Lee, commanding C. S. A.:

GENERAL: Your note of yesterday is received. As I have no authority to treat on the subject of peace, the meeting proposed for 10 A. M. to-day could lead to no good. I will state, however, General, that *I am equally anxious for peace with yourself*; and the whole North entertain the same feeling. *The terms upon which peace can be had are well understood. By the South laying down their arms, they will hasten that most desirable event, save thousands of human lives, and hundreds of millions of property not yet destroyed.*

Sincerely hoping that all our difficulties may be settled *without the loss of another life*, I subscribe myself,

Very respectfully,
Your obedient servant,
U. S. GRANT,
Lieutenant-General United States Army.

REJOICINGS.

THE VICTORY.

Thanks to God, the Giver of Victory.

Honors to Gen. Grant and His Gallant Army.

A NATIONAL SALUTE ORDERED.

Two Hundred Guns to be Fired at the Headquarters of Every Army, Department, Post and Arsenal.

[OFFICIAL.]

WAR DEPARTMENT, WASHINGTON, D. C., April 9, 1865—9:30 P. M.

Lieut.-Gen. Grant:

Thanks be to Almighty God for the great victory with which he has this day crowned you and the gallant armies under your command.

The thanks of this Department and of the Government, and of the People of the United States —their reverence and honor have been deserved— will be rendered to you and the brave and gallant officers and soldiers of your army for all time.

EDWIN M. STANTON, Secretary of War.

WAR DEPARTMENT, WASHINGTON, D. C., April 9, 1865—10 o'clock P. M.

Ordered: That a salute of two hundred guns be fired at the headquarters of every army and department, and at every post and arsenal in the United States, and at the Military Academy at West Point on the day of the receipt of this order, in commemoration of the surrender of Gen. ROBERT E. LEE and the Army of Northern Virginia to Lieut.-Gen. GRANT and the army under his command. Report of the receipt and execution of this order to be made to the Adjutant-General at Washington.

EDWIN M. STANTON,
Secretary of War.

FROM RICHMOND.

Perils and Excitements of a Voyage Up the James—Scenes and Incidents Along the River.

which greets the vision is a gaily dressed tug, with a guard of marines, having in tow Admiral PORTER'S barge with the President, on his return from Richmond, complacently seated in the stern sheets. It looks very much like a pic-nic. Following a short distance after is the President's handsome flag-ship, the *River Queen*. Not far behind is the beautiful steel gunboat *Bat*, ex-blockade runner, now general convoy to distinguished guests, and one of the fastest vessels in the navy. The *River Queen*, which took the President up the river, proceeded no farther than the obstructions at Drewry's Bluff. We are soon abreast of this historic fortification, and eager eyes scan closely its formidable walls and positions.

Here is the chief line of obstructions sunk by the rebels early in the war, and located as they are, directly under the guns of Fort Darling, subjecting every approaching thing to a terrible plunging fire, it is readily admitted that this was the impassable barrier to the naval advance on Richmond. The river here is very narrow, and the movement of large vessels attended with much danger. The obstructions were placed directly across the river, and filled it completely with the exception of a gap of fifty or sixty feet, left for the passage of the rebel fleet and flag-of-truce boats. They consist of the hulls of two or three old steamships, that formerly plyed between Richmond and New York. The wheel-houses, fast crumbling to decay, still rise above the water, and present the appearance of a melancholy ruin.

We pass so hurriedly under the guns of Fort Darling, that we have no good opportunity to observe its construction. We know it looks very strong, and on the north side it has one or two small outlying works on its flank. Our naval companions tell us that it is a casemated fortification, and with its surrounding field works, all parts of the fort itself, mounts not less than forty guns. All these, like hundreds more, are our trophies without blemish or injury.

Not far above Fort Darling lies the wreck of one of the famous rebel fleet in the James, the iron-clad *Virginia*. Whether she has been blown up or simply scuttled and sunk, cannot be ascertained from looking at her as she lies. She sank in deep water, and is careened over on her side, leaving a portion of her overhang visible above the water-line. Of the other iron-clad, the *Richmond*, we find no trace.

In the immediate vicinity of Fort Darling we pass through a very substantial bridge with a draw, used by LEE for the speedy transfer of troops from the north to the south side of the James. Ere reaching Richmond we pass two more of the same kind, though hardly so well built as the first; but all demonstrating that LEE had no pontoon bridges across the James anywhere—probably, because the rapid current rendered them unsafe, and probably, too, because he had not any pontoons to spare, when something else would answer just as well.

We have now steamed safely by all obstructions and chances of torpedoes, and the very pardonable trepidation which we felt in view of our possible danger, gives way to a feeling that just now is a moment in our lives, the significance, importance and sublimity of which cannot be justly appreciated. The City of Richmond is in view. The spires pointing heavenward; the smoke still rising from the conflagration's awful ruin, and the Stars and Stripes floating from a hundred house-tops and mastheads, all form a picture so sublimely grand and inspiring, that the human mind is simply lost in mute contem-

ances, while the Union guard outside seemed to richly enjoy the transition that the famous building had undergone, evidently having been there himself. The whirligig of time makes all things even, and the thousands of loyal officers and soldiers who have suffered the tortures and horrors of these dungeons may now contemplate their present uses with serene satisfaction, and yet without resentment.

A close inspection of Castle Thunder reveals one of the most hideous dungeons that can be conceived. We failed to see it, however, in all its filth and nastyness, for a strong force of men had been engaged two days in carrying out the accumulation of the past three years. The corporal of the guard who conducted us through, pointed out a spot on the floor on one of the main halls, not yet cleaned, where the dirt was three inches thick, and alive with vermin, *and yet on this floor, in this condition, prisoners were obliged to sleep either upon the dirt itself or upon palets of decaying straw.*

But I will not descant further upon this vile relic of the rebellion. Its career is too well known. The prisoners confined here, it will be recollected, were those against whom special vengeance was directed, prisoners of State, persons charged with harboring Union prisoners, Union officers charged with being spies, blockade-runners, &c. Well has it been said that a confinement in Castle Thunder is a forstaste of the tortures of the damned.

This building, together with the Libby belongs to the estate of JOHN ENDERS, and was leased by the rebel Government. They were originally built for stores, but subsequently turned into tabacco manufactories. But their base uses are now at an end.

This is the fourth day of the Union occupation, and the confusion in the city necessarily attendant upon such an evacuation, and such an occupation, is gradually subsiding. Could the ruins of the fire be removed from sight, Richmond would present an attractive appearance, for it is really a handsome city; but, after all, the saddest scenes are at the headquarters of the Provost-Martial, the Commissioners of Subsistence, and the office of Sanitary Commission, the latter being already established here. Gen. WEITZEL had no sooner established his headquarters here than thousands of citizens besieged him for rations. And as the city is now shut out from all supplies from the country, the crowd of applicants for subsistence is rapidly increasing. This morning there was nothing in the markets but a few small fish caught by negroes. The Capitol, the City Hall and the Capitol-square are filled with a great throng of all classes, condition, sexes and ages, with basket in hand and an appealing expression of face. What the regulations yet are in regard to the issue of rations to the citizens, I do not know, but a limited quantity is being supplied them at present.

In order to study this peculiar social feature of the rebellion, I mingled with these crowds this morning for a short time, to observe their temper, desires and condition. They were, of course, largely made up of what appeared to be the poorer classes, and many negroes were among them, some for subsistence for themselves and some as servants of families. I found many whose intelligent expression of countenance, fair features and attempted gentility of dress, indicated that they were of the higher classes, on whom the demands of want and hunger were as insatiable as upon those of less position. I noticed several ladies approach the officer in charge

The Rebel Arms, Artillery, and Public Property Surrendered.

Rebel Officers Retain Their Side Arms and Private Property.

Officers and Men Paroled and Allowed to Return to Their Homes.

The Correspondence Between Grant and Lee.

OFFICIAL.

War Department, Washington, April 9, 1865—9 o'clock P. M.

To Maj.-Gen. Dix:

This department has received the official report of the SURRENDER, THIS DAY, OF GEN. LEE AND HIS ARMY TO LIEUT.-GEN. GRANT, on the terms proposed by Gen. Grant.

Details will be given as speedily as possible.

Edwin M. Stanton,
Secretary of War.

Headquarters Armies of the United States, 4:30 P. M., April 9.

Hon. Edwin M. Stanton, Secretary of War:

GEN LEE SURRENDERED THE ARMY OF NORTHERN VIRGINIA THIS AFTERNOON, upon the terms proposed by myself. The accompanying additional correspondence will show the conditions fully.

(Signed) U. S. Grant, Lieut.-Gen'l.

Sunday, April 9, 1865.

General—I received your note of this morning, on the picket line, whither I had come to meet you and ascertain definitely what terms were embraced in your proposition of yesterday with reference to the surrender of this army

I now request an interview in accordance with the offer contained in your letter of yesterday for that purpose.

Very respectfully your obedient servant,
R. E. Lee, General.

To Lieut.-Gen. Grant, Commanding United States Armies.

Sunday April 9, 1865.

Gen. R. E. Lee, Commanding Confederate States Armies.

Your note of this date is but this moment, 11 50 A M. received

In consequence of my having passed from

[...]

Very respectfully,
Your obedient servant,
R. E. Lee, General.

THE PRELIMINARY CORRESPONDENCE.

The following is the previous correspondence between Lieut.-Gen. Grant and Gen. Lee, referred to in the foregoing telegram to the Secretary of War:

Clifton House, Va., April 9, 1865.

Hon. Edwin M. Stanton, Secretary of War:

The following correspondence has taken place between Gen. Lee and myself. *There has been no relaxation in the pursuit during its pendency.*

U. S. Grant, Lieutenant-General.

April 7, 1865.

Gen. R. E. Lee, Commanding C. S. A.:

General: The result of the last week must convince you of the hopelessness of further resistance on the part of the Army of Northern Virginia in this struggle. I feel that it is so and regard it as my duty to shift from myself the responsibility of any further effusion of blood, by asking of you the surrender of that portion of the Confederate States Army, known as the Army of Northern Virginia.

Very Respectfully,
Your obedient servant,
U. S. Grant,
Lieutenant-General,
Commanding Armies of the United States.

April 7, 1865.

General: I have received your note of this date.

Though not entirely of the opinion you express of the hopelessness of further resistence on the part of the army of Northern Virginia, I reciprocate your desire to avoid useless effusion of blood, and therefore, before considering your proposition, *ask the terms you will offer on condition of its surrender.*

R. E. Lee, General.

To Lieut.-Gen. U. S. Grant, Commanding Armies of the United States.

April 8, 1865.

To Gen. R. E. Lee, Commanding C. S. A.:

General: Your note of last evening in reply to mine of same date, asking the conditions on which I will accept the surrender of the Army of Northern Virginia, is just received.

In reply, I would say that *peace being my first desire, there is but one condition that I insist upon,* viz

That the men surrendered shall be disqualified for taking up arms again against the Government of the United States until properly exchanged.

I will meet you, or designate officers to meet any officers you may name, for the same purpose, at any point agreeable to you, for the pur-

[...]

this city,

Albany, Monday, April 10—1 A. M.

There is great rejoicing here over the news of the surrender of Gen. Lee and his army.

The news was received at about 10 P. M., and about midnight State and Pearl streets were filled with people anxiously awaiting the particulars.

The bells are ringing, cannon firing, while the multitude are indulging in fireworks.

The Governor was called up and briefly addressed the throng around his residence.

The State House and many private residences are illuminated.

Philadelphia, April 9.

The glorious announcement of Lee's surrender was received here about nine o'clock. It was telegraphed to all sections of the city, and was announced in the several churches. The *Ledger* office was illuminated in five minutes. The bell of Independence Hall was rung by the order of the Mayor. The firemen immediately assembled and blocked up the streets. Salutes were fired, and the whistles of the steam-engines and the cheers of the assembled multitudes made the whole city ring.

Worcester, Mass., Monday, April 9.

The news of the surrender of Lee and his army created an intense excitement here to-night. The bells were rung, guns were fired, bonfires kindled, the fire companies turned out, and many stores and buildings were illuminated.

Pittsburgh, Pa., Sunday, April 9.

The news to-night brought nearly the entire population into the streets. The recruiting booths were turned into bonfires, salutes were fired, speeches were made, and bands played.

Trenton, N. J., Sunday, April 9.

The glorious news was received here with cheering and ringing of bells. The people are turning out *en masse* to receive and rejoice over the glad tidings.

Providence, R. I., Sunday, April 9—Midnight.

Bells are ringing, cannon are firing, and the citizens are out rejoicing over the news of Lee's surrender. A large bonefire is burning on Weybosset bridge.

FROM THE PACIFIC COAST.

Juarez said to be Coming to Washington by way of San Francisco—French Forces in Sinaloa—French War Steamers in California Ports—The Overland Mails.

San Francisco, Friday, April 7.

The steamer *John L. Stephens*, from Mazatlan, brings $93,000 in treasure and a thousand bags of silver ore.

The Mazatlan *Times*, the Imperialist organ, give the report that Juarez was en route for Cape St. Lucas, whence he would sail for San Francisco on his way to Washington.

A French naval expedition had sailed, it was supposed, for Guaymas.

An Imperial force has moved to Sinaloa.

A correspondent of the San Francisco *Bulletin*, writing from Mazatlan, March 4, says that Juarez is still at Chihuahua with his ministers raising troops, though money, arms, and ammunition are scarce.

The French war steamer *Victoria* and transport *Du Rhine* was at Santa Barbara, on the coast of California. They hope to obtain supplies of coal at San Francisco.

The daily Overland Mail, hence to Salt Lake, resumed its trips yesterday. The first mail this way since the interruption arrived last night.

The recent meeting in behalf of the Christian Sanitary Commission, resulted in remittances, by telegraph, within the past few days, of $20,000 in gold.

The scarcity of flour and wheat continues. Extreme prices are obtained, and consequently trade does not improve much

The Union Convention of Washington Territory have nominated A A Denny as Congressional Delegate.

Military celebrations for the national victories were held throughout the State to-day

A mass meeting in aid of the Soldiers Relief Association was held here to-night.

[...]

liant rhetoric, no vivid word-painting, no oratorical eloquence can portray the sublimity and immensity of the great victory. It is almost beyond the power of the human mind to comprehend its extent, and when you begin to descend to detail, the task is simply appalling in its magnitude. Think of a line of operations, held defensively and operated from offensively with such success, *thirty-nine miles long from flank to flank, thoroughly fortified throughout its entire length!* Think of the cities captured, of the fortificationss stormed and taken, with their hundreds of guns, great and small, of the material of war now in our hands, yet beyond the possibility of computation of the terrible battles, and the overwhelming defeat, and rout of the chief army of the rebellion of the prisoners captured. Counted by the tens of thousands; of the terrified flight of the arch-traitor and his few desperate minions; of the triumphant entry of Abraham Lincoln into treason's fallen capital. Let every lover of his country depict the vast scene in his own imagination for words to fitly discribe it fails altogether.

Through the courtesy of Provost-Marshal Gen. Patrick, I enjoyed an exceedingly pleasant sail from City Point to the Richmond wharves this morning, on his fleet flag ship, the *Mattino*. Accompanying the General were Hon. C. H. Dana, Assistant Secretary of War, his wife and son, and Hon. Roscoe Conkling, member of Congress from New-York. The snake-like bends of the James between City Point and Varina Landing, were quickly passed, and at the latter place assurance was given that the river was clear for our vessel to the very docks of Richmond; but I can assure you that the navigation of the tortuous channel of the James thence to Richmond, thickly sown with obstructions and supposed torpedoes, was an exceedingly delicate task, and full of excitement. Our pilot knew the channel of old, but he knew not the warlike devices of the enemy.

We were, however, very fortunate, and the approach to the city, especially during the last eight miles from Drewry's Bluff, was full of the intensest interest, for over these waters the Union flag had never before floated during the war. When we leave Dutch Gap and that famous canal, which looks as though it might have been washed out by a billow, we at once enter upon the lines held by the enemy. Howlett House, Battery, famous for its determined resistance to our engeneering operations on the north side of the river, stands abandoned and gloomy, with its twelve large guns still in the embrasures; but all silent as we steamed rapidly by. Another long and large earthwork appears on the left bank, mounting eight or ten guns, and bearing directly upon the mouth of the canal. This, too, like the rest, is abandoned, with its armament unimpaired. We next pass the wreck of the rebel gunboat, blown up by our batteries during the effort made to run through our fleet some months ago.

The next point of interest is Fort Brady, on the north bank of the river, and the left of the position of our Army of the James What strikes one as very remarkable here is the fact that owing to the intricate windings of the James there are two rebel batteries, Howlett House and another absolutely in the rear of this former position of our army. Fort Brady is the point where Gen. Gibbon opened on the retreating rebel rams. Had there been larger guns at his disposal, the range is so good that they would have stood a poor chance of escape.

We are now fairly in that part of the river held solely by the rebels, and a knowledge of the channel and obstructions is absolutely necessary to a safe voyage. The gunboat *Monticello* is therefore hailed, and on asking for information a pilot who has been up and down is tendered with much politeness. The obstructions sunk by our own fleet are soon passed, likewise the fleet of monitors, and the next object

[...]

L. L. CROUNSE.

First Impressions of Richmond—The Great Conflagration in the City—Who Was Responsible for it?—The Libby and Castle Thunder—Suffering for Food—Distribution of Supplies—Lee's Family.

From Our Own Correspondent.

Richmond, Thursday, April 6, 1865.

So many thousand facts are presented to the mind of the visitor here in such a very short space of time, that to record them systematically is almost impossible. The great features of the evacuation, the entrance of our troops, the conflagration, the President's visit and reception, have already been forwarded to you in detail by your correspondents who came in with the troops, and I will, therefore, allude to them only in a general way.

Let me say, though, at the outset, that the best part of the city is a ruin. That the awful fire kindled by the enemy, and which at first promised to consume but a few buildigns, was so fanned by the rising wind, that before it could be got under subjection, *thirty squares, comprising not less than eight hundred buildings in the very best and most valuable business part of Richmond were in ashes.* What the pecuniary loss is no one can estimate. Nearly all the principal mills, factories, warehouses, stores, banks and insurance offices were destroyed, and the losses being so heavy, the insurance companies, perhaps insolvent already from their countenance of the rebel currency, are now more than bankrupted, and thousands of property owners, computed wealthy in their actual possessions three days ago, are now reduced to beggary. It is among the things easily discernable, that this ruin, wrought by their own friends, to whom they have given all, and to whose tyranny they have submitted, with even cheerfulness, is the cause of far deeper gloom among many than that produced by the loss of the city or the defeat of their army. It is apparent indeed that the transfer of the city to the Union flag was not only not *distasteful to a very large portion of the people, many of them among the best classes, but even highly gratifying.* No captured city, not even Savannah nor Columbia, can present the ruin apparent here in Richmond. It will carry its painful evidences for half a score of years, and the only thing which will speedily alleviate the dire distress that must prevail, and give the city a chance for a speedy recovery from its present stagnation, is immediate peace. It is Richmond's only salvation. The origin of the fire and the incendiaries are so well and positively known that no extended investigation on these points is required. It seems that *Gen. Lee was not responsible for it, but that Jeff. Davis and his Secretary of War, Breckenridge, were.* The destruction of the supplies and the arsenal involved the destruction of the city, and it was so decided by the leading citizens. Gen. Ewell and Maj. Carrington both protested against it in the most earnest manner, as did also a committee of citizens, but Breckinridge, in reply, exclaimed *that he didn't care a d—n if every house in Richmond was consumed, the warehouse must be burned.* Thus this wretched rebel, hoisted into a powerful position with no constituents, is responsible for the dreadful ruin, and his master Davis is likewise responsible, because he silently countenanced it.

The fire was started in two places, among the supply warehouses near the wharves, and at the Danville Depot, where there were 1,500 hogsheads of tobacco belonging to the Confederate Government. This consumed the Danville Depot, also the Petersburgh Depot, and the bridge over the James to Manchester. The famous Libby Prison, and Castle Thunder, as I have already informed you, were not burned. They were reserved for a far more appropriate fate. I visited them yesterday, and found Castle Thunder used as a guard-house for factious and thieving negroes, caught in acts of plunder, while the Libby contained 700 rebel prisoners, officers and privates, temporarily shut up together. They looked through the iron gratings with gloomy counte-

[...]

pect their names were as foreign to them as the hunger they now sought to appease had been in days gone by. Many of the wealthiest families, however, who had the means, have far larger supplies of provisions on hand than was consistent with the repeated appeals of Confederate officials for such to spare from their bounty to feed the army.

The exodus of prominent citizens was confined mainly to those connected with the rebel government, and a few who had made themselves very conspicuous in rebel politics—all the rebel Cabinet and their chief assistants, though not much of their clerical force, got away. The preparations for the evacuation began very quietly among the officials. At noon of Sunday the important records of the departments were boxed up and carted to the depot; but very little suspicion was excited among the citizens as to the real state of the case. A strong guard was stationed at the Danville depot, and four trains were got ready, the first of which left, with Davis on board, at seven o'clock in the evening, and the last at midnight. Davis' family had gone into the country on the Friday preceeding, but not because of any apprehension that the city was to be given up. Very few families left the city, and there are very few vacant houses, the mansions of Jeff. Davis and Gov. Billy Smith being among those now in want of tenants. The family of Gen. Lee, consisting of his wife, who is an invalid, and three daughters, are among those who remain. They occupy a stylish house on Franklin-street, and for their protection a well disciplined guard is placed at the dwelling, and the family are scrupulously protected from annoyance of any character, the staring gaze of the passer-by hardly being allowed. This is the second time that Mrs. Gen. Lee has been in our hands. She was once captured by our cavalry near White House, in 1862, and sent through our lines to Richmond under flag of truce, by order of Gen. McClellan.

L. L. CROUNSE.

Union Sentiment in Richmond—Projects of Reconstruction—Distinguished Visitors—Recruiting Negro Troops—The Truth about Rebel Enlistment of Negroes.

From Our Own Correspondent.

Richmond, Friday, April 7, 1865.

I can give you news, to-day, which will gratify the heart of every loyal American. Virginia will return to the Union, and that right speedily. Desiring to ascertain the exact truth with reference to the alleged existence of a strong Union sentiment in the city, I availed myself of an opportunity to call upon certain gentlemen here whom I had heard alluded to by Secessionists as Union men, and I must say, that I spent two of the happiest hours of my life in full and free conversation with some of the most thorough and radical Union men in the country; men of wealth and position, whose faith has never wavered for an instant, and who, slaveholders, as they are, *demand that Virginia shall be taken back into the Union "under the Emancipation Proclamation;" that no vestige of the rebellion shall be tolerated; that the usurpation State, and Confederate, which has wrecked Virginia, shall not be recognized in a single respect;* that the State Government must be organized anew, by a convention of the people, as soon as that can be properly effected, and the State and its inhabitants thoroughly purged of treason in every shape.

Union sentiments, in this strong form exist here to a far greater extent than has yet been conceived; not alone among the poorer classes,—mechanics and laborers,—*but in wealthy and influential circles, where may be found men who have never lost faith in the Union;* who have confidently anticipated its triumph, and who greeted the old flag with tears of joy. They are men of the John Minor Botts school, and they are the leaven which shall leaven the whole lump here in this venerable old commonwealth of Virginia. They will delight to see the mass of the people treated with magnanimity, but they have felt too deeply the

Continued on Eighth Page.

course was adopted; Tweed tried to amend the criminal code so as to give to judges — of whom he had several in his pocket — greatly increased latitude in deciding what was contempt of court. When this attempt failed Tweed's agents started the story that the land on which the Times Building was situated, and which had been occupied before by the Brick Presbyterian Church, had been sold under a restriction binding it for all time to church uses. The effort to eject the paper from its home also came to nothing, but it gave Jones a good deal of worry for some time.

Worse still, he had not only enemies without but some lukewarm supporters in his own camp. Raymond had been dead less than a year and a half, but already his family wanted to get rid of their stock in *The Times*. The interest of the Taylor estate could hardly be counted as hostile to Tweed, and merchants afraid of the ring had begun to withdraw their advertising from the paper, which was continuing its fight in spite of the testimony of New York's most reputable business men that the city finances were "administered in a correct and faithful manner." As a matter of fact the decline in the paper's income was not large, but it was exaggerated by rumor, and Tweed might hope that some of the stockholders would begin to put pressure on Jones.

It was evidently in the conviction that Jones either would be willing or would be compelled to withdraw from a losing fight that Tweed formed, early in 1871, a company to buy the control of *The Times* — one of the most curiously assorted companies that was ever brought together for publishing

a newspaper, or for anything else. The science and art of politics were represented by Tweed, Oakey Hall, and Sweeney; finance high and low by Fisk, Gould, and Cyrus W. Field; and the necessary flavoring of probity and rectitude was provided by Peter Cooper and Moses Taylor. Just what these gentlemen would have done with a newspaper if they had had it would be hard to say, but one thing they would certainly have done — they would have silenced the only journalistic critic of the ring. It may be that sooner or later thievery on such a grand scale would have been exposed and defeated, but there is no certainty that anything but death would have interrupted Tweed's activities. And, as it happened, the final exposure by *The Times* came just as the ring was preparing a new scheme, the Viaduct Railroad, which was to begin with a theft of five million dollars and might have gone ten times farther before it was finished. Perhaps if *The Times* had been put out of the way a champion would have been raised up in the course of time, but no candidates for the position were visible in 1871. And even two or three years more might have enabled Tweed to do as much damage to New York as could be accomplished by anything but an earthquake and tidal wave.

All this was plain enough to George Jones, and he refused to sell. And since rumors that *The Times* was to be bought and put out of the way had been widely circulated, he published in the paper, on March 29, 1871, a statement over his signature which disposed of Tweed's hopes in that direction for all time.

> No money that could be offered me [he wrote] should induce me to dispose of a single share of my property to the Tammany faction, or to any man associated with it, or indeed to any person or party whatever until this struggle is fought out. I have the same confidence in the integrity and firmness of my fellow proprietors.
>
> Rather than prove false to the public in the present crisis, I would if the necessity by any possibility arose immediately start another journal to denounce those frauds upon the people which are so great a scandal to the city, and I should carry with me in this renewal of our present labors the colleagues who have already stood by me through a long and arduous contest.

After that *The Times* continued with redoubled vigor, but without much more success until well in the summer. A new reform organization was established. It held a mass meeting in Cooper Union, it commented upon the fact that the city debt had gone up something like a hundred million dollars in two years; but the masses remained unaffected, proof of what everybody believed was not forthcoming, and Tweed and his friends looked forward with confidence to the time when, having stolen everything in New York that was not tied down, they could go on to Albany and Washington.

For the benefit of those who believe that the right is sure to triumph in the end it may be observed that the actual exposure of Tweed was due to an accident — the overturn of a sleigh in which the County Auditor, one of Tweed's most useful sub-

ordinates, was riding. This was in December, 1870; the Auditor died of his injuries some weeks later and was replaced by the County Bookkeeper, and into the Bookkeeper's office went Matthew J. O'Rourke, a political follower of James O'Brien in a Democratic faction on bad terms with Tweed. Whether the actual discovery of the thefts should be credited to O'Rourke himself, or to one Copeland, an accountant in his office, is somewhat doubtful; but at any rate there was an investigation of some of the claims which proved at once what ought to have been evident even from the most superficial inspection, that millions were being stolen. The evidence gathered in O'Rourke's office and later published in *The Times* showed that six million dollars had been spent for repairs on the county courthouse (payment being authorized by Mayor Hall and Controller Connolly), of which ninety per cent was pure graft, and that there had been frauds of almost equal magnitude in the renting and furnishing of armories. This was a dangerously large matter — too large for minor officials to handle; but the discoveries were promptly reported to O'Brien. In the somewhat discouraging history of that period, when high officers of city, state and federal governments regarded their positions as nothing more than opportunities for grand larceny, it is pleasant to come upon this instance of obscure public servants, receiving modest salaries, who apparently out of no other motive than a sense of fidelity to their trust gave away information which Tweed would undoubtedly have paid them a million dollars to conceal.

O'Brien now had the facts, but it was something of a question what he could do with them. Eventually he gave them to *The Times*, but *The Times* was not his first choice. The transcript of Connolly's books was the biggest exclusive local story ever offered to a New York newspaper; but it was offered to one newspaper which refused it. Then, realizing that nobody else would take it, he gave it to *The Times*, but at first would not give his consent to its publication. Knowledge of the facts fortified *The Times* in its denunciation of the report of the six respectable citizens, and eventually O'Brien's reluctance disappeared.

By the time he gave his consent for the publication of the evidence Tweed had found out what was going on. He had failed to scare Jones out or to freeze him out; now there remained but one recourse, to try to buy him. One afternoon in the early summer of 1871 a lawyer with whom Jones was on friendly terms asked the publisher to come to his office for a business consultation. When Jones entered he found to his surprise that only one man was in the room — Controller Connolly; and Connolly promptly came to the point and offered Jones five million dollars to suppress the news.

"I don't think," Jones remarked, "that the devil will ever bid higher for me than that." Connolly seems to have taken this as encouragement, for he at once added: "Think of what you could do with five million dollars! Why, you could go to Europe and live like a prince."

Thereupon Jones made his refusal unmistakable,

and Connolly went away sorrowing, for he had great possessions.

But before entering on a fight which with the publication of the evidence would become a death struggle Jones felt it desirable to make his own position somewhat safer. The Raymond family still wanted to sell its stock. Undoubtedly that stock could have been sold to Tweed, and the fact that it was not, directly or indirectly, is proof enough that though the Raymonds were getting out of *The Times* they were still loyal to its interests. But Jones was afraid that somehow Tweed would get control of this stock; and while it would not give him a dominating influence on the paper, it would enable him, by alleging that the interests of the stockholders were being injured by the campaign, to start litigation which could have given one of Tweed's pocket judges an excuse for appointing a receiver. Jones had to make sure that the Raymond share could be counted on the right side; and he found invaluable support in E. B. Morgan of Aurora, N. Y., who had owned two shares of stock when *The Times* was founded, had aided in the financing of the building project, and had recently taken a more vigorous interest not only in his property but in the fight which Jones was making against Tweed. On July 8 *The Times* published a long digest of some of its evidence relating to frauds in the rental of armories, and in the succeeding days there were repeated editorial attacks on the ring and promises of greater exposures to come. But Jones was not ready to go on till he had fortified his position, and that was soon done. On July 19 the editorial page of *The*

Times began with a short statement to the effect that the thirty-four shares of *Times* stock held by the Raymond estate had been purchased by Morgan, who would thereafter be associated with Jones in the management of the paper. The statement continued:

> It has been repeatedly asserted that the Raymond shares were likely to fall into the possession of the New York ring, and it is in order to assure our friends of the groundlessness of all such statements that we make known the actual facts. The price paid in ready money for the shares in question was $375,000. Down to the time of Mr. Raymond's death the shares had never sold for more than $6000 each. Mr. Morgan has now paid upward of $11,000 each for 34 of them, and this transaction is the most conclusive answer which could be furnished to the absurd rumors sometimes circulated to the effect that the course taken by *The New York Times* toward the Tammany leaders had depreciated the value of the property.

Immediately following this was a double-leaded editorial headed "Two Thieves," in which Jennings threw his hat into the air with a loud and joyous whoop and declared that evidence which *The Times* was about to publish would prove that at least two of the four leaders of the ring were criminals. Of these gentlemen, one eventually escaped conviction by flight to Europe and the other by grace of a hung jury; that both were what Jennings called them nobody has ever seriously doubted.

The next day *The Times* published another long

analysis of some of its evidence, this time relating to the furnishing of armories. This article, like its predecessor, was written by John Foord, and was accompanied by a fiery editorial by Jennings. And on the 22d *The Times* opened up with all its batteries. When it came to the evidence afforded by the Controller's books as to the money spent (ostensibly) on the new court house, the figures themselves spoke more forcibly than any summary or any comment — those very figures which had been audited and approved by the six respectable citizens. The previous articles had been published on the editorial page, running over into the page opposite; and even on the 21st the front page of *The Times* had begun, in the usual style, with a single-column head, "General News."

But on the 22d *The Times* published a chapter of figures from the Controller's books on the front page, in broad measure, and under a three-column head. So far as can be ascertained this was the first time a real display heading had ever appeared in *The Times*, but the editors felt apparently that the facts they had to set before the public deserved the aid of all the resources of the typography of the period. Jennings's editorial accompanying the first chapter of the accounts also employed full-face type for emphasizing some of the figures, and the small capitals in which then as now the names of individuals appeared in editorials were also used for some of Jennings's epithets, such as SCOUNDRELS, SWINDLERS, THIEVES and other terms which he evidently felt were synonymous with some of the personal names mentioned.

THE FOURTH TIMES BUILDING,
PARK ROW,
1888-1905.

That editorial demanded immediate criminal prosecution of some of the city officials, and it contained the observation, fully justified by the conditions of the time, that "if the public does not come to the same conclusion before we have finished our extracts from the Controller's books, then facts have lost their power to convince, and public spirit must be regarded as dead."

The facts were convincing enough. It appeared, for example, that for carpets in the courthouse enough money had been paid out to cover City Hall Park three times over with the finest carpet that could be bought in New York. A single carpenter, according to the books, had received more than $360,000 within a month for his work in repairing a courthouse which was not yet finished. Of course, the carpenter never got it. Whatever the name in which the bill was made out — and the assurance of the ring may be gauged by the fact that one of the city's creditors was put down as "Philip F. Dummey" — the checks given in payment were indorsed by members of a few firms in which Tweed and some of his accomplices were partners. Altogether, the Controller's books fully supported *The Times's* editorial assertion that a man who had a bill of $5000 against the city for work honestly done could not get it paid until he raised it to $55,000, with the balance going by one means or another to Tweed and his friends.

Readers of *The Times* were allowed one day to think over the first chapter from Connolly's books, and on the 24th another followed. There was still another before the end of the week, and on

Saturday the 29th all the evidence, with some editorial comment, was put into a special four-page supplement. This document was printed in both English and German; for the German-Americans at that time were a much more distinct racial group than at present, and one which furnished valuable aid to municipal reform. But, for various motives of which partisanship was the most worthy, the German-American press had hitherto given its support to Tweed; so *The Times* let the Germans read the evidence in their own language.

It had been announced beforehand that two hundred thousand copies of that supplement would be issued — a wholly unprecedented edition for a New York paper in those days. As a matter of fact the edition ran to 220,000, and a few hours after the presses had stopped it became apparent that this had not begun to meet the demand. The presses started again, and for a whole week were run continuously, except when getting out the regular issues of *The Times*, in printing the famous supplement. Altogether more than half a million copies were issued. The people of New York now had the proof; it remained to be seen if they were capable of defending themselves.

At first the ring was confident enough. Tweed's famous comment, "Well, what are you going to do about it?" epitomized their reaction to the exposure. Mayor Hall seemed to think that he could meet the accusations by declaring that the papers were "surreptitiously obtained from a dishonest servant," and it says a good deal for the standards of the time that the charge of dishonesty against

the man who had exposed the theft of millions by city officials was seriously received by a large part of the public. Hall further remarked that the animus of *The Times* could be found in the delayed payment for the advertising contract already mentioned. Neither he nor anybody else made other reference to the story told by the figures than an occasional remark about "alleged records" or "garbled accounts."

All over the country the revelations made by *The Times* were the chief topic of news, and of editorial comment. Only in New York City did the newspapers appear to know nothing about it. Greeley, to be sure, who belatedly remembered that he was not only a moral man but a Republican, ventured to suggest that Tweed and his associates might sue *The Times* for libel, a procedure which *The Times* earnestly invited; but the other papers did not even by this much dignify the disclosures with any comment that might be twisted into an admission that they amounted to anything. The papers of London and Paris published long editorial comments on New York politics, but the New York papers seemed to see in them only what Mayor Hall called them, "the gross attacks of a partisan journal upon the credit of the city."

Nevertheless, the public, or a part of it, was awakened. The claims, it will be remembered, which were authorized by the Board of Audit — and which, it was now apparent, contained anywhere from sixty to a hundred per cent of pure graft — were to be met by the issuance of revenue bonds payable during the year. For two years there had

been no statement of city finances. As Foord writes, "Nobody save the men in power and those in their immediate confidence knew at what figure city bonds were being negotiated, or at what rate the debt was increasing." The first consequence of the revelations was the sudden and very natural refusal of bankers to lend any more money to an administration which was getting no one knew how much, but pretty certainly was stealing most of what it got. And there, for some weeks, matters rested. Public indignation was steadily rising as *The Times* brought out more evidence; most of the tax money had been spent, and the city could no longer borrow money; municipal employés were not getting their pay. Already the summer of 1871 had seen one serious riot, when several hundred members of an Irish mob which had attacked the Orangemen's parade had been shot down by militia, and it seemed that this might be only a beginning. Now mobs of unpaid laborers gathered every day in City Hall Park; and Tweed and his friends, with the aid of his newspaper supporters, were trying with some success to transfer the blame for the shortage of city money from the thieves to the reformers who had exposed the thefts. And while there was not much money left in the city treasury, there was no guarantee that Tweed and his friends would not steal what little had escaped them. For they calmly refused to resign, and under the Tweed charter they could not be removed.

On September 4 there was a mass meeting of citizens in Cooper Union, with former Mayor William F. Havemeyer presiding, and a committee of seventy

was appointed to investigate the frauds and prosecute the criminals. But Tweed and his friends were not asleep; immediately after this meeting there was a "robbery" in the Controller's office. The vouchers which would have furnished evidence that no jury could have disregarded were taken out of the glass case which had been thought sufficient to protect them, and it was later found that they had been removed, and burned, by a Tweed official. Something desperate had to be done, and John Foley, a prominent figure in reform movements of the time, did it. Bringing suit as a taxpayer, he got an injunction on September 14 restraining the Controller from paying out any more money on claims against the city.

This meant that not only the fraudulent claims could not be paid, but the honest claims of contractors, the wages of laborers, even the wages of the police. If the four chief conspirators had had the courage to hang on and wait for the inevitable riots, it is possible that they could have escaped with no other punishment than the compulsion to be a little more moderate thereafter; for the rioters would undoubtedly have turned their attention to *The Times* and the reformers before going on to the more profitable investigation of the stores of Broadway and the residences of Fifth Avenue, leaving the homes of Tweed and his friends untouched under their guards of "shoulder hitters." But luckily the conspirators lost their nerve, and then came one more proof of the familiar fact that the principal advantage of the forces of law over the criminal classes lies in the absence of honor among thieves.

The Mayor suggested to Controller Connolly that inasmuch as his administration had been somewhat discredited by the voucher theft, he had better resign. Connolly rightly thought that resignation just then would be taken as confession, and he also concluded that Tweed, Hall and Sweeney had decided that somebody would have to be thrown to the wolves. Being in some perplexity, he asked the advice of Samuel J. Tilden and William F. Havemeyer, with whom he had been associated in the more respectable activities of the Democratic party; and they promptly told him that he had better appoint Andrew H. Green as Deputy Controller and turn over the office to him. There were few men in the city who knew more than Green about the city government, and none who was more certainly above suspicion. Connolly took the advice, and Green's appointment on September 16 marked the beginning of the end of the Tweed ring.

In the second phase of the fight *The Times* had more assistance, for reform was beginning to become not only fairly safe, but somewhat popular. But it was also less spectacular, and Green's tenure of office took the form of a long trench war against all forms of corruption, intimidation, and chicanery. The Mayor at first refused to recognize the appointment, and then tried to turn him out; the office had to be guarded by armed men. Under the injunction the Deputy Controller could pay out no city money, and the funds left in the treasury were not sufficient to meet the interest on city bonds which would be due in six weeks. While valid claims were being

sorted out from the mass of fraudulent charges no pay rolls could be met, and the danger of riot disappeared only very slowly and gradually. Before it disappeared *The Star*, a paper which had received a good deal of money from the ring, published the home addresses of Jennings and Jones, with a hardly veiled suggestion to city employés whose families were starving that these men were responsible for the stoppage of wages. When *The Times* made some comments on this *The Star* had the hardihood to declare that not *The Star* but *The Times* was inciting to riot — by trying to prevent Tweed and his friends from collecting what little was left.

Not all the newspapers of the city attempted to stir up riots, but virtually all of them were hostile to Green's administration of the city finances. The reason was simple enough; among the bills which he refused to pay until their validity had been certified were those for newspaper advertising. In consequence of this the man who actually put a stop to the thefts and brought the city finances into as near order as was possible after two years of wholesale brigandage — who had borrowed money on the strength of his own reputation for integrity to meet immediate and unavoidable obligations, at a time when he had no legal authority to make commitments in the name of the city — who eventually saw that all honest creditors got their money, and that as little as possible was paid out for suspicious claims, had to fight through the greater part of his term of office with practically no newspaper support except from *The Times*.

Green had the hardest and most thankless part

of the work; even of the papers which still opposed him some had begun before election day to denounce Tweed and all his doings except those by which the papers stood to profit. The investigations of the Citizens' Committee and Mr. Tilden's study of the accounts in the Broadway bank, showing how the stolen money was divided, had driven some of the more timorous members of the Tweed combination to seek foreign parts; and it was clear that if the election went against Tweed the ring was broken. And it did go against him. Tweed's own district sent him back to the State Senate, but almost all of his candidates elsewhere were beaten; and *The Times* jubilantly asserted that the result "justifies our confidence in the capacity of the people, even in large cities, for self-government."

That was a long time ago; men had not learned then that though St. Michael may slay the dragon on the first Tuesday after the first Monday in November, that old serpent will probably be crawling about as vigorous as ever by the middle of June. The Tweed ring, to be sure, was broken, and the consequences of the prosecution were fairly typical of what has happened in a hundred similar cases in American municipal history. Because Tweed was the chief offender, because the evils of his time had become embodied, in the popular imagination, in his person, he was pursued with vigor through a long and tortuous career of indictments, hung juries, convictions, prison terms unduly shortened by technicalities, flights to California, Spain, and Cuba, rearrests, civil suits, and finally commitment in

The New-York Times.

VOL. XIV......NO. 4230. NEW-YORK, SATURDAY, APRIL 15, 1865. PRICE FOUR CENTS

AWFUL EVENT.

President Lincoln Shot by an Assassin.

The Deed Done at Ford's Theatre Last Night.

THE ACT OF A DESPERATE REBEL

The President Still Alive at Last Accounts.

No Hopes Entertained of His Recovery.

Attempted Assassination of Secretary Seward.

DETAILS OF THE DREADFUL TRAGEDY.

[OFFICIAL.]

War Department, Washington, April 15—1:30 A. M.

Maj.-Gen. Dix:

This evening at about 9:30 P. M., at Ford's Theatre, the President, while sitting in his private box with Mrs. Lincoln, Mrs. Harris, and Major Rathburn, was shot by an assassin, who suddenly entered the box and approached behind the President.

The assassin then leaped upon the stage, brandishing a large dagger or knife, and made his escape in the rear of the theatre.

The pistol ball entered the back of the President's head and penetrated nearly through the head. The wound is mortal. The President has been insensible ever since it was inflicted, and is now dying.

About the same hour an assassin, whether the same or not, entered Mr. Seward's apartments, and under pretence of having a prescription, was shown to the Secretary's sick chamber. The assassin immediately rushed to the bed, and inflicted two or three stabs on the throat and two on the face. It is hoped the wounds may not be mortal. My apprehension is that they will prove fatal.

The nurse alarmed Mr. Frederick Seward, who was in an adjoining room, and hastened to the door of his father's room, when he met the assassin, who inflicted upon him one or more dangerous wounds. The recovery of Frederick Seward is doubtful.

It is not probable that the President will live through the night.

Gen. Grant and wife were advertised to be at the theatre this evening, but he started to Burlington at 6 o'clock this evening.

At a Cabinet meeting at which Gen. Grant was present, the subject of the state of the country and the prospect of a speedy peace was discussed. The President was very cheerful and hopeful, and spoke very kindly of Gen. Lee and others of the Confederacy, and of the establishment of government in Virginia.

All the members of the Cabinet except Mr. Seward, are now in attendance upon the President.

I have seen Mr. Seward, but he and Frederick were both unconscious.

EDWIN M. STANTON, Secretary of War.

DETAILS OF THE OCCURRENCE.

Washington, Friday, April 14—12:30 A. M.

The President was shot in a theatre to-night, and is, perhaps, mortally wounded.

Secretary Seward was also assassinated.

SECOND DISPATCH.

Washington, Friday, April 14.

President Lincoln and wife, with other friends, this evening visited Ford's Theatre for the purpose of witnessing the performance of the "American Cousin."

It was announced in the papers that Gen. Grant would also be present, but he took the late train of cars for New-Jersey.

The theatre was densely crowded, and everybody seemed delighted with the scene before them. During the third act, and while there was a temporary pause for one of the actors to enter, a sharp report of a pistol was heard, which merely attracted attention, but suggested nothing serious, until a man rushed to the front of the President's box, waving a long dagger in his right hand, and exclaiming "*Sic semper tyrannis,*" and immediately leaped from the box, which was in the second tier, to the stage beneath, and ran across to the opposite side, making his escape amid the bewilderment of the audience from the rear of the theatre, and, mounting a horse, fled.

The screams of Mrs. Lincoln first disclosed the fact to the audience that the President had been shot, when all present rose to their feet, rushing toward the stage, many exclaiming "Hang him! hang him!"

The excitement was of the wildest possible description, and of course there was an abrupt termination of the theatrical performance.

There was a rush toward the President's box, when cries were heard: "Stand back and give him air." "Has any one stimulants." On a hasty examination, it was found that the President had been shot through the head, above and back of the temporal bone, and that some of the brain was oozing out. He was removed to a private house opposite to the theatre, and the Surgeon-General of the army, and other surgeons sent for to attend to his condition.

On an examination of the private box blood was discovered on the back of the cushioned rocking chair on which the President had been sitting, also on the partition and on the floor. A common single-barreled pocket pistol was found on the carpet.

A military guard was placed in front of the private residence to which the President had been conveyed. An immense crowd was in front of it, all deeply anxious to learn the condition of the President. It had been previously announced that the wound was mortal; but all hoped otherwise. The shock to the community was terrible.

The President was in a state of syncope, totally insensible, and breathing slowly. The blood oozed from the wound at the back of his head. The surgeons exhausted every effort of medical skill, but all hope was gone. The parting of his family with the dying President is too sad for description.

The President and Mrs. Lincoln did not start for the theatre until fifteen minutes after eight o'clock. Speaker Colfax was at the White House at the time, and the President stated to him that he was going, although Mrs. Lincoln had not been well, because the papers had announced that Gen. Grant and they were to be present, and, as Gen. Grant had gone North, he did not wish the audience to be disappointed.

He went with apparent reluctance and urged Mr. Colfax to go with him; but that gentleman had made other engagements, and with Mr. Ashmun, of Massachusetts, bid him good-bye.

When the excitement at the theatre was at its wildest height, reports were circulated that Secretary Seward had also been assassinated.

On reaching this gentleman's residence a crowd and a military guard were found at the door, and on entering it was ascertained that the reports were based on truth.

Everybody there was so excited that scarcely an intelligible word could be gathered, but the facts are substantially as follows:

About 10 o'clock a man rang the bell, and the call having been answered by a colored servant, he said he had come from Dr. Verdi, Secretary Seward's family physician, with a prescription, at the same time holding in his hand a small piece of folded paper, and saying in answer to a refusal that he must see the Secretary, as he was entrusted with particular directions concerning the medicine.

He still insisted on going up, although repeatedly informed that no one could enter the chamber. The man pushed the servant aside, and walked heavily toward the Secretary's room, and was then met by Mr. Frederick Seward, of whom he demanded to see the Secretary, making the same representation which he did to the servant. What further passed in the way of colloquy is not known, but the man struck him on the head with a "billy," severely injuring the skull and felling him almost senseless. The assassin then rushed into the chamber and attacked Major Seward, Paymaster of the United States army, and Mr. Hansell, a messenger of the State Department and two male nurses, disabling them all, he then rushed upon the Secretary, who was lying in bed in the same room, and inflicted three stabs in the neck, but severing, it is thought and hoped, no arteries, though he bled profusely.

The assassin then rushed down stairs, mounted his horse at the door, and rode off before an alarm could be sounded, and in the same manner as the assassin of the President.

It is believed that the injuries of the Secretary are not fatal, nor those of either of the others, although both the Secretary and the Assistant Secretary are very seriously injured.

Secretaries Stanton and Welles, and other prominent officers of the government, called at Secretary Seward's house to inquire into his condition, and there heard of the assassination of the President.

They then proceeded to the house where he was lying, exhibiting of course intense anxiety and solicitude. An immense crowd was gathered in front of the President's house, and a strong guard was also stationed there, many persons evidently supposing he would be brought to his home.

The entire city to-night presents a scene of wild excitement, accompanied by violent expressions of indignation, and the profoundest sorrow—many shed tears. The military authorities have dispatched mounted patrols in every direction, in order, if possible, to arrest the assassins. The whole metropolitan police are likewise vigilant for the same purpose.

The attacks, both at the theatre and at Secretary Seward's house, took place at about the same hour—10 o'clock—thus showing a preconcerted plan to assassinate those gentlemen. Some evidence of the guilt of the party who attacked the President are in the possession of the police.

Vice-President Johnson is in the city, and his headquarters are guarded by troops.

Saturday Morning—1 O'clock.

The person who shot the President is represented as about 30 years of age, five feet nine inches in height, sparely built, of light complexion, dressed in dark clothing, and having a genteel appearance. He entered the box, which is known as the State box, being the upper box on the right hand side from the dress-circle in the regular manner, and shot the President from behind, the ball entering the skull about in the middle, behind and going in the direction of the left eye; it did not pass through, but apparently broke the frontal bone and forced out the brain to some extent. The President is not yet dead, but is wholly insensible, and the Surgeon-General says he cannot live till day-break. The assassin was followed across the stage by a gentleman, who sprang out from an orchestra chair. He rushed through the side door into an alley, thence to the avenue and mounted a dark bay horse, which he apparently received from the hand of an accomplice, dashed up F, toward the back part of the city. The escape was so sudden that he effectually eluded pursuit. The assassin cried "*sic sempre*" in a sharp, clear voice, as he jumped to the stage, and dropped his hat and a glove.

Two or three officers were in the box with the President and Mrs. Lincoln, who made efforts to stop the assassin, but were unsuccessful, and received some bruises. The whole affair, from his entrance into the box to his escape from the theatre, occupied scarcely a minute, and the strongest of the action found everybody wholy unprepared. The assault upon Mr. Seward appears to have been made almost at the same moment as that upon the President. Mr. Sewards wound is not dangerous in itself, but may prove so in connection with his recent injuries. The two assassins have both endeavored to leave the city to the northwest, apparently not expecting to strike the river. Even so low down

EUROPEAN NEWS.

TWO DAYS LATER BY THE EUROPA.

The Insult to Our Cruisers by Portugal.

The American Minister at Lisbon Demands Satisfaction.

Dismissal of the Commander of Fort Belan Requested.

Further Advance in Five-Twenties.

FINANCIAL AND COMMERCIAL.

Halifax, Friday, April 14.

The steamship *Europa*, from Liverpool on the 1st, via Queenstown on the 2d inst., arrived here at 2 o'clock this morning. She has 43 passengers for this port, and 30 for Boston. Her dates are two days later than those already received.

The steamship *Cuba*, from New-York, arrived at Liverpool at noon on the 1st inst.

THE STONEWALL AFFAIR.

A Lisbon dispatch, of the 31st of March, says that the American Minister at Lisbon has demanded satisfaction of the Portuguese Government for the firing upon the *Niagara* and *Sacramento* by the Portuguese forts. He also requests the dismissal of the Commander of Fort Belan, and a salute of twenty-one guns to the American flag.

Nothing as yet has been decided in regard to the matter.

A PROPHECY FROM RICHMOND.

The correspondent of the London *Times*, writing from Richmond on the 4th of March, says:

"I am daily more convinced that if Richmond falls and Lee and Johnston are driven from the field, it is but the first stage of this colossal revolution which will then be completed. There will ensue a time when every important town of the South will require to be held by a Yankee garrison, when exultation in New-York will be exchanged for soberness and right reason, and when it will be realized that the closing scenes of this mightiest revolutionary drama will not be played out, save in the times of our children's children."

GREAT BRITAIN.

Parliamentary proceedings on the 30th ult. were unimportant.

In the House of Commons, on the 31st, Lord C. Paget said that the Admiralty had received no proposal for sanctioning or supporting any fresh attempt to reach the North Pole. He was, therefore, unable to say what course the government would take if such a proposal were made.

Mr. Newdegate put some questions as to the idea

omize, but must maintain the position of Austria as a great Power.

INDIA.

A private Calcutta telegram of March 27 reports commercial affairs in much the same state as on the 25th, when slight improvement had taken place.

BRAZIL.

London, Sunday, April 2.

The Brazilian mail has reached Lisbon, bringing the following dates:

Rio de Janeiro, Saturday, March 11.

Exchange 25⅜@26¼.

Coffee.—Sales of good firsts at 6$806. Shipments 100,000 bags. Stock, 100,000 bags. Freights 50@62½.

Bahia, Saturday, March 11.

Exchange 26¼.

Cotton nominal.

Pernambuco, Saturday, March 11.

Exchange 26⅜@27.

Montivedeo has surrendered to Gen. Flores. The Brazilians now occupy the city.

LATEST VIA LIVERPOOL.

Liverpool, Saturday Evening, April 1, 1865.

The *Times* to-day has an editorial on the amended tariff law of the United States. It says:

"It is impossible to find an excuse for it. Tried by the light of reason or by the results of experience it is alike condemned."

It ironically credits the framers of the scheme with peculiar wisdom in selecting the 1st of April for its inauguration.

The *Army & Navy Gazette* says: "The work of the United States Navy has now been accomplished, and it must be confessed that in the hands of Farragut and Porter the high reputation which the officers and seamen of that Power established soon after the national existence of itself, has been greatly enhanced."

LATEST VIA QUEENSTOWN.

London, Saturday, April 1.

There is no news of importance this morning.

Paris, Friday, March 31—P. M.

The Bourse is steady. The Rentes closed at 67f. 30c.

COMMERCIAL.

LIVERPOOL MARKET.

Liverpool, April 31.—Evening.

The Market report was received per *Moravian*.

Cotton—The stock of Cotton in port is 580,000 bales by actual count, being 13,000 bales below the estimates, of which amount 48,000 bales are American.

TRADE REPORT.

The Manchester market was firmer with an upward tendency.

Breadstuffs—The market is easier. Messrs. Richardson, Spence & Co., and others, report: Flour dull and easier. Wheat quiet and quotations are barely maintained; red Western 8s.@8s. 8d. Corn, inactive, mixed 27s. 6d.

Provisions—The market is downward. Wakefield, Nash & Co., and others, report: Beef has a downward tendency. Pork heavy and declined 2s. 6d. Bacon firmer and holders demand an advance. Lard dull and easier at 58s.@61s. Butter flat and declining. Tallow downward.

Produce.—Ashes easier at 29s. 6d. for Pots, and 30s. for Pearls. Sugar, flat. Coffee, quiet and steady. Rice, quiet and steady. Clover Seed, firmer. Jute, 10s.@30s. lower. Cod Oil, quiet at 57s. Sperm Oil, no sales. Linseed Oil, steady. Resin, very dull. Spirits Turpentine, quiet at 65s.@66s.

Petroleum—Boult, English & Brandon report: Petroleum firm, at 1s. 11d.@2s. for refined; no crude in market.

LONDON MARKETS.

Flour firm; Wheat steady. Iron advancing; bars and rails, £6 10s.@£6 15s; Scotch pig, 52s. 3d. Sugar inactive. Coffee active at a decline of 1s.@2s. Tea steady at 10½d. for common Congou. Rice steady. Spirits Turpentine firm at 67s. Petroleum steady at £18 for crude, 2s. for refined. Sperm Oil nominal at £82. Tallow downward, at 40s.@43s. Linseed Oil flat.

LATEST COMMERCIAL.

... the presence of having a prescription, was shown to the Secretary's sick chamber. The assassin immediately rushed to the bed, and inflicted two or three stabs on the throat and two on the face. It is hoped the wounds may not be mortal. My apprehension is that they will prove fatal.

The nurse alarmed Mr. FREDERICK SEWARD, who was in an adjoining room, and hastened to the door of his father's room, when he met the assassin, who inflicted upon him one or more dangerous wounds. The recovery of FREDERICK SEWARD is doubtful.

It is not probable that the President will live throughout the night.

Gen. GRANT and wife were advertised to be at the theatre this evening, but he started to Burlington at 6 o'clock this evening.

At a Cabinet meeting at which Gen. GRANT was present, the subject of the state of the country and the prospect of a speedy peace was discussed. The President was very cheerful and hopeful, and spoke very kindly of Gen. LEE and others of the Confederacy, and of the establishment of government in Virginia.

All the members of the Cabinet except Mr. SEWARD, are now in attendance upon the President.

I have seen Mr. SEWARD, but he and FREDERICK were both unconscious.

EDWIN M. STANTON,
Secretary of War.

DETAIL OF THE OCCURRENCE.

WASHINGTON, Friday, April 14—12:30 A. M.

The President was shot in a theatre to-night, and is, perhaps, mortally wounded.

Secretary SEWARD was also assassinated.

SECOND DISPATCH.

WASHINGTON, Friday, April 14.

President LINCOLN and wife, with other friends, this evening visited Ford's Theatre for the purpose of witnessing the performance of the "American Cousin."

It was announced in the papers that Gen. GRANT would also be present, but he took the late train of cars for New-Jersey.

The theatre was densely crowded, and everybody seemed delighted with the scene before them. During the third act, and while there was a temporary pause for one of the actors to enter, a sharp report of a pistol was heard, which merely attracted attention, but suggesting nothing serious, until a man rushed to the front of the President's box, waving a long dagger in his right hand, and exclaiming "Sic semper tyrannis," and immediately leaped from the box, which was in the second tier, to the stage beneath, and ran across to the opposite side, making his escape amid the bewilderment of the audience from the rear of the theatre, and mounting a horse, fled.

General BARNES and his immediate assistants, were around his bedside.

The President and Mrs. LINCOLN did not start for the theatre until fifteen minutes after eight o'clock. Speaker COLFAX was at the White House at the time, and the President stated to him that he was going, although Mrs. LINCOLN had not been well, because the papers had announced that Gen. GRANT and they were to be present, and, as Gen. GRANT had gone North, he did not wish the audience to be disappointed.

He went with apparent reluctance and urged Mr. COLFAX to go with him; but that gentleman had made other engagements, and with Mr. ASHMAN, of Massachusetts, bid him good bye.

When the excitement at the theatre was at its wildest height, reports were circulated that Secretary SEWARD had also been assassinated.

On reaching this gentleman's residence a crowd and a military guard were found at the door, and on entering it was ascertained that the reports were based on truth.

Everybody there was so excited that scarcely an intelligible word could be gathered, but the facts are substantially as follows:

About 10 o'clock a man rang the bell, and the call having been answered by a colored servant, he said he had come from Dr. VERDI, Secretary SEWARD's family physician, with a prescription, at the same time holding in his hand a small piece of folded paper, and saying in answer to a refusal that he must see the Secretary, as he was entrusted with particular directions concerning the medicine.

He still insisted on going up, although repeatedly informed that no one could enter the chamber. The man pushed the servant aside, and walked heavily toward the Secretary's room, and was then met by Mr. FREDERICK SEWARD, of whom he demanded to see the Secretary, making the same representation which he did to the servant. What further passed in the way of colloquy is not known, but the man struck him on the head with a "billy," severely injuring the skull and felling him almost senseless. The assassin then rushed into the chamber and attacked Major SEWARD, Paymaster of the United States army and Mr. HANSELL, a messenger of the State

a stroke from Heaven laying the whole of the city in instant ruins could not have startled us as did the word that broke from Ford's Theatre a half hour ago that the President had been shot. It flew everywhere in five minutes, and set five thousand people in swift and excited motion on the instant.

It is impossible to get at the full facts of the case, but it appears that a young man entered the President's box from the theatre, during the last act of the play of "Our American Cousin," with pistol in hand. He shot the President in the head and instantly jumped from the box upon the stage, and immediately disappeared through the side scenes and rear of the theatre, brandishing a dirk knife and dropping a kid glove on the stage.

The audience heard the shot, but supposing it fired in the regular course of the play, did not heed it till Mrs. LINCOLN's screams drew their attention. The whole affair occupied scarcely half a minute, and then the assassin was gone. As yet he has not been found.

The President's wound is reported mortal. He was at once taken into the house opposite the theatre.

As if this horror was not enough, almost the same moment the story ran through the city that Mr. SEWARD had been murdered in his bed.

Inquiry showed this to be so far true also. It appears a man wearing a light coat, dark pants, slouch hat, called and asked to see Mr. SEWARD, and was shown to his room. He delivered to Major SEWARD, who sat near his father, what purported to be a physician's prescription, turned, and with one stroke cut Mr. SEWARD's throat as he lay on his bed, inflicting a horrible wound, but not severing the jugular vein, and not producing a mortal wound.

In the struggle that followed, Major SEWARD was also badly, but not seriously, wounded in several places. The assassin rushed down stairs, mounted the fleet horse on which he came, drove his spurs into him, and dashed away before any one could stop him.

Reports have prevailed that an attempt was also made on the life of Mr. STANTON.

MIDNIGHT.

The President is reported dead. Cavalry and infantry are scouring the city in every direction for the murderous assassins, and the city is overwhelmed with excitement. Who the assassins were no one knows, STANTON, WELLS, MCCULLOCH, SPEED and USHER are with him, as also the Vice-President, the Surgeon-General, and other Surgeons.

There is a great throng about the house, even at this hour.

2 o'clock A. M.

The President still lives, but lies insensible, as he has since the first moment, and no hopes are entertained that he can survive.

The most extravagant stories prevail, among which one is to effect, that Gen. GRANT was shot while on his was to Philadelphia, of course this is not true.

Another is, that every member of Mr. SEWARD's family was wounded in the struggle with the assassin there. This also is untrue. Mr. FRED. SEWARD, the Assistant Secretary, and Major CLARENCE SEWARD, of the army, were wounded, neither of them dangerously.

THE CONDITION OF THE PRESIDENT.

WASHINGTON, April 15—2:12 A. M.

The President is still alive, but he is growing weaker. The ball is lodged in his brain, three inches from where it entered the skull. He remains insensible, and his condition is utterly hopeless.

The Vice-President has been to see him; but all company, except the members of the Cabinet and of the family, is rigidly excluded.

Large crowds still continue in the street, as near to the house as the line of guards allows.

THE SIEGE OF MOBILE.

Fierce Bombardment of the Spanish Fort—Mobile Papers Announce the Capture of Selma.

NEW-ORLEANS, Saturday, April 8, via CAIRO, Friday, April 14.

A special dispatch to the New-Orleans *Times*, from the Spanish Fort, dated April 5, says:

"A furious fire was opened on the rebel forts last night from our entire line. During the bombardment a small magazine in the Spanish Fort exploded. The damage is unknown. Quiet prevailed on the 5th. Deserters report from 18,000 to 20,000 troops in and about Mobile, including all the State Reserves, and about 2,000 in the Spanish Fort. The loss outside the Spanish Fort up to the 4th instant amounted to about 500 killed and wounded. The rebel loss exceeds ours."

Adjt.-Gen. THOMAS arrived at New-Orleans on the morning of the 7th.

Mobile papers of the 4th inst. announce the capture of Selma, Alabama, with 23 pieces of artillery, and a large amount of Government property.

Fort Sumter Celebration in Bangor.

BANGOR, Me., Friday, April 14.

The restoration of the Old Flag to Fort Sumter was celebrated here to-day by a national salute at noon, by a display of all the flags on public and private buildings, and by the raising of the Stars and Strips one thousand feet above the city by means of a monster kite bearing the name of U. S. GRANT.

The Madrid *Bolsa* says if the Pope should leave Rome, Spain would confer upon him the Balearic Isles.

The *Politica* says the Pope would rather inhabit the Montpensier Palace at Seville.

The revenue returns for the financial year, ending March 31, show a net increase of over £104,000 on the year. Notwithstanding the great reductions in taxation, the revenue exceeds by nearly half a million sterling the estimates of Mr. GLADSTONE.

Messrs. BARING's circular says that large business has been done in 5-20 bonds, and that prices advanced early in the week to 57⅛@58, but have since relapsed to 56⅜@57—the demand being chiefly from the continent.

On Friday, the telegrams per the steamship *Cuba* were received, and 5-20s again advanced to 57¾@58⅛. Erie and Illinois Central Shares have also attracted attention, and have again advanced.

The Bank of England on the 30th ult. reduced its rate of discount to 4 per cent., at which there is a fair demand for money. This movement strengthened the English funds, and Consols are buoyant and advancing.

KELSON, TRITTON & Co., East India and general merchants, have suspended payment. Their liabilities are estimated at £900,000 sterling.

Another provincial bank has suspended, the Portsmouth and South Hants Banking Company. Their liabilities are about £170,000 sterling.

The Birmingham and Joint Stock Banking Company had agreed to take up the business of Atwood & Spooner's Bank, which lately suspended at Birmingham, and to pay the creditors 11s. 3d. on the pound.

The West India Mail steamer had arrived, with over two and a quarter millions of dollars in specie. She also brought several Captains of blockade-runners, whose occupations were gone.

THE ATLANTIC TELEGRAPH.

The French Government will probably send one or two steamers to accompany the two that are sent by the English Government with the *Great Eastern* across the Atlantic, at the time of laying the Atlantic cable, and it is hoped that the United States Government will do the same.

FRANCE.

Weekly returns from the Bank of France show an increase of cash on hand of over ten and a half millions francs.

In the French Chambers of the 30th, M. JULES FAVRE spoke upon the necessity for political liberty, but was interrupted by the President and declined to finish his speech. The amendment was rejected.

The amendment in favor of the liberty of the press was debated, but rejected by a large majority.

It is stated that NAPOLEON will leave Paris early in May, not returning until November. His physicians have recommended seven months' absence in the country air.

The Bourse is firm, 67.45.

SPAIN.

The *Epoca* states that the Minister of War tendered his resignation, and that Gen. LEORSUNDI refused to place him.

A later dispatch says the Minister of War resigned from ill health.

Gen. RIVERA succeeded to the office.

DENMARK.

The King relieved M. HELLEEN, Minister of Justice, of his functions. HELLEEN represented the alliance between the Reactionary and extreme Democratic parties. It is supposed that all members of the late Cabinet will return to their posts.

ITALY

In the allocutions delivered at the last consistory the Pope expressed surprise and sorrow at the sad events which have recently taken place in Mexico. His Holiness hoped MAXIMILIAN would abandon the course upon which he had entered, and satisfy the just desires of the Holy See. The Pope further thanked the Bishops of the Catholic world, especially those of Italy, for defending the religion and liberties of the Church, despite the decrees of the secular authorities.

PRUSSIA.

In the Military Committee of Chambers, the Deputies amendment was introduced with the object of effecting a reconciliation between the government and chamber, and proposing a maximum strength of the army at 180,000 men, which was rejected by 11 to 8. The committee also rejected the general military estimates and navy estimates and amendments, thus refusing the whole military and naval proposals of the government.

AUSTRIA.

Count MENSDORFF had made some ministerial explanation in the Lower House Reichsrath. He said the views of the government on the question of the Duchies would be communicated in the Federal Diet on the 6th of April.

As regards relations with Italy, he said the government desired to promote the material interests of the two countries, but that Italy maintained a hostile attitude to the government. He desired to econ-

BREADSTUFFS—The market is quiet and steady.
PROVISIONS—The market is dull.
PRODUCE—The market is quiet and steady. Petroleum firm at 2s.@2s. 0½d. for refined.

LONDON, Saturday, April 1—Evening.

CONSOLS closed at 89¾@90 for money.
AMERICAN STOCKS—Illinois Central Railroad 61½@62½; Erie Railroad 36½@36¾. United States Five-twenties 57⅝@58⅛.

Gen. Lee in Richmond—The Oath of Allegiance.

BALTIMORE, Friday, April 14.

The Richmond *Whig* of yesterday contains little of importance. It announces the arrival of Gen. LEE on the night previous.

The *Whig* publishes the oath of allegiance, which it says citizens will be required to swear and subscribe to. The Provost-Marshal's office is crowded with people anxious to take it, and the only question among citizens seems to be who shall be first to renew their citizenship.

Rejoicings at Cincinnati.

CINCINNATI, Friday, April 14.

Business was entirely suspended to-day. The city was universally decorated with flags, and great enthusiasm prevailed. The procession was an immense affair, comprising the entire police force, Gens. HOOKER and WALLICH, with their staffs, four regiments of National Guards, discharged veterans, ward organizations, the Fenian Brotherhood, the Fire Department, and a large number of colored citizens. All the bells in the city were rung, and salutes were fired at 6 o'clock this evening. To-night the city is brilliantly illuminated, and there is generally a display of fireworks.

Fire.

ROCHESTER, N. Y., Friday, April 14.

The cabinet warehouse of JAMES E. HAYDON, of this city, was partially destroyed by fire this morning. The stocks of HUMPHREY REEDY & Co., stove dealers, HASTINGS & MCVEAN, paper dealers, S. B. ROBY, saddlery and hardware dealers, and the agency of the American Tract Society, were damaged. Total loss, $30,000; insurance, $20,000. The origin of the fire is unknown.

The Funeral of Gen. T. A. Smyth.

WILMINGTON, Del., Friday, April 14.

The remains of Brig.-Gen. T. A. SMYTH arrived here to-day at 1 o'clock, and will be interred on Monday afternoon with appropriate ceremonies.

An Unseaworthy War Steamer.

To the Editor of the New-York Times:

UNITED STATES STEAMER MUSCOOTA, HAMPTON ROADS, Va., Wednesday, April 12, 1865.

This vessel has returned to this port, having made her fourth attempt to make a cruise to the Pacific. On each occasion she has proved herself to be an unsafe sea boat. On her last trial she narrowly escaped being lost in the Gulf Stream. Inclosed you will find a list of her officers; please publish.
Respectfully, &c.,

ARTHUR BURTIS, Jr., Paymaster.

List of officers attached to the U. S. steamer *Muscoota*, one thousand tons, 10 guns:

Commander GEO. M. RANSOM, Lieut. Thos. S. Spencer, Ass't Paymaster Arthur Burtis, Jr., Ass't Surgeon Danl. McMurtrie, Act'g Master Geo. R. Durand, Act'g Ensigns Robt. M. Clark, Jas. Courtney, John D. Thomas, Chas. A. Stewart, Second Ass't Engineers Robert H. Gunnell, Jas. H. Grasmer, Henry Snyder, Act'g Third Ass't Engineers Robt. L. Case, Geo. Taylor, Geo. Westinghouse, Jr., Masters Fred'k. A. Beatie, A. L. Spinney, Wm. Merrill, Captain's Clerk Geo. S. Dana, Paymaster's Clerk F. B. Hathaway.

Arrivals in the City.

Gov. Jos. A. Gilmore, Concord, N. H., is stopping at the Fifth avenue Hotel.

Hon. O. N. Shannon, Cincinnati; Gen. B. F. Stringfellow, Atchison; Dr. N. Greene, Louisville, and Wm. D. Griswold, Terre Haute, are stopping at the Metropolitan Hotel.

COLLISION.—The steamship *La Favorite*, while returning from a trial trip and passing up the East River, collided with the Catharine Ferry-boat *Manhassett*, as she was entering her slip on the Brooklyn side, doing considerable damage to the *Manhassett*, by tearing away a portion of the gentlemen's cabin, and somewhat injuring the hull. Fortunately nobody was hurt.

default of payment of a judgment to Ludlow Street jail, where he died. Of the other principals in the ring all in one way or another escaped jail; a few minor personages were convicted and locked up, and of the numerous millions stolen from the city a few hundred thousand dollars was recovered. And that was all.

Three years later the Tammany ticket once more swept the city. To be sure, it was a somewhat deodorized Tammany. It was ruled by Honest John Kelly, and its ticket contained so considerable an infusion of respectable men that it might be a matter of some doubt whether the tiger was a black beast with yellow stripes or a yellow beast with black stripes. But it was the same old tiger, and before long it was up to the same old tricks. In view of all this, municipal reformers may be excused if they occasionally become faint with weariness and the heat of the day; if they wonder whether their efforts really serve any useful end but their own personal pleasure, and incline to suspect that while they may be hedonists, they are certainly not utilitarians.

Nevertheless, experience has shown that this same prematurely triumphant *Times* editorial was accurate when it said that "the theory that government is only organized robbery has received its death blow." No other administration has ever been so bad as that over which Oakey Hall presided and which was ruled by Tweed. Even the worst governments of later decades did give the city some value for at least a good part of the money spent, and there has never been any parallel to the astounding robberies committed under the guise of repairs and

furnishings for the Tweed courthouse. Reform movements are bolder now; they have behind them something of a tradition of occasional victory. They are no longer beaten before they start; they need no longer fear that there is serious danger of voters being terrorized by mobs of gangsters, or of regularly elected candidates being counted out. That a majority of the residents of New York City still prefer a bad government to a good one might be assumed from election results now as ever, but some of them change their minds occasionally, and the minority which wants a decent administration no longer stays away from the polls from sheer hopeless conviction that it could accomplish nothing. No city administration of these times could dream of attempting to conceal its accounts from the public; and certainly no future Tweed, if there shall ever be any, would find that respectable newspapers are willing, as they were in 1871, to eat the bread of infamy and earn the wage of shame.

For these ameliorations, such as they are, no single man can claim the credit. They are the work of many public-spirited men working through many years. But no one man has contributed so much to this improvement as George Jones.

CHAPTER IV

National Politics, 1872–1884

THE victory over Tweed was such a success as no American newspaper had ever scored before. It raised the prestige of *The Times* to a height that had been unheard of even in the most prosperous periods of Raymond's editorship, and gave it a world-wide renown eclipsing that which *The Herald* had won by its lavishness and eccentricities, while establishing it solidly in the favor of friends of good government in the United States. In the year after Tweed's fall *The Times* received still further accessions of influence and prosperity through the defection of *The Tribune* from the Republican party. At that time, only seven years after Appomattox, partisan animosities burned with a fierceness such as Americans of a later generation can hardly realize, and even in the case of newspapers which as purveyors of the news were as good as *The Times* and *The Tribune*, a large if not a predominant part of the constituency valued the paper as a political organ rather than as a vehicle of information. When Greeley split off from his party and accepted a presidential nomination not only from the Liberal Republicans but from the Democrats, *The Tribune* suffered as *The Times* had suffered in 1866, and considerably more. In 1872 *The Times* could and did advertise itself as "the only Republican morn-

ing paper in New York," and the support of the faithful flowed to it accordingly. Its influence in the early seventies was greater than it had ever been before, and its prosperity may be judged by the fact that some of its stock sold in 1876 at fifteen times the face value.

Yet the prosperous and powerful *Times* of the seventies had a circulation only about a tenth of that enjoyed by *The Times* today. Evidence for the entire period is not available, but in the fall of 1871 — at the height of the campaign against Tweed, just before the election in which *The Times* led the reform forces to victory — the circulation never exceeded 36,000. The circulation of the supplement with the extracts from the Controller's books is, of course, an exception, and now and then on the morning after election the paper might have shown a higher figure; but on the whole it may be said that the leading Republican paper of the East at least, if not of the entire United States, in those years of prosperity sold anywhere from 31,000 to 35,000 copies a day.

It would be interesting to learn just what was the true circulation of *The Times's* contemporaries. Whatever it may have been, it was certainly not what they asserted. But statements of circulation fifty years ago belonged to the field of relativity rather than of conventional mathematics, and the circulation managers of that day have long since gone to face the final audit of the Recording Angel.

And even on this small circulation *The Times* paid regularly a dividend of eighty, ninety, or a hundred per cent on its capitalization of $100,000. There

was no reason why it shouldn't have paid dividends. Salaries were lower, as were living costs. The expense of news getting was still very moderate. During the later months of 1918 *The Times* often had a bill for cable tolls of $15,000 a week, but in the seventies $15,000 would have paid the cable tolls of all the New York newspapers for a whole year. And while the circulation of daily papers was not large, most of them had weekly editions; and the ethical standards of the time permitted papers to allow the national committees of the great parties, in presidential years, to buy and distribute the weekly edition by the hundred thousands. That source of revenue has disappeared with the disappearance of weekly editions, and with the spread of a newer conception of newspaper ethics for which the present management of *The Times* may perhaps claim some degree of credit. A similar improvement has led to the exclusion of certain kinds of advertising which in the seventies were regarded as unobjectionable.

It may be observed that the business conscience of *The Times* in the seventies was notably higher than that of some of its contemporaries. By all the standards of the time, its prosperity was well deserved, as was its political influence. Nevertheless, there was from the first a certain insecurity in this lofty position — an insecurity due to the character which Raymond had given *The Times* from its very first number; indeed, even from that prospectus which had promised that it would be free from "bigoted devotion to narrow interests." For there had been a painful degree of truth in Oakey

Hall's observation when *The Times* first published the figures from Connolly's books, that such an eminent Republican newspaper might be able to keep itself busy investigating the corruption in its own party. To the scandals which flourished in Washington, invisible to the somewhat too long-sighted eye of President Grant, the editors of *The Times* could not be blind; and seeing them they could not fail to condemn them, even though their Republican principles made them sometimes delay such condemnation rather too long in the hope that the party would do its own housecleaning. Unfortunately, the party was not so minded; and *The Times*, which had always maintained a measure of independence unusual in its day, was compelled on occasion to express itself with a frankness which met with disfavor from more extreme partisans.

So the chief interest in the history of *The Times* in the thirteen years between the overthrow of Tweed and the campaign of 1884 lies in the struggle of its editors, continually more difficult and finally hopeless, to reconcile their principles with their party allegiance. To one who studies the evidence of that struggle in the columns of the paper for those years there is apt to be suggested the simile of a loyal wife doing her best to get along with a scandalously dissipated husband. *The Times* had not exactly married the Republican party to reform it, but it did what it could to bring the party back to the strait and narrow path, and without success. Its reproaches were dignified; they never sank to the level of nagging; perhaps, indeed, they were too dignified to be effective, as *The Times's* readiness to

believe in the reformatory intentions of its errant partner was certainly too complaisant. But at last the connection became unendurable, and under the final affront of the nomination of Blaine *The Times* walked out of the party and slammed the door. After that it would have taken a miracle of miracles to bring it back.

When the Liberal Republicans met in 1872, *The Times* saw in their convention a strange assortment of well-intentioned but impractical doctrinaires, and of practical politicians who were disappointed because their rivals had crowded them away from the trough. That reform was needed *The Times* did not deny, but it could not see that it was likely to be accomplished by these gentlemen. And when the Cincinnati convention nominated Horace Greeley, the paper which had known Greeley and enjoyed his hostility for twenty years had no further occasion to seek for any concealed merits in the Liberal Republican organization. Greeley's attitude toward Tweed had weakened his standing as a reformer; and when he permitted the Democrats to accept him as their candidate the paper which Greeley had so fiercely denounced, only six years earlier, for favoring a policy of reconciliation with the South could hardly place as much faith in his sincere desire for better things as perhaps it merited. Persons so violently and assiduously sincere as Greeley in a variety of contradictory causes can hardly expect to be understood by their fellows who are less gifted in moral fervor and metaphysical tergiversation. In view of the standards of newspaper controversy prevalent at the time, it says a

good deal for the editors of *The Times* that they confined their attacks on Greeley to his political views and affiliations, and did not drag out the old scandal of Fourierism and free love.

Yet *The Times* did not deny during that campaign that something had to be done. On October 29, 1872, in the course of an editorial devoted chiefly to the prediction that the reëlection of Grant in the following week would mean the disappearance of the Democratic party, there appeared this observation:

> With the exception of one or two unfounded flings or insinuations at the present administration, there is nothing in the Cincinnati platform [Liberal Republican] to which any Republican will not heartily assent, nor on the other hand is there anything in the platform adopted at Philadelphia [by the regulars] to which any supporter of Horace Greeley can take exception.

However, it could well have seemed to honest and patriotic men in 1872 — and indeed it did seem to several millions of them — that it was safer to give the Republican organization another chance. Though *The Times* was at that time probably the strongest and most influential Republican paper in the country, though its editors could have solidified their position and made still more certain their prosperity by becoming an out-and-out party organ, they did not fail in the succeeding years to denounce the misdeeds of men in Washington, even when close to the administration.

As a collector and distributor of news, too, *The Times* maintained in the early seventies the high

EDWARD CARY,
Associate Editor,
1871-1917.

JOHN NORRIS,
Business Manager,
1900-1911.

standard of past years, and often surpassed it. The cable was now working at last, though its capacity was small. The Franco-German war had seen the first use of its facilities for the transmission of important news, and even then only two or three columns a day of condensed bulletins and official statements had come in this way, with the mails bringing the detailed accounts of the defeats of the French army, the heroism of the Defense Nationale, the fall of one empire and the rise of another.

The Times covered that war thoroughly and well. If it was somewhat outshone by *The Tribune*, it had an honorable excuse; for *The Times* in 1870–71 was giving up a good deal of its space, and of its energy, to attacks on Tweed, while *The Tribune* had no interest in this particular field of the news. Great domestic news stories of the period were also handled exceptionally well. In the case of the fires at Chicago in 1871 and Boston in 1872 *The Times* gave more than a page on each of the first two days to stories of the disaster, and at the time of the Boston fire issued special editions through the afternoon of Sunday while the fire was at its height.

Much of the credit for the excellence of *The Times* news service at this period must go to John C. Reid, who came to the paper in 1872 and served for seventeen years thereafter as managing editor. He was one of the greatest news editors of the time, a pioneer of the new age which has seen the news department take over a good deal of the predominance which formerly belonged to the editorial page. Under Reid, *The Times* performed in 1874 and 1875

a feat without parallel in New York journalism up to that time, the reporting in full of the court proceedings in the suit of Theodore Tilton against the Rev. Henry Ward Beecher for alienation of Mrs. Tilton's affections and misconduct with her. Editorial comment, at the time and later, suggests that the editors of *The Times* did not have that complete faith in the reverend gentleman's innocence which was entertained by his congregation, and the prevalence of doubt in the community was suggested by the eventual disagreement of the jury. But they handled the news with full appreciation of its value. Each day's story began with a "lead" of two columns or so, followed by a complete stenographic transcript of evidence and argument, the whole sometimes taking up as much as three pages in what was by that time a twelve-page newspaper. It was an expensive proceeding, but it was a great achievement in giving the public the news.

No doubt a good many readers of *The Times* thought that the paper was giving an undue amount of space to this chronicle of sin and suffering. Those complaints come in often enough even in these days from readers who appreciate the paper's general reluctance to display news of this sort, and wonder why a good general rule should occasionally be violated. But there was a reason in the Beecher case, as there has usually been a reason in similar affairs since. Dr. Beecher was one of the most prominent clergymen in the country; there was a natural curiosity as to whether he was practicing what he preached. One of the counsel at the trial declared that "all Christendom was hanging on its outcome."

Full reporting of its course was not a mere pandering to vulgar curiosity, but a recognition of the value of the case as news.

But always in the background was the horrendous ghost of Republican corruption and misgovernment, a ghost which refused to be laid and which was every now and then uttering hollow groans such as could not fail to be heard by the editors even of a good Republican paper. General Grant's second administration failed to be that Saturnian reign which *The Times* had hoped in 1872. The great panic of 1873, though no doubt a natural reaction from the violent expansion just after the Civil War, provided a background of economic dissatisfaction for political discontent. A bad business kept getting worse, and it was becoming apparent that the country might not be willing to wait much longer for the often-deferred reforms within the party. And a warning, strong and unmistakable, was given by the election of 1874 when the Democrats recaptured the House of Representatives, and elected governors in a number of states, including New York.

Looking back from the vantage point of half a century later, one is compelled to admit that *The Times* seems to have been somewhat unjust to Samuel J. Tilden, whose great accomplishments in exposing and prosecuting members of the Tweed group had won him the Democratic nomination for the governorship in 1874. *The Times* felt that Tilden had only climbed on the band wagon of reform when it had become safe to do so. During the early and critical

days of the struggle against Tweed, before the publication of the Controller's accounts, Tilden had given *The Times* no help; but neither had anybody else except Thomas Nast. And it could not be denied that the beginning of the end had come when Connolly turned over his office to Andrew H. Green, on Tilden's advice and insistence. This alone would have given Tilden an honorable place in the gallery of reformers, and his later services in analyzing the accounts of the Broadway Bank which showed the disposition of the plunder, and in forcing the impeachment of the worst of the Tweed-Fisk judges, had been of great and enduring value. Against this *The Times* could set off his tolerance of Tweed before the exposures, and of the undoubted fraud which had procured the Democratic victory in the state and city elections of 1868. Tilden had kept his eyes shut when they should have been open; but he was not the only man who did that in the gilded age. He had opened them at last, and opened them quite as widely as the eyes of *The Times* were open toward similar misconduct in the Republican party. He was in pretty bad company before 1871, and when he accepted the support of Kelly in 1874. But a politician who wanted to keep out of bad company in those days would have had to climb to the top of an ivory tower and pull his ladder up after him.

When Tilden was nominated for the governorship *The Times* had given cordial enough recognition of his ability and character, and its opposition to him during the campaign was directed only against his associates. Indeed, Tilden suffered like many re-

spectable candidates from the distrust of some of his supporters; and he set an excellent precedent by showing very promptly that he was his own master. Unlike many of the western leaders of his party, he was a sound-money man. He was as firm against Tammany as ever. And presently he uncovered, prosecuted, and broke up the bipartisan ring of canal grafters which had for years past maintained pleasant and profitable relations with administrations of both parties. *The Times* gave Tilden hearty support against the canal conspirators, and at the same time it was compelled to condemn the scandalous abuses which had been disclosed in Washington, abuses not only ignored by the national administration, but oftentimes actually shared in by men more or less close to the throne. In 1875 the prospect of the coming elections was enough to discourage any honest Republican. A Democratic governor of New York was sending political crooks to jail without caring what party they belonged to, while a Republican president of undoubted personal integrity was blindly standing by his friends, and every week or so brought some new evidence that his friends were profiting by his confidence.

The men who managed the Federal government behind the respectable figure of Grant could neither learn nor forget. *The Times* was compelled to repeat that the third-term movement was folly; that there was no reason for breaking an old and sound precedent for the sake of a man whose executive abilities were obviously not of a class with his military talents. The third-term movement eventually subsided, to rise again in later years; but with its subsidence came

the growth of the probability that James G. Blaine would become the Presidential candidate. And most of the editors of *The Times* were convinced that Blaine would not do. Reform was needed, was demanded; and it would be an insult to the country to pretend that Blaine was the man to bring it about.

By giving expression, even with due caution, to these opinions, *The Times* had by the beginning of 1876 fallen pretty well into the bad graces of an administration which on the whole it had supported much more steadfastly than that administration deserved, and dissatisfaction with *The Times's* independence led to another scheme to take the paper away from George Jones, whom the friends of the administration regarded as chiefly responsible for *The Times's* unwillingness to exculpate a thief merely because he was a Republican. Jones was the largest stockholder, but he was not a majority stockholder. He had been saved from a similar attempt during the fight against Tweed by the opportune assistance of E. B. Morgan, but in 1876 he had to save himself. And, unfortunately, he had enemies within the office. Louis J. Jennings, the editor-in-chief, whose Republicanism was of a more blazing and reckless type than Jones's, entered into a plan with certain Republican politicians affiliated with the Grant administration to get control of the paper and make it a real organ of the party. Apparently they had some support among the stockholders; and the ten shares belonging to the estate of James B. Taylor were now on the market and might be used to solidify the control of *The Times* in the hands of Jennings and his friends.

But on February 4, 1876, it was announced that Jones had bought the Taylor stock, thus becoming for the first time owner of a majority of the shares. The price paid for Taylor's ten shares was $150,000, and this fact had become known in financial and newspaper circles. Rivals of *The Times*, unwilling to admit that this represented the real value of the stock, had circulated the report that part of the price represented "back dividends," or that it had been unduly inflated by bidding up against the friends of Jennings. It was also said that *The Times* had spent $40,000 in reporting the Beecher trial; if so, it got it all back in increased circulation. At any rate, Jones took the occasion of the announcement of this purchase to deny all these rumors, and to inform the public that in 1875 *The Times* had paid a dividend of $100,000, or 100 per cent of the par value of its stock. At that rate $15,000 a share was a reasonable enough price.

Further the announcement informed *The Times* readers that

> at no time during the last fifteen years [that is, since the beginning of the Civil War] has the paper paid a less dividend than 80 per cent on the original capital, and in some cases the dividend has been 100 per cent. During the same period the entire indebtedness on The Times Building and property has been paid off, and the paper is now in the satisfactory position of owing no one anything.

It was added that the circulation was larger than ever before in *The Times's* history.

The conspiracy being thus defeated, and Jones left in unhampered control of the paper, Jennings resigned in the following month and went back to England, where he became a member of Parliament, and passed his later years in the writing of books about the joys of the rural pedestrian. One of the illustrated papers at the time celebrated Jennings's departure by a cartoon which represented Jones standing on the roof of the Times Building and administering to his late editor-in-chief a kick which had sent him clear across the Atlantic, so that he might be seen in the distance dropping on the sod of Great Britain. Jennings had made many enemies in New York, who were glad to see him go; but it must be said that this scurrilous caricature somewhat unduly simplified and dramatized the transaction.

John Foord, who had made his reputation by his work on the Connolly books, succeeded Jennings as editor and held that position until 1883.

So *The Times* came into the campaign of 1876 still a Republican paper, but a paper with a shade of independence unpleasing to true zealots of the party. It was a campaign in which the paper played a very important part, and in whose outcome one of its executives, acting on his own responsibility and outside of office hours, had a part which was probably decisive. *The Times's* attitude toward both the threatened nomination of Blaine, and what many have always believed to have been the election of Tilden, has been the subject of some misconception and of a certain amount of interested misrepresentation. The ac-

[illegible]	[illegible]—Paid for Repairs, &c., Check in name of C. D. Bollar & Co., indorsed by Ingersoll & Co., to Feb. 3, 1869	38,907 43
Sept.	30.—Paid for Fitting up Armories, Check in name of C. D. Bollar & Co., indorsed by Ingersoll & Co., Sept. 1, 1868	44,737 45
Sept.	20.—Paid for Fitting up Armories, Check in name of C. D. Bollar & Co., indorsed by Ingersoll & Co., July 1, 1869	32,112 78

GEORGE S. MILLER, 1869—*All the Checks Indorsed by Ingersoll & Co.*

July	2.—Paid for Repairs to Court of Common Pleas to Oct. 17, 1867	$905 51
July	2.—Paid for Repairs to Courts and Offices from Aug. 1 to Oct. 20, 1868	6,089 24
July	28.—Paid for Repairs to County Offices, Dec. 23, 1868	10,647 56
July	28.—Paid for Repairs to County Offices and Courts, Nov. 20, 1868	11,349 54
Sept.	8.—Paid for Carpenter-work, County Offices and Courts, from Nov. 12, 1868, to Dec. 12, 1868	48,833 23
Dec.	3.—Paid for Repairs to County Offices and Buildings from Oct. 21 to Oct. 31, 1868	23,038 74
Dec.	29.—Paid for Repairs and Alterations, County Offices and Buildings, July 21, 1868	27,885 04
Jan.	11.—Paid for Repairs in Armories and Drill-rooms from Nov. 27 to Dec. 19, 1868	15,415 14
Jan.	19.—Paid for Repairs in Armories and Drill-rooms from Oct. 23 to Dec. 4, 1868	14,691 78
Feb.	27.—Paid for Repairs in Armories and Drill-rooms from Jan. 14 to Jan. 30, 1869	27,937 51
May	12.—Paid for Carpenter-work in Various Armories from Jan. 30 to March 23, 1869	27,651 40
June	7.—Paid for Carpenter-work in Various Armories from April 23 to May 18, 1869	38,676 50
June	7.—Paid for Carpenter-work in Various Armories from March 30 to April 16, 1869	13,864 07
Sept.	20.—Paid for Carpenter-work in Various Armories from May 25 to June 9, 1869	14,130 36
Oct.	11.—Paid for Carpenter-work in Various Armories from May 25 to June 29, 1869	49,763 80

A. G. MILLER, 1869—*Checks Indorsed by Ingersoll & Co.*

Dec.	20.—Paid for Repairs to County Offices and Buildings, March 8, 1868	$34,785 03
Dec.	20.—Paid for Repairs to County Offices and Buildings, July 7, 1868	18,222 47
Sept.	28.—Paid for Repairs to County Offices and Buildings, July 2, 1869	48,798 63

1870. INGERSOLL & CO. 1870.

Jan.	17.—Paid for Furniture Furnished County Court-rooms and Offices, July 17, 1868	$20,655 72
Jan.	24.—Paid for Furniture Furnished County Court-rooms and Offices, May 13, 1868	33,538 36
Feb.	7.—Paid for Furniture Furnished County Court-rooms and Offices	11,186 92
Feb.	16.—Paid for Furniture Furnished County Court-rooms and Offices, Aug. 21, 1869	29,404 48
Feb.	23.—Paid for Furniture Furnished County Court-rooms and Offices, Sept. 23, 1869	51,813 77
Feb.	26.—Paid for Furniture Furnished County Court-rooms and Offices, Oct. 6, 1869	26,981 90
Feb.	26.—Paid for Furniture Furnished County Court-rooms and Offices, Sept. 3, 1869	33,037 15
May	6.—Paid for Furniture Furnished County Court-house, Dec. 10, 1869	64,954 87
May	21.—Paid for Cabinet-work County Court-house, July 23, 1869	70,117 59
May	21.—Paid for Cabinet-work County Court-house, Oct. 17, 1869	64,984 82
May	28.—Paid for Furniture County Court-house, Oct. 21, 1869	40,314 09
May	28.—Paid for Furniture County Court-house, Nov. 3, 1869	39,844 19
May	30.—Paid for Furniture County Court-house, Dec. 27, 1869	68,218 82
June	3.—Paid for Furniture Furnished in County Buildings and Offices, Feb. 5, 1870	54,030 26
June	10.—Paid for Furniture, Clocks, &c., Furnished in County Buildings and Offices, March 23, 1870	69,719 10
June	13.—Paid for Furniture and Cabinet-work in County Court-house, April 18, 1870	98,259 07
June	20.—Paid for Cabinet-work in County Court-house, Feb. 3, 1870	66,292 33
June	27.—Paid for Cabinet-work and Furniture in Armories and Drill-rooms, Feb. 27, 1869	58,330 93
June	30.—Paid for Cabinet-work and Furniture in Armories and Drill-rooms, Feb. 6, 1870	54,053 33
June	30.—Paid for Cabinet-work and Furniture in Armories and Drill-rooms, March 26, 1870	29,129 99
Aug.	1.—Paid for Furniture in Court-rooms and Offices, March 28, 1870	91,325 50
Mar.	14.—Paid for Furniture in Armories and Drill-rooms, Nov. 3, 1869	58,937 60
April	16.—Paid for Furniture in Armories and Drill-rooms, Sept. 11, 1869	28,608 68
Aug.	31.—Paid for Fitting up District-Attorney's Office, Aug. 22, 1870	30,000 00
Aug.	30.—Paid for Fitting up Commissioners of Taxes' and Receiver of Taxes' Offices, June 30, 1870	40,000 00
Aug.	30.—Paid for Fitting up Register's Office, Aug. 3, 1870	10,000 00
Oct.	26.—Paid for Fitting up Surrogate's Office, Sept. 3, 1870	12,000 00

C. D. BOLLAR & CO.—*Checks Indorsed by Ingersoll & Co.*

May	7.—Paid for Furniture, &c., Furnished in County Court-house, Sept. 16, 1869	$39,260 17
May	7.—Paid for Furniture, &c., Furnished in County Court-house, Oct. 18, 1869	35,114 08
May	13.—Paid for Cabinet-work Furnished in County Court-house, July 18, 1869	89,379 00
May	21.—Paid for Fitting up in County Court-house, March 6, 1870	39,950 18
May	21.—Paid for Fitting up in County Court-house, Jan. 20, 1870	39,614 59
May	27.—Paid for Cabinet-work Furnished in County Court-house, Aug. 23, 1869	125,830 56
June	10.—Paid for Cabinet-work Furnished in County Court-house, April 16, 1870	67,487 21
June	30.—Paid for Fitting up Armories and Drill-rooms, Jan. 7, 1870	49,208 14
June	30.—Paid for Fitting up Armories and Drill-rooms, March 13, 1870	37,072 16
Aug.	1.—Paid for Cabinet-work, &c., done in County Buildings and Offices, March 12, 1870	60,503 43

J. A. SMITH—*Checks Indorsed by Ingersoll & Co.*

May	6.—Paid for Carpets Furnished in New Court-house, June 22, 1869	$34,082 25
May	7.—Paid for Curtains and Shades Furnished in New Court-house, Sept. 23, 1869	36,083 80
May	21.—Paid for Carpets and Shades Furnished in County Buildings and Offices, Feb. 21, 1870	34,515 73
May	28.—Paid for Carpets and Shades Furnished in County Buildings and Offices, Feb. 21, 1870	73,602 46
June	3.—Paid for Carpets and Shades Furnished in County Buildings and Offices, Dec. 27, 1869	63,175 51
June	6.—Paid for Carpets &c., Furnished in County Court-house, Aug. 3, 1869	42,291 45
June	6.—Paid for Carpets, &c., Furnished in County Buildings and Offices, June 21, 1869	44,259 23
June	6.—Paid for Shades Furnished in County Buildings and Offices, Sept. 16, 1869	36,987 25
June	24.—Paid for Carpets Furnished in Armories and Drill-rooms, Dec. 22, 1869	36,441 42

and how the corporations resist collection, on the ground that they acted on the instructions of an agent of the Government in neglecting to retain the amount of the tax, and that they are not liable to sustain loss because of the reversal of the decision on which they acted. Solicitor BANFIELD has been considering their plea, and today handed the Secretary of the Treasury his opinion as to the legality of action for the collection of these taxes. The opinion will be made public to-morrow, together with the Secretary's decision based upon it. This is another case which must make Commissioner PLEASONTON aware that he is one of the Secretary's subordinates, and that he is so regarded by the President.

BRISK WORK IN THE PENSION OFFICE.

A statement was not long ago published which showed that there were about 100,000 pension claims unexamined on the files of the Pension Office. Those who are anxiously looking for action upon applications will be glad to hear that the daily average work of the Pension Office under the new Commissioner, Gen. BAKER, has been already about doubled. Yesterday 188 certificates for pensions were issued, the largest number ever issued from the office in one day. The first week in June, which was the first week after Gen. BAKER came into the office, 423 certificates were issued. Since then there has been a general constant increase and last week 915 were issued. This week the number is expected to reach 1,100, and during July 4,000 are expected to be signed. At this rate the office will be gaining on its work instead of falling further behind, and an effort will be made to bring the work up to time as soon as possible with the limited force which can be employed.

SECRETARY DELANO.

Secretary DELANO has written that his return will be delayed till Tuesday next.

Dispatch to the Associated Press.

AUSTRALIA'S IMPORTATIONS.

A statement has been compiled at the Treasury Department from the latest statistics, showing the imports into Australia and New-Zealand, as follows: From Great Britain, £17,924,420; from the United States, £1,354,385; all other countries, £3,812,478. Stated by per centage, they are as follows: From Great Britain, 77 6-10; from the United States, 5 5-10; all other countries, 16 6-10. The Parliament of New-South Wales has recently voted a subsidy of $75,000 to a monthly line of American steamers between San Francisco and Sidney. The imports of Australia and New-Zealand being largely manufactured goods, it is believed that a very large and profitable commerce will spring up with our Western Coast.

IMMIGRATION AT NEW-YORK.

The official returns received at the Bureau of Statistics show that during the quarter ending June 30, 1871, the total number of passengers arrived at the port of New-York from foreign countries was 107,114, of whom 64,213 were males and 42,901 females. Of the total number arrived, 101,015 were actual immigrants—males, 60,082; females, 40,963. Ages—Under fifteen, 19,812; fifteen and under forty, 71,056; forty and upward, 10,147. The deaths on the voyage were 92, of whom 54 were males and 38 females. The principal nationalities of the immigrants were as follows: England, 17,845; Scotland, 4,613; Wales, 399; Ireland, 26,149; Great Britain, locality unknown, 6,672; Germany, 30,814; Austria, 1,983; Sweden, 5,727; Norway, 1,286; Denmark, 1,143; France, 849; Switzerland, 1,305; Spain, 104; Italy, 8,671; Holland, 409; Belgium, 78; Russia, 295; Poland, 183; Cuba, 43; Bermudas, 77.

THE KUKLUX INVESTIGATION.

The Kuklux Committee, today, examined a witness named MCBRIDE, who testified that while a teacher of a colored school in Chickasaw County, Mississippi, a band of disguised men seized and whipped him, and insisted he should leave the country. Other colored schools were broken up in that section. Three witnesses from North Carolina are in attendance, and will testify relative to the existence of

[illegible], Minnesota, $380,000; Georgia, $861,000; Kansas, $176,100; North Carolina, $609,000; Missouri, $1,290,000; South Carolina, $258,000; Nebraska, $212,000; Texas, $145,000; Colorado, $61,000; New-Mexico, $155,000; Oregon, $137,000; Alabama, $260,000; California, $3,205. The law requires that one-half of the increased circulation shall be apportioned among the States not having an excess already, according to population, and one-half according to the existing banking capital resources and business of such State and Territory. The census returns of the valuation of property and banking capital have not yet been received, and the proportion of circulation for the States of Ohio, Indiana and Illinois cannot probably be ascertained with any accuracy until about the 1st of October. It is probable, however, that there will be sufficient circulation for all of the Southern and Western States when the full census returns are received. No additional circulation can be issued to the Eastern and Middle States.

THE ABUSED CAR-HORSES.

Inspection of Stables by Henry Bergh—Sickening Sights—Comparative Views.

Yesterday, Mr. BERGH and Mr. A. H. CAMPBELL, the President and Superintendent of the Society for the Prevention of Cruelty to Animals, accompanied by Dr. LIANTARD, of the New-York Veterinary College, and a TIMES reporter, made a tour of inspection of the principle car companies' stables to examine the horses, the condition of the stables, the quality of feed, and the general order of the homes of the best servants of mankind. The first stables inspected were those of the Fourth-avenue line. The Superintendent, Mr. MESSEROE, received his visitors very politely, and showed them over the premises. This line had lost eighteen out of ninety-four cases with the new disease. Ninety out of the ninety-four affected were mares, and the eighteen that died of the disease were mares. The hospital yesterday had sixty disabled horses in it. Only a very small portion, however, were down with the malady, the others being sick with sore feet, quittors, sore backs, and otherwise disabled. Some of the poor creatures had fearful wounds on the fetlocks, caused by their injuring themselves in the numerous switches on the line. This is reckoned the hardest road for horses of any in the City. The feed given the horses of this line is half oats and half corn. The condition of the stables is tolerable. The open windows of the stable in which the sick horses were, looked into a yard belonging to the proprietors of the Fourth-avenue stage line, and the filth and mud in this place was knee-deep. The stench must be anything but conducive to the recovery of the sick horses. The feed was examined and found of medium quality.

The stables of Messrs. WILKINS & MARSHALL, the proprietors of the Fourth-avenue stage line, were next visited. The stables were three tiers deep, and the atmosphere of the lowest was very bad. The refuse besides ran through from the top to the lower stable, rendering it altogether quite unfit for the purpose, in addition to which it is quite underground, and excepting just at the entrances quite dark. In a dirty yard were fifteen horses turned out for exercise in course of recovery from the disease. The stock consisted of 330 horses. Eighty had been attacked, out of which number eleven mares had died. One of the proprietors drew Mr. BERGH'S particular attention to one horse which had been kept from work two weeks simply because he had a sore back. Mr. WILKINS, one of the proprietors, said he felt certain that the disease was easily curable if attended to quickly. He said the first symptoms were swelling of the hind legs and running at the eyes, but Dr. LIANTARD did not at all agree with this view. The horses were fed on half corn and half oats.

The stables of the East Belt line, at Thirty-seventh-street and First-avenue, were next inspected. Here were found 400 horses, a great proportion of which were in appearance very unfit for the every day toil required of them. There were about seventy cripples in a deplorable condition, and many more with large sores and ulcers on the fetlocks. Superintendent TERRY was asked if the latter were worked, and replied that he was compelled to work such stock or he must stop the line; and besides, he thought such horses better working than standing idle. Mr. BERGH did not agree with him, and cautioned him not to use many of the suffering beasts which were noticed in the stalls. The horses go over eighteen miles every day, and the daily feed of each consisted of twelve pounds of meal and four and a half pounds of ground oats. The line had lost forty animals,

[illegible] only reported four cases of the disease, all of which were slowly recovering. He said that the Company had decided not to use in future any kiln-dried corn. After being dried it was found to have lost its virtue, and when sown it would not grow. The horses of this line had seventeen pounds of feed per day supplied to each.

The stables of the Forty-second-street, or Cross-town line, which has of late given Mr. BERGH and his officers so much trouble, were next visited. The clerk was very civil, and called the stable-keeper, A. CHALMERS, to escort Mr. BERGH and his party over the premises, but CHALMERS recognized the visitors, kept out of the way, and was found only after great trouble. He said he had received strict orders from JOHN GREEN, the President, not to show any one over the stables, and especially Mr. BERGH nor any of his officers. The reason of this refusal was quite apparent, for a more filthy, dilapidated and unwholesome-looking place, even from the outside, is difficult to conceive of. The office is dirty, and a coke-dealer would hardly deign to use it. The waiting-room is an inch deep in dirt, and the seats covered. Some half-dozen dirty-looking ruffians were squatting inside the shed, who were pointed out to our reporter as drivers and conductors of the "line." Mr. BERGH told CHALMERS he knew perfectly well the reason he was refused admittance, for he had gone over the cellars, called stables, a year ago and had found them in an awful condition. CHALMERS denied that the stables were in a bad condition. It is strange that Mr. BERGH and his party should be so cordially received and treated so well at every other stable that was visited, and invited to call at any time and point out such horses as he might feel justified in ordering to be relieved of work, and yet be refused even admission to the "sheds" of the Green line. Mr. BERGH begged that CHALMERS would request Mr. GREEN to go over the Sixth-avenue stables, and then "go and do likewise."

DESTRUCTIVE FIRE.

Several Buildings in West Forty-Seventh and Forty-Sixth Streets Destroyed or Damaged.

Another destructive conflagration occurred last evening, which was discovered at about 9 o'clock, in the two-story saw and planing mill of KINNEY & CLARK, Nos. 628 and 630 West Forty-seventh-street, and which, being first seen in the boiler-room, probably originated from the furnace. The flames spread with extraordinary rapidity, and almost before the engines arrived the entire building was enveloped, and the fire communicated to adjacent property. The mill was entirely destroyed with all its contents and the loss will probably reach $15,000. Next west was the lumber yard of JOHN W. STEVENS & BRO., where stock to the amount of about $5,000 was destroyed. Next east was a five story building, Nos. 622, 624 and 626 West Forty-seventh-street, occupied as a morocco factory, by C. P. Buckin, the top floor of which was reached by the flames and the loss will probably exceed $5,000. The fire even reached across the street to the two story dwelling of THOS. ING, whose loss is $500; also to the building No. 627, owned by JOHN DARRAGH, and the lower floor of which was occupied as a stable and the upper portion as a tenement. The Twenty-second Precinct Police got out a great portion of the furniture of the tenants and the thirty horses in the stable, so that the loss was chiefly confined to the building, which will require $1,500 for repairs. No. 629 was occupied as a stable by HENRY BENKIN, whose loss is $500, and the slaughter-house of RICHARD DONOVAN, in the rear, was also slightly damaged. The fire also extended from the rear of the houses on the south side of the street to the raw-hide establishment of WM. CARR, Nos. 641 and 643 West Forty-sixth-street, whose loss is chiefly confined to the building, which is damaged $1,500. The fire at one time threatened to destroy the entire block, and that result would have undoubtedly followed, but for the great exertions of the firemen, ably directed by Chief Engineer PERLEY and the district engineers.

Meeting of the Riot Relief Fund Association.

A meeting of the Twelfth of July Relief Fund Association was held last evening at No. 295 Third-avenue, Dr. J. C. HANNAN presiding. The General Committee already appointed was authorized to begin the collection of subscriptions, and was authorized to name a subcommittee to investigate cases of distress arising out of the late riot. The election of a treasurer was deferred to the next meeting, each member of the Committee being ordered to report to the Secretary all collections made in the meantime. The name of JAS. H. GOODMAN, attorney-at-law, was added to the General Committee, which will meet at No. 204 East Twenty-first-street next Friday evening. Our reporter was informed that the subscriptions already promised amount to $700.

compromise with their employers.

FRANCE.

The Paris Elections To-Morrow—Rumored Resignation of the Orleans Princes—German Evacuation of the Northern Departments Ordered.

PARIS, July 21.—The Radicals are actively canvassing for the municipal elections to be held next Sunday. The contest grows more and more exciting. In the Assembly, today, Minister LAMBRECHT explained that the state of siege was still maintained in Paris, because the reorganization of the Police had not yet been completed. Notwithstanding the adverse report of the Committee of the Assembly, M. THIERS intends to defend his policy of protection before the Assembly. It is rumored that the Duke D'AUMALE and the Prince DE JOINVILLE have resigned their seats in the Assembly. President THIERS will shortly leave Paris for one of the watering-places. *Le Monde*, the ultra Catholic organ, demands that the Government support the Pope in the exercise of his temporal rights. Criminal proceedings have been commenced against the *Avenir Nationale* for calumniating the Government. The Prussian troops have received orders from Berlin to evacuate the Cities of Amiens and Rouen, and the Departments of the Somme, Lower Seine and Euse. Rouen will be evacuated to-morrow.

GENERAL EUROPEAN NEWS.

Serrano Forms a New Ministry in Spain—Adjournment of the Cortes—Alsace and Lorraine—A Fleet Preparing to Convey the Grand Duke Alexis to America.

MADRID, July 20.—Marshal SERRANO has been intrusted by King AMADEUS with the formation of a new Ministry, and has already designated the following members: Minister of Justice, Señor GOMEZ; Minister of Foreign Affairs, Señor CAUDAN; Minister of Marine, Admiral MALCAMPO; Minister of Finance, Señor CAMADIO. The Cortes has adjourned tumultuously amid the protests of the minority.

VIENNA, July 21.—Count AGENOR GOLUCHOWSKI has been appointed Governor of Galicia.

BERLIN, July 21.—Several decrees are published today, organizing Courts of law in Alsace and Lorraine.

LONDON, July 21.—The Grand Duke CONSTANTINE, of Russia, has arrived in England. A naval squadron is fitting out at Cronstadt to accompany the Grand Duke ALEXIS to America.

The "Reformed" Hackmen—Opposition to the Proposed New Regulations.

The Hackmen's Association met last evening in Apollo Hall, in Prince-street, with a very large attendance. JOHN MARRION, the President, occupied the chair, and J. PHILLIPS was Secretary. A dozen new members were elected, and $149 50 was received for dues and fees.

A resolution was passed to expel any member of the association who should take passengers with the Transfer Companies' tickets. The initiation fee was changed to $5 for owners, and $2 for drivers.

The Treasurer reported that the expenses for the past week had been $217, and the cash in hand, previous to the meeting, was $215.

The new regulations proposed by Mayor HALL did not meet the views of the hackmen. Several members spoke in opposition to them. They considered them as unjust and unconstitutional; they would drive the men out of their business, and the men who had new carriages would get all the business, while those who had second rate or middling carriages would have to go to the wall. They deemed the clause which prevents the hackmen from soliciting passengers, as illegal, and they would contest it in Court if necessary. It was a job got up to benefit a few politicians who are engaged in the business, who wish to monopolize it and drive the poorer men out of it altogether. A committee was appointed to visit the Mayor and explain the view of the hackmen, and request him to modify it

FRANCE.

The Paris Elections [illegible]

[illegible]

THE ABUSED CAB-DRIVER.

[illegible]

DESTRUCTIVE FIRE.

[illegible]

GENERAL EUROPEAN NEWS.

[illegible]

[illegible]

1870. INGERSOLL & CO. 1870.

[illegible]

count which follows is based upon office tradition and the recollection of surviving members of the staff, together with a study of the files of the period.

If Blaine, whom *The Times* had shown to be clearly unfit for the Presidential chair, had actually been nominated in 1876, there would undoubtedly have been some beating of the breast in *The Times* office, but the balance of probability seems to indicate that the paper would have supported him. But the Mulligan letters disabled Blaine for the time being, and the convention set a precedent by selecting a respectable gentleman from Ohio, who was not handicapped by a record, bad or good. *The Times* supported Hayes with an enthusiasm undoubtedly enhanced by the memory of what had so narrowly been escaped, and attacked Tilden with a bitterness which can be explained only by the combination of an honest conviction that he was the less desirable candidate with a deadly fear that he was going to be elected. The sentiments of the editors concerning the great issues of the time, when those issues could be separated from questions of partisan preference and personal hostility, may be read in an editorial on November 10, headed "Republican Responsibilities." This was two days after the election. The first awful sinking of heart that had come with the early returns on election night had passed away; latest returns — at least Republican returns — from the doubtful states indicated victory; and it was not yet apparent that the Democrats would be unsportsmanlike enough to object to any measures by which the Grand Old Party that had saved the Union might find it necessary to perpetu-

ate its beneficent sway. Two days after the election Republicans could speak their honest feelings with a freedom that would have been unsafe before and afterward, and in the editorial of that day *The Times* denounced the carpet-bag governments, and declared that the party would not have had such a narrow squeak if its leaders had paid attention to the popular demand for reforms in the civil service and the national finance. That editorial of November 10, in fact, is a sound and well reasoned Democratic campaign document.

The Times's news service during the campaign was full and able. It was, unfortunately, dominated by political prejudice; but to a large degree that was the rule in those days, and though political correspondence was full of vituperation of the enemy, *The Times* was generally first with the news, good or bad. Something must also be allowed for the temperament of John Reid, the managing editor. Reid had served in the war and had spent some time in Libby Prison. According to an office tradition, a Virginian who had known him before the war observed as he was entering: "There goes John Reid. He'll never come out alive." Unfortunately, Reid overheard him, and upon coming out alive he transferred his resentment from this lone rebel to the entire Democratic party. Whatever weight may be given to this legend, Reid's partisanship was certainly rather exceptionally bitter even for those days, and was reflected to some degree in the news columns of *The Times*.

The paper had had a number of political correspondents in the South, and its readers were pretty

well informed of the conditions likely to surround the election. It was a time of bitter feeling, a trial of strength between the reviving forces of southern self-government and the carpet-bag administrations which saw themselves facing a long postponed and heavy accounting. The result of the polling at any given point would pretty obviously turn on the question whether the Ku Klux would keep the negroes away from the polls or the regular army would keep the Ku Klux away from the polls. On both sides were very earnest men, so firmly convinced of the eternal justice of their purpose that they felt that the end legitimized any means that might be necessary. So the election of 1876, all through the South, could be accurately described, in Clausewitz's famous phrase, as "the continuation of politics by other means."

Early reports from all sources on election night indicated that Tilden was winning. But early reports on election night do not always, though they do generally, furnish an accurate forecast of the result, as is evident from the recent example of 1916. The other papers conceded the election of Tilden — even *The Tribune*, which was trying to atone by excess of zeal for its heresy of 1872. But the first edition of *The Times* — which went to press at a considerably later hour in those days than is now customary — began with the headline: "A Doubtful Election."

And it was a doubtful election, some of the states being still claimed by both sides, with that pertinacity which campaign managers exhibit when they have any excuse at all. The first-edition editorial contained the statements that the re-

sult was still in doubt and that both parties had "exhausted their full legitimate strength," together with some observations on Democratic election methods in New York City and in the South, "where there is only too much reason to fear that they have been successful." Then some analysis of the electoral vote, conceding most of the South to the Democrats and ending in the conclusion that to elect Tilden the Democrats would have to carry, of the states where the contest had been hardest, New York, New Jersey, and either Oregon or Florida. New York they had beyond dispute; at the time of sending the edition to press the result in New Jersey was uncertain; Oregon had not been heard from; and Florida was claimed by the Democrats.

The final election extra, which went to press at six o'clock in the morning, contained the same statements as to the doubtful result. New Jersey was conceded to the Democrats; Oregon was claimed for the Republicans. The tabulation assigned 184 votes to Tilden and 181 to Hayes, including Oregon, Louisiana and South Carolina, with the four of Florida still in doubt; and the editorial ended with the statement that, "if the Republicans have carried that state, as they claim," Hayes would win by one vote. John Bigelow, in his life of Tilden, saw a deep and dark significance in the fact that ungenerous references to the Democratic shotgun tactics in the South, and the fear that they had been successful, had been removed from the editorial in the last edition. Having been a newspaperman once himself, Mr. Bigelow might have appreciated the fact that something had to be taken out in order to insert the tab-

ulation of the vote by states, which appeared in the last edition and not in the first, while still leaving the article of approximately the same length.

It will be seen that the essential differences between the first and last editions consist in the ascription of Oregon, previously not heard from, to the Republicans, the substitution of a Republican assertion of victory in Florida for the Democratic claim made in the earlier edition, with the final result set down as doubtful, and the transfer of Louisiana and South Carolina from Tilden to Hayes.

Any number of profound and elaborate explanations have been offered for these changes, as well as for *The Times's* assertion that the result was doubtful. One story, first published in *The Sun* in 1887, was that Zachariah Chandler, chairman of the Republican National Committee, and William E. Chandler, who seems to have been a sort of deckhand and general roustabout for that body, sent a message to *The Times* in the early morning hours instructing the paper to "claim Louisiana, Florida, and South Carolina at all hazards, through thick and thin." Aside from the fact that *The Times* was not under the orders of these gentlemen, this story is disposed of by the circumstance that at that time Zack Chandler was asleep in his room at the Fifth Avenue Hotel, and probably troubled by nightmares, while William E. Chandler was just arriving by train from New Hampshire, and reading in *The Tribune* of the great Tilden victory.

More widely circulated, and more generally believed, has been the tale that *The Times* would never have thought of casting any doubt on the election

of Tilden if Abram S. Hewitt, chairman of the Democratic National Committee, had not incautiously sent a message to the office, toward morning, asking what figures *The Times* had from Louisiana, Florida, and South Carolina. According to this version, Reid decided that if the Democratic National Committee didn't know what had happened, it might still be possible to save the sinking ship; a point of view which certainly Reid did impress on Zack Chandler after the last edition had been put to bed.

But in supposing that this message had a decisive influence on *The Times*, some chroniclers of the episode have forgotten that a newspaper office on election night receives news from other sources than national committees. It is true that about midnight Hewitt sent to *The Times* office to ask what majority the paper was conceding to Tilden, and Reid defiantly answered, "None!" As the first edition shows, the other editors were not quite so positive in their confidence; but at least this fact pretty well refutes the allegation that when the first edition went to press *The Times* had no doubt of the election of Tilden.

The other message, asking for *The Times's* figures from the doubtful states, did indeed come in from the Democratic headquarters — not from Hewitt, but from Arthur Pue Gorman — between editions; and it did undoubtedly gladden the heart of John Reid. But its influence on the men who declared in the final edition that the election was in doubt was only subsidiary. That the Democrats had no news of glorious victories in the doubtful states was a fact to be taken into consideration, but along with,

and subordinate to, the other facts which had come into the office in the telegraphic dispatches of early morning.

The truth is, in the words of an article printed in *The Times* on June 11, 1887, that

> on the morning after the election of 1876 *The Times* had the news — which no other paper in the United States had, and which the Republican National Committee did not have. It obtained it through its own enterprise and sagacity, and it paid for it.

And the news was that the result was still in doubt.

When the last edition went to press that morning, there were present in *The Times* office John Foord, the editor-in-chief, George Shepard and Edward Cary, political editorial writers, and John Reid, managing editor; besides Charles R. Miller, the present editor of the paper, who was then at the telegraph desk, and labored under the added handicap of being the lone supporter of Tilden in a company whose other members were all Republicans. The editorial council passed upon the news.

What was the news? Oregon had been heard from. An Associated Press dispatch from Portland, by way of San Francisco, reported that the Republicans claimed the state by a majority of five hundred. That was the only news from Oregon, and it is the sort of news which has been accepted provisionally, in default of better, in every newspaper office in the country on every election night. Florida was still in doubt. An early morning dispatch from Augusta, Georgia, said that the Democrats claimed Florida by a small majority; a dispatch from the

same place just before midnight had said that "both sides claim the state." If Reid's enthusiasm carried the council out of line, it was in the weighing of those two dispatches.

South Carolina had been put by *The Times* in the Republican column. An Associated Press dispatch from Charleston at 2:15 A.M. said that the election was very close, and that it seemed probable that the Republican Presidential ticket and the Democratic state ticket would win. An earlier message from the same source said that the Democrats claimed the state by four thousand, but that the result depended on some of the coast counties which could not be reached by telegraph. A special dispatch to *The Times* from Columbia reported that the Republicans had probably carried the state by 10,000, and that the Republican state committee claimed it by from 15,000 to 20,000.

Louisiana *The Times* also assigned to Hayes. A message from the chairman of the Republican state committee declared that the state had gone Republican by six or eight thousand; an Associated Press dispatch from New Orleans said that the Democrats claimed the state by 20,000, "the best informed moderate Republicans" by 4000; but that the returns were "meager and insufficient for an accurate estimate."

This was the evidence. It certainly seems that it offered reasonable ground for thinking that the election was still in doubt; and if the Democratic National Committee itself was not informed as to the result in some of the doubtful states, that fact hardly justified news editors in giving them off-hand to the

TIMES SQUARE,
WORLD SERIES BASEBALL CROWD.
© Brown Bros.

Democrats. In *The Times Jubilee Supplement* the chief influence in making this decision was assigned to Edward Cary, who was certainly not a bigoted Republican, and who could hardly be suspected of much sympathy with the sort of methods that might, and presently did, commend themselves to Zack Chandler.

To working newspapermen who know upon what slender grounds election night estimates are sometimes made up, and how generally these hazardous estimates are justified by the event, the decision of *The Times* editors will arouse little of the suspicion that was drawn upon this transaction by the proceedings of the Republican leaders in the following weeks.

Undoubtedly, *The Times* incurred unwarranted suspicion on this occasion from the enterprises subsequently undertaken, *motu proprio*, by its managing editor. But when John Reid left *The Times* office at daybreak on Wednesday, woke Zack Chandler out of his troubled sleep, and presented that surprised but delighted statesman with his own analysis of the election returns, he was acting as an unterrified Republican and not as managing editor of *The Times*. The paper can hardly be held responsible for the telegrams which he presently dispatched to Republican leaders in the doubtful states, over Chandler's signature, containing such pointed suggestions as "Don't be defrauded" and "Can you hold your state?" Those telegrams were charged to *The Times* because at the telegraph office where Reid filed them the Republican National Committee had no charge account. In the circumstances, Mr.

John Bigelow's indignant comments on the conspiracy in *The Times* office are somewhat beside the point. But then Mr. Bigelow, besides having a very real ground for indignation in the proceedings which eventually put Hayes in the White House, had perhaps, through the unhappy though innocent experience with the gold corner which ended his career as editor of *The Times*, acquired a somewhat exaggerated impression of the susceptibility of the paper to the schemes of conspirators.

Thursday's paper began with the joyful heading, "The Battle Won," and contained the declaration that Florida was Republican by 1500 or 2000. But it must be confessed that the dispatches on which this was based all came from Republican campaign managers, and it requires no very fantastic imagination to see in them the prompt response to the messages which Reid had dispatched in the name of Zack Chandler on Wednesday morning. Thereafter the paper stuck to its guns; it believed honestly that Hayes had been elected and it said so. Newspaper custom of the period did not require that the election night's news should contain any statements from the authorities of the opposition party, or any account of the manner in which the opposition candidate received the returns. On Wednesday *The Times* had published a dispatch from Columbus on Hayes's reception of the news, but not till Friday did it notice the Democrats at all, and then only to denounce as fabrications some assertions of the "outrage mill, otherwise the press bureau of the Democratic National Committee, which continued to maintain the he-

retical opinion that Tilden had been elected. On Saturday an editorial headed, "Let the Count Be Honest" expressed approval of Grant's ordering regulars to the disputed states, and echoed his statement that it would be infinitely better for the party to lose the election than to win a victory "tainted by the suspicion of fraud." There can be no doubt that the man who wrote these lines was quite as sincere as when he went on in the next paragraph to declare that an honest count would show that Hayes was elected.

The editors of *The Times* could see no merit in the proposal of an electoral commission. To *The Times* it was indubitable that the President of the Senate alone had the right to count the votes as received from the states, and that the two Houses had no more privilege in the matter than any other spectators. There was a good deal of force in *The Times's* criticisms of the electoral commission. Proposed as a method for reconciling the conflicting claims of the two Houses of Congress, it was easily reducible in fact to the shifting of the whole burden of decision to a single Justice of the Supreme Court. Not without reason *The Times* observed that it would be simpler, and equally fair, to let Tilden and Hayes cut for the high card; and the paper's disapproval of the measure as bringing the Supreme Court into politics was entirely justified by the event.

It appears, however, that objections to the electoral commission were based in some degree on the fear that some of its Republican members would double-cross Hayes. *The Times* was obviously relieved when David Davis, who was expected to be-

come the nonpartisan fifteenth member of the commission, resigned his seat on the supreme bench to go into the Senate, but it did not breathe easily till the first of the cases from Florida had been decided. *The Times* editorial the next day expressed regret that the decision had been reached by the partisan vote of eight to seven, but the explanation was easy: "Not one Democratic Senator, not even one Democratic Justice, could be found impartial enough to sustain the decision which was finally reached" — by the eight Republicans.

Though for some of President Hayes's policies *The Times's* praise could be only damningly faint, it supported him vigorously when it could in his efforts to improve the standard of public service, and it found reason for jubilation in at least one event which happened during his administration — the resumption of specie payments. *The Times* had fought so steadily and vigorously for the maintenance of sound principles of national finance and currency that it could see in this one more sign that hope for better things in public life was not wholly illusory.

One effect of Hayes's conduct of the Presidential office was to give *The Times* a higher opinion of his predecessor, and when the campaign of 1880 came in sight the paper gave some encouragement to the movement to bring General Grant in for a third term. But this support seems to have been due largely to the returning fear of Blaine, and lack of confidence in some of the other competitors for the nomination. At any rate, when the Republican convention nominated Garfield *The Times* gave him

hearty support. If the statement that he was "strong in his freedom from intrigue to gain the nomination" hardly seems as indisputable after forty years as it did when it was written, *The Times's* approval of his soundness on financial issues was as creditable to him as to the paper. And if the editorial on the civil service plank in the Republican platform was compelled to admit that the party leaders were against any reform in this direction, the editors could soothe their suspicions of the Grand Old Party by turning their eyes to the familiar spectacle of the iniquitous opposition. News dispatches from the Democratic convention were full of such violent denunciations and such bitter sneers as would not now be likely to appear even in editorial criticism of the opposition party. When Hancock was nominated *The Times* called him "a pretentious blockhead," "an inflated Franklin Pierce," and remarked that the convention had "nominated a Northern General to resurrect a Confederate government." Hayes, to the great dissatisfaction of *The Times*, as well as of a good many northern Republicans who were not yet certain that the South was back in the Union, had withdrawn the Federal troops from the southern states, and it was evident that this election could not be won either before or after the counting of the vote by the methods that had succeeded in 1876. Perhaps fear of the outcome may account for the vigor with which *The Times* derided Tilden's refusal to let his name go before the convention, and continued its attacks on "the great claimant" until Hancock was actually the candidate.

However, there was no uncertainty as to the result of the election of 1880. The story of the election of Garfield and Arthur in *The Times* of Wednesday morning, November 3, was headed "The Great Trust Renewed," and the editorial comment as usual referred to the "great responsibilities" which lay on the leaders of the Republican party. "The momentous issues of the past are decided," said *The Times*, in remarking that sectional questions were disappearing and that an election was once more turning on problems which did not depend on the climate for their impression on the voters. How true that was *The Times* itself was to show four years later.

In the quarrel over patronage in New York State which led to the fight between Garfield and Conkling *The Times* sided with the President, and made some severe criticisms of the part played in support of the New York Senators by Vice-President Arthur — whom, when he was nominated, it had described as "a man eminently worthy of a wider sphere for his abilities." That description is not usually applied to the Vice Presidency, but when Arthur exerted his abilities in the extra-official sphere of manipulations at Albany a great many people felt that this was rather beneath the dignity of the second officer of the Federal government. And then Garfield was shot.

The Times's editorial comment on the morning after very naturally pointed the moral of the evil results occasioned by the demoralization of the civil service, which had led a disappointed office seeker to shoot the President of the United States. Also

there was some rather stern castigation for political leaders whose bitter attacks on the President might have had their effect on the mind of Guiteau, which in *The Times's* opinion was "not remotely akin" to those of Conkling and Platt. The next editorial, headed "To Whom It May Concern," contained these somewhat pointed observations:

> When James A. Garfield was reported yesterday as lying at the point of death, new bitterness was added to the poignancy of public feeling by the thought that Chester A. Arthur would be his successor. . . . No holder of the vice-presidential office has ever made it so plainly subordinate to his self-interest as a politician and his narrowness as a partisan.

When Garfield died, however, *The Times* expressed approval of the correctness of Arthur's attitude during the interim in which there had been much discussion of the President's "disability." But it added:

> The moment he selects an administrative officer because the nominee is his friend, and not at all because he possesses qualities which render him obviously fit to perform certain public duties, that moment his administration will be discredited.

Arthur's record made this admonition somewhat desirable, but if it should be taken literally, one must fear that a good many administrations would have been discredited.

Arthur as President turned out a good deal better than there had been reason to fear, but by no means

as well as could have been desired; and throughout his term *The Times* was slowly drawing farther away from what politicians would call reliability. The great causes in which the paper had long been interested now absorbed still more of its attention; civil service reform, though progressing slowly, was having a hard fight against the sturdy opposition of political leaders; tariff reform was still for most of the country a matter of religious sentiment and not of common sense, as Hancock discovered to his misfortune; and prevalent through much of the country, especially those parts of the West in which a whole generation was working itself to death to bring in civilization, there was a conviction that most of the problems of poverty would be solved if by some formula men could borrow hundred-cent dollars and pay their debts in fifty-cent dollars, or in pieces of paper which the United States government might see fit to regard as dollars.

To educate the public on these issues took up much of the energy of the editors of *The Times*, and the perception that their efforts were regarded as a rule with positive hostility by the leaders of the party gradually cooled that fierce Republican enthusiasm which had burned highest in the office in 1876. Moreover, corruption at Washington was not yet a matter of ancient history; and *The Times* in 1881, by exposing the Star Route frauds, accomplished a public service which deserves to be ranked next to the overthrow of Tweed in the paper's *res gestae*.

The contracting for the delivery of mails on certain routes (marked with a star on post-office records) lying for the most part in remote and thinly settled

The New-York Times.

VOL. XXVI.......NO. 7849. | NEW-YORK, THURSDAY, NOVEMBER 9, 1876. | PRICE FOUR CENTS.

THE BATTLE WON.

A REPUBLICAN VICTORY IN THE NATION.

GOV. HAYES ELECTED PRESIDENT AND WILLIAM A. WHEELER VICE PRESIDENT—THE REPUBLICANS CARRY TWENTY-ONE STATES, CASTING 185 ELECTORAL VOTES—A REPUBLICAN MAJORITY IN THE NEXT CONGRESS.

The dispatches received since our last issue confirm the reports on which THE TIMES yesterday claimed 181 electoral votes for Gov. HAYES. On Wednesday the following States were put down as surely Republican: Colorado, California, Illinois, Iowa, Kansas, Maine, Massachusetts, Michigan, Minnesota, Nevada, Nebraska, New-Hampshire, Oregon, Ohio, Pennsylvania, Rhode Island, Vermont, Wisconsin, Louisiana, and South Carolina. Some of these States were claimed by the Democrats, but all intelligence, thus far received, not only shows that the above estimate was correct, but that Florida, which was left in doubt, has gone Republican by at least 1,500 majority—our latest dispatches say 2,000—and that the two Republican Congressmen are also elected. Encouraging reports were received from Oregon early yesterday morning, and in the afternoon came the decisive news that the Democrats conceded the State, which had given a Republican majority of over one thousand, and gained a Republican Congressman. In Nebraska the same condition of affairs was shown. There the Republican majority rose to 8,000. Dispatches from Nevada made it certain that the State had gone for Hayes. The latest news from South Carolina shows a Republican victory, the Democrats conceding the State to Hayes and the Republicans claiming 5,000 majority. Louisiana is one of the States which the Democrats have claimed; but our dispatches, coming from various sources in the State, show that it has gone Republican. The latest intelligence points to the certain election of Gov. Rutherford B. Hayes to the Presidency, and a Republican victory in the nation.

All the Congressional districts have not been heard from definitely, but the advices received destroy the Democratic majority in the present House. The indications now are that the Republicans have elected 145 members, (including those chosen in September and October,) and

2. Horatio Bisbee, Jr. (?)

GEORGIA.

1. *Julian Hartridge.*
2. *William E. Smith.*
3. *Philip Cook.*
4. *Henry R. Harris.*
5. *Milton A. Candler.*
6. *James H. Blount.*
7. *William H. Dabney.*
8. *Alexander H. Stephens.*
9. *Benjamin H. Hill.*

ILLINOIS.

1. William Aldrich.
2. *Carter H. Harrison.* (?)
3. Lorenzo Brentano.
4. William Lathrop.
5. Horatio C. Burchard.
6. Thomas J. Henderson.
7. Philip C. Hayes.
8. Greenbury L. Fort.
9. *George A. Wilson.*
10. B. F. Marsh.
11. *R. M. Knapp.*
12. *William M. Springer.*
13. Thomas F. Tipton.
14. Joseph G. Cannon.
15. *John R. Eden.*
16. E. M. Ashcroft.
17. *William R. Morrison.*
18. Benjamin L. Wiley.
19. *William B. Anderson.*

INDIANA.

1. *Benoni S. Fuller.*
2. *James H. Cobb.*
3. *George A. Bicknell.*
4. Leonidas Sexton.
5. Thomas M. Browne.
6. Milton S. Robinson.
7. John Hanna.
8. Morton C. Hunter.
9. Michael D. White.
10. William H. Calkins.
11. James L. Evans.
12. *Andrew H. Hamilton.*
13. John H. Baker.

IOWA.

1. J. C. Stone.
2. Hiram Price.
3. Theodore W. Burdick.
4. N. C. Deering.
5. Rush Clark.
6. Ezekiel S. Sampson.
7. H. J. B. Cummings.
8. W. F. Sapp.
9. Addison Oliver.

KANSAS.

1. William A. Phillips.
2. Dudley C. Haskell.
3. Thomas Ryan.

KENTUCKY.

1. *Andrew R. Boone.*
2. *James McKenzie.*
3. *John Caldwell.*
4. *J. Proctor Knott.*
5. *Albert S. Willis.*
6. *John G. Carlisle.*
7. *Joseph C. S. Blackburn.*
8. *Milton J. Durham.*
9. *Thomas Turner.*
10. *John B. Clarke.*

LOUISIANA.

1. *Randall L. Gibson.*
2. *E. John Ellis.*
3. Chester B. Darrall.
4. *J. B. Elam.*
5. John E. Leonard.
6. Charles E. Nash.

MAINE.

1. Thomas B. Reed.
2. William P. Frye.
3. Stephen D. Lindsey.
4. Llewellyn Powers.
5. Eugene Hale.

MARYLAND.

1. *Daniel M. Henry.*
2. *Charles B. Roberts.*
3. *William Kimmell.*
4. *Thomas Swann.*
5. *Eli J. Henkle.*
6. *William Walsh.*

MASSACHUSETTS.

1. William W. Crapo.
2. Benjamin W. Harris.
3. *Benjamin Dean, Con.*
4. *Leopold Morse.*
5. Nathaniel P. Banks.
6. George B. Loring.
7. Benjamin F. Butler.
8. William Claflin.
9. William W. Rice.*
10. Amasa Norcross.
11. George D. Robinson.

MICHIGAN.

14. *George M. Beebe.*
15. *Stephen L. Mayham.*
16. *Terence J. Quinn.*
17. Martin I. Townsend.
18. Andrew Williams.
19. Amaziah B. James.
20. John H. Starin.
21. Solomon Bundy.
22. George A. Bagley.
23. William J. Bacon.
24. William H. Baker.
25. Frank Hiscock.
26. John H. Camp.
27. Elbridge G. Lapham.
28. Jeremiah W. Dwight.
29. John N. Hungerford.
30. *E. Kirke Hart.*
31. *Charles B. Benedict.*
32. Elbridge Spaulding (?)
33. George W. Patterson.

NORTH CAROLINA.

1. *Jesse J. Yates.*
2. Curtis H. Brogden.
3. *Alfred M. Waddell.*
4. *Joseph J. Davis.*
5. *Alfred M. Scales.*
6. *Walter L. Steele.*
7. *William M. Robbins.*
8. *Robert B. Vance.*

OHIO.

1. *Milton Sayler.*
2. *Henry B. Banning.*
3. Mills Gardner.
4. *John A. McMahon.*
5. *Americus V. Rice.*
6. Jacob D. Cox.
7. *Henry L. Dickey.*
8. J. Warren Keifer.
9. James S. Jones.
10. Charles Foster.
11. Henry S. Neal.
12. *Thomas Ewing.*
13. *Milton I. Southard.*
14. *E. B. Finley.*
15. Nelson Van Vorhes.
16. Lorenzo Danford.
17. William McKinley.
18. James Monroe.
19. James A. Garfield.
20. Amos Townsend.

OREGON.

1. Richard Williams.

PENNSYLVANIA.

1. Chapman Freeman.
2. Charles O'Neill.
3. *Samuel J. Randall.*
4. William D. Kelley.
5. Alfred C. Harmer.
6. William Ward.
7. Isaac N. Evans. (?)
8. *Heister Clymer.*
9. A. H. Smith.
10. *Samuel S. Bridges.*
11. *Francis D. Collins.*
12. *Hendrick B. Wright.*
13. *James B. Reilly.*
14. John W. Killinger.
15. Edward Overton.
16. John I. Mitchell.
17. Jacob M. Campbell.
18. Thaddeus M. Mahon.
19. *Levi Maish.*
20. *Levi A. Mackey.*
21. *Jacob Turney.*
22. Russell Errett.
23. Thomas M. Bayne.
24. W. S. Shallenberger.
25. Henry White.
26. John M. Thompson.
27. Lewis F. Watson.

RHODE ISLAND.

1. Benjamin T. Eames.
2. Latimer W. Ballou.

SOUTH CAROLINA.

1. Joseph H. Rainey.
2. Richard H. Cain.
3. *D. Wyatt Aiken.*
4. *John H. Evins.*
5. Robert Smalls.

TENNESSEE.

1. James H. Randolph.
2. Jacob M. Thornburgh.
3. *George G. Dibrell.*
4. *Haywood Y. Riddle.*
5. *John M. Bright.*
6. *John F. House.*
7. *W. C. Whitthorne.*
8. *John D. C. Atkins.*
9. *Wm. P. Caldwell.*
10. *H. Casey Young.*

TEXAS.

1. *John H. Reagan.*
2. *David B. Culberson.*

Counties.	Hayes.	Tilden.	Grant.	Greeley.
Ontario	800	....	1531	....
Orange	....	300	756	....
Orleans	1050	....	1466	....
Oswego	2807	....	3115	....
Otsego	....	200	....	40
Putnam	200	....	369	....
Queens	....	2000	422	....
Rensselaer	....	1000	3265	....
Richmond	....	1454	187	....
Rockland	....	1000	....	211
St. Lawrence	7500	....	6940	....
Saratoga	900	....	2221	....
Schenectady	....	300*	567	....
Schoharie	....	1800	....	913
Schuyler	....	200	482	....
Seneca	....	500	33	....
Steuben	1100	....	1615	....
Suffolk	....	....	677	....
Sullivan	....	1000	193	....
Tioga	750	....	870	....
Tompkins	1000	....	949	....
Ulster	....	1561	912	....
Warren	500	....	1098	....
Washington	2000	....	2770	....
Wayne	1500	....	2396	....
Westchester	....	2485	....	236
Wyoming	1300	....	1609	....
Yates	1100	....	852	....
Total	57762	88279	83169	30675

Estimated majority for Tilden..........30517

THE ASSEMBLY.

The returns received indicate that the following candidates have been elected to the Assembly, the names of Republicans being printed in roman and of Democrats in italic:

ALBANY.

Dist.
1. *John Sanger.*
2. *Jonathan K. Herrick.*
3. *William J. Maher.*
4. *Edward Curran.*

ALLEGANY.

Sumner Baldwin.

BROOME.

Edwin C. Moody.

CATTARAUGUS.

1. Thomas J. King.
2. Edgar Shannon.

CAYUGA.

1. George I. Post.
2. John S. Brown.

CHAUTAUQUA.

1. Sherman Williams.
2. Theodore A. Case.

CHEMUNG.

Hosea H. Rockwell.

CHENANGO.

J. Hudson Skillman.

CLINTON.

Shepard P. Bowen.

COLUMBIA.

1. *Jacob H. Proper.*
2. John T. Hogeboom.

CORTLAND.

Delos McGraw.

DELAWARE.

1. William J. Welch.
2. *Isaac H. Maynard.*

DUTCHESS.

1. Thomas Hammond.
2. DeWitt Webb.

ERIE.

1. *John R. Crowley.*
2. *John C. Laugner.*
3. Edward Gallagher.
4. *Charles F. Tabor.* (?)
5. *Bertrand Chaffee.*

ESSEX.

Benjamin D. Clapp.

FRANKLIN.

John I. Gilbert.

FULTON AND HAMILTON.

George W. Fay.

GENESEE.

[illegible]

Dist.
15. *John Dimond.*
16. *Francis B. Spinola.*
17. *James E. Coulter.*
18. *Stephen J. O'Hare.*
19. *Thos. C. E. Ecclesine.*
20. *Joseph I. Stein.*
21. J. C. J. Langbein.

NIAGARA.

1. *Amos A. Bissell.*
2. *Sherburn B. Piper.*

ONEIDA.

1. James Corbett.
2. Everett Case.
3. *Benjamin D. Stone.*
4. J. Robert Moore.

ONONDAGA.

1. Thomas G. Alvord.
2. Carroll E. Smith.
3. C. Frederick Herbst.

ONTARIO.

1. *H. O. Harmon.*
2. Amasa T. Winch.

ORANGE.

1. James G. Graham.
2. *Stewart D. Durland.*

ORLEANS.

Joseph D. Billings.

OSWEGO.

1. George B. Sloan.
2. George M. Case.
3. DeWitt C. Peck.

OTSEGO.

1. *James S. Davenport.*
2. Simeon R. Barnes.

PUTNAM

Hamilton Fish, Jr.

QUEENS.

1. Samuel Willetts.
2. Jno. E. Van Nostrand.

RENSSELAER COUNTY.

1. *John H. Burns.*
2. John J. Filkins.
3. Richard A. Herrick.

RICHMOND.

Samuel R. Brick.

ROCKLAND.

George W. Weiant.

ST. LAWRENCE.

1. David McFalls.

hear from which gave last year 70 Democratic majority. The total vote will reach 80,000, the greatest ever polled in the State.

SOUTH CAROLINA REPUBLICAN.

A MAJORITY OF FULLY FIVE THOUSAND FOR HAYES—THE LEGISLATURE REPUBLICAN.

Special Dispatch to the New-York Times.

COLUMBIA, Nov. 8.—There is no doubt about South Carolina. With two Republican counties to hear from the majority for Hayes is over 3,000. The Republican Committee claim that their majority will be fully 5,000. The Democrats concede the State to Hayes. The Congressional delegation will stand three Republicans and two Democrats, a Republican loss of two. The Legislature will be Republican by a small majority.

SERIOUS RIOT IN CHARLESTON.

AN REPUBLICAN EX-MEMBER OF CONGRESS FIRED UPON BY DEMOCRATS—ONE MAN KILLED AND SEVERAL WOUNDED.

Special Dispatch to the New-York Times.

CHARLESTON, Nov. 8.—A serious riot arose here about five o'clock this afternoon in Broad street, near the *News and Courier* office, where a throng has been collected all day scanning the bulletin board for election returns. Col. E. W. M. Mackey, Republican, and ex-member of Congress, was conversing with some gentlemen about the election, he holding that Chamberlain was elected, and the group around him offering to bet that Hampton was. While thus engaged, some of the Democrats, who were listening to the talk, withdrew to the opposite side of the street, and began firing at him, but luckily missed him. The shots were heard several squares off, and hundreds of white and colored men ran toward the scene. In a short time the streets were filled with excited men, and there was imminent danger of an extensive riot. The firing continued for several minutes. The policemen on duty in the neighborhood were fired at, and one or two of them wounded. A detachment of Police armed with Winchester rifles was at once dispatched from the station-house, and succeeded in driving the mob away and quelling the riot. A young man named Walter was killed, one negro was mortally and eight others seriously wounded. A detachment of troops under Col. Hunt was marched to the station-house. There is intense excitement all over the city, and the rifle clubs have armed themselves. The feeling between the Republicans and Democrats is very strong. Efforts are being made to allay the excitement by prominent men of both parties, but the aspect is threatening.

LOUISIANA NOT IN DOUBT.

THE STATE REPUBLICAN—LARGE REPUBLICAN GAINS IN THE PRINCIPAL PARISHES.

Special Dispatch to The New-York Times.

NEW ORLEANS, Nov. 8.—Returns continue to show large Republican gains. Assumption Parish, where Nicholls resides, gives 300 against him. The same parish went Democratic in 1874. Lafourché and Iberia Parishes which also went Democratic in 1874, are carried by the Republicans. All have lost only in one parish, as far as heard from, except the five parishes selected by the Democratic committee for intimidations. Returns from the river parishes, where we have overwhelming [illegible]

publican. The entire Republican ticket in every county in the State is elected.

Dispatch to the Associated Press.

SAN FRANCISCO, Nov. 8.—A private dispatch from Virginia City, Nev., says Nevada is sure for a decided Republican majority.

SAN FRANCISCO, Nov. 8.—Scattering returns from Nevada leave no doubt that the State has gone Republican by a fair majority.

WISCONSIN SURE FOR HAYES.

A REPUBLICAN MAJORITY OF 3,000—THE CONGRESSIONAL DELEGATION.

Special Dispatches to the New-York Times.

MILWAUKEE, Nov. 8.—The Chairman of the Republican State Committee claims a Republican majority in the State of 3,000. Caswell, in the Second District, is elected to Congress, making probably five Republicans from the State.

Twenty-five Minutes Past Eight P. M.—Three hundred and forty-one towns give a Republican majority of 2,876, a Republican net gain of 7,97[illegible]. Vernon and other Republican counties still to hear from.

Fifteen Minutes Past Nine P. M.—The Republicans elect five Congressmen, as follows: Williams, in the First District, receives 5,500; Caswell, in the Second, 740; Hazleton, in the Third, 2,500; Humphrey, in the Seventh, 6,000, and Pound, in the Eighth, by a small majority. The Democrats elect Lynde, in the Fourth District, by 5,100; Bragg, in the Fifth, 5,000; Bouck, in the Sixth, 1,700. This leaves the Wisconsin delegation the same as last year. The Republican gains in the State are constantly increasing. There is no doubt of a Republican majority of over 3,000.

Dispatch to the Associated Press.

MILWAUKEE, Nov. 8.—The Congressmen elect from this State are as follows: Williams, Rep.; Caswell, Rep.; Hazleton, Rep.; Lynde, Dem.; Bragg, Dem.; Bouck, Dem.; Humphrey, Rep.; and Pound, Rep. Hayes' majority is from 3,000 to 5,000.

PENNSYLVANIA.

REPUBLICAN GAIN OF EIGHT OF NINE CONGRESSMEN AND THE LEGISLATURE REPUBLICAN IN BOTH BRANCHES—THE ABORTIVE ATTEMPTS AT FRAUD BY THE DEMOCRATS.

Special Dispatch to the New-York Times.

PHILADELPHIA, Nov. 8.—The majority in the State of Pennsylvania will be reduced considerably by the latest returns from the Democratic counties, but in other respects the victory is more complete than was anticipated. The gains in members of Congress are claimed to be eight certainly, and possibly nine, after deducting a loss of one. It turns out to-day that Payne, in the Luzerne district, is defeated by Wright. This is a Republican loss. The vacancy for the same district, existing in the present Congress by the resignation of Judge Ketchum, is filled by Mr. Jones, a Republican. The gains are Harmer, in Philadelphia; Bayne, in Allegheny City; Errett, in Pittsburg; White, in Indiana County; Campbell, in Cambria County; Thompson, in Mercer County; Watson, in Erie County; Overton, in Bradford County, and Martling, in Schuylkill County. There is doubt about the election of Mahon over Stenger. The vote will be very close, and the result is not yet positively known. There is believed to be no doubt of a net gain of 8. The majorities cannot yet be given with any accuracy. Nutting's majority will be small, and perhaps it may wholly [illegible]

in the State will run over 30,000. The Democrats elect eight Congressmen, leaving one district—the Fourth—in doubt, with a very strong probability of the election of Jorgensen, Rep., over Hunton, Dem., in that district.

NORFOLK, Nov. 8.—Returns to-night assure the re-election of Goode, Dem., to Congress, from this district, by 2,000 majority.

NEW-JERSEY.

TILDEN'S MAJORITY, 8,000—REPUBLICAN GAIN OF ONE CONGRESSMAN—THE LEGISLATURE DEMOCRATIC IN BOTH BRANCHES.

The latest returns show that Tilden's majority in the State is much less than the Democrats first claimed, and instead of being 15,000 is probably not over 8,000. Gov. Bedle, Democrat, carried the State in 1875 by 13,233.

CONGRESS.

The Congressional delegation stands three Republicans and four Democrats, as follows:

Districts.
1. Clement H. Sinnickson, Rep.*
2. Dr. J. Howard Pugh, Rep.
3. Miles Ross, Dem.*
4. Alvah A. Clark, Dem.
5. Augustus W. Cutler, Dem.*
6. Thomas B. Peddie, Rep.
7. Augustus A. Hardenburg, Dem.*

*Re-elected.

THE SENATE.

The Republicans elect their Senators in the Counties of Passaic (a gain) and Cape May. The Democrats carry both Middlesex and Hunterdon—both gains—Sussex and Burlington.

The Senate, as far as is known, is Democratic by 2, making a Democratic majority of 3 on a joint ballot. The Legislature will be very close.

ASSEMBLY.

County.	District.	Name.
Atlantic		Leonard H. Ashley, Rep.*
Bergen	1.	John H. Winant, Dem.*
	2.	Barney N. Ferdon, Dem.*
Burlington	1.	George Syres, Dem.
	2.	Edward T. Matthews, Dem.*
	3.	Samuel Taylor, Rep.*
	4.	John Cavileer, Rep.*
Camden	1.	Alden C. Scovel, Rep.*
	2.	Oliver Lund, Rep.*
	3.	Samuel T. Murphy, Rep.
Cape May		William T. Stephens, Rep.*
Cumberland	1.	Isaac T. Nichols, Rep.
	2.	George W. Payne, Rep.*
Essex	1.	Albert D. Trawhagen, Rep.*
	2.	Edward D. Pierson, Rep.
	3.	Francis K. Howell, Rep.*
	4.	S. C. Van Rensselaer, Rep.*
	5.	Joseph H. Van Wightman, Rep.
	6.	Godfried Krueger, Dem.
	7.	Elkanah Drake, Rep.*
	8.	Charles Gomer, Dem.
	9.	James Malone, Dem.
Gloucester	1.	Caleb C. Pancoast, Rep.
	2.	Samuel Moore, Rep.*
Hudson	1.	Martin M. Drohan, Dem.
	2.	Thomas J. Hamnon, Dem.*
	3.	Marmaduke Tilden, Rep.
	4.	Alexander W. Harris, Dem.
	5.	Lewis A. Brigham, Rep.
	6.	James Stevens, Dem.
	7.	Rudolph Rabe, Dem.*
	8.	Elijah T. Paxton, Dem.
Hunterdon	1.	Henry Britten, Dem.
	2.	John Hacket, Dem.
Mercer	1.	Horatio N. Burroughs, Rep.
	2.	William S. Yard, Dem.
	3.	J. V. Powers, Dem.
Middlesex	1.	John Waldron, Dem.
	2.	Charles A. Campbell, Dem.*
	3.	David Z. Martin, Dem.*
Monmouth	1.	James L. Rue, Dem.*
	2.	William H. Bennett, Dem.
	3.	James H. Leonard, Rep.
Morris	1.	Abraham C. Van Duyne, Rep.
	2.	Cummins O. Cooper, Rep.
	3.	Cornelius P. Garrabrant, Dem.
Ocean		Isaac A. Van Hise, Rep.
Passaic	1.	John W. Griggs, Rep.*
	2.	John Sanderson, Dem.*
	3.	Joseph L. Cunningham, Rep.*
Salem	1.	John S. Elwell, Dem.
	2.	Quinton Keasbey, Rep.*
Somerset	1.	James L. Bergen, Dem.*
	2.	James H. Voorhees, Rep.*
Sussex		George Gorer, Dem.

I shall frequently recall this visit during the time I shall yet live among you, with pleasure. I bid you good night.

CINCINNATI, Nov. 8.—The vote in Hamilton stands as follows: Tilden, 29,468; Hayes, 28,770; Cooper, 37; Smith, (Prohib.) 1.

ILLINOIS.

THE STATE REPUBLICAN BEYOND DOUBT—CULLOM ELECTED GOVERNOR BY 35,000 MAJORITY—A GAIN IN CONGRESSMEN.

CHICAGO, Nov. 8—11:30 A. M.—Returns have been received up to this hour from 461 towns and precincts in the State of Illinois, outside of the city of Chicago. Four hundred and twenty-six of these give Hayes 89,673; Tilden, 69,214. Thirty-five other towns, returning majorities only, give Tilden a majority of 451. These returns give Hayes a net majority of 21,021. Deducting 2,000 as the probable Democratic majority in the City of Chicago, and Hayes' net majority so far is 11,021. If the same ratio is kept up in the remainder of the State the majority will be, as compared with the vote of 1872, from 30,000 to 35,000. Cullom is undoubtedly elected Governor over the combined Democratic and Greenback vote. Gen. Farnsworth concedes the election of Lathrop, the regular Republican in the Fourth District, over himself and Hurlbut. Later returns from the Third District leave it in doubt between Le Moyne and Brentano.

CHICAGO, Nov. 8.—Complete returns from Cook County, except a few districts and Republican towns, gives Hayes 36,636; Tilden 38,648; Cooper 257. Cullom, Rep., for Governor, received 36,297, and Stewart, Dem., for Governor, 36,927. The remaining districts and towns will, it is claimed, almost certainly change the result to a small Republican majority in Cook County. The vote of the city of Chicago is: Hayes, 28,317; Tilden, 33,247; Cooper, 229.

The *Tribune* claims that the Republicans have elected their whole county ticket except Clough, the candidate for Sheriff. This claim is based on nearly complete returns in each case.

Receipts from 552 towns and precincts, outside the city of Chicago, give Hayes 110,262, Tilden 91,030; Hayes' majority 19,232. Fifty-three other towns return for Hayes a net majority of 913, making his majority 22,145. These towns show an increase in the aggregate vote of nearly fifty thousand over the vote for President in 1872.

Returns from the Congressional districts so far as received, show the election of Aldrich, Rep., in the First; Harrison, Dem., in the Second; Brentano, Rep., in the Third; Lathrop, in the Fourth; Burchard, Rep., in the Fifth; Henderson, Rep., in the Sixth; Fort, Rep., in the Eighth; Wilson, Dem., in the Ninth; Marsh, Rep., in the Tenth; A. Springer, Dem., in the Twelfth; Cannon, Rep., in the Fourteenth; Morrison, Dem., in the Seventeenth; Wiley, Rep., in the Eighteenth; and the result in the Seventh, Eleventh, Thirteenth, Fifteenth, Sixteenth and Nineteenth in doubt. The Republicans have certainly gained three Congressmen and possibly four.

CAIRO, Nov. 8.—Returns from the Eighteenth Illinois District indicate the election of Wiley, Republican, for Congress.

INDIANA.

A MAJORITY OF SEVEN THOUSAND FOR TILDEN.

INDIANAPOLIS, Nov. 8.—Returns from 383 townships and wards, which cast forty-three per cent. of the October vote, show Hayes ahead of Tilden 3,491, but which is a Democratic gain of 903. The same ratio of gain in the rest of the State would give Tilden 7,000 majority. Strong Democratic counties to hear from may increase this estimate. The townships not heard from gave 9,529 Democratic majority in October last.

MICHIGAN.

THE STATE CARRIED BY 20,000 MAJORITY—A LARGE MAJORITY ON JOINT BALLOT IN THE LEGISLATURE.

The following table summarizes the result of the election, showing the votes cast by each State in the Electoral College, and to whom they will go:

MAJORITIES FOR GOV. HAYES.

	Electoral Vote.
California	6
Colorado	3
Florida	4
Illinois	21
Iowa	11
Kansas	5
Louisiana	8
Maine	7
Massachusetts	13
Michigan	11
Minnesota	5
Nebraska	3
Nevada	3
New Hampshire	5
Ohio	22
Oregon	3
Pennsylvania	29
Rhode Island	4
South Carolina	7
Vermont	5
Wisconsin	10
Total	185

MAJORITIES FOR GOV. TILDEN.

Alabama	10
Arkansas	6
Connecticut	6
Delaware	3
Georgia	11
Indiana	15
Kentucky	12
Maryland	8
Mississippi	8
Missouri	15
New-Jersey	9
New-York	35
North Carolina	10
Tenuessee	12
Texas	8
Virginia	11
West Virginia	5
Total	184
Whole number of votes	369
Necessary to elect	185

FORTY-FIFTH CONGRESS.

ITS PROBABLE COMPLEXION—INCREASED REPUBLICAN GAIN IN MEMBERSHIP.

We present below a list of the names of the members of the next Congress thus far elected, revised by our latest advices. The names of Republicans are printed in Roman; of Democrats in italic. Candidates whose election is not assured are marked with a (?) and those whose seat will probably be contested by the abbreviation "con."

ALABAMA.
1. *F. G. Bromberg*, Ind.
2. *Hilary A. Herbert.*
3. *Jeremiah N. Williams.*
4. James T. Rapier (?)
5. *Robert F. Ligon.*
6. *G. W. Hewitt.*
7. *William H. Forney.*
8. *W. W. Garth.*

ARKANSAS.
1. *Lucien C. Gause.*
2. *William F. Slemons.*
3. John McClure.
4. *Thomas M. Gunter.*

CALIFORNIA.
1. Horace Davis.
2. Horace F. Page.
3. Joseph McKenna.
4. *P. D. Wigginton.*

COLORADO.
James B. Belford.

CONNECTICUT.
1. *George M. Landers.*
2. *James Phelps.*
3. John T. Wait.
4. *Levi Warner.*

DELAWARE.
James Williams.

FLORIDA.
1. William J. Purman.

12. *John M. Glover.*
13. *Aylett H. Buckner.*

NEBRASKA.
Frank Welch.

NEVADA.
Thomas Wren.

NEW-HAMPSHIRE.
Elects in March, 1877.

NEW-JERSEY.
1. Clement H. Sinnickson.
2. John H. Pugh.
3. *Miles Ross.*
4. *Alvah A. Clark.*
5. *Augustus W. Cutler.*
6. Thomas B. Peddie.
7. *Aug. A. Hardenburgh.*

NEW-YORK.
1. *James W. Covert.*
2. *William D. Veeder.*
3. S. B. Chittenden.
4. *Archibald M. Bliss.*
5. *Nicholas Muller.*
6. *Samuel S. Cox.*
7. *Anthony Eickhoff.*
8. Anson G. McCook.
9. *Fernando Wood.*
10. *Abram S. Hewitt.*
11. *Benjamin A. Willis.*
12. *Clarkson N. Potter.*
13. John H. Ketcham.

2. Horace B. Strait.
3. Jacob H. Stewart.

MISSISSIPPI.
1. *H. L. Muldrow.*
2. *Van. H. Manning.*
3. *Hernando D. Money.*
4. *Otho R. Singleton.*
5. *Charles E. Hooker.*
6. *James R. Chalmers.*

MISSOURI.
1. Anthony Ittner.
2. Nathan Cole.
3. *Richard G. Frost.*
4. *Robert A. Hatcher.*
5. *Richard P. Bland.*
6. Harrison E. Havens.
7. *Thomas T. Crittenden.*
8. *Benjamin J. Franklin.*
9. *David Rea.*
10. H. W. Pollard.
11. *John B. Clark.*

3. *Gilbert C. Walker.*
4. Joseph Jorgenson.
5. *George C. Cabell.*
6. *J. Randolph Tucker.*
7. *John T. Harris.*
8. *Eppa Hunton.*
9. *Auburn L. Pridemore.*

WEST VIRGINIA.
1. *Benjamin Wilson.*
2. *Benjamin F. Martin.*
3. *John E. Kenna.*

WISCONSIN.
1. Charles G. Williams.
2. Lucien B. Caswell.
3. George C. Hazleton.
4. *William P. Lynde.*
5. *Edward S. Bragg.*
6. *Gabriel Benck.*
7. H. L. Humphrey.
8. Thaddeus C. Pound.

RECAPITULATION.

	Next Congress.	Present house.
Republicans	145	110
Democrats	145	183
To be elected	3	--
Majority	Rep. 0	Dem. 73

Republican net gain, 73.

THE RESULT IN NEW YORK.

MAJORITIES BY COUNTIES ON THE ELECTORAL VOTE.

The official returns have been received from more than half the counties in the State, showing the majority given by each on the electoral vote. The subjoined table is made up from these returns, from our private dispatches, and from careful estimates based on the Presidential vote of 1872. It may be relied upon as being nearly correct. It is not probable that any later returns will greatly vary the result as now given. The complete returns of the vote on Governor have been received from only a few counties. So far as received, they show that both candidates ran slightly behind their respective Electoral tickets. In nearly all instances the Republican county tickets have been elected. In the next Legislature the Republicans will have a majority of 15 Assemblymen. The Senate holds over, but from death and resignation there were two vacancies to fill, and a Democrat and a Republican have been elected to fill them. This leaves a Republican majority of six. Of the Congressional delegation there are nineteen Republicans and fifteen Democrats, a Republican gain of four. Following is the table of county majorities:

Counties.	Hayes.	Tilden.	Grant.	Greeley.
Albany	....	2200	621	....
Allegany	2800	....	3170	....
Broome	1300	....	1397	....
Cattaraugus	1300	....	2009	....
Cayuga	3002	....	3207	....
Chautauqua	4380	....	3265	....
Chemung	....	300	622	....
Chenango	1200	....	1296	....
Clinton	600	....	481	....
Columbia	....	512	....	585
Cortland	1450	....	1229	....
Delaware	900	....	513	....
Dutchess	358	....	....	402
Erie	900	....	5363	....
Essex	1500	....	1789	....
Franklin	1167	....	1295	....
Fulton	550	....	624	....
Genesee	1000	....	1454	....
Greene	....	1000	....	263
Hamilton	....	50	....	139
Herkimer	800	....	1447	....
Jefferson	2159	....	2712	....
Kings	....	18501	....	4739
Lewis	....	200	369	....
Livingston	1043	....	1403	....
Madison	2000	....	2198	....
Monroe	1875	....	3772	....
Montgomery	300	....	371	....
New-York	....	51466	....	23147
Niagara	....	250	1006	....
Oneida	1773	....	3306	....
Onondaga	3500	....	2959	....

3. *John J. Shandley.*
4. *James G. Tighe.*
5. W. W. Stephenson.
6. *John M. Dittemeier.*
7. *Charles L. Lyon.*
8. Adrian M. Suydam.
9. *John McGroarty.*

LEWIS.
William W. Rice.

LIVINGSTON.
Jonathan B. Morey.

MADISON.
1. Albert N. Sheldon.
2. Merchant Billington.

MONROE.
1. Willard Hodges.
2. James G. Graham. (?)
3. *Wash'gton L. Rockwell.*

MONTGOMERY
Edward Wemple

NEW-YORK.
1. *James Healey.*
2. *Thomas F. Grao*
3. *William H. Roons*
4. *John Galvin.*
5. *Peter Mitchell.*
6. *Michael Healey.*
7. Isaac I. Hayes.
8. *Martin Nachtman.*
9. William H. Corsa.
10. *Christopher Flecke.*
11. Elliot C. Cowdin.
12. *Maurice F. Holahan*
13. Robert H. Strahan.
14. *Luke F. Cozans.*

SCHUYLER.
William Gulick.

SENECA.
Albert Childs.

STEUBEN.
1. *William B. Ruggles.*
2. Jerry E. B. Santee.

SUFFOLK.
Morris B. Smith.

SULLIVAN.
Thornton A. Niven.

TIOGA.
Eugene B. Gere.

TOMPKINS.
Silas B. Wickes.

ULSTER.
1. *Thomas Hamilton.*
2. Nathan Keator.
3. *Isaac W. Longyear.*

WARREN.
Robert Waddell.

WASHINGTON.
1. Townsend J. Potter.
2. Isaac V. Baker, Jr.

WAYNE.
1. *Emory W. Gurnee.*
2. Jere. Thistlewaite.

WESTCHESTER.
1. *Ambrose H. Purdy.*
2. *William F. Moller.*
3. James W. Husted.

WYOMING.
Arthur Clark.

YATES.
Mason L. Baldwin.

Republicans, 71; Democrats, 57.

FLORIDA FOR HAYES AND FREEDOM.

THE REPUBLICAN MAJORITY BETWEEN FIFTEEN HUNDRED AND TWO THOUSAND.

Special Dispatches to the New-York Times.

TALLAHASSEE, Nov. 8.—Our State ticket and the Hayes electoral ticket are safe by at least 1,500 and probably 2,000 majority. We have elected our Congressman in the First District, and probably in the Second. Perfect order prevailed throughout the State.

M. MARTIN,
Chairman Republican State Committee.

JACKSONVILLE, Nov. 8.—The Republicans will elect four Electors and two Congressmen and the entire State ticket. PETER JONES,
Secretary Campaign Committee.

JACKSONVILLE, Nov. 8.—Florida is Republican by an increased majority over the vote of 1874.

PETER JONES,
Secretary Campaign Committe.

WASHINGTON, Nov. 8.—The following dispatch has been received here by J. W. Edmunds, of the Republican Congressional Committee:

TALLAHASSEE, Nov. 8—6 P. M.

We have carried the State by not less than fifteen hundred and probably two thousand. Full returns are not yet in, but such as are received make the above figures certain.

M. MARTIN,
Chairman Republican Campaign Committee.

JACKSONVILLE, Nov. 8.—In sixteen counties the Republican majority is 6,000, an aggregate Republican gain of 2,500 over the vote of 1874. The Republican majority in the State will not be less than 2,000. PETER JONES,
Secretary Republican Campaign Committee.

Dispatch to the Associated Press.

LAKE CITY, Nov. 8.—Returns are being made up as fast as possible. Finley, Dem., for Congress in the Second District, is elected by 600 majority. Columbia County gives 195 Democratic majority, a Democratic gain of about 240. Duval County gives a Republican majority of 800, a Republican gain of 330 over the vote of 1874. Polk County gives an estimated Democratic majority of 452, a Democratic gain of 119. Madison County gives a Republican majority of 392, a Democratic gain of 77. Nassau County gives a Republican majority of 9?, a Democratic gain of 40. St. Johns County gives an estimated Democratic majority of 200, a Republican gain of 31. Monroe County gives an estimated Democratic majority of 73, a Democratic gain of 63. Baker County gives a Democratic majority of 98, a Republican gain of 2.

THE VOTE IN NEW-HAMPSHIRE.

THE REPUBLICAN MAJORITY OVER 3,000.

CONCORD, Nov 8.—Returns from 210 towns give Hayes 39,565, Tilden 36,323, with 26 towns to

reported everywhere, except in five small parishes.

Dispatch to the Associated Press.

NEW-ORLEANS, Nov. 8.—There are as yet no definite returns, and matters stand as at 11:30 last night. Both parties claim the State. Indications point to Democratic gains in the interior parishes. The Democrats elected Elam for Congress over Smith in the Fourth District. The city will probably give 10,000 Democratic majority.

The following special is from a Democratic source:

CLINTON, East Feliciana Parish, Nov. 8.—Owing to the failure of the Register to fill his appointments, a large number of voters were not registered. Seventeen hundred and forty-three registered votes were polled, of which Hayes got three and Tilden the balance. At a poll conducted under the United States Supervisor 443 voters who had been unable to register deposited their ballots in a separate box, all Democratic. The Republicans refrained from voting. There was no intimidation, and the gross number of voters was within 300 of the number at the last election. Many Democratic voters were deterred by want of registration. The whites and blacks fraternized, and all are happy and jubilant.

The above majority of 1,740 shows a Democratic gain of 2,581 over the vote of 1874. Prominent Republicans say the voting in East Feliciana was informal, and the votes will not be counted by the Returning Board, as the Registrar sent there was intimidated and run off. Other Democratic parishes will be treated in the same way for similar reasons. Charges of intimidation, fraud, &c., will be made.

Onachita Parish gives a Democratic majority of 1,087, being a Democratic gain of 1,915 over the vote of 1874, when Dubucklet, Rep., received 828 majority.

The following official and unofficial returns o parishes have been received here:

Iberia.—Republican 1,453, Democratic 1,246—a Republican gain of 377.

Calcasieu.—Democratic 1,241, Republican 95—a net Republican gain of 25.

West Feliciana—Democratic by 250 to 300 majority—a Democratic gain of 1,109.

Jackson. Democratic, 1,046; Republican, 330—a Democratic gain of 265.

Comparisons are made with the 1874 returns of the Democratic Conservative Committee. The election was peaceable and quiet. No disturbance has been reported from any quarter of the State.

THE VICTORY IN OREGON.

A CLEAN SWEEP—THE DEMOCRATS CONCEDE A REPUBLICAN VICTORY—1,000 MAJORITY FOR GOV. HAYES.

Special Dispatch to the New-York Times.

PORTLAND, Nov. 7.—Indications are we have made a clean sweep, electing our Presidential Electors and Congressmen.

G. A. STEELE, Chairman.

PORTLAND, Nov. 8.—Oregon has gone for Hayes and Wheeler, and Williams, Rep., is elected to Congress. We claim 1,000 majority; and the Democrats concede a Republican victory. JOHN H. MITCHELL,
United States Senator.

Dispatch to the Associated Press.

SAN FRANCISCO, Nov. 8.—Latest returns from Oregon show a Republican majority of 1,000. The Democrats now concede that State to the Republicans.

SAN FRANCISCO, Nov. 8—10 P. M.—Oregon is conceded Republican by a small majority. A dispatch just received from Portland says Oregon is safe for from 3,000 to 5,000 Republican majority.

NEVADA WILL VOTE FOR HAYES.

THE STATE SURE FOR A DECIDED REPUBLICAN MAJORITY.

Special Dispatch to the New-York Times.

VIRGINIA CITY, Nov. 8.—Nevada gives a majority for Hayes. O. O. BALLERMAN,
Chairman Republican State Committee.

VIRGINIA CITY, Nov. 8.—Nevada has gone Republican by 1,000 majority. Wren, Rep., is elected Congressman; Leonard, Rep., elected Supreme Court Judge. The Legislature is Re-

six to eight. The most important gains for the lower house are ten in Allegheny County, four in Crawford, two in Venango, two in Washington, five in Luzerne, two in Delaware, and two in Franklin.

The Republicans have large gains in many of their counties, the principal being about as follows: Allegheny County, 2,500; Beaver, 700; Lawrence, 600; Indiana, 600; Blair, 400; Lancaster, 1,000; Chester, 1,000; Bradford, 600; Tioga, 1,000; Warren, 600. The large Democratic gains are, in Northumberland County, 1,000; Berks, 1,000, York, 500; Green, 700; Luzerne, 1,800. The majority on the Presidential ticket in Philadelphia will be about 16,000. It now looks as though the State, outside the city, would be about even, but the returns are not complete enough to warrant a statement by counties. The extent of the majority is of little consequence, since all the fruits of a great majority are gathered. The evidence is conclusive of a profuse expenditure of money by the Democrats throughout the State, and purposes of frauds which did not have much success, except in a few localities. The discovery of the fraudulent receipts, no doubt, prevented the State going for Tilden. There are some facts in relation to frauds, and the use of money by Democrats, which it will be profitable to examine when the excitement has further subsided.

THE RESULT ON CONGRESSMEN.

Special Dispatch to the New-York Times.

BUTLER, Nov. 8.—Thompson, Rep., is elected in the Twenty-sixth Congressional District by 2,000 majority.

POTTSVILLE, Nov. 8.—Returns received up to noon indicate the election of Reilly, Dem., for Congress by 100 majority.

TOWANDA, Nov. 8.—The majority for Hayes in this county is 3,000. Col. Overton, for Congress, has 2,400 majority in the county, and 2,000 in the district.

WARREN, Nov. 8.—For Congress, Watson's majority in Warren County is 1,100, and in the district about 3,000.

ROCHESTER, Nov. 8.—Incomplete returns indicate the election of W. S. Shallenberger for Congress by a majority of 2,000 in the district.

PHILADELPHIA, Nov. 8.—In the Seventeenth Congressional District, Campbell, Rep., has a majority of 581. This district is at present represented by a Democrat.

WELLSBORO, Nov. 8.—John I. Mitchell's majority for Congress will exceed 1,000 in this district.

MISCELLANEOUS RETURNS.

PHILADELPHIA, Nov. 8—9:30 P. M.—Full returns from twenty-four counties in this State, including Philadelphia, show a net Republican gain of 2,499. This does not include Allegheny County.

The Republicans gain five members of the Legislature in the county, electing seven of the nine members.

Jones, Republican, is elected to the Congressional vacancy. Wright, Democrat, is elected to the forty-fifth Congress. The Republicans elect the District Attorney in this county, and probably Prothonotary. They also elect two State Senators, which is a gain of one.

Reilly, Dem., is elected to Congress from the Thirteenth District by a majority of 125.

MAJORITIES BY COUNTIES.

PHILADELPHIA, Nov. 8.—The following are the majorities in Pennsylvania by counties as far as heard from. All the townships are not in, but there are enough to estimate from:

County.	Hayes Maj.	Tilden Maj.	Rep. Gain.	Dem. Gain.
Allegheny	7000	....	....	....
Bradford	3000	....	....	....
Bucks	....	360	....	73
Blair	1022	....	447	....
Butler	350	....	440	....
Chester	3075	....	1065	....
Columbia	....	2345	....	231
Fayette	....	1000	....	173
Lehigh	....	2166	....	38
Montour	....	600	....	270
Pike (official)	....	962	....	340
Snyder	383	....	51	....
Wyoming	....	330	....	85
Warren	750	....	433	....
Wayne	....	800	....	519
Tioga	3000	....	1000	....
Center	....	830	550	....
Lancaster (incomplete)	7419	....	2279	....
Lycoming	....	1200	....	....
Northampton	....	3900	....	1076
Northumberland	....	570	306	....
Delaware	2234	....	233	....
Carbon	....	348	33	....
Cameron	29	....	....	47
Erie	245	....	....	....

VIRGINIA.

TILDEN'S MAJORITY OVER 30,000—EIGHT DEMOCRATIC CONGRESSMEN ELECTED.

RICHMOND, Nov. 8.—Incomplete returns from nearly every section indicate that Tilden's majority

*Re-elected.

THE COUNTY VOTES.

Atlantic County.—Hayes carries this county by 186, a Democratic gain of 218, as compared with 1872. Pugh, (Rep.,) for Congress gets 218 majority, a Republican gain of 17. Ashley, (Rep.,) is elected to the Assembly by 244, a Republican gain of 13. The whole Republican county ticket is elected by an average majority of 225.

Monmouth County.—The Republicans elect Leonard to the Assembly in the Third District of Monmouth County by 20 majority, a Republican gain of one Assemblyman and of 29 votes. The Democrats elect two Assemblymen. The official majorities in the county are—Tilden, 2,217; Ross, Dem., for Congress, 2,186.

Middlesex County. (official.)—Tilden's majority is 570; Ross, Dem., for Congress, has 480 majority; Ludlow, Dem., for State Senate, 725; Waldron, Dem., for Assembly, 285; Campbell, Dem., for Assembly, 100; Martin, Dem., for Assembly, 383. This county is a Democratic gain.

Essex County.—This county gives Hayes 1,941 majority, a Democratic gain of 3,039 over 1872, but a Republican gain of 1,679, on Congressmen, over 1874.

Passaic County. John W. Griggs, Rep., is re-elected to the Assembly from Paterson, instead of Stevenson, Dem., as first reported.

Hudson County.—Alexander M. Harris, Dem., is elected to the Assembly from the Fourth District of Hudson County, instead of H. Brannigam, Rep., as at first reported.

Morris County. (official.)—Tilden's majority is 30; Cutler's, Dem., for Congress, 176.

Union County.—Full returns from the City of Elizabeth show a Democratic gain of 350 on Mayor. The Republicans elect four Councilmen, and the Council and Board of Education stand the same as last year—Republicans 9, Democrats 7. The Democrats elect William E. Hoy Mayor by about 75 majority. The First Assembly District re-elect Egan, Dem., by a large majority. The Second District re-elects Cory, Rep., by about 70, and the Third District re-elects Vail, Rep., by 34. Elizabeth elects Democratic Freeholders, which will make the Board stand—Democrats 10, Republicans 7.

Cape May County.—This county has elected a Republican Senator and Assemblyman.

Burlington County.—Ridgway, Dem., for Senator, is elected, with two Democratic Assemblymen and one Republican, and one Assembly District remains in doubt.

Mercer County.—Hutchinson, Rep., for the Assembly, has been defeated by seven votes. The county now stands two Democrats and one Republican.

Pugh, Rep., is elected to Congress in the Second District by a majority of 500.

DELAWARE.

THE DEMOCRATIC MAJORITY IN THE STATE 2,600.

WILMINGTON, Nov. 8.—The Democratic majority in this State will reach 2,600.

ENTHUSIASM IN OHIO.

A MAJORITY FOR HAYES CLAIMED IN THE ELECTORAL COLLEGE — PERTINENT SPEECH BY THE NEXT PRESIDENT.

COLUMBUS, Nov. 8.—There is great excitement here over the announcement that Gov. Hayes is elected. His private secretary is sending out telegrams claiming a majority of one for Hayes in the Electoral College. High street, in front of the Republican head-quarters, is closely packed with thousands of people, all wild with excitement. In the midst of the general excitement, all efforts to obtain complete returns of the Ohio election by counties have signally failed. Thus far returns have only been received from nineteen counties. It is, however, conceded by both the State Committees that the Republican majority will be from 8,000 to 10,000.

After hearing the news at the Republican head-quarters, the crowd, numbering several thousand, formed into a procession and marched to Gov. Hayes' residence. In response to repeated calls Gov. Hayes appeared in the doorway and amid much cheering by the crowd spoke as follows:

MY FRIENDS: I assure you I am obliged for this hearty demonstration, but if you will keep quiet about half a moment, I will say something to you which I think it is my duty under the circumstances to say. While our present advices look favorable, we must remember that several of the States which have been considered doubtful, have a large territory remote from railroad or telegraphic communication, and it will naturally take some time to receive definite returns from them. I therefore take this call as an earnest of your loyalty to the Republican Party, and your desire for its success. If later advices should change the result from what it is announced at present, I assure you

[illegible] thousand majority for Hayes in this State, with the State ticket behind somewhat. The Legislature shows over fifty Republican majority on joint ballot, and we have carried every Congressional district except the First, which re-elects Williams, Democrat, by about twelve hundred majority.

DETROIT, Nov. 8.—Returns from 304 townships and five precincts in this city give Hayes a net majority of 12,025; a Democratic gain of 9,463 over 1872. The same towns give Coswell, Rep., for Governor a net majority of 6,631. Willits, Rep., for Congress in the Second District, has 708 majority; McGowan, Rep., for Congress in the Third District, has 741 majority. The Democrats claim the election of Williams in the First District by about 1,000.

Midnight.—Later returns indicate that the majority for Hayes in this State will be from 15,000 to 20,000. Crowell's majority for Governor will be somewhat less. The Legislature will be Republican by a majority of about 50 on joint ballot. The Republicans certainly have 7 out of 9 Congressional Districts. The Democrats elect Williams in the First District by about 100 majority. The Eighth District is claimed by both parties. Wayne County elects the entire Democratic ticket, with the exception of Durfee, Rep., who is elected Judge of the Probate Court, and possibly Coats, Rep., for Sheriff.

MINNESOTA.

A REPUBLICAN MAJORITY OF 15,000—A GAIN OF TWO REPUBLICAN CONGRESSMEN.

ST. PAUL, Nov. 8.—The total vote of St. Paul and Ramsey County gives Tilden a majority of 1,184, and Stewart, Rep., for Congress, 365 majority.

Minneapolis complete gives Hayes 335 majority and McNair, Dem., for Congress 355 majority.

The vote throughout the State, except in Ramsey County, generally shows Republican gains. Only about twenty of the seventy-two counties have yet made complete returns, but these, with fragmentary returns from other points, indicate that the Republican majority in the State will be from 15,000 to 18,000.

Dunnell, Rep., is elected in the First District by from 5,000 to 7,000 majority. Strait is elected in the Second District by 5,000 majority, and Stewart, in the Third, by 1,000 majority.

IOWA.

FIFTY-FIVE THOUSAND MAJORITY—REPUBLICAN GAIN OF ONE CONGRESSMAN.

Special Dispatch to the New-York Times.

DES MOINES, Nov. 8.—Thirty counties thus far heard from give majorities for Hayes amounting to 20,903, and two counties give Tilden 2,250. The net Republican majority is 18,882, a gain of 8,829 over the vote of last year. The remaining counties, upon the same proportionate gain, will make Hayes' majority 53,000. All the Congressmen elected are Republicans.

Dispatch to the Associated Press.

DES MOINES, Nov. 8.—Returns from seven counties, and twenty-two precincts in others, show a majority for Hayes of 9,367, a Republican gain of 4,727. The State will go at least 55,000 Republican. Every precinct shows a Republican gain.

CHICAGO, Nov. 8.—Returns from 130 Iowa towns, in sixty-seven counties, show a Republican gain of 5,869, and a Democratic gain of 341.

MISSOURI.

RETURNS FROM ALL PARTS OF THE STATE—THE VOTE IN ST. LOUIS COUNTY—A GAIN OF THREE CONGRESSMEN.

Special Dispatch to the New-York Times.

ST. LOUIS, Nov. 8.—We have carried two out of the three St. Louis Congressmen, and the county ticket. CHAUNCEY I. FILLEY.

Dispatch to the Associated Press.

ST. LOUIS, Nov. 8.—Up to 4 o'clock this morning only fifty of the seventy-nine precincts had completed the count. These precincts give Tilden 12,800, and Hayes 11,896; Phelps, Dem., for Governor, 10,229; Finkelnburg, Rep., 10,262, Thomas, Rep., for Sheriff, 11,122; Brown, Dem., 8,688. For Congress in the First District, Ittner, Rep., has 3,775, and Kehr, Dem., 3,467. In the Second District Wells, Dem., has 3,035; Slayback, Dem.,

Continued on Fifth Page.

parts of the country, had provided an opening for some enterprising grafters. The stealing had been going on for years, and the money abstracted from the public treasury seems to have amounted to something like eight or ten million dollars. The guilty officials were to be found in almost every branch of the service, and their confederates outside the department included several politicians of national eminence.

The frauds were discovered by some of those eccentric persons who, holding public office in that period, regarded it as their duty to live on their salaries and treat their offices as a public trust. Like the men who exposed Tweed, they knew there was not much use in reporting their discoveries to high officials; and like those men they offered the facts to a newspaper. The parallel goes one step farther; in each case *The Times* was the second choice. Information as to the Star Route peculations was offered to the Washington correspondent of another New York newspaper, who sent to his office a synopsis of the evidence. It was plain to the editors that the trail led pretty high up in the post-office department and in political life outside, and it seems to have been feared that in the rarefied atmosphere of those lofty altitudes investigating journalists might find the climbing uncomfortable. So the paper first selected by the discoverers declined their offerings with thanks, and they came to *The Times*.

The work of following up their leads and analyzing the methods of the conspirators was given to Frank D. Root of *The Times* Washington office, who is still with the paper. He did his work very thor-

oughly, and by way of a greeting to the new administration *The Times* in the spring of 1881 published the whole history of the frauds with appropriate comment. In the early days of the exposure, Root's stories sometimes occupied the entire front page of the paper and most of the second; and they had their effect in indictments, resignations, and a clean-up, of the department. The eventual result, of course, was not wholly satisfactory. Four years later, in editorial comment on the end of the last of the numerous prosecutions arising from the disclosures, *The Times* was compelled to record that the case had closed with "not one cent recovered and not one guilty man punished." But the stealing had been stopped, and one more piece of evidence had been offered that with the development of investigative journalism the way of the transgressor was at least a little harder than in the past.

In another instance in that same year *The Times* showed that it could crusade when it found occasion. Justice Theodoric R. Westbrook of the state Supreme Court had been lending his valuable support to Jay Gould in the financier's effort to get control of the Manhattan Elevated Railway Company. The jurist had even gone to the length of holding court in Gould's office, and had written to Gould that he would "go to the very verge of judicial discretion" in the aid of Gould's schemes. *The Times* investigated and exposed these transactions, which were promptly taken up in the Assembly in the hope of impeaching the judge. One of the leaders in the effort to get the Assembly to impeach Westbrook was a young man of good family just beginning his

official career, to whom the city editor of *The Times* furnished the evidence on which he based his first attack on a misbehaving public servant and a malefactor of great wealth. As usual, justice flashed in the pan; the Assembly, for certain devious but not very dark reasons, finally refused to bring charges against Westbrook; but the judge thereafter walked as delicately as Agag when he was dealing with Jay Gould, and Assemblyman Theodore Roosevelt found himself well started on a career as a reformer, which *The Times* always thereafter regarded with interest even when it could not give it support.

Another enterprise of the paper at about that time was of a less bellicose nature, but equally praiseworthy — the raising of a $250,000 fund for General Grant. First suggested in 1880 by John M. Forbes of Boston, it was taken up by *The Times* immediately after the election. George Jones took a deep personal interest in the campaign, and succeeded in pushing it through to complete success by the following March. Thereafter he served as one of the trustees of the fund until his death.

Accomplishments such as these, together with the general high standard of the paper's news service and editorial expression, kept *The Times* prosperous and powerful in the early eighties. New influences were coming into journalism; changes which were perhaps deplorable, but probably inevitable, were bringing papers of a different type into prominence; but *The Times* maintained its distinction as a conservative paper — a Republican paper, to be sure, but never subservient to the party managers, inter-

ested in a number of causes essentially nonpartisan and so drifting steadily away from partisan allegiance. That it would actually break away from the party nobody expected until it actually happened, but the ground was prepared by the whole history of the paper and of the party in the previous years.

By 1884 a good many men were getting ready to break away from the Republican party. Those promises of reform had been too often made and too regularly forgotten to carry much conviction. The party's reputation was no longer sufficient to carry a weak candidate; by the beginning of 1884 sensible men were beginning to realize that it would need a very strong candidate and a lot of luck. And when it became apparent that James G. Blaine, carrying all the handicap of the Mulligan letters and the rest of his past, was likely to get the nomination, and that the most hopeful of his competitors was President Arthur, it was evident that the party might have to carry a heavier load than it had borne for a number of years. The first efforts of *The Times* were devoted to a fight against either of these nominations, and all through the spring of 1884 the paper conducted an editorial campaign designed to remind Republicans who wanted to win that this year the head of the ticket might have to carry the party instead of riding free on its record.

By that time the editor of *The Times* was Charles R. Miller, who had succeeded John Foord as editor-in-chief in April, 1883, and who has held that position ever since. Mr. Miller was born in Hanover, N. H., in 1849, graduated from Dartmouth, in 1872,

and after several years on *The Springfield Republican* came to *The Times* in 1876. Though of Democratic origin, he was at that time an independent in politics. His influence must be counted as considerable in determining the course of the paper in the campaign, but most of the other editors and Mr. Jones were in agreement that this year at any rate it would be impossible to support an obviously unfit nominee. An exception should be made of the ever-faithful Reid, who continued to believe that the Republican party was the sole repository of eternal truth, and thought that even a hint of departure from its ranks was the unpardonable sin. But nearly everybody else on *The Times* felt that though the paper ought to support the Republican ticket if it could, there were circumstances in which its duty to the public demanded a different course.

The deciding voice, however, had to be that of Mr. Jones. The editors who had grown tired of apologizing for the party's record, who had felt the gradual turning away of many of the most honorable and intelligent Republicans from the leaders of the party, and who had seen with misgiving the failure of efforts to head off the drift to Blaine — these men did not own the paper. In fact, none of them had any stock in it at all, and the certain financial penalties of secession from the party must be borne by Jones. These considerations were laid frankly before the owner of the paper by its editor, and with equal frankness he declared that he could not and would not support a candidate whom he regarded as deplorably unfit for the Presidential office.

The Times published on May 23 an editorial

headed "Neither Blaine nor Arthur." The text of that sermon lay in this sentence:

> The list of men to choose from is not a long one. We do not believe that this is a year when "any good Republican will do."

But there was still hope in the office that the Republican convention would select a satisfactory candidate, and on the same page appeared an editorial calling attention to the blunders which the Democrats had committed, as usual, in the House of Representatives.

The next day the campaign was continued in an article headed "Neither Arthur nor Blaine." In this, Mr. Miller spoke aloud an opinion which a good many Republicans had been almost afraid to whisper in private, but which they knew to be true: "The party is not strong enough to elect a President by the votes of what may be called its regular members." The notorious defects of Blaine were briefly mentioned, and President Arthur was dismissed with the remark that he

> has done better than was expected, and is reported to have been a modest, quiet, inoffensive occupant of the executive office.

But this was no time for modesty and inoffensiveness; the country needed something more than that.

> Neither Blaine nor Arthur [the editorial continued] is a possible President. The choice of a candidate must start from that fact. That once clearly recognized, it ought not be difficult to find a man who can poll the full Republican vote, and with it enough

> of the independent vote to keep the government in the hands of the party which, we are convinced, is the safest and best.

When the suspicion gradually arose that *The Times* might not swallow Blaine, people began to ask questions. One of these — a query from an indignant subscriber who asked outright "if *The Times* will support the nominee of the Chicago Republican Convention" — was answered on the editorial page May 29.

> If the nominee of the Chicago Republican Convention [said the editorial reply] is a man worthy to be President of the United States, *The New York Times* will give him a hearty and vigorous support. If he shall be a man unworthy to hold that high office, a man who personally and politically, in office or out, represents principles and practices which *The Times* abhors and has counseled the party to shun, we shall watch with great interest the efforts of those responsible for such a nomination to elect the candidate, but we shall give them no help.

There it was in plain language: Raymond's paper, Jones's paper, the paper that had led the Republican journalism of the nation for a decade, would not support Blaine. That it would support the Democratic nominee was as yet by no means certain, even to its editors, and in the spring of 1884 nobody looked on the possible departure from the Republican party as anything but a temporary absence without leave; but absence of any kind, for any reason, was certain to displease a great many readers, and it was yet to be seen whether the

paper's defection would do more harm to the Republican party or to *The Times*.

At any rate, the decision was soon made. Blaine was nominated June 6, on the fourth ballot, and on the following morning a *Times* editorial headed "Facing the Fires of Defeat" announced that the paper would not support him, but would watch the party's adventures in the ensuing canvass with the interest of a friend and physician. Blaine, in the opinion of *The Times*, represented "the average of Republican principles and purposes, of Republican honor and conscience, as they now are"; and it was suggested that "defeat will be the salvation of the Republican party." The editors of a Republican paper which had just made such a difficult and costly decision might be expected to hope and believe that one sad experience would purge the party, and that thereafter intelligent and patriotic men could return to it without qualms. That *The Times* never has returned to the party, and that for the next twelve years it leaned toward the Democrats, was due partly to the unexpectedly large amount of original sin remaining in the Republican party even after the purgatorial experience of 1884, and partly to the new spirit that was coming into American politics, and was embodied by Grover Cleveland.

CHAPTER V

The Times in Transition, 1884-1896

THE campaign of 1884 definitely closed an epoch in the history of *The Times*. It is hardly likely that anybody foresaw how complete would be the break with the party which for twenty-eight years had commanded the loyal support of the paper. The Republicans had no monopoly of corruption and incompetence, and it was quite possible that the Democrats might make a nomination as bad as that of the party in power. But they did not. Cleveland was not very well known in 1884, but his good record as Governor had given the editors of *The Times* confidence in his principles and his capacity. At that time they were not personally acquainted with him; the long personal friendship between Mr. Miller and the President was a later growth. But what they knew of his public record was satisfactory, and they soon came to the conclusion that he deserved the paper's support. And they had a good deal of company; in the latter part of July a considerable number of the best men in the Republican party decided to support Cleveland, and the Mugwump campaign was on.

So, if *The Times* had left the party with which it had so long been associated, it found itself almost at once recognized as the principal spokesman for a group which represented much of the best of the old

Republican party and practically none of its undesirable elements. And for years thereafter the paper retained this position, and found its independence not only more comfortable and satisfactory than its former party allegiance, but for a time almost as lucrative. The rejection of Blaine did indeed bring losses, which were considerable but not disastrous. And as an offset to the defections the paper won many new readers who had previously found its intense Republicanism somewhat unpalatable.

The income did indeed drop a long way in that year. The net profits of the paper were $188,000 in 1883 and only $56,000 in 1884. But much of this decrease was due to the reduction in price from four cents to two, in the hope of meeting the competition of the two-cent *World* and *Sun*, which took effect in September, 1883. And within a few years *The Times*, despite the loss of circulation income which followed the change to two cents, had recovered most of the lost ground and was very nearly as prosperous as it had been in its best years of the past. The decline of its fortunes in the early nineties was due to a complex of reasons, which will be analyzed presently; but it does not seem that in the long run it lost very much by abandoning the Republican party.

What those readers missed who left it in 1884 was, it may be presumed, not so much Republican editorials as Republican news. Though deeply aggrieved by the alteration in the paper's political allegiance, John Reid stuck to the ship, and before the campaign was over the political correspondents were

speaking of the Grand Old Party in pretty much the same uncomplimentary language that had been poured out in previous years on the Democrats. Apparently political writers of the period were moved more by loyalty to the paper than by their predilections for any party.

The result of the election was a little doubtful in 1884 — not so doubtful as some of the Republican leaders pretended, to be sure, but Cleveland carried New York by only 1100 votes, and without New York he could not have won. On election night his supporters thought his majority was considerably larger, but some of the Republicans believed that Blaine had carried the state, and certain eminent stock speculators kept the wires busy with alleged news to that effect.

The judgment of *The Times* rested on the reports of its own unequaled election news service. Those reports in 1876 had indicated that the election was in doubt; and while at this distance one may believe that the Republican claims were unjustified, the evidence gathered by *The Times* correspondents did point to a conclusion borne out by the results. This was what happened in 1884. If three days after the election *The Times* insisted that there could no longer be any doubt of Cleveland's victory, it was because the reports of correspondents in whom the office had learned to have faith, and of the County Chairmen who wired their figures every night, gave New York to Cleveland by a majority of 1276. This was less than two hundred off the final and official figure; and to have come so close as that in a vote of over a million, in those more primitive days

and in such a hotly contested election, was a really remarkable feat of news-gathering.

President Cleveland turned out even better than *The Times* had hoped. He fought persistently, and in great measure successfully, for the causes in which the paper was most deeply interested — reform of the tariff and the civil service, and maintenance of sound ideas of public finance. With him, indeed, a new era began; the war was over, and the folly of partisan divisions based on memories of the war was becoming more apparent. The old names, the old forms, survived; but there were new issues and new ideas, and for the next decade *The Times* had an important part in forming the public opinion of the new day. In 1888 *The Times*, still an independent paper, gave Cleveland its support for reëlection without any hesitation; he had earned it. But David B. Hill, the Democratic candidate for governor, had not earned, in *The Times's* opinion, the support of the paper. Accordingly the paper's influence in the state campaign was thrown to the support of the gubernatorial candidacy of Warner Miller. It was *The Times's* luck to back the loser in each case; Cleveland was beaten, and Miller went down in history as "the intrepid leader who fell outside the breastworks." The Republican party was coming back hungry after a long fast, and outside the breastworks was a poor place to fall. Nothing occurred in Benjamin Harrison's administration to change *The Times's* opinion that Grover Cleveland was the most competent and trustworthy man in American public life, and in 1892 it supported his

presidential candidacy once more with the conviction born of long acquaintance and complete confidence.

In Cleveland's second term the paper had fallen on evil days, financially, and its support was perhaps no longer so powerful as it had been; but it was whole-hearted and unhesitating through a period of years when the President most needed friends. The Republicans had luckily been turned out in time to escape the blame for the panic of 1893, and were prospering by the misfortunes and division of their opponents. A good deal of the Democratic party had gone out to eat grass like Nebuchadnezzar, and the rest of it was mainly occupied in doing the work of the Republicans in the tariff struggle. The President's support was distinguished by quality rather than by quantity. But *The Times* saw a man fighting against desperate odds to preserve the credit of the nation, to win more and more of the public service away from the spoilsmen, and to keep faith with the people on the tariff issue; and it did what it could to hold up his hands.

What is perhaps even more to its credit, the paper stood by Cleveland in the Venezuelan question, when many who had supported him on domestic issues thought that his rashness was likely to provoke a needless war. *The Times* maintained throughout that crisis that Cleveland's Venezuelan message to Congress was not a war message but a peace message; that the resources of routine diplomacy had already been exhausted without result, and that decisive and arresting action was needed to prevent the dispute from drifting to a point where there

would have been nothing to do but give up the Monroe Doctrine or fight. The event showed that this view was correct. When the British government realized that America took the Monroe Doctrine seriously neither the Ministry nor the people was willing to make an issue in support of a petty intrigue of colonial policy, and Cleveland not only won his point but succeeded in making both America and England realize that they were worth a good deal more to each other than they had suspected. This happy consequence could not be foreseen at the time by most Americans, and some of the most bitter opponents of the President were men who had hitherto given him their support. The position of *The Times* was due not only to well-grounded confidence in Cleveland's insight, but to a correct interpretation of the issues; it is easy to praise it now, but it took both wisdom and courage to adopt it then.

In 1896 the paper was in something of a quandary as to the Presidential campaign. For the ideas and the principles of William Jennings Bryan it had no use; it had seen in past decades a good many Messiahs from the tall grass who promised to make two dollars grow where one had grown before. But it saw no particular reason for confidence in the party of Mark Hanna. On the tariff question the leaders of the Republican party stood for everything *The Times* abhorred, and while eventually the party and its candidate took the right position on the overshadowing issue of the currency, they were a long time in making up their minds. So *The Times* gave its support to the Gold Democratic ticket of Palmer and Buckner. In a sense, of course, its

efforts were wasted; everybody knew that Palmer and Buckner could do nothing but make a gesture of protest. But a protest was badly needed in that year.

At the end of Cleveland's second administration, on March 2, 1897, *The Times* published a six-column editorial signed with the initials of Charles R. Miller — so far as can be discovered, the only signed editorial that has ever appeared in the paper except in discussion of the paper's own affairs — reviewing the President's record. Today, when hardly anybody denies Cleveland's claim to greatness, this contemporary estimate can be studied with some profit. In the history of *The Times* there is nothing more creditable than the steadfast and loyal support which the paper gave to Abraham Lincoln and Grover Cleveland in dark days when it could not be foreseen that the faith of its editors would be approved by the judgment of posterity.

American journalism was changing fast in the eighties. The first influence in bringing in new ideas, that were destined to work more powerfully than their originators realized, was that of Charles A. Dana; the most powerful influence was that of Joseph Pulitzer. Between them, they eventually succeeded in inflicting mortal injuries on the old type of political newspaper that had flourished in the age of the slavery issue, the Civil War and reconstruction. Of the old-timers *The Times* survived longest — with the possible exception of *The Tribune*, which passed a good many years in a state of coma with only occasional signs of persisting vitality.

The modern type of newspaper in which the news side is predominant, though not to the exclusion of a vigorous editorial page, has taken form during the control of *The Times* by the present management, and it may not unfairly be said that that management has had a considerable influence in establishing the character of such papers; but in the late eighties and early nineties American journalism was headed in a different direction, and *The Times* stood out as almost the last representative of the old school. That it retained its influence in a changing world so long as it did, and indeed that it survived its extraneous misfortunes and lived to rise again, is sufficient evidence of the vitality of its old organization even when compelled to meet conditions for which it was not wholly prepared.

Though "personal journalism" in the old sense had passed, the editorial page was still for perhaps the majority of *Times* readers the most important part of the paper; but the news service was still good. As an instance may be cited an episode which was remembered in *The Times* office because of the fact that it produced the most expensive cable message which the paper has ever received. In 1884 there was under negotiation a commercial treaty with Spain, which would have an important effect on American trade with Cuba and Porto Rico. John W. Foster, the American Minister in Madrid, was conducting negotiations with the Spanish Foreign Ministry; but the provisions of the expected treaty were carefully kept a secret. Since they were of great importance to all exporters and merchants doing business with the Spanish West Indies,

The New-York Times.

VOL. XXX.......NO. 9258. NEW-YORK, WEDNESDAY, MAY 11, 1881. PRICE FOUR CENTS.

THE REPUBLICAN CAUCUS

SENATORS HOPEFUL OF AVOIDING A CONTEST.

ANOTHER LONG DISCUSSION OF THE NEW-YORK CUSTOM-HOUSE CASE—A BETTER FEELING PREVALENT—HOPES OF REACHING AN AMICABLE SETTLEMENT.

WASHINGTON, May 10.—The Republican caucus met again this afternoon about 1 o'clock, and, after a session of four hours, adjourned without deciding the question that is causing so much trouble. There seems to have been a better feeling among the Senators than was exhibited at the meeting of yesterday, and the speeches to-day were free from those acrimonious recriminations that have hitherto marked the discussions in caucus of the Robertson nomination. The debate was participated in by nearly all the Senators present, but there were no long speeches, the desire evidently being to avoid saying anything calculated to invite a controversy.

Mr. Conger made one of those humorous speeches for which he was so well known in the House of Representatives, and succeeded in getting his colleagues in the very best humor. He addressed himself mainly to Mr. Conkling, whose patriotism, ability, and great services to the country and the Republican Party he complimented in high terms. He said God had done much for Senator Conkling, but that Senator could do much more for himself, and this was his great opportunity. He should, upon this occasion, display some of that magnanimity for which he was noted in New-York and elsewhere, and waiving all feeling of pride and disappointment, all desire for vindication and revenge, come forward, fall upon the neck of the President, and extend forgiveness to that high officer for nominating Judge Robertson to be Collector of Customs at New-York. If Mr. Conkling should forgive the President, the country would forgive Mr. Conkling, and everybody, including Judge Robertson, be made happy. Mr. Conger spoke for about 20 minutes, and his humorous points were enjoyed by Mr. Conkling as well as the other Senators.

Other Senators thought it was still probable that a contest over Robertson's nomination could be avoided, and, referring to the good feeling prevailing to-day in the caucus, advised that any attempt to reach a final disposition of the case be postponed for two or three days. The effect of such a contest as is threatened, should it be decided immediately to dispose of the Robertson case, on the Republican Party in New-York and other States was talked over, and all agreed that no effort should be spared to secure harmony of action. No one attempted to reply to the speech made yesterday by Mr. Conkling, and at to-day's session that gentleman said nothing except in reply to questions propounded by Mr. Sherman and one or two others. No proposition was brought forward to-day and no formal conclusion was reached as to any action that should be had in the Senate. There is, however, a tacit understanding that during the next two or three days each Senator shall, in such a manner as to him may seem best, do what he can to bring about the result so much desired. While no definite plan of action was agreed upon, it is said that Senators, individually, are expected to consult with each other and with the President, with a view of reaching some understanding that will be satisfactory to the President and ac-

as Assistant Attorney-General for the department has been tendered, but not yet accepted by the Postmaster-General, will, it is stated, remain at the head of the law office of the department.

GEN. UPTON'S WILL.

PROVIDING FOR THE EDUCATION OF NEPHEWS AND NIECES—DISPOSING OF BATTLE SWORDS AND PAPERS.

BATAVIA, N. Y., May 10.—The will of the late Gen. Emory Upton, who died in Presidio, Cal., last March from a pistol-shot wound inflicted by himself, was admitted to probate in the Genesee County Surrogate's office, in this village, yesterday. The will was drawn by Gen. Upton on July 3, 1875, while he was visiting his parents in this town previous to starting on his tour around the world. It is a singular document. Miss Sara K. Upton, the General's sister, to whom he was greatly attached, is the Executrix and principal legatee, though his father and mother, who yet live here, and other members of the family, which consisted of 10 grown children, are all remembered. The value of the estate is estimated at $25,000, the greater portion of which is invested in a manufacturing concern at Battle Creek, Mich. The income from the copyrights of Gen. Upton's "United States Infantry Tactics" and "Tactics for Non-military Bodies" is bequeathed to his sister Sara, provided the income does not exceed $1,000. The residue of the income from these copyrights, after paying several small bequests, is directed to be held in trust by his Executors to be applied to the education of such of his nephews and nieces as desire a collegiate education, but when, in the judgment of the Executors, no more of the income is needed for the above purpose, they are empowered to apply the residue to aid such necessitous and worthy person or persons residing in Genesee County, N. Y., as may be desirous of a collegiate education and shall have passed a satisfactory examination before three competent examiners. It is stipulated that not more than $600 per annum shall be so applied, upon the further condition that one-fourth part of the money shall be repaid by the person receiving it at such a time within 10 years after its receipt as the Executor may decide. The income from these copyrights amounts to about $6,000 per year.

The steel sabre worn by Gen. Upton in the battles of Blackburn's Ford, Bull Run, Gaines's Mill, Charles City Cross Roads, Crampton's Gap, Antietam, Fredericksburg, Chancellorsville, Gettysburg, Rappahannock Station, Mine Run, Wilderness, Spottsylvania Court-house, Cold Harbor, and Petersburg is bequeathed to his brother James S. Upton, of Battle Creek, Mich., to be by him given to the first nephew or collateral relation of the name of Upton who may be graduated at West Point and enter the Army. His swords, commission, and official papers are bequeathed to his father and mother, to be by them distributed as they may think proper.

RUMORED INDIAN OUTRAGE.

A RANCH IN COLORADO SAID TO HAVE BEEN ATTACKED AND THREE MEN MURDERED.

DENVER, Col., May 9.—A telegram received by the Governor states that on May 5, in La Plata County, a ranch was attacked, 140 head of cattle were run off, and three ranchmen named Thurman, Smith, and May were killed. It is not known who were the attacking party. Some think they were Indians and others white desperadoes. The *News* furnishes the following additional information: The Governor's telegram was dated Durango, and said that Indians committed the murder, and the ranch was the property of John Thurman. Upon receipt of the telegram the Governor telegraphed its purport to Gen. Pope and also sent a courier to Durango to ascertain the truth, and, if true, what band of Indians and how many of them were engaged in the murders, and also if Chief Ignaco was at the Southern Agency with the main body of the tribe. No reply can possibly be received until to-morrow after-

DORSEY'S WORK EXPOSED

SHOWING UP THE STAR ROUTE SWINDLES IN OREGON.

THE EX-SENATOR'S IMPRUDENCE IN NOT PAYING AN AGENT—THE DIRECTIONS GIVEN FOR OBTAINING PETITIONS AND MAKING BIDS—DORSEY FULLY IDENTIFIED WITH THE BUSINESS.

SAN FRANCISCO, May 10.—A dispatch from Portland, Oregon, says: "The telegrams from Denver, Col., which have been published, giving information that legal proceedings had been commenced against ex-Senator Dorsey, of Arkansas, now Secretary of the National Republican Committee, for services rendered to obtain an increase of mail service and get additional pay therefor on the star routes in Oregon, attracted much attention here, the more, so from the fact that it was stated that the papers on which the suit had been instituted at Denver had been received there from a well-known attorney at Portland, and that the claimant was a well-known politician here. The *Oregonian* set on foot an inquiry to-day and got to the bottom of the transaction, and the history of it fully identifies ex-Senator Dorsey with the star route business. The claimant in the suit is Frank R. Wilcox, who, though formerly connected with politics in Arkansas, has not appeared prominently in politics here. He went to Arkansas from Illinois in 1869, and became acquainted with S. W. Dorsey there. He was the Secretary of the State Republican Committee of Arkansas, though he never held other office, and bore a prominent part in the election of Dorsey to the Senate. Desiring to get out of politics, he left Arkansas and came to Oregon in 1877. When Dorsey began to operate in star routes in Oregon he remembered that Wilcox had come to this State, and, as his relations with him had been of the most intimate kind, he fixed upon Wilcox as the man to help him work up to higher figures the mail routes in which he had become interested. Dorsey first telegraphed to persons in Portland to learn if Wilcox was here. Having ascertained that he was, he wrote him, stating what service he wanted performed, and directed him to go to Eugene City, giving him instructions at the same time how to get up petitions, have them signed, and make sub-contracts for carrying the mails. The petitions were to be forwarded to Washington to be used in getting service and the pay increased for the service required. Wilcox was to receive $5 a day and his expenses. Before starting for Eugene City he received the following telegram:

WASHINGTON, D. C., April 26, 1879.

F. R. Wilcox:

All my other letters written to Eugene City. Have telegraphed office. Go immediately.

S. W. DORSEY.

"Money being received for expenses, Wilcox went to Eugene City, where he received Dorsey's other letters, with memoranda directing him how to proceed. The route Dorsey first wished to operate on was out from Eugene City, across the Cascade Mountains, to

est I can get. Contract was closed at $11,000 for six trips.'

"Though Dorsey telegraphed Wilcox that he was interested only in the Bridge Creek and Looking-glass routes in Oregon, the statement is probably to be understood only as a notice to Wilcox that these were the only routes that he (Wilcox) was to work upon, for the greatest swindle of all is in the route from Dalles to Baker City, by way of Cañon City, which stands also in the name of J. M. Peck, Dorsey's brother-in-law. Already there was a route from Dalles to Baker City, and from Pendleton to Lagrange, or parallel to this one, which carried and still carries all the mails between the two points. This route from Dalles to Baker City, by way of Cañon City, was, however, under the manipulation of the ring to increase the service to six times a week, which was wholly unnecessary, and the pay was raised from $8,288 to $72,520. J. M. Peck also has another expedited route, viz., from Cañon City to Camp McDermitt, most of the way through a country without population, and incapable of sustaining any. This route was expedited from $2,888 to $21,500. J. M. Dorsey, a brother of S. W. Dorsey, has the contract on the route from Dalles to Lakeview, in Southern Oregon, which route also was expedited from $3,088 to $20,300. It is probable, therefore that Wilcox had charge of only a small part of the business of the Dorsey ring in Oregon."

The *Oregonian* of to-morrow will say of the developments in the star route frauds:

"Ex-Senator Dorsey will hardly ask the Post-master-General now to write a letter exonerating him. George A. Steele, who has been nominated for the Postmastership of Portland, was the Special Agent of the Post Office Department for Oregon, Washington, and Idaho at the time when the star service was so largely expedited, and the pay on many routes so immensely and fraudulently increased. He knew all about these transactions, as he had his attention called to them, and especially to the route from Dalles to Baker City, via Cañon City, which route was expedited from $8,288 to $42,500. It would be a pertinent inquiry to learn what was the nature of his reports to the department on these routes and what recommendation he made. Did he help the contractors to work up these routes and get their enormous increase of pay, or did he expose its iniquities to the department? Just now, since he expects to be Postmaster of Portland, these are pertinent inquiries. We venture the opinion, and that without special hazard, that, as a post official, he threw no obstacles in the way of the 'expediting' contractors."

The Portland dispatch adds: "The Dorsey suit was begun at Denver for the reason that the plaintiff was able to get service on Dorsey there. Wilcox is still in Oregon. The attorney who sent the claim from Portland to Denver to be sued is J. H. Woodward, formerly County Judge of this (Multnomah) county. The original documents printed above are here in custody of the agent of the Associated Press."

USELESS SERVICE STOPPED.

AN ORDER DISCONTINUING EIGHT STEAM-BOAT ROUTES IN THE SOUTH.

WASHINGTON, May 10.—Orders were issued to-day by the Post Office Department discontinuing steam-boat mail service forthwith on the following routes in the South and South-west: Memphis, Tenn., to Wittsburg, Ark., 140 miles; cost of service, $12,133 per annum. Camden, Ark., to New-Orleans, 671 miles; cost of service, $30,000. Jacksonport, Ark., to Batesville, Ark., 50 miles; cost of service, $3,959. Little Rock to Fort Smith, Ark., 260 miles; cost of service, $9,000. Service on the following steam-boat routes will be discontinued on Aug. 1: Elizabeth City to Fairfield, N. C., 100 miles; cost of service, $5,374 per annum, and from Elizabeth City to Williamston, N. C., 120 miles; cost of service, $11,779. Point Clear to Gasque, Ala., 47 miles; cost of service, $3,584. Mobile to Selma, 310 miles;

AFFAIRS IN FOREIGN LANDS

THE MARCH OF EVENTS IN THE RUSSIAN EMPIRE.

SIGNIFICANCE AND EXTENT OF THE RISING AGAINST THE JEWS—THE UKASE MODIFYING PEASANTS' RENTS AND PROVIDING FOR TRANSFERS TO THE WORKING CLASSES.

ST. PETERSBURG, May 10.—The *Official Messenger* says: "Disturbances at Kieff began at noon on the 8th inst. Several Jews were injured and some booths and shops were pillaged. The military restored order and arrested 500 persons. The disturbances were renewed on Monday, but were suppressed by the troops, when a woman was killed and several other persons were injured.

The *Journal de St. Petersburg* states that the Russian troops escorting the family of the Ameer, Abdurrahman Khan, will only proceed as far as Nasari Shereef, the first frontier town.

The ukase relative to peasants' rents, the terms of which have been settled, is expected to be issued in a few days. Gen. Melikoff and M. d'Abaza have been its principal promoters. Experience of 20 years has shown that the payments imposed upon peasants for land received at the time of the emancipation of the serfs brought much more benefit to the landed proprietors than to the peasants. In many cases these payments amount to more than the whole income capable of being derived from the land. The ukase will decree that proprietors and peasants may come to a voluntary agreement for the complete transfer of ownership to peasants until Jan. 1, 1883, when the period of obligatory transfer will begin. In the meantime, the annual payments will be reduced forthwith to a rate which the peasants are able to pay, and assistance will be afforded them to redeem their holdings. The Government will assume the payment of 9,000,000 rubles annually to indemnify the proprietors for the reduced payments received from the peasants, which will be taken from the accumulated profits of the State Bank, now amounting to about 100,000,000 rubles.

Prof. Dragemanoff writes to the *Pall Mall Gazette* from Geneva: "The significance of the recent anti-Jewish rising in Russia is much underrated. It extends through the Ukraine, which is full of Jews, between whom and the peasantry there has been an undying hatred for centuries. The trouble does not originate in religious animosity. It is purely social. It is the beginning of a social war, long foreseen by those familiar with the condition of the Ukraine. It may assume frightful proportions. Of the 3,000,000 Jews in Russia, an immense majority are crowded together in the towns and cities of the South and West. In many towns they form a majority of the population. Through their hereditary vocations as usurers, spirit dealers, traders, &c., they have made themselves masters alike of the indebted landlords and of the unfortunate peasants. It is the deep-rooted detestation of the peasant for the money-lender which is breaking out in the Ukraine."

The Russian imperial yacht Livadia has left Ferrol for Gibraltar.

LONDON, May 11.—A correspondent at Paris telegraphs a letter from a well-informed correspondent in Russia, who says it would be vain to attempt to describe the situation at Elizabethgrad. The town looks as if it had been devastated by a hurricane. Whole streets are literally razed. All the Jews' houses and shops have been sacked. Bonds have been stolen and destroyed. People hitherto well off are beggars. Thousands of Jews are homeless and are subsisting on charity. Many were

be fatal to Mr. Dillon. Mr. Gladstone supported Mr. Forster's refusal, and said the Government would be prepared to meet a direct indictment, but objected to being led into a vague discussion on a motion for adjournment. After a general discussion, in which Mr. Joseph Cowen, Radical Reformer, joined the Irish members in condemning the Government, the motion for adjournment was agreed to.

Mr. John Bright, in his speech in the House of Commons last night, said that if a great fleet assembled at Cork or Galway, offered free passage to the whole population of Connaught, (not Ireland,) it was probable that all, certainly half, would find their way to the United States.

The *Daily News* says: "There is great dissatisfaction among the Irish in London at Cardinal Manning's order forbidding any Catholic club-rooms to be used for meetings of the Land League. Some public expression regarding the matter is probable."

The transport Holland, which arrived at Portsmouth to-day, has been ordered immediately to convey three companies of marines to Ireland.

DUBLIN, May 10.—The *Gazette* declares that the metropolitan district of Dublin, Belfast, and the Baronies of Upper and Middle Dungannon have been proclaimed under the provisions of the Arms act.

At the Land League meeting here to-day, the receipt was acknowledged of £2,900 during the past week, all of which was from America, except £500. Secretary Brennan said it was decided that a convention should be held as soon as the Land bill passed its second stage.

Mr. Parnell has written to Archbishop Croke that he would have hesitated to recommend abstention from voting on the Land bill, but it was abundantly clear that it would not endanger the bill. In the absence of any suitable declaration by the Government, he was bound to urge the maintenance of the attitude of abstention and take care that the just claims of his party were not compromised by the too easy acceptance of an imperfect, and, in some cases, perhaps, mischievous measure.

CURRENT FOREIGN TOPICS.

CAPETOWN, May 10.—The *Cape Times* has a telegram stating that the Basutos have rejected the award of Sir Hercules Robinson.

NEWCASTLE, Natal, May 10.—The Royal Commission, appointed to consider and settle all points left in abeyance at the treaty of peace with the Boers, has formally opened its session. It has been decided to exclude representatives of the press from the sittings of the commission.

LONDON, May 10.—Adelina Patti has recovered from her recent illness, and has arrived in London for the opera season.

The brooch lost by Baroness Burdett-Coutts at the Queen's "drawing-room" on Tuesday last has been found at Buckingham Palace.

The papers warmly praise the tone and matter of Mr. Gladstone's speech in the House of Commons yesterday on moving a memorial to Lord Beaconsfield.

The party installed in power by the proclamation of Prince Alexander of Bulgaria is Russian and Conservative. The dismissed Ministers are the leaders of the Radical Young Bulgarian Party.

The London correspondents of the provincial press renew the rumors about Mr. Gladstone's partial or complete retirement. The rumors are probably occasioned by his recent illness.

For the Chairmanship of the Congregational Union of England and Wales, which has occasioned a heated contest, the Rev. J. A. Mac-

DINING WITH MERCHANTS

SPEECHES OF THE CHAMBER OF COMMERCE GUESTS.

SECRETARY WINDOM ON RECENT SUCCESS WITH BONDS AT THREE AND A HALF PER CENT.—REMARKS BY POSTMASTER-GENERAL JAMES—LETTERS AND OTHER SPEECHES.

The one hundred and thirteenth anniversary of the Chamber of Commerce of the City of New-York was celebrated last night by the usual annual dinner of the chamber at Delmonico's, Twenty-sixth-street and Fifth-avenue. The large banquet-hall on the second floor was decorated in a manner befitting the occasion. The walls were draped with American flags, and the tables were set off by baskets of flowers, bouquets, and pieces representing the industries of the nation. The main table, reserved for the presiding officer and the more distinguished guests, was spread on the west side of the hall, running north and south. Over this hung the great seal of the Chamber of Commerce, and upon it rested baskets of flowers and two set pieces, one representing an elevator, with a canal-boat anchored at its side, and the other a train of cars passing over a rocky promontory. The balcony in which the band was stationed was draped with the American flag, and in addition to this a forest of evergreens rose from its railing, completely hiding the musicians from sight. At each cover a button-hole bouquet was neatly entwined in the folds of the napkin, and these small bunches of flowers, combined with the baskets which were distributed all over the tables, made the air fragrant with perfume. Five long tables, running east and west from the main table, were lettered A, B, C, D, and E, and each accommodated 45 guests. The main table was presided over, in the absence of President S. D. Babcock, by James M. Brown, Vice-President of the chamber. On his right were the Hon. William Windom, Secretary of the Treasury; the Hon. Levi P. Morton, the Rev. Dr. W. F. Watkins, the Hon. Henry S. Sanford, Chauncey M. Depew, W. H. Draper, M. D., the Hon. Nathaniel Shipman, Gen. S. L. Woodford, Judge A. R. Lawrence, and Parke Godwin. On the left were Postmaster-General Thomas L. James, Judge Noah Davis, the Hon. S. B. Chittenden, the Rev. Dr. W. M. Taylor, Prof. J. J. White, the Rev. Dr. G. D. Wildes, the Hon. Marshall Jewell, Judge Enoch L. Fancher, and Controller Allan Campbell. The following are among the gentlemen who occupied the five other tables: James H. Stebbins, Daniel Drake Smith, Jackson S. Schultz, Benjamin B. Sherman, Jerome B. Wheeler, Daniel S. Appleton, Gen. Anson G. McCook, Morris K. Jesup, William E. Dodge, Jr., Joseph H. Brown, M. W. Cooper, Postmaster Henry G. Pearson, Daniel C. Robbins, Clinton B. Fisk, Elliott F. Shepard, Henry C. Robinson, John Austin Stevens, Asa W. Tenney, Horace Porter, Thomas Hillhouse, C. R. Agnew, M. D., David Dows, Josiah M. Fiske, David M. Stone, Erastus Brooks, Silas W. Burt, Gen. Edwin A. Merritt, J. Nelson Tappan, Charles L. Tiffany, George Jones, Francis B. Thurber, A. S. Sullivan, Frederick L. Talcott, John T. Agnew, Franklin Edson, Gustav Schwab, Luther Kountze, Adrian Iselin, Gen. B. H. Bristow, John H. Starin.

The invited guests began to assemble in the parlor at 6:30, and a half-hour was passed in social converse before the march to the dining-room began. At 7 o'clock the gentlemen entered the banquet hall. James M. Brown, the Vice-President, led the procession, with Secretary Windom on his arm, and the rest of the guests followed in regular

...night, although the most industrious inquiry fails to discover that there is anything tangible on which to base the apparent confidence now exhibited in a satisfactory adjustment. A report is being circulated to the effect that it was suggested in the caucus to-day that harmony might be secured by withdrawing the names of Judge Robertson and William E. Chandler and then nominating the latter for Collector at New-York and the former for Solicitor-General. A proposition of this kind was made some time ago to the President by Senator Blair, of New-Hampshire, but it did not receive any consideration from the President. It may have been brought forward in the caucus to-day by Mr. Blair, but if so it made no impression, and it is certain that the proposition is not what has excited the hope that the threatened contest may be avoided. No time was fixed for another meeting of the caucus, and as several Republican Senators will leave the city to-morrow for the remainder of the week, it is not likely that another meeting will be called before next Monday or Tuesday.

At the meeting yesterday Mr. Edmunds offered a resolution to postpone the consideration of Robertson's nomination until December, and supported it in an earnest speech. To-day Mr. Edmunds withdrew his resolution and the Administration Senators say he did so for the reason that he became convinced that it would be defeated. These gentlemen say further, that a careful poll of the Republican side has been made, and that the result shows that fully three-fourths of the entire number of Republican Senators will vote to confirm Robertson's nomination.

THE SUPREME BENCH VACANCY.

MR. MATTHEWS'S NOMINATION LIKELY TO BE CONSIDERED TO-DAY.

WASHINGTON, May 10.—The nomination of Stanley Matthews to be Associate Justice of the United States Supreme Court, which was adversely reported yesterday by the Committee on the Judiciary, is expected to be taken up by the Senate for consideration to-morrow. There is an understanding among Senators on both sides that this nomination shall be fairly and fully considered, and that while no captious opposition shall be manifested on the one hand, no attempt shall be made on the other to take any advantage to force a vote, until the fullest opportunity has been given to consider the general fitness of Mr. Matthews for a seat on the Supreme Bench. Some of the strongest men on both sides of the chamber will oppose Mr. Matthews's confirmation, and among these Messrs. Edmunds and Bayard will be prominent. The opposition to Mr. Matthews is mainly based on his well-known opinions touching the questions at issue between the United States and the subsidized railroad companies, which opinions are in favor of the corporations, and were advanced with all Mr. Matthews's force and ability in the Senate when a member of that body. The contest over this nomination is likely to be continued through two or more sittings of the Senate. The friends of Mr. Matthews are confident that he will get through by a small majority. Gov. Foster, of Ohio, is here, working earnestly to secure his confirmation.

NOTES FROM WASHINGTON.

WASHINGTON, May 10, 1881.

The national bank notes received for redemption to-day amounted to $432,000.

The receipts from internal revenue to-day were $275,134 66, and from Customs, $654,259 13.

The Secretary of the Treasury has written a letter to Thomas H. Wells, Chairman of the Committee of Hoop-iron Manufacturers, at Youngstown, Ohio, in which he adheres to the decision of ex-Secretary Sherman in 1881, on the subject of duty on cotton-ties.

It is understood at the Post Office Department that the President and Postmaster-General have decided, since Mr. Grier declined to accept the position of Third Assistant Postmaster-General, not to make the contemplated changes in the offices of Third Assistant Postmaster-General and Assistant Attorney-General for the Post Office Department. The nomination of Mr. Hazen to be Assistant Attorney-General for the department will, it is understood, be withdrawn, and he will remain in his present position. Judge Freeman, whose resignation

...answered the Governor, saying the report seems incredible, as Durango is only 14 miles from Fort Lewis, where four companies of infantry and one of cavalry are stationed, and if an outbreak had occurred as far back as May 5 he would have been given notice by Commander F. N. Lewis, and states that reports received by him to-day from Uncompahgre, at the White River Agencies, indicate everything peaceable. Nine companies of regular troops left Kansas City for Uncompahgre to-day.

MRS. LOCKWOOD IN MARYLAND.

A CARROLL COUNTY JUDGE REFUSES TO ADMIT HER TO PRACTICE.

BALTIMORE, May 10.—Mrs. Belva Lockwood, the Washington female lawyer, yesterday applied for admission to the Bar of the Carroll County Court, at Westminster, Md. To-day Judge Hayden, presiding, denied her application for admission and reviewed the law of the State upon the subject. Mrs. Lockwood, in her argument for her admission yesterday, rested her case upon section 6 of article 59 of the Revised Code, which says that upon the application of any lawyer, who may have practiced or have been licensed to practice in any other State, District or Territory of the United States, for admission to practice in the courts of this State, it shall be the duty of the court to whom he shall apply to admit him upon the same terms that a citizen of Maryland would be admitted to the courts of the State, District, or Territory in which such applicant may have practiced. In this section the words "he" and "him" are used, and upon this point Mrs. Lockwood referred the court to rule 6 of the rules of interpretation of the Code, to the effect that "the masculine includes all genders, except where such construction would be absurd and unreasonable." Judge Hayden ruled adversely to her application, on the ground that it would be absurd in this section to make the pronouns he and him refer to any but the masculine gender. This decision created much comment, as Mrs. Lockwood has already been admitted to practice in the United States District Court at Baltimore and in the Circuit Court of Frederick County, in this State.

SMALL-POX IN A DELAWARE CITY.

WILMINGTON, Del., May 10.—The small-pox is prevalent in this city to an alarming extent, and at the opening of the May term of the Newcastle County criminal courts here, yesterday, the Judges were officially informed by the Trustees of the Poor of the state of affairs, in order that they might adjourn the court without doing any business if they deemed it proper. The Trustees, in a letter to the Chief-Justice, called attention to the fact that a large number of cases were now under treatment at the hospital connected with the Almshouse, and that there were about 75 cases in various parts of the town, and expressed fear that the assembling of a large crowd of witnesses and spectators, belonging in large part to the lower classes, among which the disease is principally raging, would tend to spread the pestilence through the rural districts and uninfected parts of the city. The court concluded to proceed with business as usual. A panic was created among the waiting crowd before the court opened by the presence of a man believed to have been suffering from small-pox in a light form. A boy who lives in a house where there are several cases of the disease was also noticed in the court-room. Both were immediately removed.

A MURDER LEFT IN MYSTERY.

SCRANTON, Penn., May, 10.—The Coroner's jury was busy here all day investigating what is pronounced a mysterious murder. The victim was found Sunday morning in Washington-avenue, in the most central part of the city, with his skull cracked. A woman on her way to early mass was the first to see him. Although alive, he was unable to speak, and the Police took him to the Lackawanna Hospital, where he died last evening. Nobody knows who he is or how he came to his death, although the testimony given before the jury to-day as to the nature of his wounds goes to show that he was foully dealt with. His pockets were empty, and nothing was found on his person to furnish a clue to his identification or show where he came from. The jury did not complete its labors to-day, as the authorities are determined on making the investigation as thorough as possible.

ELECTION AT LONG BRANCH.

LONG BRANCH, N. J., May 10.—There was a heated contest for Mayor and Commissioners to-day. The "regular" ticket was successful. The Mayor and Board of Commissioners chosen embrace the old board, namely, Mayor Thomas R. Woolley, and Commissioners Thomas McKenna, Benajah Layton, and R. V. Breece. According to the Long Branch charter, three Commissioners to represent the property-holders who are non-residents are appointed by the Justice of the Supreme Court. The appointed Commissioners are R. J. Dobbins, Charles Brown, and George W. Brown.

...tures were to be obtained and forwarded to the Postmaster-General:

'We, the undersigned citizens of Bridge Creek, Oregon, beg to earnestly recommend to your favorable consideration an increase of mail service between Eugene City and this place to a daily line, and ask that the speed be greatly increased. This route supplies a large and rapidly increasing population, and is the sole means of conveying intelligence to a great portion of Southern Oregon. We believe the public interest will be greatly subserved by an early increase of this service, and we earnestly recommend it.'

"To this Dorsey added the following words of instruction to Wilcox:

'Of course you want the wording as well as the handwriting of each person to be as different as possible.'

"Dorsey next proceeded to instruct Wilcox how to sub-let routes, as the following telegram shows:

WASHINGTON, April 23, 1879.

To F. R. Wilcox, Eugene City:

Make contract for Bridge Creek route for speed of four and a half miles an hour, three trips a week—no sub-contract to be filed, but payment to be guaranteed by me personally. Make the same contract on the Looking-glass route. Send result to S. W. DORSEY.

"The following was the next telegram received by Wilcox:

WASHINGTON, April 28, 1879.

To F. R. Wilcox:

Make no compromise with sub-contractors; must be absolutely new contract, with amounts specially stated. Telegraph fully upon closing contracts. S. W. DORSEY.

"Fearing that Wilcox would not fully understand, Dorsey at a later hour on the same day telegraphed as follows:

WASHINGTON, April 28, 1879.

F. R. Wilcox:

New contract becomes necessary because the old firm is dissolved and business passes into new hands. Must have new contract or no pay. Make contract on Bridge Creek route for three, six, and seven trips on schedule of four miles an hour; also, the same on Looking-glass route. Telegraph me fully before closing any contract. Deal with responsible men. S. W. DORSEY.

"Here the old trick is apparent. The old firm is dissolved, that is, the straw bidder was pushed out of the way, and the ring was now making its next move. Here is the next telegram:

WASHINGTON, D. C., May 3, 1879.

To F. R. Wilcox:

I have no interest in the star route except the Bridge Creek and Looking-glass contracts. On Bridge Creek, one, three, six, and seven times a week, on a schedule of 50 hours. On the prices named in my letter of the 16th, the department demands four miles an hour speed, and you must make a contract covering that speed or more. Do not leave out the following: Three times, $8,000; six times, $15,000; seven times, $16,500. Telegraph me fully before you close the contract.

S. W. DORSEY.

"The following is the last telegram sent to Wilcox at Eugene City:

WASHINGTON, May 3, 1879.

F. R. Wilcox:

I presume you understand you must make contracts before you try to get up papers for increase.

S. W. DORSEY.

"As a result of these operations by Dorsey in the Oregon mail contracts, he got the compensation for carrying the route from Eugene City to Bridge Creek increased from $2,468 to $21,460. The contract stands in the department as received from Eugene City to Mitchell, and is in the name of J. M. Peck, a brother-in-law of S. W. Dorsey. The Looking-glass route, so frequently referred to in the above dispatches, was 'expedited' under Dorsey's management from $1,800 to $13,475 a year.

"The next question was to get the route in Washington Territory 'expedited.' This was the route from Wallula to Pleasant Grove, on the Upper Yakima. Under directions from Dorsey, Wilcox went to Wallula on an errand similar to that which he had performed at Eugene City, where Dorsey telegraphed him as follows:

WASHINGTON, June 10, 1879.

F. R. Wilcox, Wallula:

Have you done anything with the Wallula and Pleasant Grove route? Answer.

"To this Wilcox returned the following:

WALLULA, Washington Territory, June 10, 1879.

Hon. S. W. Dorsey, No. 1,121 I-street, Washington, D. C.:

Have been over the route from Wallula to Pleasant Grove. Your figures are impossible. The lowest solid bids are $2,500 for two trips, $6,000 for three trips, $11,000 for six trips, $12,500 for seven trips. What shall I do? F. R. WILCOX.

"To this the following answer was returned:

WASHINGTON, D. C., June 11, 1879.

To F. R. Wilcox:

You may give $1,800 one trip, $5,000 three trips, $8,400 for six trips, and $9,000 for seven trips.

S. W. DORSEY.

"Wilcox replied on the same day.

'Your figures impossible. Mine of yesterday low-

...can be satisfactorily performed over the star routes alone by simply extending them in a few localities. These extensions can be made in every instance at a very slight expense, compared with the cost of the steam-boat service, which will be discontinued. The aggregate cost of the service on these eight steam-boat routes is nearly $82,000 per annum, and it is estimated at the department that the extension of the star routes necessary to cover the points not now touched by them will not cost more than $7,000, and thus a yearly saving of $75,000 will be effected. In addition to the routes mentioned, a score or more of short routes in the South and South-west, which have been maintained at a cost varying from $100 to $500 per annum, will be discontinued at an early date. Other and larger reductions of what the department regards as unnecessary routes in various sections of the country may be expected from time to time.

THE SILVER PROBLEM.

DISCUSSIONS IN THE PARIS CONFERENCE—INDIA'S POSITION.

PARIS, May 10.—Signor Luzatti, Italian delegate, who was the chief speaker at the Monetary Conference to-day, while highly complimenting M. Pirmez, Belgian delegate, on his knowledge of finance, pointed out that the view he expressed at Saturday's sitting on the monetary situation of England, Germany, and the British Indies was, in some respects, a mistaken one. The present state of the money market, Signor Luzatti said, amounted to a monetary crisis. While the value of silver has been depreciated by the laws of the various countries, it was clear that gold was not sufficiently abundant to be adopted by all civilized nations as a single standard. He reviewed the causes of the power of the United States for absorbing gold, and rectified some inaccuracies which had been committed in estimating the losses which the action of bi-metallism had entailed upon France.

MM. Burckhard and Bischoff dwelt upon the disappearance of gold from Switzerland, and urged the necessity for improving penal legislation.

M. Thoerner, Russian representative, advocated monometallism, but said he recognized the necessity for a subsidiary employment of silver. M. Ruscons advocated bi-metallism.

Thirty-four delegates were present, including Sir Louis Mallet. The next meeting will be held on Thursday, when M. Cernuschi, Mr. Dana Horton, and Signor Seismit-Doda will speak.

LONDON, May 10.—The *Times* says: "The suggestion at the Monetary Conference by M. Cernuschi, French delegate, that an international subscription should recoup Germany the sum of £4,000,000 lost by selling silver caused amusement in banking circles."

In the House of Commons to-day Mr. Gladstone, in reply to a question, said India was represented at the Monetary Conference after America and France had accepted the terms under which she was willing to be represented, namely, that she would not thereby be committed to any resolution taken, but all proposals would have favorable consideration with a view to the re-establishment of the value of silver.

MR. BRADLAUGH AGAIN EJECTED.

HE DEMANDS TO BE SWORN AND IS EXPELLED BY A VOTE OF THE HOUSE.

LONDON, May 10.—In the House of Commons to-day Mr. Bradlaugh again advanced to the bar to be sworn. The Speaker ordered him to withdraw. He refused to do so, when the Sergeant-at-Arms, at the Speaker's request, approached and touched Mr. Bradlaugh on the shoulder. He still refused to withdraw. Sir Stafford Northcote then moved that he be excluded from the precincts of the House until he promised that he would not further disturb the proceedings of the House. Mr. Gladstone said that Mr. Bradlaugh had a statutory right to come to the bar of the House. Mr. Labouchere, (Advanced Liberal,) member for Northampton, said he would like to know the real meaning of Sir Stafford Northcote's resolution. Sir Stafford Northcote explained that he proposed that Mr. Bradlaugh should not be permitted to enter the door until he gave an undertaking not to disturb the proceedings of the House. The motion was put and carried without a division. Mr. Bradlaugh then left the House.

A GALA DAY AT THE AUSTRIAN CAPITAL—THE WEDDING PROCESSION AND CEREMONIES.

VIENNA, May 10.—The marriage of the Crown Prince Rudolph, of Austria, and the Princess Stephanie, of Belgium, was most imposingly solemnized at the Church of St. Augustine to-day. An immense multitude collected in the streets through which the imperial and royal personages proceeded to the church.

The weather was cold, but not rainy. At 11 o'clock the procession started from the palace and proceeded to the church in the following order: The Archdukes and foreign Princes, in full uniform, walking in pairs, followed by Prince Rudolph in the uniform of a Major-General. Then came the Emperor Francis Joseph, having on his right the King of the Belgians, both being in Generals' uniforms. Then came the bride, with the Empress of Austria and the Queen of the Belgians on either hand. The trains of the three ladies were borne by the principal ladies-in-waiting. Princess Stephanie wore a magnificent robe of cloth of silver, with a train elaborate in embroidery, orange blossoms arranged in bunches looping up the dress, and a veil of Brussels lace specially made for the occasion. Her mother, the Queen, wore a blue velvet dress, trimmed with lace, and the Empress wore a pale gray dress, trimmed with Brussels point lace. The trains of the foreign Princesses and Archduchesses were borne by pages and ladies of the palace. Another group of officers completed the procession.

An hour before the commencement of the ceremony the church was densely crowded by a brilliant assembly. A *fanfare* of trumpets signaled the arrival of the bridal party at the church door, where they were received by Cardinal von Schwarzenberg at the head of his clergy. Their Majesties took seats under a canopy over a throne. The bridal pair proceeded to the places before the sanctuary rails, where they offered a short prayer. After a brief address from the Cardinal, the marriage ceremony was proceeded with. At the moment the rings were exchanged peals broke forth from the bells of the city and salvos of artillery were fired. At the conclusion of the ceremony a Te Deum was sung, after which the Hofburg choir executed an old German march. The newly married pair, accompanied by the other imperial and royal personages, then returned to the City Palace of the Hofburg.

The Church of St. Augustine, where the marriage ceremony was performed, is the church of the imperial household.

In commemoration of the marriage the Emperor Francis Joseph has founded 22 scholarships at various schools and has given 100,000 florins for the free admission of 10 pupils to the establishment for the education of the daughters of officers. He has also granted complete or partial amnesty to 331 persons imprisoned for various offenses.

All the diplomats, Generals, and other dignitaries assembled in the Hofburg this afternoon and were presented to Prince Rudolph and his bride, who later in the day departed for the Château of Laxenberg, where they arrived at 7 o'clock this evening. They were enthusiastically welcomed by the people, and the town was illuminated. The Prince and Princess of Prussia bade them farewell during the afternoon, and will leave for Berlin to-morrow. The Prince of Wales will proceed to Pesth, to be present at the entry of Rudolph and Stephanie.

The bridal procession walked from the Hofburg Palace to the Church of St. Augustine through the Argus Passage, which route is always used on such occasions. The display in the church was magnificent; daylight was excluded and the sacred edifice was lighted with countless small gas-jets around the pillars and walls. Their Majesties were much affected when they embraced the bride and bridegroom after the ceremony. The Archbishop of Vienna and Primate of Hungary assisted Cardinal Schwarzenberg.

THE TROUBLES OF IRELAND.

A REFUSAL TO EXPLAIN DILLON'S ARREST—ENFORCING THE ARMS ACT.

LONDON, May 10.—In the House of Commons to-night Mr. Parnell asked the Government to state the precise acts for which Mr. Dillon was arrested. Mr. Forster, Chief Secretary for Ireland, refused to make such an exception in favor of Mr. Dillon. Mr. Parnell then moved an adjournment of the House, and declared that lengthened confinement would probably

...quired concerning the recent rumors of his resignation, saying he does not differ from his colleagues regarding the oath question; does not believe that the House of Commons ought to set up a test against any particular individual, and does not see how the House of Commons can refuse to grant the same option to affirm as is now granted by law courts.

The *Globe* says of the different methods of Booth and Irving, that the latter's are more imaginative and impulsive and Booth's more finished and correct. There is scarcely a point of resemblance between them. Booth's Othello is more virile and conceivable, and Irving's more ideal and sympathetic. Booth's Iago is more human in his villainy, while Irving's has a grotesque quasi-imaginative diabolism suggestive of an origin scarcely more human than Caliban's.

Alexander Jonas, editor of the New-York *Volks Zeitung*, was recently arrested at Dresden. He was suspected of traveling in the interest of the Socialists. His baggage was searched, his private papers taken, and he was not allowed to leave Dresden. After nine days, however, his papers were restored, as no proof of the alleged suspicion was found. He has now applied to Mr. White, United States Minister at Berlin, for redress. Mr. White has submitted the matter to the Berlin Foreign Office.

A dispatch from Rome says the rumors that the French troops are close to Tunis have caused extraordinary excitement in Parliamentary circles. Signor Cairoli has conferred with the other leaders of the Left. Party differences for the moment are dissipated.

TUNIS, May 10.—The Bey has sent a circular to the provincial authorities stating that the dispute with France will be settled by diplomacy, and announcing that he is occupied with the matter in concert with the Porte and the powers.

LONDON, May 11.—The *Post* says: "Adelina Patti intends to give farewell performances in London and on the Continent next season and conclude her operatic career with an eight months' tour in America."

A Newcastle, Natal, correspondent says the question of punishment for acts contrary to civilized warfare was the first subject which came before the Royal Commission. The Boers and natives have commenced hostilities on the western border.

The *Times* says: "On the whole we are inclined to place Booth's Iago above Irving's as a work of art and a piece of technical skill. The parts cohere better, the colors are more skillfully blended. It is, perhaps less startling and brilliant, perhaps, to minds imbued with a yearning for novelty tamer, but, as a whole, we think, more artistic. Irving's soliloquies, however, are superior."

SUICIDE OF A MORPHINE-EATER.

MEMPHIS, Tenn., May 10.—At 4 o'clock this afternoon William Simms, formerly employed as a druggist, went to Father William Walsh, who resides in the parsonage adjoining St. Bridget's Church, at Third and Overton streets, and related a story of trouble between himself and his wife. After patiently listening to him, and as Simms was laboring under great mental excitement, Father Walsh told him to lie down on a sofa in the study and said he would go and see Mrs. Simms and arrange matters between them. Simms complied, and Father Walsh, after locking the door to prevent him from being disturbed, called on Mrs. Simms. Returning an hour later, Father Walsh was horrified, on entering the study, to find Simms lying dead on the floor with his throat cut from ear to ear. The deceased man was a confirmed morphine eater, and was under the influence of that drug when he committed the act.

WILLIAM PENN'S REMAINS.

HARRISBURG, May 10.—In the State Senate to-day a resolution was unanimously agreed to, and sent to the House for concurrence, looking to the transfer of the remains of William Penn from Jordan Meeting-house grave-yard, Buckinghamshire, England, to Philadelphia. The resolution also provides that copies be sent to Peter Penn Gaskell, of Ireland, and William Stewart, of England, representatives at law of William Penn, asking their co-operation in the matter, and requests the co-operation of the President of the United States, if necessary, in securing this object.

THE COWPENS MEMORIAL.

SPARTANBURG, S. C., May 10.—Senator Hampton and the Hon. T. W. Higginson, of Massachusetts, arrived here to-day, and will speak at the unveiling of the Cowpens monument to-morrow. Gov. Hagood is also here and will speak. The unveiling is to be done by young ladies descended from the heroes of the battle. The city is full of people, including many distinguished persons, and crowds are still pouring in.

...which Delmonico has spread during the present season. This required nearly three hours. At 9:30, Vice-President Brown called the gentlemen to order, and after expressing his regrets at the absence of President S. D. Babcock, he read a letter from him explaining that an attack of severe hoarseness prevented him from being present. After the reading of this letter the Rev. Dr. George D. Wildes made a brief speech, apologizing for the absence of President Babcock, and offering as a toast "the better health of the President of the Chamber of Commerce." This toast was drunk amid great enthusiasm. Acting President Brown then offered the first regular toast of the evening—"The President of the United States—now the chief magistrate of fifty millions of people." In answer to this the band played "Hail to the Chief," and Mr. Brown read the following letter:

EXECUTIVE MANSION,
WASHINGTON, April 30, 1881.

GENTLEMEN: It is with regret that I find it will be impossible for me to accept your kind invitation to be present at the one hundred and thirteenth anniversary banquet of the Chamber of Commerce at Delmonico's, on the 10th of May. Very truly yours,

J. A. GARFIELD.

SECRETARY WINDOM'S SPEECH.

The next toast was "The National Treasury—best honored in the integrity of its administration," and Secretary Windom arose to respond. He was greeted with a burst of applause which endangered the stability of the tables. Secretary Windom said:

"I am profoundly grateful to you for this kindly expression of feeling, and I am grateful to you also for the invitation to be present on this occasion. It is due to you, as well as to myself, however, to say that the extreme pressure of public duties which has been upon me for the last two or three weeks has utterly prevented anything like preparation of a speech such as I should otherwise be glad to deliver. It will, however, be to your interest, perhaps, that I have been thus pressed; for, had I found the opportunity to prepare it, I should probably have made a speech that would take me some minutes to deliver. As it is, having had no chance whatever to think upon the subject—for I have been engaged during the last three or four weeks discussing questions of appointments to clerkships in the Treasury Department—I shall be very brief.

"I appreciate, Mr. President and gentlemen, the opportunity of appearing before the merchants of New-York and participating with you in this magnificent banquet. For several years past I have devoted a great deal of attention to the industrial and commercial interests of the country, and I am intensely interested in everything that looks to their promotion. When I remember what a country we have, and the magnificence of its commercial metropolis, and when I look forward a little into the future and forecast what middle-aged men will live to see—that this is, I believe, now to be the greatest nation on the face of the earth, and New-York the leading commercial metropolis of the world. [Applause and loud cheering.] I say when I look forward to this event, which, I think, is in the near future, and remember that I am now in the presence of an organization 118 years old, outnumbering the days of the Republic, I feel a sense of pride and gratification which I cannot adequately express. I avail myself of this opportunity, however, to speak a little more directly to the subject of the toast to which I am called to respond—"The Treasury of the United States." When the present Administration came into power on the 4th of March it found a maturing debt of nearly $700,000,000, $200,000,000 of which (or $195,000,000 and over) bore 6 per cent. interest, and was payable on the first day of July next. About $470,000,000, bearing 5 per cent. interest, became redeemable on the first day of May, the present month, but not absolutely payable. The Administration found itself without any funding bill provided for the purpose of refunding this large amount of indebtedness. Two questions presented themselves.

First, shall an extra session of Congress be called for the purpose of meeting the emergency which would arise within two or three months, or shall some other mode be adopted which will obviate the necessity of an extra session of Congress and make the requisite provision for this debt? The President of the United States—and I think we all agree with him very well on that subject—recognized the fact that an extra session of Congress is a very expensive luxury; expensive not in the money cost, perhaps, but in the fact that during an extra session of Congress the business of the country is usually unsettled and deranged, and that business men dislike to embark in enterprises requiring large investments because they do not know what the effect of legislation may be upon the investments. But I need not tell you why an extra session of Congress is not regarded as very desirable, especially in midsummer. [Laughter.] It was, therefore, thought desirable to obviate it if possible, and then a plan must be adopted which would meet these bonds and preserve the credit of the United States. The plan adopted was one which would not disturb any of the business interests of the country, not jostle them nor jar them in the least, and which would not cost any considerable amount of money. It was a sort of self-acting, self-regulating process, and I am happy to announce to you to-night, Mr. President and gentlemen, the grand success which has followed the adoption of that policy. [Applause.] That $195,000,000 of 6 per cent. bonds, which would fall due on the 1st of July, were called, as you are aware, with the promise of payment on that day, but permission was given to the holders to come forward, if they desired to do so—as a favor to them—and accept 3½ per cent. interest, instead of having the

all the papers had been trying hard to find out the contents of the treaty in Washington and Madrid; but both governments were extremely reticent. At last it became known that the treaty had been completed, and that Minister Foster was bringing it home for presentation to the Senate.

Early in December, 1884, *The Times* received information that certain persons in Madrid were able, and would be willing, to communicate the text of the treaty, which they seem to have obtained through financial connections, to an American newspaper. At once *The Times* cabled a credit of $8000 to these men to cover cable tolls, necessary expenses, and whatever personal remuneration might be found suitable. The full text of the treaty was cabled back to *The Times*, at a cable rate of 66 cents a word, translated in the office, and published on December 8. It occupied five columns of the front page; and the rest of the page was taken up with as many expressions of opinion from business men as could be obtained on Sunday.

John W. Foster, on that morning, woke up in the downtown hotel to which he had been driven from the pier the night before, and upon opening his copy of *The Times* dived hastily under the bed and looked in his bag. To his certain knowledge the only copy of that treaty in the United States had been brought in by him the night before, and he could explain the publication in *The Times* only on the theory that somebody had gone through his baggage in the night. But his copy of the treaty was still there; and it was duly taken to Washington and laid before the Senate. By that time, however, men who had studied the

treaty had come to the conclusion that it did not give sufficient protection to American commercial interests; and its rejection by the Senate may be taken as the result principally of the prompt and full publication in *The Times*.

Another foreign news story on which *The Times* beat the town was the revolution in Brazil which overthrew the Emperor, Dom Pedro II. A feature of *The Times* which its readers could count on every Sunday was Harold Frederic's cable letter from London. In those simpler days only exceptional events in Europe were reported at any length as soon as they happened; the daily cables carried only a sort of skeleton of the news, and every New York paper depended on the weekly cable letters from London and Paris for general interpretative discussion of foreign affairs. In this field, of great importance in those days, Harold Frederic was in the eighties and nineties without superior, and his correspondence from London was one of the great features of *The Times*.

Toward the very end of Mr. Jones's life — in the early summer of 1891 — *The Times* undertook another crusade, this time against certain abuses in the New York Life Insurance Company. W. C. Van Antwerp, then a member of *The Times's* Wall Street staff and later president of the Stock Exchange, followed up a tip which had come to the paper with such amazing exposures that before long the officers of the company had filed personal libel suits against Jones and Miller for millions of dollars. These suits, naturally, had no consequence except to make *The Times* more diligent in proving its case; and the

affair ended in the board of directors of the company coming in a body to the office of the editor of *The Times*, and asking him to tell them how to clean house. As a result of this visit John A. McCall was elected president of the company and the necessary reforms were carried out.

The building which in 1857 had seemed preposterously expensive and unnecessarily large for a newspaper office was by this time too small. Construction of the second building erected by *The Times*, and the fourth home of the paper—which, like the first, was in its day the finest newspaper structure in the country—was begun in 1888 from designs by George B. Post, and involved an engineering feat which aroused much astonishment at the time. It was found impossible to move out temporarily while the old building was razed and a new one erected on the same spot, and it became necessary to tear down the old building and put up the new one at the same time, while the work of getting out the paper continued in the midst of the wreckers and rebuilders. Thus as the old building disappeared the new one gradually took shape in its place, and by April, 1889, the work of reconstruction was completed.

Mr. Jones was fond of saying in his later years that this building would be his monument. He was mistaken in that; it was soon surpassed in size and splendor by new skyscrapers, and before long it passed out of the control of *The Times*, though it continued to house the paper for a decade after it had ceased to be in fact the Times Building. He may have thought that the paper itself would be

another monument, but in that, too, he was mistaken; *The Times* fell into misfortune and had to be rebuilt by other men. His true monument is a house not made with hands; it is to be found in a better informed public opinion, a higher standard of public morality; in a city and a nation where workers for good government are no longer hopeless or afraid.

He died on August 12, 1891, at the age of eighty, having spent the last half of his life in *The Times* office. In the editorial appraisal of his work which appeared in the paper after his death it was said that

> his wish was that the newspaper should pay more attention to the worthy than to the unworthy side of human nature, that it should commend itself to right-thinking persons of some seriousness of mind and judgment rather than strive to satisfy the desire to know what the sinful and frivolous are about.

Further in that editorial it was stated that "no writer of *The Times* was ever required or asked to urge upon the public views which he did not accept himself." This ought to be true on every newspaper, and it is true on a good many — on more today than thirty years ago.

To the best of the knowledge and belief of the oldest members of the staff, it has always been true on *The Times*.

It is often supposed that the decline in the financial prosperity of *The Times* which set in in the early nineties had its origin years earlier, in the loss of Republican readers in 1884 and the reluctance of

Jones to adopt the new methods of a new age. As already suggested, there does not seem much ground for this belief. The ground lost in 1884 had been pretty nearly recovered within three or four years. What really started *The Times* downhill was the heavy expense of the new building. The annual profit dropped from well over $100,000 in the middle eighties to only $15,000 in 1890.

It was true that the business system of *The Times* was out of date. It had done well enough in the sixties and seventies, when making a newspaper was a much simpler and less expensive matter; but times had changed. Expenses — necessary expenses — were rising every year. Competition was keener, abler, and more vigorous than ever before; and *The Times* was at a disadvantage with some of its competitors whose methods of advertising themselves, and of gathering and presenting the news, were not handicapped by any ethical scruples. A business organization of the modern type the paper had never had — and had never needed so long as George Jones was alive. There was no sound system of cost accounting; nobody knew just what the paper was getting out of the money it spent. But if the machine was antiquated and rusty, Jones knew every peculiarity of its workings, and so long as he lived to run it he could get results. When he died and a new man took the wheel, the defects of the mechanism became painfully apparent.

The great majority of *The Times* stock was owned by Mr. Jones at his death, and left by him to his children, with the injunction, embodied in his will, that the paper should never be sold. Its active

direction was assumed by his son Gilbert, and his son-in-law, Henry L. Dyer. Gilbert E. Jones had been trained in *The Times* office for twenty years, but there are some things about newspaper management that cannot be learned, but must come by the gift of God. In one respect, indeed, Gilbert Jones was an expert. He knew a great deal about newspaper mechanics; but neither he nor Dyer could operate an outworn business mechanism and recover the money that had been sunk in the new building.

Also, *The Times* under George Jones had paid so well that his children were left with a good deal of property outside their stock in the paper. Naturally, when *The Times* began to lose they were somewhat reluctant to throw into it the money which would enable them to live on in independence and comfort aside from any consideration of its fortunes. It is hardly surprising that when it became apparent that the new management could not make the paper pay, the heirs began to think of disregarding the stipulation that they should hold on to the paper whether it proved to be a source of profit or a drain upon the fortunes of the family.

The reduction of the price to two cents, in 1883, had not brought the expected increase in circulation and had materially reduced the income. The two-cent *Times* was soon forced to compete with one-cent papers; and the stroke of genius which saved *The Times* in 1898 by reducing the price to one cent, and discovering a new army of readers in a field where it had been supposed there was no appetite for anything but the variegated and somewhat too highly flavored menu offered by some of the other papers,

was beyond the vision of the heirs of George Jones. The best they could do was to raise the price, and it was set at three cents in December, 1891. The result was a further loss in circulation, and before Jones had been dead a year his children were preparing to get rid of a property which had been a gold mine in his hands, but which they found only a burden.

It came to the knowledge of the editors of *The Times* late in 1892 that the paper was likely to be sold, and sold to a gentleman who, whatever his good qualities, could hardly be regarded as an entirely desirable chief by the men who had served Raymond and Jones. There were men on *The Times* who understood and valued its great traditions, who had given the best part of their lives as a contribution to its work, and who were unwilling to let that work come to nothing; and it was as a desperate resort that they undertook to buy the paper themselves, with the aid of their friends.

On April 13, 1893, *The Times* was sold to the New York Times Publishing Company, of which the president was Charles R. Miller, the editor of the paper. Mr. Miller and his associates, Edward Cary and George F. Spinney, had been the organizers of the new company. Some of the men associated with them in the ownership had come in because of personal friendship, others because they appreciated the continuing need for such a paper as *The Times*.

The price paid to the Jones estate was $1,000,000, and it bought virtually nothing but the name and good will of the paper. The real estate was transferred to another company controlled by Mr. Jones's

heirs, and his newspaper continued as a tenant in the building erected with its profits and its credit. In order to recoup themselves for the losses sustained in the past two years, Jones and Dyer had also retained the outstanding accounts receivable. The presses were old and dilapidated; the linotype machines were only leased. A million dollars was a good deal of money to pay for the privilege of continuing the business at the old stand, but the men who paid it were those who knew, loved, and appreciated the merits of the paper. The heirs of Mr. Jones were naturally more interested in getting a price which would set them back in the position they had occupied before they had essayed to publish *The Times* themselves, while its editors were chiefly concerned to prevent it from being "sold down the river." This difference in purpose also accounts for the fact that the new owners were willing, when they found it necessary, to pay cash. As a matter of fact, one man who had promised and expected to invest $50,000 in the enterprise found at the last moment that he could not get the money, so Jones and Dyer, appreciating the loyalty of the men who wanted to continue George Jones's paper and who could not possibly scrape together more than $950,000, decided to accept that sum.

Though the editors of *The Times* held only a small minority of the stock in the new company, it was understood that they were to undertake the editorial and business management of the paper. Unfortunately, it could not be managed without money. All

the money still due *The Times* was to be paid to the Jones estate; and the editors had put into the purchase price every cent they had or could raise among their friends. They had no outside properties such as would have enabled Jones and Dyer to carry the paper, for a time, at a loss. And then came the panic of 1893.

Not only did that panic make it all but impossible to find money to carry on the paper, but it led to a great and ruinous decrease in advertising — especially financial advertising, in which *The Times* had always been preëminent. The new company never had a chance to get started; the only surprising feature of its history is that it managed to hold on for three years. Eventually it managed to sell $250,000 of debenture notes, and the money thus received carried the paper along; but it was losing more heavily every day. As it lost money it became less able to incur expenditures for the gathering and presentation of news; and becoming thus a less valuable newspaper it lost still more money. The editorial page was as good as ever, and its valiant support of President Cleveland is one of the brightest spots in the history of *The Times;* but it is the only bright spot between 1893 and 1896.

For the restoration of the paper to its former state various schemes were devised by the men who had invested in the new company, but none of them gave much ground for confidence, and it began to seem that the great institution built up by Raymond and Jones might fall into unworthy hands, or lose its individuality by consolidation with another paper. Hope that *The Times* could be restored

while retaining its character had almost vanished, when there appeared in New York a small-town newspaperman from Tennessee, who became interested in the problem and presently set himself to find a solution. This was Adolph S. Ochs, of Chattanooga.

PART II

CHAPTER I

Restoration of The Times, 1896–1900

THE history of *The New York Times* since 1896 should properly be written with a somewhat different emphasis and from another viewpoint than the story of the paper under Raymond and Jones. In their day, a newspaper was first of all a vehicle of political opinion; and, as has been noted, *The Times* retained that character longer than most of its contemporaries. The art of gathering and presenting news was primitive in Raymond's day, and indeed in Jones's day; and the ideal of impartial and disinterested news was less generally respected. So the history of *The Times* before 1896 must in large part be the history of a political newspaper, and its interaction with the changing feelings of the period.

In the story of *The Times* as it is today, a paper which was born again in 1896, discussion of political views takes a secondary position. For most newspaper readers of the present the news department is of more importance than anything else, and in the modern history of the art of getting and presenting news *The Times* has a prominent part. Another department of the paper, subordinate but essential, also claims a share of interest. In the time of Raymond and Jones the volume of business even of the most successful paper was small, by modern

standards, and its organization had none of the intricacy of development essential for the paper of today. Nor were the ethical standards of the mid-nineteenth century as exacting as those of today. The modern newspaper has to find revenue, free from subvention of any kind and particularly in the shape of political patronage, to provide for the enormous expenditures for news. The history of the development of the business affairs of *The Times* in the past twenty-five years offers a good deal of instruction and interest; it is the story of the rise of a paper exemplifying certain principles from destitution to a degree of prosperity almost without parallel, and one which seemed to a good many newspapermen beyond the reach of a paper conducted on those principles.

Moreover, the editorial character of *The Times* has always been pretty much the same, in prosperity and in adversity. In 1851, in 1871, in 1884 and in 1921 it was a sober, conservative, dignified paper, always American, with its special position in the esteem of readers who valued sobriety of discussion and intelligent and balanced judgment. The principal interest in the history of the modern *Times* lies in the process by which this paper, which in its best days of old had seldom had more than 35,000 subscribers, came to appeal to more than ten times that number. Its rise surprised even its conductors; the best they hoped, twenty-five years ago, was that a paper conducted on the principles which they held might attain as large a circulation as 50,000.

The story of this astounding rise to prosperity and influence has been told by other writers, but only in

fragments. This history will attempt for the first time to tell it as a whole, and with fuller and more authentic details than have previously been presented to the reader, in the belief that it will be found instructive by men engaged in making newspapers and of some interest even to the general public, which believes more and knows less about newspaper making than about almost any other business on earth. The story is unfinished; its action is still going on; its chief actors, or most of them, are still on the stage. This fact perhaps imposes some restraint on the historian, but it is his belief and the belief of the conductors of *The Times* that no relevant detail of the story has been omitted. Because it is an unfinished story, however, the narrative must be treated as a record rather than as a critical history. It is too early for detached judgment on most of the work of the past twenty-five years in *The Times* office, and in any case the men who have done that work, and whose views are represented in this part of the narrative, are not the men to pass judgment on what they themselves have done. The rise of *The Times* possesses, to a rather unusual degree, that romance which attaches to the growth of most great business enterprises; but that side of the story must be left for treatment by persons outside the institution. It could, moreover, easily lead to a distorted view of some of the phases of that growth. The fact that *The Times* was often, in past years, desperately hard up, has some romantic and dramatic value; but for the purposes of this narrative the fact, which may be assumed, is less important than the policies pursued

by the management of the paper in that situation. Essentially, then, this story must be something in the nature of a report of a laboratory experiment, presented by those who have done the work for the critical judgment of the public outside.

Adolph S. Ochs, publisher of *The Chattanooga Times*, who came into the history of *The New York Times* in the spring of 1896, had been first actively interested in New York City papers by a hasty summons from a friend in New York, who had telegraphed, "The opportunity of your life lies before you." This opportunity, it was presently discovered, was the business management of *The New York Mercury*, a publication which maintained a rather precarious existence in somewhat the same field as that now occupied by *The Morning Telegraph*. The great free silver campaign of 1896 was about to begin, and a group of "silver Senators" had planned to buy *The Mercury* and establish it as a free silver daily in New York.

Mr. Ochs's informant was a personal friend, Leopold Wallach, a prominent member of the New York bar, who later was for many years, until his death, legal adviser of *The Times*. He, though hostile to the free silver cause, had become acquainted in a professional way with some of these gentlemen, and when he learned that they were seeking an experienced newspaperman as business manager of the enterprise he at once thought of his friend in Chattanooga.

To the execution of this plan, however, there was an insuperable obstacle. Mr. Ochs believed in the

The New-York Times,

PUBLISHED EVERY DAY IN THE YEAR.

Offices.

Publication....Printing House Square, New-York
Up-Town................1,269 Broadway, (32d St.)
All American District Telegraph Offices.
Washington....................515 Fourteenth St.

Subscription Rates—Specimen Copies Free.

	1 Yr.	6 Mos.	3 Mos.	1 Mo.	1 Wk.
Daily, with Sunday..	$10.00	$5.00	$2.50	$ .90	$ .25
Daily without Sunday	8.00	4.00	2.00	.75	.20
Sunday edition only..	2.00	1.00	.50	.....	.05
Any one day (except Sunday)	1.50	.75	.40	.....	.03
Weekly edition.......	1.00	.50	.30	.....	.03

Postage prepaid to all points in the United States, Canada, and Mexico, except in New-York City, where the postage is 1 cent per copy; in all other countries, 2 cents per copy per day, payable by the subscriber.

The Times will be sent to any address in Europe, postage included, for $1.50 per month. It is sold in Europe as follows:

London: Low's Exchange, 3 Northumberland Av.
Geneva, Switzerland: Librairie, Georg & Co.; Librairie, A. Cherbuliez, Rue Bovy, Lysberg.
Mainz, Germany: Saarsbach's News Agency, agency for Germany and Austria.
Rome, Italy: Loescher & Co.

The address of subscribers will be changed as often as desired. In ordering a change of address both the old and the new address MUST be given.

Cash in advance always. Remittances at the risk of the subscriber, unless made by Registered Letter, Check, Money Order, or Express Order, payable to "The New-York Times Publishing Co."

ADVERTISEMENTS may be left at either of The Times Branch Offices, at any District Messenger Office in New-York City, and at regularly authorized newsdealers' offices, where they will be taken at the same rate as at the Publication Office. Rate cards mailed on application to the publisher. Estimates promptly given.

COMPLAINTS.—Subscribers who fail to receive a single copy of The Times should immediately notify the publishers. Readers who are unable to purchase The Times at any news stand or on any railroad train or steamboat will oblige us by promptly reporting that fact.

TWELVE PAGES.

NEW-YORK, WEDNESDAY, AUG. 19, 1896.

The Times does not undertake to return rejected manuscripts. In all cases where a return of manuscript is desired postage must be inclosed.

To Readers Going Out of Town.

The New-York Times will be mailed, daily and Sunday, for 90 cents per month, and the address changed as often as desired.

BUSINESS ANNOUNCEMENT.

The New-York Times Publishing Company, proprietor of THE NEW-YORK TIMES, has been reorganized. The new organization assumes the ownership to-day. Mr. ADOLPH S. OCHS of Chattanooga, Tenn., in the interest of the new owners, becomes the publisher and general manager. Mr. CHARLES R. MILLER will continue to be the editor.

that his election is not expected and that the success of his policy is not looked for.

Another inference is that the speculators who bought silver bullion in the belief that the silver craze would at least for a time be general enough to promote a rise in price, have abandoned that belief and are either unloading or threatening to unload.

There are, of course, other causes, purely commercial, which affect the price of silver as that of any other commodity is affected. With these it is not now necessary to concern ourselves. Mr. BRYAN refuses to recognize their existence, and those who understand them are regarding them without reference to politics.

THE NATIONAL DEMOCRATIC ADDRESS.

"For more than a century no man was ever in doubt as to what constituted Democracy." This is the basis of the statement of the Executive Committee of the National Democratic Party just issued from Chicago. The statement founded upon it is admirably simple and complete. Not only every Democrat, but in all essential regards every sensible and patriotic citizen, can accept it. "Every Democrat believed," says the address, "in the rule of law and the rule of an impartial law, in the unhesitating protection not only of the lives of citizens, but of private rights of property, and in the enforcement of obedience to duly constituted authority."

While every Democrat believed this, "he profoundly disbelieved in the ability of Government, through paternal legislation or supervision, to increase the happiness of the Nation." "He believed that it is the function of Government to provide the people with an honest and stable medium of exchange, thus enabling them to transact their business safely and conveniently in every market of the world. He reprobated every attempt to supply to money by means of legislation that value which it can possess only by return of those qualities that render it acceptable to the world when unsupported by legislative fiat."

What can a Democrat with these beliefs and disbeliefs have to do with the Populist policy represented by BRYAN, SEWALL, and WATSON? Every feature of that policy violates some honored Democratic principle. Its chief measure, the free and unlimited coinage of silver at 16 to 1, as proposed, openly defies nearly all those principles. It invades private rights by forcing inferior money on every man to whom a dollar is owing, from the capitalist to the wage earner. It destroys the right of contract. It assumes power in the Government which JEFFERSON would have abhorred. It is class legislation for the direct profit of the mine owners solely. It threatens public credit and private security.

The address declares, and justly, that amendment, but the general lines of the charter for the Greater New-York ought really to be fixed in the Constitution instead of being left liable to continual disturbance by legislative action at Albany. As it is now, the whole charter in its outlines and in its details is a matter of legislation, subject to amendment at any time.

THE BOY ORATOR AND THE MAN ORATOR.

There has very seldom been offered in New-York a more pointed and instructive contrast than was furnished in Madison-Square Garden a week ago to-night and last night. The contrast was not only in the speeches, but in the audiences and in the arrangements. Last night the arrangements both on the part of the organizers of the meeting and of the police were immeasurably improved from the previous occasion. Nobody who was furnished with a ticket had any considerable delay or trouble in finding his seat. The queer and picturesque element added to the Bryan meeting by the intense heat was absent last night, the spectacle of a coatless crowd relieving itself by the waving of fans. But the management provided an efficient substitute for it last night by furnishing every seat with a little American flag, which produced an effect equally bizarre and more attractive.

But the main contrast was in the speeches themselves. Nobody who was at both meetings needs to be told that this contrast was so frightfully to the disadvantage of Mr. BRYAN that he will be not only very bold, but very ill advised, if he presumes again during the campaign to confront an audience in this part of the "enemy's country." He was known on his first appearance, apart from his character of the chosen champion of repudiation, as the "Boy Orator of the Platte" and as the man whose sudden eloquence had stampeded into nominating him a body, if not of entirely sane persons, at least of adult males who were at large. To hear the eloquence which had performed such a feat was the motive which assembled the most respectable of his auditors. These connoisseurs of oratory were the most disappointed and the most resentful of all his hearers, except those who had their money on him, so to speak, the men who expected either commercial profit or political preferment in the event of his election, and had made sacrifices of money or of reputation in view of that event. How the connoisseurs in oratory felt, who had gone to hear him in the hope of receiving the sensation that eloquence gives, without regard to the sentiments it adorns, we tried to explain the next morning. The simplest expression is that they felt deceived and imposed upon, and that it would be quite impossible to get any of them to hear BRYAN again.

The most conclusive criticism of him ... was the fact that he made him, insomuch that he leaves it doubtful whether he really regards "BRYAN" as a dissyllable. What is more to the purpose, the Milesian "twinkle" is eminently his, the welling drollery of which the Populist candidate has not a single trace. Moreover, his language, instead of being the bald commercial English of the Nebraskan, is the English of a scholar, full of unexpectedness and allusion. In short, Mr. BOURKE COCKRAN is an orator who would be alluring on the wrong side, and Mr. BRYAN a proser who would be intolerable on the right. If the sound-money Democrats could inveigle the Populist candidate into a joint debate with his critic, of which there is unluckily no hope, what would be the wonder of the hearers of that debate at the reflection that it was on account of his oratorical powers that Mr. BRYAN was a candidate for the Presidency of the United States?

WANTED—POLICEMEN.

It was the simple notion of our old-fashioned forefathers that the office should seek the man. For something like two generations the politics of this country have, in great degree, been run on exactly the opposite principle, often with results that no sane and honest American could look upon without disgust. Even at the highest tide of patriotic feeling that the Republic has ever known Mr. LINCOLN was wont to declare that the office hunters bothered him as much as the insurgents in arms. And only a dozen years ago the men who believed that the sound rule of the fathers was practicable were sneered at as theorists, idealists, and amateur politicians.

Among the men whom these sneers in no way disturbed was THEODORE ROOSEVELT, then a member of Assembly from this city. To his energy, zeal, and skill the State largely owed the civil service law, the chief object of which was to put an end to the use of offices as the spoils of political victory. At that time and until very recently there was no department of the city or State service in which party politics of the worst sort had so much and such mischievous influence. To-day Mr. ROOSEVELT, speaking for the Police Commissioners, gives public notice that in the next four months 800 appointments will be made to the police force, and invites young men who are fit for these places to enter competition for them. "There probably never has been," he says, "such a chance offered in New-York for the employment of young men of good intelligence, of bodily vigor, and of good character. We desire all such to enter our examinations. If they pass them, they will be admitted strictly on their merits and without regard to personal or political influence of any kind."

Every word of this statement is absolutely true. It shows such a change as the most sanguine believers in reform did not dare five years ago to hope for. And ... about these changes is

agement of the banks, and the cost of management, in receiving, safekeeping, investing, and repaying the funds, is only one-third of a cent on the dollar. No savings-bank depositor who understands his own interest can cast a vote in favor of debasing the standard of value and producing financial disturbance.

Mr. BRYAN seems to be no more concerned about the accuracy of his quotations than the originality of his metaphors. In his speech at Barrytown he made bold to say that "SOLOMON said he desired neither riches nor poverty." In fact, the quotation which the Boy Orator was groping at reads "neither poverty nor riches." But waiving that, and waiving also the question raised by modern criticism whether SOLOMON had anything whatever to do with the compilation of proverbs that have his name, it is evident that he had nothing to do with this particular saying. It is expressly credited, in the King James version, at the beginning of the chapter to "AGAR, the son of JAKEH," and it is always known, in and out of the pulpit, as "the prayer of AGAR." That Mr. BRYAN is ignorant of this raises a painful suspicion that he does not know much more about his Bible than he does about bimetallism or the intentions of the American people regarding himself.

"This campaign is characterized by more thinking than we younger men have ever seen," says Mr. BRYAN. This sounds as if Mr. BRYAN were unused to thinking. Men as young as he can recall the campaign of 1876, when the hold of the Republican Party, as the great war party, was broken; the campaign of 1884, when independence became a powerful element in National politics; the campaign of 1892, when for the first time in a generation a definite adverse verdict on extreme protection was given at a Presidential election. No, the quantity of thinking is not so extraordinary as Mr. BRYAN thinks. It is the result of it that puzzles him, and will puzzle him more and more.

Of course the Park Commissioners will not grant special privileges in Central Park to the well-meaning folks who are going to drive all sickness out of America by introducing Father KNEIPP's barefoot cure. If the advocates of KNEIPP are to have favors bestowed upon them, the advocates of all other systems of medicine must be treated with the same indulgence, and presently Central Park will be an open-air sanitarium, with lawns kept continually damp for barefooted invalids to walk over, with mud baths and blood baths and water-cure pavilions innumerable. Generations come and go, creeds change, political parties rise and fall, the world moves on, but the misunderstanding of the design and purpose of our beautiful Park, a place of recreation and flower garden for all, not particularly for poor or rich or moderately well-to-do, is persistent and unchanging.

CAMPAIGN LITERATURE DEMANDED

The Two Congressional Committees Have Their Hands Full of Business.

WASHINGTON, Aug. 18.—Since the opening of the campaign the Republican Congressional Committee has sent out a little more than 13,000,000 of documents. On Saturday alone 337,000 copies of various speeches were started on their way. So great has been the demands for literature that the committee has been compelled to again enlarge its ... The speech for which there is

SILVER HAS RETARDED PROGRESS.

Responsibility Rests on It for the Panic of 1893.

To the Editor of The New-York Times:

The civil war ended in 1865. Personal liberty was then established throughout this broad land. From that date down to the year 1892 the industrial progress of this country has been continuous, subject to temporary retardations, such as may always occur in the ordinary conduct of business. In 1893 that progress suddenly stopped, enterprise ceased, and from that time to the present day there have been financial chaos, depression, disaster, and compulsory idleness. Although specie payment was suspended from 1865 to 1869, every one had confidence in the ultimate redemption of every promise of the United States in gold coin of the legal standard.

It may be judicious to give the facts proving progress not only in National and personal wealth, but in individual welfare, and to that end the following statement of facts is submitted, covering the period in part from 1865, or an earlier period, to 1890, and in part to 1892.

Relative progress in population and in the principal elements of wealth and welfare compared at various periods:

	Per Cent.
1. Gain in population—1865, 34,748,000; 1892, 65,520,000....	88½
2. National expenditures per capita, 1879 to 1882, average $5.18; 1889 to 1892, 5.03. Excess in first period..........	3
3. National taxation per capita, 1865, $15.73; 1892, $5.43. Excess in 1865...	190
4. National debt per capita, 1865, $76.98; 1892, $12.85. Excess in 1865.........	500
5. The combined imports and exports of the United States were, in 1865, $404,744,883; in 1892, $1,857,680,610. Increase	361
6. The cost of moving a bushel of wheat from Chicago to New-York, by lake and rail, from 1865 to 1868, was 26 6-10 cents; in 1892, 5 61-100 cents. Excess in first period.................	352
7. The charge for moving merchandise over the New-York Central Railroad in 1865 averaged 3.31 cents per ton per mile; in 1892, average, 0.70 cent per ton. Excess in 1865......................	370
8. The postal receipts of the United States in 1865, $14,556,159; in 1892, $70,930,475. Increase........................	387
9. Appropriations for common schools, in 1865, $60,107,612; in 1892, $155,000,000. Increase	158
10. Production of grain, corn, wheat, rye, oats, barley, and buckwheat, in 1865 to 1868, inclusive, an average of 1,312,761,319 bushels; in 1889 to 1892, an average of 3,109,115,463 bushels. Increase	136
11. Production of cotton, the crops of 1865 to 1869, averaged 2,386,000 bales; in 1888 to 1892, averaged 7,982,000 bales. Increase	234
12. Production of pig iron, 1865, 931,582 tons; 1892, 10,255,840 tons. Increase.	1,100
13. Production of steel, 1865, 13,627 tons; 1892, 4,927,581 tons. Increase	3,606
14. Property insured against loss by fire, assuming that in 1865 the insurance covered only one-half the value of the insured property, and in 1892 three-quarters, the insurance contracts indicate a value in 1865, $3,362,511,218; in 1892, $26,580,728,193. Increase	690
15. Railway mileage, 1865, miles in operation, 35,085; 1892, miles in operation, 175,000. Increase	400
16. New-York Central Railroad, 1865, tons freight, 1,275,299; 1892, tons freight, 20,721,752. Increase	1,525
17. St. Mary's Ship Canal, 1865 to 1868, average tonnage passing, 464,283; 1889 to 1892, average tonnage passing, 8,681,064. Increase	1,770
18. Purchasing power of a dollar: equal quantities of the same kind of food, fuel, and materials for clothing—in 1865 one dollar in paper would buy 1.80 portions; in 1892 one dollar in gold would buy 3.33 portions. Increase	85
19. Workmen in a New-York gasworks—Firemen's wages, 1845 to 1850, inclusive, were $1.20 per day; 1885 to 1890, $3. Increase....................	150
20. Weavers in a woolen mill—In 1850, Adult men and women worked in a Rhode Island woolen mill fourteen hours a day at 4 3-10 cents an hour, earning 60¼ cents a day. In 1892 weavers worked in the same mill ten hours a day at 13 16-100 cents per hour, earning $1.34½ per day.	
Increase per hour	212
Increase per day	123
21. Mechanics' Earnings—The average earnings of carpenters, machinists, ...	

NAVY YARD ACCIDENT INQUIRY

Sunken Caisson and Commandant's Barge Raised.

The caisson of Dry Dock No. 2 in the Brooklyn Navy Yard, which was sunk in the recent accident there, by which the Commandant's barge was wrecked and the torpedo boat Ericsson was damaged, was raised yesterday morning as was also the barge, which was sunk in the dry dock. A careful inspection of the caisson will be made to-day, to ascertain the cause of the accident, if possible.

The official inquiry into the accident was continued yesterday. Assistant Naval Constructor F. W. Hibbs was present at the morning session, with a table of calculations, from which he figured that the weight of the caisson was 96.7 tons. Civil Engineer Menocal had testified that its weight was estimated by its builders at 104 tons. Mr. Hibbs declined to state his opinion as to the cause of the accident.

"Would you," he was asked, "attempt to replace the ballast in the caisson in the manner in which it was being done prior to the accident?"

"Not knowing anything more than I do at present, and having had no experience in removing ballast from caissons, I should say I would not have attempted it," he replied.

He added that had he been engaged in the work, he would have left a considerable margin for safety.

Mr. Hibbs said the dock and caisson were in good condition before the accident.

Naval Constructor Bowles said he did not know the weight of the caisson. He did not think the warm weather was responsible for the accident. He did not recollect having held a conversation with Civil Engineer Menocal about the weight of the caisson. He did not know how much stone ballast was in the caisson.

Assistant Naval Constructor Zam said he told Mr. Menocal it would be safe to remove all the ballast from the caisson, and he was still of that opinion.

The Board of Inquiry will hold another session at 10 o'clock to-day, though no more testimony may be taken.

LORD RUSSELL IN SARATOGA.

He Will Attend the Meeting of the Bar Association To-day.

DOBBS FERRY, N. Y., Aug. 18.—Lord Chief Justice Russell of England and his party left Mr. Willard's residence this morning for Hudson, N. Y. The party embarked on J. Pierpont Morgan's yacht Corsair. The party on arriving at Hudson took a train for Saratoga.

ALBANY, Aug. 18.—Lord Chief Justice Russell of England and party visited the State Capitol building this afternoon. Superintendent Eaton had kept the forces of orderlies at their posts, and had the party shown through the building. A committee of the National Bar Association accompanied the distinguished party, which, after its tour, left for Saratoga at 7:15 to attend the annual meeting of the American Bar Association there. Among the Bar Association committee which accompanied the party were James C. Carter, ex-Minister Edward J. Phelps of Vermont, Charles Claflin Allen, and United States Attorney General Harmon.

SARATOGA, Aug. 18.—The nineteenth annual meeting of the American Bar Association will open here to-morrow. The presence of Lord Russell of England has awakened a widespread interest, and many of the most distinguished men of the country will attend. Senator Gorman of Maryland, Senator Gray of Delaware, Judge I. E. Wales of Wilmington, United States Judge C. P. Shires of Iowa, Judge L. D. Brewster of Danbury, Conn., and Judge Howe of New-Orleans have arrived, and others are coming in by every train. It is expected that the attendance will be fully three times as large as that of any previous year. Lord Russell and party are at the United States Hotel, where they have engaged cottages.

Much Good It Will Do the Mar...

From The London News.

It has been decided, with the ...

... to conduct a high-standard newspaper, clean, dignified, and trustworthy, requires honesty, watchfulness, earnestness, industry, and practical knowledge applied with common sense, I entertain the hope that I can succeed in maintaining the high estimate that thoughtful, pure-minded people have ever had of THE NEW-YORK TIMES.

It will be my earnest aim that THE NEW-YORK TIMES give the news, all the news, in concise and attractive form, in language that is parliamentary in good society, and give it as early, if not earlier, than it can be learned through any other reliable medium; to give the news impartially, without fear or favor, regardless of party, sect, or interests involved; to make of the columns of THE NEW-YORK TIMES a forum for the consideration of all questions of public importance, and to that end to invite intelligent discussion from all shades of opinion.

There will be no radical changes in the personnel of the present efficient staff. Mr. CHARLES R. MILLER, who has so ably for many years presided over the editorial pages, will continue to be the editor; nor will there be a departure from the general tone and character and policies pursued with relation to public questions that have distinguished THE NEW-YORK TIMES as a non-partisan newspaper—unless it be, if possible, to intensify its devotion to the cause of sound money and tariff reform, opposition to wastefulness and peculation in administering public affairs, and in its advocacy of the lowest tax consistent with good government, and no more government than is absolutely necessary to protect society, maintain individual and vested rights, and assure the free exercise of a sound conscience.

ADOLPH S. OCHS.

NEW-YORK, Aug. 18, 1896.

THE PRICE OF SILVER.

Silver touched 66 cents per ounce yesterday for certificates. At this rate the bullion in the dollar that Mr. BRYAN advocates would be worth 51 1-6 cents. This is a fall of about 2 cents since the Populist candidate was put in the field, or a decline of nearly 4 per cent.

There are several inferences to be drawn from this. One is practically forced upon us by Mr. BRYAN himself. It is his professed belief that his election and the policy he sustains would bring the market value of silver to $1.29 an ounce and the value of the silver in a dollar to 100 cents. The fall in price may, therefore, be regarded as evidence ... Democratic Party are at stake."

We are quite ready to concede that even the radical errors of the Populists may sincerely be supported by those who believe in them, but they have no claim on the support of Democrats as such. To these they are simply party treason, and party loyalty joins with patriotism in demanding their utter condemnation and rejection.

THE GREATER NEW-YORK COUNTIES.

It seems to us desirable, if it is practicable, to do away entirely with the separate county organizations within the limits of the Greater New-York when a common Municipal Government is established. The mere declaration in the act providing for the consolidation that it was not its intent to affect the boundaries or government of counties is no bar to future action by the Legislature if it is deemed expedient and is within the Constitutional authority of that body.

There is no doubt about the power of the Legislature to set off a part of one county and add it to another, though it cannot in doing so change the boundaries of legislative or judicial districts, which are fixed by the Constitution. This was decided in the case of the last annexation of a part of Westchester County to the City and County of New-York. The only county divided by the proposed consolidation is Queens, and it would be competent for the Legislature to add the portion left out of the enlarged municipality to Suffolk.

But could it then consolidate the four Counties of New-York, Kings, Queens, and Richmond into one? The counties are not created by the Constitution, but their existence is recognized and they are all enumerated in the provisions relating to the apportionment of representation in the two branches of the Legislature. The decision in the Westchester case makes it plain that the Senate, Assembly, and judicial districts must remain as described by county lines when the Constitution was adopted, but it does not follow that the county boundaries must remain for county purposes.

It is desirable to get rid of the county division if possible, because otherwise not only will the Boards of Supervisors of Queens and Richmond have to be retained, but those of New-York and Kings will have to be revived, as neither would any longer have the same boundaries as a city. The counties would also have a separate debt-incurring capacity. So far as other county officers are concerned—Sheriffs, clerks, District Attorneys, and Registers—there seems to be no reason why their offices might not be consolidated as well as those of the municipality with proper provision for branches and deputies. The county question is a somewhat awkward factor in the consolidation problem, and it is possible that it can only be eliminated by a Constitutional ...

... at the beginning and three times as large at the end, knew, that Mr. BOURKE COCKRAN knew how to talk. But those who had not heard him before and who had heard BRYAN were scarcely prepared for the full force of the contrast that was impressed upon them. The orator's affluent eloquence flowed on, interrupted only by applause as spontaneous as the applause for BRYAN was perfunctory and managed, and by the hearty laughter which BRYAN did not once elicit, and there must have been many who remembered with dim and remote wonder how they had suffered less than a week before in the place in which they were now delighted, and marveled at the vastness of the difference between an orator and a bore.

The difference is indeed very wide. The old saying about a poet being born and an orator made seems to need revision in view of such a contrast, and to be corrected by the statement that "temperament" counts for as much with an oratorical as with a musical artist. Perhaps that is the difference. The oratorical temperament Mr COCKRAN evidently has in abundant measure, and Mr. BRYAN, so far as can be judged from his essay in New-York, has it not at all. The meaning of the saying "orator fit" we may take to be that any man may by application arrive at the power of clear expression. That may be conceded to the industrious, or, as they used to say about preachers, the "painful" Mr. BRYAN. For, if he was not clear at all points in his speech, it was partly because there were points in it about which it was not prudent for him to be clear. The trouble with him as an orator is that he is so intensely average, to use the vulgar saying, as common as a yellow dog. This remark applies to his appearance, to his manner to his gesticulations, so far as his attention to his manuscript allowed him any to his language, and to his thought. It was all hopelessly humdrum and dog-trot, and utterly without distinction or individuality. Anybody could have written it and anybody could have spoken it.

It seems that a man born so can no more acquire eloquence than he can add a cubit to his stature. And it seems so even more vividly when one has had a chance of hearing the genuine article. Mr BRYAN appears to have two phases, one of extravagant rhetoric and one of bald monotony of statement or misstatement. Mr COCKRAN decorates, without effort or parade, a substantial and serious staple of thought. He has every advantage of stature, expressiveness of face and voice, and becoming gesture, which Mr BRYAN lacks. His voice is remarkably rich and expressive. Mr BRYAN'S name denotes that he is of Irish origin, but nothing in his speeches bewrays him. Mr COCKRAN'S race, on the other hand, is quite unmistakable. The remains of a rich Milesian brogue still abide with ...

... department of this State on the condition of the savings banks for the year ending with June 30 comes as a timely argument in favor of sound money. It shows that the number of depositors is considerably larger than the number of voters in the State. Many of them are women and children and other non-voters, but it is not unlikely that they include a majority of the voting citizens. Of the effect upon the value of the savings-bank deposits of degrading our currency to the silver basis by free coinage we have frequently spoken, but this report suggests various considerations for the contemplation of the community.

The total amount of resources, including the surplus held in excess of deposit accounts, is more than $800,000,000. Where is all that capital? Very little of it is lying idle in bank vaults, for it would earn no interest for depositors there. A very large proportion of it has been invested in mortgages on real estate; in other words, has been advanced to purchasers of land and builders. It is part of the invested capital of the community, the value of which and the returns from which depend upon the stability of the currency. Another part is invested in securities paying interest, which would be largely reduced in actual value by a debasement of the money standard.

What does it mean that, notwithstanding the hard times of the last year, the number of depositors has increased and the amount of new deposits was greater than the amount of withdrawals? In part it means that it has been hard to make use of capital in business or in any form of investment that will pay more than the savings-bank rate of 3½ per cent., and there has been a disposition to hoard as well as to save, due to uncertainty about the future. That the sole decrease in the figures is to be found in the aggregate surplus of the banks is significant. It shows that the investments have been less easy to make and less profitable than before, and that in order to keep up the rate of interest it has been necessary to draw upon previous accumulations. This indicates at once the importance of having the surplus and the financial difficulty caused by fear of a currency disturbance. The calamity of any policy that would reduce by nearly one-half the purchasing power of this vast capital, accumulated in investment, but distributed in ownership among more people than there are separate families in the State, can hardly be estimated.

Superintendent KILBURN does well to remind the people of what the well informed in this State knew before—that interest in this vast fund is chiefly that of the depositors. The savings banks are not money-making corporations. They have no stockholders or bondholders, and their Trustees are allowed to have no pecuniary interest in their transactions or investments. No officer is paid anything but for actual services in the man...

... exhausted, and another is on the press. Another popular tract that has been printed by the hundred thousand is written in a conversational vein, and is entitled "Three Evenings with Money."

One of the most popular things issued by this committee is a speech made on the stump in Texas by Judge Aldridge. Singularly enough, this comes to them under the franking privilege through the agency of a Democrat—Senator Caffery of Louisiana, who in a speech in the Senate on the financial question incorporated this Texas speech. The committee has lifted it and made a separate document of it.

Over at Democratic headquarters the committee finds it impossible to keep up with the demand that comes from all sections of the country. The State of Arkansas, the home of Chairman Jones, admitted on all sides to be absolutely certain for the Democratic ticket by a very handsome majority, is clamorous for free-silver literature, and the names of hundreds of Republicans are being sent in with the request that this sort of thing be mailed to them. The Middle Western States are consuming vast quantities of free-silver literature, and the printers having contracts with the committee are forced to operate their works to the limit to come anywhere near getting the work out. In Ohio alone tons of literature have been distributed, and every line of it pertains solely to the financial problem. Thousands and thousands of Republicans whose names are secured by Democratic workers are regularly supplied with this food, and the increasing demands for it in letters written by the recipients themselves is one of the things that leads the committee to believe that the State is to be overturned at the coming election.

The Chairmen of both committees agree that never before was there such a "reading" campaign. The Republican preparation of this literature for distribution will cost hundreds of thousands of dollars. No one is refused, and every letter asking for information at headquarters is referred to some particular individual and an answer written. If it can be replied to with printed matter such is used; if not, a written letter is sent. Thus the committee is kept in touch not only with the political worker, but with the voter himself. The mailing rooms of the two committees are vast beehives, where every employe puts in from eight to ten hours' work a day, and frequently another force is engaged until midnight on the same work.

TO BUY THE WALLACE HOUSE.

It Was Washington's Headquarters at Somerville, N. J.

NEWARK, N. J., Aug. 18.—The Executive Committee of the Revolutionary Society of New-Jersey held a meeting in the office of John Whitehead, Prudential Building, at noon to-day, and contemplated the purchase of the old Wallace House, at Somerville, where Gen. Washington had his headquarters during the Winter and Spring of 1778-9. The Sullivan campaign against the Indians was planned at this place, and near it the Pluckamin fête celebrating the treaty with France was held.

Mr. Whitehead moved that the Executive Committee, at its judgment, be authorized to procure a refusal of the Wallace House until Jan. 1, 1897. The price set upon the house is $6,500. As the Revolutionary Memorial Society is the outgrowth of the Society for the Preservation of Washington's Headquarters at Rocky Hill, and as negotiatoins for the Berriam house at that place did not culminate, a circular was directed to be sent to all original subscribers, notifying them of the proposed change of location.

A meeting of the historico-patriotic societies of New-Jersey will probably be held at Somerville on Sept. 19, to commemorate the centennial anniversary of Washington's farewell address to the people of the United States. President Stevens of the socity is Chairman of the committee, and six others to be named later, are to be associated with him.

... 4.29 portions, in 1892, 8.66 portions. Increased value of a day's wages.......... 106

22. Standard freight locomotive—1865, price in paper, $21,000; 1892, price in gold, $7,350. The engine of 1892, 50 per cent. more effective. Excess of price in 1865.......... 186

23. Steel stubble plows—The price of a low-grade steel plow in 1865 was $24 in paper; a high-grade steel plow in 1893, $13.50. Excess of price in 1865.......... 78

The average earnings of all the workmen in a large plow works in Illinois were, in paper, in 1865, $1.80; in gold, in 1893, $1.98. The purchasing power of the wages in 1893 in equal quantities of the same kinds of food, fuel, and materials for clothing increased.. 111

Compiled and computed from various authorities, April, 1893.

The proofs of every one of these statements, with the citation of the authorities on which the proofs rest, may be found in the great work upon the "United States of America," edited by Prof. N. S. Shaler, Vol. II., Chapter 1, to which reference may be had.

The foregoing proofs of progress in every department of industry and in every line of National importance were compiled from various authorities in the Spring of 1893. A little later the whole course of events was altered by force of legislation. The subtle poison of the coinage of silver dollars of full legal tender from bullion purchased by means of a forced loan which increased the demand debt of the United States by nearly $500,000,000, culminated in that year in the doubt of the credit of the Nation and in the distrust of the credit of every individual firm or corporation therein.

This crime brought what had been long anticipated by the few—industrial paralysis, financial panic, a stop to constructive enterprise, and a reversal of the progress of the country. No other term will suffice to describe the cause of the financial chaos, the compulsory idleness, and the stop to enterprise since that date. The conspirators who have taken advantage of political power and who secured a force bill for the purpose of forcing bad money upon the people of this country must be held guilty at the bar of public opinion and are about to be condemned.

I use strong words. Let the offer be made to give the advocates of the free coinage of silver at 16 to 1 free coinage, provided they ask nothing else, and they will refuse it. What they want is to be empowered by law to force bad money into circulation, instead of good money, and they delude honest men by trying to make them believe they will get higher prices. The mere threat and danger of their success brought on the panic of 1893. They forced down prices by stopping credit, stopping constructive energy, and to-day, while the grain rots or wastes in the bins of the farmers, and cannot be sold at the cost of production, thousands and thousands of industrious workmen are standing idle throughout the country, in want of this very food. The distress has been brought upon them by men of the mining States, who have taken advantage of their number in the Senate to threaten both political parties. They have been ejected, and, in their effort to discredit the Nation, they are themselves discredited, if not disgraced.

EDWARD ATKINSON.

BOSTON, Aug. 18, 1896.

JEFFERSON CLUB'S ANNUAL OUTING

Prominent East-Side Democrats Spend a Day at Roton Point.

The residents of Avenues A, B, C, and D turned out in large numbers yesterday morning to assist at the departure of the Jefferson Club on its annual clambake and outing. The Jefferson Club is the leading Democratic association of the Eleventh Ward and is a very popular organization. Its guiding spirit is ex-County Clerk Patrick Keenan.

The club went to Roton Point, Conn., for its day's enjoyment. As early as 7:30 o'clock the excursionists began to assemble at the clubhouse, 247 Seventh Street. About 300 members marched to the dock at the foot of Eighth Street and embarked on the steamboat Isabella. At the head of the line marched Mr. Keenan, on either side of him Judges Giegerich and Newburger. In the front rank was Aaron Hanover, who is known on the east side as the "Mayor of Avenue C."

Others who went were Judge Goldfogle, Henry Bloch, Alderman William Tait, Senator Ahearn, Congressman Sulzer, Assemblyman Benjamin Hoffman, William Hanna, Moses Newhaus, Lawyers Friend and House, Nathan Heller, Abraham Lazarus, Dr. M. Liebeman, Thomas J. Doran, Jerold Fitzgibbon, "Tim" Campbell, Morris Blumenthal, Theodore Koch, and George Widder.

... placed in the south aisle of the church. The material for the pedestal will be contributed from quarries in England, Ireland, and Wales, and the cross itself will be of Scotch granite. Inscriptions in Armenian by a distinguished Gregorian ecclesiastic, and in English by a member of the committee, will record the circumstances of the Orfe and of the massacres. Cardinal Langenieux, Archbishop of Reims, has been invited to write the Latin inscriptions.

Nansen Reaches Hammerfest.

HAMMERFEST, Norway, Aug. 18.—The members of the Conway expedition, accompanied by Dr. Fridjoh Nansen, whose failure to reach the north pole by drifting in the steamer Fram was lately chronicled, have arrived here.

The Conway expedition, which included Sir William Martin Conway, D. Trevor Battye, Dr. Gregory E. Garwood, and H. E. Conway, went to explore Central Spitzbergen.

YESTERDAY'S TEMPERATURES.

From THE NEW-YORK TIMES'S thermometer, on the face of THE TIMES Building, 6 feet above the street level, and from the thermometer of the Weather Bureau, 285 feet above the street level. Both records show the changes of temperature for the 24 hours ended at midnight, and that of the Weather Bureau gives the temperature on the corresponding date last year:

	Weather Bureau. 1895.	Weather Bureau. 1896.	TIMES. 1896.
3 A. M.	73	66	65
6 A. M.	71	60	65
9 A. M.	75	66	68
12 M.	80	70	74
4 P. M.	83	68	72
6 P. M.	82	59	65
9 P. M.	76	61	65
12 P. M.	73	60	63

Average Temperatures Yesterday.

Printing House Square.......... 67.13
Weather Bureau.......... 65.00
Weather Bureau corresponding date 1895.......... 77.00
Weather Bureau corresponding date for last twenty years.......... 72.00

Probabilities for To-day

In this city: Fair, Cooler

Complete "Weather Forecast" Page 12, Column 1.

Index to Classified Advertisements.

Amusements This Evening.

CASINO—In Gay New-York—8:10. Roof Garden.
EDEN MUSEE—Waxworks and Concerts—2:30 and 8:00 P. M.
GARRICK—Thoroughbred—8:30
GRAND CENTRAL PALACE ROOF GARDENS—Vaudeville—8:00.
HAMMERSTEIN'S OLYMPIA—Roof Garden—Vaudeville—8:15.
KOSTER & BIAL'S—Vaudeville—8:00. Roof Garden
MADISON SQUARE ROOF GARDEN—Vaudeville—8:15 to 12:00.
MANHATTAN BEACH—Orchestral Concert—3:30 and 7:15. Rice's Evangeline—8:45. Rice's Circus Carnival—3:30 and 9:00. Fireworks—8:15.
POLO GROUNDS—Baseball—New-York vs. Chicago—4:00.
PROCTOR'S PLEASURE PALACE—Vaudeville—12:00 to 12:00.
SCHUETZEN PARK, Union Hill, N. J.—Plattdeutsche Volksfest—Day and Evening
TERRACE GARDEN—Der Polengraf

See Amusement Advertisements—Page 7.

gold standard, and his newspaper, *The Chattanooga Times*, was its most consistent advocate in the southern states at a time when most of the southern Democrats were making a fetish of 16 to 1. When he learned the nature of the enterprise, after arriving in New York, he declined to consider the offer; and for various reasons the plan was presently abandoned. The owner of *The Mercury*, however, was still eager to get rid of his property; and after some conversations with Mr. Ochs he offered to sell it to him. Mr. Ochs saw what he thought was an opening in New York City for a small strictly news paper at one cent. Although he was not particularly interested in *The Mercury* as it then was, it seemed to him that *The Mercury* might be transformed into a newspaper of this sort, for it was a client of the associated newspapers of New York and received their full service. This service was at that time quite complete, as *The New York Sun*, *Times*, *Herald* and *Tribune* were directing the United Press organization in a bitter contest with the Associated Press, which at that time was composed chiefly of western papers. But the negotiation for the purchase of *The Mercury* came to nothing when the owner found he could not give an assurance for a continuance of the press association news service of the other New York dailies. *The Mercury* shortly thereafter ceased publication, but the negotiations had caused Mr. Ochs to make several trips to New York, and in the meantime a rather academic interest which he had previously expressed in the affairs of *The Times* had been awakened.

It happened that in 1890 Harry Alloway, a mem-

ber of *The Times* Wall Street staff, had been entertained by Mr. Ochs while on a trip through the South and had heard him remark that *The New York Times* offered the greatest opportunity in American journalism. Long after this — on March 12, 1896, Mr. Ochs's thirty-eighth birthday — he received a telegram from Mr. Alloway saying that if he was interested there seemed likely to be an opportunity of acquiring *The New York Times* with no very large outlay of money. Alloway knew of the financial difficulties of *The Times*, and of some plans for its reorganization, and telegraphed to Mr. Ochs purely as a friendly act, without authority from any one. Mr. Ochs did not take the matter very seriously; but it happened that the next day he had occasion to go to Chicago. While there he took lunch with his friend, Herman H. Kohlsaat, publisher and proprietor of the Chicago *Times-Herald*, to whom he incidentally mentioned the telegram from Alloway. A general discussion of the New York newspaper situation ensued, and Mr. Kohlsaat observed that he thought *The Times* was Mr. Ochs's opportunity. To this Mr. Ochs objected that he didn't think he was a big enough man for the job. "Don't tell anybody," Mr. Kohlsaat advised him, "and they'll never find it out."

Arriving in New York a few days later, Mr. Ochs met Mr. Alloway and learned from him the information he had gathered about the situation in *The Times* office — that a plan of reorganization was being discussed, that several newspaper managers in New York had been approached with the suggestion that they try to rebuild *The Times*, and that

for an investment of $250,000 it might be possible to secure control. Mr. Ochs having displayed interest, Mr. Alloway arranged an interview with Charles R. Miller, the editor-in-chief. Mr. Ochs and Mr. Miller met for the first time that evening at Mr. Miller's residence. The interview had been arranged for a few minutes after dinner, as Mr. Miller had an engagement to accompany his family to the theatre. Two kindred souls met. The discussion of the situation of *The Times* and of Mr. Ochs's ideas of newspaper making was so absorbing that the family went ahead to the theatre on the understanding that Mr. Miller would join them later. The performance ended, they returned and found the discussion still in progress. It lasted until midnight, and resulted in convincing Mr. Miller that the man from Chattanooga had some pretty sound ideas about the reconstruction of *The Times*.

Mr. Miller arranged for Mr. Ochs to meet the next day the men who were working out a plan of reorganization for which they had secured some promises of new capital. Charles R. Flint and Spencer Trask, who were at the head of this movement, were both favorably impressed, and invited Mr. Ochs at once to join the syndicate they were forming, which had only a day or so left to make its plans operative and hold the tentative subscriptions. But the plan required more money from Mr. Ochs than he could command, or would have cared to endeavor to secure. When he declined to become financially interested, Mr. Flint had acquired such confidence in his ideas that he offered Mr. Ochs the management of the proposed reorganized company,

and intimated that a salary of $50,000 a year was not beyond the possibilities. In other circumstances Mr. Ochs might have been willing to go down in history as the first Tennessean who ever got such a salary, but he was of the opinion that if he tried to manage *The Times* for somebody else the most probable result would be the speedy disappearance of the job, the salary and *The Times*.

The failure of this plan left the way clear for that faction of the stockholders which wanted to consolidate *The Times* with *The New York Recorder*, a daily newspaper on which several millions had been spent in a fruitless effort to establish it. They had even gone so far as to file at Albany application for a charter for "The Times-Recorder Company," with a capital of $2,500,000, when Charles R. Miller and Edward Cary, who were the chief editors of the paper and members of its Board of Directors, obtained the appointment of a receiver and circumvented this plan.

All those interested in the reorganization who had met Mr. Ochs seemed agreed that he was the man *The Times* needed, and the receiver, Mr. Alfred Ely, was selected by those friendly to Mr. Ochs. But it should be remembered that before his appearance it had been the conviction of most of those interested in *The Times* that it needed a man experienced in New York journalism to do the work. Every ambitious managing editor in town had long ago been approached and invited to attempt the restoration of *The Times*, and with one accord they had all made excuses. Not till the whole field of metropolitan journalism had been searched in vain for a

rescuer, not till every one of the men who ought to have known had declared that *The Times* could not be restored, did Mr. Ochs get his chance. These experienced men, with intimate knowledge of the New York newspaper situation, were of one opinion—that it would require several million dollars to resuscitate *The Times* and place it in a position to compete with *The Herald*, *The World*, *The Journal*, *The Tribune* and *The Sun*, all having men of great wealth as owners or interested in their success.

Mr. Ochs's experience, to be sure, had been varied enough. He was thirty-eight years old; he had started in the newspaper business at the age of eleven as a carrier of papers, had graduated from that position to printer's devil, and had worked up through every position which either the news, the editorial, or the business department of Tennessee journalism had to offer until at the age of twenty he had become proprietor and publisher of *The Chattanooga Times*. In eighteen years he had brought this paper to a degree of prosperity remarkable in a city of that size, and to a position in public confidence perhaps still more unusual — for the obstacles to journalistic virtue are perhaps most formidable in the smaller cities. Among southern newspaper men he was already widely known, but Chattanooga is a long way from New York; and the gentlemen who were trying to dig *The Times* out of the drifts were slow to admit that a problem which was by this time too much for them, and which had been politely evaded by some of the ablest newspaper managers in New York, could be solved by an unknown from a small town. Fortunately, Mr. Ochs was able to

gather a formidable volume of letters of recommendation. They came from the President of the United States, from Senators, Governors and bishops; from bank presidents, railroad presidents, editors of rival newspapers and people who had known him in Chattanooga. That he was able to produce so many of them was perhaps due to the fact that he had been semi-officially recognized as the entertainer of distinguished visitors to Chattanooga, and thus had become fairly well acquainted with a wider circle than the ordinary newspaper man of the interior could know. At any rate he had many letters and their tone was convincing. They served to reinforce the confidence which had gradually been established by personal contact.

It was expected that the receivership, which was a friendly one, would be required for only a few days, pending the adoption of a plan of reorganization fathered by Mr. Spencer Trask. But this scheme also miscarried, and with Mr. Trask's encouragement Mr. Ochs submitted a new plan which he presented personally to nearly every stockholder and creditor of The New York Times Publishing Company. It was approved and accepted, and Mr. Trask consented to act as Chairman of the Reorganization Committee, whose other members were Marcellus Hartley, Alfred Ely, James T. Woodward, and E. Morā Davison. The plan was declared operative on July 2, 1896.

It was a pretty large undertaking for Mr. Ochs to buy control of *The Times*, even though he was buying it mostly with his ability rather than his money; but it was not much larger, in proportion,

than the effort he had made eighteen years before, when, not yet old enough to vote, he had bought *The Chattanooga Times* by paying $250 in cash — borrowed — and assuming its debt of $1500. It seemed to him that the principles which had succeeded in Chattanooga might succeed equally well in New York; at any rate they were the only principles which he felt competent to put into practice. Only one new resolution did he make on coming to New York — a firm resolve not to have any other outside interest, but to give all his attention, and employ all the resources of his credit, for the interests of *The Times*.

The plan of reorganization has already been told in various publications, but may perhaps here be given in outline. A new organization, The New York Times Company, was formed, with a capital of 10,000 shares of par value of $100. Two thousand of these shares were traded in for the 10,000 shares of the old company. The holders of the outstanding obligations of *The Times*, amounting to some $300,000, received in exchange an equal amount of 5 per cent bonds of the new company; and perhaps the most exacting part of the financing of the reorganization was accomplished when $200,000 more of these bonds were sold at par, to provide that operating capital the lack of which had been so severely felt in past years. As a persuasive, fifteen shares of stock were offered to each purchaser of a $1000 bond. Mr. Ochs himself, scraping together all the money he had or could borrow, bought $75,000 of these bonds, receiving with them 1125 shares of stock. Of the remaining capital stock of

the company 3876 shares were put into escrow, to be delivered to Mr. Ochs whenever the paper had earned and paid expenses for a period of three consecutive years. Thus he would have — and within less than four years did have — 5001 of the 10,000 shares and $75,000 in bonds, the whole acquired by the payment of $75,000 for the bonds and by his personal services. That $75,000 was the financial investment, and the only investment, aside from his own labors, which the controlling stockholder of *The Times* made for his majority interest.

The company thus organized bought *The Times* at public sale on August 13, 1896. The receivership was terminated by court order; on August 18, 1896, the property was formally transferred to the reorganized company, with Mr. Ochs as publisher in unrestricted control; and the saddest chapter in the history of *The Times* was closed.

It may be well at this point to puncture a few bubbles of fantasy which have been widely blown about. *The Times* probably has the distinction of having been more generally misrepresented than any other newspaper in the United States. Some of these misrepresentations are due to malice, some to the somewhat painfully widespread inability of members of the human race to believe in the honesty of their fellows; a good many of them, one must suppose, have no other origin than the myth-making instinct whose pervasiveness is perhaps not fully appreciated by any but newspaper men. The rejuvenated *Times* succeeded so rapidly and so brilliantly that people who could not understand its success

ADOLPH S. OCHS,
August 18, 1896.

found it most convenient to suppose that great sums of money had been poured into it from some secret and probably discreditable reservoir. Ignorance was soon reinforced by hostility; persons who disagreed with the conservatism of *The Times* editorial policy, and who were quite unable to conceive the idea that a man, and even a newspaper, might honestly believe in conservative principles, thought that the explanation could be found in the theory that *The Times* had been bought by Wall Street bankers. It is unfortunately true that a large percentage of the all too human race can find no explanation for disagreement with its opinions except that those who disagree have been bought by somebody. And the ascription to various eminent financiers of the honor of being the man behind the throne on *The Times* is probably due quite as much to credulity as to malice. It is more romantic and entertaining to suppose that a newspaper is the mouthpiece of a mysterious malefactor of great wealth, who gives his orders to its editors in a few pregnant monosyllables, than to accept the prosaic truth that it represents the views of its owners and conductors.

In more recent years the legend of British gold offered a convenient explanation of *The Times's* attitude on the Great War to Irish and German enthusiasts who were used to the idea of subsidized newspapers, but the force of this view was somewhat diminished when the Irish and Germans extended it from *The Times* to all other American newspapers which failed to see in Sinn Fein and Kaiserism the sum of human perfection. The secret ownership or control of *The Times* has been ascribed to so many

different men that one might suppose some doubt would have arisen in the minds of the most credulous; at any rate they couldn't all own it at once. But the number of people who can be fooled all the time is regrettably large.

A few of the more important myths will here be cited and explained, in so far as they can be explained by anything except the credulity of human nature. It is not to be supposed that the explanations will be accepted by Sinn Feiners, admirers of the late Kaiser or devotees of the principles of Karl Marx or Nikolai Lenin. To convince these gentlemen is beyond the power of human logic. But some explanation may perhaps be of interest to the large number of readers of *The Times* who have heard these various rumors and have perhaps been inclined to believe them because the paper has not thought them worthy of explicit denial.

President Cleveland, for example, did not bring Mr. Ochs up from Chattanooga to set a good Democratic paper on its feet. Mr. Cleveland had no more idea, when Mr. Ochs came to New York, that he was going to buy *The Times* than did Mr. Ochs himself. The only possible basis for this legend lies in the fact that when Mr. Ochs found New Yorkers somewhat reluctant to accept the views of a man about whom they knew nothing, he collected a large number of letters of recommendation, as noted above, from everybody whose endorsement seemed likely to be of value. Naturally a recommendation from Mr. Cleveland, then in the White House, would carry a good deal of weight. The President wrote that

> * * * * * in your management of *The Chattanooga Times* you have demonstrated such a faithful adherence to Democratic principles, and have so bravely supported the ideas and policies which tend to the safety of our country as well as of our party that I would be glad to see you in a larger sphere of usefulness. * * * * *

This was Mr. Cleveland's sole contribution to the reorganization of *The Times.*

Of the various bankers who have been mentioned as the controlling influence in *The Times*, August Belmont has perhaps the distinction of having been named most often. Mr. Belmont, as a matter of fact, owned $25,000 of the debentures of the old company, which he exchanged for bonds of the new organization, and these bonds were bought by *The Times* long ago, at par, and retired.

The assertion that he controlled *The Times* was some years ago spread rather widely by the Hearst papers, which eventually retracted it when its untruth was demonstrated. It is doubtless often repeated by persons who do not realize how it came to be diffused.

Before the inventive German propagandist supplied the more brilliant explanation of British gold, it was a favorite doctrine of Socialist thinkers that *The Times* was an organ of the Morgan firm. J. P. Morgan & Co. held $25,000 of the debentures of the old company, like Mr. Belmont, and like him accepted for these obligations an equal amount of the bonds of the new company, which were also bought and paid for by *The Times* at par value and retired

years ago. Numerous other financiers, traction magnates and politicians, shady and otherwise, have also figured in these romances, but none of them ever owned a dollar's worth of The Times Company stock or in any manner had the power to influence the policies of *The Times*, editorial or other. Nor did any of them ever get anything out of *The Times* except such information as they may have obtained from its news columns or such moral elevation as they may have derived from the study of its editorial page. And it might be added that none of them was ever in a position to control, influence or affect the paper's policies.

But theorists who have been unwilling to display favoritism by believing that any one man was the secret master of *The Times*, when so many have been mentioned, have cherished the belief that the paper was dominated by its bondholders as a group. It is not. The outstanding bonds amount to less than $600,000. The name of every person or institution holding more than 1 per cent of this not very formidable amount may be found on the editorial page of the paper, twice a year. These bonds represent the residue of an issue of $1,200,000 put out some years ago in financing the construction of The Times Building after retiring the bonds of 1896. The bonds were bought, just as any other bonds are bought, by people who thought they were a good investment; who believed, that is to say, that *The Times* would be able to pay interest and principal. It will be noted that more than half that issue has already been retired out of earnings.

As *The Times* grew and moved into new quarters

it had to make heavy investments in real estate and machinery. The Times Building, like any other new building, was mortgaged during its construction. The mortgage was placed like any other mortgage — because those who made the loan thought that the Times Building was a safe risk. It is being constantly reduced, and is now less than a million dollars — on property worth several times that amount. So bonds and mortgage, the total indebtedness of the company, amount to something like $1,500,000. The cash resources of the company are more than sufficient to pay this off at any time. The value of the company's real estate and paper-mill properties, entirely apart from plant, good will and other resources, is several times the indebtedness. So virtually *The New York Times* as a newspaper entity is free of any indebtedness of any kind or description.

Where did the money come from which built up the institution? Aside from $100,000 of the $200,000 of new capital provided by the sale of bonds in 1896, it came out of the earnings. Of the money which the paper has earned during the last twenty-five years, in round figures $100,000,000, 97 per cent has been put into the operation and development of the property and 3 per cent has been kept for the owners in dividends. There have been commercial borrowings from time to time, as in any business; but the loans have always been paid promptly, and in no case were the lenders influenced by any other consideration than the belief that they would be paid promptly.

Indeed, why should the owners of *The Times*

submit to outside influence? They own a large and prosperous institution, out of debt, which brings them in all the income they can reasonably require. Quite aside from moral considerations and the reluctance which many men feel to sell their souls, the owners and controllers of *The Times* have no particular use for "British gold," or Wall Street gold, or any other gold that might be offered for the control of the paper. They have all the "gold" necessary for their requirements.

It is perhaps a tribute to the prosperity of *The Times* that it is rarely accused of being controlled by its advertisers. It is accused of about everything else, but this charge would be too obviously ridiculous. It may be in order to observe, however, that even in the days when it was struggling desperately *The Times* was never controlled by its advertisers. Certain advertisers, on occasion, may have made efforts to influence the business policy of the paper. They never succeeded; sometimes they withdrew their advertising, but they nearly always came back, and came back knowing that they were buying advertising space and nothing more.

The Times is sometimes called the organ of the investing classes. The concept of a class organ is somewhat more familiar in Europe than in the United States, where about its only true exemplars, aside from trade journals, can be found in those socialist papers which speak for the modest number of sectarians who consider themselves the whole working class. *The Times* can be called the organ of the investing class only in the sense that most investors

read it because of the volume and reliability of its financial news. Because most investors read it, it is the favored medium for financial advertising. But financial advertising, like any other advertising, buys only advertising space. As a matter of fact, the belief that newspapers as a class are controlled by their advertisers is a popular delusion not much more respectable than the belief that breaking a mirror brings bad luck. Breaking some mirrors does bring bad luck — in restaurants and barrooms, for example; and some newspapers may be controlled by their advertisers. The proportion is considerably smaller than it was twenty-five years ago, and it is growing smaller every year.

No, *The Times* is not owned or controlled by Lord Northcliffe or Wall Street bankers or traction interests or the owners of department stores. It is owned by the men and women whose names appear in the list of stockholders, officially published every six months, and controlled by the owner of its majority stock, Adolph S. Ochs.

As has been said, the $200,000 obtained by the sale of bonds for cash was supposed to provide the working capital for the newspaper. Mr. Ochs discovered after taking charge that unfunded obligations of the paper would eat up half that sum. He had, then, about $100,000 to go on; and that is all the fresh capital that has been put into *The Times* since 1896. It has paid its way out of its earnings.

The purpose of the new management was announced in the following salutatory published on

the editorial page over Mr. Ochs's signature on August 19, 1896:

> To undertake the management of *The New York Times,* with its great history for right-doing, and to attempt to keep bright the lustre which Henry J. Raymond and George Jones have given it is an extraordinary task. But if a sincere desire to conduct a high-standard newspaper, clean, dignified and trustworthy, requires honesty, watchfulness, earnestness, industry and practical knowledge applied with common sense, I entertain the hope that I can succeed in maintaining the high estimate that thoughtful, pure-minded people have ever had of *The New York Times.*
>
> It will be my earnest aim that *The New York Times* give the news, all the news, in concise and attractive form, in language that is parliamentary in good society, and give it as early, if not earlier, than it can be learned through any other reliable medium; to give the news impartially, without fear or favor, regardless of any party, sect or interest involved; to make of the columns of *The New York Times* a forum for the consideration of all questions of public importance, and to that end to invite intelligent discussion from all shades of opinion.
>
> There will be no radical changes in the personnel of the present efficient staff. Mr. Charles R. Miller, who has so ably for many years presided over the editorial page, will continue to be the editor; nor will there be a departure from the general tone and character and policies pursued with relation to public questions that have

> distinguished *The New York Times* as a non-partisan newspaper — unless it be, if possible, to intensify its devotion to the cause of sound money and tariff reform, opposition to wastefulness and peculation in administering public affairs and in its advocacy of the lowest tax consistent with good government, and no more government than is absolutely necessary to protect society, maintain individual and vested rights and assure the free exercise of a sound conscience.

It will be seen that this platform was in large degree a reaffirmation of the traditional principles of *The Times*. From the ideal of impartiality of news and of discussion the paper had indeed departed considerably in its most Republican days, but it had returned after its declaration of independence in 1884. The emphasis upon certain features of this newspaper policy, however, was dictated by conditions of the times. Reference to *The Times's* appeal to "thoughtful, pure-minded people" and the promise that news would be given "earlier than it can be learned through any other reliable medium" were the first guns in the aggressive war against "yellow journalism," which *The Times* now undertook, and which it carried through to entire success. But at the outset that fight seemed all but hopeless. "Yellow" journalism was a good deal more powerful in the nineties than today; and it was a good deal yellower.

Mr. Pulitzer, who had awakened the eighties by his development of *The World*, had been followed and imitated in the early nineties by Mr. Hearst, who

made prodigal expenditures of money and was not hampered by any of the restraints which modified some of the enterprises of his rival. If in some details of outward appearance the journals then called "yellow" are in our day even more excruciating, their character is not so offensive — and it must be remembered, of course, that *The World* has undergone such a development in the last two decades that it long ago lost the character of a "yellow" journal as that phrase was understood when the "Yellow Kid" cartoons first brought it into currency. *The World* and *The Journal* in 1896 were considered quite deplorable from most points of view. But they were prosperous; they sold for one cent, and had enormous circulations as circulations went in those days; they made a great deal of noise about themselves and about each other, and attracted a corresponding amount of attention; they spent money wildly for new features, or even to get news. And they embellished the news with such unsavory details as are perhaps less often given to the public today, and in any event are less offensive to the somewhat broader tolerance of our time than they were in the nineties.

The consequent reaction of a considerable part of the reading public was very much the same as forty-five years before, when Raymond had set out to conduct a paper which should be welcomed into the homes which found no interest in the trivialities of *The Sun*, and were repelled by the vulgarity of *The Herald* and by what was regarded as the insidious immorality of *The Tribune*. A good many homes, schools and clubs deliberately excluded *The World* and *The Journal* in 1896; but their fierce rivalry,

their reckless expenditure, and even in some degree the quality of the brains which they had been able to obtain, gave them a certain advantage over their competitors. Of the other papers of the period, *The Sun* was brilliantly written, and was read chiefly by people who liked brilliant writing. It printed as much news as its reporters and correspondents, in the pressure of more important business, had time to get, and as its make-up men found it necessary to admit to the columns as an offset to literature. Aside from that, its energies were principally devoted to the contentions that New Yorkers could never be persuaded to ride in subway trains, and that Whitelaw Reid had driven Horace Greeley to the madhouse and the grave. *The Herald* was a daily directory, had an excellent foreign service, but otherwise had no particular claim on the attention of readers unless they happened to be interested in the doings of a somewhat curiously defined "society" or in premature burial, dogs, and more dubious topics of interest. *The Tribune* carried a small but genteel stock of Republican ideas, most of which had lain for a considerable time on the shelves. There was room for a paper whose first object was to get the news promptly and publish it with due attention to its relative value — a paper so conducted that nobody need be ashamed to be seen reading it, but containing all the solid content which intelligent readers wanted, and for which, in desperation, they sometimes had to burrow in the muck heaps of the "yellows."

This ideal of *The Times* was presently expressed in the motto "All the News That's Fit to Print,"

first published on the editorial page on October 25, 1896, and carried in a box on the front page from February 10 of the following year down to the present day. Probably no newspaper motto has ever aroused more discussion or more obstinate difference of opinion — a difference, it may be observed, which is to be found in *The Times* office as well as outside. In its most literal and narrowest interpretation it of course suggests that terrible crime widely discussed under the title of "suppression of news." This phrase itself is something of a begging of the question, for no newspaper is large enough to publish accounts of all happenings even if anybody would read them. In every newspaper office every day there must be a selection of the most interesting or important happenings, as many of them as can be crowded into the paper. In the sense that the less interesting or important items have to be left out there is "suppression of news" in every newspaper office all the time, as many self-admiring persons have discovered.

"All the News That's Fit to Print," however, has been criticised, even by more or less friendly commentators, as implying the exercise of editorial judgment as to what news may be too horrible or obscene for the public — a right which, it is assumed, no editor possesses. But no newspaper ever published all the harrowing details of the Armenian massacres, for instance. The essential facts were published; the decorative trimmings could well be left to the imagination. It has been argued that if it is news of sufficient importance it is fit to print. *The Times* has never held otherwise. The fact of

an atrocious crime or a deplorable scandal is news. The sordid particulars have sometimes a legitimate news value, but more often their only appeal is to the salacious curiosity.

The motto has often been contrasted with Dana's remark that "whatever Divine Providence permits to occur I am not too proud to report." But there are certain details of events permitted by Divine Providence which have never been and will never be printed in *The Sun*, even though mention of the events in a general way may be published as news. It is a question of methods, of treatment, of emphasis — a fact which may easily be proved by the protests which *The Times* often receives against items published in its columns which seem to some of its readers unfit to print. There is often a difference of opinion among editors of *The Times* as to whether the unassailable general principle that what is news should be printed justifies the inclusion of certain details which are of dubious fitness; and no doubt the practice of the paper occasionally fails to agree altogether with this excellent principle. But the influence of the motto is present none the less. It has been described as "a silent monitor at the copy desk"; and in the course of years its influence has been sufficient to keep a good deal of contaminating and worthless material out of the paper.

If it be held that a doctrine so difficult to define precisely is a rather unsafe guide, it should be remembered that it was first adopted in somewhat unusual circumstances. In effect, "All the News That's Fit to Print" was a war cry, the slogan under

which the reorganized *Times* fought for a footing against the formidable competition of *The Herald, The World* and *The Journal.* What it meant, in essence, was that *The Times* was going to be as good a vehicle of news as any of those papers, and that it would be free from their indecency, eccentricity, distortion or sensationalism. The publisher of *The Times* once answered a question as to what news is unfit to print with the brief definition, "What's untrue." A great deal of the so-called news published by some of *The Times's* contemporaries in 1896 was untrue — sometimes, though not very often, deliberately invented; more frequently mishandled, edited or colored until it conveyed an entirely inaccurate impression. There was to be none of this sort of thing in *The Times*, and so far as its editors are humanly able to live up to their good intentions, there never has been. Moreover, the columns of *The Times* were not to be filled with matter which depended for its interest to the public purely on its appeal to prurient cravings or to unwarranted suspicion. The motto selected in 1896 might have been restated as "The news, all the news and nothing but the news." This was the sort of paper, and the only sort of paper, which the new publisher of *The Times* would or could produce; it was still to be seen whether he was right in believing that New York in the nineties offered a living for such a paper, and the experiment was begun under a heavy handicap — with an outworn plant, a tradition of misfortune and a discouraged staff, to say nothing of the general opinion that the new venture had little chance of success.

The new publisher was quite as well aware as anybody else of the difficulties which he had to face, but he was of the opinion that there were some counterbalancing advantages which had been overlooked by some of the men who had thought *The Times* beyond hope of recovery. In the first place, it did have a great tradition. Within the memory of many thousands of newspaper readers — indeed until a few years previously — it had been one of the great newspapers of the country. Its name and standing had by no means been destroyed by its comparatively brief period of misfortune. In a sense, the good will was still there.

It was not on the surface, of course; it would have to be dug out and cultivated, as the experience of the previous management showed. Nevertheless, the gentlemen who had sold the name and good will of the paper for a million dollars in 1893 had, perhaps, given better value than they realized. *The Times* had fallen into a situation from which it could work out only by showing merit, but once that merit was shown it would find a welcome in many homes where it had been a valued friend in the past. A new paper with a new name would have had to spend an enormous amount of money to establish this friendly disposition which the new management of *The Times* would find ready to welcome it — if *The Times* could succeed in recovering the attention of these readers.

And it should be observed that the reconstruction of *The Times* involved no change in the essential character of the paper. The new publisher indulged in no eccentric experiments, no efforts to emulate

prominent and profitable features of rival publications. It is perhaps fortunate that his capital was so small, for he did not have the money to do this sort of thing, even if he had wanted to. He felt that the chief asset of *The Times* was its character, its tradition, its good will. That character was to be preserved. The remnant of old readers who continued to buy *The Times* because they liked that kind of paper were not to be driven away by any sudden alteration of the paper's character in the vain effort to emulate its competitors. *The Times* was to be the same kind of paper as of old, a kind of paper which a large part of the reading public was known to like; the changes under the new management were intended only to make it a better paper of that kind.

Another item of value was the paper's staff. The new publisher intended to make no changes unless experience showed him that change was necessary, for he had a high admiration for the staff as he found it. Indeed, the men then getting out *The Times* were, on the whole, the men who had produced and edited it in the days of its greatness. They were no longer getting the results which they had got then; but this was due to a complex of reasons in which the inexperience of the heirs of George Jones, the bad luck of their successors in taking over the paper without any working capital on the eve of a financial panic, and the lack of a sound business organization were most important. Given even a little breathing space from importunate financial obligations, and a somewhat better direction of energy, and they could make it a great paper once more.

THE TIMES EDITORIAL COUNCIL.

Left to right: Osmond Phillips, Edward M. Kingsbury, John Corbin, Rollo Ogden, Charles R. Miller, E. A. Bradford, F. C. Mortimer, John H. Finley, F. T. Birchall, Adolph S. Ochs, Carr V. Van Anda, Elmer Davis, H. E. Armstrong, Julius O. Adler, Louis Wiley, Arthur Hays Sulzberger and Ralph H. Graves.

Nevertheless, the situation was bad enough. When Mr. Ochs assumed the control of *The Times*, an old and trusted employé, to whom had been confided some of the details of the paper's management too painful to be widely disseminated, took him into his office, unlocked his rolltop desk, and with tears in his eyes imparted to the new publisher his shameful secret. *The Times* was printing 19,000 copies a day, and 10,000 of them were coming back unsold. The net circulation was 9000, and it was growing smaller every day. Mr. Ochs said something to the effect that he thought the circulation would be increased before long. "Increased!" said his astounded hearer. "Increased! Mr. Ochs, if you could keep it from going down any further you'd be a wonderful man."

However, the new publisher set to work to see what he could do. One item of waste which was soon reduced, though it was a long time before it was entirely eliminated, was the printing of papers that came back to the office old paper bin from the news stands where they had vainly waited for purchasers. While staying in New York and making arrangements for the purchase of *The Times* Mr. Ochs had noticed that at the news stand he patronized he was always offered *The Sun*. At first he felt rather flattered at the idea that the keen-eyed newsdealer had judged him to be the sort of man who would want *The Sun;* for this was in the height of Dana's fame as a producer of newspaper literature, and to be seen reading *The Sun* was, at that time, a mark of intellectual distinction. But inquiry discovered that the newsdealer was actuated by a more sordid

motive. *The Sun* circulation system allowed no returns; and in consequence the first thing the newsdealer thought of was to sell off his stock of *Suns.* When they were gone he could turn to the distribution of the other papers with the restful assurance that such copies as he could not sell could be sent back to the office and would cost him nothing. It seemed to Mr. Ochs, upon reflection, that the papers which permitted the return of unsold copies were in effect supplying the capital for the promotion of *The Sun.*

So *The Times* first reduced the return privilege to 10 per cent, presently abolished it entirely for the Saturday issue with the literary supplement, and eventually eliminated it altogether. Thereafter the bills for print paper could be paid with the consoling assurance that, at any rate, *The Times* was paid for every copy sent out to the newsdealers. Meanwhile the new publisher had been finding his way about the office. He had the idea that the essentials of successful newspaper publishing were pretty much the same in New York and in Chattanooga; that, as he afterward expressed it, the best policy was "no policy" — a reliance on honesty, industry and unhampered judgment. In time this doctrine proved its worth by its practical success, but it seemed so strange at the time that years afterward the editor of another New York paper said that Mr. Ochs had come to town and "taught us something new." It did not seem so to him; he thought he had merely reminded New York newspaper men of something they had forgotten.

In a sense, of course, that statement could be

applied to the rise of almost any successful newspaper. Perhaps the history of journalism could be expressed in a formula of rotary motion. Every twenty years or so somebody achieves a great success by digging up an old truth that had been discarded. One truth rediscovered on *The Times* in the nineties, however, has perhaps a more generally useful application than the secrets of the success of other newspapers. This is the ancient but still somewhat surprising fact that thorough knowledge and unremitting diligence are likely, barring accident, to bring results. The new publisher of *The Times*, who had come from the interior of the country to undertake the solution of a problem which to veterans of New York journalism seemed entirely hopeless, was regarded by a good many observers as a man with more money than brains — a judgment which, in view of the actual state of his fortunes, was anything but complimentary. But he knew every department of the newspaper business from the ground up.

It was his opinion that *The Times* staff, as it then existed, was as competent and well equipped a body of men as could be found on any newspaper in the country, and that the paper could be rehabilitated by those men. What they needed was more coordination and a little more enthusiasm. Too many of the subordinates had allowed themselves to slip into a groove and were conducting their own particular duties in a routine grown familiar with years of practice without paying much attention to the relation of their work to the whole. Men were apt to stick to themselves and ignore what went on about them.

The arrival of the new publisher brought a good deal of encouragement to men at the top who had become acquainted with him and had caught something of his enthusiasm, but for most of the staff enthusiasm had to wait for acquaintance. When Mr. Ochs came in with the intention of turning *The Times* around and starting it uphill the majority of the staff watched him with interest, but at first without any great amount of confidence. He was a new man and unknown, and he had undertaken a job which seemed to be too much for anybody. He was welcome, because the ruin of the paper, without some new stimulus, seemed only a question of time; but it was still to be seen if he could give it that stimulus.

As for the publisher, he experienced a certain diffidence as he began to familiarize himself with his new associates. He was now set as commanding officer over men, a good many of them older than himself, of whom he had been hearing for years with a certain amount of awe. These great names of New York journalism had resounded rather thunderously in Chattanooga, and it required a considerable time for Mr. Ochs to get over his conviction that they were persons of a somewhat different order of professional eminence, or that, at any rate, they were New Yorkers, while he was fresh from a small town. Nevertheless, he set to work to invigorate the staff, to inspire it with new courage, and to find out in the meantime what was the matter with *The Times*. Much was done from the very first in bringing the members of the staff together; but it may serve as an illustration of the necessity of beginning pretty much from the ground up that the publisher found

that one of his first tasks was to educate the staff into reading the paper.

They were induced to read *The Times* by the somewhat roundabout expedient of giving to each man the task of comparing each day's issue of *The Times* with one of its contemporaries. The publisher had discovered that the writers had preferences among the other morning papers, and he assigned each man to find out every morning what his pet paper had discovered that was unknown to *The Times*. It perhaps goes without saying that this task of comparison was already part of the work of the news department; it was laid upon the editorial council for purely educational reasons. And it worked. Before long the men who were reading *The Times* because they had to know if it had been beaten on the day's news found themselves compelled to admit that there was a good deal in it that was worth reading.

This instance may illustrate the work which had to be done in coördinating the work of the various members of *The Times* staff. The work was done, because there was a directing influence to see that it was done; and before long *The Times* had an organization, still rudimentary, but more deserving of the name than anything it had ever known before. There was a man at the head who understood the work of every department from his own experience, and who not only knew whether that work was being well done, but had been able to inspire the workers with a more vivid interest in the welfare of the whole institution. And another element in their confidence, perhaps of slower growth, was the realiza-

tion that the new chief was in complete and absolute control, unhampered by any external influences whatever. It is unfortunately true that outside influence on many newspapers has been — a past tense is used because this condition though still existing in some newspaper offices, is much less general now than it used to be — so strong that a good many newspaper men of wide experience find it hard to believe that it is not universal. *The Times* has had a good deal of difficulty in persuading some of its employés that news is not to be handled in deference to editorial policy, just as it had trouble in the nineties in convincing them that news was not to be treated with a view to the supposed prejudices of influential outsiders. The new publisher was to a certain extent regarded for a time as the representative of the men who had sunk their money in *The Times* a few years before; and it took time for the employés to realize that he was conducting it himself, without any orders from outside. When they did realize it, as he took care they should, it gave a tremendous impetus to the industry of a staff which had been afraid of shadows for some time past, and now at last began to realize that they were only shadows.

Meanwhile there had been some experiments with the contents of *The Times*. Certain departments had continued for years by the force of inertia, and it was suspected by the new publisher that they no longer served any useful purpose. One of the daily features of the paper was a feuilleton, which Mr. Ochs suppressed as soon as he took charge. The paper happened on that dav to be publishing the

next to the last instalment of a continued story. Mr. Ochs did not want fiction, and he insisted that the story stop right there, but was persuaded to let the concluding chapters appear next day.

It is true that the largest newspaper circulation in the world has been built up by the *Petit Parisien* on the basis of serial fiction and human interest, and it is true that even so dignified a paper as the *Temps* lately gave up much of its scanty space to the serial publication of Florence Barclay's novel, "The Rosary." But, aside from the question of the difference in French and American ideas of a newspaper, it must be remembered that the American institution of the popular fiction magazine is unknown in France. The newspapers are both newspapers and fiction magazines, in effect. Whatever may or may not have been the increment in circulation gained by various American newspaper magazine sections through the publication of fiction, it may be doubted if any American paper ever accomplished much by printing fiction in its daily issue, unless it be that peculiar type of fiction which is written for and found only upon the woman's page of evening newspapers. At any rate, *The Times* never suffered from its abandonment of the popular fiction field to the new venture of Mr. McClure, which was just then opening a new epoch in American magazine history.

Another department which was abolished was the detailed report of prices in the commodity markets. Again Mr. Ochs found dissent from his opinion that these had no place in *The Times*, and that people who were interested in this item were a good deal more likely to get it out of the trade papers. So

strong was the opposition of the circulation department to the abandonment of this feature that the publisher finally decided to try dropping out these reports a little at a time. A stick here and a stick there, the space given to commodity markets was reduced without any expected clamors of protest from readers who had learned to look for it every morning. At last, when four whole columns of what is technically known as "punk" had been excised from the paper, *The Times* did hear from a subscriber at Haverstraw, who wrote that he missed the quotations on naval stores. And that was all. It was demonstrated to be a sheer waste of valuable space.

Some of this material eventually found its way back into the paper, but in better form. Where the new management found a legitimate field of the news which existing papers had left uncovered it took up and gave some attention to it, but there was to be no more competition with trade journals on their own ground. And when "punk" came back, the deadening routine which had gradually deprived these old departments of their usefulness had disappeared. It is probable that by the publication of the complete court calendars, for instance, *The Times* has gained a considerable number of readers, and the great development of the page of business news, which began early in the history of the present administration but grew gradually through many years, has made *The Times* the favorite daily of many men in businesses which are served by extraordinarily good trade papers. But the entire process, both of subtraction and of addition, has been a matter of special judgment in individual cases. If

an existing department seemed to be serving no useful purpose, it went out; if the addition of a new department promised to justify the effort and expense, it was introduced. How to decide what was needed and what could be abolished? Well, it is betraying no trade secret to say that this was a matter of judgment based on experience.

But the mere cutting out of dead wood was only a part, and a small part, of the work. The rise from 9000 to 350,000 was not accomplished by mere elimination of useless items, nor by tightening up the business office, establishing a sound accounting system and cutting losses. There had to be some positive achievements. One of the most useful of these was the wide advertisement of the policy expressed in the motto, "All the News That's Fit to Print." That motto, when adopted, aroused a good deal of discussion which was fostered and abetted by the management of the paper. For some months a huge electric sign at Twenty-third Street and Broadway made known to the passing throng the legend of *The Times*. There were some editorial expositions of the ideals expressed by the motto, and after these had made *Times* readers familiar with the intentions of the new publisher a prize of $100 was offered for any ten-word motto which seemed better to express those ideals. Richard Watson Gilder, editor of the *Century*, was asked to act as judge in the contest, which brought out some 20,000 suggestions, of which 150 were thought good enough to publish. The prize was given to "All the World's News, but Not a School for Scandal"; but to the editors of *The Times* this did not seem as satisfac-

tory as their own device, so though the inventor of this motto got his $100, "All the News That's Fit to Print" continued to be the motto of the paper. All this attracted a certain amount of attention to the new methods on an old paper, and a certain number of readers were drawn to buy *The Times* and find out what all the disturbance was about. It is hardly necessary to say that the advertisement would have been useless if they had not discovered, on examining *The Times*, that it was living up to its promises; that it was giving the news and presenting it with sanity and decency.

Meanwhile some new and valuable features had been added to the paper. The first of these, and one of the most important, was the illustrated Sunday magazine, first published as part of the Sunday paper on September 6, 1896, three weeks after Mr. Ochs took control. Newspaper Sunday magazines in that day were distinguished chiefly by the so-called comic supplement — a feature which *The Times* has never had, never needed, and never desired. The magazine section, in the narrower sense of the word, was also influenced chiefly by the "yellow" journals; the type is still represented by some belated survivals, rather less flamboyant than twenty-five years ago. Against this *The Times* offered a pictorial supplement printed on good coated paper and illustrated with half-tone photographs. It was as great an advance in its day as the more recent rotogravure pictorial supplement, and it gave a real illustrated news magazine to the New York newspaper public.

This magazine was popular from the very first.

Perhaps its greatest accomplishment was the publication of the pictures of Queen Victoria's jubilee in 1897. Fifty photographs of the procession on June 22 were bought at 10 guineas apiece from the official photographer and rushed to New York; and on July 4 *The Times Illustrated Magazine* published sixteen pages of them. They were not only published in *The Times* before any other New York paper had them, but they were well printed so that the reader could see what they were — something which a reproduction on ordinary newsprint could hardly have accomplished. That feat, which cost altogether $5000 — a considerable sum to *The Times* of 1897 — is still remembered in the office as one of the first of a long series of beats, and it added greatly to the reputation of the illustrated magazine. But week in and week out that magazine was widely prized; and when it was discontinued in September, 1899, after three years of existence, chiefly because *The Times* had attained so large a circulation that the magazine could no longer be produced by the inadequate plant then available, it left a good many mourners, who only in recent years have found an adequate substitute in the present pictorial and magazine supplements of the Sunday paper.

Perhaps the most important service of that magazine in the long run was its effect on other newspapers, many of which were inspired to imitate it. This was true in a still higher degree of the next feature of the rejuvenated *Times* — the Saturday Review of Books, first published on October 10, 1896, and edited then and long afterward by Francis W. Halsey. In this publication was carried out an idea

of the publisher of *The Times* that a newspaper book review should be a literary newspaper, treating newly published books as news and containing besides other news of literary happenings. While open to criticism from several standpoints, the treating of books as news is certainly more in accordance with the function of a daily newspaper, as well as somewhat easier to do well, than more serious effort at literary criticism. And in *The Times Saturday Review* the news of the literary world was assembled and presented better than ever before in an American daily. Moreover, the new tabloid form, with the excellent typography and good quality of paper used, attracted the attention of readers to book news which they might have passed by in the columns of the regular edition.

As an example of the conviction of students of literature that it did meet a long-felt want may be cited the action of Professor C. Alphonso Smith, then at the Louisiana State University, who required all members of some of his classes in English literature to take *The Times Book Review* in order to keep up with current events in the literary field. This publication, too, has since been imitated, and in some instances improved upon, but in 1896 it was a new idea which once more made the New York public realize that something was happening on *The Times.* Its ultimate service to the cause of book reviewing in the United States — a cause which still needs all the help it can get, but which is considerably better off than it was in 1896 — was perhaps even greater than its contribution to the well-being of *The Times.*

For a considerable time, indeed, it seemed that

this new publication was to be a gratuitous and disinterested contribution to American letters. It found immediate favor with readers, but not with advertisers. Book publishers argued that when the book reviews were embodied in the regular news columns of the paper, as had previously been the custom, they and the adjacent advertising would be seen by the general reader; whereas if they were segregated in a special supplement they would receive the attention only of the limited and presumably impecunious section of the reading public which was interested in books. Only very slowly did the publishers realize that people who were interested in books were more likely to buy books when they had any money to buy them with than those who irritably turned over the sheet in order to escape from the book reviews to the sporting news on the next page. After the first publisher tried the experiment of advertising in the Book Review others soon followed, and before long the publication was paying its way.

There were disadvantages about the publication of the literary supplement on Saturday. It had to be in the form of loose sheets, folded into the rest of the paper. If the reader did not want the Book Review he merely opened up the paper and let the sheets flutter out — and they fluttered well. The Saturday morning paper, naturally, was read by people on their way downtown to work. Those who didn't care to carry the Book Review about with them — they rarely failed to "look over" it — let it blow away in the wind, so one morning the management of *The Times* was attracted, and rather ag-

grieved, by a cartoon in *Life* entitled "The Littery Supplement," and depicting a citizen desperately trying to struggle out of an elevated station through a heap of discarded sheets of *The Times Saturday Book Review.*

This was publicity, though not of the most favorable sort; but it was finally decided that the Book Review would go better with the Sunday paper, in most instances delivered at the home, where it could be conveniently laid aside for reading at leisure. Once more, however, the book publishers were disturbed by the change. Some of them had scruples against advertising in a Sunday paper. One or two publishers held out for a little while and insisted on advertising only in the regular issue of Saturday; but their rivals soon began to get results which gradually drew all the book advertising into the Book Review supplement to the Sunday edition.

The more recent history of *The Times Book Review* is another matter. Superficially, its combination with the magazine section may seem to be a reversal of the principle on which the literary supplement was originally separated from the body of the paper; but the present-day *Book Review and Magazine* is still in a process of development whose event, it is hoped, will justify the belief of the management of *The Times* that a still better literary newspaper is attainable than has ever yet been produced. If the history of the various transformations of *The Times* literary supplement shows anything, it shows that books are, generally speaking, bought by the people who like to read about books; and that literary advertising will bring results if

placed alongside literary news, wherever that may be.

Still another feature was added to *The Times* on November 8, 1897, in the weekly financial review which was published for a number of years thereafter as a supplement to the Monday morning paper. Each of these additions to the paper brought new readers, and others were constantly being attracted by the slow and steady improvement of the quality of the paper.

Another innovation of the new management was the giving over of much of the space allotted to letters from readers to the views of those who disagreed with the editorial opinions of the paper. This was not wholly a novelty in American journalism, but *The Times* now began to do it on a scale previously unknown. Not so very many years before 1896 most American newspapers (*The Times* among them) had been reluctant to print even news which did not accord with editorial policy. That time had passed, and the new management of *The Times* now made a point of opening its columns to the presentation of views on any side of any subject, as a matter of news and as a contribution to the formation of well-grounded opinion. Almost all decent newspapers do that now, but it was a novelty in the nineties.

It has, perhaps, some perils; certain inveterate self-advertisers have nothing to do but flood the columns of all newspapers with their letters, and if the editors occasionally feel that other people have a right to be heard these correspondents at once conclude that they are being suppressed for unworthy reasons. Also, if a book review opens its

correspondence page to all comers, that page is likely to be filled with complaints from authors who feel that the reviewers did not do justice to their works. Nevertheless, the practice is now universally recognized as useful and necessary, an opinion which was a rarity in the days when *The Times* first began to invite letters from people who disagreed with it.

The editorial page was as good as ever. In the campaign of 1896, when the paper supported the Gold Democratic ticket of Palmer and Buckner, *The Times's* editorial arguments for sound money were powerful and effective. The publisher and the editors took the issues of that campaign so seriously that they all marched in the great gold parade, the biggest New York had ever known; and they had the satisfaction of feeling at the end of the campaign that *The Times's* editorial attitude had counted for a good deal in the sound money discussion. The improvement of the news columns in the direction of impartiality, which had made much progress since the secession of *The Times* from the Republican Party, was carried still further under a new publisher who was interested in politics only as an external observer and good citizen. The loss of subscribers had been stopped; in the first year and a half of the new management the circulation had more than doubled; and the deficit was now rapidly approaching the vanishing point.

Advertising was coming to the paper in increasing amounts. It had been the boast of Mr. Jones that no man had ever been asked to subscribe to *The Times* or to advertise in *The Times*. If he chose to do either, that was his own affair; but nobody

CARR V.
VAN ANDA,
Managing
Editor.
© Underwood &
Underwood.

LOUIS WILEY,
Business Manager.

would give him any provocation. Whatever the merits or demerits of this attitude, the time for it had passed by 1896. If a newspaper owner of that period chose to regard his paper as something which he published for his own personal pleasure there was considerable danger that the public would respect his reticence. The new management of *The Times* had space to sell for legitimate advertising, which in its opinion would satisfy the purchaser and give him his money's worth, and they did not regard it as beneath their dignity to tell him about it.

Nevertheless, certain types of advertising were from the first carefully excluded. While not all patent medicines are kept out of *The Times's* advertising columns, the rules adopted under the new management were so strict that almost all of this matter was automatically rejected. Patent medicine advertising was much more general, of course, twenty-five years ago; today it survives in a few metropolitan journals of somewhat antediluvian standards, and is a welcome guest of many publications in the smaller towns. Some of it is legitimate advertising, but so much of it is not that *The Times* felt that its publication could do no good, while in many instances it did positive harm.

Word puzzles and similar schemes in which prizes were offered for something which looked easy, but was generally impossible of accomplishment, were also excluded. Persons who offered something for nothing, who guaranteed the cure of illnesses or the payment of large dividends, also found themselves compelled to display their wares in other papers. It was and is the conviction of the publisher of *The*

Times that honesty is the best policy, and that business success cannot be securely founded on misrepresentation and fraud. There is doubtless a considerable part of the public which will always be too stupid to know that it is being deceived, or too listless to care; but *The Times* was not aiming at that class of readers.

It has sometimes been objected that discrimination against objectionable advertising should logically be carried to the point of investigating all advertising before publication. *The Times* does not do this. It does investigate all advertisements as to which it has any reason to entertain suspicion; and if the suspicion remains after investigation, even though nothing is proved, the reader is given the benefit of the doubt and the advertising is excluded. The principles above mentioned result in the wholesale exclusion from *The Times* of those classes of advertisements in which there is most likely to be misrepresentation. In other fields a sharp watch is maintained for fraudulent advertising, with results which may be fully appreciated if *The Times's* financial advertising, for example, be compared with that of some of its contemporaries.

Elimination of questionable material is, of course, considerably easier in financial than in mercantile advertising. In this latter field it has seemed to *The Times* that the exercise of ordinary vigilance is about all that can be expected of a newspaper. The newspaper may do a good deal in the suppression of improper claims by advertisers, but it cannot do all the reader's thinking.

Two instances of rejection of advertising by *The*

Times, very early in the history of the present management, deserve special notice. As permitted, though not enjoined, by the election laws of 1896, the Board of Aldermen in that year voted that the complete canvass of the vote in the city should be published in six daily newspapers. *The Times* was one of the six papers selected, but it promptly attacked the decision as a waste of public money and urged that publication be confined to the one paper mandatory under the law — which would not have been *The Times*. This report was of enormous volume, and its publication, at the ordinary rates, would have brought to every paper carrying it some $33,600 — a total of over $200,000. *The Times* needed $33,600 rather badly just then, but it declined the advertisement in an editorial which called the election canvass "a waste of public money." The members of the Board of Aldermen professed to be startled and horrified by the discovery that the expense would be so heavy. Certainly they were horrified by this proclamation to the public that so much money was being thrown away, and the publication was finally reduced to the smallest amount permitted by law, none of which came to *The Times* — a result, of course, which had been expected.

Some months later all the regular advertising of the city government was unexpectedly offered to *The Times*. This amounted to about $150,000 a year, a sum which would have made a tremendous difference to *The Times* of that period. Moreover, assurances were brought to the management of the paper by a gentleman who was a friend both of the

publisher and of the Tammany leaders that this offer was made with absolutely no strings. It was neither the expectation nor the desire of Tammany that *The Times* should feel itself influenced in any way, and it was understood that the allotment of the advertising did not in any way involve a modification of *The Times's* general hostility to Tammany in local politics. The only reason for this sudden windfall, said the gentleman who brought the news, was the conviction of the Tammany leaders that it was a good thing for the general interests of the Democratic Party to have a conservative Democratic paper maintained in New York City. That paper's feelings about Tammany did not enter into the case.

The publisher of *The Times* had entire confidence in the good faith of the gentleman who gave him these assurances, and saw no need for questioning the good faith of the Tammany leaders. For whether or not their intentions were honorable, their proposal was unacceptable. It was asking too much of human nature to suppose that thereafter when *The Times* had reason to attack Tammany, as it certainly would (its exposures of graft payments for gambling-house protection were not very far in the future), the subconscious, if not the conscious minds of those in *The Times* office might be affected by the thought that $150,000 was at stake. By that time the paper might have got accustomed to living on a higher scale, and would have missed the $150,000 more than if it had never had it. Moreover, *The Times* was still far behind its rivals in circulation. If this considerable revenue were suddenly awarded to the smallest in circulation of New York

morning papers, everybody would believe that Tammany had bought *The Times,* no matter how pure the motives of the organization or of the paper's management. The shadow was as bad as the substance, in this case; from any point of view the offer was unacceptable.

Years later, in Mayor McClellan's administration, *The Times* was designated for a large part of the city advertising — the greater part mandatory in connection with condemnation proceedings in the matter of the Ashokan water supply. By that time the paper's circulation was large, and was growing by leaps and bounds. Its revenues were also large and increasing; there could no longer be any serious suspicion that *The Times* had reason to sell its soul for advertising patronage, and its selection as an advertising medium was a natural choice, for that selection had in the meantime been made by great numbers of private advertisers who had found that advertising in *The Times* would sell their goods.

Principles of this sort temporarily cost the paper a good deal of money. But on the whole it was fighting its way slowly back to prosperity. In its antagonism to "yellow" journalism it was beginning to find a good many friends. It was not alone in its attack upon the methods of *The Journal* and *The World; The Sun* and *The Press,* for example, made much more of a crusade out of it. But their effort was chiefly destructive; they devoted a good deal of space to attacks upon the personalities and practices of the "yellow" press. *The Times* was less concerned in holding up to the public view infamies already quite apparent to those who were capable

of being disturbed by them than in demonstrating to persons who did not like "yellow" journalism that *The Times* was the sort of paper they wanted.

The "yellows" fought back, of course. *The World* graciously referred to some of its journalistic critics as "doomed rats struggling in a pit," and endeavored to make it clear that a monopoly of journalistic purity was possessed by *The World*. In *The World's* opinion, *The Times* was owned by the trusts; it had been bought up by Wall Street speculators for their own selfish purposes. The basis of this legend, started in a quarter where it would probably be promptly repudiated today, was the very moderate amount of obligations of *The Times* held by certain bankers mentioned in the earlier part of this chapter. *The World*, of course, saw some advantages in circulating the suspicion that Mr. Ochs was not solely directing *The Times*, and it chose to regard him, and to speak of him, as "caretaker of the deficit."

The Times was making its way, slowly, but with increasing sureness among those who were disturbed by the tendencies of *The World* and *The Journal*. It was advertised by the assertion that "It does not soil the breakfast cloth." And this negative virtue no less than its positive excellences was winning it new readers all the time. Mr. Jason Rogers of *The New York Globe* has said that "If ever a newspaper was built brick upon brick, through the recommendation of one reader to a friend who was not yet reading, *The New York Times* was so built." This description, which could be generally applied to the growth of *The Times* in the last twenty-five years, is especially accurate as a description of the paper's

recovery in its first year and a half under the new management. It might have gone on growing at this steady pace, with no sudden mutations of fortune, had it not been for an event which, if not exactly unforeseen, could hardly have been provided against, which subjected the paper to an almost ruinous strain, and put it in jeopardy from which there was no escape but by the desperate expedient that, almost overnight, made its fortune. This event was the Spanish War.

The very first issue of *The Times*, on September 18, 1851, had carried an editorial on the Cuban question. Crittenden's filibusters, who had gone to aid the Lopez rebellion, had lately been captured and shot, and the rising itself had been put down. *The Times* saw in the failure of the Lopez rising proof that the Cubans did not want independence, and it opposed the annexationist agitation of that day on very solid grounds. For of course the Cuban question, in the fifties, was only part of the larger question of the slave empire of the Golden Circle. Annexation was desired by those who wanted another slave state, and opposed in the North precisely because that was the motive of those who wanted it. Even the article above referred to took a couple of paragraphs to explain that Americans would always sympathize with any people struggling to be free.

By 1898 the Cuban question was on a wholly different basis. Cuba was no longer a partisan interest in American politics, nor was there any doubt as to the popular support of the revolution which had be-

gun in 1895. *The Times* had held in Cleveland's Administration, and in the first year of McKinley's, that the distress and disorder in the island must be ended, and that if they could not be ended by Spain on a basis satisfactory to Cuba there might be need of American intervention. As the situation became more critical *The Times* editorial page discussed the right of intervention according to international law, coming to the conclusion that the United States Government would undoubtedly be justified in taking that step, should it prove impossible to settle the Cuban question by other means, on the ground of safeguarding the peace and safety of our own people who could not be persuaded to sit quietly by while the Cubans were fighting for freedom. President McKinley afterward acknowledged that these articles had been of great value in helping him to clarify his own views about the rights and duties of our Government in the crisis. In the weeks leading up to the declaration of war *The Times* had maintained a temperate attitude, hoping that some satisfactory solution might be reached without hostilities, but insisting that the Cuban question must now be settled, and finally settled. When the course of the war brought unexpected acquisitions of territory in the Pacific and the Caribbean, *The Times* could see little merit in the arguments of the anti-imperialists. In its opinion there was not much use talking about the desirability of expansion. Expansion had happened; it had come as an incident in an apparently inevitable historical development; and it had to be accepted as a fact. Mr. Bryan's zealous anti-imperialism only rein-

forced in the minds of the editors of *The Times* the impression that his attitude on the currency had already created, and his personality and the two major issues which he had selected led *The Times* to give its support to the Republican Presidential ticket in 1900, for the first time in sixteen years.

But if *The Times's* editorial reaction to the issues of the Spanish War honorably carried on the traditions of the paper's history, the other departments found the war all but disastrous. Advertising fell off ruinously in the spring and summer of 1898, when a good many excitable persons expected to be awakened any morning by the roar of Cervera's guns bombarding Coney Island. This loss, borne by all the papers, naturally fell with particular weight on the one which was just beginning to struggle back to financial security. *The Times*, indeed, managed to enliven the early period of the conflict by a private war of its own with certain advertisers. The North German Lloyd Steamship Company had sold a vessel to the Spanish Government, for use as a troopship or converted cruiser. *The Times* observed editorially that whatever the legal aspects of this sale of war material to the enemy, it was pretty poor business in the North German Lloyd thus to affront the people which was its best customer. This observation stirred up a too zealous official of that company not only to withdraw his own advertising from *The Times*, but to endeavor to persuade other steamship lines to follow his example, on the ground that this was unwarranted and intolerable criticism of a foreign transportation company.

This coming to the attention of *The Times*, its

editors were moved to the comment, several times repeated on the editorial page, that this transaction involved something which looked very much like criminal conspiracy. The right of the North German Lloyd to withdraw its own advertising was conceded, but when it attempted to form a combination against *The Times* it was taking a pretty long chance. The German line had chosen a highly unpopular issue, and before long friends of its managers were coming to *The Times* office and begging the paper to let up on them. The attempted combination was abandoned. Even if the German line had been successful, the loss of steamship advertising would have made no very great diminution in the income of any newspaper; but just then, in 1898, *The Times* needed all it could get — and indeed a good deal more.

Nor was it able to recover any of the lost ground on the basis of enormous increases in circulation. Some increase there was; *The Times* was growing from week to week — but growing slowly. And the war had suddenly forced it into a situation where it could not hope to compete against its more prosperous rivals.

The Spanish-American War was probably, from the viewpoint of a certain type of newspaper man, the most convenient war ever fought. It was a little war; it was a short war, and it was near at hand. Nor had there been any great conflicts in recent years which might have overshadowed it or enabled the country to view it in proper perspective. And, though the fighting was on a small scale, the issues were indeed important — important to the whole country. Here was a war, almost on the front door-

step, in which a people which had been at peace for a third of a century had an overwhelming interest. This alone made it a tremendous news story. Moreover, it did not last long enough for the enthusiasm of the early weeks to be cooled. It was brilliantly successful; there were no defeats to sober the country, no long casualty lists to divert attention. Its history could be, and was, what was called a few years later a "glory story."

And, above all, it was a war on a small scale. It was not so big that the doings of the armies overshadowed the competitive enterprise of the newspapers. As a happy hunting ground for war correspondents it has seldom been equaled. The armadas of dispatch boats loaded with reporters, feature writers and photographers sent down by some of the New York papers were about as formidable as Sampson's fleet, and their doings took up pretty nearly as much space in dispatches. As for the campaigns ashore, the readers of some papers might justifiably have been in doubt whether the war was primarily a field for the doings of eminent personages who had volunteered from civil life or a convenient arrangement for exploitation of the famous correspondents who happened to write about the eminent personages. The fact that a battle had been fought, and that we had won it, was less important than that Mr. A, the renowned politician, and Mr. B, the noted Yale halfback, had taken part in the battle; and this again was of less consequence (according to some newspapers) than that the doings of Mr. A and Mr. B had been reported by the famous correspondent X, and depicted by the cele-

brated artist Y. And before the public had time to tire of this sort of thing the war was over, and everybody but the few thousand victims of "canned horse" and the Cuban climate had come home.

In all this *The Times* had no part, for the painful reason that it had no money. It was laboriously paying its way; it could manage to meet current expenses, but it could not plunge into any of the wild expenditures undertaken by the more prosperous New York papers. As an example of what those papers which could afford it were doing may be mentioned *The Herald's* dispatch of some 2000 words on the night of July 3, which alone of special dispatches to individual newspapers brought, in time for publication next morning, the details of the destruction of Cervera's fleet. It was filed at Port Antonio, Jamaica, for transmission via Kingston and Panama, and to take precedence of the hundreds of thousands of words of press dispatches piled up at the Port Antonio telegraph office it was sent at double the commercial rates, prepaid, the total cost being $3.25 a word, paid in gold.

The Times could not do this or anything like it. Even dispatch boats and special cables were an impossible luxury. When the news came *The Times* displayed it as intelligently and satisfactorily as anybody, and its editorial comment on the news was sound and well informed; but the news itself was everybody's news — it came from The Associated Press. *The Times* did, indeed, have a little mail correspondence, but that counted for nothing in a time when the victories of Schley and Shafter were less important in themselves than the oppor-

tunities which they afforded for shrieking headlines, signed cablegrams in twelve-point full face and smudgy pictures by staff artists. *The Times* was still a good newspaper, but it couldn't compete in calling the attention of the public to its excellence.

So the end of the war found the management of *The Times* facing the possibility that the work of the past two years had been in vain. The meagre hundred thousand dollars of operating capital with which Mr. Ochs had started was gone, and the receipts of the paper, though gradually improving, were not sufficient to make it up. It was apparent that something had to be done, but when the publisher put forward his idea of the proper remedy many people thought that it meant sudden and irretrievable ruin. He proposed to cut the price to one cent. It had been forty-seven years since *The Times* had sold at that price, and the one-cent field among morning newspaper readers had long been left to *The World* and *The Journal.* It had come to be the general opinion that that was the sort of thing people wanted for one cent; that those who thought that no newspaper was worth more than that would be quite content with what was offered them and had no appetite for anything else.

The publisher thought otherwise. It was his belief that a great many people who found the difference between three dollars and ten dollars for a year's newspaper bills sufficient to be worth considering were reading *The World* and *The Journal* only because they were cheap. Give them a choice and a good many of them might prefer a paper of the character which *The Times* had established. It was not

to be doubted that there were a good many objections to the proposal. There would be an immediate and considerable decrease in circulation revenue, though at the low price of paper in those days it would still be possible for *The Times* to get more than enough income from a one-cent circulation to pay for the paper on which the news was printed. The question, of course, was whether the circulation would increase sufficiently to bring in advertising. There was a danger that advertisers who had been used to regarding *The Times* as appealing to a constituency small in quantity but high in quality would come to the conclusion that it had merely lowered the quality without corresponding increase in quantity. What *The Times* hoped to do was to increase the quantity while retaining the same quality.

In other words, it did not expect to cut in on the natural field of *The World* and *The Journal*. It was not going to be a "yellow" journal; it was not going to compete for the favor of those who wanted "yellow" journals. Mr. Ochs said in an interview published in a trade paper a few months later (January, 1899):

> Such papers as *The World* and *The Journal* exist because the public wants them. I hold that some of their features are open to criticism, but each of them has done infinitely more good than harm.

It was quite clear to the publisher of *The Times* that there was a large part of the one-cent public which wanted precisely what it was getting for one cent. The question which could be decided only by trial was whether there might be also a part of the

one-cent public that wanted something of a different sort. And *The Times* resolved to find out.

In the editorial announcement of the change of price on October 10, 1898, some of the aspects of the matter as they appeared to *The Times* management were stated as follows:

> It is the price of the paper, not its character, that is changed. In appealing to a larger audience *The Times* by no means proposes to offend the taste or forfeit the confidence of the audience it now has, already large, discriminating, and precious to it as lifelong friends. That statement we make in full sincerity and with firm resolution. We wish to make it with all possible emphasis, so that no reader of *The Times* in the past need scan the columns of this morning's issue, or of any subsequent issue, with the least misgiving or apprehension lest the reduction in price may be concurrent with a lowering in tone and quality. The old readers of *The Times* and the new shall find it a clean, truthful, carefully edited newspaper at one cent, a paper that recognizes its obligation to give its readers all the news, but values its own good name and their respect too highly to put before them the untrue or the unclean, or to affront their intelligence and their good taste with freaks of typographic display or reckless sensationalism. . . .
>
> During the past two years *The Times* has made a large advance in circulation. . . . No paper, however, ever increases in circulation fast enough to satisfy its conductors. It has seemed to the management of *The Times* that while the growth of its

> sales was steady and substantial, it was too slow; that, while its circulation has reached a large figure for a newspaper of its character, it ought to be larger. . . .
>
> The proposition that many thousands of persons in this city of three and one-half million souls buy and read one-cent newspapers chiefly on account of their price and not on account of their character and quality seemed sound. We believe these thousands would like to read a newspaper of the character and quality of *The Times* in preference to, or let us generously suppose in conjunction with, the papers they have been reading. *The Times* has determined to extend its appeal beyond those readers with whom quality is indispensable and price a matter of no consequence to the presumably much larger number of persons to whom both price and quality are of consequence.

This emphasis on the unaltered character and quality of the paper now offered at one third of the former price was terribly necessary. Many readers would be certain to feel that only a "yellow" paper could be produced for one cent and would look with cynical eagerness for the expected deterioration in quality. Indeed, this view seems to have been held by some people in *The Times* office. On the night the change was announced one of the reporters came in with what he joyfully heralded to the night city editor as "a beautifully sensational story." It did not appear in the paper; indeed, the publisher afterward observed that he wouldn't have had a "sensational" story in that day's issue for any consideration. And, little by little, doubting readers

THE PRESENT HOME,
THE TIMES ANNEX,
WEST 43RD ST.—TIMES SQUARE.

of *The Times* became convinced that their fears were needless. It was the same paper they had been getting; nothing had been changed but the price.

Some unfriendly comment, however, was occasioned by the change, and for other reasons. It must have been known to anybody in the newspaper business in New York that the editorial observation of October 10 that "it has seemed to the management of *The Times* that while the growth of its sales was steady and substantial, it was too slow," was certainly not an overstatement. Newspaper men pretty generally suspected what was indeed the fact, that *The Times* had virtually been driven to the step; and there were some who ungenerously attributed it to base reasons. A gubernatorial campaign was going on at the time, and the newspaper was supporting Augustus Van Wyck, the Democratic candidate. The suspicion not unnaturally sprang up in many minds that this reduction of income was only possible because there was some compensating revenue which had suddenly been opened to the paper. Only one newspaper, *The Evening Mail*, came boldly out and said that *The Times* had been subsidized by Tammany; and when *The Times* promptly called that paper to account, it as promptly apologized. But the suspicion persisted among some readers, and one of them, who was frank enough to express his opinions in a letter to the editor, was answered by an editorial statement which pointed out that it would be rather transparently stupid to take this step in the middle of a political campaign if its reason were that which the political position of the paper might suggest.

Stronger than the conviction that *The Times* had sold out to Tammany was the belief of most practical newspaper men that this meant the beginning of the end. The changes of price in the eighties, which had such unhappy results, were recalled, and it seemed to be the general conviction that *The Times* would find it impossible to retain its quality at one cent. *The Tribune* and *The Herald*, whose comments on the change were in a friendly tone which bore evidence of the more civilized spirit which was coming into New York journalism, nevertheless expressed their conviction that high quality could not long be given at low price. One may surmise that their conviction was perhaps strengthened by the fear that if it were possible, their own readers might wonder why they couldn't do it; and though the suspicion is perhaps ungenerous, one cannot help feeling that the friendly tone of their references to the subject was perhaps due to the conviction that this meant the speedy disappearance of an old rival.

More gratifying to *The Times*, among the numerous remarks on the change in other papers, were those of *The Philadelphia Record*, which expressed a belief based on its own experience that *The Times* would find, as *The Record* had found, that it was possible to be both decent and cheap. Since *The Record*, selling at one cent, was at that time one of the most profitable newspaper properties in the country, this encouragement was welcome as a hopeful token of what might be ahead of *The Times*.

And *The Record's* prediction was right. At first the reduction applied only to sales in the city; out-

of-town customers still paid three cents, as they had paid before. But with the announcement came an immediate demand from these subscribers for a reduction of *The Times* to two cents out of town, which was the price charged in those parts for *The World* and *The Journal*. It had been the intention to make this change eventually; it had been delayed because the presses were barely able to take care of the increased city circulation anticipated from the reduction. But the protests of out-of-town subscribers made it apparent almost at once that there was opportunity to make great gains in that field also. The change was made one week after the original announcement, with the assistance of other papers who lent *The Times* the use of part of their mechanical plant until its own could be appropriately expanded. It might be remarked for the benefit of the nonprofessional reader that newspapers have always, even in the days of their most bitter vituperation of each other, been ready for such reciprocal assistance in case of any really serious need — a fact which might have suggested to their readers long before the smoke began to blow away that a good deal of the harsh language was emitted merely for the joy of battle.

The Times's circulation began to jump. It no longer climbed slowly and laboriously; it vaulted from pinnacle to pinnacle. Less than a month showed that the reduction of price had done all that had been hoped, and it continued to do more in the following months. The most skeptical eventually had to admit that the quality of *The Times* was as good as ever — indeed, better than ever, for the re-

newed prosperity of the paper made it possible to spend more money for news. And the gain in circulation was astounding. In September, 1898, the daily average circulation was 25,726. In September, 1899, one year later, it was 76,260. There are few if any parallels to this sudden rise in American newspaper history.

The gain in advertising was commensurate. In 1898 the advertisements printed amounted to 2,433,193 agate lines. In 1899 they had risen to 3,378,750. And the increase had not been accompanied by any loss in character. Some of the advertisers supposed that the drive at a one-cent circulation meant reduction of rates, since the increase in circulation might be offset by the lower buying power of the new readers. It did not seem so to the management of *The Times;* in a single month, shortly after the change, more than $50,000 worth of advertising was refused because it was offered below the regular rates of the paper. *The Times* was preparing to build up a high-class constituency at a low price. It succeeded amazingly, and long before it had achieved the full measure of its intent the late Andrew Carnegie, as shrewd a judge of values as ever came from Scotland, pronounced it "the best cent's worth in the world."

It may be admitted that when the change was made it was not supposed by the management of *The Times* that the one-cent price would be long retained. Newspapermen in the latter part of 1898 knew that *The World* and *The Journal,* by their enormously expensive competition, which came to a climax in the covering of the Spanish War, had

eaten heavily into their profits. The fight was beginning to cost more than it was worth, and it was generally understood that the papers were preparing, by agreement, to raise their price to two cents. When that time came, *The Times* was going to two cents with them; but the management believed that it would be more profitable to come up to two cents than down to it — that most of the readers who had learned to like *The Times* at one cent would stay with it when the price was increased, especially as there would be no one-cent morning papers left. But *The World* and *The Journal*, faced with this sudden and amazingly vigorous competition in their own field, did not dare to try it; they were quite possibly afraid that if they went to two cents *The Times* would stay at one cent and attract many of their readers. As suggested above, the publisher of *The Times* was not of this opinion; but since his competitors stuck to the old price he did the same, and there was no change until the unprecedented expenses of the World War, nearly twenty years afterward, forced all the morning papers to go back to two cents.

From the morning of October 10, 1898, the prosperity of *The Times* was assured. It had turned the corner and the old penniless days were soon to become only a memory. It was thereafter only a question of the degree of the paper's success, and it presently increased beyond the dream of any one in the office. Of the fact of success there was never, from the end of 1898, any doubt.

Though the rate of progress was slower for a few years after that, the progress was without inter-

mission. So well was *The Times* getting ahead that the paper was able in 1900 to undertake at an expense of $50,000 the publication of a special edition at the Paris Exposition. This younger sister of *The New York Times*, to which it bore a very strong family likeness, was published within the Exposition grounds in June, July, August, September and October under the editorship of George W. Ochs, a brother of the publisher. It showed the French a good deal about American newspaper methods and aroused their respect, even if it did not excite their emulation, and it furnished American visitors to the Exposition with a plentiful supply of home news and world news such as they were quite unable to get from the old established competing publication which devoted most of its space to the doings of the European aristocracy and the mathematical perplexities of the Old Lady from Philadelphia. It was a good newspaper, and it was an excellent advertisement for *The New York Times*.

By this time, however, *The Times* was getting to the stage where it hardly needed any longer to advertise itself. Its reputation was attending to the advertising. The general belief among the newspaper men of 1896 that *The Times* could not be revived had been so strong that some of the paper's competitors did not realize that it was catching up with them until it was some distance ahead.

The old United Press, which had been maintained at heavy expense by *The Sun*, *The Herald*, *The Tribune* and *The Times*, and whose drain on *The Times's* resources had done a good deal to bring

the paper into its financial misfortunes, went to pieces soon after the new management assumed control of *The Times*. *The Times*, *The Herald* and *The Tribune* at once applied for admission to The Associated Press, then incorporated under the laws of Illinois, and *The Herald* and *The Tribune* were admitted with full rights and privileges, but *The Times* was able to get in only as a sort of stepchild, on what was known as a Class B membership, with no right of protest. Fortunately for the paper, the Supreme Court of Illinois decided in 1900 that The Associated Press was a public utility and compelled to furnish its news to anybody. This forced a reorganization under the laws of New York. Mr. Ochs, through his *Chattanooga Times* membership, was one of the leading members of The Associated Press and had been active in the work of the organization. Now that there was to be a reorganization in New York, *The Times* received full membership, and he was welcomed to the councils of the leaders and became one of the charter members of the new body. And for twenty years past he has been a member of the Board of Directors and of its Executive Committee.

By that time the prosperity of *The Times* was securely established, and the reorganization committee was dissolved on July 1, 1900. The 3876 shares which had been held until the publisher should have made the paper pay its way for three consecutive years were transferred to him. The experiment, regarded as hopeless by all the experts, had succeeded in less than four years, and it was already evident that bigger things were ahead. In

this recovery many men played their parts, but the contribution of the new publisher may be suggested by the remark made, years later, by one of the veterans of *The Times* staff: "He found the paper on the rocks, and made them foundation stones."

"All the News That's Fit to Print."

The New York Times.

THE WEATHER.
Warmer, increasing cloudiness to-day; showers to-morrow.

VOL. LVIII...NO. 18,856. * * * NEW YORK, THURSDAY, SEPTEMBER 9, 1909.—TWENTY PAGES. ONE CENT In Greater New York, Jersey City, and Newark | Elsewhere, TWO CENTS.

COOK NOT NEAR POLE, SAYS PEARY; PROOFS STILL HELD BACK BY COOK

Two Eskimos Cited by Cook Told Peary He Never Went Far from Land.

SAYS "I HAVE COOK NAILED"

Cables His Wife Not to Worry About the Doctor's Claim to the Pole.

COOK TO ASK FOR AN INQUIRY

Says He Will Submit His Observations to Competent Scientists.

DOUBT OF HIS STORY GROWS

Cook's Supporters Here and Throughout Europe Greatly Worried by His Failure to Refute Peary.

This message from Commander Peary to The New York Times was received at 4:57 o'clock yesterday morning:

INDIAN HARBOR, via Cape Ray, N. F., Sept. 8.—Cook's story should not be taken too seriously. The Eskimos who accompanied him say that he went no distance north. He did not get out of sight of land. Other men of the tribe corroborate their statements. Kindly give this to all home and foreign news asso-

proofs that he had visited the north pole on April 21, 1908. Those proofs were convincing and would in due time be given to the world.

Doesn't Fear Public Clamor.

When it was suggested to him that his chances of proving his case might be ruined unless he made a satisfactory statement immediately, he smiled—his usual quiet smile, and asked how could a man be ruined by popular clamor calling him an imposter when he had proofs in his case which could and would be published, as he had oftimes repeated, when they were in proper form to be given out.

Dr. Cook told Capt. Sverdrup and another friend the day after he landed here that he hoped there would be no unpleasantness over supplies with the Peary party; that he had found some of Peary's men in possession of one of his depots and had turned them out unceremoniously.

It is settled that Cook will send a ship back to bring to America the two Eskimos who accompanied him on the last stage of his journey to the pole, as well as some of the party who were sent back when the start of the last stage began. Capt. Sverdrup may command the expedition. It is Dr. Cook's desire that he shall do so, and they conferred for some hours to-day regarding the details of the expedition.

Dr. Cook's purpose in bringing his Eskimo comrades to America is to have them relate their stories of the trip to the pole. He proposes to have them examined by any men familiar with the arctic and the Eskimo, including the members of Commander Peary's party, if they wish. Dr. Cook's apparent confidence is the greatest factor working in his support in Copenhagen. Those who have had the opportunity to talk with him are only of one mind, that he is an absolutely sincere, simple man, or deserves a pedestal in history as one of the greatest of actors.

PROOFS TO-DAY, SAYS COOK.

But Grave Doubt Is Felt That He Can Supply Them.

By PHILIP GIBBS.

Special Cable to THE NEW YORK TIMES.
Dispatch to The London Daily Chronicle.

everything, and I shall prove the truth of my story to the world."

To these words I say Cook cannot prove his story to-morrow or the day after. Cook has no proof in Copenhagen to give the university, and if the committee which is to make the examination says, "We are satisfied," then I say beforehand they will be satisfied without proof, without any trustworthy evidence whatever, as Prof. Stromgren was satisfied without proof or evidence, because I had evidence to-day still further proving that Cook cannot produce proof to-morrow. I had that evidence from one of the most distinguished men of science in Europe, whose word cannot be doubted, and who still believes, or tries to believe, in Cook, and I had that evidence from Frederick Cook himself. I will give briefly the gist of two remarkable interviews, first with Dr. de Querlain Chief of the Swiss-German expedition and joint Director of the Swiss Central Meteorological Institute. This interview was before three witnesses and the special correspondent of a London journal, Comte de Lesdain, and myself. The following questions were asked and answered:

"Do you know Cook well?"

"I was four weeks with him! Upon his return, coming back with him in the Hans Egede, we had long conversations."

"Did he show you any of his observations?"

"No; but he said he would show them to me. I pointed out to him the importance of putting forward proofs to satisfy public opinion, and it was for that reason I suggested he should show me his observations, as, of course, I have had long training experience in these matters."

"And did he?"

"No. I regret to say that when I asked him again he said he would prefer not to do so."

No Observations on Hans Egede.

"Are you sure he had any observations on board?"

"I could not be sure. He had a box on board in which he said he had papers. Most of his books went by boat—Whitney's boat—from Greenland to America."

COMMANDER PEARY'S PRELIMINARY ACCOUNT OF HIS SUCCESSFUL VOYAGE TO THE NORTH POLE

He Sends to The Times by Wireless a Summary, to be Followed by His Full Report—Record of His Swift Progress to the Utmost North.

FROM CAPE COLUMBIA UP IN 37 DAYS, BACK IN 16 DAYS

Prof. Ross G. Marvin, of Cornell, Drowned on April 10, Forty-five Miles North of Cape Columbia, While Leading the Supporting Party.

BATTLE HARBOR, Labrador, Via Wireless Cape Ray, N. F., Sept. 8.—As it may be impossible to get my full story through in time for to-morrow's TIMES, partly as a prelude which may stimulate interest and partly to forestall possible leaks, I am sending you a brief summary of my voyage to the North Pole, which is to be printed exactly as written.

SUMMARY OF NORTH POLAR EXPEDITION OF THE PEARY ARCTIC CLUB.

The steamer Roosevelt left New York on July 6, 1908; left Sydney on July 17; arrived at Cape York, Greenland, August 1; left Etah, Greenland,

at Cape Columbia March 1; passed British record March 2; delayed by open water March 2 and 3; held up by open water March 4 to 11; crossed the 84th parallel March 11; encountered open lead March 15; crossed 85th parallel March 18; crossed 86th parallel March 23d; encountered open lead March 23d; passed Norwegian record March 23d; passed Italian record March 24th; encountered open lead March 26th; crossed 87th parallel March 27th; passed American record March 28; encountered open lead March 28; held up by open water March 29; crossed 88th parallel April 2; crossed 89th parallel April 4; North Pole April 6.

All returning left North Pole April 7, reached Cape Columbia April 23, arriving on board Roosevelt April 27.

The Roosevelt left Cape Sheridan July 18; passed Cape Sabine August 8; left Cape York August 26; arrived at Indian Harbor with all members of expedition returning in good health except Prof. Ross G. Marvin, unfortu-

"Via Cape Ray, N. F., Sept. 8.

"Good morning. Delayed by gale. Don't let Cook story worry you. Have him nailed.

"BERT."

COOK DEMANDS A TRIBUNAL.

Still Declares He Has Proofs—Withholds Them, Despite Urging.

COPENHAGEN, Sept. 8.—This is Dr. Cook's reply to Commander Peary:

"I have been to the north pole. As I said last night when I heard of Commander Peary's success, if he says he has been to the north pole, I believe him.

"I am willing to place facts, figures, and worked-out observations before a joint tribunal of the scientific bodies of the world. In due course I shall be prepared to make public an announcement that will effectually dispel any doubt, if there can be such, of the fact that I reached the pole. But, knowing that I am right and that right must prevail, I will submit at the proper time my full story to the court of last resort—the people of the world.

Won't Enter Into a Controversy.

"I will not enter into any controversy over the subject with Commander Peary, further than to say that if he says I have taken his Eskimos my reply is that Eskimos are nomads. They are owned by nobody and are not the private property of either Commander Peary or myself. The Eskimos engaged by me were paid ten times what they agreed to accompany me for.

"As to the story that Commander Peary says I took provisions stored by him, my reply is that Peary took my provisions, obtaining them from the custodian on the plea that I had been so long absent that he was going to organize relief stations for me in case I should be alive. For this I have documentary proof."

Concern in Copenhagen.

Coming so quickly upon other dramatic incidents of the week, Commander Peary's dispatch denying that Dr. Cook had achieved the triumph for which he has been fêted and honored in Copenhagen beyond the lot of any other private person, has been read here with feelings of amazement and concern.

But Dr. Cook himself seems in no wise disturbed. He was perfectly cool and apparently unmoved when confronted to-light with telegrams from the United States saying that Commander Peary had denounced him as an imposter. His demeanor has not changed in the slightest from the day he landed at Copenhagen.

Dr. Cook's friends had urged him to their utmost to make any statement possible for the public, but he had said repeatedly that all he had to say for the present was that he possessed

... wildly improbable and unsupported by a shred of scientific facts, that those many explorers who were present in this city of explorers and who stood by Cook now felt shattered in their belief. Some of them went to Cook early this morning and told him that unless he produced the strongest evidence of his claim within twenty-four hours they would denounce him as an impostor. To this he said:

"I will produce my proofs within twenty-four hours."

Immediately after that declaration Peary's telegrams were published in Copenhagen. The effect was immediately seen in the Danish newspapers. They had upheld Dr. Cook, and had denounced me personally for my daily criticism of Cook's story. Now they come out with articles headed "Is Cook an Impostor?" and Danish journalists came to interview the English journalist who had been alone in his disbelief. That was the only amusing thing in a day which had been too exciting and too strenuous. I had many things to do. I had first of all to see Cook himself and ask him what he had to say about Peary's words. He said:

"I shall say very little about what Peary says. It does not matter to me. Wait a little while and you will see."

I must now say that this man Frederick Cook is the most remarkable, most amazing man I have ever met. He calls me his enemy, but I have no personal animosity against him, and I will say honestly that I am filled with a sense of profound admiration for him. If he is an impostor he is also a very brave man—a man with such iron nerve, such miraculous self-control, and such magnificent courage in playing his game, that he will count for ever among the greatest impostors of the world. That and not the discovery of the north pole shall be his claim to immortality.

Here was this man doubted by all who had acclaimed him a hero, with his story strongly discounted by Peary, pursued by circumstantial evidence, and threatened within twenty-four hours by the almost certain possibility of final exposure, and yet he faced the world, defied criticism, and smiled and smiled again.

I was in the same room with him for two hours to-day, a drawing room into which came a stream of distinguished people, full of suspicion about him. But, ceremoniously polite, he stood among them haking hands and bowing and smiling. He was haggard, and there were deep lines upon his face, but his hand was perfectly steady as he took a cup of tea and still he smiled.

Now what is Cook's answer to the challenge of Peary; to that ultimatum given by the explorers and scientists of Denmark? His answer is:

"I will produce my observations and records and instruments before the university to-morrow. They shall see

"Was this sextant an ordinary one?"

"He told me it was a better sextant than the ordinary one used in the navy."

"Has he brought his instruments to Copenhagen?"

"No, he sent them to America."

"But is it not necessary to test these instruments before the value of the observations can be proved?"

"Strictly speaking, that is so."

After this interview, in which every answer was drawn painfully and reluctantly from a man desiring to shield his friend but compelled by conscience to tell the truth, Dr. de Querlain signed a document in which he made this remarkable statement. The following are his exact words:

"I recognize that Cook, with whom I passed several weeks on board the Hans Egede, has given me the impression of a man who understands quite well how to take observations. Moreover, Knud Rasmussen, who passed some time with Cook after the return of the latter from the pole, has received favorable evidence of Cook's story from Eskimos who knew two men who accompanied Cook and believes Cook had been to the pole.

Didn't Tell of Meeting Rasmussen.

The later part of his statement is startling. Cook never referred to his meeting with Rasmussen upon his homeward journey. Rasmussen's letter to his wife suggests a direct contradiction of Cook upon a material point, and from the lips of Mrs. Rasmussen and Mr. Freuken, an explorer in whose hands I first saw this letter, I heard the words that Mr. Rasmussen does not believe in Cook's claim. They have repeated that to others.

This, however, is not part of my main evidence. The essential point in the above interview is Cook's refusal to show Querlain his observations after his promise to do so, and Querlain's statement that Cook's instruments and most of his books have been sent to America by way of Greenland. I now come to Cook himself. This morning I put the following questions to him in the presence of Comte de Lesdain.

"Have you any original observations in Copenhagen?"

"At first Cook refused to answer this question. He then said:

"I have in Copenhagen results of my observations only, but my instruments and the working out of my observations have been packed with great care and are on their way to America."

"Why have you not shown your observations and instruments to any Danish or other scientist?"

"I have not done so because I prom-

Continued on Page 3.

Latest Shipping News.

Arrived—Steamer Pennsylvania, Hamburg, Aug. 28.

... ruary 15, 1909, and started for the North. Arrived

... the supporting party.
ROBERT E. PEARY.

MAP SHOWING PEARY'S ROUTE TO THE POLE

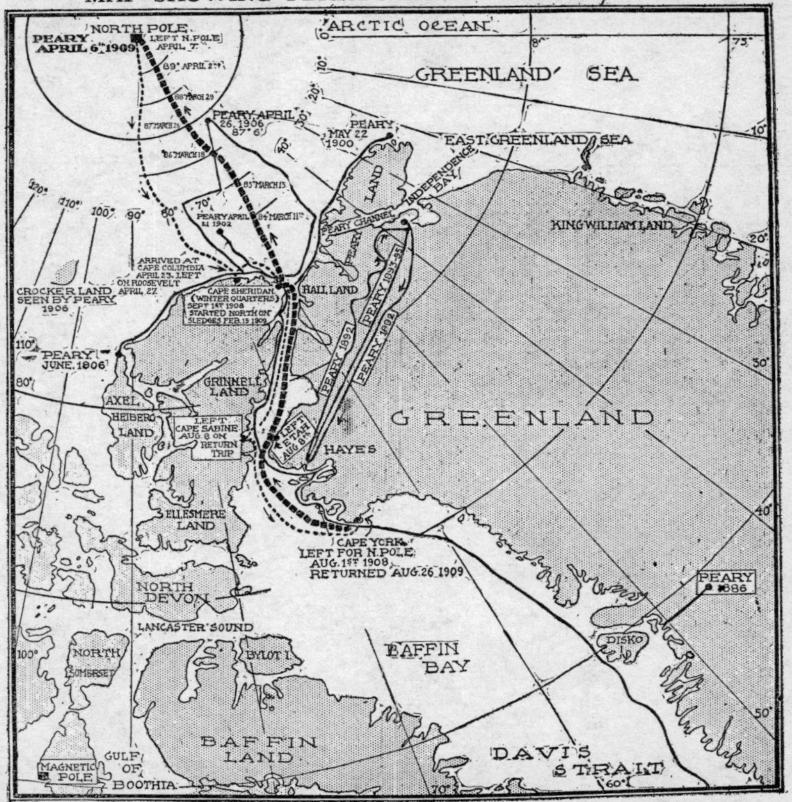

CHAPTER II

Conservatism, Independence, Democracy: 1900-1914

ON September 18, 1901, *The Times* celebrated its golden jubilee, which was commemorated on September 25 in a special historical supplement whose publication was deferred for a week on account of the funeral of President McKinley. The advertisements published in that supplement, 224 in number, were all representative of firms which had been doing business in New York City on September 18, 1851, and ever since, a convincing demonstration that even in this city of rapid and enormous changes there was still a commercial substratum of old traditions with prospects of something like permanence. In the editorial comment on the anniversary there was of course some discussion of the changes in the character of journalism between 1851 and 1901, the chief of which was the extensive publication by papers at the beginning of the twentieth century of what may be called "personal news," the chronicle of happenings in the lives of individuals themselves of no great importance. The reading public had become interested not only in the big news, in public affairs and events of great importance, but in the reporting of things on which the reader could make the comment, "That might have happened to me."

It might have been supposed in 1901 that the

development of the art of news-getting in future decades would be chiefly in this same direction. But the editors of *The Times* suspected even then that this was not wholly true, for in their editorial remarks on the future of the paper they gave their principal attention to the "alliance for mutual benefit" which had just been concluded with *The London Times* — an arrangement of which more will presently be said — by which *The New York Times* obtained all rights to the world news service of its English contemporary. Said a *Times* editorial article on the jubilee day:

> The occasional triumph known in the lingo of journalism as a "beat" may shed a fleeting lustre on the name of a newspaper. Of those *The Times* has had its share in the half century of its life. But the daily habit of gathering into its columns from the four corners of the earth all the news which vigilance and faithful effort can obtain and in which intelligent minds are likely to be interested gives enduring character and reputation and determines the public judgment.

And indeed the remarkable growth of *The Times* in the following years was largely due to its diligence in obtaining, and sound judgment in handling, the big news, much of it foreign news. This had been notably true even before the outbreak of the war of 1914–1918 gave to American journalism a test from which *The Times* emerged perhaps more brilliantly than any of its competitors. Even so early as 1901 it was apparent that the American people were in the world, whether they liked it or not;

that the long introversion of the decades after the Civil War had at last come to an end. The world was visibly drawing into a closer interrelation, and the years between 1901 and 1914 were to see the development of a peaceful internationalism, an assimilation of all nations, or at least of the upper and middle classes of all nations, to a common standard of life, such as had not been known since the Roman Empire broke down.

It was to be the destiny of *The Times* to find its most brilliant opportunities in responding to the demands of this new age for news from far wider fields than those in which the majority had had any interest in the latter part of the nineteenth century. The isolation of the seventies and eighties, an isolation always more apparent than real, had ended when Dewey's guns boomed in Manila Bay. "Personal news" had reached its utmost popularity in the nineties; with a new era of international peace it may once more come back, as it has begun to come back since the war, to overshadowing importance; but the editors of *The Times* in 1901 judged rightly the tendencies of the age which was beginning. For a third of a century the American people, like some orders of mediaeval monks, had been trying to find peace by gazing at its own navel, and it was just awakening to the discovery that the world contained sights of somewhat more absorbing interest.

The Times set forth upon this new era in the enjoyment of a higher degree of material prosperity than it had ever known in its best days of old. Its paid circulation in its jubilee month averaged

102,472 per day — a stupendous figure by the standards of Raymond and Jones, but one which the conductors of the paper could already see was only a beginning. Even they hardly realized in 1901 that the circulation of *The Times* would reach the figures of today, which are seldom much below, and often above, those of its most aggressively "popular" contemporaries in New York morning journalism. That some New York papers have a circulation of 300,000 or 400,000 a day is not surprising; the only surprising circumstance is that they do not sell a million a day, for there is nothing in them which anybody cannot understand. That a paper such as *The Times*, which, though not aiming expressly at a limited number of intelligent readers, does give up its pages rather to the news of general interest and high importance than to items which tickle the fancy, should have a circulation of 350,000 is somewhat more remarkable, and those who produce *The Times* may be pardoned if they regard it as rather encouraging for the future of a democracy which is likely to get into a good deal of trouble unless it knows what is going on.

The Times in 1901 was firmly on its feet; it had won back its old position and somewhat more. The history of that recovery has been told; the chronicle of the years that were to come before the outbreak of the World War is a somewhat different story, the story of the paper's emergence from the crowd, so to speak, to a position which may at least be described as that of a *primus inter pares* in the prompt and reliable presentation of the news of the world. Some of the war cries of the earlier years

were to be heard less frequently in the future. The crusade against "yellow" journalism, for example, gradually died away. There was no longer so much need for a crusade, for the bright orange journalism of the nineties was, in some quarters at least, slowly fading into a somewhat more respectable color.

The Times had of course contributed a good deal to the war against "yellow" journalism, but its war aims were of a somewhat different sort from those of its associates. To use a terminology familiar to present-day readers, it was not fighting a war of conquest or annihilation. It might aspire to some disannexations of those portions of the reading public which had been attracted into the sphere of influence of the "yellow" journals, though they rightfully belonged to *The Times*, but that had been accomplished by the reduction of price in 1898. Its conductors never had the desire which was apparently cherished by some of their contemporaries to blot out certain others.

The object, and the only object, of *The Times's* criticism of "yellow" journalism was to familiarize every newspaper reader with the fact that *The Times* would give him what its conductors regarded as the good elements that were to be found in their more sensational contemporaries, and would give them at the same low price, without the other features which many readers found objectionable. It was their purpose to see that nobody should read the "yellows" under the misapprehension that there and there alone could he get the news, and get it for one cent. When this fact had been advertised, when everybody knew what *The Times* offered, then

it was the reader's business to decide what kind of paper he wanted. After that *The Times* was content with the steady growth that came year by year as more and more readers came to find *The Times* more satisfactory than the papers which had previously been their favorites.

The history of this intervening period between 1900 and 1914 can perhaps best be told in compartments; by taking up first the editorial views of *The Times* and their reactions on the public, then the development of the news side of the paper, and finally some episodes in its business history which are pertinent to the story of the paper's rise to power, and interesting also as having some bearing on the rising ethical standards of the newspaper business.

The Times's position as an independent Democratic newspaper was maintained in the early years of the twentieth century, with the qualification that it was somewhat more independent than Democratic. For Mr. William Jennings Bryan *The Times* has never had much admiration, except in so far as it welcomed him as imparting to politics something of that character, at once hilarious and consecrated, which the Rev. Dr. Billy Sunday gives to religion. *The Times* supported the Republican Presidential ticket in 1900 because at last the Republican Party had been driven into genuine support of the sound money issue, and because the Republicans, though by no means united in their opinion on the future duties and responsibilities of the United States as a world power, were free from that academic sort of

anti-imperialism which pleased Mr. Bryan. Mr. McKinley, though by no means a giant among statesmen, was learning more about the business of being President, and his latest utterances indicated that he understood some of the demands of the day a little better than the gentleman who so soon was to succeed him.

For Mr. Roosevelt's character, energy and patriotism *The Times* always had the highest respect, and its editors would not deny that on the whole he was an immensely valuable asset to the America of his time. But the President of the United States has to be not only the worshiper and preacher of ideals but an official performing certain functions. For many of Mr. Roosevelt's actions *The Times* had only praise, but its editors were inclined to think that the effect of much of his radical teachings went a good deal further than he himself would have liked to believe, and they could not fail to note that one of the great problems of the time, tariff reform, was an issue when he came into office and an issue that had got no further forward when he went out.

The Democratic Party in 1904 had repudiated most of the heresies which Mr. Bryan had raised to the level of dogmas, and seemed to be turning back toward the sounder positions of Cleveland's day. *The Times* accordingly supported Alton B. Parker. As in 1872 and 1880, the people were once more inclined to trust the Republican Party, and unhappily the Democratic leaders seemed to think after the defeat of 1904 that the only way to overcome Roosevelt's popularity was by adopting

his doctrines. When Mr. Bryan was once more the Democratic candidate in 1908, *The Times* supported Taft, but the betrayal of pledges by the Republican Party which followed immediately drove away from it all its independent supporters, as well as a considerable fraction of the party membership. In the agitation which beset the Democratic Party during the years when every aspiring politician had his eye on a nomination that carried more prospect of election than those of previous campaigns, *The Times* was chiefly interested in keeping the party from running off the track. In the preconvention campaign of 1912 it had no favored candidate, but when it became apparent that the nominee must be either Woodrow Wilson or Champ Clark *The Times* declared its opinion that Mr. Wilson was as well equipped for the Presidency as any man the party could nominate, and considerably better equipped than any one else whose nomination could be regarded as a possibility. After the convention Mr. Wilson believed, and said in a telegram to the publisher of *The Times* that that editorial had greatly contributed to his nomination. His record as Governor of New Jersey, his speeches during the preconvention campaign, and the character of much of his support had marked him as a radical candidate. Some of the leaders in the Baltimore convention believed, or allowed themselves to be convinced by enemies of Mr. Wilson, that the conservative elements in the party would not support him if he was nominated. These fears were blown away by this editorial in *The Times*. If the leading conservative paper in the party, a paper which had shown its

independence by supporting the Republican candidate in two elections out of the last three, was satisfied with Mr. Wilson, there could be no fear of any serious bolt.

The Times was not wholly in sympathy at that time with Mr. Wilson's ideas of government, but its conductors realized that the choice lay between him and Champ Clark. Speaker Clark's conservatism, in the opinion of *The Times*, consisted rather in a certain antiquity of manner, and a resolute indifference to things that had happened in recent decades, than in any real understanding of conservative ideas; and Mr. Wilson's intellectual equipment was so far superior that *The Times* thought it wiser to trust a man competent to fill the Presidential office, who might be expected to learn as he went along.

The subsequent history of *The Times's* editorial support of President Wilson is sufficiently well known. No newspaper ever gave an administration more loyal support; no favors were received in return and none would have been accepted. *The Times* has never been willing to pose as an amplifying transmitter for whispers from the lips of authority. To become recognized as the mouthpiece for any administration would have meant the surrender in some measure of the paper's independence, or at any rate of its reputation for independence; it would have required a somewhat different attitude on the part of its conductors, a complaisance toward tendencies in the administration with which they were dissatisfied, a willingness to shut their eyes to some things that existed, and to pretend to see things that were mere figments of the imagination.

But it may be said by critics of the Wilson administration that on the major issues of these eight years the paper supported the President. It did so in many cases because it happened to agree with the President. The Underwood-Simmons tariff *The Times* regarded as the most satisfactory that had been enacted in many years, and for Mr. Wilson's services to the country in obtaining the passage of the Federal Reserve act it felt that no praise could be too high. There was much room for criticism and dissatisfaction in Mr. Wilson's first year, but, as a rule, on minor points. Mr. Bryan's disruption of the diplomatic service, for example, was deplorable in itself, but it was part of the price of the Federal Reserve act. Had Mr. Bryan been left outside the administration that enactment might have been impossible over his opposition.

In the principal crises of the later years of Mr. Wilson's administrations *The Times* supported the President because the choice was not between Mr. Wilson and ideal perfection, but between Mr. Wilson and concrete alternatives which seemed less desirable. In the opinion of its conductors he was a President who rose to most of the unusually heavy responsibilities laid upon him, and on the dominant issues of his day took a position against which nothing could be said except that he was perhaps a few years ahead of the average voter. And in its editorial summary of his eight years in office, on February 27, 1921, *The Times* took the position that Mr. Wilson had been a great President, whose true importance and usefulness would be increasingly apparent as time went on. As was said in that article:

> It made a world of difference whether throughout the war and at the end of the war we had in the White House a common man, or a man above the common. A President content to patch up the shattered world and set it spinning again in the old grooves would have been overlooked altogether. He never would have helped the nation to find its soul, he would not have found his own. . . . As if by predestination, when the war came, one was at the post of duty and of trial who, by his gifts and abilities, seemed to be designated above all others for a service such as no American had ever before been summoned to undertake.

Yet, because the paper was not always able to agree with the administration, it incurred the usual inconveniences of those who see some right on both sides. To most Republicans it was a rabid Democratic paper, to be abhorred for its partisanship; and by thick-and-thin, for-better-for-worse adherents of Mr. Wilson, it was accused of damning the administration with faint praise.

Most of the matters, however, on which *The Times* criticised those in office between 1913 and 1921 were questions outside the President's own field of activity. The election of 1912 had brought not only Woodrow Wilson but the Democratic Party into power, and on many issues the President was wiser than his party. The criticism has been made that *The Times* was a consistent supporter of Wilson, yet was opposed to almost everything that Wilson did. That is a mistake. *The Times* was a consistent supporter of Wilson, though disagreeing with his

attitude on some of the less important issues of his administration; its opposition was for the most part directed against the eccentricities of the Democratic majority in Congress, which the President was often compelled, for political considerations, to ignore, or to meet with an acquiescence which must at times have come hard.

It may be asked, then, why *The Times* in recent years has consistently supported the Democratic Party. The answer is, first, that the publisher of *The Times* is a Democrat not by geography — though Mr. Ochs spent his early life in Tennessee, his father had been a Captain in the Union Army — but by conviction, and so is its editor-in-chief, Mr. Miller, who comes from New Hampshire. But that answer, after all, does not explain much, for there are no longer very many Democrats left in the Democratic Party. That party once meant something; it meant that one of the great political organizations of the country believed that the people in a democracy could better be trusted, in the long run, than any group whatever of benevolent oligarchs, and that the federal organization of the United States was more than a mere historical accident — that it met the needs of a numerous people occupying a country of enormous extent, with wide differences in natural conditions and in the public sentiment of far distant localities. In that sense the conductors of *The Times* are among the few Democrats surviving. And it might be added that this fundamental concept of the Democratic Party's philosophy explains the fact that the two chief Democratic papers of the country, *The Times* and

The World, can both be Democratic while disagreeing on most details. *The World* is liberal and *The Times* conservative, but they are agreed in the opinion that the union of these states is and of a right ought to be a Federal union, as well as in the view that political wisdom and capacity for government, even if not bestowed very liberally on the people at large, are not to be found more highly concentrated in any particular economic, religious or geographic subdivision of the people.

These doctrines were once the distinguishing mark of a Democrat. They are now conspicuous chiefly by their rarity; about the only distinction between a Democrat and a Republican today is that the Democrat is generally out of office. The centralizing movement of recent years, which has pretty well blotted out state lines and tended to turn over the control of Government more and more to bureaucrats, has been promoted quite as much by Democrats as by Republicans. The Republicans, to be sure, have been inclined to favor oligarchies whose claim to superiority was their possession, real or pretended, of executive ability; while the Democrats have generally bowed down before oligarchies of pretended superiority of moral virtue. But whether the favored few are protected manufacturers or officials of the Anti-Saloon League, the effect is the same.

What is the duty of a Democrat in such a time? It might be held that his motto should be, "My party, right or wrong; if right, to keep it right; if wrong, to make it right." *The Times* has not been able to go quite so far as this; sometimes the Demo-

cratic Party has been so wrong that the only way to make it right was by supporting the Republican ticket. But, generally speaking, the conductors of the paper have believed that the Democratic Party needed all the intelligent support it could get and all that could conscientiously be given by those who hold to the old Democratic doctrines. So long as old-fashioned Jeffersonian Democrats and conservative Democrats found it possible to stick to the party they could act as a brake on the exuberant and misdirected energies of those Democrats whose chief representative in recent history has been Mr. Bryan. By clinging to the party and doing their best to remind it that it is, or ought to be, something more than a mere aggregation of jobless politicians, these Democrats could perhaps do a real service to the country in holding the party to certain standards, and thus making it a really effective check on the Republicans.

For the genius of the Democratic Party shines best in adversity. Out of office the party often displays public spirit and sometimes real statesmanship. Once in control of the Government, the Democrats are likely — in the opinion of the management of *The Times* — to forget their own principles and become mere imitators of the Republicans. Opinions may differ as to whether it is admirable to be a Republican, but certainly it is better to be a real Republican than a poor carbon copy. Republicanism can best be practiced by men who are Republicans year after year, in office or out, and not by diluted imitations who no sooner find themselves in control of the Government than they begin to wonder,

rather frantically, how the Republicans would do it, and then try their best to do the same.

Ninety years ago the Democratic Party, or that controlling faction of it led by Andrew Jackson, really meant something in national affairs. When it came back after the misfortunes under Van Buren and the Whig interlude that followed, it had bound itself to the service of a sectional oligarchy, and it remained in bondage till the Civil War. Since then the party has always been, in effect, the opposition. Even the great vote that ought to have carried Samuel J. Tilden to the White House was largely a protest vote. By undeserved good luck the Democratic Party had as its leader in the '80s and '90s one of the strongest and wisest statesmen of American history. What did it do with him? It nominated him, to be sure, and renominated him twice, but that was because Grover Cleveland had shown that he could be elected, and no other Democrat since the war had been able to do that. When he was once in office some of his own followers were the first to stick their knives in his back.

But whether or not the country would be best served by a condition in which the Republicans, perpetually in power, would be prodded into virtue and efficiency by a Democracy perpetually in opposition, such a condition is impossible. Ambitious young men join the party which has the offices at its disposal. A few Democrats have to be elected now and then to encourage the others. This may perhaps explain why *The Times*, though Democratic, is apt to be more critical of the Democrats in office than of their opponents. Nothing surprising or out of the ordinary is to be ex-

pected from the Republican Party — except under such unusual leaders as Roosevelt, and, after all, Roosevelt kept the country expecting great and wonderful things for seven and a half years, few of which happened. In ordinary times everybody knows what the Republican Party is; good or bad, it is a fixed quantity. There is more exhilaration in supporting and criticising the Democrats, whose worst can be incredibly bad, whose best is sometimes surprisingly good, and who are just as likely to display the one as the other. At any rate, there is always the possibility that with the proper support, and the proper amount of well-timed castigation, the Democrats may be driven to do something which ordinarily would be entirely beyond their vision — the Federal Reserve act, for instance. It is the difference between marrying a domestic disposition and an artistic temperament.

So it will be observed that *The Times* is Democratic both because its principal personages believe in the traditional Democratic doctrines, and because they think the public welfare is best served by giving the paper's support to the Democratic Party in the hope that, being constantly reminded of its basic principles, it may occasionally go back to those doctrines. This attitude would in itself make it impossible for *The Times* ever to become the organ of an Administration even if other and decisive considerations did not prevent it. And it may be noted that *The Times* has never, under the present management, had a candidate whom it pushed vigorously for the nomination. Its support of Wilson during the 1912 convention was, as explained above,

HONOR ROLL

★ HAROLD J. BEHL
★ WILLIAM BRADLEY
★ JOYCE KILMER
★ W. S. MANNING
★ EDWARD B. PIERCE

A. R. ADDISON
JULIUS OCHS ADLER
ABRAHAM FRANK AGMAN
RICHARD ALDRICH
EDWARD ROSCOE ALLEN
ROBT. K. ALLISON
RICHARD F. AMES
CHARLES WALTER ATKINSON
EDWARD A. ATKINSON
CARL E. BARTLETT
WALLACE A. BAWER
W. BERRYMAN
H. M. BJORCK
GORDON BLAIR
JOS. F. BLAND
THOMAS S. BOSWORTH
FRANCIS J. BOYLAN
FREDERICK A. BOYD, JR.
CHARLES W. BOYLE
FRED BRAZONG
MICHAEL BRIENZA
WILLIAM F. BROSNAN
LEE D. BROWN
H. M. BUGGELYN
E. BURQUIST
JESSE S. BUTCHER
ARTHUR G. CAMPBELL
S. M. CHAMBERS
ANTHONY CITRO
ROBERT C. COCHRANE
WILLIAM D. COLGAN, JR.
WALTER H. COLLINS
THOMAS COOK
GEORGE COOPER
WALTER COULTER
CHARLOTTE HOLMES CRAWFORD
BENJAMIN CULLEN
EDW. B. CUMMERFORD
JOHN WEBSTER CURLEY
LEE CURTIS
GEORGE CUSACK
CHARLES DALY
CLARENCE H. DEBAUN
LOUIS DECOLLE
PATRICK S. DELANEY
EDWIN F. DELANO
JOSEPH DIXON
EDWARD DOYLE
HUGH PENTLAND DUNN
ALBERT ELDRED
HERBERT ELLUM
EDWARD WALDO EMERSON
MORRIS FACTOR
C FARRELL
JOHN FEY
HAROLD FINCH
EARL N. FINDLEY
JOHN FINN
EDWARD J. FITZSIMMONS
GEORGE H. FLANAGAN
SIMEON T. FLANAGAN
GERALD E. FORCE
ROBERT J. FORESMAN
BENTLEY J. GEIGER
ARTHUR GORTON
CHARLES GOTTSCHALK
JEANETTE C. GRANT
FRANK B. GRISWOLD
EDWARD GROSS
WM. A. GROTEFELD
L. A. GUNDERSON
GUSTAV HANSON, JR.

HONOR ROLL—Continued

H. HARMAN
ROLAND H. HARPER
ALFRED HARRIS
EDWARD J. HARRIS, JR.
A. E. HARTZELL
FRANKLIN A. HARWOOD
HAROLD B. HAVILAND
WILLIAM J. HEGARTY
ELLIOTT P. HENRY
THOS. J. HERLIHY
JOHN HIMPLER
ULRICH HOFELE
PHILIP D. HOYT
C. F. HUGHES
L. HUGHES
MICHAEL A. HUGHES
HOWARD HUMPHREY
GEORGE E. HYDE
CHAS. JENKS
CARL O. JOHNSON
W. R. JOYCE
RUDOLPH C. KARR
EDWARD J. KEAN
ROBERT F. KELLEY
WM. JAY KELLEY
JOHN F. KIERAN
JOHN KIMBALL
EDWARD KLAUBER
MORTIMER J. KROLL
MAURIC LANGERMAN
WM. LANIGAN
WM. LEARY
GEORGE LEHMAN
GEORGE LEONARD
GERSON LEVY
JOSEPH LISSON
G. C. LOHSS
CLARENCE E. LOVEJOY
WILLIAM H. LUBRECHT
ALLEN LUTHER
WILLIAM F. LYNCH
WRIGHT McCORMICK
JAMES McCANN
THOMAS McCANN
NEIL MacNEIL
ANDREW E. MAGNUSON
CHARLES P. MAILE
AUSTIN M. MALONE
EDWARD F. MANNIX
LOUIS J. MERRELL
JAMES D. MILLS
ROBERT C. MORTON
EDWARD MOTIZZ
MATTHEW J. MURPHY
PATRICK J. MURPHY
WILLIAM MURPHY
FRANK L. NELSON
JOHN NELSON
JAMES E. NIX
JACK NYDICK
GEORGE F. O'CONNER
JAMES W. OSBORNE, JR.
FRANCIS XAVIER PAVESICH
GEORGE PAYNE
ARTHUR H. PENNEY
JOHN PETERS
EDW. J. POLOQUIN
MICHAEL PROZAN
RAPHAEL J. REARDON
EDWARD REYNOLDS
ROBERT H. ROESEN
MARTIN L. ROMAN
GEORGE L. ROONEY
R. ROWAN
REGINALD G. RUSSOM
TRACY J. RYAN
OSCAR SALVAIL
J. J. SANFORD
J. ARNOLD SAVAGE
GEORGE H. SCHNEIDERMAN
SAMSON H. SHAHBOODAGHIAN
CHARLES J. SHARKEY
J. SHARKEY
JOHN SIMONS
A. LEONARD SMITH, JR
JAMES JOSEPH SMITH
WILLIAM SMITH
R. J. SPRAGUE
EDWARD J. STEWART
JOSEPH F. SULLIVAN
ARTHUR HAYS SULZBERGER
WILLIAM A. SWANSON
PAUL LELAND SWIGART
JAMES M. TAYLOR
GROVER C. THEIS
FREDERIC D. THOMAS, JR.
BERNARD S. THOMSON
BERNA D TRACEY
CHARLES B. VOLCKENS
H. H. WALKER
CHARLES J. WALSH
C. C. WEAVER
H. C. WEAVER
SAMUEL WEISS
MICHAEL WEISSMAN
E. B. WELLS
JAMES A. WHITEHOUSE
S. T. WILLIAMSON
EDWARD A. WIRTH
ALEXANDER WOOLLCOTT
RICHARD B. WRIGHT
EZRA WRIGHT

THE RIGHT IS MORE PRECIOUS THAN PEACE
WE SHALL FIGHT FOR THE THINGS WHICH WE HAVE ALWAYS
CARRIED NEAREST OUR HEARTS
TO SUCH A TASK WE DEDICATE OUR LIVES

due to specific circumstances which had not been present in the pre-convention campaign.

In the Spring of 1920, to be sure, *The Times* did suggest John W. Davis as a man worthy of the consideration of the Democratic National Convention. But it was a suggestion and no more, and inspired chiefly by a desire to remind the delegates that all the talent of the party was not embodied in the persons of William G. McAdoo, James M. Cox and A. Mitchell Palmer. Mr. Davis was not personally known to the conductors of *The Times;* but he was, as Baedeker says, well spoken of. He was suggested to the party without much expectation that he would be nominated — and indeed it would have been rather unfortunate to waste him in a year when no Democrat could have been elected. He was mentioned in the hope that some Democrats might be stirred to remember that their party had after all more talent than its leadership often allowed to become visible.

The more important aspects of the editorial position of *The Times* in recent years are, however, those lying outside of party affiliations or partisan doctrines. It will probably be generally admitted that *The Times* for years past has been regarded as the most eminent champion of so-called conservatism in the American press. This is by no means the same thing as saying that it is the most conservative newspaper; it is not, by a good deal. But its wide circulation, its consistency of doctrine, its vigorous adherence to views which have often been unpopular, have given it a certain primacy among those

marshaled on the conservative side. This position became more clearly defined, perhaps, during the World War and in the discussion of subsequent issues; but it was established years before that. And its conservatism is partly, though not wholly, responsible for the distinction which *The Times* undoubtedly enjoys — and that word is used advisedly — of being more thoroughly hated by Communists, Socialists and radicals, to say nothing of pro-Germans and Irish extremists, than any other newspaper in the United States.

It is not to be supposed that the editors of *The Times* are so eccentric as to take pride in a measure of intellectual isolation, or so inhuman as to derive a fiendish pleasure from the disapproval of their fellows. If they are proud of their enemies, it is because they believe that the widespread antagonism to the editorial views of the paper is in more ways than one directly due to its merits. The readers of *The Times* represent a far wider range of political opinion than the ordinary newspaper constituency. A great many people who cordially despise the political and economic opinions of its editors feel that they have to buy the paper in order to get the news. If any one doubts this, let him observe that the radical weeklies, for example, cite *The Times* news columns as authority for most of their statements of fact. There is no doubt a certain crafty precaution in this; if the news report should happen to be wrong, the radical commentator can offer the apology that he was misled by the untrustworthy "capitalist" press. Nevertheless, the radical weeklies continue to get their news from *The Times*. Simi-

larly, many stalwart Republicans and convinced opponents of the League of Nations have in the past two years started the day by hating *The Times* over the breakfast grapefruit; but they find that they have to have it in preference to papers which might better reflect their own political opinions, and thus start them to the office with a pleasant sense of the rightness of the world. Forty years ago, when newspapers were chiefly political, these men would not have taken *The Times;* today, when a newspaper is first of all a newspaper, they feel that they have to have it to find out what is going on.

A second reason for the dislike for *The Times* which is felt among radicals, at least, is that *The Times* stands for something. When the Socialist orator comes to the congenial theme of the iniquity of the "capitalist" press, he thinks of *The Times* as its most prominent representative. *The Times* is frankly and pretty consistently conservative — not so consistently, of course, as radicals seem to think; no human institution could be so regularly of one mind as that — but on the whole always to be found on the Right (it being understood that for obvious reasons of delicacy this word is used in the sense familiar in European politics, and not necessarily with an ethical implication). Certain newspapers, which need not be mentioned, represent pretty nearly the same general opinions on politics and economics as *The Times*, but nobody ever wastes much hostility on them. There are other journals whose political views are so variable, or so negligible, that you might as well hate the city directory. Much of this antipathy to *The Times* is, then, mere

recognition of the fact that the paper has opinions of which it is not ashamed, and which it advocates with all the vigor that its editors are able to command. In the frequent denunciations of its policies, which its editors read with interest, there are many which are quite obviously not directed at *The Times* as an individual newspaper, but at *The Times* as the most prominent, powerful, and easily recognizable representative of a whole school of opinion.

Furthermore, a great many critics of *The Times* are persons of whose friendship the paper would be ashamed. It is sufficient to cite in this connection the bitter attacks made upon it during the war by German agents or their Irish sympathizers. But even before the war *The Times* had many critics whose hostility it could not regard as anything but a badge of merit. Not all of them, by any means, could be included in this classification, but a sufficient number to explain the fact that almost any radical orator can move his audience to wild cheers by a few maledictions on *The Times*. The paper has never had much confidence in efforts to remove all human evils overnight by a magic formula. It has distrusted patented and proprietary remedies for political and economic ills. In both minor and major matters it has usually managed to awaken the fiery hostility of the long-haired. It has not believed and does not believe in socialism, Fourieristic, Marxian or Leninist; in Greenbackism, Free Silver, or the political-economic system of the Nonpartisan League; in putting the Government into business; in the medical sociology of anti-vivisection or the artistic philosophies of dadaism. And since it is

the common peculiarity of most of these gospels that their devotees become somewhat intolerant and think that unbelievers might as well be hurried to the stake, those who are moved to cast doubt on the saving virtues of the new doctrine naturally come in for a good deal of denunciation.

Yet this conviction throughout all the various divisions of liberalism and radicalism that hatred for *The New York Times* is one of the essentials of salvation is in large measure a somewhat recent growth. Why was not *The Times* so cordially disliked fifty years ago? It was, of course, by Democrats; but this was an ordinary manifestation of partisan animosity and involved no real conviction on the part of the enemies of the paper that it was Satan's right arm. And however poor an opinion its editors may entertain of their antagonists of today, there is no doubt that these antagonists, or nearly all of them, are wholly sincere. Why this difference? It is largely due, perhaps, to a change of emphasis in the issues; the violence of political opinion has been steadily dying away in the United States ever since the end of the great political upheaval of the Civil War. It is not all gone, but it has been growing less every year since the impeachment of Andrew Johnson. People who hate violently today are apt to do so for economic reasons, or for reasons which, though partly political, racial, or temperamental in origin, they have been taught to regard as economic.

Yet *The Times's* general position on economic questions has always been pretty much the same. In economics as in politics, it has never thought it advisable to burn the barn in order to get rid of the

rats. No doubt those who think ill of the paper might represent this general continuity of doctrine on *The Times's* editorial page by saying that the paper has stood still while the country has moved on. But neither of these statements would be true. The paper has stood still only on certain fundamental issues, such as that two and two make four, or, at any rate, have made four in all past human history, and that it is somewhat unlikely that by virtue of some mystic gospel from Kansas, North Dakota or Russia, two and two can be made to add up to six and a half. Nor is it true that the rest of the country, or the rest of American journalism, has moved away to the Left while *The Times* remained in splendid isolation in its old position just beyond the Right Centre.

Radicalism is nothing new in America; not even economic radicalism. But there has been a considerable change in the character, if not in the volume, of American radicalism, due largely to the changing racial composition of the American people. Economic radicalism in the early days of *The Times* was largely a matter of agrarian or easy-money agitation. It was conducted, as a matter of course, chiefly by native Americans; recent immigrants, less numerous than now and mostly of a different racial provenance, were too busy graduating from the pick and shovel to capitalistic comfort to stop and remember that America was the country where no poor man had a chance. Dilettante radicalism of the wealthier classes had not yet appeared, or rather had sunk out of sight after its manifestation by such men as Jefferson in the early days of the Republic.

The radical movements in the earlier days of *The Times* found most of their support among farmers; they were native products; and their votaries usually recovered their balance after two or three good crop years. The general characteristic of these delusions was a conviction that economic evils could be ended by the printing of unlimited paper money, or the validation of unlimited token money; and this conviction usually disappeared as men and the country grew older, and the specific grievance faded away in periods of prosperity. Passing of hard frontier conditions brought better times to the prairie states; young men who had followed some peerless leader of the day in the earnest conviction that poverty could be cured by happy improvisation often discovered, as they grew older, that in default of more palatable remedies poverty could be cured by work. Radicalism in those days was apt to be only a form of wild oats.

But the newer radicalism is different in quality. It is not a question of removing specific grievances, real or fancied; the whole world, to the contemporary radical, is only one great grievance. And the cure of this painful condition must be exactly thus and so, otherwise it is no cure. This radicalism is a matter of dogma — at least the most popular and conspicuous of its manifestations, Marxian Socialism, is a matter of dogma. The world is divided into the true believers and the infidels; and the infidels shall not see salvation.

The influence of socialist intolerance even on non-socialist radicalism has probably contributed a good deal to the conviction of most radicals that no man

can honestly be conservative. Those who disagree with the radicals are actuated only by the desire to continue grinding down the faces of the poor, or to preserve their ill-gotten gains from those who would like to pass them around. And it should not be forgotten that these doctrines, and most of their adherents, came from parts of the Continent of Europe where the give-and-take of political activity has been unknown till quite recent years. Granting the numerous faults of Anglo-Saxon institutions, it remains true that the races who have lived for a considerable time under those institutions are able to find other explanations for difference of political opinion than the innate and total depravity of the opposition.

It may be conjectured that these considerations explain, in large measure at least, the embittered tone of most current radicalism. All conservatives, of course, are the targets of its wrath; *The Times* happens to be a conspicuous target, standing out above the crowd. Also, the reasons suggested above for the paper's unpopularity among opponents of its political views are valid in considerable measure in the field of economic controversy. Some Socialists prefer to get the news from their own sectarian organs; but a good many of them, with praiseworthy eagerness to find out what is happening, look for pleasant as well as unpleasant information in the columns of *The Times*. It may be held, indeed, that only a devout Bolshevik can get full pleasure out of reading *The Times;* for after he has read the news he can turn to the editorial page and enjoy a complete catharsis of the emotions, ending with the gratify-

ing conviction that *The Times* editors are a gang of scoundrels and that his own moral purity is positively dazzling by contrast.

In the period now under discussion *The Times* gradually won its way to this position of conservative leadership. It had and still has a conviction, which the little experience available has justified, that the Government is about as poor a business manager as can be found.

During the trust prosecutions, which offered such lavish and innocuous entertainment to the public for a decade or so, *The Times* was inclined to regard each case on its merits. In some few of these cases the paper was of the opinion that misconduct had been proved and that the offending corporation should suffer the penalty, such as it was, of dissolution; but it was unable to admit that size alone was a crime, or that the power to do evil was to be regarded as no less criminal than the actual doing of evil; and the view on this point has since been accepted by the courts. It seems probable that on both of these issues the position taken by *The Times* is much more generally accepted today than a few years ago. For several years *The Times* labored to show that bench and bar had fallen under the spell of an ancient legal phrase, "restraint of trade." The courts have now come to the view that the restraint must be actual, not potential.

The direct primary, the initiative and referendum, the recall of Judges and other officials, and similar mechanical devices by which, it was widely believed ten years ago, the purity of political life could be automatically safeguarded, also found *The Times*

somewhat incredulous as to their merits. This incredulity, it may be observed, was based principally on a study of politics not only in the present but in the past, and on the conviction that political improvement must usually be effected by raising the standard of civic consciousness in the electorate. It is one of the misfortunes of most radicals that they think, or appear to think, that the beginning of the world was contemporaneous with the beginning of their consciousness of the world. Very often that is why they are radicals; it is unknown to them that their panaceas have already been tried on the patient without producing much improvement. Conservatism, in its literal meaning, implies an inclination to preserve the good that has come down from the past, and a reluctance to discard institutions that have worked at least well enough to survive until there is strong reason to believe that substitutes would be more satisfactory. But American conservatism, thanks to the character of most of the opposition, has rarely been forced back to this defensive line. Most of its campaigns have been in the nature of outpost fighting; its principal work has been to remind the public of the existence of the past when so many thinkers of contemporary public life appear to believe that history begins with the Communist Manifesto.

The Times's attitude toward socialism, syndicalism, and similar movements is sufficiently well known to need no particular mention here. On other issues, however, it should be remarked for the sake of the record that the conservatism of the paper has not been so unvarying as some of its critics seem to

think. At the time of the State Constitutional Convention of 1915, for example, *The Times* thought there was need of a far more extensive revision of the fundamental law than the convention even attempted. The document finally produced, though it seemed to *The Times* a rather inadequate response to the opportunity, nevertheless received the paper's support on the ground that it was a considerable improvement over the Constitution of 1894, and made some much needed changes in the direction of simplification and economy, and making the government of the State more easily controlled by the voters. On this occasion the mass of the electorate was considerably more conservative than *The Times*, preferring the old Constitution with all its imperfections to a new one against which no serious argument was ever attempted except that it had been made by a body in which Elihu Root was one of the leaders.

In the matter of prohibition the paper has expressed a good deal of dissatisfaction with the theory of Constitutional prohibition as well as with the practice of the Volstead act. The basis of this is not so much a belief that in questions such as this action by the several states is more likely to result in an approximation of the popular will, though some of the editors of *The Times* do believe that. Whatever the merits of our Federal system, it is dying; every day the states are losing more of such power as is left them to a centralizing Federal Government, and not very many people seem to care. The doubts of *The Times* about the wisdom of prohibition arise rather from a skepticism as to the

readiness of the people for any such drastic measures, and a belief that it is poor policy to make such a sweeping change practically irrevocable by its embodiment in the Constitution.

The judgment of history is at best a somewhat uncertain criterion, even after some centuries have afforded opportunity for inspection of the results of political action and reaction. To appeal to the judgment of history, after a decade, is a little too hazardous. The archaeologist from the Island of Yap, excavating the pyramidal ruins of Manhattan in the year 4921, may perhaps understand just where the United States was headed in the beginning of the twentieth century; he will certainly know whether or not it got there. Contemporary observers can only guess. Still, taking the evidence for what little it is worth, the editors of *The Times* may feel that there is no great reason to fear that their position on the issues of these years was mistaken.

This period, between the Spanish War and the World War, was the age of muckraking; the day of a great emotional revival in American public life; of a new infusion of morality into politics, and of politics into morality.

The Times during this carnival of purity was compelled to preserve its attitude of conscientious skepticism, and consequently was as unpopular with followers of the new gospel as the village infidel at protracted meeting; for it steadfastly refused to stagger down to the mourners' bench. And now the revival is over, and most of those who hit the sawdust trail have fallen from grace and gone back to walk in darkness till the next day of Pentecost. *The Times*

contemplates their side-slips without exultation; rather with a certain sadness. It would be a wonderful thing if life were what the reformers thought it was, but experience has shown that it is not. It was the painful duty of *The Times*, at the height of the revival, to remind the reformers of the lessons of experience; to express its doubts as to the value of measures which introduced new evils without curing the old; and to suggest that neither was the past as black as it was painted, nor could the future reasonably be expected to be one unspotted smear of rose-color. This is what conservatism means, and *The Times* is not ashamed of it.

The attitude of *The Times* toward union labor has been pretty widely misrepresented. *The Times* believes in trades unionism as a valuable contribution to the national well being. It does not think, however, that the followers of the organized trades are the whole people, or a specially privileged part of the people. It believes that the American Federation of Labor has rendered very great services to the nation at large as well as to the men enrolled in it, but it believes that the members of the Federation are part of the people, and that their interests cannot be considered apart from the general interest.

For those movements, mostly outside the Federation, which tend toward syndicalism *The Times* has no sympathy, for it believes that syndicalism is morally and economically unsound. When the railroad brotherhoods hold up the Government as they did in 1916, the Government is more to blame than the railroad brotherhoods; but *The Times* has been un-

able to regard the railroads as existing solely for the interest of their employés.

The Times does not pretend to have a patented cure for industrial ills, nor to know where that cure can be found. It does have a pretty strong suspicion, however, as to where it cannot be found. Socialists and syndicalists object to the trades union philosophy that it implies a constant state of industrial war, or at best of industrial truce, between employer and employé. *The Times* has not found it so in practice.

When the new publisher took over *The Times* in 1896 he discovered that the composing room was heavily, even ruinously, overmanned. The publisher felt that as a matter both of right and of expediency this condition should be discussed with the union officials, and a conference with the then head of Typographical Union No. 6 made it plain that that gentleman's ideas of a fair day's work for a fair day's pay coincided with those of the publisher of *The Times;* so the payroll of the composing room was reduced $1000 a week without any lessening of its efficiency. The composing room has since found plenty of work for several times the number of men then employed, but relations have always been good, and such differences as arose have always been settled in an amicable manner.

CHAPTER III

Modern News-gathering, 1900–1914

SO much for the editorial policies from 1900 to 1914. The period under discussion was, however, above all a period of development in the news service of *The Times*. All the newspapers in New York had a better idea of what was news in 1914 than they had in 1900, all of them knew more about what to do with news when they had it, and though they made less noise about the getting of the news than they had been inclined to do in the nineties, they got more news and more reliable news than they had ever done before. In this gradual improvement *The Times* led the way. Whatever its relative position in New York journalism — which is a matter of opinion, perhaps — that position was higher in 1914 than in 1900. It was to become higher still during the war, but in the years before the war was laid the foundation of the great organization for getting and publishing the news which is the chief distinction of *The Times* today.

The history of the paper's growth in this period is not easy to tell, for it is not a matter of isolated "beats," of great individual achievements rising from a level plain of daily routine, of great crusades or magnificent exposures. *The Times* has had plenty of "beats" and has shown its enterprise in digging up more than one neglected field of the news. but

its real preëminence is a matter of high average rather than of scattered peaks of achievement. Day in and day out it gets more news, and handles it more intelligently, than any paper knew how to do a decade or two ago; and this implies, obviously, the slow assembling of an especially competent staff, the indoctrination of every man with a gradually evolved set of principles, as well as unusually efficient direction from above. *The Times* as a newspaper is far from perfect; its conductors know that better than anybody else. Its news-gatherers may overlook some things; its editors may make mistakes in dealing with what they have to give the public. But there can be no very serious doubt that *The Times* makes fewer mistakes of this sort than its contemporaries.

In the building of this news organization credit must be given to the men at the top — to Henry Loewenthal, at present in charge of the business news department, whose connection with *The Times* began in 1875 and who was managing editor from 1896 to 1904; to Arthur Greaves, city editor from 1900 to 1915; to William C. Reick, who from 1906 to 1912 was associated with the general management of the paper, and chiefly to Carr V. Van Anda, who has been managing editor since 1904 and has been most directly concerned with the extraordinary development of the news department and with reaching its highest peak. Under all these men *The Times* was steadily coming into prominence as a paper which, while giving less attention than some of its contemporaries to spectacular demonstrations of its enterprise, was learning how to get

"All the News That's Fit to Print."

The New York Times.

THE WEATHER.
Unsettled Tuesday; Wednesday, fair, cooler; moderate southerly winds, becoming variable.
For full weather report see Page 23.

VOL. LXI...NO. 19,805. NEW YORK, TUESDAY, APRIL 16, 1912.—TWENTY-FOUR PAGES. ONE CENT In Greater New York, Jersey City, and Newark. | Elsewhere, TWO CENTS.

TITANIC SINKS FOUR HOURS AFTER HITTING ICEBERG; 866 RESCUED BY CARPATHIA, PROBABLY 1250 PERISH; ISMAY SAFE, MRS. ASTOR MAYBE, NOTED NAMES MISSING

Col. Astor and Bride, Isidor Straus and Wife, and Maj. Butt Aboard.

"RULE OF SEA" FOLLOWED

Women and Children Put Over in Lifeboats and Are Supposed to be Safe on Carpathia.

PICKED UP AFTER 8 HOURS

Vincent Astor Calls at White Star Office for News of His Father and Leaves Weeping.

FRANKLIN HOPEFUL ALL DAY

Manager of the Line Insisted Titanic Was Unsinkable Even After She Had Gone Down.

HEAD OF THE LINE ABOARD

J. Bruce Ismay Making First Trip on Gigantic Ship That Was to Surpass All Others.

The admission that the Titanic, the biggest steamship in the world, had

Biggest Liner Plunges to the Bottom at 2.20 A. M.

RESCUERS THERE TOO LATE

Except to Pick Up the Few Hundreds Who Took to the Lifeboats.

WOMEN AND CHILDREN FIRST

Cunarder Carpathia Rushing to New York with the Survivors.

SEA SEARCH FOR OTHERS

The California Stands By on Chance of Picking Up Other Boats or Rafts.

OLYMPIC SENDS THE NEWS

Only Ship to Flash Wireless Messages to Shore After the Disaster.

LATER REPORT SAVES 866.

BOSTON, April 15.—A wireless message picked up late to-night,

tional Mercantile Marine, conceded that probably only those passengers who were picked up by the Cunarder Carpathia had been saved. Advices received early this morning tended to increase the number of survivors by 200.

The admission followed a day in which the White Star Line officials had been optimistic in the extreme. At no time was the admission made that every one aboard the huge steamer was not safe. The ship itself, it was confidently asserted, was unsinkable, and inquirers were informed that she would reach port, under her own steam probably, but surely with the help of the Allan liner Virginian, which was reported to be towing her.

As the day passed, however, with no new authentic reports from the Titanic or any of the ships which were known to have responded to her wireless call for help, it became apparent that authentic news of the disaster probably could come only from the Titanic's sister ship, the Olympic. The wireless range of the Olympic is 500 miles. That of the Carpathia, the Parisian, and the Virginian is much less, and as they neared the position of the Titanic they drew further and further out of shore range. From the Titanic's position at the time of the disaster it is doubtful if any of the ships except the Olympic could establish communication with shore.

Titanic Sank at 2:20 A. M. Monday.

In the White Star offices the hope was held out all day that the Parisian and the Virginian had taken off some of the Titanic's passengers, and efforts were made to get into communication with these liners. Until such communication was established the White Star officials refused to recognize the possibility that there were none of the Titanic's passengers aboard them.

But by nightfall came the message from Capt. Haddock of the Olympic to Cape Race, Newfoundland, telling of the foundering of the Titanic and of the rescue of 655 of her passengers by the Cunarder Carpathia, which, the wireless message said, reached the position of the Titanic at daybreak. All they found there, however, was lifeboats and wreckage. The biggest ship in the world had sunk at 2:20 o'clock yesterday morning.

Mr. Franklin admitted late last night that the Parisian and the Virginian, though they were among the first to answer the Titanic's calls for help, could not have reached the scene before 10 o'clock yesterday morning, seven and a half hours after the big Titanic buried her nose beneath the waves and pitched downward out of sight. The Carpathia, so the wireless dispatch from Capt. Haddock to Cape Race announced, reached the scene of the Titanic's foundering at daybreak, several

CAPT. E. J. SMITH,
Commander of the Titanic.

hours before the expected arrival of the Virginian and the Parisian.

1,465 Lives Lost First Report.

It is unbelievable, so White Star Line officials were compelled to concede finally, that the Carpathia should have failed to pick up every lifeboat which still floated on the waves. If they failed to pick up more than 655 passengers, it was because the others of the ship's complement had gone with her to the bottom.

But it was not until nearly nightfall that the extent of the disaster was realized. Before that the reassuring nature of the bulletins issued by the White Star line was sufficient to quiet the fears of those who had relatives or friends aboard the unfortunate ship and to prevent widespread belief in a serious disaster.

Capt. Haddock's message from the Olympic, which is printed in another column of THE TIMES, strongly indicated that none but the 655 taken from life boats by the Carpathia had been saved. This message was re-

THE PROBABLE LOSS.

Number Aboard.	
First cabin	325
Second cabin	285
Steerage	710
Crew, (estimated)	800
Total	2,120
Saved.	
By the Carpathia	866
Probably drowned	1,254

layed immediately to the White Star offices, but Mr. Franklin positively declined to make the text of the message public. He offered still the hope that passengers were aboard the Parisian and the Virginian, and even when the admission was wrung from him that there seemed little hope of the saving of any others than the 655 aboard the Carpathia, he clung to the hope that in some unexplained way there were other passengers abroad the two Allan liners.

First Reported Titanic in Tow.

Throughout the day there had been reassurances that the Titanic was being towed to port by the Virginian,

PARTIAL LIST OF THE SAVED.

Includes Bruce Ismay, Mrs. Widener, Mrs. H. B. Harris, and an Incomplete name, suggesting Mrs. Astor's.

Special to The New York Times.

CAPE RACE, N. F., Tuesday, April 16.—Following is a partial list of survivors among the first-class passengers of the Titanic, received by the Marconi wireless station this morning from the Carpathia, via the steapship Olympic;

Mrs. JACOB P. ——— and maid.
Mr. HARRY ANDERSON.
Mrs. ED. W. APPLETON.
Mrs. ROSE ABBOTT.
Miss G. M. BURNS.
Miss D. D. CASSEBERE.
Mrs. WM. M. CLARKE.
Mrs. B. CHIBINACE.
Miss E. G. CROSSBIE.
Miss H. ROSEBIE.
Miss JEAN HIPACK.
Mrs. HY. B. HARRIS.
Mrs. ALEX. HALVERSON.
Miss MARGARET BAYS.
Mr. BRUCE ISMAY.
Mr. and Mrs. ED. KIMBERLEY.
Mr. F. A. KENNYMAN.
Miss EMILE KENCHEN.
Miss G. F. LONGLEY.
Mrs. A. F. LEADER.
Miss BERTHA LAVORY.
Mrs. ERNEST LIVES.
Miss MARY CLINES.
Mrs. SINGRID LINDSTROM.
Mr. GUSTAVE J. LESNEUR.
Miss GIORGETTA A. MADILL.
Mme. MELICARD.
Mrs. TUCKER and maid.
Mrs. J. B. THAYER.
Mr. J. B. THAYER, Jr.
Mr. HENRY WOOLMER.
Miss ANNA WARD.
Mr. RICHARD M. WILLIAMS.
Mrs. F. M. WARNER.
Miss HELEN A. WILSON.
Miss WILLARD.
Miss MARY WICKS.
Mrs. GEO. D. WIDENER and maid.
Mrs. J. STEWART WHITE.
Miss MARIE YOUNG.
Mrs. THOMAS POTTER, Jr.
Mrs. EDNA S. ROBERTS.
Countess of ROTHES.
Mr. C. ROLMANE.
Mrs. SUSAN P. ROGERSON. (Probably Ryerson).
Miss EMILY B. ROGERSON.
Mrs. ARTHUR ROGERSON.
Master ALLISON and nurse.
Miss K. T. ANDREWS.
Miss NINETTE PANHART.
Miss E. W. ALLEN.
Mr. and Mrs. D. BISHOP.
Mr. H. BLANK.
Miss A. BASSINA.
Mrs. JAMES BAXTER.
Mr. GEORGE A. BAYT—
Miss C. BONNELL.
Mrs. J. M. BROWN.
Miss G. C. BOWEN.
Mr. and Mrs. R. L. BECKWITH
Miss RUTH TAUSSIG.
Miss ELLA THOR.
Mr. and Mrs. E. Z. TAYLOR.
GILBERT M. TUCKER.
Mr. J. B. THAYER.
Mr. JOHN B. ROGERSON.
Mrs. M. ROTHSCHILD.
Miss MADELEINE NEWELL.
Mrs. MARJORIE NEWELL.
HELEN W. NEWSOM.
Mr. FIENNAD OMOND.
Mr. E. C. OSTBY.
Miss HELEN R. OSTBY.
Mrs. MAMAM J. RENAGO.
Mlle. OLIVIA.
Mrs. D. W. MERVIN.
Mr. PHILIP EMOCK.
Mr. JAMES GOOGHT.
Miss RUBERTA MAIMY.
Mr. PIERRE MARECHAL.
Mrs. W. E. MINEHAN.
Miss APPIE RANELT.
Major ARTUR PEUCHEN.
Mrs. KARL H. BEHR.
Miss DESSETTE.
Mrs. WILLIAM BUCKNELL.
Mrs. O. H. BARKWORTH.
Mrs. H. B. STEFFASON
Mrs. ELSIE BOWERMAN.

The Marconi station reports that it missed the word after "Mrs. Jacob P." In a list received by the Associated Press this morning this name appeared well down, but in THE TIMES list it is first, suggesting that the name of Mrs. John Jacob Astor is intended. This supposition is strengthened by the fact that, except for Mrs. H. J. Allison, Mrs. Astor is the only lady in the "A" column of the ship's pasenger list attended by a maid.

NAMES PICKED UP AT BOSTON.

BOSTON, April 15.—Among the names of survivors of the Titanic picked up by wireless from the steamer Carpathia here to-night were the following:

Mr. and Mrs. L. HENRY.
Mrs. W. A. HOOPER.
Mr. MILE.
Mr. J. FLYNN.
Miss ALICE FORTUNE.
Mrs. ROBERT DOUGLAS.
Miss HILDA SLAYTER
Mrs. P. SMITH.
Mrs. BRAHAM.
Miss LUCILLE CARTER.
Mr. WILLIAM CARTER.
Miss CUMMINGS.
Mrs. FLORENCE MARE.
Miss ALICE PHILLIPS.
Mrs. PAULA MUNGE.
Mrs. JANE ———
Miss PHYLLIS O. ———
HOWARD B. CASE
Miss MINEHAN.
Miss BERTHA ———

and when Capt. Haddock's message proved this to be untrue only the admission was made at the White Star offices that the Titanic had sunk. Mr. Franklin said that Capt. Haddock's message was brief and "neglected to say that all the crew had been saved." But the inference was not that all the passengers had been saved. Rather it was that many of them had died, and presently Mr. Franklin admitted the fear that there had been a terrible loss of life on the Titanic.

This version of Capt. Haddock's wireless had been given at the White Star offices.

Capt. Haddock of the Olympic sends a wireless message to the White Star offices here that the steamer Titanic sank at 2:20 A. M., after all the passengers and crew had been lowered to life boats and transferred to the Virginian. The steamship Carpathia, with several hundred passengers of the Titanic, is now en route to New York.

At 9 o'clock, however, he modified this statement, declaring:

As far as we know the situation, there have been rumors from Halifax that three steamers were at the scene of the Titanic's sinking, namely, the Virginian, the Parisian, and the Carpathia. We have heard from Capt. Haddock of the Olympic, who says that the Titanic sank at 2:20 o'clock this morning. Haddock also informs us that the Carpathia has 675 survivors on board. It is very difficult to say whether the Virginian and the Parisian have any survivors on board until we can get a report from those vessels.

Fears Serious Loss of Life.

We have asked for that report from Capt. Haddock, and we are expecting a reply at any time. The Carpathia is proceeding to New York direct. We very much fear that there has been serious loss of life, but it is impossible for us to say definitely concerning this sad part of the situation until we are able to reassure ourselves whether or not any of the Titanic's passengers are aboard the Allan liners.

We are hopeful that the rumors which have reached us by telegraph from Halifax that there are passengers aboard the Virginian and the Parisian will prove to be true, and that these vessels will turn up with some of the passengers. It is the loss of life that makes this thing so awful. We can replace the money loss, but not the lives of those who went down.

Another version of the message from the Olympic was current last night and included the sentence: "Loss likely total 1,800 souls." This sentence was not in the message received by THE TIMES from Cape Race nor in that sent to the White Star line offices.

Continued on Page 2.

They are mostly women and children, the message said, and it concluded: "Grave fears are felt for the safety of the balance of the passengers and crew."

Special to The New York Times.

CAPE RACE, N. F., April 15.—The White Star liner Olympic reports by wireless this evening that the Cunarder Carpathia reached, at daybreak this morning, the position from which wireless calls for help were sent out last night by the Titanic after her collision with an iceberg. The Carpathia found only the lifeboats and the wreckage of what had been the biggest steamship afloat.

The Titanic had foundered at about 2:20 A. M., in latitude 41:16 north and longitude 50:14 west. This is about 30 minutes of latitude, or about 34 miles, due south of the position at which she struck the iceberg. All her boats are accounted for and about 655 souls have been saved of the crew and passengers, most of the latter presumably women and children.

There were about 2,100 persons aboard the Titanic.

The Leyland liner California is remaining and searching the position of the disaster, while the Carpathia is returning to New York with the survivors.

It can be positively stated that up to 11 o'clock to-night nothing whatever had been received at or heard by the Marconi station here to the effect that the Parisian, Virginian or any other ships had picked up any survivors, other than those picked up by the Carpathia.

First News of the Disaster.

The first news of the disaster to the Titanic was received by the Marconi wireless station here at 10:25 o'clock last night [as told in yesterday's New York Times.] The Titanic was first heard giving the distress signal "C. Q. D.," which was answered by a number of ships, including the Carpathia,

the news wherever it happened and about as soon as it happened, and to present it to the public with some appreciation of its relative importance and interest.

A business connection which has already been mentioned deserves somewhat more detailed notice here, for in the earlier years of this period it proved of considerable value. This was the "alliance for mutual interest and advantage" with *The London Times*, begun on September 2, 1901. No doubt this alliance has been the pretext — it could hardly be called the excuse — for much of the belief that *The New York Times* is owned or controlled by Lord Northcliffe. In fact, it was precisely what it was called at the time, an alliance for mutual benefit. The alliance consisted only of this — that *The New York Times* bought the full rights for publication in North America of *The London Times* news service, *The London Times* receiving reciprocal rights to *The New York Times* news service for publication in England. It was an arrangement of the same general character as those which the paper now maintains with *The London Daily Chronicle*, the Paris *Matin* and *The Chicago Tribune*. To suppose that it involves ownership of *The New York Times* in England is very much the same as saying that a man is owned by the restaurant where he occasionally dines.

As for Lord Northcliffe, a genius in newspaper making, he had nothing to do with *The London Times* when this contract was concluded. That paper was then owned by the Walter family, and managed by the Walters and Moberly Bell. The arrangement was

continued for some years after Lord Northcliffe bought *The London Times*, but relations with him were sharply broken off at the beginning of the World War because of some difference of opinion between him and the management of *The New York Times* with respect to news exchange arrangements. This has been told so often that very few of those who still repeat the story of a Northcliffe influence on *The New York Times* have even the poor excuse of ignorance.

Aside from its effect in furnishing nonexplosive ammunition for credulous Sinn Feiners, the connection was on the whole a useful one. It was most useful at the beginning, when the relative position of the two papers was not quite what it is today. In the early years of the twentieth century it gave *The New York Times* a connection with a worldwide news service of much intrinsic value and still greater reputation, which proved particularly valuable in the Russo-Japanese War. Later on it was less important, for *The New York Times* was becoming able to collect the news of the world on its own initiative; not so much by means of a widely traveling staff of special correspondents as by a few centralized offices which had learned how to get the earliest reports from almost anywhere.

Much of the development of *The Times* news department has a purely technical or intramural interest, but a good deal of it has such bearing on the general improvement in journalistic methods that it deserves to rank almost as a public service. This is especially true of the paper's share in the

development of wireless telegraphy. To Marconi and the other men who were perfecting that invention in the early years of the twentieth century *The Times* gave not only publicity and encouragement but sometimes a rather insistent support which drove them on to do more than they would ever have dreamed they could do if there had been nobody there to tell them. The war would undoubtedly have forced the development of long-distance wireless in any case, but it is due in some degree to *The New York Times* that the art was so far advanced as it was when the war began.

In the early years of wireless the interest of *The Times* was chiefly, if not wholly, that of a newspaper eager to give the news. Marconi's announcement on December 14, 1901, that transatlantic communication had been established between Poldhu, Cornwall, and St. John's, Newfoundland, received the display in the news columns, and the enthusiastic comment in the editorial columns, which its importance warranted. But these first transmissions went no farther than the sending across the Atlantic of a single letter — S — whose three dots in the Morse code, repeated at stated intervals, did indeed convince the inventor that he could send a message from Europe to America, but left him far short of the goal of a service which would be commercially useful. His experiments were continued, without much publicity; and by a curious accident *The New York Times* was deprived of the news of one of the most interesting of these experiments, the dispatch of the first transatlantic wireless press message.

On December 16, 1902, Dr. (afterward Sir) George

R. Parkin, then one of the correspondents of *The London Times*, visited Marconi at his new station at Glace Bay, Nova Scotia. By this time Marconi was able to send matter eastward across the Atlantic with fair success, though he had had little luck with westward messages. Dr. Parkin wrote out and sent a twenty-five-word Marconigram to *The London Times*, expressing the sentiments proper to the occasion, and then came back to New York and told for the first time the thrilling story of the epoch-making event, of the successful transmission of a message, without wires, across the Atlantic, and of the progress Marconi was making. The conductors of *The New York Times*, however, were deeply interested in what Marconi was doing, and they were delighted to learn that Dr. Parkin had written an account, some two thousand words in length, of what he was the first newspaper representative permitted to witness.

Since the alliance between the two papers was hen in force, Dr. Parkin had the story typed on *New York Times* stationery and mailed it himself, in a plain envelope, to his paper in London. A carbon copy was left in *The New York Times* office, to be published simultaneously with the London publication; *The New York Times* was to be advised by cable of *The London Times's* receipt of the story. The editors waited for days and weeks and the message did not arrive. And at last Dr. Parkin's original story came back through the dead letter office, refused at *The London Times* office because of insufficient postage calling for the payment of surtax refund. Years later one of the managers of *The*

London Times explained this by saying that that paper received an enormous amount of unsolicited correspondence from all over the world, and that such of it as did not have enough postage paid was declined. Whatever Lord Northcliffe may have done to *The London Times*, it is probable that its mail no longer goes back to the Post Office unopened.

It was years later before Marconi was able to open up a regular transatlantic service, and in the meantime *The New York Times* had so unfailingly displayed its confidence in him that when regular service was begun between Clifden, Ireland, and Glace Bay, Nova Scotia, on October 17, 1907, the first message accepted for transmission westward came to the paper from its London office. Of the ten thousand words or so sent by wireless that night a good deal was *New York Times* news, and one of the dispatches from the Paris office carried a message of greeting from Georges Clemenceau, then Premier for the first time. Naturally *The Times* made a great display story of the opening of regular wireless communications, and among the "follows" which it printed the next morning was Dr. Parkin's account of his experience nearly five years before.

For some years thereafter a considerable proportion of *The Times* European news for the Sunday issue came through by wireless, but the delays in transmission were so great that the most important news was generally sent by cable. When the regular Marconi service was first opened most of the cable company officials had taken it rather lightly, and some were incredulous. Others professed to believe that its competition would not be dangerous;

and for a matter of four years they were justified. Some of them foresaw that eventually wireless might carry a much higher percentage of transatlantic messages than it could handle in 1907, but they were optimistic enough to think that there would be plenty of business for all. And they were right; the war and the continuing interest in European news which survived the war have kept both wireless and cables busy enough.

But from 1907 to 1912 the wireless service could not be depended on for sure and speedy transmission of important news. Since the wireless rate was only five cents a word, and the minimum cable rate on press messages was double that, the wireless was used wherever possible. In those days *The Times* published two or three pages of general European news in one of its Sunday sections — society and fashion notes, the movements of American tourists, and such similar items as occupied most of the little attention that was given by Americans to European affairs before the war — and the wireless was useful and cheap for this sort of service. A story written on Thursday did not need to get to the office on Friday if it was intended for the Sunday paper. In those days *The Times* did a great deal more for the wireless companies than the wireless companies did for *The Times;* every dispatch was carefully marked "By Marconi Wireless Telegraph," and the value of this acknowledgment was undoubtedly great.

Still the wireless remained distinctly a secondary matter; anything urgent had to be put on the cables. And this might have continued indefinitely if *The Times* had not been moved to some reflections, early

in January, 1912, by the chance consideration of a wireless message which had come through from London in five hours. This was considerably less than the average time required for ordinary press messages by the Marconi service, and on reflection no reason was seen why there should be even this much delay. The Hertzian waves traveled fast enough for any taste; the delays, then, must be in the land connections from European capitals to Clifden, and from Glace Bay to New York.

It was the old story of the early days of news-gathering, when the utmost speed in getting European news to Cape Race might be nullified by the indolence of a telegraph operator in the Maine woods. Once smooth out the land connections and there was no reason why wireless could not come as fast as cables. So *The Times* suddenly informed the officials of the Marconi company that on an appointed date, about two weeks ahead, it would give them its entire London business. Suggestions for the prompt handling of this business were offered by *The Times*. Wires to Glace Bay were arranged for by the paper, and after much insistence by *The Times* the Marconi officials managed to get better service to Clifden. At the time named the new service was begun, and was a success from the start. From the middle of January, 1912, to the outbreak of the war virtually all of *The Times* dispatches from London came by wireless; they arrived in good time; and in the beginning nobody was so surprised at the achievement as the officials of the wireless company.

Present-day readers of *The Times* will remember

the page — usually the third or fourth — headed "By Marconi Wireless Telegraph to *The New York Times*" — which in those days contained each morning all the European news of interest to American readers, except in the cases when something was important enough for the front page. If the wireless companies were startled, the cable companies were scandalized. The suspicion that this matter did not come by wireless at all was rather widely expressed; every cable company thought it was sent over the lines of its competitors. One of the chief cable experts in Germany, with truly German inability to realize that what had once been true was not necessarily still true, insisted weeks after the new plan was adopted that *The Times* was still getting all its foreign news by cable. There were men in Germany, however, who understood well enough the possibilities of the wireless telegraph, and the time was not far away when Germany was to make more use of it than anybody ever dreamed in 1912.

When the war broke out the military importance of the wireless telegraph caused considerable restrictions to be placed on its use, but it proved invaluable, particularly to American correspondents in Germany before 1917. It would probably have come into general use during the war in any case, but its importance would not have been so promptly recognized if *The Times* had not demonstrated two years earlier that the wireless was capable of doing a great deal of work in very good time. It is not pretended that the paper's motives in giving invaluable advertising and a very necessary stimulus to the wireless com-

BEN. C. FRANCK.

MAJOR JULIUS OCHS ADLER.
© Underwood & Underwood.

ARTHUR HAYS SULZBERGER.
© Underwood & Underwood.

KATE L. STONE.

ASSISTANTS TO THE PUBLISHER.

panies were entirely altruistic; when it had shown the wireless experts what they could do it got its European news at half the price of cables. As soon as other newspapers woke up sufficiently to realize what could be and was being done, they shared in the benefit.

In other uses of the wireless *The Times* was again a pioneer. The naval fighting off Port Arthur in the Russo-Japanese War was covered for *The London Times* and *The New York Times* by Capt. Lionel James in a dispatch boat equipped with the De Forest wireless, through which he maintained communication from 150 miles out at sea with the cable station at Wei-Hai-Wei. The naval battle of April 13, 1904, for instance, in which the Russian flagship *Petropavlovsk* was sunk, was reported to *The Times* from both land and sea — the official Russian version from Port Arthur coming by way of Petrograd, and Captain James's eyewitness reports sent by wireless from his boat and cables from Wei-Hai-Wei. Throughout the fighting around Port Arthur *The Times* thus had a long lead over its competitors — for though the Japanese Army was the first to break the long domination of war by the correspondents who wrote about it, and to introduce the modern idea that the war correspondent's place is in the home, their naval authorities had not yet sufficiently realized the importance and possible danger of wireless communication to put any restriction on James's activities. Perhaps, too, in that particular war the Japanese felt a certain reluctance to hamper the correspondent who represented the leading newspaper of an allied country, and what

was becoming one of the most important papers in the most friendly neutral nation.

The C Q D call from the White Star liner *Republic*, sinking in collision on January 23, 1909, which brought up other ships in time to save her 1600 passengers, may have been obliterated from the memory of most readers by the greater and more spectacular marine disasters of more recent years; but it was a great news story in its day, and the more so since it was the first prominent instance in which wireless had proved of immense value in saving life at sea. All the papers had that story, of course, though the *Republic's* wireless operator as a matter of course sent his story to *The Times*. If *The Times* handled the news somewhat better than some of the others, it was only because by that time *The Times* was learning the art of handling big stories with a thoroughness which had not yet been known in New York journalism. As a matter of fact, the first actual wireless call for help had come nearly three years earlier — from the *Nantucket* lightship, battered by storms, on December 10, 1905. There again it was everybody's story. But *The Times* shares with *The Chicago Tribune* the distinction of having printed the first news story sent by wireless of a rescue at sea. The freighter *St. Cuthbert*, afire off Cape Sable, on February 2, 1908, was sighted by the liner *Cymric*, which managed to rescue in a heavy sea thirty-seven of her crew of fifty-one. A correspondent of *The Chicago Tribune* aboard the *Cymric* sent the story to his own paper as soon as the liner was near enough to shore for the short-distance wireless of those days to com-

municate with shore stations, and having sent the news he remembered that *The New York Times* was interested in anything connected with wireless telegraphy, and accordingly sent a query by wireless to find out if the paper wanted the story. It did, and it got it.

These episodes of the past seem commonplace enough today, when the wireless is as much a matter of course as the telegraph; when *The Times* has, as it has had for more than a year past, its own receiving station just off the news room on the third floor of the Times Annex, and receives there in addition to its own dispatches everything else that comes through the air, even from such a distance as the Russian frontier, where the Bolshevist wireless operators are sending out the daily fiction feuilleton of the Soviet Government. But in their day they were considerable achievements, requiring not only a good deal of work but a good deal of imagination and faith.

Somewhat similar to certain of these demonstrations of the possibility of wireless telegraphy was the round-the-world cable message sent by *The Times* to itself on August 20, 1911. The Commercial Cable Company had then lately opened its Pacific line, and *The Times* wanted to see just what could be done in the way of getting a message from New York across the country, across the Pacific, up through the Indian Ocean and the Mediterranean and back to New York. A brief dispatch was received in the office sixteen and a half minutes after it was sent, and this without any preliminary smoothing of the way such as speeds the congratulatory messages of Kings and Presidents opening a new line. To the nonprofessional reader this may seem pur-

poseless, a mere advertising of *The Times* and incidentally of the cable companies. But it was not. It was a test of the possible speed of transmission of messages under ordinary conditions; it gave the editors of *The Times* some data by which they could estimate what ought to be expected in the case of real news, and thereby would necessarily keep the cable companies somewhat more alert to see that in the sending of news messages there would be no inexplicable delays.

Perhaps, to complete the record of *The Times* interest in wireless telegraphy, it should be mentioned that the publisher of *The Times* bought some shares of stock in the American Marconi Company. He bought them at the market price, of course; bought them partly because he believed in the future of wireless telegraphy and thought they would be a good investment, and largely because he wanted to promote the development of an industry that promised increased facilities and reduced rates for international communications. This stock he eventually sold at a considerable loss. It deserves mention here only because the incident was distorted to make it appear that Mr. Ochs was in some mysterious way "involved in the English Marconi scandal." And although he never owned, bought or sold a single share of English Marconi stock, there are no doubt some people who have believed the story. As has been observed above, the people who will believe anything are regrettably numerous.

Another of the modern arts in whose development *The Times* took a keen interest was aviation. In the

decade before the war, indeed, aviation and wireless were the two chief special interests of the office. *The Times* published more news about their progress than its contemporaries, and gradually acquired a sort of special position in both aviation and wireless news, which attracted to it automatically a good deal of information about the progress of these arts. But in aviation as in wireless *The Times* did more than merely give publicity to what was going on. It promoted and inspired a good deal of the development in the early years of the new invention, and more than once was able to incite the experts to the accomplishment of things which of their own accord they would never have attempted. For in those days the art of aviation and of airplane construction was rather primitive. An airplane was a dangerous and incalculable machine, just how dangerous and incalculable fliers alone knew. Editors of *The Times*, who did not have to do the flying, were perhaps rather insistent that the aviators should crowd their luck and see how far they could develop their art; but the fact remains that many of these enterprises would not have been attempted if the aviators had not been prodded — and none of them met with any misadventure while working for *The Times*.

One of the first big display stories about aviation which *The Times* printed dealt with an exhibition promoted by another paper. On May 29, 1910, Glenn Curtiss flew from Albany to New York for a prize offered by *The World*. With an entirely reasonable caution, Mr. Curtiss was rather slow in getting away — so slow that *The World* apparently lost faith in him and announced that another aviator

was on the way to Albany and would probably make the flight before Curtiss did. *The Times* had more confidence in Curtiss, as well as a fuller realization of the importance of this demonstration of the powers of the airplane; so when Curtiss did start, *The Times* was right under him with a special train and covered the whole story much more fully than *The World*. A fortnight later, on June 13, 1910, Claude Hamilton flew from New York to Philadelphia and back in a single day for a prize offered by *The Times*. Eleven years have brought such progress in aviation that it is hard to realize what an achievement this was at the time; as a matter of fact, Hamilton's machine broke down in Jersey on the return trip, had to be patched up, and was brought back to New York at very great risk to the flier.

In October of the same year *The Times* and *The Chicago Evening Post* promoted an aviation meet at Chicago, at the end of which there was to be a race from Chicago to New York for a $25,000 prize offered by the two papers. The meet was a great success, artistically and financially; so great a success in the latter respect that the aviation company which got the gate receipts was rather reluctant to hazard its machines and its fliers on a trip to New York even for $25,000. At last, however, on October 10, Eugene Ely did make the attempt, only to come down just over the Indiana line. Aviation engineers tinkered with his engine for days and finally concluded that it was impossible to go on; not till later was it discovered that nothing was the matter with it except that a clot of mud had stopped up an air valve and prevented ignition. But for that,

there is a chance that the flight from Chicago to New York — possibly even a non-stop flight — might have been completed without mishap.

It was six years before *The Times* again tried to promote a flight from Chicago to New York. This time it was to be a non-stop flight, with Victor Carlstrom of the Curtiss staff trying it alone. In that interval the war had forced aviation to an unexpected development, and fliers in Europe were doing things that could not have been dreamed of three or four years earlier. But once more the attempt was unsuccessful as a non-stop flight, and again because of a trivial mishap — a loose nut on a feed pipe which had somehow escaped the attention of the battalion of engineers and mechanics who had examined the machine. Carlstrom spent the night at Hammondsport, N. Y., and finished the flight to New York next day. This episode is notable also in that the American Telephone and Telegraph Company developed for *The Times* a quite efficient news service, having instructed all its agents along the line of Carlstrom's flight to keep watch for the aviator and report instantly when he appeared.

Always in those years *The Times* was eager to find out what aviators were doing, and to encourage them to do still more. Among its other endeavors to promote aerial navigation may be mentioned the offer of a cup for a flight from Boston to Washington in July, 1911, which was won by Harry Atwood, and its promotion of an air race around Manhattan Island in October, 1913, in connection with the Aeronautical Society's meet. Not long after that the war broke out, and aviation was forced to a devel-

opment which no longer needed any journalistic stimulus.

The two great special interests of *The Times* were combined in an enterprise which the paper promoted in conjunction with *The London Daily Telegraph* and *The Chicago Record-Herald* in October, 1910 — Walter Wellman's attempt to fly across the Atlantic in a dirigible balloon. Wellman succeeded in flying about a thousand miles, but unfortunately not in a straight line, as a northeast wind caught him off Nantucket and drove him down to the latitude of Hatteras, where he and his companions were rescued by a passing steamer. Though the attempt to cross the Atlantic was unsuccessful, Wellman's dirigible, of course infinitely more primitive than the airships which finally did make the flight in 1919, made a record creditable enough for that period. In the first hours of the flight Wellman kept in communication with *The Times* by wireless — the first time, as far as can be learned, that an aviation story was covered by wireless from the air — and the wireless again brought the news of his rescue out at sea, though in this case the messages were dispatched from the rescuing steamer.

The automobile business was at this period going through the transition from a dangerous sport of the idle rich to a basic industry meeting the needs of the proletariat. Automobile news for a long time was prominent in every paper, more prominent than it is now, because the automobile attracted both a sporting and a commercial interest. Its promotion, however, was being taken care of by so many people

that *The Times*, though publishing very full and trustworthy automobile news, had no occasion to do in this field anything like its work in aviation and wireless. One event, however, it did promote — a New York-to-Paris automobile race, in collaboration with the Paris *Matin*, early in 1908.

If one single news story published in *The Times* in this period were to be marked out as more famous than all the rest, it would have to be Admiral Peary's story of the discovery of the North Pole. Before Peary started north on his final trip *The Times* had arranged for exclusive news publication of his story in New York and had agreed to act as his agent in selling other rights. It had advanced $4000 to him, as he needed that much to make the expedition possible, to be repaid out of the profits from the use and sale of the rights to Peary's story of the trip. As it turned out, Peary's story sold so well that he realized through *The Times* nearly three times this amount.

It was, accordingly, a good deal of a disappointment to the conductors of *The Times* when early in September, 1909, Peary being still absent beyond communication in the north, the little known Dr. Frederick Cook suddenly appeared en route to Copenhagen and announced that he had discovered the Pole on April 21 of the previous year.

The Times's reaction to the news was, however, about the same as the reaction of nearly everybody else. It was inclined to give Dr. Cook the benefit of the doubt, and, when more details of his alleged exploit began to come in and proved to be vague,

confusing and rather suspicious, *The Times* was still, like most other people, inclined to wait for proof before discrediting the story.

But all this was changed when on September 6, while Cook was dining with the King of Denmark and receiving all the honors that Copenhagen could bestow, Peary reached Indian Harbor and sent word to *The Times* by wireless and cable that he had found the Pole. Everybody believed Peary; he was an explorer and scientist of the highest standing, and the whole world took his word. The trouble began a day or two later when Peary informed his family, and the public, that Cook's story need not be taken seriously. By that time Cook had sold the right of publication of his narrative to *The New York Herald*, which had syndicated it everywhere. It turned out to be a bad bargain for *The Herald*, but it was an excellent bargain for Cook in more ways than one. Aside from the price he received — which, according to rumor, was, through a mistake in cable transmission, ten times what he had asked, but which to James Gordon Bennett seemed not exorbitant for what Cook had to offer — he found at once a large number of newspapers enrolled on his side and compelled in their own interest to advocate his claims to the very last.

It may be said that *The Times* was in luck and *The Herald* was out of luck. But it was not a question of luck; *The Times* had reason for putting up money for Peary's story before he started north, for he was the most experienced and probably the most renowned of Arctic explorers. In so far as success in reaching the Pole was not a matter of chance,

Peary was a better bet than anybody else. Bennett's purchase of Cook's story, after Cook had asserted that he had discovered the Pole, was natural enough, for nobody knew much about Cook then. It must be regarded as an unfortunate lapse from impartiality of judgment, however, that the papers which had published Cook's story for the most part felt that they had to believe it, or at any rate to pretend that they believed it.

Peary's detailed story came through by wireless rather slowly, and was published in *The Times* on September 9, 10 and 11, 1909. In the meantime a correspondent of *The London Chronicle*, Philip Gibbs, who was to become famous as a war correspondent a few years later — and more famous through the American publication of his work in *The New York Times* and papers which bought the news from *The Times* than even his home paper made him — had subjected Dr. Cook and his story to an intensive study, and had come to the conclusion that there was nothing in it. For a few days Gibbs was almost alone in saying this outright, but Peary's heated denunciations of Cook forced the issue and the world-wide civil war was on. In the promotion of domestic strife in every nation, in the setting of households against each other and bringing not peace, but a sword to every breakfast table, Cook and Peary did better than Lenin and Trotzky ever dreamed of doing.

That war is ancient history, and there is no longer any doubt as to who was right. *The Times*, which had obtained the North Pole story on its own initiative, was equally successful in obtaining the ac-

counts of the two discoveries of the South Pole by Amundsen and Scott, though in both cases it could do no more than buy the American rights from British owners — in the case of Scott, the Central News; in the case of Amundsen, *The London Chronicle.* Of course, exclusive rights to American publication of great news stories of this sort were not any too widely respected. The narratives of Amundsen and Scott were stolen and published by other newspapers, though *The Times* owned the copyright. Naturally, *The Times* sued all the New York newspapers that republished these stories without permission. The suits failed on technical points. The common-law sanction of a right of prior publication by the purchaser or gatherer of news, finally established in the litigation by which The Associated Press compelled the Hearst services to stop the practice of "lifting" Associated Press bulletins, had not yet been established when these cases were tried, and *The Times* got no material compensation from those who had infringed its rights. But its lawsuits did have one important and valuable result; at each successive stage of the suits, when technical decisions went against *The Times*, the appropriating newspapers gleefully announced their victory, telling their readers over and over how *The Times* had bought the news but they had been able to take it and "get away with it." This unintentional advertisement of *The Times* was quite helpful.

Of the great news stories of the period to which everybody had access, and in dealing with which an individual newspaper could distinguish itself only by specially competent treatment, the one most vividly

remembered in *The Times* office is the sinking of the *Titanic* in April, 1912. *The Times* was more fortunate than other papers in handling that story correctly from the moment when the news of the first wireless call for help was received in newspaper offices. "More fortunate" is the proper term, for the general conviction that the *Titanic* was unsinkable was so strong, and so gallantly maintained for twenty-four hours after the disaster by the officials of the White Star Line, that there was good excuse for reluctance to believe that the disaster had been serious.

It happened that *The Times* by careful comparison of the first dispatches about the collision with the iceberg and by repeated inquiries of its own promptly made up its mind that the *Titanic* was gone. It held to that view all through the confused reports of the next day, even though officials of the line still asserted that there was no news confirming the suspicion; and it was right.

When the *Carpathia* landed with the survivors *The Times* covered the story more completely than any other New York paper, though they all did their best. One feature, the stories told by the *Titanic's* two wireless operators, though arranged for by wireless before the *Carpathia's* arrival, could not have been obtained when the ship docked but for the opportune assistance of Senator Marconi; but the rest of the news was gathered by the diligence of *The Times's* own reporters, who performed feats of interviewing on that night which showed the high standard of news-getting ability to which the staff had been brought. Altogether, the paper

printed fifteen pages of news about the *Titanic* the next morning. Its work on this famous story excited widespread admiration, and members of *The Times* staff visiting the offices of European newspapers have been gratified to learn that some of them had considered copies of *The Times* of that period worthy of preservation as models to be studied. Even certain New York editors wrote to friends in *The Times* office expressing ungrudging admiration.

The Times's political news in this period was steadily gaining wider recognition for trustworthiness. Like everything else on *The Times*, the political correspondence was less spectacular than that of some other papers, but in the long run it was apt to be more trustworthy. There were, however, a number of outstanding feats of news enterprise which supplied the spectacular element from time to time. Such was, for example, the publication in advance of the draft of the Republican national platform of 1908, as drawn up by the leaders of the Roosevelt forces at the convention. President Roosevelt at once went into eruption upon seeing this news in *The Times*, and declared that it was not a correct version. But when the platform was adopted and made known to the world it was found to differ only in half a dozen minor points of phraseology from the version printed in *The Times* — which, of course, was presented as nothing more than the draft agreed on by the dominating Roosevelt faction at the time of publication. This achievement set a precedent to which *Times* political reporters have managed to live up ever since; in most subsequent

campaign years *The Times* has managed to obtain the platform of one or the other national conventions before it was formally given out to the press at large.

Accomplishments such as this are the result of long preparation; they imply a well-organized staff of veteran political reporters with a wide acquaintance, with many friends in high place, and with qualities that command confidence. An illustration of the competence of *The Times* political staff under different circumstances was afforded at Mr. Taft's inauguration in 1909. It may be remembered that in that year a blizzard suddenly descended on Washington on the night of March 3, and by the time the inauguration ceremonies had been concluded the next day practically all the telephone and telegraph wires leading out of the town were out of commission. The stories of the day's events written by *The Times* staff were prepared in quintuplicate. One copy was kept on file in the office of the Washington correspondent of *The Times*, and all through the evening desperate but unavailing efforts were made to get this through on the leased wires or by telephone. Another was filed with the Western Union for transmission on any other wires they might be able to open. Two more were dispatched by messengers on trains for New York. Both trains were held up by snowdrifts, but one of them reached Philadelphia late at night and the copy was telegraphed on by *The Times* correspondent there. But before it reached the office, most of the news had already arrived. *The Times* managed to find a telegraph wire open from Washington to New Orleans,

and the fifth copy of each story was sent over that wire to New Orleans, thence to Chicago, thence to Albany, and finally into the office in New York, circling the area devastated by the blizzard. *The Times* had all its special dispatches about the inauguration in its first edition the next morning.

The Times was able on occasion not only to get news from politicians but to send news to politicians. During the Democratic National Convention at Baltimore in 1912 special trains brought down every morning the city edition of *The Times*, so that before the morning sessions had begun the delegates were reading the news of what they had been doing up to four or five o'clock that morning — and since the work of national conventions is mostly done after midnight in smoke-filled rooms, there is a big difference between the first edition and the last edition in convention week. It might be mentioned here that during the Republican convention at Chicago last year *The Times* sent a moderately late edition, carrying news received up to three A.M., to Chicago by airplane.

In 1903 Thomas A. Janvier wrote for *The Times* a series of articles on the early history of New York, and the paper announced a competition for the school children of the city in the writing of essays based on Janvier's articles. The interest aroused by this was enormous. In thousands of homes the entire family was excited by the son's or daughter's effort to win one of the prizes or medals offered for the best compositions, and the result was not only an increase in the circulation of *The Times*, which, of

LAYING THE CORNERSTONE,
TIMES BUILDING, JANUARY 18, 1904.

TIMES SQUARE,
THE CENTRE FOR NEWS.

course, was the principal purpose of the competition, but the educating of a great many children, and a great many parents, in the past of a city whose history is less known to its inhabitants than probably any other in America. It hardly needs to be said that the increase in circulation created by this competition would have been only temporary and illusory if new readers attracted to *The Times*, who first read it in order to see what chance Johnny or Gladys was likely to have of getting a medal, had not found that it was worth reading all the time. The contest was a good piece of advertising, but it would not have brought results if the merchandise advertised had not been satisfactory.

The results which it did bring were so gratifying that *The Times* has done the same thing on several occasions since then — notably in 1909, when in commemoration of the Lincoln centenary there was a competition of essays based on a series of articles on the life of Lincoln by Frederic Trevor Hill. But though these competitions were always useful, both to *The Times* and to those who participated in them, none of the later ones had the effect of the first. For in 1903 the idea had been new and striking in its novelty; and it was so effective that all the other papers soon imitated it.

But the story of those years is, after all, the story of a steadily improving news service, a staff constantly more alert for news, and better educated in the handling of news. There are other stories, many of them, that were important enough at the time, but are hardly relevant to the history of *The Times*

as a whole. One or two of them may be mentioned as indicative of certain tendencies which have become more prominent in the character of *The Times* in more recent years. When Theodore Roosevelt, returning from Africa, made his famous speech at the Guildhall, London, on June 18, 1910, *The Times* had a verbatim report of it sent by cable. The idea that the public would be interested in every word of a speech delivered at a great distance was then a novel one; it was still novel years later, in the war, when *The Times* developed the habit of publishing in full the speeches of Lloyd George, of Bethmann-Hollweg, Hertling and Czernin, and other leaders of the European Governments. In this process, which may be described as the documentation of current history, *The Times* has always maintained a long lead over its rivals. Other papers may think that the public does not want to read long speeches, and will be satisfied with a summary and a few quotations. *The Times* has found that at least in such a crisis as the World War a large part of the public is interested in long speeches, verbatim speeches; that on some occasions every word of such speeches is news. Roosevelt's Guildhall speech was news, and deserved to be printed in full. As a matter of fact, the idea that a speech which would be printed in full if it were delivered in New York, with an advance copy sent to the city editor, can be dismissed with a column summary if it is delivered in London or Paris, has no sound foundation. It rests on a tradition coming down from the days when cables were few and press cablegrams necessarily brief and expensive. With modern facili-

ties of communication, there is no reason why news from London, Paris and Berlin cannot be handled as its importance deserves.

The great development of *The Times* sporting news has come since the end of the war, but on certain occasions before the war it covered big sporting events rather more fully than was its custom. One of these was the Jeffries-Johnson fight at Reno in 1910, when the stories sent by regular members of *The Times* staff were supplemented by expert criticism contributed by John L. Sullivan. Mr. Sullivan, though then appearing for the first time as a journalist, knew enough about prize fighting to make, and defend, the prediction that Johnson was going to win; which, being contrary to the wish and belief of a majority of the public, brought to *The Times* a considerable volume of protest. However, Sullivan was right. On the value of these occasional contributions from outside experts there may be divergent opinions; but at any rate the paper which published the first literary works of Henry Adams and John L. Sullivan may be credited with a certain breadth of taste, as well as with a keen realization of the variety of belletristic talent produced in Boston.

Perhaps two matters of special interest to *The Times* may here be mentioned, although their most notable development falls in a later period. One of the hobbies of the paper has been the protection of the city parks. Special interests of this sort are more in the line of some other New York papers; in general *The Times* has not given much attention to

them, for while realizing that they offer considerable opportunities for public service it considers them outside the field of straight newspaper work to which it is devoted. Its interest in the parks, however, has seemed necessary, since it is a duty which has been neglected by others.

The number and variety of the schemes for the invasion of city parks, especially Central Park, would be inconceivable to those who have not had occasion to study them. From such magnificent schemes as the cutting up of the whole park into building lots down to trivial incursions, ostensibly for special or temporary purposes, almost every use has been suggested for Central Park by persons who call themselves practical men. It has seemed to the management of *The Times* that the most practical use of Central Park, or any other park, is to keep it as a park — as a place where residents of the city may get into the open air and make some effort to get back to a sort of nature. Some of the other plans for using the park space have been well enough intended, but *The Times* has always thought that New York needed it as a park more than as an athletic field, a site for public buildings, or anything else.

The most notable incident in this long and measurably successful struggle to preserve the park against encroachments, and the most difficult, because the aims of those who wanted to invade the park were excellent in themselves, was the "park trench" episode in the spring of 1918. The members of the Liberty Loan Committee, then in the fourth loan campaign, had allowed themselves to be persuaded by an enthusiastic publicity man that

popular interest could be aroused by the exhibition in New York of a model trench sector such as those in which American soldiers were fighting in France — which was correct — and that the place for this exhibition was the Sheep Meadow in Central Park — which to *The Times* seemed entirely erroneous. The damage that would have been done to the park by the digging of trenches, though considerable, could have been repaired; the harm done to the idea of the integrity of the park could not have been repaired. For that was in the palmy days of drives — drives for all sorts of causes, most of them worthy. The Liberty Loan campaigns being the greatest and most obviously necessary drives, minor enterprises were inclined to follow their lead. Had the precedent once been established of using the park for visual education of this sort, every drive that followed would have come forward with the same demand; and it would have been as difficult to draw the line between drives which wanted to get into the park as it was later found to discriminate between campaigners who wanted space on the steps of the Public Library, or the privilege of soliciting contributions in the public schools.

The fight to keep the trenches out of the park is perhaps remembered chiefly because it produced Mayor Hylan's memorable remark about "art artists." But it is worthy of remembrance because it succeeded in keeping the trenches out of the park. In the course of the campaign *The Times* had occasion to do a good deal in the way of educating the public in the elementary philosophy of parks — a task it had undertaken before, but never at such

length or with such earnestness. It may be hoped that this effort was not without effect, and that a somewhat larger percentage of the population of New York City now understands that the purpose of setting aside land for a park is to have a park, and not to provide a convenient building site for some structure intended for a worthy purpose, whose promoters do not want to pay the current prices of real estate.

The defense of the parks is a matter in which *The Times* has felt under obligation to take up a public duty neglected by others. The other special interest of the paper mentioned above is still more peculiarly its own, for it was invented by the publisher of *The Times*. This is the annual Christmas appeal for the Hundred Neediest Cases, chosen from the lists of four of the leading charitable societies in the city. The appeal was first made in 1912, and aroused an interest that increased from year to year. By 1920 the individual contributions had mounted into the thousands, and a total of more than $111,000 was raised—every cent of which goes directly to the relief of the cases whose history is told in *The Times*, or others like them, and only less needy, when the first hundred have been relieved; for in several years the response was sufficient to cover more than two hundred cases, comprehending about a thousand persons each year. The administrative expenses come out of the general funds of the charitable societies, so that all the money raised by the appeals goes directly for relief. The total of contributions in each year's appeal is here tabulated:

1912	$ 3,630.88
1913	9,646.36
1914	15,032.46
1915	31,819.92
1916	55,792.45
1917	62,103.47
1918	81,097.57
1919	106,967.14
1920	111,131.00

What has been accomplished by this appeal? First of all, of course, the relief of hundreds of destitute families — the raising of hundreds of thousands of dollars, most if not all of which would never have been contributed to charity if *The Times* had not, day after day, in the weeks before Christmas of each year, presented the stories of these families who were in desperate need. With few exceptions, the cases selected for presentation in these appeals have been families, or individuals, who needed only temporary help in order to get back on their feet again and become able to pay their way. That this result has been achieved in hundreds of instances is proved by the records of the charitable societies. Many orphan children have been adopted into kindly homes. Some of those who were aided in the earlier years have since been listed among the contributors to the fund. More and more of them will appear in this character as time goes on, and children who have been aided to get an education, or whose disabled parents have been enabled to bring them up properly, become self-supporting members of society.

But the wider usefulness of the annual campaigns lies in the education of the public. Many people

who have never given to organized charity before are stirred by this Christmas appeal; and when they have once begun to learn something about the destitution which is always to be found in New York City, their interest is apt to continue and they become regular contributors. Some of them go further and give personal attention to charitable work; and all of them learn something about the nature of that work, and the conditions which it is trying to improve. The conductors of *The Times* do not know the solution of the problem of poverty, nor even if there is a solution; but they think that a solution is more likely to be found if everybody studies the problem.

These considerations were in large part responsible for the refusal, by the management of *The Times*, of the offer of $1,000,000 as a standing endowment, the interest on which should be applied to the relief of the Hundred Neediest Cases, on condition that *The Times* should undertake the investigation of the cases and the administration of the fund. A sufficient reason for refusing this offer was the fact that *The Times* is a newspaper and not a charitable society, and that its conductors find that getting out a newspaper takes all their time and ability. It was felt that the gentleman who made this offer could do more effective work for the relief of poverty if he allowed his money to be handled by the people who have given a lifetime of study and practice to relief work.

Such a magnificent gift might have inclined other possible contributors to think that the need had already been met. And it can never be fully met,

"All the News That's Fit to Print."

The New York Times.

THE WEATHER
Generally fair today and Monday; gentle to moderate south winds.
For full weather report see PAGE 5, SPORTS SECTION.

VOL. LXIII...NO. 20,644. NEW YORK, SUNDAY, AUGUST 2, 1914.—88 PAGES, In Seven Parts, Including Picture and Rotogravure Section, Real Estate Directory, and Review of Books. PRICE FIVE CENTS.

GERMANY DECLARES WAR ON RUSSIA, FIRST SHOTS ARE FIRED; FRANCE IS MOBILIZING AND MAY BE DRAWN IN TOMORROW; PLANS TO RESCUE THE 100,000 AMERICANS NOW IN EUROPE

Transports for Refugees Being Considered by State Department.

MAY CHARTER VESSELS

Appropriation Will Probably Be Asked from Congress to Rescue Stranded Americans.

MIGHT SEND OVER GOLD

To Relieve Those Unable to Get Cash on Paper or to Obtain Passage.

FEW WARSHIPS NOW THERE

Consuls Being Confronted with Many Urgent Calls for Assistance.

ANXIOUS INQUIRIES POUR IN

Washington Can Only Reply That Our Representatives Are Instructed to Give All Possible Aid.

ENGLAND HESITATES WHAT COURSE TO TAKE

Grey Wants to Throw the Weight of Great Navy at Once in Favor of Russia and France.

Special Cable to THE NEW YORK TIMES.

LONDON, Sunday, Aug. 2.—Great Britain's rôle in the European war now begun is now a great question. THE TIMES correspondent learns on good authority that the Cabinet is practically divided into equal parts on the question whether to take immediate action or await developments in the hope of remaining outside of the struggle.

Sir Edward Grey, according to this information, heads the party which believes that it is England's duty and interest to throw the weight of her navy at once into the scales on behalf of France and Russia.

Lloyd George leads the other faction, which believes that this country can with honor and advantage hold itself outside and not engage in a European conflict.

One statement, which is given for what it is worth, is that the Chancellor of the Exchequer thinks that England and the United States can together intervene at a propitious moment in such fashion as to reduce to some extent the horrors of a Continental Armageddon. In passing it may be mentioned that the wildest reports have been current on all aspects

France Orders Mobilization After Germany Asks Her Intentions.

DELCASSE WAR MINISTER

Germany's Old Enemy Heads Army Organization — Once Nearly Caused Conflict.

CLEMENCEAU IN CABINET

President and Cabinet Issue a Manifesto to French Nation.

PLAIN WORDS TO GERMANY

"You Are Mobilizing; We Know It," Says Prime Minister to German Envoy.

ORDERS TO FOREIGNERS

Americans May Stay on Getting Permits—Austrians and Germans Liable to Arrest.

PARIS, Aug. 1.—An official decree

Poincare Orders Mobilization, Telling France It Is Not War Yet

PARIS, Aug. 1.—President Poincaré and the members of the Cabinet today issued the following joint proclamation to the French nation:

For some days the States of Europe have been considerably aggravated, and, notwithstanding the efforts of diplomacy, the horizon has darkened. At the present hour a greater part of the nations have mobilized their forces. Even the countries protected by neutrality conventions have deemed it their duty to take this measure as a precaution.

The powers whose constitutional or military legislation differs from ours have, without issuing a decree of mobilization, begun and carried on preparations which, in reality, are equivalent to mobilization, and are but the anticipated execution of it.

France, who always has affirmed her desire for peace, who on many a tragic day has given to Europe counsels of moderation and a living example of decorum, and who has multiplied her efforts to maintain the peace of the world, has now prepared herself for all eventualities, and has taken from henceforth her first indispensable dispositions for the safeguarding of her territory.

But our legislation does not permit the completion of these preparations without a decree of mobilization. Conscious of its high responsibility, and feeling that it would fail in its sacred duty if it did not take this measure, the Government has signed the decree.

Mobilization is not war. Under the present circumstances it would appear, on the contrary, to be the best means of assuring peace with honor.

Strong in its ardent desire of arriving at a peaceful solution of this crisis, the Government under cover of these essential precautions will continue its diplomatic efforts, and still hopes to succeed. It counts upon the coolness of the people not to give itself up to unjustified emotion. It counts upon the patriotism of every Frenchman, and it knows that there is not a single one who is not ready to do his duty at this hour.

There are no longer any parties. There is an eternal France—a France peaceful and resolute. There is a fatherland of peace and justice, all united in calm vigilance and dignity.

main unchanged. We wish peace, and the best proof we can give you of this is that at the present moment the French Parliament has not been convoked. Under our constitution we should be compelled to convoke it if our intentions were not peaceful."

Baron von Schön said: "But frontier incidents are unfortunately to be feared."

Premier Viviani replied:

"How can you suppose such things? Our troops are five miles from the

KAISER SIGNS ORDER MOBILIZING HIS ARMY

"Let Your Hearts Beat for God and Your Fists on the Enemy," Cries Chancellor.

BERLIN, Aug. 1.—Emperor William, at 5:15 o'clock this evening,

Germany's War Challenge Delivered to Russia at 7:30 Last Evening

EMBASSY THEN DEPARTS

Enrollment of Reservists Begun Throughout the Czar's Vast Empire.

STIRRING SCENES ATTEND IT

Hardly a Family but Loses a Protector, Yet They Take the Call Submissively.

FRANCE HAS TILL MONDAY

Reply to Germany Due Then, but Issue May Be Forced Earlier.

ITALY REMAINS NEUTRAL

Triple Alliance Obligations Not Touched, She Says—Feared a Revolution.

Chronology of Yesterday's Fateful Events

12 Midnight—Germany demands that Russia cease mobilization and gives a twelve-hour limit.

2 A. M.—King George of England, after an audience with Premier Asquith, telegraphs to the Czar, making a strong appeal for peace.

12 Noon—The time limit of Germany's ultimatum to Russia expires.

5:15 P. M.—Emperor William signs an order for the mobilization of the German Army.

7:30 P. M.—The German Ambassador at St. Petersburg delivers to the Russian Government a declaration of war in the name of Germany and leaves St. Petersburg.

First Shots Fired in the Russo-German War.

BERLIN, Aug. 1.—A German patrol near Prostken was fired on this afternoon by a Russian frontier patrol. The Germans returned the fire. There were no losses.

Prostken is a village of 2,300 inhabitants, in East Prussia. It is situated about two and one-half miles west of the international boundary line, on the Konigsberg & Lyck Railroad. The nearest Russian village is Grajevo, about three miles across the international boundary.

Kaiser Forgives Enemies, Prays for Victory.

BERLIN, Aug. 2.—The Emperor again spoke from a window of the Castle tonight to a crowd of 50,000 beneath, who cheered and sang patriotic songs until he appeared. He said:

"I thank you for the love and loyalty shown me. When I enter upon a fight let all party strife cease. We are German brothers and nothing else. All parties have attacked me in times of peace. I forgive them with all my heart. I hope and wish that the good German sword will emerge victorious in the right."

The speech was thrice interrupted by vociferous cheering. At its conclusion the Kaiser bowed in all directions, retiring amid a frenzied demonstration.

The Imperial Chancellor also addressed the assembly, saying:

"All stand as one man for our Emperor, whatever our opinions or our creeds. I am sure that all the young German men are ready to shed their blood for the fame and greatness of Germany. We can

they will confer again and get the opinion of the bankers who usually serve the State Department abroad in normal times.

If necessary the Washington Government is prepared to send American vessels abroad with gold for the relief of Americans. Immediately after the conference with the President Mr. Bryan cabled all consulates, legations and embassies to spare no pains in caring for Americans who remain in the war zones, and to give every facility to those who wished to leave.

State Department officials admitted that a most serious problem was confronting them in the plight of Americans abroad. They estimated that at least 100,000, and possibly as many as 300,000, were scattered throughout Europe. The disorganization of European exchange has made it practically impossible to cash checks or letters of credit. American consulates, legations and embassies are devoid of funds for the emergency which has suddenly confronted them. They are being besieged on all sides with requests for financial assistance.

With the cancellation by several steamship lines of their sailings many Americans find themselves unable to get passage on the overcrowded boats of American register. American warships would be of little use, as they have hardly any capacity for passengers. Naval officers have suggested that the Government could charter immediately some of the big ocean liners of foreign register to bring Americans home.

By special arrangement, officials believe the American Government could obtain the use of foreign ships, securing exemption from seizure if used only for transportation of Americans.

The only American warships in European waters are the little gunboat Scorpion, station ship at Constantinople, and the battleship Maine at Villefranche, with Annapolis midshipmen and the officers and crew of the battleship Idaho taken over at that port by the Greek Government. The Maine will leave Villefranche today for Annapolis.

A special appropriation would be required to charter steamships to bring Americans home. Congress always has acted promptly in such emergencies, and is expected to do so again.

Many applications were received at the State Department from persons in the United States desirous of having American Consuls investigate and report upon the safety of their friends and relatives in Europe. The State Department is returning the uniform answer that under their general instructions the Consuls will look after and report the case of any Americans in distress in their respective districts, and consequently that no special instructions are needed.

till then, and none is going out of reach. Some hope to get a day's golfing as a respite.

The Cabinet Council sat for two and a half hours yesterday. Sir Edward Grey left in the middle of the proceedings for the Foreign Office.

With reference to the Cabinet's position, The Observer this morning says:

"France and Germany have cast the die on their frontiers. Before nightfall, or even before these lines see the light may be fired in the western and decisive theatre of war the first shots of a tremendous struggle that will decide the destinies of the Old World for generations. The first great actions may decide the final issue, first in the West and then in the Near East.

"If after the lamentable wavering of last week, we hesitate one day more we shall be too late to influence an arbitrament which indirectly but surely will decide our own fate no less than that of France. Our hours are numbered. If the Ministry decides today to desert France, then they will strike us out of the list of nations that any power can trust."

Fleet Ready for a Blow.

It is said that the Cabinet is likely to reach a decision tonight. One factor that will probably influence the decision is the total absence of indications of any of that anti-German sentiment which has been a feature of the spurious agitation of recent years. In the event of the Cabinet deciding upon war, speculation is rife as to what the fleet will do first.

The First Home Fleet, which sailed under sealed orders, is believed to be off the coast of Holland or in the neighborhood of Denmark. A high official of the Admiralty said to THE TIMES correspondent tonight:

"It is idle to speculate. Only three men in England know what its orders are."

Thanks to the recent Spithead review by the King, Great Britain's navy is practically ready for war, and a proclamation of mobilization would only really affect the second line. Its ability to strike a sudden, serious blow is not doubted in England, and, as is evident from the orders given to German liners, the blow is apprehended in Germany.

The Admiralty is, of course, in wireless touch with the commanding officers, and to prevent any possibility of interference with the radio communications stringent instructions have been issued that all amateur or private wireless systems must be stopped.

bodies of men, formed into regular companies in ranks ten deep, paraded the streets, waving the Tricolor and other national emblems and cheering and singing the "Marseillaise" and the "Internationale," at the same time throwing their hats in the air.

Here and there the cry, "On to Berlin!" was raised.

On the sidewalks were many weeping women and children. All the stores and cafés were deserted.

Relations Not Yet Severed.

The decree of mobilization of the French Army, which was followed by a proclamation by the President and the Cabinet to the nation, has, however, not terminated diplomatic relations between France and Germany. Conversations between the powers, notably between Russia and Austria and between France and Germany, continued this evening.

Up to a late hour tonight, it was stated, the German Ambassador was still in Paris.

A rumor in circulation here tonight was to the effect that there were some waverers in the Cabinet yesterday on the question of ordering the mobilization, but that the views of those who asserted that it would be suicidal to allow Germany to put France to further expense with regard to war preparations without actual mobilization prevailed.

The course of diplomatic events since yesterday afternoon can be stated briefly as follows:

Baron von Schön, the German Ambassador to France, called on the French Premier, René Viviani, at 7 o'clock last evening and formally notified him that Germany had addressed an ultimatum to Russia, desiring to know by noon today whether the St. Petersburg Government would discontinue the mobilization of the Russian Army.

Baron von Schön was directed by his Government to ask what were the intentions of France should Russia's reply to Germany be a refusal to demobilize.

The German Government fixed "before 1 P. M. today" as the period within which France must answer. Baron von Schön called at the French Foreign Office at 11:40 A. M. to receive France's reply. Premier Viviani made an earnest appeal to the German Ambassador, asking if Germany could not yet do something to avert war.

The Baron promised to communicate with Berlin and to return to the Foreign Office at 4 P. M., which he did.

"You Are Mobilizing, We Know It."

In the course of their second interview today Premier Viviani said to the German Ambassador:

"You are mobilizing. We know it."

Baron von Schön did not reply, and M. Viviani continued:

"This attitude of your Government has dictated ours. We were compelled to take precautions similar to yours. Our peaceful intentions re-

very foot of the frontier posts, and said he concluded from this that if incidents occurred they could only be provoked by the German military forces.

The German reply was submitted to a French Cabinet Council, which, within a few minutes afterward, ordered a general mobilization of the French Army.

The date of the mobilization was set for tomorrow, but it really begins immediately. The men are called out in classes at intervals of days, according to the year in which they entered the army. Precise instructions are always in the possession of every man, so that he may know what to do when a general mobilization is posted.

Reservists Obey Instantly.

The response to the order of mobilization was instant, and the stations of all the railways, particularly those leading to the eastward, were crowded tonight with departing reservists. Many women accompanied the men until close to the stations, where, the women softly crying, farewells were said.

The Russian Ambassador, M. Iswolsky, called on Premier Viviani at 11 o'clock tonight and informed him that Germany had declared war on Russia.

Nothing is known among the general public as to what is going on behind the screen which fell along the German frontier at about 4 o'clock yesterday afternoon.

Arrangements were made last night by Myron T. Herrick, the American Ambassador, acting under instructions from Washington, to take over the affairs of the German Embassy, while Alexander H. Thackara, the American Consul General, is to look after the affairs of the German Consulate.

All foreigners may leave Paris or France before the end of the first day of mobilization by train, but not by automobile. Those deciding to leave France may do so by certain trains, the time tables of which are posted on the walls of Paris tonight, or by sea.

American citizens or British subjects may remain in France, except in the regions on the eastern frontier and near certain fortresses, provided they make declarations to the police and obtain special permits.

No foreigner will be permitted to leave France after the first day of mobilization without a passport signed by a Prefect. Americans, Englishmen, and other foreigners may remain in Paris by obtaining special permits from the police.

Delcasse War Minister.

LONDON, Aug. 1.—A Paris dispatch to the Central News by indirect route reports that Premier Viviani has made changes in the Cabinet.

Théophile Delcassé becomes Minister of War, and Georges Clemenceau, the ex-Premier, joins the Ministry.

M. Delcassé is one of the bitterest enemies of Germany among French statesmen. He nearly caused a war with that country in 1905.

Cabinet Council in Session Till 4 A. M.

PARIS, Sunday, Aug. 2.—The Council of Ministers, which held a late night session to discuss the European situation, adjourned shortly after 4 o'clock this morning. It will continue its discussion of the situation this afternoon. No announcement of the result of the deliberations has been given out.

strictions, therefore, on the postal, telegraph, and railway services are inevitable, owing to the requirements of the military authorities.

It was officially announced that the time limit of the German ultimatum to Russia expired at noon.

An official communication published in the North German Gazette says the Russian Emperor on July 29 telegraphed to Emperor William urgently requesting him to help in averting the misfortune of a European war and to try to restrain his ally Austria-Hungary from going too far.

Emperor William replied that he would willingly take up the task of mediator, and accordingly diplomatic action was initiated in Vienna.

While this was in progress the news that Russia was mobilizing arrived in Berlin, and Emperor William telegraphed to the Emperor of Russia that his rôle as mediator was by this endangered, if not made impossible.

The communication adds that a decision was to have been taken in Vienna today in regard to the mediation proposals in which Great Britain had joined Germany, but that meanwhile Russia had ordered the full mobilization of her forces. Upon this Emperor William addressed a last telegram to Emperor Nicholas emphatically declaring that his own responsibility for the safety of the German Empire had forced him to take defensive measures.

War Speech by Chancellor.

The German Imperial Chancellor, Dr. von Bethmann-Hollweg, addressed a huge procession of demonstrators today from the window of his official residence, making a stirring speech, in which he said:

"At this serious hour in order to give expression to your feelings for your Fatherland you have come to the house of Bismarck, who with Emperor William the Great and Field Marshal von Moltke welded the German Empire for us.

"We wished to go on living in peace in the empire which we have developed in forty-four years of peaceful labor.

"The whole work of Emperor William has been devoted to the maintenance of peace. To the last hour he has worked for peace in Europe, and he is still working for it. Should all his efforts prove vain and should the sword be forced into our hands we will take the field with a clear conscience in the knowledge that we did not seek war. We shall then wage war for our existence and for the national honor to the last drop of our blood.

"In the gravity of this hour I remind you of the words of Prince Frederick Charles to the men of Brandenburg:

"'Let your hearts beat for God and your fists on the enemy.'"

Enthusiastic cheers and the singing of the national anthem greeted the close of the Imperial Chancellor's speech.

The news reached here in a Reuter telephone message from Brussels at 4 A. M. New York time.

Luxemburg is a neutral State southward of Brussels, with its borders on Germany and France. A straight line drawn between Berlin and Paris would pass through the heart of the Duchy of Luxemburg.

Special Cable to THE NEW YORK TIMES.

LONDON, Sunday, Aug. 2.—The news that Germany had declared war against Russia reached London from St. Petersburg late last evening, only half an hour after a Central News dispatch from Paris had raised the hopes of all by the statement that Germany had extended for forty-eight hours, that is, until Monday noon, the period in which Russia and France could reply to the German ultimatums.

The first of these ultimatums was one demanding that Russia cease the mobilization of her army in twelve hours.

The second was a note presented by Baron von Schoen, the German Ambassador in Paris, to Foreign Minister Viviani calling upon France to inform Germany whether in the event of the outbreak of war between Germany and Russia, France would remain neutral.

These notes were regarded as diplomatic skirmishing, designed to cover the hard fact that Germany was bending all her energies to the delivery of the first blow, which might affect the whole course of the war, now officially begun.

In the history of modern warfare an official declaration of war is either accompanied or preceded by an actual stroke of war.

In London this morning it is believed Germany would not officially declare war upon Russia unless her plans for a rapid attack had been entirely completed. Where or how the first blow will be struck is a matter of the widest speculation.

France Next to Be Involved.

France's reply to the German request as to the former's attitude in case Germany engaged in war with Russia is stated to have proved unsatisfactory to Berlin. It was bound to be. Germany could count confidently on it being so. Therefore, according to speculation in London this morning, the eventual news is likely to show that Germany has taken an unsatisfactory reply from France for granted, and while declaring war on Russia has struck or has made her chief preparations to strike at [redacted]. This, of course,

is for what it is worth.

The established facts, bearing on the crisis in yesterday's developments, are important to note. The first is that the effort made by King George to bring influence to bear on the Czar in favor of peace failed of effect.

The terms of the King's telegram are guarded as the strictest secret. All information THE TIMES correspondent could obtain was that the message was of a highly personal and confidential nature. It followed an interview with Premier Asquith at 2 o'clock yesterday morning.

Italy Feared a Revolution.

The second development was a confirmation of the report that Italy would remain neutral as long as she was assured that her interests were not menaced.

From an official source THE TIMES correspondent learns that the Italian Government was practically forced to this decision by the apprehension that the taking up of arms on behalf of Austria in a quarrel, precipitated by the hereditary enemy of Italy, would have caused an immediate revolution in Italy.

Italy's abstention is a serious blow to the Triple Alliance and may yet prove an important factor in determining, if not the issue of peace or war, at least the duration of the conflict.

One of the ways suggested to prevent the outbreak of war was that Italy and Great Britain should combine and declare themselves on the side of France and Russia. The suggestion utterly disregarded the treaty by which Italy was bound to the Triple Alliance, but it was given some color of vraisemblance by the fact that the British and Italian Ambassadors in various capitals have been working together in a manner which indicated that the Italian Government preferred any peaceable solution of the war to the treaties which bound her to Germany and Austria.

The third important development of the night was the news that the French Government had issued orders for general mobilization.

This came a few hours after the severance of telephonic communications between London and Paris. The French Government informed the British authorities that the telephone was cut for ordinary communication in order to prevent any leakage of news.

Up to 2 o'clock this morning practically no news beyond the announcement of the mobilization had been received here from Paris.

The fullest confirmation of the general mobilization was obtained in London by the issue of a notice to the French Embassy here. This called upon all Frenchmen liable to military service to return to France within twenty-four hours. The news speedily became known in Soho, the French quarter of London, and this morning bands of enthusiastic Frenchmen paraded through Leicester Square.

The almost complete severance of telegraphic and telephonic communication with Paris was shown by the

obtain a special wire, under a guarantee that nothing in the nature of leakage of military secrets could possibly occur, had not received a word out of Paris up to 3 o'clock this morning.

Telephonic and telegraphic communications with the Continent were generally interrupted.

GERMANY'S DECLARATION.

Served by the Retiring Ambassador as Russian Enrollment Begins.

ST. PETERSBURG, Aug. 1.—The German Ambassador, in the name of his Government, sent a declaration of war to the Russian Minister of Foreign Affairs at 7:30 o'clock this evening. Count von Pourtales and the entire staff of the German Embassy then left St. Petersburg.

Martial law has been proclaimed in the capital and its suburbs.

Announcement of the declaration of war was made to the people two hours after it had been received. The city immediately presented a spectacle of extraordinary animation. The Nevsky Prospect, and all the leading thoroughfares are filled with war-frenzied people marching in processions, carrying portraits of the Emperor, with flags waving and torches blazing. From time to time there is an outburst of cheering, followed by singing.

Speakers fired with patriotic fervor harangue the crowds. In front of the Kazan Cathedral each procession halts and a sudden hush falls over the processionists, then the strains of the national anthem, sung in perfect harmony by a section of the procession, are heard, and the crowds listen silently with bared heads. On the conclusion of the hymn the procession moves forward and the demonstrations are resumed with greater ardor.

Enrollment of the reservists started at a hundred centres in St. Petersburg at 6 o'clock this morning and was accompanied by stirring scenes. Crowds of women and children accompanied their husbands and fathers to the assembling stations, while priests everywhere blessed the reservists as they marched through the streets singing hymns.

The Municipal Council of Warsaw has voted 1,000,000 roubles (about $500,000) for the Red Cross service of Russia and friendly powers.

The Fateful Red Posters.

Special Cable to THE NEW YORK TIMES.

ST. PETERSBURG, Aug. 1.—All attention is now concentrated on the mobilization of the troops. During the night bills were posted in all parts of the city summoning the whole of the reservists to the colors, and the population awoke to read the startling news on posters printed in red.

Women wept, but the men took it for the most part quietly and seriously, in sad submissiveness.

"I don't care for my life," said one peasant to me, "but I am sorry for the children."

Such expressions are frequent on all hands. Hardly a hour, hardly a fam-

at least not until everybody in New York has come to understand it. The educational value of the annual campaigns has certainly been great, and is greater every year. Indeed, they have already won their place in literature; Mr. Robert W. Chambers presented as the heroine of one of his recent novels an orphan who had been adopted by a wealthy gentleman after he had read her story as one of the Hundred Neediest Cases.

On April 1, 1913, *The Times* abandoned the seven-column page which it had presented to its readers for the past forty-eight years and went to eight columns. The change was chiefly due to a conviction that the narrower column was somewhat easier to read, but it was also based in some degree upon the need of getting more reading matter into the paper without increasing the size of the page. Already the number of pages had increased, though it was not yet foreseen that the time would come when the paper would print forty pages on a week day, as happened occasionally in 1919.

But *The Times*, increasing the quantity of its offering to readers, had maintained the same quality which it had always presented. It was still the same solid, dignified, reliable paper; the only difference was that it was appealing to more and more readers every year.

The average circulation, which had been more than 102,000 in the jubilee year, rose gradually to 143,460 in 1907; leaped the next year to 172,880; passed 200,000 in 1911; reached 225,392 in 1912, and was around the quarter-million mark at the out-

break of the war, when the great achievements of *The Times* news service sent it leaping once more.

Though its worldwide renown was chiefly a growth of the war years, *The Times* was already recognized as one of the great newspapers of the country, great not only in circulation and volume of business, but in character. A good many people did not like the kind of paper which *The Times* was and always had been, but they had to admit that it was an excellent paper of the kind, and more and more people every year were coming to prefer that kind.

In the articles on New York journalism written by Will Irwin for *Collier's Weekly* in 1911 *The Times* was called a "commercial newspaper" — a somewhat curious epithet, since all newspapers are conducted with the purpose, even if that object is not always attained, of making a profit. Mr. Irwin was compelled, however, to admit that *The Times* came "the nearest of any newspaper to presenting a truthful picture of life in New York and the world at large," and indeed his only criticism was that it did not crusade. This, of course, was during the muckraking epoch, and it is a striking tribute to *The Times* that in that day when every institution was being violently assaulted a muckraker could find nothing to say against the paper except that it did not wield the muckrake.

The great news feats mentioned above all played their part in attracting attention to the paper and winning new readers, but it cannot be repeated too often that in the newspaper business as in any other business customers who are attracted by advertising can be held only by the quality of the merchan-

dise. For whatever reason people began to read *The Times*, they continued to read it because they found it an enterprising and trustworthy newspaper. The essay competitions had taken it into the public schools, where in many cases it came to be regarded as the best guide to current events. And in private schools, too, *The Times* was always welcomed where some of its competitors were regarded with a suspicious eye. The proprietor of its ablest rival in the morning newspaper field once graciously called attention to the fact that *The Times* was the only morning newspaper taken at the select school which his daughter attended.

CHAPTER IV

Some Aspects of Business Policy

THE *TIMES* had begun to gain circulation very soon after the new publisher took charge. With this, of course, went an enormous increase in the business of the paper. There was built up an unusually efficient business department, managed for many years past by Louis Wiley and previously by the late John Norris. Within four years after the assumption of control by the new management the circulation of *The Times*, at the beginning of the new century, had reached 100,000; ten years later it had passed 200,000, and now in the twenty-fifth year of the present management it circulates an average of 330,000 copies on week days and 500,000 on Sundays.

And this is a genuine circulation. There are no return privileges which permit of subtle distinctions between the number of papers distributed and the number sold, nor has the circulation been padded or inflated by any irregular methods. Some illustrations of the principles of *The Times* on this point may here be offered with apologies to the well-intentioned friends of the paper with whose ideas the management was unable to agree.

One day during the Presidential campaign of 1900 the Republican National Committee happened to be meeting in New York. That morning *The Times*

carried an editorial on the issues of the campaign which struck the Republican managers as about the most forcible presentation of the case which they had seen anywhere. Mr. Luther Little of the Committee was accordingly instructed to call on the publisher to express the Committee's thanks and appreciation and to order one million copies of that issue for distribution.

To his profound surprise, the publisher of *The Times* refused to accept the order. He felt that the wide free distribution of a marked newspaper might easily create, in the minds of many who received it, a false impression to the effect that the appearance of the article and the purchase of the copies might be in some way a bargain. *The Times*, of course, would not receive payment of any sort for what appeared in its reading columns, and it did not want to incur even the suspicion. Mr. Little argued, not without plausibility, that *The Times* must have printed that editorial hoping that people would read it, and here a million more readers were offered. But the publisher of the paper felt that readers of that sort would do the paper little good, while the accompanying suspicions would do positive harm.

The conductors of *The Times* were publishing a paper for the people who liked the sort of paper they were publishing. They did not want it forced on anybody's attention or given away free because it contained something which happened to strike the fancy of gentlemen who were able to order and distribute a million copies. Circulation of such character, it was felt, could do the paper no good and might do a great deal of harm. The only readers

The Times sought were readers who would buy the paper because they wanted it. They did not wish it to be classed with the sort of campaign literature that is distributed free.

A somewhat similar issue arose in the same campaign when the Republican State Committee of New Jersey wanted to buy 20,000 copies of *The Times* every day during the last three months of the canvass. This proposal also was declined. This sort of thing had been a commonplace of the political journalism of an earlier period. The weekly editions of such New York newspapers as had strong partisan sympathies, in the sixties and seventies had been in campaign years little more than campaign pamphlets, full of praise of the party's candidates, violent attacks on the opposition, and argument in defence of the party's position; and for their circulation in those years they had depended largely on the party committees, which bought and distributed many thousands of copies.

This, of course, was in effect a subsidy from the party to the paper, but according to the journalistic ethics of past years there was nothing irregular about accepting it. By 1900 newspaper standards in some quarters were somewhat higher, but still the action of the management of *The Times* surprised a good many newspaper men, as well as the party managers, who had supposed that the paper would regard the proposed arrangement as advantageous to both sides.

The reluctance of *The Times* was not due simply to the fact that it was not a Republican paper and did not want to become identified in any way with the party leadership. Its conductors felt that *The*

Times had no right to accept compensation in any form for its editorial opinion, even though that compensation was after the fact and the opinion had been formed without any expectation of it.

This question has been raised several times since in somewhat different form, and without political connections. A number of requests have been made for a considerable number of copies of the paper for free distribution on account of an article appearing in the editorial or news columns. Always the request has been refused, though permission to reprint articles from *The Times* for distribution has been freely granted, on condition that the reprint contain some statement making it clear that *The Times* had no hand in the distribution. It has been the publisher's opinion that this policy prevented the growth of mistaken opinions not only outside, but more particularly within *The Times* office. He was seeking the confidence of the public, but he regarded as still more essential the confidence of those who were associated with him in making the newspaper. Mr. Ochs has always felt that he need not be concerned about public opinion with respect to *The Times* if its editors believe in his sincere desire for clean, honest work.

Some years ago a prominent Western manufacturer wrote to *The Times* and ordered the paper sent daily for a year to fifty clergymen in his town. His reason was that he regarded *The Times* as a good newspaper, in fact, the best newspaper, and he thought that ministers in a small city of the interior might have their outlook on the world broadened by the study of its pages.

The Times refused to send the papers to the addresses he had forwarded. The publisher held that the orders could be filled only if they came with the knowledge and consent of the recipients, that is, if they really wanted the paper. *The Times* was not to be forced on anybody who had not asked for it, and it was not to be distributed in quantity by outsiders, thereby perhaps incurring the suspicion that it was in some way an organ or a mouthpiece for the views of the individuals or classes accelerating its distribution.

More recently the same question was raised by a banker in South Carolina, who admired *The Times* financial news and its editorial discussions of financial problems. He thought that the bankers of his state, inclined to be absorbed in their own local affairs, would be better off for learning something about world trade and world finance, and, accordingly, ordered *The Times* sent regularly to 450 of them at his expense. In this case, again, *The Times* could not but regard this as a compliment, and had no doubt whatever of the correct intentions of the man who wanted to pay for the papers. But again the publisher felt that, while it might be good for South Carolina bankers to read *The Times*, it was not good for *The Times* to be distributed gratis.

The banker who had made the offer still thought that his colleagues needed education, so when *The Times* refused to fill his order he attempted partially to carry out his purpose through the medium of a Charleston newsdealer. The sudden increase of 450 copies in this dealer's order at once aroused suspicion in the office, and when this suspicion was verified

ROLLO OGDEN,
Associate Editor.

JOHN H. FINLEY,
Associate Editor.

The Times, although rather gratified by this evidence of the persistent conviction of the banker that it was a good paper, refused to fill the order.

It may be added that in the belief of the management these principles are not in conflict with the action of certain large hotels which see advantage to themselves in providing each guest in his room with a copy of *The Times* every morning.

It can be assumed from these illustrations that there is nothing artificial about *The Times's* circulation. Its subscribers are people who desire it, who want it, and who know why they want it.

Of course, the increase in circulation brought with it a great increase in advertising. The volume of advertising published in 1896 had been more than quadrupled by 1914, and the rates were several times increased during this period. *The Times* has not been always a single-rate paper in the strictest sense of the word, but it has always been a single-rate paper to the extent that everybody paid the same price for the same service.

The advertising rates have been very slowly advanced with the greatest consideration for the advertiser's problem in adjusting his appropriation for space in *The Times* to the increased rates. And whereas the net return to *The Times* per column in 1896, with a circulation of less than 20,000, was $45, in 1921 the rate for a circulation of 340,000 — more than seventeen times larger — was only $150.

The management of *The Times* has always felt that all good advertising, that is honest advertising, has a certain news value. It is information for the

public, of some interest and advantage to the public. In discriminating between advertisements, when limitations of space compelled discrimination, it has been the policy to give preference so far as possible to advertising which possessed news interest in a higher degree.

It is not to be supposed that anybody seriously believes any longer that *The Times* is in any way controlled or influenced in its editorial policies by its advertisers. Some papers may be so influenced, though it may be doubted if this could be said of any important one in New York City. The papers which are too tender of advertisers' feelings are, naturally, poor papers, financially poor, which cannot afford to lose advertising. In recent years *The Times* has sometimes been compelled to refuse advertising, offered for insertion in a single day, the total amount of which would have filled many pages and yielded perhaps $20,000, because it did not have room enough to hold all that was offered; so no sane man is likely to suppose that its policies are affected by the wishes of any advertiser.

However, *The Times* has not always been prosperous. In poverty as in affluence, none the less, it has always held the same principles, and in consequence it has had a number of disagreements with advertisers who thought that somehow their business dealings with *The Times* gave them the privilege of complaining of its editorial positions, its news publications, or its business policies.

In one instance, at least, and a rather important one, in the early history of the present management twenty years ago, an advertiser came into conflict

with the paper on a point of advertising policy. A regular advertiser called the attention of *The Times* to the advertisement of a competitor which in his opinion was so misleading as to be downright fraudulent. Investigation showed that in this particular case he was right, and the objectionable advertisement was refused thereafter. But the complainant, not satisfied with this, began to ask some humiliating promises from the management of *The Times* with respect to its policies. The conductors of *The Times* were even more anxious than this overzealous advertiser to keep their columns free from undesirable matter, but they were unwilling to enter into an argument with an advertiser about the policies of the paper. The position taken by the management of the paper was set forth in the letter given below, which closed the incident until years later the gentleman found it desirable, in the interests of his business, to bring his advertising back to *The Times* without asking for anything more than space in the paper.

The publisher of *The Times* set forth his views in this letter as follows:

THE NEW YORK TIMES
OFFICE OF THE PUBLISHER
NEW YORK, NOV. 21, 1901.

* * * * * * *

You must excuse me from discussing with you the policy of *The New York Times*. It is a subject we do not care to discuss with an advertiser. We consider it a privilege to any one to be permitted to make an an-

nouncement in the columns of *The Times* aside from the fact that our rates for advertising space are far from commensurate with the service rendered. If *The New York Times* as it appears every day is not a sufficient recommendation for the use of its columns by advertisers (such as we will accept), assurance otherwise would be of little or no value.

We do not want to sail under false colors. *The New York Times* is not published solely for the purpose of attracting advertisers. We hope, however, to attract by the number and the class of our readers. We are seeking to secure the good-will and confidence of intelligent, discriminating newspaper readers. The advertiser is a secondary consideration. We take great pride in the knowledge of the fact that we have succeeded in impressing the honesty of our efforts upon the largest number of the best citizens of this city, representing both readers and advertisers. Of course, there are some exceptions. Among the latter class a conspicuous example is yourself. You seem to wish that *The New York Times* should go about as a mendicant, begging for advertising patronage. We will never do anything of the kind and are happy to say there is no occasion for our doing so.

This all leads to the statement that if your advertisement remains out of *The New York Times* until you have some assurance other than the paper as it appears every day, as to the policy of the publisher, *The Times*, as long as it is under its present management, will endeavor to get along without your business.

* * * * * * *

Some of the differences of opinion with the book publishers have already been told. A later episode, however, involved something far more serious than a mere disagreement on the advertising value of *The Times* literary supplement; it was, indeed, perhaps the most formidable attempt ever made by advertisers to coerce *The Times*. The Book Publishers' Association threatened to withdraw, and then withdrew, all of its members' advertising from *The Times* because of the insertion of cut-rate prices of their books in the advertisement of a department store.

While admitting that the competition of a department store selling certain articles at cut rates offered some formidable problems to business men dealing only in these articles, the publisher of *The Times* had occasion to ask the publishers how it happened that the store could get these books. That was a matter between the book publishers and the store; the advertising of the dealer's wares was the affair of the store and *The Times*. Indeed, the management of the paper observed that if the fact was not advertised that books could be purchased at lower prices than those charged by the publishers, it would deserve to be given to the readers of *The Times* as news.

This concept of a paper's responsibility as being first of all to its readers rather than to any advertiser or group of advertisers was somewhat novel to the book publishers, but they presently found that *The Times* could not be moved by the loss of their advertising, and that in fact they were hurting nobody but themselves. After a few weeks they came back, con-

tent to let the paper run its own business without further interference and recognizing the wisdom of *The Times's* attitude.

Another heavy advertiser's custom was lost, in this case forever, through a difference of opinion on the relative value of advertising and news. This gentleman had arranged for the publication of what he considered an important announcement in a half-page advertisement on June 16, 1904, the morning after the burning of the excursion steamer *General Slocum*, with the loss of more than a thousand lives. At that time the mechanical facilities of *The Times* did not permit the printing of more than sixteen pages. The advertisement was omitted on the ground that the space was needed for news and that the paper's duty to its readers demanded that news be given the right of way.

Perhaps the most notable difference with advertisers was a disagreement with one of the largest and best advertisers in the country, who withdrew his advertising from *The Times* because of a personal grievance, arising out of an incidental publication in another paper controlled by the publisher of *The Times*. This item was mistakenly attributed to the publisher, and some exacting demands were accordingly made which could not be complied with. Although it involved the loss of more than a million dollars' worth of the most desirable advertising, the management of *The Times* was adamant in its refusal to make the publication requested. After ten years' absence the advertiser returned to *The Times* without any conditions, and good relations were happily restored.

It was in a later period, in 1915, that an attempt was made to control *The Times's* dramatic criticism by somewhat different methods. A producer conceived the mistaken impression that the chief dramatic critic of *The Times* was prejudiced against his productions, and in spite of the fact that very few of the reviews responsible for this impression had been written by the critic in question, the producer suddenly refused to admit him to his theatres. For a time the critic managed to review the producer's plays under the protection of an injunction, but this was presently vacated. While the doors of the theatres were closed to *The Times* critic, the advertising columns of *The Times* were closed to the producer, and publication of his offered announcements was refused.

In the legal fight the paper was beaten. It was developed that while the laws of New York regard the theatre as a public institution to the extent that its owner cannot exclude classes or racial groups of the public, it is sufficiently private to permit him to keep a man out if he does not like him. The lessee of a theatre cannot refuse to admit a negro, but he can refuse to admit a critic, provided the critic is white. Having no colored critics on its staff, *The Times* was compelled to continue to ignore the producer as the producer ignored *The Times;* and after the ignoring had gone on for several months the producer discovered that he was cutting off his nose to spite his face. Consequently the critic was readmitted to the theatre, and the advertising was readmitted to *The Times*. It need hardly be said, however, that this restoration of peace bv joint resolution did

not imply any change in the critic's attitude. He continued to judge these productions, as all other productions, on their merits as he saw them; and by that time the producer had cooled off and recognized that his notion that the critic was prejudiced had no foundation. So that even in this case, when beaten in the courts, *The Times* achieved the substance of victory.

These are old, unhappy far-off things. It is now established and well known that *The Times* will not accord special favors to advertisers, nor permit them improperly to influence its news, editorial or busines policies; it is so well known that in recent years nobody has tried it. But it was not so well known in the past, and the management of the paper sometimes paid pretty heavily for the retention of its independence. In this matter, too, however, the conductors of the paper have always felt that good business and good morals were identical. If it is morally dishonest to permit advertisers to dictate the policies of the paper, it is likewise commercially ruinous in the long run — at least for a paper such as *The Times*. There are readers who can be fooled all the time, but *The Times* does not appeal to very many of that class.

The unexpectedly rapid growth of the paper had very early begun to make it uncomfortable in its cramped quarters in the old Times Building, and its conductors presently began to look around for a new building site. While they were looking they had to move (in 1904) to temporary new quarters at 41 Park Row, around the corner from the site which *The Times* had occupied for forty-six years. The old

Times Building was still owned by the estate of George Jones. A difference with it about the terms of the lease compelled the paper to move, but it was known that this change was only for a short time until a new and greater Times Building could be erected.

The Times Building is a landmark in the history of the paper no less than in the course of Broadway. The move uptown was one of Mr. Ochs's intuitions; and the building which was erected was a monumental piece of architecture, and gave invaluable publicity to the paper. Its construction involved some important and interesting engineering problems, and incidentally it put a heavy strain upon the resources of *The Times*. But the perilous paths were traversed successfully without *The Times* forming any embarrassing associations or commitments; and the enterprise required the expenditure of several millions in cash.

In a history of this character, however, the Times Building can be given little more than passing mention. *The Herald* had set the example in moving uptown from Park Row, but the publisher of *The Times* showed an accurate prevision of the direction of growth of the city's uptown centre by selecting for his new building the triangle between Broadway, Seventh Avenue and Forty-second Street. What is now the Times Square district was then a region of no particular importance or distinction, occupied for the most part by lodging houses and flats, with some few hotels and restaurants, mostly second or third class, scattered among them. Broadway — the Broadway of tradition — still had its centre of grav-

ity somewhere between the Flatiron Building and Herald Square. Yet it was evident that the corner where the Interborough subway, then under construction, met several surface car lines would become the pivotal point of transportation distribution whenever the subway was opened. The conductors of *The Times* were right in their judgment of the future of the Times Square district, but a very brief experience was to show that they had fallen far short of foreseeing the great development that was coming to *The Times*. If they had known in the early years of the century how the paper was going to grow they would never have put up the new building on that narrow plot of ground, which allowed so little space on each floor that *The Times* had outgrown the building almost before it was settled in it.

However, the erection of that building offered serious problems enough. Part of the land was purchased in fee simple from the Subway Realty Company, part had to be obtained by the purchase of a long-term lease from Charles Thorley. But the purchase of the land was only a beginning; the building had to be erected in a sense straddling the subway, for some of the pillars supporting it are planted right between the old subway tracks. This called for a good deal of engineering ability and implied a good deal of expense; and the construction involved an endless series of annoyances to the owners of *The Times*.

The building cost several hundred thousand dollars more than was anticipated, as buildings have a way of doing, and at one time it looked as if, while the seventeen stories of the building proper could be

completed, there would be no money left to finish the tower which gave to the structure its chief architectural distinction. It was suggested to the publisher that he had room enough in the building as it stood, and that he could finish the tower later. But he felt that to leave the tower unfinished was only a proclamation to the whole town that he had bitten off more than he could chew. By desperate effort the money was raised; and the building, the cornerstone of which had been laid with the collaboration of Bishop Potter on January 18, 1904, was occupied by the paper on January 1, 1905.

It had cost a great deal of money, and a great deal of effort to get the money, but it was worth it. It filled one of the most commanding positions in the landscape of New York City with a structure adequate in every way. At the time of its construction it was the tallest structure in town, except the Park Row Building — and taller than that if extension beneath the pavement were included. But it was more than a tall building — it was a beautiful tall building, and erected in a period when very few architects had come to realize that a skyscraper could just as easily be beautiful as well as useful. C. L. W. Eidlitz and Andrew C. Mackenzie, who designed the building, had found their inspiration in Giotto's campanile at Florence, and their plans provided not only for splendid lines but for ornamentation which was effective — and expensive. It was hard to build and hard to finance, but it was a magnificent signpost calling attention to the paper, at a point which was soon to become the centre of midtown business and of the night life of the city. Everybody in New York

saw the Times Building when they came into the midtown district; it was a standing reminder that the paper was doing great things.

A still greater advertisement was given to the paper when in 1904 the Board of Aldermen gave the name of Times Square to the previously nameless open space between Forty-third and Forty-seventh Streets at the intersection of Seventh Avenue and Broadway. Some name was needed, for the subway had two stations on Forty-second Street and had to differentiate between them somehow; and the precedent already set by the naming of Herald Square led the city authorities and the owners of the subway to agree that this new centre of the city's life deserved to be named for the paper which was doing so much to develop the neighborhood and contributing an architectural monument to the city. Naturally, this change passed unnoted by the other morning newspapers, most of which to this day ignore the fact in the geography of New York City which is obvious to anybody who has ever been in the neighborhood and prefer the name of Longacre Square, which never had any official standing. It was a local designation like San Juan Hill, owing its origin to the fact that some carriage builders who formerly had shops on the square named it after the London Street where carriage factories predominate.

As an advertisement it is believed that the Times Building has been worth every cent it cost, and more, besides the reward that comes from the consciousness that its erection, in that place and at that time, was a public service. Times Square fulfilled

all the expectations which the management of the paper had entertained when selecting it as the location of the paper's new home. It became and has remained the pivotal centre of the city and is the hub of its transportation systems.

But the conductors of *The Times*, accurately estimating the future development of New York, had far underestimated their own future. The paper grew so fast that the Times Building was soon cramping it. The next move was to a site as near as possible to Times Square, to the structure known as the Times Annex. This building, of 147 feet front, at 217-229 West Forty-third Street, was designed by Mortimer J. Fox, and if not so architecturally ambitious as the Times Building, was considerably more extensive. When virtually all departments of the paper were moved into it, on February 2, 1913, it was the largest, finest and most completely equipped newspaper home in North America. It is probably architecturally unsurpassed by any newspaper building in the world, except the magnificent structure which houses *La Prensa* at Buenos Aires. But, though it was planned on such a large scale that when the paper first moved in, five of its thirteen floors had been set aside as a reserve for growth — though the men who had had to move twice in ten years thought that this time they would make sure of allowing room for all the expansion likely to be needed in many years to come — after eight years this building is already far too small, and some departments of *The Times* have overflowed into temporary quarters in five reconstructed apartment houses next door, which *The Times* has purchased anticipating further growth,

while those that remain are beginning to be cramped and crowded.

The years before the war and the early months of the war saw the establishment of some subsidiary publications of The New York Times Company which in effect cover more fully certain outlying fringes of the newspaper field which had previously been handled by the newspaper itself. The weekly financial review was in January, 1913, raised to the dignity of an independent magazine, *The Annalist*, appearing every Monday, dealing with commerce, economics, and finance. After eight years it has a larger circulation than any other magazine in its field.

In April of the same year the paper for the first time began the publication of *The New York Times Index*, which from that time on was much more complete than it had ever been before, and which, published quarterly in convenient form, provided a chronological guide to the news which has become absolutely indispensable to students of contemporary history, and is a useful index, as to dates, for any American morning newspaper.

The war caused the production, in August, 1914, of *The Current History Magazine*, which began as a mere repository for long articles on the war, some of them reprinted from *The Times* and others too extensive for publication in a newspaper. But as it developed it became a sort of reservoir of documentary exhibits on current history, and in its present form it includes a review of the month's news from every country in the world, comments descriptive,

explanatory, or apologetic on the news by experts or by partisan pleaders (and both kinds have their use), and finally a collection of original records and documents which make it perhaps the most valuable of periodical source books.

A great development in pictorial illustration was made possible by the introduction in April, 1914, of the rotogravure presses. A German newspaper containing pictures printed by this process, then unknown in America, came by chance to *The Times* some months before that, and the management was at once struck by the fact that this method made possible much better reproductions of photographs than any then in use. A special trip to Germany resulted in the purchase of rotogravure presses and their installation in *The Times* office. The superiority of the pictorial supplement printed by this process was so apparent that other papers soon followed *The Times's* example. *The Times*, however, which was the first in the field, developed a greater interest in pictorial illustrations than it had had before that time. The paper has never done much in the way of printing photographs in its news section on ordinary newsprint paper, and consequently had never needed the staff photographers who were so important a part of other newspaper organizations. But the rotogravure presses not only gave the conductors of *The Times* a greater interest in the Sunday pictorial supplement; they made possible the establishment of a new and independent publication of The New York Times Company, *The Mid-week Pictorial*, first issued in September, 1914. This, like *The Current History Magazine*, began as a war publi-

cation and has survived the war as a pictorial weekly newspaper. To serve the increasing needs of the Sunday and mid-week pictorials The Times Wide-world Photo Service was organized in 1919, under the direction of Charles M. Graves, and already has some notable feats to its credit.

In at least one use of the rotogravure presses *The Times* is still without competition. *The Annalist* and *The Times Sunday Book Review and Magazine* are now printed by this process, which makes possible an excellence of typography otherwise unattainable in such publications, and a fineness and fidelity in the reproduction of photographs which had never previously been achieved in any newspaper supplement.

THE TIMES BUILDING,
ILLUMINATED FOR VICTORY
© Brown Bros.

CHAPTER V

The Times in the War, 1914–1918

TO the biggest news story of modern times the American press as a whole reacted in a manner highly creditable. It would almost be safe to say that there was not a single newspaper in the country which was not a better paper, from the technical point of view, at the end of the war than at its beginning. That is to say, its editors knew more about what news was, how to get it, and how to present it to their readers. Also, the great majority responded honorably to the secondary but sometimes highly important duty of interpreting and clarifying the news by editorial comment. Most of the influential papers of the country understood at the outset at least the general causes of the war, and were able to assess rightly the responsibility for its outbreak.

In general, the service of *The Times* during the war consisted in its doing what the other papers, or most of the other respectable papers, did, but doing it better. The merit of its war news is sufficiently well known. It was thanks chiefly to the excellence and the universal scope of its news service that the circulation of the paper, which was about 250,000 at the beginning of the war, had risen to some 390,000 at its close. But it should not be forgotten that *The Times* in editorial analysis of the causes of the war was amazingly accurate from the very outset,

so accurate that it brought down on itself almost at once the wrath of the Germans and their sympathizers, and within a few months had earned the honorable distinction of being the principal focus of the vituperation which the Germans and pro-Germans fired at an unsympathetic American press.

The news department of a paper should not be, and that of *The Times* is not, influenced by editorial policies. But it is sometimes forgotten by amateur critics of journalism that the editorial page has a function going somewhat beyond the mere assertion of opinion. It is often the duty of the editorial writers to interpret the news, to discriminate between the probable and the improbable, the tendentious and the more or less impartial, in the great volume of news reports which come to the office. Since human nature is fallible, it has been found advisable to print all the news and leave to the editorial page the assessment of its relative worth, rather than exercise discrimination at the news desk and suppress everything that fails to accord with the news editor's judgment of the probabilities.

The general reader may disagree with the editorial interpretation. That is his privilege, for it is presented only as an interpretation. But editorial writers are somewhat better informed than the average reader. They probably know more of the news than he does, for they read half a dozen papers a day where he reads one or two; a newspaper prints all the news it gets, so long as that news is not libelous, but a single paper does not always get it all. But the editorial writers have read much outside of the daily papers; they have a background

of solid information which enables them to understand a good deal that is dark to the man in the street. Elucidation based on wider and more thorough knowledge is probably the most important function of the editorial page today.

There has rarely been a better example of the performance of this function than *The Times's* editorials on the outbreak of the war. Information available then was far from complete; it consisted only of vague and scanty official statements on the diplomatic exchanges. The accounts of the secret conferences in which every Government of Europe was going over the situation in the last week of July, 1914, as well as the story of much of the actual diplomatic negotiation, did not come to public knowledge till much later. But after the lapse of seven years, despite all the voluminous publication of secret archives which since the armistice has informed the world of what went on behind the scenes in those days, there is not one line of *The Times* editorial analysis of the responsibility for the war, written in the days when the war was being made, which would have to be retracted today.

The Times, to be sure, like all the world, was slow to believe that the conflict that had been so long expected that it had come to seem impossible was at last at hand. It held the same hope that everybody held in the summer of 1914 in the moderating influence of financiers and business men, and above all it believed, until belief was no longer possible, that the German Emperor had the will to avert the war as he undoubtedly had the power. But the events of the week leading up to the declaration of war

convinced *The Times* that Austria was responsible for the war in the sense that the criminal recklessness of Austrian statesmen had deliberately provoked it, and that Germany was responsible in that if the Kaiser had forbidden it there would have been no war.

On July 27, 1914, when Austria had refused to accept the Serbian reply to the ultimatum and had stood out before the world as plainly determined to fight, *The Times* said in an editorial article:

> It will be freely said that Count Berchtold has seized what seemed to him a most propitious moment for dealing a blow at Pan-Slavism and strengthening Pan-Germanism, and incidentally reviving the German party in Austria. . . . The only hope of peace seems to be in the awakening of the German conscience.

Four days later, when it was evident that the German conscience either had not awakened or was unable to affect the consciences of the rulers of Germany, *The Times* observed:

> Now is the very best of all times for taking account of the frightful wrong involved in governmental systems which permit great and prosperous peoples to be dragged into the war without consulting their will and their welfare.

On August 2 *The Times* pronounced the famous speech of the German Emperor about the sword which had been forced into his hand "a piece of pompous humbug," and after deploring the fact that evidently some European peoples, even those

which had been regarded as highly cultured, were no more than a dumb herd which could be driven, physically and psychologically, where the leaders willed, went on to say that

> there is a possibility, historically justified, that a general European war would be followed by changes which would make the herd vocal.

Four days later it resumed this same argument, going so far as to make the prediction, later sustained in every particular, that the war was very likely to result in revolution in Russia, revolution in Germany and the break-up of Austria-Hungary.

Again, on August 6 *The Times* observed that while every nation going into the war found plenty of excuse for justifying its course of action,

> the historian will have no trouble in placing his finger on the cause of the war, and there are men in Vienna today whose descendants for many generations will redden at the verdict.

The peculiar German mind was of course not so well understood in those days. It takes a good deal to make the average German redden, even today, as the trials of war offenders at Leipzig showed. Nevertheless, even the Germans are likely to accept the truth of this judgment in time; the rest of the world has already ratified it. But in the summer of 1914 it did not command universal acceptance, even though the majority of Americans thought Germany in the wrong. The chief public service of *The Times* in the war was that from the very beginning it

understood where the rights and wrongs of the conflict lay, it was able to justify its position by sound argument, and it never ceased to maintain that position with all the vigor which its editors were able to command. The furious hostility toward the paper which the Germans and their sympathizers soon displayed is the best measure of its success in performing this duty.

However, there was an equally important duty to be performed in giving to the public every bit of information as to the underlying causes, as well as the immediate occasion, of this vast and multiplex conflict. It is not too much to say that before the war had been going on three months *The Times* had become the principal forum for debate on the issues of the war. Despite the fact that its editors were firmly convinced that Germany was in the wrong, *The Times* realized the necessity of hearing everything that could be said on both sides. As was said on the editorial page a few months after the war began, "access to its columns has been denied to no German sympathizer, if reputable, responsible and literate." Some of them, indeed, were neither reputable nor responsible, but if they seemed to have anything of value to contribute to the discussion *The Times* heard them.

The principal item in this discussion was unquestionably the publication in full of the arguments of the various European Governments — the White Papers, Yellow Books, Orange Papers and so on, consisting of the diplomatic correspondence leading up to the outbreak of the war, or as much of it as the several governments were inclined to give out to the

public. Long extracts from these were, of course, sent to *The Times* by cable as soon as they were issued, but it seemed to *The Times* that the importance of the issue made it imperative to present the whole case, or as much of it as the governments themselves had given out.

The first copy of the British White Paper was brought to this country at the end of August, 1914, by the Rev. Dr. Frederick Lynch, who had received it in advance of publication from an official friend just as he was boarding his steamer at Liverpool. He gave it to a *Times* reporter, and it was published in full on the following Sunday. The presses were still printing it when, in the small hours of Sunday morning, Frederic William Wile, Berlin correspondent of *The Times*, arrived with a copy of the German White Paper. A corps of translators was set to work at 2 A.M.; by 10 o'clock Sunday evening they had finished their task, and the document was printed in full in Monday morning's *Times*. Thus early in the war *The Times* presented to its readers on two successive days all that was obtainable from official sources on both sides of the case. The two documents were reprinted in pamphlet form and distributed at cost to some hundreds of thousands of eager readers throughout the United States and Canada.

After the British and German statements came the official documents of the French, Russian, Austrian and Belgian governments, giving to the world what each saw fit to publish of its diplomatic records, and having set the precedent *The Times* published them all, in full. Again they were repub-

lished in tabloid form, and before the end of 1914 *The Times* was in effect running an extension university on the issues of the war. At that time its war news was on the whole about the same as the war news of other papers, so far as related to the actual fighting; but from the very start it surpassed all its competitors in giving the news about the reasons for the war.

Here was the official brief of each government; it seemed to the management of *The Times* that the next thing was argument from the briefs. An attempt was made to have eminent American lawyers discuss the White Papers as attorneys for the two governments, but this proved to be impossible for the somewhat significant reason that the three or four American lawyers known to be sympathetic with Germany, or inclined to entire neutrality, who were asked to present the German side of the argument refused to argue the German case if they were restricted to the evidence put forward in these official documents. Clearly they were able to realize that the German White Paper presented a pretty poor case. When it proved impossible to present this debate, the publisher of *The Times* finally persuaded James M. Beck to analyze alone all the arguments, not as a representative of either side, but as an impartial reviewer.

Mr. Beck was a former Assistant Attorney General of the United States and was one of the leaders of the New York bar, but his discussion of the case presented by the White Papers before "the supreme court of civilization" made him internationally famous. Arguing from the briefs presented by the

"All the News That's Fit to Print."

The New York Times.

EXTRA
5:30 A. M.

Weather Today and Sunday Fair.

VOL. LXIV...NO. 20,923. NEW YORK, SATURDAY, MAY 8, 1915.—TWENTY-FOUR PAGES. ONE CENT In Greater New York, Jersey City and Newark. Elsewhere TWO CENTS.

LUSITANIA SUNK BY A SUBMARINE, PROBABLY 1,260 DEAD; TWICE TORPEDOED OFF IRISH COAST; SINKS IN 15 MINUTES; CAPT. TURNER SAVED, FROHMAN AND VANDERBILT MISSING; WASHINGTON BELIEVES THAT A GRAVE CRISIS IS AT HAND

SHOCKS THE PRESIDENT

Washington Deeply Stirred by the Loss of American Lives.

BULLETINS AT WHITE HOUSE

Wilson Reads Them Closely, but Is Silent on the Nation's Course.

HINTS OF CONGRESS CALL

Loss of Lusitania Recalls Firm Tone of Our First Warning to Germany.

CAPITAL FULL OF RUMORS

Reports That Liner Was to be Sunk Were Heard Before Actual News Came.

Special to The New York Times.

WASHINGTON, May 7. — Never since that April day, three years ago, when word came that the Titanic had gone down, has Washington been so stirred as it is tonight over the sink-

SOME DEAD TAKEN ASHORE

Several Hundred Survivors at Queenstown and Kinsale.

STEWARD TELLS OF DISASTER

One Torpedo Crashes Into the Doomed Liner's Bow, Another Into the Engine Room.

SHIP LISTS OVER TO PORT

Makes It Impossible to Lower Many Boats, So Hundreds Must Have Gone Down.

ATTACKED IN BROAD DAY

Passengers at Luncheon—Warning Had Been Given by Germans Before the Ship Left New York.

Only 650 Were Saved, Few Cabin Passengers

QUEENSTOWN, Saturday, May 8, 4:28 A. M.—

crisis in the international relations of the United States.

It is pointed out that the sinking of the Lusitania is the outcome of a series of incidents that have been the cause of concern to this Government in its endeavor to maintain a strictly neutral position in the great European war.

Nation's Course in Doubt.

It is impossible to say tonight what effect the loss of American lives on the Lusitania will have on the Government. Judged from the little that can be learned it is a safe prediction that President Wilson will endeavor to ascertain all the facts, including evidence as to whether a German submarine was responsible for the sinking of the vessel, before proceeding to determine the course to be pursued. The news that many lives had been sacrificed, probably as many as a thousand, was given to him at the White House about 10 o'clock this morning, but no word came from him as to what effect this intelligence had on him.

The State Department tonight sent instructions to the American Embassy in London to send the names of any Americans who might have been killed or injured in the disaster. A bulletin from THE TIMES, saying probably 1,000 lives had been lost, was sent to the White House as soon as received and laid before President Wilson. The news that two torpedoes had been fired into the Lusitania by a submarine and that the Lusitania sank fifteen minutes afterward was also sent to the White House, but reached there after the President had gone to bed. The President retired about 11 o'clock.

On account of the many inquiries it had received from friends and relatives of passengers on the Lusitania and the intense public interest in the tragedy, orders were given tonight to the telegraphers and cipher clerks in charge of the telegraph office in the State Department to remain at their posts all night. They also had instructions to make public any messages bringing official details regarding the Lusitania's passengers. Usually the telegraph office closes at midnight.

Rumors of Congress Session.

There were reports this evening that Congress would be called in extra session, but these were not justified, and the most that can be said is that while the Government is greatly concerned over the situation, it has shown no inclination toward excitement or taking hasty action.

Senator W J Stone, Chairman of the Committee on Foreign Relations, said tonight

"I cannot comment on a supposed

Continued on Page 4.

Nothing Heard from the Well-Known Passengers on Board—Story of Disaster Long Unconfirmed While Anxious Crowds Seek Details.

Official news of the sinking of the Lusitania yesterday reached New York in fragmentary reports, and several hours elapsed between the first unverified rumor of the disaster and the cable messages that told at night of the saving of some of the passengers and gave meagre details of the most sensational incident of its kind in the war

The early accounts that indicated all on board had been saved reassured hundreds of friends and relatives of passengers. Later it was made known that lives had been lost and probably many persons had been injured

Among the prominent passengers rescued was George A Kessler The list of those of whom no word was received included A G Vanderbilt, Charles Frohman, Charles Klein, Justus Miles Forman, and Elbert Hubbard, besides persons widely known in society

A cablegram sent to Farley Hopkins of The Yale News staff at New Haven, by his father who was aboard the Lusitania, stated that the vessel was sunk not beached, that three hundred persons had been already landed, and that the rest in small boats were making for shore The message reached New York at 8.15 o'clock and was signed "Lee, Higginson & Co., London"

Word of the safety of Charles E. Lauriat, Jr., of Boston Mass, a member of the firm of Charles E Lauriat & Co., booksellers, who was a first-cabin passenger reached relatives there in a cablegram early this morning The message, dated at Queenstown, 2 40 A. M Read simply

Charles E Lauriat Jr safe and well

For more than half a century it was the boast of the Cunard Line that it never had lost a life The Oregon was sunk in collision near Fire Island in 1886, but no lives were lost until five passengers were swept off the Campania's forward deck by a wave on Oct. 5, 1903. The sinking of the Lusitania is the first big disaster the Cunard Line has had

Message to Cunard Office.

The first word of the sinking of the Lusitania received here reached the local offices of the Cunard Line, 21 State Street, at 11.41 o'clock yesterday morning, but was not made public until late in the afternoon The message, which was sent from the head office in Liverpool, read:

The Lusitania, we regret to advise, an unconfirmed report states to have been torpedoed by a submarine at 2 P M., Friday, ten miles from Kinsale and sunk at 2 30 There is no news as to the safety of passengers or crew

Following this dispatch there was a message which had been picked up by the wireless station at Land's End evidently a distress call from the liner, which said:

Come at once. Big list. Position ten miles west Kinsale.

A third dispatch from Queenstown stated:

All available craft in harbor dispatched to assist. Weather here beautifully fine. Wind southeast, light.

By 3 o'clock in the afternoon the news of the sinking of the Lusitania had been spread in the city and the Cunard offices were besieged by relatives and friends of the passengers on board. Owing to the alterations in and additions to the passenger list on sailing day, last Saturday, it took some time to get the correct figures, which were finally given out as 290 first, 601 second, and 362 third class passengers. Of the cabin passengers thirty-six had been transferred from the Cameronia on Saturday morning. This delayed the Lusitania's departure from 10 o'clock to 12:28.

1,918 Persons on Board.

The officers and crew numbered 665 men instead of the usual complement of 950, on account of fewer men being carried in the engineers' and stewards' departments. Thus there were in all 1,918 persons on board

The Cunard agents told all inquirers that they would give out the messages as fast as they were received and had no intention of keeping back the news from the public. Several bulletins were received from the Liverpool office, but few of them contained any definite statements and they were cancelled, in some instances, within an hour One received at 4 P M read

Motor fishing boats towing two boats filled with passengers, probably fifty. Tug Stormcock making Kinsale Some passengers on board. Many rescue vessels are now apparently making Queenstown

The first dispatch stating positively that the Lusitania had sunk reached the Cunard office at 5 P. M. It read:

Old Head Kinsale Station reports about twenty boats, all belonging to Lusitania, are in vicinity where sunk. About fifteen boats are making for the spot to resume.

An unconfirmed report was received late in the afternoon that all the passengers and crew had been saved in small boats and rafts This information was given out to the people waiting in the Cunard office, and many of them went home. It was estimated that fully 300 inquiries were received by telephone and telegraph in the afternoon from relatives and friends of passengers on board Long-distance calls were received from St Louis, Atlanta, Montreal, and Toronto.

The next bulletin made public at the Cunard office was the following:

Liverpool, May 7.
1 51 P M., (New York Time.)
Following received by Admiralty, Galley Head 4 25 P M. Several boats, apparently survivors, southeast nine miles. Greek steamer proceeding to assist.

The next bulletin was:

Liverpool, May 7.
2 23 P M (New York Time.)
Queenstown wires Old Head: Large steamer just arrived in vicinity, apparently sending assistance Tugs, patrols &c.

Continued on Page 3

Vanderbilt and Frohman Reported Lost

LONDON, Saturday, May 8, 5:30 A. M.—The Press Bureau has received from the British Admiralty at Queenstown a report that all the torpedo boats and tugs and armed trawlers, except the Heron, which went out from Queenstown to the relief of the Lusitania have returned.

These vessels have landed 595 survivors and forty dead. Fifty-two more survivors are reported aboard a steamer, while eleven others and five bodies have been landed at Kinsale, making the total number of survivors 658, besides forty-five dead. The numbers will be verified later, and it is considered possible Kinsale fishing boats may have rescued a few more

Among the survivors is the Captain of the Lusitania, William T Turner Some of the survivors at Queenstown say that Alfred Gwynne Vanderbilt was drowned. Every effort to find Mr. Vanderbilt and Charles Frohman, the theatrical manager, among the survivors has failed.

The Central News says that the number of the Lusitania's passengers who died of injuries while being taken to Queenstown will reach 100

QUEENSTOWN, Saturday, May 8, 4:45 A. M.—The list of the Lusitania's survivors, as far as compiled, follows:

TURNER, Captain.
MATHEWS, A. T., Montreal.
ABRAMOWITZ, S.
LANE, G. B.
MEYERS, W G. E.
TRIMMINS, J. T
WITHERBEE, Mrs. A F
MACKWORTH, Lady
ADAMS, Mrs. HENRY, Boston
RANKIN, ROBERT, New York
SHARP, SAMUEL.
BYRNE, M. B., New York
DAVIS, EMILY.
WALKER, ANNIE.
HOUSNELL, E.
CROSS, A. B.
YOUNG, PHILIP, Montreal
VASSAR, W. A F., London
STEELE, GEORGE.
CROSLEY CYRUS.
PARKER, JAMES
COLEBROOK, the Rev. R. †
MORRIS, H C S
FISH, Mrs., and two children.
MARTIN, Miss R.
GAUTLETT, F J., New York
MAYCOCK, Miss MAY
HENDERSON, VIOLET
MARDERUD, UNO.
LEVIN, THOMAS D
THOMAS, D. A., Cardiff, Wales
EVANS, T. J M
CLARKE, A. R
BURGESS, W G
CHARLES, J H. and daughter, Toronto.
LONEY, Miss, New York
HERRIS, JOHN
HOLLAND, Miss
BRANDELL, Miss JOSEPHINE, New York
PERRY, F. K A
GRAB, O. H.
MOSLEY, G G., New York
BROOKS, J H., New York
JEFFRY, A. M
CAIRNS, M
HAMMOND, O. H New York
MANLEY, A.
NEATH, H
NORTH, Miss.
WINTER, Miss.
WINTER, Miss.
DUGUID, GEORGE
MOORE, DANIEL.
McCONNELL, JOHN W., Memphis, Tenn.
SHARPE, Miss
CONNER, Miss.
DALY, H M
CLIFFE, PATRICK
BOHAN, JAMES, Toronto
CROSLEY, Mrs CYRUS
BRETHERTON, Mrs CYRIL H and two children Los Angeles Cal.
HOPKINS, A L. New York
LASSETTER, Mrs. H B. of Sydney, Australia, wife of General Lassetter
LASSETTER Master F
LAURIAT, CHARLES E., Jr., Boston, Mass.
PAYNTER, Miss IRENE, Liverpool, England.

KINSALE, Ireland, May 8.—Eleven survivors of the Lusitania have been landed here, together with the bodies of five persons who were dead. Among the survivors are:

SMITH, J. RESTON, New York
BOTTOMLEY, FREDERICK
BOYLE, N. L
HOTCHKISS, CHARLES.
HARRIMAN, CORNELIUS
LIVERMORE, VERNAR.
SULLIVAN, Mrs. F.

Consul's List of Saved.

WASHINGTON, May 8.—Consul Lauriat at Queenstown sends this report:

"Total saved of all nationalities, 700. The following are American survivors of Lusitania. Other names will follow:

CRAB, O. S.
PEARL, Major and Mrs., and two children.
SMITH, Mrs. JESSIE TAFT
HARDWICK, CHARLES C
EARL, STUART D
PEARL, AMY
STANLEY, Mrs.
LINES, L. B
HILL, C. T
RANKIN, ROBERT.
LONEY, Miss.
DOHERTY, Mrs. WILLIAM and infant.
PHILLIPS, THOMAS.
McADAMS, WILLIAM.
HOUGHTON, J. H.
SWEENEY, JOHN M.
HAMMOND, OADEN H.
BROOKS, J. H
JEFFRY CHARLES T
LUND Mrs. C. H.
SHEPPERDSON, ARTHUR
MOORE Dr D. V
BERNARD, CLINTON.
LIGHT, HERBERT.
LINNSON, J., Jr
WILLIAMS, EDITH.
LEARY JAMES J
SLIDELL THOMAS.
WOLFENDEN, Mrs. JOHN
HOLLAND, Mrs. NINA.
MESH, Mrs. THOMAS
KESSLER, GEORGE A
McMURRAY, L.
KAY ROBERT
LOCKHART, R. B
CANNON, OWEN
HARRIS, DURIGHT C
JUDSON, FRED S.
COLLIS, ED M.
WRIGHT, R. C
GAUNTLET, F J.
KNOX, S. N
O'DONNELL, PATRICK.

and Watched Torpedo as It Struck Ship

Ernest Cowper, a Toronto Newspaper Man, Describes Attack, Seen from Ship's Rail—Poison Gas Used in Torpedoes, Say Other Passengers.

Queenstown, Saturday,
May 8, 3:18 A. M.

A sharp lookout for submarines was kept aboard the Lusitania as she approached the Irish coast, according to Ernest Cowper, a Toronto newspaper man, who was among the survivors landed at Queenstown.

He said that after the ship was torpedoed there was no panic among the crew, but that they went about the work of getting passengers into the boats in a prompt and efficient manner

"As we neared the coast of Ireland," said Mr Cowper, "we all joined in the lookout, for a possible attack by a submarine was the sole topic of conversation

"I was chatting with a friend at the rail about 2 o'clock when suddenly I caught a glimpse of the conning tower of a submarine about a thousand yards distant. I immediately called my friend's attention to it. Immediately we both saw the track of a torpedo followed almost instantly by an explosion. Portions of splintered hull were sent flying into the air, and then another torpedo struck. The ship began to list to starboard

"The crew at once proceeded to get the passengers into boats in an orderly, prompt, and efficient manner Miss Helen Smith appealed to me to save her. I placed her in a boat and saw her safely away I got into one of the last boats to leave.

"Some of the boats could not be launched as the vessel was sinking. There was a large number of women and children in the second cabin. Forty of the children were less than a year old."

Poison Fumes from Torpedoes.

From interviews with passengers it appears that when the torpedoes burst they sent forth suffocating fumes which had their effect on the passengers, causing some of them to lose consciousness.

Two stokers, Byrne and Hussey of Liverpool, gave a few details. They said the submarine gave no notice and fired two torpedoes, one hitting No. 1 stoke hole and the second the engine room. The first torpedo was discharged at 2 o'clock. In twenty-five minutes the great liner disappeared.

Signals have been received at Queenstown that an armed trawler, believed to be the Heron, and two fishing trawlers are bringing in 100 more bodies.

The Cunard Line agent states that the total number of persons aboard the Lusitania was 2,160

Loss of the Lusitania Fills London With Horror and Utter Amazement

Special Cable to THE NEW YORK TIMES.

LONDON Saturday May 8.—Stupefaction is the word which best describes the first impression created by the news of the sinking of the Lusitania People seemed unable to realize that at this stage of the world's progress such a deed could be committed as an act of war

"I have no words for it," said Lord Rosebery and everywhere one found the same sentiment repeated.

It was some hours between the time

Continued on Page 2.

rescued were saloon passengers.

Official Confirmation.

WASHINGTON, May 8.—A dispatch to the State Department early today from American Consul Lauriet at Queenstown stated that the total number of survivors of the Lusitania was about 700.

LONDON, Saturday, May 8.—The Cunard liner Lusitania, which sailed out of New York last Saturday with 1,918 souls aboard, lies at the bottom of the ocean off the Irish coast.

She was sunk by a German submarine, which sent two torpedoes crashing into her side at 2:30 o'clock yesterday afternoon while the passengers, seemingly confident that the great, swift vessel could elude the German underwater craft, were having luncheon.

The great inrush of water caused the liner to list heavily to port, so that she could not launch many of her lifeboats.

About 1,260 of those on board the great ship, including many Americans, apparently went down with her, as a statement issued late this morning by the Admiralty says the total number of survivors is only 658.

There were 1,253 passengers on board the steamship, including 200 who were transferred to her from the steamer Cameronia. The Americans totaled 188. The crew numbered 665.

It is believed that only a few first class passengers were saved as they thought the ship would remain afloat, and made little effort to escape.

There appears to be a large proportion of the ship's crew among the survivors landed at Queenstown. Only a few offi-

[illegible] Torpedo [illegible] Struck Ship

Ernest Cowper, a Toronto Newspaper Man, Describes Attack Seen from Ship's Rail. Former [illegible] Used in Torpedoes, Say Other Passengers.

[illegible]

Loss of the Lusitania Fills London With Horror and Utter Amazement

[illegible]

Nothing Heard from the Well-Known Passengers on Board—Story of Disaster Long Unconfirmed While Anxious Crowds Seek Details

[illegible]

several governments, he reached the conclusion that Germany was in the wrong, and supported his opinion by an able and searching analysis. First presented in *The Times* of Sunday, October 25, 1914, his articles were reprinted in pamphlet form under the title of "The Evidence in the Case," by several governments, notably the English, and millions of copies distributed over the world in many languages. Extracts and summaries of his argument were published the world over, and gave to millions of readers the foundation for opinions which had been somewhat confused by the volume and the obscurity of the official documents.

Second only in importance to the White Papers and their like were the innumerable arguments conducted in the columns of *The Times* by sympathizers of the two sides. All papers had their share of such discussions, of course, but *The Times* had more of them, and of more distinguished authorship. Notable among these were the letters exchanged between Charles W. Eliot and Jacob H. Schiff, published in *The Times* in December, 1914; the arguments presented by G. K. Chesterton and various other British authors on the side of the Allies, and those of Dr. Bernhard Dernburg, Arthur von Briesen, Professor William Milligan Sloane and Professor John W. Burgess on the German side. Throughout most of the war military experts, usually officers either active or retired of the United States Army, analyzed each day the military operations from the technical standpoint. German sympathizers in the fall of 1914 complained that the military critic showed too much partisanship for the Allies, so for some months

The Times published frequent comments on the military situation by a former officer of the German Army.

All these discussions, of course, took place either on the editorial page or in the Sunday magazine, and were supplementary to the voluminous arguments which were part of the news of the day. There were in addition a number of important contributions on the war as affecting purely American interests, of which the most notable were a series by Theodore Roosevelt in the fall of 1914 on "What America Should Learn From the War," the articles contributed toward the end of 1916 by a publicist who concealed his identity under the signature of "Cosmos," and the later series signed by "An American Jurist," who, as has since been announced, was Robert Ludlow Fowler, Surrogate of New York County and one of the most accomplished scholars on the bench. In quieter times Judge Fowler's series of brilliantly written articles would have been generally accepted as something of a classic.

Of course, partisans of each side were often indignant that any space should be given to the other side; and because the Germans were Germans their indignation was most violent, and most inclined to the imputation of base motives. Before the war was two months old a group of more or less authentic Americans in Munich saw fit to send to the German press a protest against the "prejudiced and unfair" attitude of *The Times*, which was duly sent abroad by the industrious German wireless. Before long the most notorious German propagandists in America were accusing *The Times* of suppression of news, and

beginning that vast campaign of calumny which was taken up by the Socialists and Sinn Feiners when prudential motives imposed silence on the Germans, later in the war, and joyfully resumed by the whole crew when they came out of their holes after the armistice. Every honest and patriotic American newspaper was the target of these attacks; the assertion that the whole American press had been bought by British gold seemed reasonable enough to persons who were unfamiliar with the idea of any but a purchased press; and these accusations against any paper were only proof that that paper was honestly and fearlessly doing its duty. But *The Times* was probably honored by more denunciation than any other paper in the country, though *The World* and *The Tribune* were close behind it in this honorable competition. Fortunately, the American people were making up their minds, and most of them knew exactly what all this Teutonic clamor was worth.

However, not all the criticism came from one side. Just as half a century before some superheated northern patriots had accused *The Times* of sympathy with secession because it had a correspondent who sent the news from Charleston, so in the World War some sympathizers with the Allies could see nothing but sympathy with Germany in any inclination to give the Germans a hearing. In November, 1914, for instance, a reverend clergyman wrote to *The Times* that he couldn't stand "such dishes of German arrogance and insolence as you are serving daily to your readers." His emotional reaction was wholly creditable, but he and some others like him

forgot that it was highly important that the American people should learn what the Germans really were and learn it by the most convincing and convicting evidence, that which proceeded out of their own mouths.

It is possible that in the early months of the war *The Times* gave up nearly as much space to German arguments as to those of the opposition, for the Germans saw from the first that the balance of opinion was against them, and they made desperate efforts in their tactful way to turn the scales. These arguments were apt to be convincing, but in the opposite direction; and, anyway, the actions of the Germans always spoke louder than their words. Even before the *Lusitania*, the Germans had realized that their cause before American public opinion was lost, and had already begun to supplement their arguments and persuasions with sabotage and violence. What part the editorial columns of *The Times* may have had in the formation of American public opinion can best be determined by those outside the office, but attention may be called to one editorial, one of the most forceful and important which has ever appeared in *The Times*, which deserves special mention as an example of historical and political insight. This article, two columns in length, was written by Charles R. Miller, the editor in chief, and appeared on December 15, 1914. It was headed "For the German People, Peace with Freedom."

That editorial began with the flat statement, "Germany is doomed to sure defeat." It analyzed the military situation, the probabilities of the future;

but its argument was founded chiefly on moral considerations, on the belief that the world would not let Germany win; that a German victory meant the negation of all human progress, and that every free people, if forced to the issue, would find itself compelled to resist the German attack on civilization. "Yet," the article continued, "the downfall of the German Empire may become the deliverance of the German people, if they will betimes but seize and hold their own." And then it analyzed the situation of the German people, paying all the cost of the war, sure to endure the consequence of defeat, yet unable to win anything from victory in a conflict which they had undertaken at the command of their rulers and whose issues, even if successful, would profit those rulers alone.

"If," the article continued, "Germany chooses to fight to the bitter end, her ultimate and sure overthrow will leave her bled to exhaustion, drained of her resources, and under sentence to penalties of which the stubbornness of her futile resistance will measure the severity. We could wish that the German people, seeing the light, might take timely measure to avert the calamities that await them."

The article created a sensation. It was republished and commented on throughout the world, and is generally regarded as one of the greatest editorials ever appearing in an American newspaper. It is reproduced in full in an appendix to this volume.

This analysis of the issue raised by German aggression, of the relations between the German masses and the oligarchy that ruled them, of the only possible escape for the Germans and the

inevitable consequences of refusal to take that way of escape, was justified in every detail by the history of the next four years. Some two years and four months later the President of the United States came around to these opinions, which he expressed in his speech of April 2, 1917; and a year and seven months after that the German people were at last convinced of the soundness of this reasoning, by the only argument they were able to understand — and, unfortunately, too late to be able to escape the penalties of delay.

This editorial may stand as a summary of *The Times's* position on the war, so far as it was purely a European war. New issues were raised in the spring of 1915, both by the sinking of the *Lusitania* and by Germany's transference of the war, so far as possible, to American soil; but before that had happened *The Times* had recognized German aggression as a menace to the whole world, and though continuing to publish all the arguments on the German side, was using all its influence to convince the American people that the world could not let Germany win the war. As has been said, the German propagandists and their American sympathizers already looked on *The Times* as their chief antagonist, and were flinging at it every accusation, old and new, which their active imaginations could devise. To most of the readers of the paper these charges were evidently only a satisfying proof that the Germans felt that *The Times* was dangerous. But a good deal can be forgotten in three or four years, and already memory of the ways of German propagandists before 1917 is

fading, as well as the recollection of the influence which they had, for a considerable time, in circles where they should have been better understood.

The culmination of these attacks upon *The Times* came in March, 1915 — not in a meeting of German singing societies or the Clan-na-Gael, but in a hearing before a committee of the United States Senate, where all the enmity that had been aroused by *The Times's* criticisms of impromptu statesmanship flared into open view, and all the calumnious whispers that had been spread abroad by persons unable to imagine that any man or any newspaper could advocate any opinions except for a cash consideration were dignified by the attention of eminent Senators.

This episode deserves extended notice, for it is important not only in the history of *The Times* but in the history of modern journalism; perhaps, even, it has some interest as an illustration of recent tendencies in the United States Senate. Because the editors of *The Times* had expressed their opinions on some questions of public policy, opinions not altogether in agreement with those of the Senators on the committee, they were summoned to Washington and asked if anybody was paying them for those opinions, and if so, who. The pretext for this inquisition — in view of the course taken by the committee, it can hardly be called anything else — was *The Times's* opposition to the administration bill for the purchase of foreign ships interned in American harbors. The paper opposed this because it opposed the intrusion of the government into business, and because it had its doubts whether the

purchase in time of war of ships interned to escape capture by the enemy was valid in international law. There was much, and reasonable, opposition to this measure; *The Times* had no monopoly of its opinion. But the Senate appointed a committee to inquire "if influence had been exerted" against the bill. The possibility that there might be room for two honest opinions on the subject did not seem to occur to the Senators.

However, this suspicion, if not very creditable to the collective intelligence of the Senate, was at least more legitimate than some of the innuendoes with which the members of the committee decorated the sessions devoted to questioning editors of *The Times*. For the information of the Senators, who displayed a great deal of curiosity about the ownership of *The Times*, the managing editor furnished not only the list of all persons owning more than one per cent of the capital stock, which was published anyway twice a year, but a table showing how much each one of them owned. The discovery that the publisher of *The Times* owned 62 per cent of the stock, that its editor owned something more than 14 per cent, and that nearly half the residue was owned by other persons who had no occupation excepting contributing their bit toward getting out *The Times*, was apparently something of a disappointment to the committee; but the Senators still had a good many questions to ask.

The next session of the committee, in which the editor-in-chief was examined, began very much in the form of a class in elementary journalism. The Ship Purchase bill was forgotten; Senators asked

MAIN ENTRANCE TIMES BUILDING.

THE TIMES BUSINESS OFFICE.

Mr. Miller why *The Times* opposed parcel posts; why it thought this and that about the railroads and about the trust prosecutions; why certain stories were not put on the front page. *The Times* by that time was virtually on trial for all its opinions, and its editor no doubt experienced some weariness as he laboriously explained that the editors of a newspaper advocate certain policies because they believe them best for the public interest, that not all the news can be put on the front page, that the relative value of different news stories is a matter of judgment and that the judgment of all newspapers is not always identical.

Having got through this, however, the committee took up another line of argument. Senator T. J. Walsh of Montana, its Chairman, asked if *The Times* had "any business connections of any character in England." Mr. Miller said that it had none aside from maintaining its own correspondents there. Then Senator Walsh wanted to know if Mr. Ochs had "any financial support of any kind in England." Mr. Miller said that he had none whatever, whereupon Senator Walsh explained, rather apologetically, "I asked because I was informed that that was the case."

Mr. Miller's denial was made still more emphatic by an editorial next day, on March 17, which contained this statement:

> That there may be no cause to believe that Mr. Miller's answer to the impertinent inquiry about Mr. Ochs's private affairs does not fully and satisfactorily end the inquiry, Mr. Ochs wishes to make the asser-

> tion as broad and sweeping as language will permit that he is in possession, free and unincumbered, of the controlling and majority interest of the stock of The New York Times Company, and has no associate in that possession, and is not beholden or accountable to any person or interest in England or anywhere else in the world, nor has he ever been beholden or accountable in any form, shape or fashion, financial or otherwise, for the conduct of *The New York Times*, except to his own conscience and to the respect and confidence of the newspaper-reading public, and particularly the readers of *The New York Times* — and more particularly to the respect and confidence of those who are associated with him in producing *The New York Times* and expressing its opinions.

The conductors of *The Times* could say no more on the question of English ownership, but they still had something to say about Senator Thomas J. Walsh, who "had been informed that that was the case." Who had informed him? *The Times* asked this question, rather insistently, and bit by bit the truth came out. Just before that session of the committee opened there had come a letter, addressed to "The Hon. Chairman," signed by a name which Senator Walsh read as "Arthur M. Abbey." The writer said that he had just come back from England, where he had heard at the Junior Constitutional Club in London that "a well-known Englishman has been backing Mr. Ochs with money to get control of *The New York Times*," and that "I understand that Mr. Miller is also mixed up in some

way with this Englishman." So that nobody would go astray, the writer added, "the name of Lord Northcliffe was mentioned," and he threw in for good measure that "Mr. Ochs has also been mixed up in the English Marconi scandal."

The Times again denied each and every one of these charges and asked for more information about "Arthur M. Abbey." Who was he? What did Senator Walsh know about him, that he regarded his communication as sufficiently important to spread on the record of a Senate committee the suggestion that *The Times* was controlled by foreigners? At the Junior Constitutional Club in London he was unknown; and it presently appeared that he was equally unknown to Senator Walsh. The Senator finally sent *The Times* the original letter, and in the office the handwriting and style were soon recognized as identical with those of a whole series of scurrilous letters which had been coming regularly to *The Times* office from New York — and not from London. Of the hardly legible signatures to these letters some seemed to resemble "G. M. Hubbell" and others "A. M. Abbey"; some of the letters were not signed at all. But they were all abusive, all plainly the work of one writer, and all the work of the same man who had informed Senator Walsh that "such was the case."

No doubt this spreading of the facts upon the record did something to weaken the legend of British ownership of *The Times*. This fiction continued to be one of the staples of German, Irish and Socialist argument; but it is significant that the next attack made on *The Times* from a source pretending to

reputability, more than five years later, began with the rejection of all suspicion of outside influence and developed the entertaining theory that the editors of *The Times* were simply constitutionally incapable of understanding the truth. It was admitted that they, like all men, needs must love the highest when they see it, but it was argued that they were pretty poor judges of altitude. Perhaps not all enemies of the paper are so generous, but belief in the Northcliffe ownership has in general been confined, in recent years, to circles where it is still asserted that President Wilson was owned by Wall Street and that Germany fought a defensive war.

However, the chief importance of this incident does not lie in its bearing on the reputation of *The Times*. As was said in the paper's editorial columns at the time:

> This is not a personal issue. It is a question of the extent to which a government's machinery may be privately misused to annoy and attempt to discredit a newspaper whose editorial attitude has become distasteful and embarrassing.

And it was in the name, not of *The Times*, but of the whole American press — a press which for nearly two centuries had been free from governmental control — that Mr. Miller, at the close of his interrogation by the committee on *The Times's* editorial attitude toward every subject of public interest, addressed some remarks to the committee:

> I can see no ethical, moral or legal right [he said] that you have to put many of the questions you put to me today. Inquisi-

> torial proceedings of this kind would have a very marked tendency, if continued and adopted as a policy, to reduce the press of the United States to the level of the press in some of the Central European empires, the press that has been known as the reptile press, that crawls on its belly every day to the Foreign Office or to the Government officials and Ministers to know what it may say or shall say — to receive its orders.

Questions of that kind, he said, "tend to repress freedom of utterance and to put newspapers under a sort of duress." Nor was it to be supposed that newspapers would be free from all restraint if a Senatorial committee did not now and then turn aside to give publicity to the commonplaces of German propaganda. "We appear before the jury every day," said Mr. Miller.

> We appear before the grand inquisition, one of the largest courts in history; we are judged at the breakfast table. We feel that, if we were improperly influenced by anybody outside of the office, there is none so quick to discover that as the reader of the paper.

That *The Times*, in this case, was fighting for the freedom of the entire American press was pretty generally recognized. There was much editorial comment on Mr. Miller's statement and on the committee's procedure. *The World* called the questions "a public inquisition without an open arraignment"; *The Baltimore American* said that the hearing was "the most extraordinary exhibition of bad judgment, peevishness or evil motives the country has had from a Senate committee for years."

Bad judgment and peevishness, no doubt, had more to do with it than evil motives. For more than a year thereafter Congress, a timorous body at best, was extraordinarily sensitive to the compulsions of bought-and-paid-for German propaganda, as witness the Gore and McLemore resolutions. Only very slowly, in response to the obvious feeling of the country, and under the leadership of a few men of patriotism and courage, did Congress gradually recover the hardihood to call its soul its own. The chief criticism against this particular committee is that it was willing to believe, and to give currency to, anything it heard from anybody, anonymous or otherwise.

No doubt the Senators took a certain very human joy in getting newspaper editors up before them and putting them through a third degree; no doubt they felt entirely justified by the argument that newspaper editors often criticise Senators. But no newspaper ever accused a Senator of selling his soul to foreigners, on no better evidence than an anonymous letter.

From the sinking of the *Lusitania* the war became a domestic issue. On that issue *The Times* consistently supported President Wilson. The election of 1916 proved that the President had judged public sentiment pretty well. There will always be room for argument as to how the country would have responded if the *Lusitania* issue had led to war in the spring of 1915. But it should be remembered that the President's middle-of-the-road policy was being assailed from two sides, as too pusillanimous and as

too aggressive. *The Times* stood with the President against those who for one reason or another thought that the *Lusitania* incident ought to be passed over in silence, in the full confidence that he would not be unduly precipitate, but would not yield on essential issues of American rights.

It was theopinion of *The Times* that in the spring of 1915 the American public, as a whole, was not ready to fight over the *Lusitania.* Whatever may have been the effect of the German arguments based on the fact that the ship carried some ammunition in her cargo, and that the passengers had been warned, it was not believed by the conductors of *The Times* that the mass of the people, particularly in the West and in the rural districts, had as yet sufficiently appreciated the fundamental issues of the war to make them willing to fight Germany. It was doubted if Congress could be persuaded to declare war, and, even if it could have been, the conductors of *The Times* felt that the division of public sentiment, and the evidently lukewarm feeling of a good part of the public, would have given much aid and comfort to the enemy. Besides, America was notably unprepared for war in the spring of 1915. By 1917 great war industries had been built up, and two years of prosperity had given the nation financial and industrial strength which made its intervention decisive. These conditions were not present when the *Lusitania* was sunk, and *The Times* felt that the President should be supported in his efforts to preserve peace, so long as that was honorably possible.

It took nearly two years more of the demonstra-

tion of German methods to convince the majority that America could not honorably and safely keep out of the war. Through those years *The Times* supported the President, holding, as he did, that there must be, after the war, some sort of world organization which should, in so far as possible, prevent this thing from happening again. *The Times* had opinions far more decided than the President's on the need for a righteous settlement of this war as a foundation for any durable peace, and by 1917 the President had got around to this view. The little evidence available suggests that the editors of *The Times* had perhaps a more logical interpretation of the President's position in 1915 and 1916 than he had himself; but from 1917 on, at any rate, there was rarely occasion for disagreement. Perhaps one exception should be made to this. In the winter of 1917-18 *The Times*, though it did not exactly support Senator Chamberlain against the President, supported the substance of Chamberlain's views that more energy was needed in the executive departments if the war was to be won.

The Times realized, however, what a good many even of the friendly critics of the Wilson administration forgot in those days, that public officials are human beings and have to be accepted more or less as they are, failings and all. Its editors believed not only that President Wilson was a trustworthy and able leader, but that he was on the whole more trustworthy and more able than any other man in sight. Above all, he was President, he was the head of the State, the nation's leader; and in war times it is the duty of every citizen to support the leader.

"All the News That's Fit to Print."

The New York Times.

THE WEATHER
Fair, colder today; tomorrow warmer, probably rain; wind northwest.
For full weather report see Page 23.

VOL. LXVI...NO. 21,619. NEW YORK, TUESDAY, APRIL 3, 1917.—TWENTY-FOUR PAGES. ONE CENT In New York City. | TWO CENTS New England and Middle States. | THREE CENTS Elsewhere.

PRESIDENT CALLS FOR WAR DECLARATION, STRONGER NAVY, NEW ARMY OF 500,000 MEN, FULL CO-OPERATION WITH GERMANY'S FOES

ARMED AMERICAN STEAMSHIP SUNK; 11 MEN MISSING

The Aztec Is First Gun-Bearing Vessel Under Our Flag to be Torpedoed.

SURPRISE ATTACK AT NIGHT

12 Navy Men and Their Chief Among 17 Survivors Picked Up by a Patrol.

11 IN A LIFEBOAT THAT SANK

Liner St. Paul, with Cannon, Reaches British Port in Safety—Had 61 Passengers.

PARIS, April 2.—The American steamer Aztec has been sunk by a submarine near an island off Brest. Some of the crew were rescued and are being brought into Brest. A number of the men are missing, and little hope is held that they can be saved, as the steamer was torpedoed at night while a heavy sea was running.

[illegible] picked up nineteen

Text of the President's Address

Gentlemen of the Congress:

I have called the Congress into extraordinary session because there are serious, very serious, choices of policy to be made, and made immediately, which it was neither right nor constitutionally permissible that I should assume the responsibility of making.

On the 3d of February last I officially laid before you the extraordinary announcement of the Imperial German Government that on and after the first day of February it was its purpose to put aside all restraints of law or of humanity and use its submarines to sink every vessel that sought to approach either the ports of Great Britain and Ireland or the western coasts of Europe or any of the ports controlled by the enemies of Germany within the Mediterranean. That had seemed to be the object of the German submarine warfare earlier in the war, but since April of last year the Imperial Government had somewhat restrained the commanders of its undersea craft, in conformity with its promise, then given to us, that passenger boats should not be sunk and that due warning would be given to all other vessels which its submarines might seek to destroy, when no resistance was offered or escape attempted, and care taken that their crews were given at least a fair chance to save their lives in their open boats. The precautions taken were meagre and haphazard enough, as was proved in distressing instance after instance in the progress of the cruel and unmanly business, but a certain degree of restraint was observed.

The new policy has swept every restriction aside. Vessels of every kind, whatever their flag, their character, their cargo, their destination, their errand,

[illegible]

submarines are in effect outlaws, when used as the German submarines have been used against merchant shipping, it is impossible to defend ships against their attacks as the law of nations has assumed that merchantmen would defend themselves against privateers or cruisers, visible craft giving chase upon the open sea. It is common prudence in such circumstances, grim necessity indeed, to endeavor to destroy them before they have shown their own intention. They must be dealt with upon sight, if dealt with at all.

The German Government denies the right of neutrals to use arms at all within the areas of the sea which it has proscribed, even in the defense of rights which no modern publicist has ever before questioned their right to defend. The intimation is conveyed that the armed guards which we have placed on our merchant ships will be treated as beyond the pale of law and subject to be dealt with as pirates would be. Armed neutrality is ineffectual enough at best; in such circumstances and in the face of such pretensions it is worse than ineffectual; it is likely only to produce what it was meant to prevent; it is practically certain to draw us into the war without either the rights or the effectiveness of belligerents. There is one choice we cannot make, we are incapable of making; we will not choose the path of submission and suffer the most sacred rights of our nation and our people to be ignored or violated. The wrongs against which we now array ourselves are no common wrongs; they cut to the very roots of human life.

With a profound sense of the solemn and even tragical character of the step I am taking and of the grave responsibilities which it involves, but in unhesitating obedience to what I deem my constitutional duty, I advise that the Congress declare the recent course of the Imperial German Government to be in fact nothing less than war against the Government and people of the United States; that it formally accept the status of belligerent which has thus been thrust upon it; and that it take immediate steps not

[illegible]

the 26th of February. Our object now, as then, is to vindicate the principles of peace and justice in the life of the world as against selfish and autocratic power, and to set up among the really free and self-governed peoples of the world such a concert of purpose and of action as will henceforth insure the observance of those principles.

Neutrality is no longer feasible or desirable where the peace of the world is involved and the freedom of its peoples, and the menace to that peace and freedom lies in the existence of autocratic Governments, backed by organized force which is controlled wholly by their will, not by the will of their people. We have seen the last of neutrality in such circumstances. We are at the beginning of an age in which it will be insisted that the same standards of conduct and of responsibility for wrong done shall be observed among nations and their Governments that are observed among the individual citizens of civilized States.

We have no quarrel with the German people. We have no feeling toward them but one of sympathy and friendship. It was not upon their impulse that their Government acted in entering this war. It was not with their previous knowledge or approval. It was a war determined upon as wars used to be determined upon in the old, unhappy days, when peoples were nowhere consulted by their rulers and wars were provoked and waged in the interest of dynasties or of little groups of ambitious men who were accustomed to use their fellow men as pawns and tools.

Self-governed nations do not fill their neighbor States with spies or set the course of intrigue to bring about some critical posture of affairs which will give them an opportunity to strike and make conquest. Such designs can be successfully worked out only under cover and where no one has the right to ask questions. Cunningly contrived plans of deception or aggression, carried, it may be, from generation to generation, can be worked out and kept from

[illegible]

because we know that in such a Government, following such methods, we can never have a friend; and that in the presence of its organized power, always lying in wait to accomplish we know not what purpose, can be no assured security for the democratic Governments of the world. We are now about to accept the gauge of battle with this natural foe to liberty and shall, if necessary, spend the whole force of the nation to check and nullify its pretensions and its power. We are glad, now that we see the facts with no veil of false pretense about them, to fight thus for the ultimate peace of the world and for the liberation of its peoples, the German peoples included; for the rights of nations, great and small, and the privilege of men everywhere to choose their way of life and of obedience.

The world must be made safe for democracy. Its peace must be planted upon the tested foundations of political liberty. We have no selfish ends to serve. We desire no conquest, no dominion. We seek no indemnities for ourselves, no material compensation for the sacrifices we shall freely make. We are but one of the champions of the rights of mankind. We shall be satisfied when those rights have been made as secure as the faith and the freedom of nations can make them.

Just because we fight without rancor and without selfish object, seeking nothing for ourselves but what we shall wish to share with all free peoples, we shall, I feel confident, conduct our operations as belligerents without passion and ourselves observe with proud punctilio the principles of right and of fair play we profess to be fighting for.

I have said nothing of the Governments allied with the Imperial Government of Germany because they have not made war upon us or challenged us to defend our right and our honor. The Austro-Hungarian Government has, indeed, avowed its unqualified indorsement and acceptance of the reckless and lawless submarine warfare, adopted now without disguise by the Imperial German Government, and it has

MUST EXERT ALL OUR POWER

To Bring a "Government That Is Running Amuck to Terms."

WANTS LIBERAL CREDITS

And Universal Service, for "the World Must Be Made Safe for Democracy."

A TUMULTUOUS GREETING

Congress Adjourns After "State of War" Resolution Is Introduced—Acts Today.

Special to The New York Times.

WASHINGTON, April 2.—At 8:35 o'clock tonight the United States virtually made its entrance into the war. At that hour President Wilson appeared before a joint session of the Senate and House and invited it to consider the fact that Germany had been making war upon us and to take action in recognition of that fact in accordance with his recommendations, which included universal military service, the raising of an army of 500,000 men, and co-ope[illegible]

depositions of survivors of the disaster

Bluejackets and Officer Saved.

WASHINGTON, April 2.—French Admiralty dispatches to the French Embassy here tonight announcing the sinking without warning of the first Armed American merchantman, the freighter Aztec, by a German submarine, said apparently Lieutenant W. F. Gresham and twelve American bluejackets, constituting the armed guard of the vessel, had been saved, but that eleven of the crew were reported missing.

The Admiralty report said the Aztec, bound from New York to Havre, was torpedoed without warning yesterday off Ouessant. The torpedo struck squarely amidships, emitting a powerful gas and putting the wireless out of commission. The guard with the Captain and three other members of the crew in the second boat to put off apparently were picked up by the French patrol boat Sirrius after three hours. Eleven men are thought to have been drowned when the first boat to put off was smashed.

The third boat, containing the second officer and eighteen men, is not directly accounted for, but the fact that only eleven are reported missing leads to the belief that it must have been picked up.

The Navy Department tonight gave out the names of the navy members on the Aztec as follows:

Officer in charge—Lieutenant William F. Gresham of Tennessee.

Crew—John I. Eopolucci, boatswain's mate; mother, Annie M. Eopolucci, 649 I Street, Southeast, Washington.

Jacob J. Hilfiker, electrician; father, Jake Hilfiker, 2,208 Preston Street, Baltimore, Md.

Thomas E. Dillon, Quartermaster; father, Thomas I. Dillon, 78 Boyd Avenue, Jersey City, N. J.

William H. Douglas, coxswain; mother, Sarah D. Douglas, 1,4[illegible] South Second Street, Terre Haute, Ind.

Adolph Hendrickson, coxswain; father, Charles Hendrickson, 3,034 Eleventh Avenue, Minneapolis, Minn.

Samuel Earl Israel, seaman; mother, Annie Israel, Kellerman, Ala.

Clarence H. Kelley, Quartermaster; mother, Margaret Kelley, 454 South Broad Street, Trenton, N. J.

Joseph Klewinsky, seaman; father, John Klewinsky, Rural Free Delivery, Route 3, Box 40, Newburg, W. Va.

William F. Rominger, gunner's mate; brother, Donnie Rominger, Elizabethton, Tenn.

Joseph A. Rucker, seaman; guardian, Joseph W. Rucker, Roanoke, Ala.

Clarence W. Whitney, Quartermaster; father, James H. Whitney, Front and Broadway, Cincinnati, Ohio.

All the naval crew were taken from the United States dispatch boat Dolphin at Washington to be placed on the Aztec.

Officials tonight said the disaster would not affect the policy of arming ships, which would be continued in the most efficient manner possible.

First Armed American Ship Sunk.

The American steamship Aztec, the third armed merchant vessel to sail from

Continued on Page 24.

by unmistakable marks of identity, have been sunk with the same reckless lack of compassion or of principle.

I was for a little while unable to believe that such things would in fact be done by any Government that had hitherto subscribed to humane practices of civilized nations. International law had its origin in the attempt to set up some law which would be respected and observed upon the seas, where no nation has right of dominion and where lay the free highways of the world. By painful stage after stage has that law been built up, with meagre enough results, indeed, after all was accomplished that could be accomplished, but always with a clear view, at least, of what the heart and conscience of mankind demanded.

This minimum of right the German Government has swept aside, under the plea of retaliation and necessity and because it had no weapons which it could use at sea except these, which it is impossible to employ, as it is employing them, without throwing to the wind all scruples of humanity or of respect for the understandings that were supposed to underlie the intercourse of the world.

I am not now thinking of the loss of property involved, immense and serious as that is, but only of the wanton and wholesale destruction of the lives of noncombatants, men, women, and children, engaged in pursuits which have always, even in the darkest periods of modern history, been deemed innocent and legitimate. Property can be paid for; the lives of peaceful and innocent people cannot be. The present German submarine warfare against commerce is a warfare against mankind.

It is a war against all nations. American ships have been sunk, American lives taken, in ways which it has stirred us very deeply to learn of, but the ships and people of other neutral and friendly nations have been sunk and overwhelmed in the waters in the same way. There has been no discrimination.

The challenge is to all mankind. Each nation must decide for itself how it will meet it. The choice we make for ourselves must be made with a moderation of counsel and a temperateness of judgment befitting our character and our motives as a nation. We must put excited feeling away. Our motive will not be revenge or the victorious assertion of the physical might of the nation, but only the vindication of right, of human right, of which we are only a single champion.

When I addressed the Congress on the 26th of February last I thought that it would suffice to assert our neutral rights with arms, our right to use the seas against unlawful interference, our right to keep our people safe against unlawful violence. But armed neutrality, it now appears, is impracticable. Because

order that our resources may so far as possible be added to theirs.

It will involve the organization and mobilization of all the material resources of the country to supply the materials of war and serve the incidental needs of the nation in the most abundant and yet the most economical and efficient way possible.

It will involve the immediate full equipment of the navy in all respects, but particularly in supplying it with the best means of dealing with the enemy's submarines.

It will involve the immediate addition to the armed forces of the United States, already provided for by law in case of war, of at least 500,000 men, who should, in my opinion, be chosen upon the principle of universal liability to service, and also the authorization of subsequent additional increments of equal force so soon as they may be needed and can be handled in training.

It will involve also, of course, the granting of adequate credits to the Government, sustained, I hope, so far as they can equitably be sustained by the present generation, by well conceived taxation.

I say sustained so far as may be equitable by taxation, because it seems to me that it would be most unwise to base the credits, which will now be necessary, entirely on money borrowed. It is our duty, I most respectfully urge, to protect our people, so far as we may, against the very serious hardships and evils which would be likely to arise out of the inflation which would be produced by vast loans.

In carrying out the measures by which these things are to be accomplished we should keep constantly in mind the wisdom of interfering as little as possible in our own preparation and in the equipment of our own military forces with the duty—for it will be a very practical duty—of supplying the nations already at war with Germany with the materials which they can obtain only from us or by our assistance. They are in the field and we should help them in every way to be effective there.

I shall take the liberty of suggesting, through the several executive departments of the Government, for the consideration of your committees, measures for the accomplishment of the several objects I have mentioned. I hope that it will be your pleasure to deal with them as having been framed after very careful thought by the branch of the Government upon whom the responsibility of conducting the war and safeguarding the nation will most directly fall.

While we do these things, these deeply momentous things, let us be very clear, and make very clear to all the world, what our motives and our objects are. My own thought has not been driven from its habitual and normal course by the unhappy events of the last two months, and I do not believe that the thought of the nation had been altered or clouded by them. I have exactly the same things in mind now that I had in mind when I addressed the Senate on the 22d of January last; the same that I had in mind when I addressed the Congress on the 3d of February and on

faith within it or observe its covenants. It must be a league of honor, a partnership of opinion. Intrigue would eat its vitals away; the plottings of inner circles who could plan what they would and render account to no one would be a corruption seated at its very heart. Only free peoples can hold their purpose and their honor steady to a common end and prefer the interests of mankind to any narrow interest of their own.

Does not every American feel that assurance has been added to our hope for the future peace of the world by the wonderful and heartening things that have been happening within the last few weeks in Russia? Russia was known by those who knew her best to have been always in fact democratic at heart in all the vital habits of her thought, in all the intimate relationships of her people that spoke their natural instinct, their habitual attitude toward life. The autocracy that crowned the summit of her political structure, long as it had stood and terrible as was the reality of its power, was not in fact Russian in origin, character, or purpose; and now it has been shaken off and the great, generous Russian people have been added, in all their naive majesty and might, to the forces that are fighting for freedom in the world, for justice, and for peace. Here is a fit partner for a League of Honor.

One of the things that has served to convince us that the Prussian autocracy was not and could never be our friend is that from the very outset of the present war it has filled our unsuspecting communities, and even our offices of government, with spies and set criminal intrigues everywhere afoot against our national unity of counsel, our peace within and without, our industries and our commerce. Indeed, it is now evident that its spies were here even before the war began; and it is unhappily not a matter of conjecture, but a fact proved in our courts of justice, that the intrigues which have more than once come perilously near to disturbing the peace and dislocating the industries of the country, have been carried on at the instigation, with the support, and even under the personal direction of official agents of the Imperial Government, accredited to the Government of the United States.

Even in checking these things and trying to extirpate them we have sought to put the most generous interpretation possible upon them because we knew that their source lay, not in any hostile feeling or purpose of the German people toward us, (who were, no doubt, as ignorant of them as we ourselves were,) but only in the selfish designs of a Government that did what it pleased and told its people nothing. But they have played their part in serving to convince us at last that that Government entertains no real friendship for us, and means to act against our peace and security at its convenience. That it means to stir up enemies against us at our very doors the intercepted note to the German Minister at Mexico City is eloquent evidence.

We are accepting this challenge of hostile purpose

take the liberty, for the present at least, of postponing a discussion of our relations with the authorities at Vienna. We enter this war only where we are clearly forced into it because there are no other means of defending our right.

It will be all the easier for us to conduct ourselves as belligerents in a high spirit of right and fairness because we act without animus, not with enmity toward a people or with the desire to bring any injury or disadvantage upon them, but only in armed opposition to an irresponsible Government which has thrown aside all considerations of humanity and of right and is running amuck.

We are, let me say again, the sincere friends of the German people, and shall desire nothing so much as the early re-establishment of intimate relations of mutual advantage between us, however hard it may be for them for the time being to believe that this is spoken from our hearts. We have borne with their present Government through all these bitter months because of that friendship, exercising a patience and forbearance which would otherwise have been impossible.

We shall happily still have an opportunity to prove that friendship in our daily attitude and actions toward the millions of men and women of German birth and native sympathy who live among us and share our life, and we shall be proud to prove it toward all who are in fact loyal to their neighbors and to the Government in the hour of test. They are most of them as true and loyal Americans as if they had never known any other fealty or allegiance. They will be prompt to stand with us in rebuking and restraining the few who may be of a different mind and purpose. If there should be disloyalty, it will be dealt with with a firm hand of stern repression; but, if it lifts its head at all, it will lift it only here and there and without countenance except from a lawless and malignant few.

It is a distressing and oppressive duty, gentlemen of the Congress, which I have performed in thus addressing you. There are, it may be, many months of fiery trial and sacrifice ahead of us. It is a fearful thing to lead this great, peaceful people into war, into the most terrible and disastrous of all wars, civilization itself seeming to be in the balance.

But the right is more precious than peace, and we shall fight for the things which we have always carried nearest our hearts—for democracy, for the right of those who submit to authority to have a voice in their own Governments, for the rights and liberties of small nations, for a universal dominion of right by such a concert of free peoples as shall bring peace and safety to all nations and make the world itself at last free.

To such a task we can dedicate our lives and our fortunes, everything that we are and everything that we have, with the pride of those who know that the day has come when America is privileged to spend her blood and her might for the principles that gave her birth and happiness and the peace which she has treasured.

God helping her, she can do no other.

The War Resolution Now Before Congress

This resolution was introduced in the House of Representatives last night by Representative Flood, Chairman of the Foreign Affairs Committee, immediately after the President's address:

JOINT RESOLUTION, Declaring that a State of War Exists Between the Imperial German Government and the Government and People of the United States and Making Provision to Prosecute the Same.

Whereas, The recent acts of the Imperial German Government are acts of war against the Government and people of the United States:

Resolved, By the Senate and House of Representatives of the United States of America in Congress assembled, that the state of war between the United States and the Imperial German Government which has thus been thrust upon the United States is hereby formally declared; and

That the President be, and he is hereby, authorized and directed to take immediate steps not only to put the country in a thorough state of defense but also to exert all of its power and employ all of its resources to carry on war against the Imperial German Government and to bring the conflict to a successful termination.

Representative Flood and Senator Martin, both of the President's birth-State, Virginia, and they are the strongest declarations of war that the United States has ever made in any war in which it has been engaged since it became a nation. They are the Administration resolutions drawn up after conference with the President, and in language approved and probably dictated by him, and they will come before the two Foreign Affairs Committees at meetings which will be held tomorrow morning and will be reported at the earliest practical moment.

Unreservedly With the Allies.

Before an audience that cheered him as he has never been cheered in the Capitol in his life the President cast in the lot of America unreservedly with the Allies and declared for a war that must not end until the issue between autocracy and democracy has been fought out. He recited our injuries at Germany's hands; but he did not rest our cause on those; he went on from that point to range us with the Allies as a factor in an irrepressible conflict between the autocrat and the people. He showed that peace was impossible for the democracies of the world while this power remained on earth. "The world," he said, "must be made safe for democracy."

We had learned that the German autocracy could never be a friend of this country; she had been our enemy while nominally our friend, and even before the war of 1914 broke out. He called on us to take our stand with the democracies in this irrepressible conflict, with before our eyes "the wonderful and heartening events that have been happening in the last few weeks in Russia." He reaffirmed his hope for peace and for freedom, and looked to the war now forced upon us to bring these about; for, he said, a world compact for peace "can never be maintained except by a concert of the democracies of the

The objects for which we said, are democracy, the righ[...] who submit to authority to h[...] in their own government, th[...] liberties of small nations, [...] sal dominion of right, the [...] free peoples to bring peace [...] to all nations, and to make [...] free. These have always [...] ideals, and to accomplish ther[...] cept the war Germany has m[...] us. In fighting it we must r[...] raise an army and increase the [...] but must aid the Allies in all [...] financial and other, and so order [...] own preparations as not to inter[...] with the supply of munitions they [...] getting from us.

Trouble-making Pacifists Barred.

The President delivered this speech before an audience that had been carefully sifted. All day Washington had been in the hands of belligerent pacifists, truculent in manner, and determined to break into the Capitol. They tried to take possession of the Capitol steps, up which the President must go when he entered, and met the same fate that Coxey's rioters fell in with twenty-three years ago at the hands of the police, who dispersed them.

A handful of them fell upon Senator Lodge and assaulted him. Others en-

[illegible]

The War Resolution Now Before Congress

This resolution was introduced in the House of Representatives last night by Representative [illegible] immediately after the President's address:

JOINT RESOLUTION Declaring that a State of War Exists Between the Imperial German Government and the Government and People of the United States and Making Provision to Prosecute the Same.

Whereas, The recent acts of the Imperial German Government are acts of war against the Government and people of the United States;

Resolved, By the Senate and House of Representatives of the United States of America in Congress assembled, That the state of war between the United States and the Imperial German Government which has thus been thrust upon the United States is hereby formally declared; and

That the President be, and he is hereby, authorized and directed to take immediate steps not only to put the country in a thorough state of defense but also to exert all of its power and employ all of its resources to carry on war against the Imperial German Government and to bring the conflict to a successful termination.

[illegible]

Mr. Wilson had a way of doing more seasonably, better and more efficiently than they ever dreamed of, the things his critics blamed him savagely for not doing. His injustice to Chamberlain in the beginning of 1918, like his desertion of Garrison in the beginning of 1916, might create a very bad impression; but it did not prove that in the long run either Chamberlain or Garrison could have done better than Wilson, even had they been in a position to try.

During 1918 *The Times* editorial page, continuing its general policies on the war and support of the administration, opened up one or two special lines of discussion. It gave rather more room than other papers to consideration of the political readjustments in Europe that might be expected to follow the end of the war, and to presentation of the claims and possibilities of the various nationalistic revolutionary movements. It took, too, the most prominent place in denunciation of the behavior of the Russian Bolsheviki. It is sometimes forgotten that the Bolshevist revolution in Russia first affected the world as a phase of the war. Western Europe and America might have afforded to stand off and watch the Bolsheviki reconstruct society, if they had not begun by destroying the eastern front and releasing hundreds of thousands of German troops for service in France, and if they had not at once begun to talk of promoting revolutions in the countries fighting Germany. To be sure, they were going to start a revolution in Germany as well, but Brest-Litovsk showed how little they could or would accomplish against the German military group. In Germany, as in Russia, they began their revolution only after

the imperial power had been broken by a less radical revolution; and in Germany only after the way had been prepared by Foch's armies.

So when *The Times* argued, as it did with vigor and persistence in 1918, for the sending of allied troops to Siberia, it was chiefly in the hope that they might get through to reëstablish an eastern front. For Bolshevism as a political and economic gospel *The Times* had no use, but it regarded this aspect of the movement as less important than Bolshevism as a practical factor in a war whose decision was still in doubt.

Toward the end of the war occurred an incident which brought *The Times* more criticism, probably than anything else in its history — the publication on September 16, 1918, of an editorial favoring the consideration of the Austrian proposal for a "preliminary and non-binding" discussion of peace terms. The opinion which found expression in this article was first, that the Austrian proposal meant the beginning of the end — which was true; and second, that it was worth considering, on the theory that when conferences had begun the enemy would rapidly give way to complete surrender. Whether that would or would not have happened is, of course, a question to which there can be no answer. If the shiftiness of the Germans in their subsequent negotiations with Mr. Wilson suggests that this preliminary conference might have given opportunity for a good deal of intrigue, it is true on the other hand that the rapid caving in of the German morale in the fall of 1918 might have led to exactly the same

result as did occur. It was not generally foreseen in the middle of September that the war would be over in less than two months; but the editor of *The Times* had become convinced from his study of the German press, and the other sources of information available, that Germany was on the verge of collapse, and was confident that if peace delegates once met, the people of the Central Powers would insist on peace at any price. In the Austrian proposal he recognized evidence that Austria and Germany were exhausted and would soon be ready to surrender on any terms at all. And *The Times* declared that the Allies must insist on such peace terms as were finally imposed on Germany at Versailles. It was convinced that if negotiations began Germany would soon be forced to accept whatever terms the Allies might lay down.

That may have been a mistake, but it was at least a tenable view. It was, unfortunately, a somewhat too long-sighted view for the popular mind in the tenseness of the time, when everybody's blood was at fever heat and there was general apprehension that peace negotiation might lose the fruit of victory. The deviousness of German diplomacy was well known, and the exhaustion of German endurance was not generally understood. Perhaps some of the phrases in the editorial were chiefly responsible for the unfavorable criticism, phrases expressing a feeling such as everybody exhibited a few weeks later on armistice day. If the editor of *The Times* gave premature expression to that feeling, it was because he saw further ahead than most people and knew that this appeal meant that peace was near.

It must be added that the wide discussion of this editorial, and the unfavorable reaction to it, was in considerable part the work of other New York newspapers, who talked of "*The Times's* white flag" and even ventured on some insinuations about "Austrian gold," against the paper which every German propagandist for four years past had been accusing of subserviency to British gold.

No doubt these competitors of *The Times* were inspired in part by vigilant patriotism, but other motives may have had something to do with their agitation. *The Times* had been making enormous gains in circulation. It was within a very few thousands of the largest circulation in New York, and it had already distanced all the other morning papers. *The Herald* — then, of course, a different paper and under different ownership than at present — undertook a great circulation campaign to win over *Times* readers under such slogans as "Read an American Paper." As had happened fifty-two years before, when Raymond took the unpopular step of advocating conciliation of the beaten South, *The Times's* spotless record for loyalty during the war was ignored by journals which had found it a dangerously successful business rival. But this loyalty, and the leadership in news and opinion which *The Times* had won, was not forgotten by the public. The circulation of the paper was not affected, the clamor soon died away, and the assaults of jealous and failing competitors were as futile as they were groundless.

At the outbreak of the war the military authorities of all the nations engaged had the idea, correct

enough from a purely military viewpoint, that the newspapers and the public need know nothing about what was going on until it was all over. The success of the Japanese in keeping war correspondents out of the way in Manchuria had shown other army officers what could be done, and the strategic advantage that was to be derived from doing it. Some months passed before it began to be apparent to the various governments, and in time even to the military commanders, that every nation wanted to know what was going on, and would fight better if it knew. In the early months the task of news getting was hard enough, and the news that was obtained was mostly official and open to considerable suspicion.

Eventually, of course, all this was changed. Before the end of the war the correspondent had become a personage universally respected — if not, like MacGahan and Forbes and Russell and the men of their day, respected because he was more important than the war he was covering, at any rate respected and treated with some deference because Ministers and Generals knew that the public wanted to know what was happening and that this man was going to tell it.

The New York Times at the outbreak of the war was getting its war news from *The London Daily Chronicle*, and from its own correspondents in London and Paris. It was unable to get the other side of the case from its own correspondent in Berlin, for the German Government had locked up and then expelled this gentleman on the ground that, though an American citizen, he was correspondent not only

for *The Times* but for *The London Daily Mail*, and consequently might be engaged in espionage. But the war was only a few weeks old when *The Times* got another correspondent into Germany, a correspondent who through school and family acquaintances had unusual facility of access to German military circles, and who, during 1914, 1915 and 1916, succeeded in presenting probably the best picture given in the American press of the operations of the German Army on all fronts. This correspondent was Cyril Brown, at present *The Times* correspondent in Berlin, who almost at the beginning of his career in Germany managed, partly by his own ingenuity and partly by the assistance of a trainman whom he had met while covering a strike in Jersey City some years before, to get to German Great Headquarters at Mezières-Charleville and send to *The Times* the first account anywhere published of the scenes there. Brown's subsequent operations took him to every German battle front, and in addition, with the assistance of Joseph Herrings, he covered the political news from Berlin.

Other American correspondents in Germany performed a brilliant and useful work in interviewing the leaders of the German Government and sending out to the world their opinions on the progress of the war, though it is to be regretted that some of them eventually came to believe a good deal of what was said to them; but Brown, while doing comparatively little of this sort of thing, outdistanced all other American writers in his reporting of the German Army in action.

Now and then he had assistance, as for example

during Mackensen's Serbian campaign in the fall of 1915, and in the early days of the Verdun offensive, when *The Times* obtained by special arrangement the reports of the staff correspondents of several Berlin dailies in addition to the news gathered by its own men. To make sure that nothing going on in Germany was overlooked, *The Times* sent Garet Garrett in 1915 and Oscar King Davis at the end of 1916 to write special articles on the economic situation and the wearing qualities of German morale.

Besides getting the news out of Germany, *The Times* now and then got some news into Germany — notably in February, 1917, when the German Government had been aroused by rumors that Ambassador Bernstorff was being detained in America after the rupture of diplomatic relations and that all German ships in American ports, and their crews, had been seized. These false reports had inspired the German Government with the idea that Ambassador Gerard and all Americans in Berlin might be detained by way of retaliation. A private message from the managing editor of *The Times* to O. K. Davis, correcting these false impressions, was shown by the correspondent to the German Foreign Office and was chiefly responsible for the release of the Americans in Berlin.

On other fronts, as the war went on, *The Times* was better and better served. Of the numerous and usually able correspondents of *The London Chronicle* the most distinguished was Philip Gibbs, whose dispatches from the British front in the later years of the war were perhaps the most generally popular war correspondence of the period. Gibbs's peculiar

talent happened to meet a very general psychological need of the public in 1917 and 1918; and he was more widely read, and probably on the whole more generally admired, in America than even in England.

Of *The Times's* own correspondents with the allied armies Wythe Williams, head of the Paris office in the early days of the war, wrote a number of excellent stories from the battle-fronts in France and Italy. Edwin L. James, at present Paris correspondent of *The Times*, was the principal correspondent with the American armies in 1918, and supplied thrilling accounts of their achievements. Walter Duranty brilliantly described the successful resistance of the French armies to the German onslaught of 1918. Charles A. Selden sent the political news from Paris in the same year. Charles H. Grasty of the executive staff of the paper, possessing a wide acquaintance among both soldiers and statesmen, wrote a great deal from the British, French and American battle-fronts, though the greater part of his correspondence was political. Of the many others who at various times and from various fronts sent dispatches to *The Times*, perhaps special mention should be given to Georges Le Hir, who wrote from Verdun in the spring of 1916 some of the best battle pictures of the war.

The news from the battle-fronts was constantly supplemented by all kinds of news about the war from the writers, newspapers, and press agencies of every country in Europe presented each morning for what it was worth to the readers of *The Times*. The most important contribution to the assembling of this news was that of the London office, headed

VIEWS OF THE COMPOSING ROOM.

A VIEW OF THE NEWS ROOM OF THE TIMES.

by Ernest Marshall, which without making much parade of its merits acquired an extraordinarily high standard of all-round efficiency. Mention should be made also of Enid Wilkie, correspondent at The Hague, who was responsible for most of the news about what was going on in Germany after America declared war.

The amount of news received by *The Times*, by cable and wireless, from its own correspondents, on a number of days in the latter part of the war surpassed in the total number of words the dispatches of the largest news associations, and often exceeded all the special dispatches to all other American newspapers combined. The handling of this mass of news in the office naturally involved problems unexampled in magnitude if not new in kind, and in the delicate technical question of make-up, the arrangement of news with due consideration of its relative importance, as well as of the appearance of the page on which it is printed, *The Times* in the course of the war developed a general style to which many of its competitors paid the compliment of imitation. It was impossible, in the war period, to get all the big news on the front page, but *The Times* usually got more of it there than other papers, and in an arrangement which was at once pleasing to the eye and calculated to make it easy for the reader to see at once what had happened, as well as to give him some idea of the importance of the various dispatches.

The war make-up involved a considerable development in the art of headline composition. The limitation of the width of the column is one of the

chief technical difficulties in the presentation of news to a public which has learned to look for headlines that tell the story. And even when the head is extended to two or three columns, or seven or eight, the wider room for display does not remove all the difficulties. *The Times* in its headlines tries, and its conductors hope with a fair degree of success, to be fair and accurate; to pack the substance of the story, without prejudice, into the four or five words which may be all of the story that some readers will ever read.

Carr V. Van Anda, the managing editor, was in charge not only of the great organization which was collecting the news all over the world, but of the no less intricate and efficient organization within the office which had the work of arranging and presenting the news. In this latter field he was ably assisted by F. T. Birchall, assistant managing editor. The mechanical department under the very competent supervision of Charles F. Hart successfully responded in those days to a heavy strain and made an important contribution to the success of the paper.

From the day the *Lusitania* was sunk the war was no longer a European question, and thereafter, week in and week out, it pretty steadily dominated the news in every New York paper. Even then, of course, most papers of the interior found it less important than events closer home, and continued to give it rather limited space until America came in. As the war went on more and more of the most intelligent class of readers all over the country found that if they really wanted news about the war they

could find it in greatest volume and most satisfactorily presented in *The Times.*

The first award of the Pulitzer gold medal for "disinterested and meritorious service" by a newspaper was made by the School of Journalism of Columbia University to *The New York Times* in June, 1918, "for publishing in full so many official reports, documents, and speeches by European statesmen relating to the progress and conduct of the war." The editors of *The Times* believed that their circulation contained an unusually high proportion of readers who were willing to give the time to reading long speeches and long documents, not necessarily because they had superfluous time on their hands, but because they realized that in a war of this kind full understanding required careful study, and that study of the evidence was the most important business of any intelligent man. The editors thought, too, that *The Times* more than any other paper was read by people who were capable of forming their own opinions from study of the original evidence in full, and who would rather have every word available for their own study than accept a summary made by somebody else.

An illustration of the methods of *The Times* in getting together these documents from the most widely scattered sources may be found in the history of the publication of Prince Lichnowsky's famous memorandum on German diplomatic methods and the outbreak of the war. Parts of this had been published in various German and Swedish papers, and in The New Europe of London, and

many extracts from these publications had been cabled to the American press. But the document was for the first time printed in full in *The New York Times*, the text having been laboriously assembled from the five or six partial publications in Germany, Sweden and England. Something like this *The Times* was doing constantly during 1918, and by industry and vigilance succeeded in piecing together a good deal of evidence which other publications, both in America and abroad, had been content to accept in fragmentary form.

Every one was calling on his reserves in 1918, from Foch and Ludendorff down to the humblest citizen on the internal front who was setting his teeth and accustoming himself to new privations, and the human race as a whole was probably living more intensely and putting more of its potential abilities into action than ever before. It is perhaps natural, then, that *The Times* was at its best in this last year of the war. Its conductors are not conscious of any particular deterioration since that time, but there was more opportunity for excellence to display itself in the conditions of this last war year.

In the interchange of speeches that made up the most visible though by no means the only phase of the "peace offensives" of the winter of 1917–18 *The Times* had scored again and again by printing the addresses in full, by a make-up and typography which put the news out where the reader could see it and gave him some hints about its relative importance, and in the case of speeches delivered by German or Austrian statesmen very often by getting the news a day earlier than the other papers. The peace of-

fensive broke down and Ludendorff began a new offensive of a different kind on March 21, 1918. In *The Times* office it was recognized on the evening of that day that this was the great and decisive conflict of the war, although elsewhere, and even in London, it was some days before the magnitude and importance of Ludendorff's operations was perceived. From that time on *The Times* was generally a day ahead of the crowd. Every correspondent had been instructed on the evening of March 21 thenceforward to spare no expense or effort to get his news into the office promptly. The result was that day after day *The Times* was the only American paper which had its own dispatches describing the fighting of the day before. The Associated Press news arrived on time, for the Associated Press had, properly enough, received special facilities for getting its news through. Other American papers had special dispatches from their own correspondents, but for two or three months they generally got them and published them a day late. Within a few weeks after March 21 *The Times* was able to announce that since that date it had scored more than one hundred beats, including such items of news as Foch's appointment as generalissimo, the removal of General Gough after the defeat of the British Fifth Army, and Count Czernin's speech against Clemenceau, which had the result of bringing to the light the Austro-French peace negotiations of the previous year.

The official censorships of the various European governments interfered considerably, of course, with

the news dispatches of *The Times*, as they did with those of all other papers. No effort was made to circumvent these censorships, but in one instance the censorship was evaded by a sort of impromptu code, with the result that *The Times* beat all other papers, in America and elsewhere, on two highly important news stories. Under cover of the ostensible discussion by cable of some changes in *The Times's* European staff information was obtained of the decision to supplant Joffre as generalissimo of the French armies, of the consideration of various men for his position and finally of the appointment of Nivelle. A few months later the same formula brought to *The Times* office, again in advance of the official announcement, the news that Nivelle was to be replaced by Pétain.

Like all other newspapers, however, *The Times* tolerated foreign censorships because it had no choice, and not because it liked their methods or admired their results. When America came into the war and the first draft of the Espionage Act contained a provision for an American censorship, *The Times* was one of the most vigorous opponents of any such measure. The experience of European governments had shown that, while censors may occasionally be necessary, they are always stupid, and the likelihood that personal or political considerations would influence a censor in Washington was quite as strong as the certainty that such considerations had already played their part in Europe.

Eventually the clause was deleted from the Espionage Act, and in place of Government regulation came the "voluntary censorship," by which Ameri-

can newspapers refrained from printing news that might be of military advantage to the enemy.

One hundred and eighty-nine members of *The Times* staff, including two women, served in the armed forces of the United States during the war. Of these the following five were killed or died in service:

MAJOR WILLIAM SINKLER MANNING,
of the Washington Bureau;

LIEUTENANT WILLIAM BRADLEY,
of the business office;

SERGEANT JOYCE KILMER,
of the Sunday magazine staff;

PRIVATE HAROLD J. BEHL,
proofreader;

PRIVATE EDWARD B. PIERCE,
of the composing room.

CHAPTER VI

The Times Today

THE end of the war found *The Times* at the height of its influence and power, but the peak of its business prosperity was still to come. In the boom of 1919 and the early months of 1920 *The Times* at last expanded in size from the 24-page issue which had been the limit for the week-day paper up to the end of the war, and often since then has printed 32, 36 or even 40 pages a day. Even so, the volume of advertising offered was so great that day after day much of it had to be refused on account of lack of space. Yet the total printed in 1920 was more than 23,000,000 agate lines — nearly 80,000 columns, and almost ten times the amount printed in the first year of the new management. The greatest volume of advertising ever carried in the paper was on Sunday, May 23, 1920, when *The Times* printed in all 767 columns of advertisements. The paper on that day contained altogether 136 pages, including 24 pages of rotogravure pictorial supplement and 16 pages of tabloid book review. It weighed two pounds and ten ounces, and no doubt it felt like ten pounds and two ounces to the weary householder who picked it off the doorstep; but experience has shown that even in a paper of that size there is nothing that a good many readers do not want.

"All the News That's Fit to Print."

The New York Times.

THE WEATHER
Fair today and Tuesday; diminishing northwest winds.
For weather report see next to last page.

VOL. LXVIII...NO. 22,206. NEW YORK, MONDAY, NOVEMBER 11, 1918. TWENTY-FOUR PAGES. TWO CENTS Metropolitan District 50 Mile Radius | THREE CENTS Within 200 Miles | FOUR CENTS Elsewhere

ARMISTICE SIGNED, END OF THE WAR! BERLIN SEIZED BY REVOLUTIONISTS; NEW CHANCELLOR BEGS FOR ORDER; OUSTED KAISER FLEES TO HOLLAND

SON FLEES WITH EX-KAISER

Hindenburg Also Believed to be Among Those in His Party.

ALL ARE HEAVILY ARMED

Automobiles Bristle with Rifles as Fugitives Arrive at Dutch Frontier.

ON THEIR WAY TO DE STEEG

Belgians Yell to Them, "Are You On Your Way to Paris?"

Kaiser Fought Hindenburg's Call for Abdication; Failed to Get Army's Support in Keeping Throne

By GEORGE RENWICK.

Copyright, 1918, by The New York Times.
Special Cable to The New York Times.

AMSTERDAM, Nov. 10.—I learn on very good authority that the Kaiser made a determined effort to stave off abdication. He went to headquarters with the deliberate intention of bringing the army around to his side. In this he failed miserably.

His main support consisted of a number of officers, nearly all of Prussian regiments, who formed themselves into two regiments and placed themselves at his Majesty's disposal. To do anything with such support was seen, of course, to be Gilbertian.

During the night the Kaiser called the Crown Prince, Hindenburg, and General Gröner to him, and the consultation lasted a couple of hours. Both officers strongly pressed the Kaiser to bow to the inevitable, and Hindenburg informed him that any more delay in coming to a decision to abdicate would certainly have the most terrible consequences and lead to serious events in the army. For those consequences Hindenburg said he must refuse responsibility.

The Crown Prince, it is said, was the first to give way. General Gröner fully supported Hindenburg's view, but when the conference broke up the Kaiser remained unconvinced of the advisability of abdication. He is said to have come to his final decision an hour or so later, after several communications had reached him from Berlin and after another short and stormy talk with Hindenburg.

Meanwhile, his son-in-law, the Duke of Brunswick, for himself and his heir, had abdicated. "Brunswick's Fated Chieftain" was forced without fighting to abdicate. Reports have it that the republican movement in Brunswick, which long before the war was chafing under autocratic conditions, began to be noticed even before it was set in motion at Kiel.

BERLIN TROOPS JOIN REVOLT

Reds Shell Building in Which Officers Vainly Resist.

THRONGS DEMAND REPUBLIC

Revolutionary Flag on Royal Palace—Crown Prince's Palace Also Seized.

GENERAL STRIKE IS BEGUN

Burgomaster and Police Submit—War Office Now Under Socialist Control.

LONDON, Nov. 10. — The

Socialist Chancellor Appeals to All Germans To Help Him Save Fatherland from Anarchy

BERNE, Nov. 10, (Associated Press.)—In an address to the people, the new German Chancellor, Friedrich Ebert, says:

Citizens: The ex-Chancellor, Prince Max of Baden, in agreement with all the Secretaries of State, has handed over to me the task of liquidating his affairs as Chancellor. I am on the point of forming a new Government in accord with the various parties, and will keep public opinion freely informed of the course of events.

The new Government will be a Government of the people. It must make every effort to secure in the quickest possible time peace for the German people and consolidate the liberty which they have won.

The new Government has taken charge of the administration, to preserve the German people from civil war and famine and to accomplish their legitimate claim to autonomy. The Government can solve this problem only if all the officials in town and country will help.

I know it will be difficult for some to work with the new men who have taken charge of the empire, but I appeal to their love of the people. Lack of organization would in this heavy time mean anarchy in Germany and the surrender of the country to tremendous misery. Therefore, help your native country with fearless, indefatigable work for the future, every one at his post.

I demand every one's support in the hard task awaiting us. You know how seriously the war has menaced the provisioning of the people, which is the first condition of the people's existence. The political transformation should not trouble the people. The food supply is the first duty of all, whether in town or country, and they should not embarrass, but rather aid, the production of food supplies and their transport to the towns.

Food shortage signifies pillage and robbery, with great misery. The poorest will suffer the most, and the industrial worker will be affected hardest. All who illicitly lay hands on food supplies or other ... the means of transport necessary for

WAR ENDS AT 6 O'CLOCK THIS MORNING

The State Department in Washington Made the Announcement at 2:45 o'Clock.

ARMISTICE WAS SIGNED IN FRANCE AT MIDNIGHT

Terms Include Withdrawal from Alsace-Lorraine, Disarming and Demobilization of Army and Navy, and Occupation of Strategic Naval and Military Points.

tion is De Steeg, near Utrecht.

The former German Emperor's party, which is believed to include Field Marshal von Hindenburg, arrived at Eysden, [midway between Liége and Maastricht,] on the Dutch frontier, at 7:30 o'clock Sunday morning, according to Daily Mail advices.

Practically the whole German General Staff accompanied the former Emperor, and ten automobiles carried the party. The automobiles were bristling with rifles, and all the fugitives were armed.

The ex-Kaiser was in uniform. He alighted at the Eysden station and paced the platform, smoking a cigarette.

Many photographs were taken by [of?] the members of the Imperial party. On the whole the people were very quiet, but Belgians among them yelled out "En voyage a Paris." (Are you on your way to Paris?)

Chatting with the members of the staff, the former Emperor, the correspondent says, did not look in the least distressed. A few minutes later an imperial train, including restaurant and sleeping cars, ran into the station. Only servants were aboard.

The engine returned to Visé, Belgium, and brought back a second train, in which were a large number of staff officers and others, and also stores of food.

The preparations began for the departure at 10 o'clock this morning, but at 10:40 o'clock the train was still at Eysden. The blinds of the train were all drawn.

The Daily Mail remarks that, if the party arrived in Holland armed, all of them must be interned.

While other dispatches con-

Continued on Page Three.

... Philipp Scheidemann, who was a Socialist member without portfolio in the Imperial Cabinet, was handed to the Emperor. He read it with a shiver. Then he signed the paper, saying:

"It may be for the good of Germany."

The Emperor was deeply moved. He consented to sign the document, only when he got the news of the latest events in the empire.

The ex-Kaiser and former Crown Prince were expected to take leave of their troops on Saturday, but nothing had then been settled regarding their future movements.

GERMAN DYNASTIES BEING WIPED OUT

King of Wuerttemberg Abdicates—Sovereign of Saxony to Follow Suit.

PRINCES MAY BE EXILED

Socialists Are Demanding That Every Sovereign in the Empire Shall be Dethroned.

LONDON, Nov. 10.—A Havas dispatch from Basle says:

"Wilhelm II., the reigning King of the monarchy of Würtemberg, abdicated on Friday night."

A Wolff Bureau dispatch from Stuttgart, by way of Amsterdam, says that the King has issued a proclamation saying that his person would never serve to hinder the development of the wishes of the people.

According to a report received from Berne, the German Socialists are demanding that every dynasty in Germany be suppressed and all the Princes exiled. It is reported that the Kings of Bavaria and Saxony intend to abdicate soon.

Here is a list of the rules, until several days ago, of the various parts of the German Empire. Those who have abdicated and those reported to be on the point of abdication are marked by an asterisk

ANHALT—Duke Edward, son of the late Duke Friedrich of Anhalt and of Princess Antoinette of Saxe-Altenberg. Succeeded his brother April 18, 1861.

BADEN—Friedrich II., succeeded to

Continued on Page Two.

MORE WARSHIPS JOIN THE REDS

Four Dreadnoughts in Kiel Harbor Espouse the Revolutionary Cause.

GUARDSHIPS ALSO GO OVER

Those Protecting Mines in the Great Belt and the Baltic Abandon Their Posts.

LONDON, Nov. 10.—The crews of the German dreadnoughts Posen, Ostfriesland, Nassau, and Oldenburg, in Kiel Harbor, have joined the revolution, says a Copenhagen dispatch. Marines occupied the lock gates at Ostmoor and fought down a coast artillery division which offered resistance.

According to the British Wireless Service three German destroyers have anchored outside of Stockholm. All the guardships in the Baltic, it is said, have joined the revolutionary movement.

Six more cruisers flying the red flag arrived at Hamburg last night, says a Wolff News Agency dispatch received in Copenhagen.

An Amsterdam dispatch states that the Berlin Vossische Zeitung and Vorwärts confirm the fact that the inception of the revolution at Kiel was mistaken for the idea that a cruise had been ordered and that it was intended to give battle to the British fleet.

Up to Friday night the number of persons killed at Kiel was twenty-eight, according to information re-

Continued on Page Three.

... of the situation. The revolt is spreading throughout Germany with great rapidity.

Dispatches received in London today announce these startling developments. The Workmen's and Soldiers' Council is now administering the municipal government of the German capital.

The War Ministry has submitted, and its acts are valid only when countersigned by a Socialist representative. The official Wolff telegraphic agency has been taken over by the Reds.

The red flag has been hoisted over the royal palace and the Brandenburg Gate. The former Crown Prince's palace is also in possession of the revolutionists.

There was severe fighting in Berlin between 8 and 10 o'clock last night and a violent cannonade was heard from the heart of the city.

Burgomaster and Police Join.

A Copenhagen dispatch states that Dr. Liebknecht, the famous Socialist, who spent many months in prison for antagonizing the German Imperial Government and who was recently released, has issued the following announcement in Berlin in behalf of the Workmen's and Soldiers' Council:

"The Presidency of the police, as well as the Chief Command, is in our hands. Our comrades will be released."

A dispatch from Berne states that the Burgomaster of Berlin has placed himself and his staff at the disposal of the new Government.

Some German newspapers describe the movement as Bolshevism. The people are shouting "Long live the Republic!" and singing the "Marseillaise."

Officers Shelled by Reds.

When revolutionary soldiers attempted to enter a building in Berlin in which they supposed that a number of officers were concealed shots were fired from the windows. The Reds then began shelling the building. Many persons were killed and wounded before the officers surrendered.

When the cannonade began the people thought the Reichsbank was being bombarded, and thousands rushed to the square in front of the Crown Prince's palace. It was later determined that other buildings were under fire. Among those killed in the fighting at the "Cockchafer" Barracks was one of the workmen's leaders known as "Comrade" Habersroth.

The Reds, at last reports, were maintaining order.

Berlin was occupied by forces of the Soldiers' and Workmen's Councils on Saturday afternoon, according to a Wolff Bureau report received in Copenhagen. News of Emperor William's abdication was received in the city on that afternoon with general rejoicing, which was tempered by the fear that it had come too late.

Russians Aid in Outbreak.

How far the example of the Russian Bolsheviki influenced the German upheaval is an interesting question. Red flags figured frequently in the various risings and Chancellor Ebert's motor car floats the international emblem.

The shoulder straps were torn from the uniforms of officers in a number of German cities and even the soldiers' insignia were stripped from them. Russian prisoners played a part in the demonstrations in two or three towns.

Delegates of the revolutionary German navy arrived in Berlin on Friday, according to a dispatch from Copenhagen. They conferred for several hours with the Minister of Marine and with members of the Reichstag majority parties.

It is stated that Hugo Haase, a Socialist leader in the Reichstag, has the situation at Hamburg in hand.

It is officially announced from Berlin, according to a Copenhagen dispatch, that the War Ministry has placed itself at the disposal of Chancellor Ebert. This action was for the purpose of assuring the provisioning of the army and assisting in the solution of demobilization problems.

Serious food difficulties are expected in Germany, owing to the stoppage of trains. The Council of the Regency will take the most drastic steps to re-establish order.

In the new German Government there will be only three representatives of the majority parties, namely, Erzberger, Gothein, and Richthofen, says a dispatch from Copenhagen. The other posts will be occupied by Socialists and independents.

Reds Announce Success.

BERLIN, Nov. 9, (German Wireless to London, Nov. 10)—(Associated Press.)—The German People's Government has been instituted in the greater part of Berlin. The garrison has gone over to the Government.

The Workmen's and Soldiers' Council has declared a general strike. Troops and machine guns have been placed at the disposal of the Council. Guards which had been stationed at the public offices and other buildings have been withdrawn.

Friedrich Ebert (Vice President of the Social Democratic Party) is carrying on the Chancellorship.

The text of a statement issued by the People's Government reads:

In the course of the forenoon of Saturday the formation of a new German People's Government was initiated. The greater part of the Berlin garrison, and other troops stationed there temporarily, went over to the new Government.

The leaders of the deputations of the Social Democratic Party declared that they would not shoot against the people. They said they would, in accordance with the People's Government, intercede in favor of the maintenance of order. Thereupon in the offices and public buildings the guards which had been stationed there were withdrawn.

The business of the Imperial Chancellor is being carried on by the Social Democratic Deputy, Herr Ebert.

It is presumed that, apart from the representatives of the recent majority group, three independent Social Democrats will enter the future Government.

Scheidemann Exhorts Calm.

Deputy Scheidemann, (leader of the majority Socialists in the Reichstag,) in a speech today, said:

"The Kaiser and the Crown Prince have abdicated. The dynasty

Continued on Page Four.

...mation:

Fellow-Citizens: This day the people's deliverance has been fulfilled. The Social Democratic Party has undertaken to form a Government. It has invited the Independent Socialist Party to enter the Government with equal rights.

hand, and the allied Governments and the United States, on the other, has been signed.

The State Department announced at 2:45 o'clock this morning that Germany had signed.

The department's announcement simply said: "The armistice has been signed."

The world war will end this morning at 6 o'clock, Washington time, 11 o'clock Paris time.

The armistice was signed by the German representatives at midnight.

This announcement was made by the State Department at 2:50 o'clock this morning.

The announcement was made verbally by an officila of the State Department in this form:

"The armistice has been signed. It was signed at 5 o'clock A. M., Paris time, [midnight, New York time,] and hostilities will cease at 11 o'clock this morning, Paris time, [6 o'clock, New York time.]

The terms of the armistice, it was announced, will not be made public until later. Military men here, however, regard it as certain that they include:

Immediate retirement of the German military forces from France, Belgium, and Alsace-Lorraine.

Disarming and demobilization of the German armies.

Occupation by the allied and American forces of such strategic points in Germany as will make impossible a renewal of hostilities.

Delivery of part of the German High Seas Fleet and a certain number of submarines to the allied and American naval forces.

Disarmament of all other German warships

The impression is widely prevalent that as the paper increases in size the publisher loses money on account of the high price of newsprint. This, however, is a mistake. The advertising rates include the cost of the paper on which advertisements are printed, so that the increased cost involves only pages devoted to news. The only danger in increasing the size of the paper is that it may possibly become so bulky as to dissatisfy the reader, and *The Times* has not yet felt that handicap. Some of its readers complain that it is too large, but nobody complains that it prints too much news about the things in which he is interested. The man whose chief interest is in the stock market may think there is too much news about sports, and vice versa; but there is not too much financial news for the investor, nor too much sporting news for the follower of sports. From the four-page paper of six short columns which Raymond got out in 1851 to *The Times* of forty eight-column pages which has occasionally appeared in recent years is a long jump; but no greater than the increase in the extent of the intelligent reading public, nor in the variety of that public's interests.

The most important feature of *The Times's* editorial policy since the war has been its championship of the League of Nations, a cause in which its editors were interested long before the armistice, and which they regard as destined to ultimate triumph in some form — most probably in a form very much like that which was adopted by the Paris peace conference. Throughout that conference *The Times*

steadily supported the general policies of President Wilson, though it could not agree with him on some details. Its editors felt that it was a mistake for him to go to Paris in person, but later they came to the conclusion that the President had been right, and that by his presence at the conference he had obtained some results which would have been impossible for any negotiator of less eminence. They thought, and still think, that he made a mistake in not taking with him representative leaders of the Republican party, as well as in showing too plainly an opinion reasonable enough in itself of the endowments and the character of some eminent Senators. On some of the territorial, political or economic items of the peace settlements, too, *The Times* could not accept the President's views.

But its conductors thought that these objections were all of minor importance and irrelevant to the principal issues. With the President's opinion that the League was all-important they were in entire accord, as well as with his position on most of the territorial and economic questions in dispute. They thought the Treaty of Versailles was not ideally perfect, but about the best treaty that could have been obtained. And they held the opinion, none too common in the United States in 1919, that after all the President was the representative of the entire American people at the peace conference, that it was impossible for him to get his way on every point of difference with the other delegates, and that an enlightened view of national interest, to say nothing of those more general considerations of universal welfare which his opponents so vehemently dis-

claimed, made it advisable for the American people to forget trivial objections and give their consideration rather to the things the President had done. He had, after all, won the chief points for which he was contending as the constitutionally designated negotiator for the American people, and won them, if at the price of some concessions, over strenuous opposition. It was unlikely that any other American official would ever be able to impose American views so extensively on the other great powers of the world.

There can be no doubt that much of the antagonism which finally wrecked Mr. Wilson's peace plans was due to his personality rather than his accomplishments, to his methods rather than his results. It seemed to *The Times* that ordinary common sense might suggest that the people whom he represented should give first consideration to the work which he had done, and to the effect of that work upon their own interests, rather than to their opinions of Mr. Wilson as an individual. No doubt, some conscientious opponents of the League took this point of view, and based their opposition to the Treaty on an honest conviction that it was harmful to American interests. But there is evidence everywhere in plain sight that a good many people opposed the Treaty merely because they disliked the President.

Throughout the fight in the Senate and through the campaign of 1920 *The Times* gave its utmost support to the cause of the League and to those public men who promised to support that cause. The violent debate within the Republican Party as to whether the election of Mr. Harding meant a victory for the League or the utter rejection of the

League it viewed with sympathetic but detached interest, convinced that the logic of facts would presently bring to reason those Republican leaders who are capable of reason. Until that time shall come *The Times's* view of the particular accomplishments of the Republican Administration is determined by its judgment of their specific merits and not by general or doctrinal considerations.

Yet, in spite of its conviction that the League is necessary and indeed inevitable, in spite of its support of the Democratic ticket in the 1920 campaign, *The Times* has given its support to many of the policies of President Harding. This does not mean that *The Times* is always an administration paper. It does mean, however, that the conductors of *The Times* realize that the President of the United States is the President of the whole people and not of a single party, that his public acts affect the whole people and that it is to the interest of every citizen to get as effective and competent an administration as possible. With the type of partisanship which sees the entrance of the opposition into power as meaning nothing but opportunity for criticism *The Times* has little sympathy. It preferred Mr. Cox to Mr. Harding; but Mr. Harding having been elected it realized that he was going to be the Chief Magistrate of the United States for the next four years, and that sensible citizens would do well to encourage all the praiseworthy policies which his administration might pursue without stopping to fear that they might bring prestige to the Republican Party.

Whether Republican, Independent or Democratic, *The Times* has never been able to convince itself that

opposition must mean consistent hostility to everything done by the party in power. Its conductors regard the interests of the nation as somewhat more important than the record of any party, and they have been genuinely glad to be able to commend many of the works accomplished or attempted by President Harding and the leading members of his Cabinet. With some of the elements in the Republican Party *The Times* is entirely out of sympathy, and had representatives of those factions been chosen to direct the executive functions of the government, the paper would no doubt have had occasion to criticize their conduct rather severely; but, considering the record of the administration purely on its merits, the editors of *The Times* have been pleased to be able to recognize the fact that its performance, in the early months at least, has been meritorious in a rather high degree.

Several changes in the personnel of the paper in recent years may call for special mention. Mr. George McAneny resigned as President of the Board of Aldermen on February 1, 1916, to become executive manager of *The Times*. His duties were chiefly confined to the study of the newsprint paper situation which gave so much concern to all American papers during the war period and which is *The Times's* chief item of expenditure. In 1920 *The Times* spent for print paper $5,963,839.42. In 1897, the first full year under the present management, that item cost only $45,955.63. On January 1, 1918, the Tidewater Paper Company, of Bush Terminal, Brooklyn, with a capacity of 30,000 tons of newsprint per year, was

acquired by the New York Times Company in order to insure a supply of paper in New York free from outside interruptions by strikes, weather, etc.

With *The Times's* paper supply contracted for and assured for the next five years, Mr. McAneny withdrew from the *Times* organization in March, 1921, and soon afterward was appointed chairman of the Transit Commission.

Mr. Samuel Strauss, well known as one of the liveliest of magazine critics of current affairs, was with *The Times* as treasurer of the company from 1912 to the end of 1915. Mr. Rollo Ogden, editor-in-chief of *The New York Evening Post* for many years, came to *The Times* on May 15, 1920, as associate editor; and Dr. John H. Finley, Commissioner of Education of the State of New York, resigned that office and joined *The Times* staff, also as an associate editor, on January 17, 1921.

Note may be made here of the following members of *The Times's* staff who died either in its service or after long years with the paper:

EDWARD CARY, for forty-six years an editorial writer and for much of that period associate editor; died May 23, 1917.

THEODORE LAWRENCE PEVERELLY, for forty-three years a member of the business staff; died February 4, 1904.

ARTHUR GREAVES, city editor from 1900 and a reporter for many years before; died October 19, 1915.

CHARLES WELBORNE KNAPP, treasurer of The New York Times Company and formerly publisher of *The St. Louis Republic;* died January 6, 1916.

EDWARD AUGUSTUS DITHMAR, whose forty years

of service as dramatic critic, London correspondent, literary editor and editorial writer, ended with his death on October 16, 1917.

MONTGOMERY SCHUYLER, for twenty-four years an editorial writer; died July 16, 1914.

JACOB H. THOMPSON, for thirty-seven years with the paper, much of the time as exchange editor; died Septembeı 8, 1905.

JOHN HEBARD PAINE, for fourteen years with *The Times*, the last four years as night city editor; died October 2, 1920.

JOHN NORRIS, for many years business manager, died March 21, 1914.

BARNET PHILLIPS, whose thirty-three years of service included editorial work on the Sunday edition and book reviewing; died April 8, 1905.

LEOPOLD WALLACH, general counsel of *The Times* from August 18, 1896, to his death on January 25, 1908.

ELBRIDGE G. DUNNELL, Washington correspondent of *The Times* from 1879 to 1902; died February 3, 1905.

LEONARD B. TREHARNE, on *The Times* staff for twelve years, most of that time as night city editor; died October 17, 1904.

MAJOR JOHN M. CARSON, in *The Times* Washington office from 1874 to 1882 and 1902 to 1905, and for several years chief Washington correspondent; died September 29, 1912.

GEORGE BUTLER TAYLOR, for twenty-six years a reporter, died November 2, 1905.

FIELD LYNN HOSMER, forty years in service as reporter and editorial auditor; died January 8, 1914.

George B. Moyer, for twelve years superintendent of *The Times* buildings, died December 9, 1915.

As to the news service of *The Times* there is little to add to what has been written in the last two chapters. It has continued as it was during the war, though perhaps with a somewhat higher degree of efficiency, due to experience. The Peace Conference was covered for *The Times* by members of the paper's own staff — Richard V. Oulahan, head of the Washington Bureau; Ernest Marshall, head of the London office; Charles A. Selden and Edwin L. James, of the Paris office, and Charles H. Grasty of the executive department — and by Gertrude Atherton, until she fell ill and had to return to America. They scored a number of "beats," notably on the occasion of President Wilson's threat to abandon the Peace Conference, but most of the leading American papers scored "beats" during the negotiations. As before, the excellence of *The Times* was rather in a higher average than in outstanding single achievements. Indeed, it could be said that the war and the Peace Conference both proved the value of the American system of newspaper training. Generally speaking, the best war correspondents and the best political correspondents at the Peace Conference were men who had gone through the ordinary routine of the American reporter, rather than experts who had specialized in war correspondence or international politics all their lives. Most American reporters found that they could learn what they needed about war and international politics; while the sense of news values,

THE FIRST PRESS OF THE TIMES,
1851.

A VIEW OF THE TIMES PRESSROOM,
With a Capacity of 360,000 24-Page Papers Per Hour.

and the diligence in getting news, which is developed by the ordinary reportorial training in America, and which, of course, had been very highly developed in the men who were selected for the important assignments of the war and the peace negotiations, cannot be improvised by specialists when they are suddenly faced by extraordinarily keen competition.

Perhaps there should be special mention of the Washington correspondence of *The Times*, which is probably not only more voluminous, but more impartial, than that of any other paper. The practice of coloring the news to suit editorial policy, which was once too common in the American press, has pretty generally disappeared in recent years except in a minority of papers. But it has tended to survive longest in the Washington correspondence, where there is still, in the case of most newspapers, a tendency to hunt out first of all such news as agrees with the paper's prejudices.

This does not involve suppression of news, nor even distortion. The relativity of truth is a commonplace to any newspaper man, even to one who has never studied epistemology; and, if the phrase is permissible, truth is rather more relative in Washington than anywhere else. Now and then it is possible to make a downright statement; such and such a bill has passed in one of the houses of Congress, or failed to pass; the administration has issued this or that statement; the President has approved, or vetoed, a certain bill. But most of the news that comes out of Washington is necessarily rather vague, for it depends on the assertions of statesmen who are reluctant to be quoted by name, or even by

description. This more than anything else is responsible for the sort of fog, the haze of miasmatic exhalations, which hangs over news with a Washington date line. News coming out of Washington is apt to represent not what is so but what might be so under certain contingencies, what may turn out to be so, what some eminent personage says is so, or even what he wants the public to believe is so when it is not.

For an illustration one need go no further back than the various semi-official assertions on high authority of the intentions of the Harding administration about coöperation with Europe, which turned out to be pretty nearly 100 per cent untrue. The explanation is that most of these assertions came from irreconcilable Senators who honestly thought they could speak for the administration and who were accepted by correspondents as speaking for the administration; but who, as a matter of fact, knew less about the real intentions of the administration than the White House doorkeeper.

Obviously, then, the Washington correspondent has a pretty wide field of choice. On almost any question he can get directly opposite opinions — and most "news" from Washington is a matter of opinion — from equally high authority, and from authority which he is not permitted to identify. It is not strange that between two stories of apparently equal merit he is inclined to prefer the one which will be most welcome in the office. Generally speaking, *The Times* Washington correspondence has been very little open to criticism on this point. No paper supported the League of Nations more

vigorously than *The Times;* its editorials consistently favored the League, and its columns once more, as during the war, became the principal forum for the debates of publicists. Yet it was evident through the entire discussion, to those who read *The Times* Washington correspondence, that there was little chance of the League finding favor in the Senate. *The Times* supported Cox in the 1920 Presidential campaign, but its political correspondence made it fairly plain long before the election that Harding was certain to win.

It should be added that *The Times*, alone of prominent Democratic papers, denounced as false, slanderous and contemptible the "campaign of whispers" against Mr. Harding during the last weeks of the campaign.

The year 1919 gave *The Times*, always so keenly interested in aviation, a chance to cover very fully the news of the first flights across the Atlantic. Its interest in wireless telegraphy had already been vindicated, and at present all newspapers are enjoying wireless service which might have been somewhat longer delayed if *The Times* had not been so fully convinced of the possibilities of this art a decade ago. The end of the war brought, of course, an increase in the amount of space devoted to local news, which had been somewhat reduced in the days when the dispatches from the battle-fronts were of supreme importance; as well as a great expansion in *The Times* sporting department, responding to the great increase of interest in sports which followed the coming of peace.

The Times was the only paper in the United States, or in the world, which printed the full text of the draft of the peace treaty. As will be remembered, the document was given to Senator Borah on June 9, 1919, by a correspondent of *The Chicago Tribune*, and by vote of the Senate was spread upon the Congressional Record. That night the Washington correspondents of *The Times* got proof sheets from the government printers as fast as the copy was set up, and dispatched the text to New York on twenty-four telegraph and telephone wires obtained for the occasion. On the morning of June 10 *The Times* had all of it — sixty-two columns, occupying most of the first eight pages of the second section of a forty-page paper.

The news service of *The Times* today is pretty well known to several hundred thousand readers who prefer *The Times* to any other paper. If anything further is to be said about its quality it may best be said by the mention of one or two instances of *The Times's* methods and their results. During the political conventions of 1920 *The Times* pretty regularly had more news and more reliable news than the other papers, and had it first. These conventions were covered by a staff of nine men, all regular employés of the paper. *The Times* saw no need for hiring renowned experts, humorists, or fiction writers to supplement the work of its own men; and if any of its readers missed these features they did not say so.

The Democratic National Convention at San Francisco offered some technical problems of exceptional difficulty. Because San Francisco is 3000

miles west of New York, and because New York saves daylight while San Francisco does not, San Francisco time is four hours earlier than that of New York. That meant that the first edition of most New York morning papers was going to press at a little past midnight, only a few minutes after the night sessions of the Democratic Convention were beginning in San Francisco. Despite this fact, *The Times* had some news from the beginning of the night sessions in its first edition on every night of the convention, and its second edition, coming off the presses shortly before 2 o'clock, had about as much news as other papers were able to get on the streets at daylight.

Another difficulty in getting the news out of San Francisco was due, or rather seemed likely to be due, to the limited telegraphic facilities. Even the highest officials of the Western Union and the Postal did not realize, in advance, just how much their local organizations were going to be able to accomplish. As it turned out, the Western Union wire arrangements were more than sufficient to handle all the news of the convention; but this was not known beforehand. As a matter of precaution *The Times*, which was unable to obtain the lease of direct wires into its office from the telegraph companies, finally made a roundabout connection through Canada. A telephone wire was leased for night service from San Francisco to Vancouver and another from New York to Montreal. Between these two cities connection was established by a lease of a Canadian Pacific railroad telegraph wire, and the whole circuit was operated by telegraph with a "relay" at Vancouver — operated

so well that news dictated to a telegraph operator in the convention hall at San Francisco was in *The Times* office in New York within two minutes.

The long-distance telephone was used every night during the convention, and was responsible for the publication in the first edition, on the final night, of news which foreshadowed Palmer's withdrawal a little later in the evening.

All these are things such as all papers do, now and then, and the only distinction of *The Times* is that it does them more regularly, more smoothly and, on the whole, with more success. As a final instance of the operation of *The Times* news service today may be mentioned the handling of the news of the German reparations proposals of April 26 last — proposals which, it will be remembered, were sent to the United States Government in the vain hope of obtaining American mediation in some form, and which embodied the last German effort at compromise before the surrender to the allied demands, which took place a few days later.

The American declaration that all previous German offers were unsatisfactory reached the German Cabinet at 11 A.M. on April 26 — that is, 5 A.M. New York time. It was known that the answer would be prompt; that, as a matter of form, it would be sent to the American government; but that, since Mr. Harding and Mr. Hughes would not even transmit to the allied governments any proposal which those governments were likely to receive with disfavor, there would be informal inquiries, as soon as it was received, to find out if it were acceptable. If not, it would wither and die in a Wash-

ington pigeonhole, so far as official transmission was concerned.

The German note came to Washington on the evening of Wednesday, April 26, and a vague and general intimation as to its contents was given out to all the correspondents there. A summary of the note was also given to The Associated Press in Berlin, and on the morning of Thursday, April 27, that was all that the other New York Papers had about the German offer.

But *The Times* realized that the text of the note might be available not only in Berlin, where it was written, and in Washington, where it was received, but also in London and Paris, where the governments would be informally acquainted with its text before the note was officially transmitted. Consequently *The Times* correspondents in Washington, London, Paris and Berlin were all instructed to try to get the note verbatim. In Washington and Berlin only inadequate summaries were obtainable; the summary given out by the German government was in one or two points seriously misrepresentative and tended to represent the offer as larger than it actually was.

But *The Times* correspondents both in London and in Paris obtained and cabled the full text of the note on Wednesday night, the Paris copy arriving first, but only ten minutes ahead of that from London. *The Times* alone of New York papers published it in full on Thursday morning. *The Times* alone of New York papers published the fact that the French government had officially refused to consider the offer and had notified Secretary Hughes of its decision to

this effect. Two other papers in New York had Paris dispatches predicting, on the basis of Premier Briand's speech in the Chamber that afternoon, that the French Government would reject the note; the others had not even that much. *The Times* was also the only New York paper which printed on Thursday morning the comments of the Paris press in their issues of the same day — comments, of course, which could be transmitted only because of the five-hour difference in time, but which no other New York paper received in time for publication.

Thus on one of the most important pieces of world news in the year 1921 *The Times* alone, except for the papers which purchase *The Times's* news service for publication in other cities, published the contents of the German proposal and the fact of the French refusal to consider it. An achievement of this sort tells a good deal more about the quality of a paper than the exclusive publication of a single story acquired by the wide acquaintance of some member of its staff. It is a feat which cannot be performed on the spur of the moment; it implies an intricate and highly trained organization. That organization is the chief distinction of *The Times* today.

The story of the modern *Times* has been told — inadequately and imperfectly, but as fully and impartially as it can be told by its own family. In those twenty-five years *The Times* has gone further and grown faster than even the men who controlled it foresaw, and its growth is not yet ended. There is room for improvement, and the men who get it out every day are constantly trying to improve it; there

Section 1

"All the News That's Fit to Print."

The New York Times.

THE WEATHER
Generally fair today and Monday, except possible local thunder showers.
For full weather report see Page 23.

Section 1

VOL. LXIX...No. 22,786 ••• NEW YORK, SUNDAY, JUNE 13, 1920. In Nine Parts, including Rotogravure Picture Sections and Book Section. FIVE CENTS In Manhattan, Bronx, and Brooklyn | Elsewhere TEN CENTS

HARDING NOMINATED FOR PRESIDENT ON THE TENTH BALLOT AT CHICAGO; COOLIDGE CHOSEN FOR VICE PRESIDENT

The New York Times
"All the News That's Fit to Print."
PUBLISHED EVERY DAY IN THE YEAR BY THE NEW YORK TIMES COMPANY.
NEW YORK, SUNDAY, JUNE 13, 1920.

THE NOMINATION OF HARDING.

Upon a platform that has produced general dissatisfaction, the Chicago convention presents a candidate whose nomination will be received with astonishment and dismay by the party whose suffrages he invites. WARREN G. HARDING is a very respectable Ohio politician of the second class. He has never been a leader of men or a director of policies. For years a protégé of FORAKER, he rose to a subordinate office by favor of "Boss" COX of Cincinnati. Beaten by JUDSON HARMON in the contest for the Governorship in 1910, he has never shown independent strength in his own State save when he was named for Senator in 1914, having a majority of a little more than 100,000 over his Democratic competitor; and outside of Ohio he has only such strength as he now derives from his place at the head of the Republican ticket. Senator HARDING'S record at Washington has been faint and colorless. He was an undistinguished and indistinguishable unit in the ruck of Republican Senators who obediently followed Mr. LODGE in the twistings and turnings of that statesman's foray upon the Treaty and the Covenant.

The nomination of HARDING, for whose counterpart we must go back to FRANKLIN PIERCE if we would seek a President who measures down to his political stature, is the fine and perfect flower of the cowardice and imbecility of the Senatorial cabal that charged itself with the management of the Republican Convention, against whose control Governor BECKMAN so vehe-

HOW THE CONVENTION DID IT

Delegates Had Word Early That Leaders Were for Harding.

RECESS HASTENED CHANGE

Two Ballots Taken After Reassembling Brought Ohio Man's Nomination.

PENNSYLVANIA CLINCHED IT

Big Block of New York Votes Also Helped to Decide the Struggle.

Special to The New York Times.

CHICAGO, June 12.—The afternoon session of the Republican National Convention on its fifth day, which reached a climax in the nomination for the Presidency of Senator Warren G. Harding of Ohio, was more like a rehearsal than a star performance in the great national political drama.

Not a single time-honored device was neglected in the effort to give the per-

REPUBLICAN NOMINEE FOR PRESIDENT
SENATOR WARREN G. HARDING
OF OHIO

4 NAMED FOR SECOND PLACE

But Tired Delegates Turn To Coolidge and First Ballot Is Decisive.

LENROOT NEXT IN FAVOR

Votes Cast Also for Johnson, Allen, Anderson, Pritchard and Gronna.

DELEGATES EAGER TO LEAVE

Adjourned at 7:30 P. M., Many Leaving the Hall Before Roll Call Was Ended.

Special to The New York Times.

CHICAGO, June 12.—Governor Calvin Coolidge of Massachusetts was nominated for the Vice Presidency by the Republican Convention tonight by an overwhelming vote on the first ballot. The nomination was immediately made unanimous.

As soon as the Presidential nomination had been made, the call for Vice Presidential nominations was made by Chairman Lodge.

Medill McCormick went to the speakers' stand, and in a short address nomi-

REPUBLICAN NOMINEE FOR VICE PRESIDENT
GOVERNOR CALVIN COOLIDGE
OF MASSACHUSETTS

ARRANGED DURING RECESS

Deal for Harding, Goes Through When Lowden Frees Delegates.

BIG GAIN ON NINTH BALLOT

When the New York Delegates Swing to Him the Shouting Begins.

URGED AT NIGHT COUNCILS

But Leaders in the Race Refused to Yield at That Time—Later the Break Came.

Special to The New York Times.

CHICAGO, June 12.—Senator Warren G. Harding of Marion, Ohio, was nominated for President of the United States by the Republican Party represented by its delegates assembled in national convention at the Coliseum this evening. Calvin Coolidge, Governor of Massachusetts, was nominated for Vice President.

The nomination of the Presidential candidate came on the tenth ballot. In the ninth ballot the whole trend of the

WADSWORTH THREW | JOHNSON IS SILENT | HARDING DECLARES | PROPHESIED HOW

of white-livered and incompetent politicians. If Republican leadership had not fallen into the hands of pigmies the chief men at Chicago would have told BORAH to bolt and be hanged, just as upon the issue of the League they would have defied JOHNSON to do his worst. But they ran like a frightened flock, surrendered everything, Mr. LODGE finally throwing off all disguises and standing out as the open foe of the Covenant of the League of Nations, even with his own reservations.

What has befallen the Republican Party of the early days, the party of sixty years ago, when it was possessed of moral purposes, or of forty and thirty years ago, when it could still profess to have them and find believers?

Where are its leaders that can be compared to MORRILL, SEWARD, HALE, PLATT of Connecticut, OLIVER P. MORTON, SUMNER, BLAINE, CONKLING and a dozen others who rose to high places in the party councils? And, if the question be not too unfeeling, where and what are its principles, if any it have? Party control, exercised by a group of Senators, is divided between LODGE on the one hand and BORAH and JOHNSON on the other. None of them, none of their accomplices in party degradation, would have come within hailing distance of the foremost rank of party chiefs in the brilliant days of Republicanism. And for principles, they have only hatred of Mr. WILSON and a ravening hunger for the offices.

Governor COOLIDGE for Vice President really shines by comparison with the head of the ticket. He at least is a man of achievement, he is known to the party and to the nation. When the police force of Boston went on strike he showed himself to be a man. He met that menace to the public safety with courage and determination, and the nation rang with praise of him. It is fortunate that not a word is to be said against the character of either candidate. They are irreproachable. But that does not compensate for the lack of achievement, for the colorlessness of the candidate for first place, or for the manner in which his nomination was brought about. It will be felt and said everywhere that the Democrats at San Francisco have received from their opponents at Chicago the gift of a splendid opportunity

tachments—to revive it failed.

Just as the limp, wet, worn men balloting in the pit waited until they were sure the tide really was running strong, so did the throng of spectators wait to make very sure.

Harding Boom Starts Early.

The suddenly revivified Harding boom started at the morning session. From that moment to the end it was a process of very slow and orderly rising enthusiasm to which gratitude at getting a hot and tedious job done contributed no mean element.

None of the stampede tricks of time-honored reliability worked this time. The crowd and the delegates in their separate ways seemed deliberately to prepare themselves for the finale.

As soon as it was recognized in high places that Senator Harding was to be the victor, the proper sort of stage management was set in motion. The galleries, in which were many of Mayor William Hale Thompson's supporters, who were Johnson men out of antagonism to Lowden and Wood, were glad enough to lend themselves to the task of furnishing an appropriate setting for the drama. But with all the stage management and all the willingness of the crowd to do what was expected to the best of its ability when the switching of big delegations made it a certainty, as the ninth ballot was being tallied, that Senator Harding was to be the nominee, and later, when the tenth ended the tiny remaining speck of suspense, the performance lacked great enthusiasm.

Victory Outburst Soon Over.

Perhaps two-thirds of the delegates got to their feet. Maybe a hundred climbed on chairs. A few women waved damp handkerchiefs in a valiant effort to add the orthodox feminine touch to the first national convention in which they had participated.

But there was no frenzy, no hat-smashing, no parading worthy of the name, and so little cheering that three minutes after the nomination was announced those on their feet, including virtually every one in the spectators' parts of the Coliseum, were standing listlessly.

It is a safe assertion that if Senator Lodge had elected to pound once with his cumbersome gavel, which looked to have been destined originally to be a potato masher, the Hall would have been hushed in an instant.

Announced Lowden by Mistake.

There was just one touch of humor—though the coatless, sopping delegates didn't see it in that way. In announcing that Senator Harding had the necessary majority the Secretary inadvertently used the name of Lowden instead of that of the successful candidate. There was a howl of protest and very manifestly even the Lowden men didn't think the mistake was funny.

Senator Lodge made the formal announcement that the Ohio Senator had become the party choice in a tired voice that reflected the weariness in his pale cheeks and dark-ringed eyes. It didn't penetrate through the remnants of the din that the real, genuine Harding men were struggling desperately to accelerate into at least the semblance of a great occasion.

Senator McCormick of Illinois then strode to a point of strategic advantage under the mechanical amplifying de-

Continued on Page Four.

Ballot, Acting with Senate Leaders.

20 REMAINED UNBOSSED

Organization Men Assert That They Alone Prevented Wood's Nomination.

Special to The New York Times.

CHICAGO, June 12.—The delegates from New York kept up a show of independence until the last hour of today's convention session, but then, when orders were given by the leaders of the organization, sixty-eight responded to the lash and voted for Harding. Their choice lay elsewhere, but they followed instructions. That was more votes than the organization leaders needed, yet they could have obtained several additional delegates had they been necessary. After Harding's nomination was assured these delegates were not asked to make the sacrifice.

Among the unbossed delegates who stood out on the final ballot were six Wood men: Robert L. Bacon of the First District, Henry L. Stimson of the Sixteenth District, George Henry Payne, alternate for George Z. Medalie of the Twenty-second District, and Lansing G. Hoskins and John Taber of the Thirty-sixth District. They voted for Wood throughout and refused to yield to the wishes of Barnes, Wadsworth and the other leaders.

In the same class was Fiorella H. LaGuardia, President of the New York Board of Aldermen. His choice was Lenroot, and he voted for him to the last.

Other delegates who were not called upon to support Harding were two who favored Butler—Miss Katherine Hammer, alternate from Butler's district, and William Brice Thompson, one of

Continued on Page Three.

Something to Say Today on Combination.

THANKS HIS SUPPORTERS

Says There Is No Rancor and That Their Hands Are Clean—Borah Also Refuses Comment.

Special to The New York Times.

CHICAGO, June 12.—Senator Hiram W. Johnson, a deeply disappointed man, refused to comment tonight upon the nomination of Senator Harding, but, according to his close friends and associates, he will not bolt the Republican nominee.

Mr. Johnson was approached during the noon recess of the convention by emissaries from the Harding camp with an offer to nominate him for Vice President. He is said to have turned down this offer very testily and to have said that he was after the Presidency, not the Vice Presidency. His remarks, however, are said to have indicated that he will support Senator Harding.

The news that the Vice Presidential nomination had been offered to Mr. Johnson was in line with the report, after the adoption of the foreign relations plank, that he (Johnson) could have about anything he wanted in the convention except the nomination for President. His friends said tonight that he would make a statement concerning Senator Harding's nomination tomorrow.

When Johnson stepped before the "Battalion of Death" at his headquarters tonight to bid them good-bye he was greeted with "For He's a Jolly Good Fellow." The crowd sang lustily and with no signs of depression. When the demonstration had died down Johnson said:

"There are no tears to be shed. There is no rancor. We come out of this fight

Continued on Page Three.

Lowden Defends Release of Delegates; Hert Says Wood Would Have Won Otherwise

CHICAGO, June 12.—Fear of a deadlock which he believed would prove detrimental to his party caused Governor Lowden to release his delegates on the convention floor at today's session, according to a statement made by him tonight. Governor Lowden said:

"After the eighth ballot, upon which I received a plurality of all votes cast, it was represented to me that the delegates were becoming restive under the delay. Fearing a protracted deadlock, which I believed would have been detrimental to the interests of the country, I decided to release all delegates and advised them to use their best judgment as to whom they should support. I have great confidence in the ability and character of the successful candidate, shall support him with all heartiness and believe the ticket will be elected. The Republican Party has not had such an opportunity for service in half a century.

"For the friendships formed during this campaign and for the loyal support of so many fine patriotic men and women I shall never cease to be grateful."

"Governor Lowden withdrew in the interest of party harmony," A. T. Hert, National Committeeman from Kentucky and one of the Lowden leaders, said tonight. Hert was a prime mover in transferring the Lowden votes to Harding and cast Kentucky's 26 for the victor.

Asked if he believed Lowden had reached the height of his strength on the eighth ballot, Hert said:

"It is my judgment that Wood would have been nominated had Lowden stayed in the fight."

York and ex-Governor Herrick for Ohio.

The Chairman of the Oregon delegation placed in nomination Governor Calvin Coolidge of Massachusetts, and the Kansas delegation nominated Governor Henry J. Allen of Kansas. The convention presented a scene of disorder while various delegations were endavoring to make themselves heard to second the nomination. Massachusetts started a demonstration for its Governor. The Virginia delegation presented the name of Colonel Henry J. Anderson of Virginia for the post, in the hope that the Republicans would turn to the South for second place on the ticket.

The most enthusiastic demonstration was for Coolidge. The delegates were worn by the hard day's work behind them, and the nomination for the Vice Presidency did not seem to give much of a thrill. Those who attempted to make seconding addresses received scant attention. It was evident that what the delegates wanted most of all was to get away. In fact, many left the hall before the rollcall on the nomination was complete.

Coolidge had a runaway for the Vice Presidential nomination as soon as the balloting began. The big Eastern States, Massachusetts, New York and Pennsylvania, were lined up solidly for him, and he also got a heavy vote in the Middle West.

When Wisconsin was polled it cast two votes for Lenroot and twenty-four for Senator Gronna of North Dakota. Coolidge gained a lead so rapidly that the result was soon a foregone conclusion. When it became obvious that Coolidge would win the States down on the roll call followed the lead of the others.

The vote was:

Vote for Vice President.

State.	No. of Delegates	Coolidge	Lenroot	Allen	Anderson	Johnson	Pritchard	Gronna
Alabama	14	2	12	..	..	..	..	..
Arizona	6	6	..	..	..	..	..	..
Arkansas	13	13	..	..	..	..	..	..
California	26	19	..	2	1	..	..	..
Colorado	12	..	..	12	..	..	..	..
Conn.	14	13	..	..	..	..	..	..
Delaware	6	1	5	..	..	..	..	..
Florida	8	8	..	..	..	..	..	..
Georgia	17	9	8	..	..	..	..	..
Idaho	8	8	..	..	..	..	..	..
Illinois	58	36	4	1	..	16	..	..
Indiana	30	16	11	3	..	..	..	..
Iowa	26	17½	3	4½	1	..	..	..
Kansas	20	..	..	20	..	..	..	..
Kentucky	26	1	24	..	1	..	..	..
Louisiana	12	12	..	..	..	..	..	..
Maine	12	12	..	..	..	..	..	..
Maryland	16	16	..	..	..	..	..	..
Mass.	35	35	..	..	..	..	..	..
Michigan	30	30	..	..	..	..	..	..
Minnesota	24	24	..	..	..	..	..	..
Mississippi	12	12	..	..	..	..	..	..
Missouri	36	8	21½	..	..	6½	..	..
Montana	8	1	7	..	..	..	..	..
Nebraska	16	16	..	..	..	..	..	..
Nevada	6	6	..	..	..	..	..	..
N. H'shire	8	8	..	..	..	..	..	..
N. Jersey	28	25	2	..	1	..	..	..
N. Mexico	6	1	5	..	..	..	..	..
New York	88	59	21	8	..	..	..	..
N. Car'lina	22	9	4	7	..	..	1	..
N. Dakota	10	10	..	..	..	..	..	..
Ohio	48	10	9	10	9	..	10	..
Oklahoma	20	20	..	..	..	..	..	..
Oregon	10	10	..	..	..	..	..	..
Penn'nia	76	76	..	..	..	..	..	..
Rh. Island	10	10	..	..	..	..	..	..
S. Car'lina	11	11	..	..	..	..	..	..
S. Dakota	10	10	..	..	..	..	..	..
Tennessee	20	20	..	..	..	..	..	..
Texas	23	22	..	1	..	..	..	..
Utah	8	7	1	..	..	..	..	..
Vermont	8	8	..	..	..	..	..	..
Virginia	15	..	..	..	15	..	..	..
W'hington	14	7	7	..	..	..	..	..
West Va.	16	16	..	..	..	..	..	..
Wisconsin	26	..	2	..	..	..	..	24
Wyoming	6	6	..	..	..	..	..	..
Alaska	2	2	..	..	..	..	..	..
Dist. of C.	2	2	..	..	..	..	..	..
Hawaii	2	..	..	..	..	..	..	..
Philippines	2	2	..	..	..	..	..	..
Porto Rico	2	2	..	..	..	..	..	..
Total	984	674½	146½	68½	28	22½	11	24

Absent—California 4, Connecticut 1, Illinois 1.

Not voting—Hawaii 2.

Total vote 984

The Illinois delegation moved that

Continued on Page Three.

Proud to Receive This Great Honor from the Republican Party."

COOLIDGE ACCEPTS PLACE

Taft, Hughes, Hoover and Others Congratulate Head of Ticket.

Special to The New York Times.

CHICAGO, June 12.—Senator Harding, General Wood and Governor Lowden were in rooms adjoining the Coliseum during the final balloting today. They were in different parts of the Coliseum Annex. The result of each ballot was delivered to them by messengers.

It was a bulletin flash for a press association that gave Mr. Harding the thrill of his life. It read:

"Harding nominated."

When the news was given to the first editor ever nominated by the Republican Party for President he did not lose his equanimity. He said he was "very happy."

Later he said:

"I am very proud, as any American would be, to receive this great honor from the Republican Party. I am not unmindful of the obligations and responsibilities that come with it."

Manager Predicts Harmony.

Henry M. Daugherty, national manager for Senator Harding, issued the following statement late tonight:

"On behalf of the Republicans of Ohio, and especially on behalf of Senator Harding, his family and friends, I desire to express to Republicans of the country, men and women, our sincere gratitude for the confidence expressed in this wonderful man by nominating him as the candidate of the party for the Presidency.

"We entered this campaign with considerable reluctance because Senator Harding did not desire to make a high-powered organization campaign for the Presidency. Our plan, as is now well known, was carried out, whereby we conducted rather a modest campaign and left the selection to the Republicans of the country without too much pressure.

"We have throughout the campaign had the highest respect for opposition candidates and for their supporters. At no time have we made any attacks upon any candidate or any candidate's supporters, and Senator Harding will receive the support no doubt of every man and woman in the country who desires to vote the Republican ticket. The ticket will be elected overwhelmingly in November."

Harding Receives Correspondents.

With his accustomed simplicity of manner Senator Harding received the newspaper correspondents tonight on the fifth floor of the Hotel La Salle, in a hall adjoining his rooms. With him were a number of old friends, including Will H. Hays, just re-elected Chairman of the Republican National Committee, who will direct the Harding campaign.

The Senator made it plain that he realized the new responsibilities which

Continued on Page Four.

Daugherty, His Campaign Manager, Said Fifteen Tired Men Would Put Him Over.

SENATE "JUNTA" MADE DEAL

Attended All Conferences Behind Scenes and Blocked Move to Let Wood Bolster Forces.

Special to The New York Times.

CHICAGO, June 12.—"At the proper time after Republican National Convention meets some fifteen men, bleary eyed with loss of sleep and perspiring profusely with the excessive heat, will sit down in seclusion around a big table. I will be with them and will present the name of Senator Harding to them, and before we get through they will put him over."

This statement, substantially as written here, was made by Harry K. Daugherty, campaign manager for Senator Warren G. Harding, Ohio, shortly before the Presidential primaries were held in that State. Daugherty afterward entered the primaries as a candidate for delegate at large, pledged to support Senator Harding. He was beaten but the utterance which led the Republican voters in his own State to oppose him in view of unfolding events at the national party gathering here, appears to have been full of prophetic meaning.

The sweltering crowd which sat down in the Coliseum this morning gazed on the usual picture of a national convention bent on getting through with its business of nominating a candidate for the President of the United States and preparing to go back home. That picture may have appeared to many of the onlookers as one fraught with unusual interest and importance, but the history of this final day of Republican Convention was really made behind the scenes and very much after the fashion suggested in Daugherty's statement.

Two days ago Senator Harding's fight was looked upon as a forlorn hope by practically every trained political observer at the convention. In fact, up to the very moment the convention took its adjournment last night his prospects were not regarded as rosy. As recently as last night Senator Harding himself could not have entertained much hope of a successful issue, for at three minutes before midnight he filed with the Secretary of State at Columbus, Ohio, the necessary papers to qualify him as a candidate for re-election to his present position in the United States Senate.

Conferences Held Friday Night.

The conference at which steps were taken to break the deadlock by steering the convention toward Harding were begun soon after it finished its big day's job yesterday. During the night the conferees divided into several small groups, which kept in communication with each other by members intervisiting, in two Chicago clubs and at the Blackstone and the Congress Hotels.

While the convention was sitting today a dozen or so leaders met on the ros-

Continued on Page Three.

Senator Harding's nomination was the outcome of a complex situation that did not begin to clear until last evening. After four ineffective ballots yesterday the convention had adjourned until this morning. Four additional ballots in the forenoon and early afternoon of today had developed Harding strength, but General Leonard Wood and Governor Frank O. Lowden had remained in the lead. A recess was taken for two hours, and during that short period combinations were formed that made Harding's nomination certain.

The real stampede of delegates to Harding began when Governor Lowden, abandoning his intention to address the conveintion, issued instead a formal announcement that his delegates were released from their pledges to him.

Interesting, and even thrilling, as the open proceedings in the convention were, moves behind the scenes, of which most of the convention knew nothing, had their dramatic side. The nomination of the candidate for President was arranged in conferences in hotel rooms. The prediction made in Washington weeks ago that the convention would get into a deadlock over candidates that would necessitate a combination arranged by a comparatively few of the party's dominating spirits was fulfilled to the letter.

Johnson's Strength Disintegrated.

Johnson's strength in the convention, never very potent, had begun to disintegrate this morning, under the influence of the understanding that Harding was the choice of the leaders represented by the Senate group. All along it had been taken for granted that when Johnson saw that he could not be nominated he would ask his supporters to go to Knox. In conferences in which he took part last night, however, he failed to intimate that he was willing to abandon his candidacy, and no efofrt was made to persuade him.

In the two-hour recess this afternoon pressure seems to have been brought upon Johnson to throw his influence to Knox or some other aspirant for the Presidential honor. It is the understanding that at this juncture Johnson indicated that he was not satisfied with Knox's views on taxation, and perhaps on other public questions. So Johnson failed to place his indorsement on the Knox boom.

Senator Borah entered the conference of the conservative group of Senators and asked them to consider Knox. He was asked if he came from Senator Johnson. Borah answered that he acted only for himself. Thereupon various objections to Mr. Knox as a Presidential candidate were raised. He was too old. It was said that he was not in good health. He had voted against woman suffrage and for prohibition. He was from a State that did not need a favorite son at the head of the Presidential ticket to keep it in the Republican Party. And the Knox boom died then and there.

Thought Out of the Race.

Harding gained the Presidential nomination within twenty-four hours after he was looked upon as out of the race. He had made a poor showing in convention balloting yesterday and just before midnight last night papers had been filed at Columbus entering him as a candidate for re-election to the United States Senate.

These papers had been prepared in advance and were left with friends in Columbus to whom Senator Harding gave discretion to file or not to file as they saw fit. These friends, probably ad-

is room for still greater increase in prosperity and influence.

No more than anything else on earth will American journalism ever again be the same as before 1914. What the opportunities and demands of the future will be no newspaper man can see very clearly, though some of them think they can see after a fashion; but it is safe to say that they will require a higher standard of merit from all newspapers than that which was sufficient from 1865 to 1914. It will probably be impossible for American newspapers of the future to achieve greatness, or even much notoriety, by mere vigorous expression of partisan political views. No New York paper, at least, will ever again become great and prosperous by excellence merely in local news. Newspapers of the future must give the news, and the news of the world. They must combine in proper proportion the covering of the news in their home town, as they have learned that art in the last half century, with the presentation of the news from every continent as some of them have learned to present it since 1914.

Modern science has made news-gathering more difficult in the sense that it has broadened immeasurably the possibilities of getting news and thus enabled the most enterprising newspapers to set a very high standard for their competitors. The example given above will suggest that when a news story may be covered simultaneously by cable, wireless or telegraph, in London, Paris, Berlin and Washington, the paper which expects to cover it merely by a telegram from the Washington office is sometimes going to be left behind. A good newspaper of today needs a

larger, more intricate, more efficient and more expensive organization than the best editors of twenty years ago could have imagined.

It is possible that the progress of invention will make competition still keener in another direction. Last year, during the Republican Convention at Chicago, *The Times* sent its city edition out by airplane mail and delivered it at Chicago in the course of the afternoon. Before many years have gone this may be a matter of course; and thus for the first time it may be possible to have in America something approaching a really national newspaper. There can never be national newspapers in this country as in France and England, because of the limitations our vast distances impose upon delivery; but when New York papers are delivered everywhere east of the Mississippi on the day of publication, as they certainly will be within a decade or so, they will have an opportunity for taking on a good deal more of a national character than they have ever had in the past.

Undoubtedly *The New York Times* today approaches the character of a national newspaper more nearly than any other in America. It does so, of course, because of its copious presentation of general news, national and international, which is made possible by the fact that *The Times* is fortunate enough to have in the city where it is published a large clientele which will be interested in this news. One of the obstacles in the way of establishing a sort of generalized national newspaper such as is sometimes talked of by doctrinaires is the fact that every newspaper has to be printed and published

somewhere; that the difficulties of distribution make it inevitable that a very large proportion of its reading public will be local; and that most people want to find in their paper a good deal of news about the town in which they live. *The Times* attempts to cover the local news as adequately as its competitors, but it is fortunate in being the favorite with that part of the New York reading public which is also keenly interested in the news of the world. It is, accordingly, able to devote a great deal more of its space to the presentation *in extenso* of news of general interest, and consequently has a larger circulation outside the metropolitan district than any other New York paper. It is widely read in Washington; and in California it probably has a larger circulation than all other New York papers combined.

It is only a guess, but probably a safe guess, that *The Times* is also more generally read over the world than any other American paper. It has mail subscribers in the Aland Islands, in Mauritius, and all over the South Seas; in almost every state or colony of Africa; in Sivas of Anatolia, in Tarsus of Cilicia, in Bagdad and in Bandar Abbas. And by no means all of its Asiatic subscribers are wandering Americans; even outside of Japan and China, a good many of them are Asiatics who find something of interest in *The New York Times*.

The newspaper business in the future will not be a game for pikers. *The Times* today has some 1800 employés; its daily pay roll exceeds $10,000; it uses a daily average of nearly 200 tons of paper. The cost of news-getting may be surmised from the fact that

some $25,000 was spent by *The Times* in covering the two national conventions of 1920. It would be rather hazardous to assert that nobody could come into the New York newspaper field today on a "shoestring," as Mr. Ochs did in 1896, and succeed — hazardous, because even in 1896 all the experts said that he could not rehabilitate *The Times* without spending millions of dollars. But at least it seems quite unlikelv that anything like this could be done now.

In the past twenty-five years five New York papers have died. *The Advertiser*, *The Mercury*, *The News* and *The Press* have all disappeared. Neither *The Herald* nor *The Sun* has disappeared in name, but at any rate there is only one morning paper where both *The Herald* and *The Sun* grew before. Of the papers which were in existence in 1896 and are still appearing today some have survived because they have made money, and some because they are owned by wealthy men who can stand the loss. And it is significant that the only new daily paper which has been established in New York in the past twenty-five years — a paper, it should be observed, which is of a somewhat specialized character, predominantly a "picture paper," and can be produced much more cheaply than a daily of the ordinary type — is owned by the wealthy corporation which publishes *The Chicago Tribune*, and which could not only supply *The Daily News* with its telegraph and cable news and its features without added cost, but could put up the money to keep it going till it got on its feet.

The increased cost of production has reduced

the number of papers in most of the other cities of the country as well as in New York. It takes money not only to start a paper but to keep it going if it does not pay its way — more money than was needed twenty-five years ago. The natural result is concentration, the absorption of failing papers by their more prosperous competitors. That perhaps may not be altogether in the public interest, especially in a city of secondary rank which used to support two or three morning papers and now has only one. Even Chicago has now only two morning newspapers in the English language. It is conceivable that in a city of two and three quarter million people there are a good many readers who are not wholly satisfied with either of those papers, but to start another in successful competition would require both unusual ability and a great deal of money.

New daily papers, unless supported by men who are quite willing to go on throwing millions into them until they get on their feet in competition with established papers whose annual income already runs into the millions, are more likely to renounce all hope of competing with those already established in the covering of general news, and restrict themselves to particular interests. Even that will imply some serious disadvantages; for example, with two or three such publications competing with newspapers of the more usual type there is bound to be a good deal of waste in advertising. With certain newspapers confining their energies to only a part of the field, advertisers will be in doubt just how to reach the public they want, and a good deal more of their

money will be required. In the opinion of the management of *The Times*, advertising which does not bring results is disadvantageous not only for the advertiser, but for the newspaper; and the most satisfactory situation for both is that in which the actual situation of every newspaper both as to quantity and quality of circulation is well known.

These dangers may not be imminent, in view of the high cost of establishing a newspaper of any kind in a large city; but in somewhat modified form evils of this general character exist in present-day advertising. In the opinion of the publisher of *The Times* the most widespread defects of advertising today are lost motion and low visibility; and it may be in order to quote some of his thoughts on this subject delivered to the Associated Advertising Clubs of the World in their convention at Philadelphia on June 26, 1916:

> It may startle you if I say that I doubt if there is any business in the world in which there is so much waste of time, money, and energy as in advertising and its correlative instrumentalities. It may be rank heresy for *me* to say this, yet I affirm that more than 50 per cent of the money spent in advertising is squandered, and is a sheer waste of printer's ink, because little thought and less intelligence are applied, and ordinary common sense is entirely lacking; too frequently the dishonesty stamped on its face is about all the intelligent reader discerns.
>
> The first essential of successful advertising is something to advertise; the next, to know how to advertise, and when and

where. Too many advertisers have naught to advertise save their impotence and their folly. Too often the impelling reason is vanity — to see their names in print — and the greatest damage results when business prudence is dethroned and the advertising is done for ulterior reasons, either to favor some individual or to promote some sinister purpose. But it is not of that kind of wastage I wish to speak, for we have no interest in that sort of advertiser. I have in mind some well-intentioned advertisers' lost motion and consequently low visibility.

I say *some* advertisers — though I should say *many* advertisers. To my mind the worst evil is the thoughtless and careless method in buying advertising space. If the advertiser wishes to build a house or a factory he investigates and informs himself; employs an architect; usually invites proposals and awards the construction to a responsible builder. When he buys his supplies he studies the markets; he informs himself; he engages efficient assistants. To sell his goods or products, he concentrates all his faculties to study the trade and meet competition. But when he comes to advertising, his business judgment seems atrophied; his conceit predominates; his prejudices have full sway; favoritism and personal feelings are potent influences. The care and scrutiny he exercises in all other branches are woefully lacking in his advertising department. The attitude assumed toward the publication favored — I use the word favored advisedly — is one of benevolence.

Let me illustrate the advertiser's lost motion by an example. He decides to adver-

tise. He consults various agencies; he too often selects the cheapest — lost motion. A list of publications is selected; too often the controlling factors are extra commission or rebate, personal friendship, low rates — lost motion. In the preparation of copy: little time and poor talent employed — lost motion. Finally, cheap papier-maché impressions of the advertisement are sent to the publications instead of good electrotypes, resulting in bad printing — lost motion, and certainly low visibility, if any visibility at all.

There are few acts of advertisers more stupid than to give time and thought to the preparation of copy, to fuss and fume with artists and compositors for an effective display, pay large sums for space, and then, to save a few pennies or a little time, mar the whole effect by supplying the publication a matrix from which to make a stereotype plate. You often see evidence of that kind of advertising shortsightedness, for it stands out like a sore thumb.

Now, about lost motion and low visibility by the advertising agent. The most glaring fault is when the agent uses his credit and standing beyond his personal resources and speculates in the result of his client's business. That's low visibility, for if he would look beyond his nose he would discover breakers ahead and about them frightful wreckage of some of the stoutest ships, even when steered by the ablest mariners. It is the exception that proves the rule if an advertising agent, departing from his legitimate business, avoids disaster.

An agent mars his reputation as a safe adviser and counselor when, for the small

A VIEW OF THE TIMES ROTOGRAVURE PRESSROOM,
Which Prints About 2,000,000 Rotogravure Supplements Per Week

THE AUTOMOBILE TRUCKS
Which Hauled More Than 50,000 Tons of Paper to The Times During the Year 1920.

immediate profit in sight, he takes the business of an advertiser who has nothing to advertise except, perhaps, a bad name; or one whose advertising a tyro in the business should know would bring no results. Here's where truth should prevail, and the proposed advertiser warned against wasting his money.

"I only handle advertising which my expert knowledge and experience cause me to believe will justify the expenditure." What a drawing card that would be for an agent if he could succeed in making those interested know its truth.

Now, as to the publisher — the third party to the transaction. How about his lost motion and low visibility? I cannot even begin to catalogue his delinquencies under that head; it would consume too much time. But this I will say, that there is no other business in which there is so much lost motion and low visibility as in the publishing business. The wastage is frightful, appalling, and disheartening to those who have the temerity to acquaint themselves with the facts.

I refer especially to newspaper publishers, and it is of their bad practices I shall say a few words, for I cannot trust myself to unloose my pent-up feelings on that subject, in fear lest it largely partake of self-condemnation.

In the matter of advertising rates there seems to be only one established rule, viz., "All the traffic will bear." There seems to be no standard, no basis from which to begin, and consequently rates are altogether arbitrary. Common sense and ordinary rules of logic play little part. Rates are

fixed in the easiest way; that is, along the line of least resistance. Is it any wonder that the advertiser is disquieted and not trustful when he is asked to sail the uncharted seas?

The besetting sin is low rates. If you wish to see intelligent advertising, effective advertising, advertising that attracts the reader, where there is the least lost motion in space and words, you will find it in the publications maintaining what the advertiser considers high rates; and, on the other hand, the thoughtless, worthless advertising predominates where the rates are low.

I am not comparing largely circulated publications with those of small circulation. I have in mind publications of relatively the same circulation. When rates, in a desirable medium, are what the advertiser thinks comparatively high, he must consider quality, and nine times out of ten the quality or character of the circulation is the deciding factor. Cheap rates destroy more advertising than they create, for they encourage useless and profitless advertising.

I have a theory that the basic rate should be one cent a line per thousand circulation, in a publication where the advertising columns are given the consideration to which they are entitled, and the advertising placed to the best advantage for results with regard to the publication's good reputation and the reader's interest. There may be less advertising space in the publication, but what there is would be better done and more effective. I am discussing advertising in its broadest aspect; cases in which there is something to advertise

and advertising space is purchased with a view to the result of its direct appeal.

I wish to make clearer what I have just said regarding the placing of advertising with reference to the publication's good reputation and the reader's interest. I mean the advertisement should not be disguised; the reader should recognize it as an advertisement; no sailing under false colors. Advertising that cannot pay one cent a line per thousand circulation is hardly worth doing.

Newspapers have a variety of rates, usually the highest for the business that naturally comes to them, and the lowest for such as prefer another medium; not infrequently this discrimination is against the interests of the best clients.

The ideal newspaper advertising rate is a flat rate — one rate for all kinds of advertising; no time or space discount; a space limitation and extra charge for permissible exceptions and preferences.

There is no good excuse for reducing the rate because the advertisement has news value, for the greater the news value the stronger the justification for remunerative rates.

A word with reference to the belief in some quarters that the advertiser bears too great a proportion of the expense of publication. This creates the popular delusion of an unequal division of the expense between advertisers and readers. An established newspaper is entitled to fix its advertising rates so that its net receipts from circulation may be left on the credit side of the profit and loss account. To arrive at net receipts, I would deduct from

the gross the cost of promotion, distribution, and other expenses incidental to circulation. I affirm this on the principle that the advertiser wishes to encourage the widest distribution, for without impairing its merits the less costly the publication the larger its circulation, hence the more valuable and less costly the advertising; so, the less the reader pays, the less the advertising costs, and if circulation augments profits the publisher is rewarded for stimulating it. To assert that therefore the newspaper is solely or dangerously dependent on the advertiser is to declare that advertising has no value, that advertisers have no intelligence, and that the publisher does not know independence when he enjoys it. It is an axiom in newspaper publishing—"more readers, more independence of the influence of advertisers; fewer readers and more dependence on advertisers." It may seem like a contradiction (yet it is the truth) to assert: the greater the number of advertisers, the less influence they are individually able to exercise with the publisher.

A lot of nonsense is circulated about the advertiser's control of the newspaper. A newspaper improperly controlled by an advertiser is the exception that proves the rule.

There are some compensations for those disadvantages which modern conditions have brought. The high cost of establishing a newspaper or of conducting an unsuccessful newspaper makes it rather unlikely that in the future papers will be maintained, as they have sometimes been in the

past, for ulterior reasons — that is, with some other purpose than the presentation of the news. Financial or political interests are not likely to buy papers to support their views if they are going to have to spend millions on this type of publicity — a type which is apt to be unremunerative, since a paper subservient to external interests is usually very soon recognized for what it is, and loses all standing in consequence. Nor will it be so easy in the future as it has been in the past for wealthy men to buy newspapers as playthings.

The larger scale of present-day journalism has some other advantages. It has pretty nearly removed some of the temptations, such as subservience to advertisers or to political subsidies, which were constantly present with the publisher of past years. The perils of journalism today are those of most other human activities — slackness, routine, over-confidence, shortsightedness. They are most serious, perhaps, on the most successful papers, where the temptation to ride on a great reputation is most seductive. If American newspaper history teaches anything, it teaches that riding on a reputation is the surest road to ruin. Every paper in New York can read that in its own record.

For these consolations, such as they are, all newspaper men who take their business seriously should be thankful. In a sense, perhaps, the newspaper business is a public utility, but it differs from other public utilities in that competition is essential to its usefulness. Theoretically, there can be too much competition in the newspaper field, but there is not likely to be in the next few decades. And it is a bad

thing for any business to become so expensive that only a rich man can even dream of coming into it and shaking it up, for experience has shown that men who have acquired wealth in other occupations rarely provide very formidable competition when they go into the newspaper business; and, like all other businesses, it needs shaking up now and then. In the larger cities at least the newspaper field is virtually closed, restricted to those who now occupy it. The responsibility on them is all the heavier, for unless they do their work well it will not be done. And it has to be done in a democracy.

The recovery of *The Times* since 1896 is without parallel in modern newspaper history, and for the reasons given above it is likely to remain without parallel. Yet it may be that its history has some useful lessons for newspaper makers. What those lessons are any reader may infer from the story which has here been told. In the opinion of the management of *The Times*, perhaps the most important lesson is that integrity, common sense and good judgment are more likely to bring success than wild extravagances, constant experimentation and the frantic following of each new fashion. The fact that a particular policy or a particular feature has been a success on one paper is no guarantee that it will be successful everywhere. In the newspaper business, as in most other businesses, the surest road to success — in the opinion of the management of *The Times* — is to know what you want to do and know how to do it. If the new publisher who took charge of *The Times* in 1896 had tried to imitate *The Herald*, *The*

World or *The Journal*—the three brilliantly successful papers of the day—he would merely have accomplished his own ruin; and he could not have rebuilt *The Times* if he had not known his business from the ground up. Contrary to the opinion held in some quarters, newspaper making is skilled labor; it cannot be performed by any well-intentioned amateur.

Twenty-five Years' Record of Advertising Growth of "The New York Times"

YEAR	AGATE LINES
1896	2,227,196
1897	2,408,247
1898	2,433,193
1899	3,378,750
1900	3,978,620
1901	4,957,205
1902	5,501,779
1903	5,207,964
1904	5,228,480
1905	5,958,322
1906	6,033,457
1907	6,304,298
1908	5,897,332
1909	7,194,703
1910	7,550,650
1911	8,130,425
1912	8,844,866
1913	9,327,369
1914	9,164,927
1915	9,682,562
1916	11,552,496
1917	12,509,587
1918	13,518,255
1919	19,682,562
1920	23,447,395

Twenty-five Years' Record of Circulation Growth of "The New York Times"

YEAR	COPIES
October, 1896	21,516
" 1897	22,456
" 1898	25,726
" 1899	76,260
" 1900	82,106
" 1901	102,472
" 1902	105,416
" 1903	106,386
" 1904	118,786
" 1905	120,710
" 1906	131,140
" 1907	143,460
" 1908	172,880
" 1909	184,317
" 1910	191,981
" 1911	197,375
" 1912	209,751*
" 1913	230,360*
" 1914	259,673*
" 1915	318,274*
" 1916	340,904*
" 1917	357,225*
" 1918	368,492*
" 1919	362,971*
" 1920	342,553*
April 1921	352,528*

* Average net paid daily and Sunday circulation reported to the Post Office Department for the six months immediately preceding, in accordance with Act of Congress August 24, 1912.

The New York Times
"All the News That's Fit to Print."

NEW YORK, TUESDAY, DEC. 15, 1914.

FOR THE GERMAN PEOPLE, PEACE WITH FREEDOM.

Germany is doomed to sure defeat. Bankrupt in statesmanship, overmatched in arms, under the moral condemnation of the civilized world, befriended only by the Austrian and the Turk, two backward-looking and dying nations, desperately battling against the hosts of three great Powers to which help and reinforcement from States now neutral will certainly come should the decision be long deferred, she pours out the blood of her heroic subjects and wastes her diminishing substance in a hopeless struggle that postpones but cannot alter the fatal decree. Yet the doom of the German Empire may become the deliverance of the German people if they will betimes but seize and hold their own. Leipsic began and Waterloo achieved the emancipation of the French people from the bloody, selfish and sterile domination of the Corsican Ogre. St. Helena made it secure. Sedan sent the little NAPOLEON sprawling and the statesmen of France instantly established and proclaimed the Republic. Will the Germans blindly insist on having their Waterloo, their Sedan—their St. Helena, too? A million Germans have been sacrificed, a million German homes are desolate. Must other millions die and yet other millions mourn before the people of Germany take in the court of reason and human liberty their appeal from the imperial and military caste that rushes them to their ruin?

They have their full justification in the incompetence and failure of their rulers. German diplomacy and German militarism have broken down. The blundering incapacity of the

Kaiser's counselors and servants in statecraft at Berlin and in foreign capitals committed Germany to a war against the joined might of England. France and Russia. BISMARCK would never have had it so. Before he let the armies take the field, before he gave Austria the "free hand," he would have had England and Russia by the ears, he would have isolated France, as he did in 1870. The old Emperor, a man not above the common in capacity, surpassed the wisdom of his grandson in this, that he knew better than to trust his own judgment and he was sagacious enough to call great men to his aid. WILHELM II. was wretchedly served at Vienna by an Ambassador blinded by Russophobia, at St. Petersburg by another who advised his home Government that Russia would not go to war, and at London by the muddling LICHNOWSKY, whose first guesses were commonly wrong and his second too late to be serviceable. Germany literally forced an alliance for this war between England and Russia, two Powers often antagonistic in the past and having now no common interest save the curbing of Germany. The terrible misjudgment of the General Staff hurled Germany headlong into the pit that incompetent diplomacy had prepared. The Empire went to war with three great nations able to meet her with forces more than double her own.

Then the worth of that iron military discipline and of the forty years of ceaseless preparation to which Germany had sacrificed so much of the productive power of her people was put to the test. Again the colossal imperial machine broke down. It was not through incompetence. The German Army was magnificent in its strength, in equipment, and in valor. It was overmatched, it had attempted the impossible. That was the fatal blunder. The first rush upon Paris

was intended to be irresistible; that was the plan of the General Staff; France crushed, Russia could be sent about her business. It was not irresistible, it was checked, it was repulsed. When the invaders were driven back from the Marne to the Aisne and the Belgian frontier Germany's ultimate defeat was registered in the book of fate and heralded to the watching world. Germany's battle line has been forced back to where it stood when it first encountered the French. Calais is freed from her menace, Tannenberg was but an incident to the swarming hordes of Russia. What boots it if she enters Lodz, if she seize Warsaw, what even if by some unlooked for turn of fortune she again approach the walls of Paris? KITCHENER's new million of trained men will be in France before the snows have melted in the Vosges, and Russia is inexhaustible.

There is within the German view an even more sinister portent. The world cannot, will not, let Germany win in this war. With her dominating all Europe peace and security would vanish from the earth. A few months ago the world only dimly comprehended Germany, now it knows her thoroughly. So if England, France and Russia cannot prevail against her, Italy, with her two millions, the sturdy Hollanders, the Swiss, hard men in a fight, the Danes, the Greeks and the men of the Balkans will come to their aid and make sure that the work is finished, once for all. For their own peace and safety the nations must demolish that towering structure of militarism in the centre of Europe that has become the world's danger-spot, its greatest menace.

The only possible ending of the war is through the defeat of Germany. Driven back to her Rhine strongholds, she will offer a stubborn resistance. Even with the Russians near or actually in Berlin she would fight on.

But for what? Why? Because the German people, the very people, are resolved to get themselves all killed before the inevitable day of the enemy's triumph? Not at all. The weary men in the trenches and the distressed people merely obey the orders given by imperial and military authority. For the men in those high quarters defeat would be the end of all. Desperation, with some possible admixture of blind confidence, will continue the war. But why should the German people make further sacrifice of blood to save the pride and the shoulder straps of German officialdom? It means a million more battlefield graves. It means frightful additions to the bill of costs and to the harshness of the terms. Since the more dreadful ending is in plain view, why not force the better ending now?

But this is revolution. That may be so; call it so. Definitions are useful, they are not deterrent. Is there in all history any record of a whole people rising against their rulers in the midst of a great war? Let the historians answer the question. Is it conceivable that the loyal German people, made one by the love of the Fatherland and devoted to the accomplishment of the imperial ideals, could be stirred to revolt while still unconquered? That concerns the prophets. We are concerned neither with precedents nor with prophecy. We have aimed here to make clear the certainty of Germany's defeat and to show that if she chooses to fight to the bitter end her ultimate and sure overthrow will leave her bled to exhaustion, drained of her resources, and under sentence to penalties of which the stubbornness of her futile resistance will measure the severity. We could wish that the German people, seeing the light, might take timely measures to avert the calamities that await them.

It may well be doubted that they

will see the light. But have not the men of German blood in this country a duty to perform to their beleaguered brethren in the old home? Americans of German birth or of German descent should see and feel the truth about the present position of Germany, the probability for the near, the certainty for the remoter, future. At home the Germans cannot know the whole truth; it is not permitted them to know it. It will be unfraternal and most cruel for German-Americans further to keep the truth from them, or to fail in their plain duty to make known to them how low the imperial and militaristic ideal has fallen in the world's esteem, and to bring them to understand that the enemies they now confront are but the first line of civilization's defenses against the menace of the sword that forever rattles in its scabbard. The sword must go, the scabbard, too, and the shining armor. If the Germans here have at all the ear of the Germans there, can they not tell them so? They have come here to escape the everlasting din of war's trappings; they have come to find peace and quiet in a land of liberty and law, where government rests on the consent of the governed, where the people by their chosen representatives, when there is a question of going into the trenches to be slain, have something to say about it. Have they ever tried to get into the heads of their friends in the Fatherland some idea of the comforts and advantages of being governed in that way? Instead of vainly trying to change the well-matured convictions of the Americans, why not labor for the conversion of their brother Germans?

The State is Power, said TREITSCHKE. He would have written TENNYSON's line "The individual withers, the State is more and more." In the German teaching the State is everything, to the State the individual must sacrifice everything. With us the State is the

social organization by which men assure to themselves the free play of individual genius, each man's right in peace and security to work out his individual purposes. If the German-Americans prize the privileges they have enjoyed under our theory of the State, ought they not to tell the Germans at home what it means for the individual to be free from quasi-vassalage? There is no people on earth more worthy to enjoy the blessings of freedom than the Germans. Germany has taken her place in the very front of civilization, freed from the double incubus of imperialism and militarism the German genius would have a marvelous development. It is not in the thought of Germany's foes to crush the German people, the world would not let them be crushed. It has for them the highest esteem, it will acclaim the day when it can resume friendly and uninterrupted relations with them. But the headstrong, misguided, and dangerous rulers of Germany are going to be called to stern account, and the reckoning will be paid by the German people in just the proportion that they make common cause with the blindly arrogant ruling class. When representative Americans and men of peace like Dr. Eliot and Andrew Carnegie insist that there can be no permanent peace until an end has been made of German militarism, sober-minded Germans, here as well as in Germany, ought not to turn a deaf ear to such voices, for they speak the opinion of the world. The bill of costs mounts frightfully with every month's prolongation of the war and the toll of human lives is every day ruthlessly taken. It may be a counsel of unattainable perfection to say that the German people ought now to end the war. But for their own happiness, for their own homes, for their interests and their future, it is true. The truth of the counsel is unconquerable.

Roster of The New York Times Company

Adolph S. Ochs	President
Charles R. Miller	Vice-President
Julius Ochs Adler	Vice-President
Arthur Hays Sulzberger	Vice-President
Julius Ochs Adler	Treasurer
Ben. C. Franck	Secretary

BOARD OF DIRECTORS

Adolph S. Ochs   Charles R. Miller   Ben. C. Franck
G. W. Ochs Oakes   Iphigene Ochs Sulzberger

PUBLISHER

*Adolph S. Ochs

Executive Council

Adolph S. Ochs   Charles R. Miller   Carr V. Van Anda
Julius Ochs Adler   Louis Wiley   Arthur Hays Sulzberger

Assistants to the Publisher

Julius Ochs Adler   Arthur Hays Sulzberger   *Ben. C. Franck
*Kate L. Stone, Secretary to the Publisher

Secretaries and Clerks

ALICE M. JENKINS   MAURA L. O'SULLIVAN   C. R. SAFFORD
PETER BROWN   JOHN R. HOUSTON   ANDREW JORDAN
JOHN O'BRIEN   JOHN O'DONNELL   ANNA CARROLL
J. BENTLEY SQUIER, JR.

Attorney

Alfred A. Cook, General Counsel
George Norris, Associate Attorney

* Twenty-five years or more with *The Times.*

ROSTER OF THE NEW YORK TIMES COMPANY

EDITORIAL DEPARTMENT

*Charles R. Miller, Editor-in-chief
Rollo Ogden, Associate Editor
John H. Finley, Associate Editor

Editorial Staff

Henry E. Armstrong *E. A. Bradford John Corbin
Elmer Davis Edward M. Kingsbury *F. C. Mortimer
Frank D. Root Charles H. Grasty

NEWS DEPARTMENT

Carr V. Van Anda, Managing Editor

Frederick T. Birchall	Assistant Managing Editor
Alden March	Day News Editor
Osmund Phillips	City Editor
David H. Joseph	Assistant City Editor
J. W. Phoebus	Night City Editor
Ernest V. Chamberlin	Assistant Night City Editor
Joseph F. Tebeau	Telegraph Editor
Wilson L. Fairbanks	Assistant Telegraph Editor
John F. O'Neil	Make-up Editor
H. J. Learoyd	Assistant Make-up Editor
Ralph H. Graves	Sunday Editor
Henry Irving Brock	Assistant Sunday Editor
Charles M. Graves	Editor Rotogravure Pictorial
Victor W. Talley	Asst.Ed.Rotogravure Pictorial
Alfred D. Noyes	Financial Editor
Franklin K. Sprague	Assistant Financial Editor
*Henry Loewenthal	Business Editor
Bernard Thomson	Sports Editor
William J. Slocum	Assistant Sports Editor
Clifford Smythe	Book Review Editor
James B. Stewart	Real Estate Editor
Richard Aldrich	Music Editor
Alexander Woollcott	Dramatic Editor
Wilbur Finley Fauley	Society Editor
Elizabeth Luther Cary	Art Editor
Edward N. Dart	Director Art Department
Edwin Marcus	Cartoonist
Laurence V. Updegraff	Editor Correspondence
Charles V. Vanderhoof	Manager Syndicate News
Walter Littlefield	Foreign Publications
Harry T. Smith	Foreign Publications
*R. W. Welch	American Publications
Jennie Welland	Manager Library and Index
Thomas Bracken	Manager News Index
Irving E. Pfeiffer	Subject Index
Frederick Meinholz	Manager Wireless Station
Richard V. Oulahan	Manager Washington Office
Hal. H. Smith	Asst. Mgr. Washington Office
Ernest A. Marshall	Manager London Office
Edwin L. James	Manager Paris Office

* Twenty-five years or more with *The Times.*

ROSTER OF THE NEW YORK TIMES COMPANY

News and Editorial Staff

*ABRAHAMS, MICHAEL B.
ACKERMAN, JOHN D.
ANDREWS, HENRY V.
AUSTIN, FREDERICK A.
BARCLAY, GEO. E.
BEAN, RODNEY
BECAN, JOHN
BELL, JEFFERSON G.
BERONOWSKI, ANDREW
BLAKE, GEO. W.
BLANPIED, RALPH D.
BLYTHE, WALTER E.
BOND, F. FRAZER
BRADY, EDWARD
BRANNAN, DANA
BROADWELL, ARTHUR
BROWN, CYRIL
BROWN, JOHN
BROWN, PERCY
BURGESS, ARTHUR
BUTCHER, JESSE S.
CAMPBELL, JOHN R.
CASARIO, EUGENE
CHASE, W. B.
CHESTERTON, GEO. L.
CLARKE, HAZEL
CLARKE, VINCENT
COLLINS, WILLIAM
CONNERY, TIM
CORTESI, ELIZABETH
CORUM, MARTENE W.
CRANE, F. W.
CROUCH, H. C.
CURLEY, JOHN W.
DAVIDSON, CHARLES M.
DAWSON, JAMES
DAWSON, ROBERT P.
DAY, JOSEPH T.
DELANO, EDWIN F.
DE NARDO, ANTHONY
DE PUY, FRANK A.
DICKEY, CARL
DONLON, J. S.
DURANTY, WALTER
EATON, MALCOLM
EVERETT, ETHEL W.
FARDON, JAMES
FELD, ROSE C.
FELLEMAN, HAZEL
FINCH, TOLITA MAY

FISCHER, ELIZ. M.
FISKE, D. W.
FOLEY, MAURICE
FORD, COREY H.
FOX, ARTHUR
GLEASON, LILLIAN
GOBETZ, ARTHUR
GODDARD, PERCIVAL S.
GORDON, JOHN J.
GORMAN, HERBERT S.
GRANT, J. C.
GROVE, J. H.
HAGERTY, JAMES A.
HAGGERTY, MICHAEL F.
HALLIGAN, EDWARD
HAMBIDGE, C. G.
HAMEL, GASTON
HAMILTON, THOMAS C.
HARDING, JOHN W.
HARRIS, FRANCES D.
HARRISON, JAMES R.
HAYS, GENE
HEATH, ELIZ. M.
HEDDEN, GEORGIANA
HERTEL, H. H.
HINTON, HAROLD B.
HIRSCHEL, IRVING
HIRSCHEL, TOBIE
HOLLAND, JAMES
HOLME, LEONARD R.
HOYT, PHILIP D.
HUGHES, CHARLES F.
HUNTER, FRANK
HUNTINGTON, WM. R.
HUTCHISON, PERCY A.
IRWIN, JR., F. N.
IVERSON, REGINALD
JAEGER, FRED A.
JANNET, ADY
JOHNSTON, ALVA
JONES, WATKIN
KAUFMAN, GEO. S.
KEARNEY, AGNES
KEARNS, FRANK
KEENAN, WALTER M.
KELLY, MRS. F. F.
KELLY, JOHN
KEPPLE, ERNEST P.
KING, EARL
KLAUBER, EDWARD

KNOX, PURVES T.
KROLL, MORTIMER J.
KURTH, JR., OTTO
KURTZ, HENRY
LANE, MILTON
LARITY, THOMAS
LARNED, RICHARD M.
LAVIN, JOHN
LAWSON, WILLIAM E.
LEA, J. H.
LEWIS, HENRY N.
LINN, JR., THOMAS C.
LONG, E. JOHN
LOTT, ELLA K.
LYMAN, LAUREN D.
MacNEIL, NEIL
MARSHALL, FRANCES W.
MARTIN, WALTER T.
MASON, JOSEPH
*MCCAHILL, W. J.
MCDONALD, ANNA
MCDONALD, GEORGE
MCDOWELL, R. K.
MCGINITY, LEO A.
MCGILL, FRED W.
MCMANUS, JOHN
MCSWEENEY, EDWARD
MICHAEL, C. R.
MILLAR, H. PERCY
MORAN, STEVE
MUELLER, LOGAN E.
MUENCH, FRED
MULLER, WILLIAM
NAINOR, ANDREW
NETZER, JACK
NIXON, WILSON K.
O'CONNELL, JOHN J.
O'CONNOR, F. J.
OWEN, JOHN
OWEN, RUSSELL D.
PHILIP, P. J.
PORTER, R. S.
PRAET, JAMES J.
RAE, BRUCE
RAUCH, MAY
RICHARDSON, WILLIAM D.
RIDDELL, BEATRICE
ROBINSON, F. H.
ROBINSON, JOHN E.
ROSENBERG, R.

* Twenty-five years or more with *The Times.*

News and Editorial Staff — *Continued*

ROSENTHAL, DELPHINE
ROWLAND, EDITH
RYAN, JOHN
SACKETT, WILLIAM E.
SAPIA, JANE
SCHLOSSER, WILLIAM
SCHOCH, WALTER
SCHUMANN, CHARLES
SCHWARTZ, SADIE
SHAPS, JACK
SNYDER, FRANCES
SOULE, H. P.
SPEARING, JAMES O.
SPEERS, L. C.
SPENCER, H. S.
STARK, LOUIS
STAUB, WILLIAM
STEFFEN, CHARLES
STEFFEN, J. HAL.
STEPHENS, DOLORES
STEWART, EDWARD J.
STRUSINSKI, NICHOLAS
SUETTER, BENJAMIN
SULLIVAN, JOS. F.
SWARTZ, ARTHUR
TAFT, MARY A.
TALLEY, TRUMAN H.
THOMPSON, C. W.
THORNE, VAN BUREN
TURPIN, RUFUS E.
VAN NESS, FRED A.
VULTEE, L. H.
WADE, MARGARET
WALL, FLORENCE
WALSH, LEONARD
WAMSLEY, WILBUR F.
WARN, W. A.
WATERS, JOSEPH
WEAVER, JOS. A.
WEBER, ABRAHAM
WELDON, M. L.
WHITE, EDITH
WHITNEY, C. H.
WIDLIZKA, ANTAN
WILKIE, ENID
WILL, ALLEN S.
WILLIAMS, FLORENCE E.
WILLIAMS, T. W.
WILLIAMSON, S. T.
WILSON, WILLIAM R.
WIMBROUGH, A. C.
WOOD, LEWIS
WRIGHT, JEAN
WRIGHT, WILLIAM C.
YERION, RUTH
YOUNG, JAMES C.
ZOLOTOW, SAMUEL

BUSINESS DEPARTMENT

*Louis Wiley, Business Manager

Edwin S. Friendly	Assistant Business Manager
Hugh A. O'Donnell	Bus. Manager Representative
B. T. Butterworth	Advertising Manager
Harris H. Walker	Assistant Advertising Manager
Frank W. Harold	Advertising Censor
Arnold Sanchez	Manager Credit Department
James M. Kirshner	Manager Charge Department
R. Alexander Lawe	Manager Bookkeeping Department
William W. Miller	Classified Advertising Manager
Irma Kory	Assistant Classified Advertising Mgr.
*Charles A. Flanagan	Circulation Manager
Louis O. Morny	Subscription Manager
William Johnson	Chief Circulation Inspector
Michael A. O'Reilly	Chief Circulation Bookkeeper
William A. Hurley	Manager Annex Publication Office
Edward H. Taylor	Supervisor Branch Offices
Edward B. Wells	Mgr. Times Building Publication Office
William Kean	Manager Downtown Office
A. H. Mandelberg	Manager Harlem Office
Chester M. Goode	Manager Brooklyn Office
Bernard Van Camp	Manager Messenger Department
Sadie L. McNulty	Incoming Mail Department
Anna Groh	Outgoing Mail Department
Mildred L. Bischof	Manager File Department
Anna Kottman	Circulation Manager Index
Katherine Maguire	Chief Telephone Operator

* Twenty-five years or more with *The Times.*

ROSTER OF THE NEW YORK TIMES COMPANY

Business Department — *Continued*

ADAMS, WALTER C.
AGOADO, JOSEPH
ALLUISI, GEORGE
APPLEGATE, GERTRUDE G.
ARDELL, HERBERT S.
ASTON, HENRY H.
BABCOCK, FRANCIS M.
BACHRAN, JOHN E.
BACON, MRS. HATTIE
BALL, E. SULLIVAN
BANGS, GILBERT M.
BANKS, HARRIET D.
BARNETT, GEORGE F.
BASILOWITZ, MICHAEL
BAXTER, IRVING C.
BECK, AUGUSTUS
BEERE, SEYMOUR
BELL, ROBERT
BENDER, WILLIAM
BENNETT, MAE V.
BERGEN, MARGARET
BERGEN, PHILIP
BERGER, HELEN
BERKERY, ROSE
BIGELOW, BURT M.
BIGGS, RICHARD
BISSETT, WILLIAM
BLOCH, LENA
BOEHM, HULDA M.
BOLEI, EVELYN
BOND, FRANK
BRADLEY, MARGARET
BRENNEN, CATHERINE
BRENNEN, CHARLES J.
BRENNEN, MAY
BROSNAN, AGNES
BROWN, HARRY W.
BRUMER, FRANCES
BUCHOLZ, CLAIRE
BURKE, ANNA
BURNES, MARJORIE
BZENAK, ANNA
CAHILL, JOSEPH
CAMERON, WILSON
CANFIELD, THOMAS
CANSE, EDWARD
CARMODY, AGNES
CARVILLE, ARTHUR J.
CAVANAGH, JAMES T.
CHESTON, ESTHER
CLARK, ELIZABETH
CLARK, GRACE
CLARK, HELEN M.
CLARK, MARGARET E.
CLARK, NOBERN C.
CLARKE, JAMES J.
COCHRANE, ROBERT C.
COHEN, GEORGE
COLLIER, EDNA
COLLINS, HAZEL
CONNELL, ANNA
CONNELL, MARY
CONNORS, HELEN
COOPE, JOSEPHINE
COSTOSA, RAYMOND
COX, HARRY F.
COX, HARRY S.
CUNNINGHAM, FLORENCE
CUSACK, GEORGE J.
DALGIN, BEN
DALTON, GERALD J.
DALTON, MRS. G. J.
DALY, JOSEPHINE
DAMON, ALBERT H.
DAVIS, PAUL
DE COSTA, LUCILLE
DE GWECK, GRACE
DELANEY, WINIFRED
DE MARRAIS, JOSEPH A.
DEMPSEY, KATHERINE
DENNY, VICTOR J.
DE ZAYAS, HENRIETTA
DIX, ADELAIDE B.
DOESSERECK, WILLIAM
DONAHUE, CLAIRE
DONNELLY, ELIZABETH
DONOVAN, KATHERINE
DORGAN, JOHN
DOWLEY, MAY
DU BLAN, CARMEN
DUFFY, JOHN T., JR.
DULLAGHAN, DOROTHY
DUNN, HUGH P.
DUNN, MARY A.
EGAN, CATHERINE
EISEL, THERESE C.
ELFERS, HERBERT
EMERIC, RAYMON
ENGLANDER, BLANCHE
ERB, CATHERINE
EVANS, H. WILSON
FANCIULLI, ROMOLA
FARRELL, THOMAS
FINNEY, CHARLES A.
FITZMAURICE, ANNA
FOOTE, ANNA
FOOTE, IRENE
FOX, ELEANOR
FRANK, MINNIE
FRY, BERNARD H.
FRYER, THOMAS H.
FURY, JOSEPH
FYBUSH, ELBERT
GALL, CLARA
GALLAGHER, CATHERINE
GAW, JOSEPH
GOERICKE, HARRY
GOLD, EVA
GOLDFINE, JEANNETTE
GOMBAR, FRANK
GORDON, HELEN
GRAHAM, ROSE
GRETSCHEL, CHARLES
GRISWOLD, FRANK B.
GROSS, EDWARD A.
HAGEN, MABEL
HAHN, GEORGE M.
HAINES, EDNA
HALLIGAN, FLORENCE
HAMBERGER, FLORENCE
HAMILTON, JOHN K.
HAMMERMAN, ELIZABETH
HANDBURY, MILDRED
HARLAN, ANNA S.
HARTMAN, ALICE
HERLEHY, FRANCES
HESLIN, MATTHEW J.
HETFIELD, JAMES
HICKEY, MARGARET
HICKEY, ROSE
HOLBERT, A. RUGGLES
HOLLAND, JOHN
HOLLOWAY, MURIEL
HOLMES, AGNES
HOOPER, DUDLEY R.
HORAN, ALICE
HORAN, MRS. J. J.
HORAN, WINIFRED
HUBBARD, CARLETON S.
HUGHES, MICHAEL
HULL, MRS. GERTRUDE
HUNT, EDWARD
HUTCHINSON, LAURA C.

Business Department — *Continued*

HYNES, IRENE
IZAGUIRRE, LORETTA
JACKSON, CHARLES J.
JAEGER, HENRY
JAGELER, JOHN
JAROS, CHARLES
JOHNSON, ANNA W.
JOHNSON, JOHN
JOHNSON, MRS. MATILDA
JONAS, STELLA
JUDGE, MARY G.
KALB, AUBREY
KAUFER, OLIVE
KAUFMAN, HENRY
KENNEY, HUGH J.
KING, WILLIAM W.
KINGSMORE, HOWARD P.
KIRCHER, BERTHA B.
KIVLAN, FRANK J.
KRAMPETZ, HELEN
KRASNER, ROSE
LACEY, ROSE
LAURI, ROSE
LEAHY, THOMAS
LECK, ANNA
LEDBETTER, WILLIAM
LEEMAN, GEORGE
LEIPSIG, ROSE
LIGHTENBERG, ISAAC
LIVINGSTON, BELLE
LOCKARD, MRS. RAY
LOW, ETHEL
LYNCH, WILLIAM
MCALOON, JOHN
MCAVOY, META
MCCANN, LUCINDA
MCCOY, JOSEPH
MCDERMOTT, MARY
MCDOWELL, WM. J.
MCGAHAN, FLORENCE
MCGOWN, HENRY
MCGRAM, HELEN
MCGRANN, ALFONSO
MCGRAW, WILLIAM
MCGUINNESS, JOHN
MCINTOSH, MCQUEEN
MCINTYRE, EWEN C.
MCKENNA, JOS. L.
MCMAHON, JOHN
MCNAMARA, ALBERT
MCNAMARA, ELIZABETH
MCNAMEE, FRANCIS
MCNEILL, JOHN
MCNULTY, FRANK L.
MacDONALD, JOSEPH
MAHER, BEATRICE L.
MAHNKEN, MRS. A.
MAINARDY, FRANK
MALONE, RICHARD A.
MALONEY, HARRY
MARABLE, JUNIUS
MARKS, SARA
MASSEY, GEORGIANNA L.
MATTIMORE, ANNA
*MAUBORGNE, EUGENE C.
MAYER, MARGARET
MEIERS, WALTER
MERZ, HARRY
MEYERS, FLORENCE
MEYERS, GERTRUDE
MEYERS, HELEN
MOFFETT, MARY
MONT, ROBERT
MOONEY, FLORENCE
MOOREHOUSE, ISA J.
MORGAN, ALFRED
MUDSE, ANTHONY J.
MUHLKER, HERBERT C.
MULCAHY, MARY
MULLANEY, MARIE A.
MUNROE, ALBERT E.
NAUGHTON, WILLIAM J.
NEEL, WILLIAM H.
NEUMANN, ANTHONY
NICHOLS, GERTRUDE E.
NICOLL, EMANUEL
NIEMAN, CHAUNCY W.
NILSON, FRANK
NOBLE, WALTER H.
NOLAN, WARREN C.
NORTON, ELLEN
O'BRIEN, LILLIAN
O'CONNELL, THOMAS
O'CONNOR, JOSEPHINE
O'LEARY, JOSEPH R.
O'NEILL, ALBERT
O'NEILL, DONALL
O'NEILL, JAMES
OLDSEN, MINA
OLMSTEAD, ALFRED H.
PACCIONE, MARY F.
PATTERSON, MARGARET
PETERS, CARL
PHILLIPS, HARRY S.
PICCIRILLO, MAE
PORTENAR, ABRAHAM J.
POWERS, RAY M.
QUINNELL, EDNA
RABEY, DOROTHY
REDMOND, JOHN
REED, LORA H.
REGAN, HELEN
REGAN, THOMAS D.
REILLY, HELEN
REILLY, JOHN H.
REILLY, JOHN
REINHARDT, LEON
RENNEISEN, MILDRED J.
REYNOLDS, HELEN
RICHARDS, VERNON
RIORDAN, JULIA
RITTER, HARRY E.
ROBINSON, JAMES J.
RODGERS, DAVID S.
RODRIGUEZ, GERTRUDE
ROSENBERG, NELLIE
ROSS, ADOLPH R.
ROTHMUND, CATHERINE
RUGGER, MAY
RYAN, HELEN
RYAN, JOHN A.
SAMBORN, JOHN A.
SANDLER, JACOB K.
SANSEVERINO, GODFREY
SAUSE, EMMA
SCHATTELES, SAMUEL
SCHERB, LILLIAN
SCHULTZ, P. RICHARD
SCHWAB, ELIZABETH
SEIDLER, CARLTON
SERVER, EDWARD A.
SETZER, ABRAHAM M.
SEWING, ALMA
SHAW, SAMSON H.
SHEEHAN, KATHERINE
SHEEHY, MABEL E.
SHEPPARD, STANLEY R.
SLOCUM, WILLIAM W.
SMITH, CHARLES
SMITH, CLARA M.
SMITH, CLEVELAND G.
SMITH, EDITH
SMITH, HARRY W.

* Twenty-five years or more with *The Times*.

BUSINESS DEPARTMENT — *Continued*

SMITH, LAURA M.
SMITH, THOMAS M.
STANDISH, CLIFFORD
STEERS, ROBERT
STORER, ELEANOR M.
SUCHARIPA, FRANCES
SUFFIN, SIMON
SULLIVAN, JAMES
SUPPLE, JULIA
SUTCLIFF, BEATRICE M.
SVEC, FRANK
SWORMSTED, WOODBURN
TAUSTINE, IRVING
THOMPSON, CAREY R.
THORNE, FLORENCE
TIMMONS, MARY
TROUT, MILDRED F.
TRUEPER, JOHN H.
UBERROTH, VIOLA
VAN SLYKE, WINFRED
VAN WENKLE, FANNY D.
VOS, ANDREW V.
WALSH, F. BAGLEY
WALSH, RAYMOND
WALTERS, ANNA
WARD, ETHEL
WEINBERG, FLORENCE
WEISHAAR, AUGUST
WEIS, RUTH
WELCH, ESTELLE
WELLS, PAULINE R.
WHITEHOUSE, LOUISE M.
WIGGINS, MRS. DONNA
WILD, MATILDA
WILLIAMS, WILLIAM
WILSTRUP, ALEXIS
WOLFF, HEDWIG
ZANDER, STANLEY C.
ZANK, DAVID
ZUCHTMANN, VERA

MECHANICAL DEPARTMENTS

CHARLES F. HART, Superintendent
LEWIS COCHRANE, Assistant Superintendent

Annex Building and Mechanical Department

WALTER S. BARNES . . . . Superintendent Annex Building
WALTER E. PALMER . . . . Chief Electrician
JOHN CONNELL . . . . Chief Stationary Engineer
JUDSON DUNLOP . . . . Master Carpenter
JAMES MCCAULEY . . . . Chief Watchman
GLENN DONALDSON . . . . Head Porter
WILLIAM DURRANT . . . . Foreman Machinist
ELSIE TAUSSIG . . . . Chief Stencil Department

ADAMS, CLAUDIE
BELL, DEE
BLAKE, PERCY
BLANKEN, CHARLES
BLUMENFIELD, ELSIE
BLUNT, RICHARD
BOLDEN, JOHN
CALLAHAN, LILLY
CHANDLER, LEDGER
CHISHOLM, WILLIAM
CHURCHMAN, GEORGE
CLARK, AGNES
COLEMAN, JAMES
COLLEARY, MARY
CONLON, LILLY
CROCKETT, JOHN
CROKE, THOMAS
CUMMINGS, GEORGE
CURCIO, LOUIS
CURTIN, PATRICK
DALTON, MARY
DALY, FLORENCE
DART, JAMES
DE NICOLA, HARRY
DINSENBACHER, JOSEPH
DOUGHERTY, JOHN
DU BOIS, JESSIE
EIDENBERG, TILLIE
ELLIS, LULU
ENGLISH, WILLIS
EVANS, JOHN
FARLEY, FRANCIS J.
FENN, CATHERINE
FENTON, JAMES
FRANCIS, RUPERT
FREEMAN, LILLIAN
GALLAGHER, MARY
GEEHAN, JOSEPH
GEOGHAN, PATRICK
GORDON, PETER C.
GRADEL, ELIZABETH
GRAVES, ROBERT
HANSBURY, CLIFFORD
HARD, CATHERINE
HART, KATE
HEILIG, MARGARET
HEINS, ALICE
HOUSTIN, JOHN
HUGHES, PHILIP
HUMPHREY, HOWARD
ISAACS, ROSE

Mechanical Departments — *Continued*

JOHNSON, HENRY
JOHNSON, JOSEPH
JOHNSTON, EUGENE
JOHNSTON, JAMES
KAPLAN, VICTORIA
KARZAN, HENRY
KELLY, MARY
KENNEDY, MOSES
KILKENNY, MICHAEL
KOCH, FRIEDA
KRAUS, CHARLES
KUSTER, ALBERT
LATIGUE, AUGUST
LEE, ALICE
LENTIN, REBECCA
LEY, JOHN
MARSHALL, JABEZ
MCDERMOTT, ALLEN
MCGARRY, PATRICK
MCGARY, MARY
MCGINLEY, JAMES
MCINERNEY, TIMOTHY
MEILLY, N.
MINSTER, ROSE
MUNZER, JOHN
MURRAY, TAYLOR
PALMER, WARREN E.
PEARSALL, EUGENE
PETERSON, ANDREW
REEVES, JOHN
REID, FRANK L.
RHODES, HENRY
ROBERTSON, FRANK
ROTH, SARAH
SAVAGE, JOHN
SCHURMAN, ARTHUR
SCOTT, ROBERT
SHEA, CATHERINE
SHORT, SAUL
SIMPSON, YANCEY
SMIDILI, PAOLO
SMITH, GEORGE
SMITH, JOHN
SMITH, MARY
SMITH, WILLIAM
STARKS, JOHN
STERLING, JAMES
TAYLOR, ERNEST
TEDESCO, MINNIE
TRIBBETT, GEORGE
UTZ, EVA
VANDERVALL, JAMES
VAN NEST, MARY
VOIGTLANDER, ERNEST
WALKER, GEORGE
WALSH, TIMOTHY
WESSON, WILLIAM
WESSTROM, ISAAC
WHITTAKER, M.
WIPFLER, LOUIS
WILLIAMS, CHAS. C.
WILLIAMS, JAMES L.
WILLIAMS JOHN W.
WILLIAMS, JOSEPH
WILSON, JAMES
WOLPERT, IDA
WOODBY, GEORGE
YOUNG, ALBERT

Composing Room

*WILLIAM A. PENNEY, Superintendent

*THOMAS J. DILLON . . . . Foreman Night Shift
CHARLES I. WILLEY . . . . Foreman Day Shift
JAMES A. BAIRD . . . . Foreman Third Shift
HARRY W. DAIL . . . . Foreman Ad Room
*WILLIAM G. DEVERICKS . . . . Assistant Foreman Ad Room
*CHRIS. FADUM . . . . Foreman Machinists
WALTER C. JOHNSON . . . . Assistant Foreman Machinists
*JOHN F. MCCABE . . . . Foreman Proof Room, Day
WILLIAM H. MICHENER . . . . Foreman Operators
HARRY WILLIAMS . . . . Foreman Proof Room, Night

ABRAHAM, BEN
ADLE, RICHARD
ALEXANDER, EDW.
AMEND, JOSEPH
APOSTLE, CARL
APOSTLE, NICK
ASHE, FRED R.
ASHLEY, HARRY
BAER, LOUIS
BARNETT, CHARLES
BARNEY, RALPH
BARRETT, HARRY
BEATTY, JAMES
BECKER, WM. H.
BENNETT, A. B.
BENSON, RAYMOND
BILLMAN, FRED H.
BLOOM, S.
BOEDECKER, WM. C.
BOWERMAN, HARRY C.
BOYCE, ARTHUR J.
BOYD, JOSEPH J.
BRADY, ROBT. J.
BRILEY, JAMES C.
BRUSH, ROBT.
BUCKINGHAM, A. C.
*BURR, FRED. E.
CAIRNS, A. G.
CAMP, WILBER E.
CAMPBELL, ALEX.
*CARROLL, MARTIN J.
CARSON, JOS. E.
CARSWELL, WM. D.

* Twenty-five years or more with *The Times*.

Composing Room — *Continued*

CARVER, WM.
CITRO, ANTHONY
CLARK, BEVERLY
CLARK, JOSEPH
CLASS, PAUL T.
CLEMMITT, EDWARD B.
CLIFTON, LEO
COLANGELO, PETER
*COLE, WM. B.
COMERFORD, W.
CONWAY, D. F.
COOGAN, P. G.
COWLEY, WM. J.
CROSBY, THOS. N.
CROSS, FRANK G.
CURRAN, THOS. F.
DAVIDSON, CHAS.
DEANE, JOHN A.
*DESMARAIS, OSCAR
DEW, JOHN S.
DILLON, JOS. F.
DILLON, THOS. M.
*DITCHIE, FRED.
*DOYLE, EUGENE
*DUGAN, PATRICK
DUGAN, WILLIAM
DUNNE, FRANCIS
EBY, SAM. C.
ECKART, CHAS.
ECKERLEIN, ALFRED
EDWARDS, A. H.
*EDWARDS, EDWARD
ENDERES, A. G.
FARRELL, WM.
FERGUSON, EDWARD
FISHER, FRANK J.
FISHER, WALTER
*FITZPATRICK, JOHN M.
FITZPATRICK, JOS.
FLEMING, J. S.
FLYNN, CLARENCE
FOSTER, FRANK L.
FRANCK, RUSSELL
FRANK, JULES
FRUCHTER, MAX
GALVIN, EDWARD
GALVIN, PATRICK
GANNON, J. R.
GARRAMONE, ROBT.
GEIGER, BENTLEY J.
GEORGE, ROBERT
GERSTINE, BENJ.
*GOUGH, MARTIN
GRADY, WM.
GRAHAM, JOS.
GRANAT, WM.
*GREEN, PAUL
GREENSTONE, G.
GREGORY, STANLEY
GRESKIEWICH, JOS.
GRIFFIN, E.
GUARD, JACK
GUNTHER, CHAS.
HAGOOD, EARL V.
*HALL, ALBERT G.
HAMILTON, P.
HANSELMANN, FRED.
HARRIS, DANIEL
HATCH, JOHN M.
HEARN, JOHN E.
HEGARTY, GEO.
HEGARTY, WM. H.
HENRY, WM.
*HESSON, HORACE W.
HIGGINS, RAYMOND
HILL, WALTER
HOLMAN, E. J.
*HOLMGREN, CHAS.
*HOLZER, JOHN C.
HOREY, MADELEINE
HUNTER, GEO. R.
JAEGER, CHAS.
JAMES, EUGENE W.
*JENSEN, PETER
JOHNSON, E. W.
JOHNSTON, WILLIS
JORDAN, THOMAS J.
JOUBERT, ANDREW
KARRER, CONRAD
KAUCHER, GEO. L.
KELLY, ENOS J.
KELLEY, JAMES
KENNEDY, DAVID
KENT, TIMOTHY
KIRCHNER, JOS.
*KLEIN, DAVID
LAFFERTY, FORREST
*LAUER, THEODORE C.
LAVERTY, EDGAR
LAWLOR, JOHN T.
LEACH, SAM
LEEPER, J. W.
LEMENTRY, WALTER
LEY, WILLIAM
*LOCKWOOD, CHARLES
LUSHBAUGH, EDWARD B.
MCCANN, THOMAS J.
MCCONNELL, MICHAEL
*MCCRANEY, JAMES
MCELDARY, JOSEPH
MCGING, P.
*MCGINN, JOSEPH
MCKEAN, WILLIAM S.
MCMONAGLE, ROGER P.
MCNAMEE, MICHAEL
MCPARTLAND, FRANCIS
MCPHERSON, JOHN W.
MCWILLIAM, HENRY
MacDONALD, EDGAR
MacKENZIE, CARRIE
MABBETT, A. W.
MALONE, AUSTIN
MALONEY, J.
MARKEY, E. J.
MARTELL, RICHARD
MARTIGNETTI, PHILLIP
*MARTIN, ALFRED D.
MAURICE, RICHARD S.
MEACHAM, LAWRENCE
MEADE, CHARLES
MEIKLE, JOHN K.
*MEINERT, GUSTAVE
MELLEN, WILLIAM
MENSHON, W.
*MERZ, FRED.
MINNAUGH, JOSEPH
MITCHELL, ROBERT B.
MONTGOMERY, VIRGIL
MORGAN, A. J.
MORTON, ROBERT C.
MOSS, GEORGE A.
MOYER, CHARLES
MOYNIHAN, DENNIS
MULLER, J. HERBERT
MURRAY, CHARLES T.
NEALE, R.
NOWLAN, FRANK
*O'BRIEN, JOSEPH
O'CONNOR, CHARLES
O'GORMAN, EDWARD L.
O'GORMAN, LAWRENCE T.
*O'ROURKE, DANIEL
OLSON, OSCAR

* Twenty-five years or more with *The Times*.

COMPOSING ROOM — *Continued*

ORF, ULRICH	SALVAIL, OSCAR	TOBIN, ROBERT B.
OWENS, A. E.	SAUDER, HARRY	TOURK, HARRY M.
PASSUTH, GEORGE	*SCHUYLER, FRED J.	TULLY, JOSEPH
PATON, WILLIAM	SCOTT, EDWARD C.	*TURNEY, JACOB M.
PATTON, ALFRED	SHIELDS, ROBERT	VAN BENSCHOTEN, F.
PEFUND, JOHN	SIMON, CHARLES	VOGEL, WILLIAM
PENNEY, HORACE	SIMONS, JOHN	WAAGE, FRED W.
PEYTON, CHARLES	SINGER, LUCIAN	WALWORTH, RUSSEL B.
*PIERCE, H. CLARK	SINGLE, HERBERT	WARMINGHAM, G. H.
PIKE, ALFRED	SOKEL, EMIL G.	WASHBURN, FRED E.
POHL, JOSEPH	*SPOTH, JOHN C.	WEEKS, FRED M.
POIRIER, HECTOR	*STACK, EDWARD	*WELLS, ARTHUR
POLLOCK, NATHANIEL	STAFFORD, JOHN	WHEELHOUSE, WILFRED.
POLOQUIN, EDWARD	STALLEY, RICHARD	WHITE, F.
PYM, PERCY A.	STASNEY, EMANUEL	*WHITE, WILLIAM H.
*RANDOLPH, CLARENCE	STOCKER, RALPH	WHITEHEART, JAMES A.
*REAGAN, JOHN T.	SUTHERLAND, ALAN	WILLEY, LEWIS A.
ROACH, WALTER	*SWICK, FRED N.	WILSON, HARRY
ROBERTS, A. E.	*SYMMONS, JACOB	*WISEMAN, EDWARD
ROCHE, DAVID	TALBOYS, GEORGE	WOLFF, ADA
ROONEY, PATRICK	TAYLOR, IRA C.	WOLTZ, WILLIAM H.
ROSLOFSKY, A.	TAYLOR, JAMES	*WOODS, WILLIAM
RUBINSTEIN, ALBERT	TAYLOR, THOMAS	ZOGRAPHOS, M. E.
RUDOLPH, THEODORE	TENAGLIA, LOUIS	ZOGRAPHOS, PYTHAGORAS
*RYAN, FRANCIS	THAYER, E. J.	

Stereotype Room

JOHN H. DUNTON, Superintendent

EDWARD T. DUFFY . . . . Assistant Foreman

BERNHARD, ADOLPH	JOHNSON, DAVID	RICHARDSON, GEO.
BOYLE, CHAS. W.	KRAENGEL, WM. P.	ROBINSON, W. E.
ENSWORTH, GEO. P.	MCMAHON, JAS. A.	SHEHAN, MICHAEL R.
ESTEY, GEO. L.	MACK, JOS. A.	STEIBER, SAUL
FARMER, HARRIS	MANN, THOS.	STOPPLEWORTH, LOUIS
FREESTONE, JAS.	MURRAY, R. S.	VOGLER, JOHN N.
HENDERSON, IRVING	O'BRIEN, WM. A.	WEAVER, WM.
HOPE, JOS. J.	O'CONNOR, JAS. A.	WHITE, J. W.
HUMPHREY, NAT.	RAUNICKER, ROBT.	WINSLOW, D. E.

* Twenty-five years or more with *The Times.*

ROSTER OF THE NEW YORK TIMES COMPANY

Press Room

JOHN R. HAYS, Superintendent

FREDERICK VAN TASSEL . . . . Assistant Superintendent
*ROBERT LICHENSTEIN . . . . Foreman
JOHN BLINT, JR. . . . . Foreman
HARRY F. ALBECK . . . . Foreman
EDWARD J. DOLAN . . . . Foreman
DECATUR F. MARMION . . . . Assistant Foreman

ADOLPH, FRED
ALBECK, CHAS.
ALBECK, WALTER
AMSTER, SAMUEL
ANDERMAN, HENRY
ATKINSON, EDWARD
AUBER, WILLIAM
AYERS, CHAS.
BAKER, LOUIS
BARRINGER, HERBERT
BENNETT, WILLIAM
BERNDT, HERMAN
BIRCH, JOSEPH
BISHOP, CHARLES
BLANEY, RUSSELL
BLINT, JOHN, SR.
BODUKY, JOSEPH
BOGAN, WILLIAM
BOYD, J.
BOYLAN, FRANK
BRANDON, JOHN
BRANT, CHARLES
BRODERICK, ARTHUR
BRODERICK, JOHN
BROSNAN, WILLIAM
BURK, THOMAS
BURNS, JAMES
BUTLER, JOHN
CAMPBELL, ARTHUR
CAMPBELL, LESTER
CASEY, HAROLD
CASSIDY, EDWARD
CLARK, GEORGE
CLIFFORD, CORNELIUS
CONNERS, MICHAEL
CONROY, JOSEPH
COOPER, GEORGE
COTTER, EDWARD
COTTER, THOMAS
COULTER, WALTER
COYNE, EDWARD
DALY, CHARLES
DEACON, DAVID
DeCOLLE, LOUIS
DELANEY, PATRICK
DELVENTHAL, ARTHUR
DELVENTHAL, FRED.
DERBY, JOSEPH
DIODINE, FRANK
DONNELLY, DANIEL
DONOHUE, JAMES
DONOHUE, PETER
DONOHUE, PHILIP
DONOVAN, EDWARD
DRISCOLL, DAVID
ECKEL, CHARLES
ELLISON, CHARLES
ERHARDT, BARTHOLOMEW
FERRY, GEORGE
FEY, EDWARD
FEY, JOHN H.
FINNERTY, MARTIN
FINNERTY, THOMAS
FISHER, OTTO
FITZGERALD, EGBERT
FITZGERALD, J.
FITZSIMMONS, EDWARD
FLANNIGAN, GEORGE
FLINN, HENRY
FOLEY, JOSEPH
FOLEY, STEPHEN
FRANKLIN, JULIUS
FRENCH, JAMES
GAMMON, WALTER
GERRITY, GEORGE
GERRITY, JAMES
GILL, THOMAS
GOLD, EDWARD
GORVEN, JOHN
GRAHAM, THOMAS
GROTE, LOUIS
HAASE, HARRY
HANSON, C.
HARDY, RAYMOND
HARRIS, ALBERT
HARRIS, EDWARD
HENDERSON, GEORGE
HENDERSON, GEORGE I.
HEYER, JOSEPH
HEYER, JOSEPH F., JR.
HEYER, LAWRENCE
HIMPLER, JOHN
HIRSHBERG, I.
HOGAN, JOSEPH
HOGAN, WALTER
HOLLAND, GEORGE
HOPKINS, HENRY
HORAN, EDWARD
HORN, WILLIAM
HORNER, LOUIS
HUNGERFORD, CHAS.
HYSLOP, WILLIAM
JENNINGS, JOHN
JOHNSON, FRANK
KALMAN, HARRY
KARR, RICHARD
KEAN, ELWOOD
KEARNS, GEORGE
KEENAN, OWEN
KENNEDY, JOHN
KENNELLY, DANIEL
KENNELLY, JAMES
KENNENGEISER, GEORGE
KENNY, WILLIAM
KEYSER, E.
KUHN, JOHN
LANE, ALBERT
LANIGAN, KENNETH
LAVERY, DANIEL
LEAHY, JOHN
LEAHY, WILLIAM
LEONARD, GEORGE
LOGAN, GEORGE
LYONS, WILLIAM
MacDONALD, JOSEPH
McCARTHY, EDWARD

* Twenty-five years or more with *The Times.*

Press Room—*Continued*

MCEVOY, EDWARD	NORRIS, WILLIAM	SIEGEL, ALFRED
MCGUIRE, ARTHUR	O'CONNOR, GEORGE	SMILEY, FRANK
MCKEE, JOHN	O'CONNOR, MICHAEL	SMITH, J.
MCLAUGHLIN, B.	O'DEE, THOMAS	SMITH, WILLIAM
MCPARTLAND, RICHARD	O'HARA, JOHN	SPENCE, JOHN
MCQUADE, JOHN	O'MALLEY, MALARCKI	STEELE, WILLIAM
MACKIN, CHARLES	O'SULLIVAN, PAUL	STENGER, LOUIS
MALLON, THOMAS	PARDEE, ARTHUR	STOESSER, LEONARD
MALONEY, FRANK	PEPERSACK, JOHN	SULLIVAN, FRANK
MANN, JAMES	PETERS, CHARLES	SULLIVAN, J.
MARR, DAVID	PFISTER, FRANK	SULLIVAN, LEO
MAXWELL, JOHN	PIASECKI, ED.	SWIGART, PAUL
MAZZIE, ROBERT	POWERS, MICHAEL	TIERNEY, JOHN
MEILLY, JOHN	PURCELL, THOMAS	TOOMEY, JOSEPH
MOORE, MATHEW	QUINN, THOMAS	TOOTH, NATHAN
MOORE, PIERCE	RANDELL, GEORGE	VALANTI, JAMES
MORITZ, EDWARD	REDMOND, CHARLES	VOLCKENS, CHAS.
MUFFIN, FRANK	REDMOND, PHILLIP	WALSH, CHAS.
MULLANE, JOHN	REILLY, FRANK	WALSH, JOHN
MULQUEEN, JOHN	REYNOLDS, CLARENCE	WATSON, JOSEPH
MURICE, PATRICK	ROMMENS, LAWRENCE	WEBB, ROYAL
MURPHY, CHARLES	ROWE, JAMES	WEBSTER, FRANK
MURPHY, WILLIAM	SCHNEIDER, JACOB	WESTON, CHARLES
MURRAY, RICHARD	SCOTT, JAMES	WHITEHORNE, GEORGE
MYERS, LOUIS	SHARKEY, CHARLES	WHITEHOUSE, JAMES
NEUMAN, THOMAS	SHARKEY, JAMES A.	WILSON, ALBERT
NIX, JAMES	SHARKEY, JOHN F.	WOODARD, CLEMENT
NOLTING, GEORGE	SHARKEY, JOHN, SR.	WRIGHT, WILLIAM

Roto Etching Department

Eugene F. Ellis, Superintendent

Frank Dimmock . . . . Assistant Superintendent
John Hutchinson . . . . Foreman
John B. Johnson . . . . Foreman

ANDRIE, FRED A.	HARPER, ROLAND H.	PATTERSON, DAN J.
BARRETT, WILLIAM	HERRINGTON, RAY	PAYNE, GEORGE
COOPER, RAY	JOHNSON, W.	QUANN, JOHN
CULLEN, PAT	LANDO, FRANK	SCHWARTZ, JEAN
DANIELS, THOS. V.	MAGNUSON, ANDREW	SCHWENGER, FRED
DEFOUR, JEAN C.	MILES, FORDHAM C.	SHEA, THOMAS
DIXON, JOS. C.	MOONEY, CHRIS E.	TIERNEY, CHARLES
ERLER, CHARLES	MORGAN, WALTER A.	VOELKER, ALBERT C.
GILLICK, JOHN	MUNZ, HAROLD	
HANDWERK, HUGO	NIEDERLE, MAX	

Mail Room

DAN CORCORAN, Superintendent

EDWARD MCARDLE	Assistant Superintendent
JOHN BROWN	Night Foreman
JAMES GORDON	Day Foreman
WM. WEBSE	Foreman Hustler
DAN QUINN	Assistant Foreman Hustlers
MAX GREENBAUM	Assistant Foreman Hustlers
MOE PERLSTEIN	Foreman Chauffeurs

ARIS, JOHN
ASTWOOD, EDWIN
BARTLETT, CARL
BEAVER, WILLIAM
BECKER, CHARLES
BEGGINS, CHRIS. J.
BELABIN, LOUIS
BENDER, CHARLES
BEROLDT, MEMO
BIDEAUX, LOUIS
BIMMINGER, ERNEST
BLACK, HARRY
BOSS, ED. J.
BOYCE, J. N.
CAFFERTY, EARL P.
CANGRO, JACOB
CANTOR, HARRY
CANTOR, LEO
CASALASPRO, ANTHONY
CASALASPRO, LOUIS
CASALASPRO, MICHAEL
*COCHRANE, DAVID
COFFEY, JAS. J.
CONNERS, JOHN
CONNERS, THOMAS
DALY, JOHN
DICKSON, RICHARD
DIGNEY, FRANK
*DONOHUE, MICHAEL
DONOVAN, ANDREW
DONOVAN, JOHN A.
DOUGHTY, CLARENCE
DROGE, GEO., SR.
DROGE, GEO., JR.
EICHENBUSH, JOHN
FARLEY, JOS.
FERRIS, JOHN
FLANAGAN, WM. J.
FLETCHER, GEORGE
FOLEY, J.
FRAZEE, JOHN
GALLAGHER, MIKE
GLADMAN, ARTHUR
GLEICH, LOUIS
GOLDMAN, EMIL
GOLDMAN, JOS.
GORDON, SIDNEY
GORELICK, PHIL
GRAY, WILLIAM J.
GREENHAUSE, ABE
GROSS, CHAS.
GROSS, HARRY
GROSS, MAX
GROSSMAN, ALEX
GROVES, ED.
HAUFF, DAVID
HENRY, MICHAEL O.
HINCK, HENRY
HOFFSCHMIDT, WALTER
ISAACS, JACOB
JOHNSTON, ED.
JONES, ROBERT
KAST, JOHN
KEOUGH, JOS. A.
KIMBELL, JOHN
KINWALD, SAM'L
KLEIN, GUS
KRENTZMAN, DAVE
KRENTZMAN, SAM'L
LARESCH, MICHAEL
LARSON, RICHARD
LEVY, ISIDOR
LOCKARD, C.
MCCAFFERTY, THOS.
MCELROY, THOMAS
MCSHERRY, WM.
MAJER, CHAS.
MARKS, MARKEY
MARTIN, CLAUDE
MAYHEW, CHAS.
MAYROSE, WM.
MILLER, REX
MOONEY, JOHN
MUIR, WM. F.
MULLER, ALEX.
MURPHY, ED.
MURPHY, PATRICK
MYERS, C.
O'KEEFE, DENIS
PALTER, HARRY
PATRICK, RAY
PERREM, PAUL
PETRY, PAUL
PLUNKETT, JOHN
POWERS, JOHN
REDA, ANTHONY
RODGERS, JULIAN
ROHRBACKER, GEO.
ROSE, WILLIAM
ROSOFF, SAM'L
ROWAN, RAY
RUBENSTEIN, DAVID
SCHWEITZER, FRED J.
SCOFIELD, CHAS.
SEMRICK, CARL
SHAINE, LOUIS
SIMON, SAM'L
SNIZEK, ANTHONY
STERN, DAVID
STETTNER, THEO.
STOLOFF, ABE
STONE, CHAS.
TAUSTINE, EMANUEL
TULLY, FRANK
VALENTINE, JOS.
VER PAULT, GEO.
WATSON, SAM'L
WEED, ROY
WEISMEYER, CHAS.
WHITEMORE, FRANK
WILLINS, MICHAEL
WINDSOR, CHAS.
WOLF, LOUIS
WOLFSON, MICHAEL

* Twenty-five years or more with *The Times.*

ROSTER OF THE NEW YORK TIMES COMPANY

Transportation Department

THOMAS TALLON, Superintendent

BARNEY MCTAGUE . . . . Foreman of Dockloaders
JAMES SHERRY . . . . Foreman of Day Paper Handlers
MAURICE O'CONNELL . . . . Foreman of Night Paper Handlers

BACKUS, JAMES
BACKUS, WM.
BOTTINY, WALTER
BRADBURY, J.
BUCKLEY, MICHAEL
BURNES, ARTHUR
BYRNE, HARRY
CARROLL, J.
CLARK, FRANK
CONOLLY, FRANK
DAWSON, ROBT.
DOIG, HARRY
FALLON, JAMES
FISHER, JOHN
FITZSIMMONS, N.
GAVIGAN, JOHN
GRADY, WM.
GRAHAM, THOS.
HOPKINS, JOHN
JOHNSON, FREDERICK
KEARNS, JAMES
LANE, JOSEPH
LENNON, PATRICK
LENNON, WM.
MCELWAIN, PATRICK
MCKENNA, PATRICK
MORIARITY, PATRICK
OLSEN, CHRIS.
SHEEHY, MICHAEL
SULLIVAN, DENNIS
WOODS, FRANK
WOODS, PETER

Times Building and West 43rd St. Addition

GEO. L. ECKERSON, Agent and Manager

FRED BRAZONG . . . . Foreman Elevators
MICHAEL FALLON . . . . Chief Stationary Engineer

ARCHER, JOSEPH
ARMSTRONG, SAM
BARRETT, KATE
BICKEL, ANTON
BOOTH, ELIJAH
CARLEY, MINNIE
CHAPMAN, E.
CONNELLY, JAMES
COUGHLIN, ELIZ.
CRONIN, ANNIE
CUNNINGHAM, MARY
DALTON, JAMES
DEHATE, MAIGON
DOCKERY, STEPHEN
DURKIN, MARGARET
FARROLL, MARY
GRANT, J.
HIGGINS, THOMAS
JENKINS, BERT
JACOBI, CHARLES
JOHNSTON, NELLIE
KENNEDY, BRIDGET
KILKENNY, PATRICK
LEARY, CATHERINE
LEONARD, JOHN
LORUM, GEO.
MCCARTHY, JOHN
MCCORMACK, EDWARD
MCCUTTE, NELLIE
MCGUIRE, JOHN
MCKIERNAN, HUGH
MCTAGUE, NELLIE
MANCHESTER, ANNIE
MENDRLA, MARIE
MERZ, JOHN
MILLER, LOUISA
MINOGUE, EDWARD
MONAHAN, JAMES
MCDONNELL, THOS. J.
O'NEILL, PATRICK
O'TOOLE, PATRICK
PATTERSON, ANNIE
PATTERSON, MARY
RYAN, FRANK
SMITH, AGNES
SNOW, M.
SULLIVAN, PATRICK
WALSH, RICHARD
WARD, THOS. P.

ROSTER OF THE NEW YORK TIMES COMPANY

AUDITING DEPARTMENT

HARRY H. WEINSTOCK, Auditor

RUDOLPH WEINACHT	Mgr. Auditing Staff
EDWIN L. FINCH	Mgr. Editorial Payroll Dept.
LOUIS FISHMAN	Mgr. Accounting Dept.
CLIFFORD H. PYLE	Mgr. Payroll Dept.
THOMAS ROCHE	Mgr. Receiving Dept.
FRANK SCHMIDT	Mgr. Paper and Ink Dept.

ABEL, MARGARET
AGMAN, ABRAHAM
BELMAR, MAURICE
BERLINGHOFF, WILLIAM
BROWN, WILLIAM B.
COHN, MYRON
CONNOLLY, HUGH
CULLEN, JOHN C.
DAWSON, ALLAN
DUNLOP, JOSEPH
ENGLANDER, BENJAMIN
FRANK, MIRIAM
GLASSBERG, PHILLIP
GOLDSTONE, EVELYN
JOHNSON, OSCAR
KABAKOW, MINNIE
KAISER, GEORGE
KATZ, JOHN
LAKE, SAMUEL
LAWLER, EDWARD
LEHRHAUPT, MORRIS
LEWIS, ALFRED
LEWIS, ELSIE
MATTISON, EDWARD
MENZER, NETTIE
MILLER, HARRY
MOORE, WALTER
NETZER, ANNA
OEHLER, RICHARD
PEMBLETON, FRED
ROTH, JOSEPH
SCHENK, EDWARD
SCHLEICHER, ANNABELLE
SKINNER, ARTHUR
SMITH, HELEN
SOLOMONS, HARRY
STANGER, MARGARET
STERLING, CAMILLA
STRAIN, SAMUEL
STROBEL, LOUISE
TEAGUE, CRESTWELL
TERRIBERRY, NATHAN
THOMPSON, WILLIAM
VOGEL, HERMAN
WAGNER, STANLEY
WASSERMAN, DAVID
WASSERMAN, HARRIET
WEINBERGER, DOROTHY
WHEELER, FREDERICK
WHITTAKER, JOSEPH
WORMSER, LEON

GENERAL DEPARTMENTS

LUCIEN FRANCK	Purchasing Agent
CARL HOTOPP	Assistant Purchasing Agent
EDWARD A. HEGI	Cashier
MILDRED C. SMITH	Assistant Cashier
WILLIAM M. JACKSON	Manager Personnel Department
WALTER A. MADIGAN	Manager Restaurant

ALVAREZ, JOHN
BRONDOLO, TONY
BROWN, WILLIAM
COLGAN, WILLIAM D.
DE PASS, ADRIAN
FAHERTY, MARY A.
FLASCH, SYLVIA
FONTANA, LOUIS
FOYE, HARRY, JR.
FOYE, HENRY P.
GEHRIG, GEORGE
GERSHENSON, L.
HEGEDUS, HENRICH
JACOBUS, PHEBE
JUPITER, EDWARD
KEARNEY, CATHERINE
LEMMER, ANNA
LORENZEN, ELIZABETH A.
MCDERMOTT, JOHN
MCNEELEY, MARY
O'SHEA, WILLIAM J.
SCHNURRER, CHRIS.
SCHUTTINGER, KATHERINE
SHEEHAN, KITTY
SMITH, B.
TORCHIO, LAWRENCE
TORINO, JOSEPH
TUCKER, KENNETH
WAKELEY, DELBERT
WALTERS, HILLIS
WEAVER, MRS. JOSEPHINE
WINSTON, ANDREW
ZIMMERMAN, ALBERT

ROSTER OF THE NEW YORK TIMES COMPANY

CURRENT HISTORY, MIDWEEK PICTORIAL AND WAR VOLUMES

GEORGE W. OCHS OAKES . . . . Editor and Manager

Editorial Staff

BLYTHE, WALTER E.
DUFFIELD, J. W.
KURTH, OTTO
PRESTON, THOS. B.
SHUMAN, EDWIN L.
SNOW, DR. F. H.
WALSH, MATTHEW J.
WATERBURY, IVAN C.
WHITE, CAPT. MICHAEL A. E.

Business Office

KRESGE, HOMER D. . . . . Manager
BURGESS, FRANK T. . . . . Sales Manager
HECHELHEIM, LOUIS . . . . Bookkeeper

ADAMS, ARTHUR R.
ALBERT, MIRIAM
ALLAN, MURIEL
ANDERSON, HILDA
BARRETT, ADELE V.
BERGLING, ANNA
BLOOMER, W.
BOLSTAD, EDW.
BOTNER, PAULINE
BROWN, WM. M.
BURKETT, R. M.
BURNS, EDW. M.
CONVISER, ELLA
CORRELL, JOHN I.
CRAIG, LILLIAN
DICKINSON, CARRIE
DONAHUE, ELIZABETH
EDMUNDS, L. M.
ERGER, LOUISE
ESPOSITA, MARGARET
EZECHEL, KATHERINE
FECHNER, LEON
FERNEEKES, ELSA M.
FINGER, SHIRLEY
FINKHOUSER, FRED A.
FINKHOUSER, JAS. A.
GREEN, CHAS. J.
HALL, GERTRUDE
JACKSON, MORRIS
LAMB, VINCENT D.
LASHER, MORRIS
LAUBER, SAMUEL
LEVY, ROBT. SAM'L
LOCKLEY, ROSE
LYNCH, G. M.
MCELDARRY, MAY
MELLINGER, EDW. D.
MORRIS, KATHERINE
NEUMANN, J. A.
O'BRIEN, MARION
O'SULLIVAN, MARGARET
QUINN, S. T.
RODENBERG, G.
ROSE, LILY
SALCEDO, WM.
SUSSMAN, MOE
TALIMER, BERNARD
VRADENBURG, ARTHUR
WARNOCK, M. C.
WEISS, SAMUEL

ANNALIST

EDWARD G. RICH, Editor

LOUIS O. MORNEY . . . . Manager Business Office

ALDEN, JOHN
AMES, RICHARD
CULLUM, WELCOME H.
HARMS, AUGUST A.
POLLOCK, JOHN

WIDE WORLD PHOTO DEPARTMENT

CHARLES M. GRAVES, Manager

JULES DUMAS . . . . Sales Manager

CANFIELD, JOHN
DEVLIN, JAMES
GLUCKMAN, RAE
GOTTLEIB, GERALD
LEVY, ARTHUR
LUBBEN, PAUL
METZGER, JOHN F.
NESENSOHN, C. D.
NESENSOHN, JOHN A.
NEWTON, WILLIAM
O'MEARA, JAMES
PEYROULET, JOHN
ROSE, RICHARD
STERN, NATHAN
TAYLOR, M. M.

ROSTER OF THE NEW YORK TIMES COMPANY

TIDEWATER PAPER MILLS COMPANY
Brooklyn, N. Y.

ADOLPH S. OCHS	President
ARTHUR HAYS SULZBERGER	Vice-President and Treasurer
BEN. C. FRANCK	Secretary
ARTHUR F. ALLEN	General Manager
JOHN B. WEST	Superintendent
ROBERT O. STERNBERGER	Plant Engineer
IRWIN H. COPELAND	Pulp Expert
A. F. McCOY	Chemist
F. P. ASHWORTH	Purchasing Agent
W. S. CHAMBERLAIN	Cashier
A. E. DAVIES	Master Mechanic
A. MERCIER	Chief Millwright
JOHN J. LEE	Chief Electrician
WM. BROWN	Chief Steam Engineer
VAN A. SEEBER	Boss Machine Tender
WM. COLE	Boss Machine Tender
P. J. KILAWEE	Boss Machine Tender
H. BAKER	Beater Engineer
F. E. VINING	Beater Engineer
D. J. MURPHY	Beater Engineer
L. J. WALZ	Foreman Shipping Room
GEO. A. LEAVITT	Yard Superintendent

BARNEY ALFONZA
J. BAJGERT
THOS. BATES
M. BEKAN
FRED BLAKE
CARL BOND
HUGH BOYLE
EDW. BRATT
CHRIS BREGENZER
E. S. BRINKLEY
ARTHUR BROWN
ARTHUR F. BROWN
THOS. BROWN
J. CAPEN
ALEX CLARK
THOS. COCHRAN
JOHN CORLISS
ROBERT CORNWALL
T. COSTENO
JOHN COUGHLIN
GUS CARLSON
PATRICK DALEY
THOS. DALEY
JAS. W. DAVIS
J. E. DAVIS
JEAN DeCARLE
EDW. DeLUCCA
JOS. C. DENNINGER
JOHN DEVENEY
GEORGE DOLL
JOHN DONOVAN
RICHARD DONOVAN
JULIUS DWIGHT
M. DZYOVNES
THOS. J. EVERS
FRANK FABER
THOS. FEWER
M. FOGARTY
PETER FRAGENT
VINCENZO FRAGNITO
WALTER FREDERICKSON
JAMES GAIGOL
JAS. GALLANAUGH
ROCCO GERVASE
THOMAS GIBBONS
JAMES GRANT
J. GRAVES
IGNATZ GREGOR
ROBERT HAMMINGTON
HENRY J. HITT
THOS. ILLINGWORTH
JOHN JACKAS
J. JANEWITCH
CHARLES JOHNSON
JOHN JONES
STEVE KARANECKY
GUS KEMPF
STENLI KEIRMARSKI
JOHN KENNY
FRANK KINGSTON
T. KINGSTON
WALTER KONAPACKI
STANLEY KURARSKY
MOSES LANCTO
PETER LANGMAN
M. LINDEMANN
LEON McDOUGAL
FRANK McGEENEY
DANIEL McLOON
A. MAELES
S. MAESTR
E. M. MASKELL
GEORGE MAYHEW
FAHECK MEHMED
CHAS. MERKELS

TIDEWATER PAPER MILLS COMPANY — *Continued*

L. C. MERRITT
JOHN MILLER
HENRY MULLEN
M. NADLER
CHRIS NAGEL
GEORGE NEWBY
EDW. NORDENBERG
PETER OSMANSKI
JAMES PETERSON
T. PETTONE
JOS. PITTULE
STEVE POLICKEL
CHARLES PROSSER
F. RHOOP
JNO. RIORDAN
BENJ. ROSS
A. J. RUDOLPH
ALFRED RUEL
ALBERT SAGATAS
AUGUST SANDSTROM
AUGUST SCEMEL
JOHN SCHICK
CARL SCROXTON
E. F. SEEMS
GEORGE SEILER
FRANK SHIMSAW
P. J. SIMON
GEORGE SLATER
ORVILLE SLATER
T. STANKOWITZ
HARRY STRINGER
NICK TROICKY
GEORGE TURNER
T. VELCH
J. WALSH
D. WARD
L. W. WHETSTONE
O. WHITMAN
A. T. WILLIAMS
JOHN WILLE
T. WILLISITISKI
I. WYEROSKI
JOHN WYZLINSKI

INDEX

INDEX

INDEX

INDEX

INDEX

INDEX